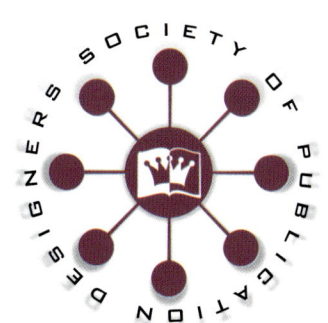

SOCIETY OF PUBLICATION DESIGNERS

BEST
MAGAZINE

DESIGN

TWENTY-NINTH

S P D

PUBLICATION DESIGN

ANNUAL

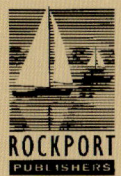

ROCKPORT
PUBLISHERS

ROCKPORT PUBLISHERS, ROCKPORT, MASSACHUSETTS
DISTRIBUTED BY NORTH LIGHT BOOKS, CINCINNATI, OHIO

ACKNOWLEDGEMENTS

OFFICERS

President
Walter Bernard
Principal
WBMG, INC.

Vice President
Don Morris
DON MORRIS DESIGN

Treasurer
Karen Bloom
Manager, Public Relations
Westvaco Corporation

Executive Director
Bride M. Whelan

BOARD OF DIRECTORS

Robert Altemus
Principal
ALTEMUS CREATIVE SERVICENTER

Tom Bentkowski
Director of Design
LIFE

Caroline Bowyer
Art Director
ELLE DECOR

Malcolm Frouman
Art Director
BUSINESSWEEK

Michael Grossman
Design Director
MEIGHER COMMUNICATIONS

Greg Leeds
Design Director
THE WALL STREET JOURNAL

Sue Llewellyn
Art Director
STEREO REVIEW

Rhonda Rubinstein
Principal
RHONDA RUBINSTEIN DESIGN

Fo Wilson
Creative Director
STUDIO W

Lloyd Ziff
Principal
LLOYD ZIFF DESIGN GROUP INC.

Ex Officio:
Phyllis Richmond Cox
Art Director
BRIDE'S & YOUR NEW HOME

Society of Publication Designers
60 East 42nd Street, Suite 721
New York, New York 10165
Tel. (212) 983-8585
Fax (212) 983-6043

COMPETITION CO-CHAIRS

Tom Bentkowski
Director of Design
LIFE

Gael Towey
Art Director
MARTHA STEWART LIVING

JUDGES

Richard Baker
Art Director
US

David Barnett
Design Director
BARNETT DESIGN GROUP INC.

Patricia Bradbury
Creative Director
NEWSWEEK

Phyllis Richmond Cox
Art Director
BRIDE'S & YOUR NEW HOME

Matthew Drace
Art Director
TRAVEL & LEISURE

Carole Erger-Fass
Art Director
ADWEEK

Teresa Fernandes
Art Director
SELLING

Janet Froelich
Art Director
THE NEW YORK TIMES MAGAZINE

Malcolm Frouman
Art Director
BUSINESS WEEK

Everett Halvorsen
Art Director
FORBES

Gregory Heisler
Photoghapher
GREGORY HEISLER STUDIO

Nigel Holmes
Graphics Director
TIME

John Korpics
Art Director
PREMIERE

Diana LaGuardia
Design Director
CONDÉ NAST TRAVELER

Duane Michals
Photoghapher
DUANE MICHALS STUDIO

Hans Teensma
Principal
IMPRESS, INC.

Pamela Berry Vitale
Art Director
ITALIE

Richard Wilde
Chairman of Visual Communications
SCHOOL OF VISUAL ARTS

Lloyd Ziff
Art Director
LLOYD ZIFF DESIGN GROUP, INC.

Mary Zisk
Principal
MARY ZISK DESIGN

THE GALA

The Society wishes to thank the New York Times Company Foundation for its generosity to the New York Public Library, which has enabled the Society of Publication Designers to hold its annual awards Gala in this very special place.

THE EXHIBITION

All winning entries were exhibited in conjunction with The Visual Communications Expo, at the Jacob Javits Convention Center, New York City in October 1994.

THE SPONSORS

The Society thanks its corporate sponsors for their continuing support:

American Express Publishing
Apple Computers, Inc.
Applied Graphics Technologies
Champion Paper Co.
Condé Nast Publications, Inc.
Dow Jones & Company, Inc.
Hachette Filipacchi Magazines, Inc.
Hearst Magazines
IBM
Meredith Corporation
Newsweek
The New York Times
Wenner Media
Time Inc.
U.S. News & World Report
Westvaco Corporation
The SPD 29th Annual

THE SPD 29TH ANNUAL

Jacket and book designed and produced by Robert Altemus of the Altemus Creative Servicenter.

First published in the United States of America by:
Rockport Publishers, Inc.
146 Granite Street
Rockport, Massachusetts 01966
Telephone: (508) 546-9590
Fax: (508) 546-7141
Telex: 5106019284 ROCKORT PUB

Distributed to the book trade and art trade in the U.S. and Canada by:
North Light, an imprint of F & W Publications
1507 Dana Avenue
Cincinnati, Ohio 45207
Telephone: (513) 531-2222
Other Distribution by:
Rockport Publishers, Inc.
Rockport, Massachusetts 01966

The Society of Publication Designers, Inc.
60 East 42nd Street #721
New York, NY 10165
Telephone: (212) 983-8585
Fax: (212) 983-6043

ISBN 1-56496-054-4

10 9 8 7 6 5 4 3 2 1

Printed in Hong Kong

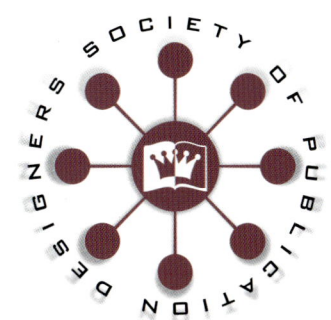

SOCIETY OF PUBLICATION DESIGNERS

BEST
MAGAZINE
DESIGN

TWENTY-NINTH

S P D

PUBLICATION DESIGN

ANNUAL

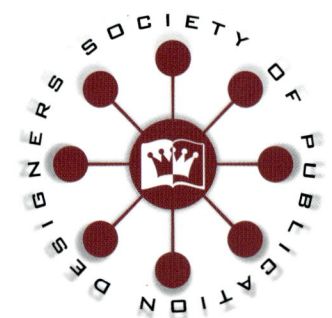

SOCIETY OF PUBLICATION DESIGNERS

BEST
MAGAZINE
DESIGN

TWENTY-NINTH

S P D

PUBLICATION DESIGN

ANNUAL

CONTENTS

PRESIDENT'S MESSAGE

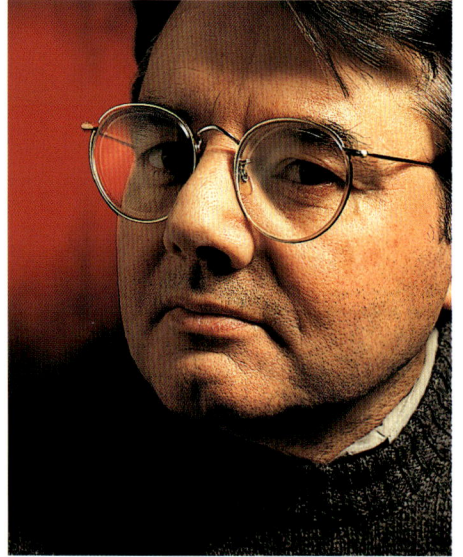

WE HAVE A LOT TO CELEBRATE IN THIS BOOK.

The first is all of the art directors, designers, photographers and artists whose work has won a place in our competition this year. While styles continually change and technology opens up new possibilities, the best work still exhibits an intelligence and craftsmanship that has always been the hallmark of excellence in design.

Secondly, we are proud to honor Ruth Ansel with the Herb Lubalin Award. You will delight in seeing her work on the following pages and learning about her amazing career.

I would also like to salute the SPD Board of Directors, all of whom have given their time and effort to a variety of tasks this year. In particular, Sue Llewellyn, art director of *Stereo Review,* who has created and supervised an extraordinary series of monthly speaker's lunches at the 60 East Club. Ms. Llewellyn and Fo Wilson, principal, Studio W, the chairperson of our speaker's evening programs, deserve special thanks. These programs, among others, have been supported by generous contributions from the leading publishers in our industry. This support is a recognition of the value placed on the designer's role in the success of their magazines.

Salutes also to Tom Bentkowski, and Gail Towey, co-chairs of the 29th annual competition, to Robert Altemus, the producer and designer of this book, and to Bride Whelan and Karen Bloom for their hard work and good cheer.

Finally, we dedicate this annual to B.W. Honeycutt, the art director of *Details* Magazine who passed away earlier this year. B.W. was co-chairman of last year's competition, and a member of our Board of Directors. He will be greatly missed. With this book, we celebrate him, too. ☀

Walter Bernard
President

ABOUT THE SOCIETY

ESTABLISHED IN 1965, THE SOCIETY OF PUBLICATION Designers was formed to acknowledge the role of the art director/designer in the creation and development of the printed page. The art director as journalist brings a visual representation to the editorial mission to clarify and enhance the written word. This graphic design skill is developed and specialized, presenting endless challenges in the current technological advancements of the publishing industry.

The Society provides for its members a monthly Speaker's Luncheon; a Speaker's Evening series; a bimonthly newsletter, GRIDS; the publication design annual; the Design Exhibition held annually at the Jacob Javits Center in conjunction with the International GRAFIX EXPO; studio and magazine tours for art directors and designers, and an annual SPOTS Competition and Exhibition for illustrators. It also actively participates in related activities that bring together members of the numerous design communities in the New York area.

The Society of Publication Designers Annual Competition draws several thousand entries from the United States and abroad. A jury of top designers, chosen for their distinguished expertise in design, judge the submitted works in seventy-five categories.

Once the finest works have been selected to appear in the Exhibition and the publication design annual, the jury awards Gold and Silver medals, the highest awards for editorial design. The remaining winners receive the distinction of merit and create, by their diversity, a compendium of the best-designed pieces from the submitted entries in design, photography, and illustration.

The Publication Design Annual, published by Rockport Publishing, is a volume containing the award-winning designs from the yearly competition. It is an invaluable reference for designers, educators, students, corporate communicators, editors, publishers, and all others engaged in the various aspects of editorial design. ☀

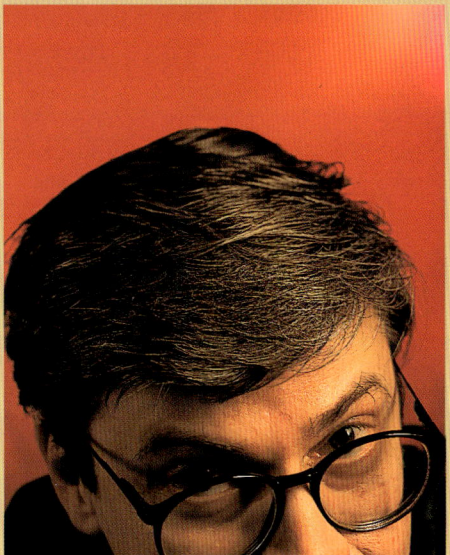

Judges' photographs by Steve Freeman

Tom Bentkowski
Director of Design
LIFE

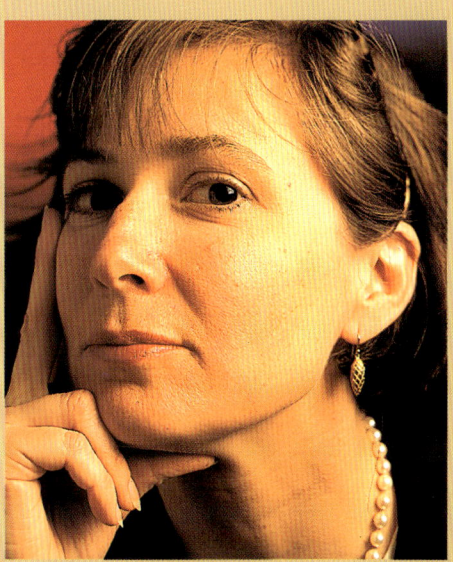

Gael Towey
Art Director
MARTHA STEWART LIVING

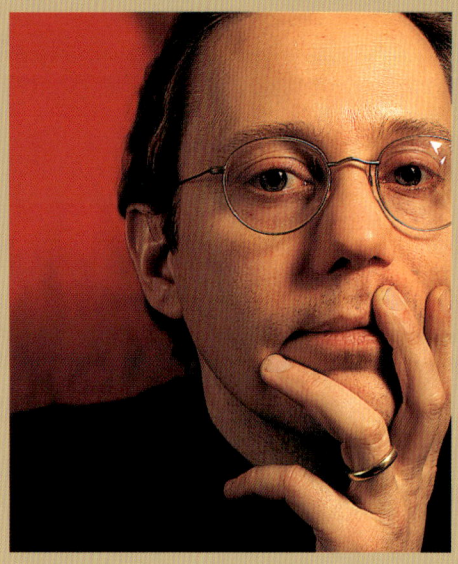

Don Morris (Chair)
Principal
DON MORRIS DESIGN

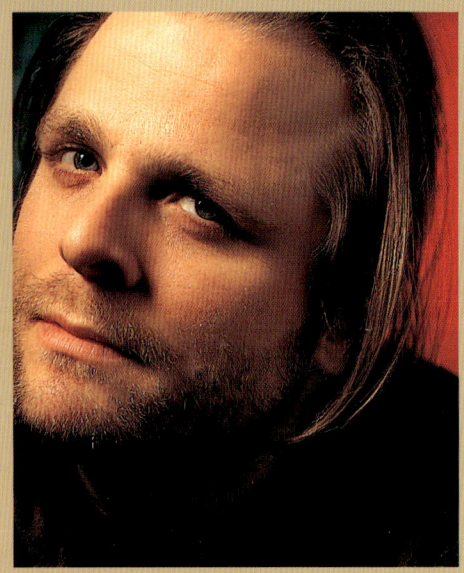

John Korpics
Art Director
PREMIERE

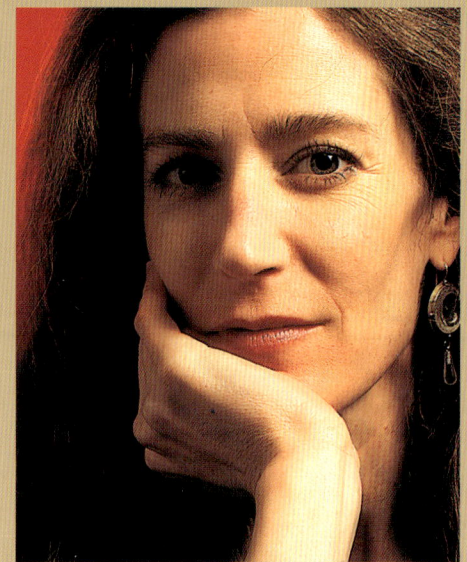

Patrica Bradbury
Creative Director
NEWSWEEK

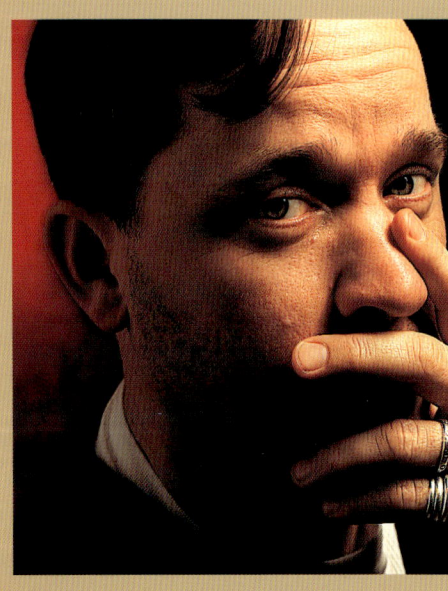

Matthew Drace
Art Director
TRAVEL & LEISURE

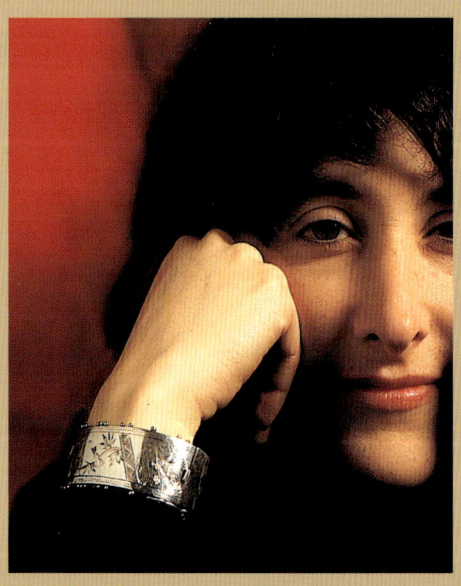

Carole Erger-Fass
Art Director
ADWEEK

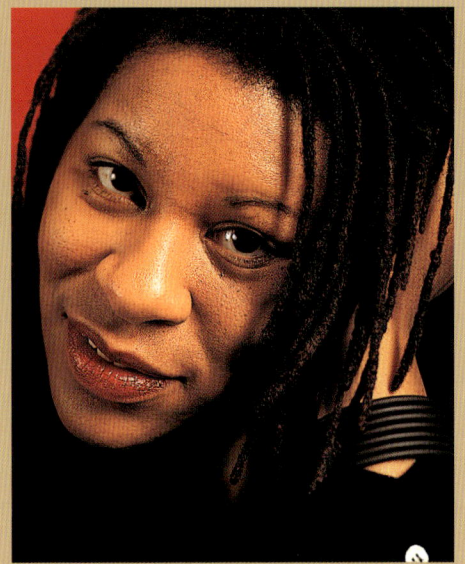

Fo Wilson (Chair)
Principal
STUDIO W

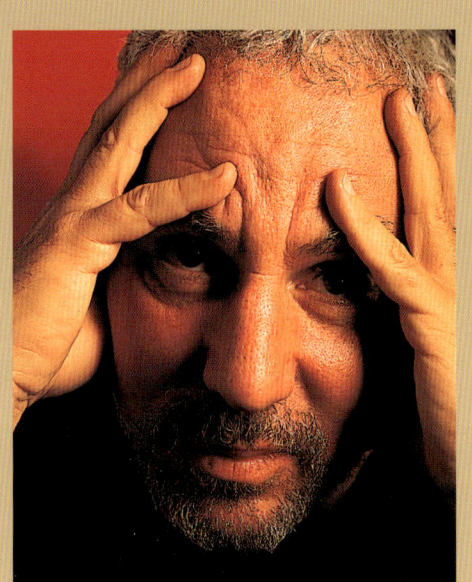

Lloyd Ziff
Principal
LLOYD ZIFF DESIGN

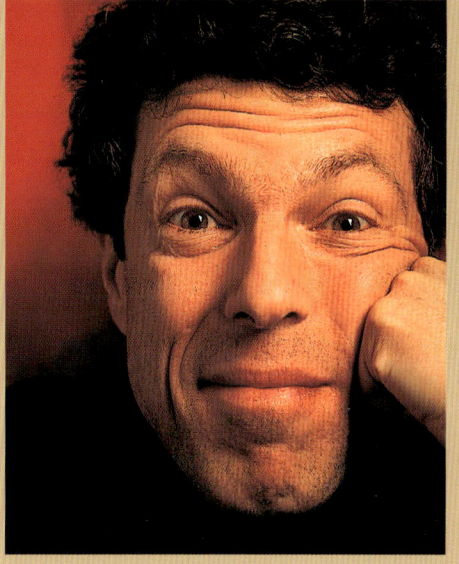

Malcolm Frouman
Art Director
BUSINESS WEEK

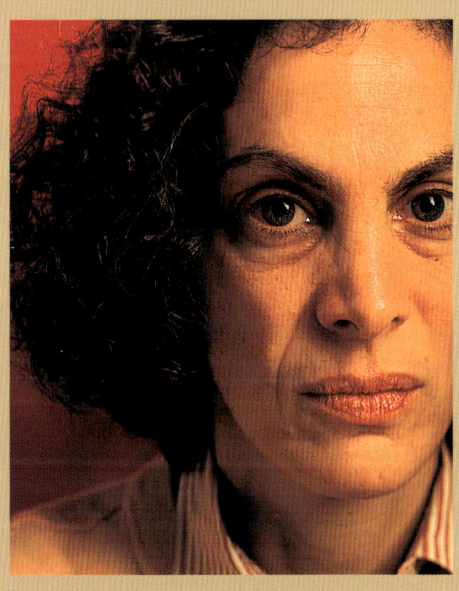

Janet Froelich
Art Director
NEW YORK TIMES MAGAZINE

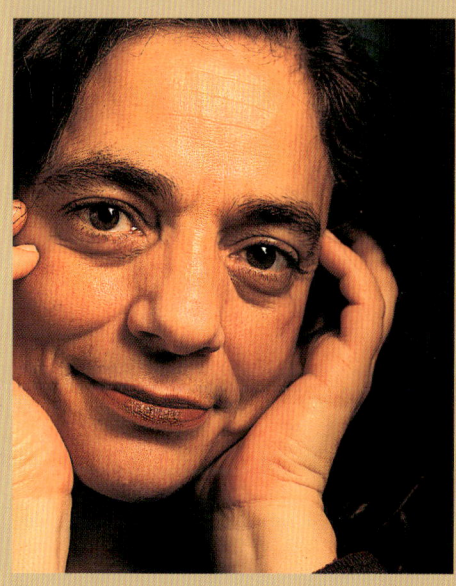

Diana LaGuardia
Design Director
CONDÉ NAST TRAVELER

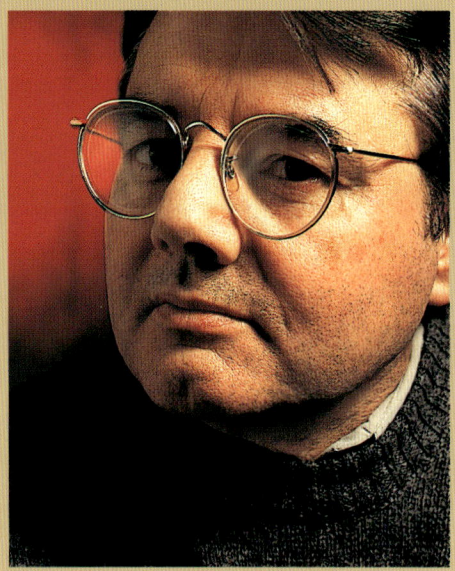

Walter Bernard (Chair)
Partner
WBMG

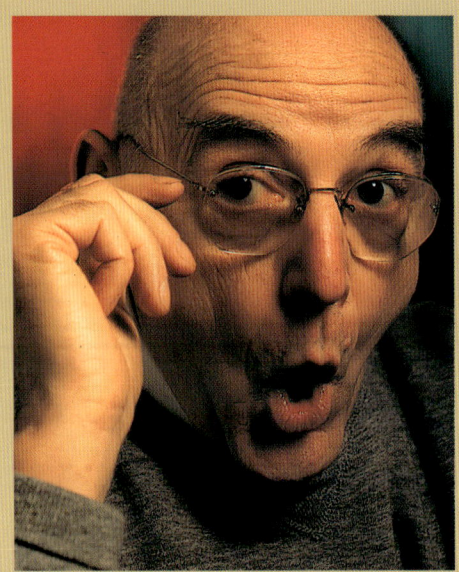

Duane Michals
Photographer
DUANE MICHALS STUDIOS

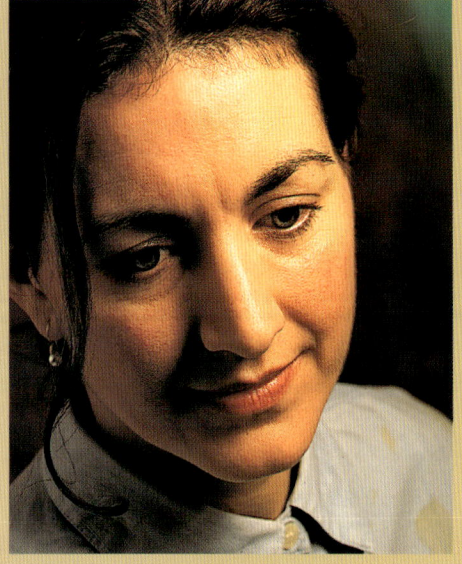

Pamela Berry
Art Director
Us

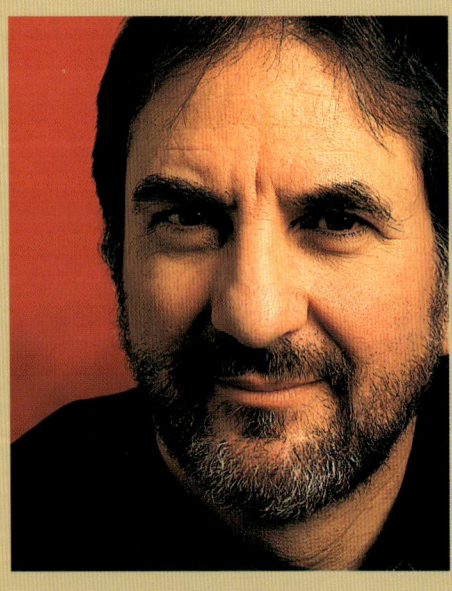

Richard Wilde
Chairman, Visual Communications
THE SCHOOL OF VISUAL ARTS

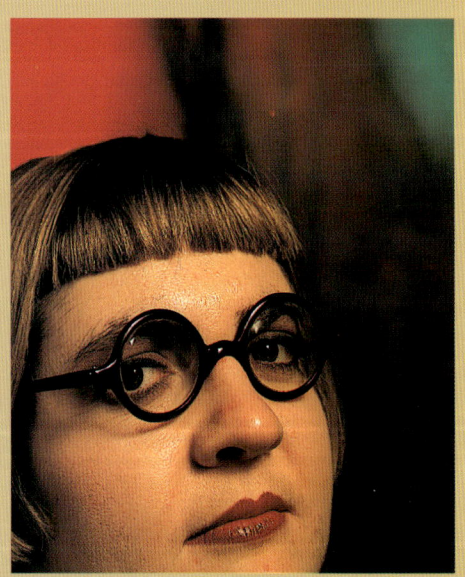

Teresa Fernandes
Art Director
SELLING

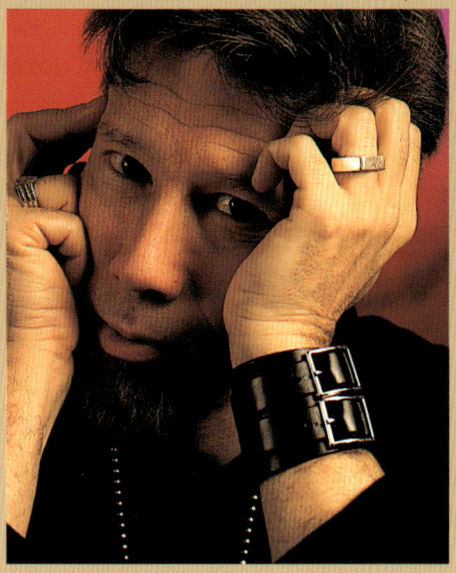

Robert Altemus (Chair)
Principal
ALTEMUS CREATIVE SERVICENTER

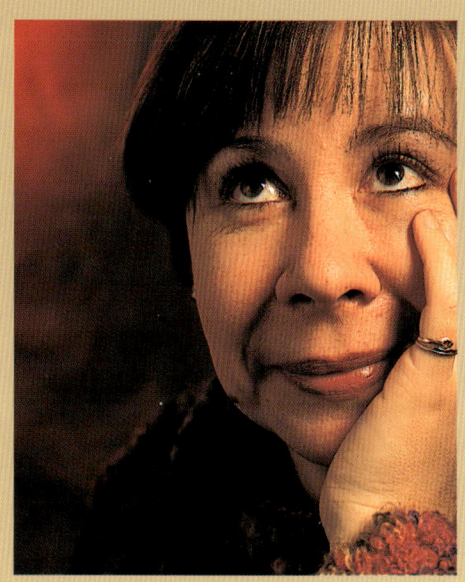

Mary Zisk
Principal
MARY ZISK DESIGN

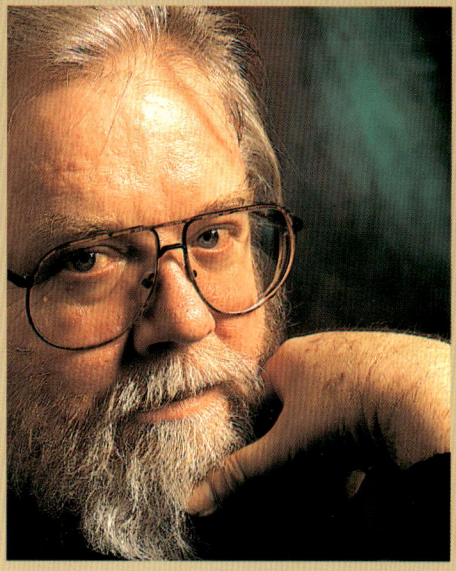

Everett Halvorsen
Design Director
FORBES

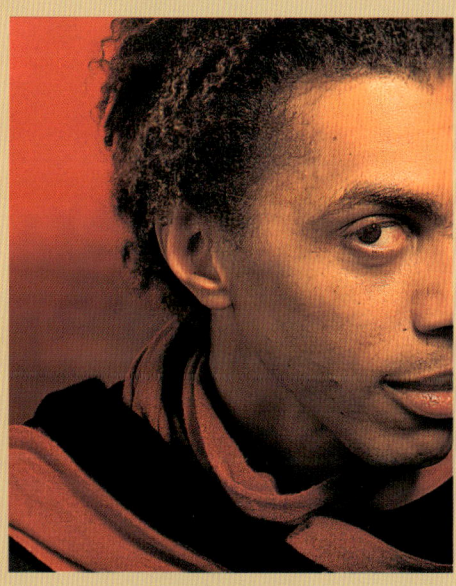

Richard Baker
Art Director
VIBE

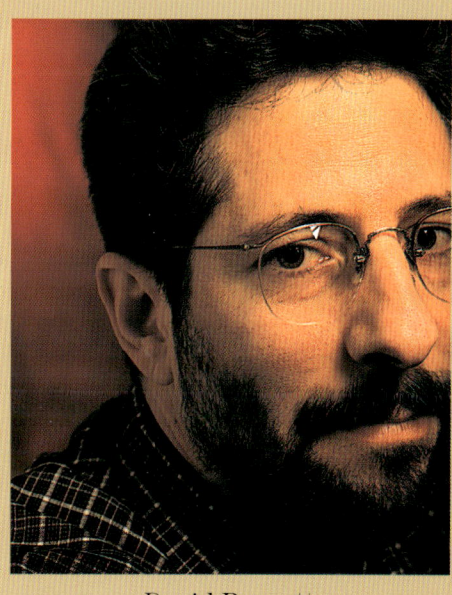

David Barnett
Principal
BARNETT DESIGN GROUP, INC.

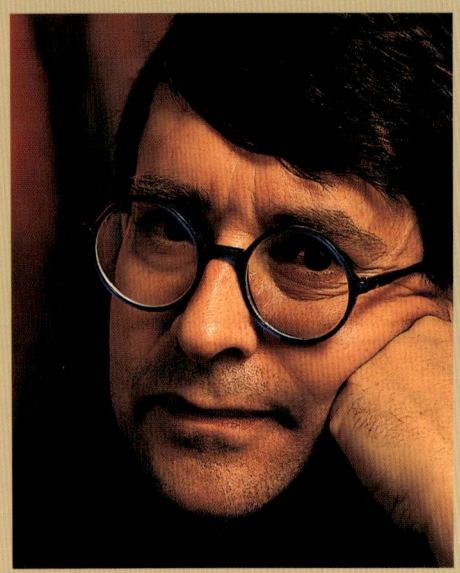

Nigel Holmes
Graphics Director
TIME

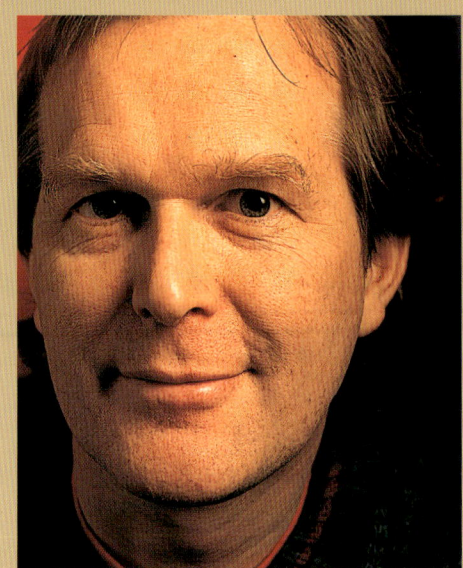

Hans Teensma
Principal
IMPRESS, INC.

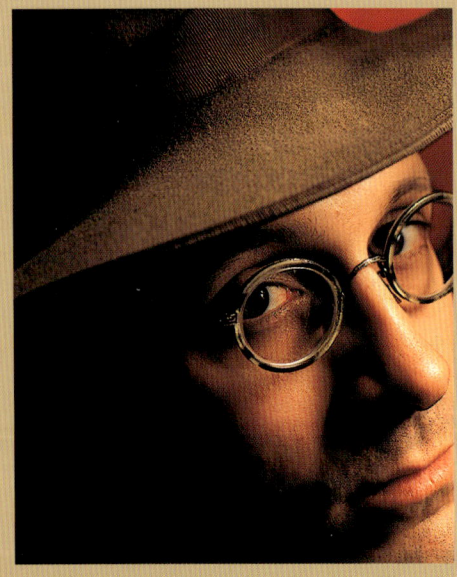

Gregory Heisler
Photographer
GREGORY HEISLER STUDIOS

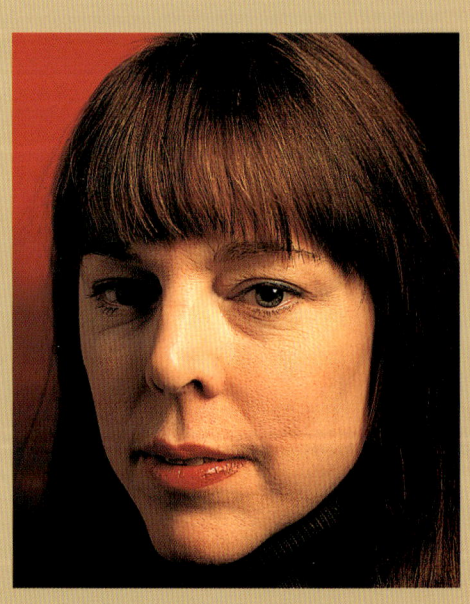

Phyllis Richmond Cox
Art Director
BRIDES & YOUR NEW HOME

HERB LUBALIN
AWARD WINNER

RUTH ANSEL

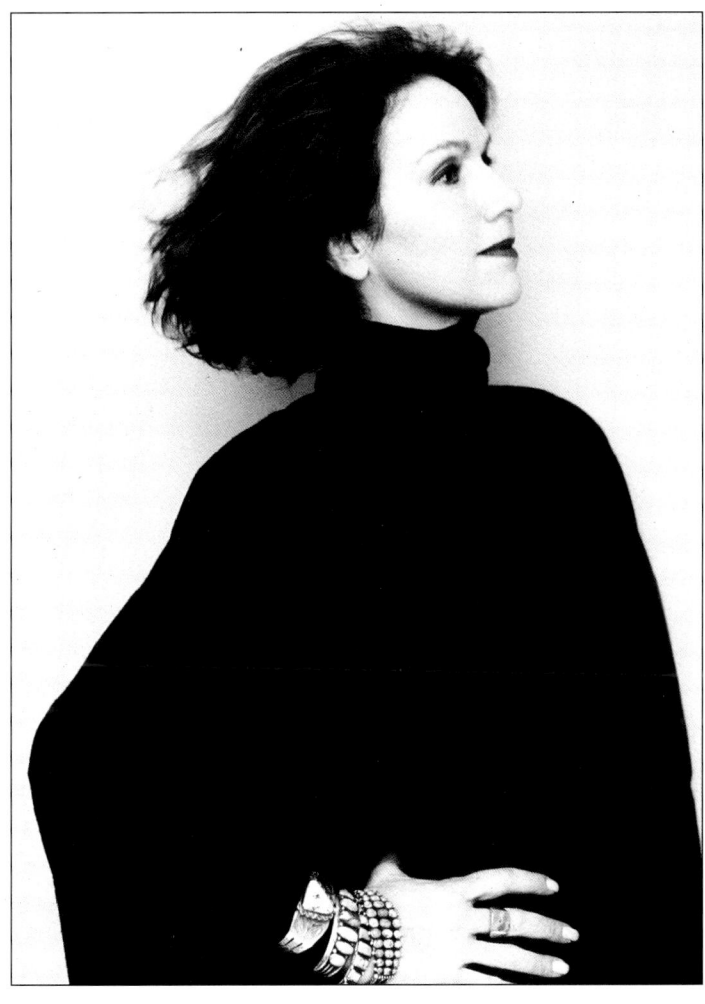

"As an Art Director, I try to have no preconceptions. I'm always looking for surprising yet accessible visual solutions that are just a little ahead of their time. Something that captures the essence of the clients message, while entertaining and informing the audience." RA

RUTH ANSEL'S UNIQUE EXPERIENCE IN PUBLICATION design started in 1962 at *Harper's Bazaar*. With Bea Feitler, she became part of a legendary young art directing team under Marvin Israel. She then joined *The New York Times* Sunday Magazine as Art Director and helped develop a new journalistic style for the 1970's. In 1982 she was appointed Editorial Design Director for Condé Nast's *House & Garden* and created a complete redesign of the magazine. A short time later, she was called upon to develop and conceive a fresh look for *Vanity Fair*. As Creative Director at Condé Nast with Alexander Liberman, she collaborated with him in the revamping of *Vogue*. She later returned to the newly named *HG* to help reshape and develop the original, updated design. In January 1992, Ruth Ansel was recruited by *Mirabella* to revitalize and update the magazine's cover and editorial layouts. As Consulting Creative Director, Ruth redesigned the covers, and instilled a new sophisticated energy to the magazine's image, creating bold new creative directions for the editorial layout.

Ruth designed fashion advertising campaigns for both Gucci with celebrated photographer Bruce Weber, and a highly innovative campaign for Karl Lagerfeld. Most recently, Ruth designed and art directed the Fall 1993 exclusive Carolyne Roehm catalogue, photographed by Oberto Gili.

Ruth's book designs include: *The Tiffany Touch* for Tiffany & Co.; Peter Beard's *The End of the Game;* and *The White Oak Dance Project*, Annie Leibovitz's photographic essay of Mikhail Baryshnikov's and Mark Morris collaborative dance performance. Ruth also joined with Annie Leibovitz in the unprecedented book entitled *A Demand Performance* for Design Industries Foundation for Aids (DIFFA). This venture brought together the greatest names in dance, music, theater and fashion who have collaborated and joined forces to show their commitment to solving the tragedy of Aids.

Ruth has created film titles for the movie *My Dinner with Andre*, directed by Louis Malle, museum posters and billboards for Richard Avedon and The International Center of Photography. She also designed the weekend section for *The Paris International Tribune* newspaper.

Ruth Ansel has received Gold and Silver Medals from the Art Directors Club in New York, awards of Merit and Distinction from the American Institute of Graphic Arts (AIGA), the Society of Illustrators, and the Society of Publication Designers (SPD). She has also judged at the Type Directors Club and SPD design competitions. Recently, Ruth was selected by the International Center of Photography (ICP) to be a judge for the 1994 10th Annual ICP Infinity Awards.

The Society of Publication Designers is proud to present her with their most prestigious award. ❖

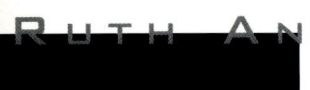

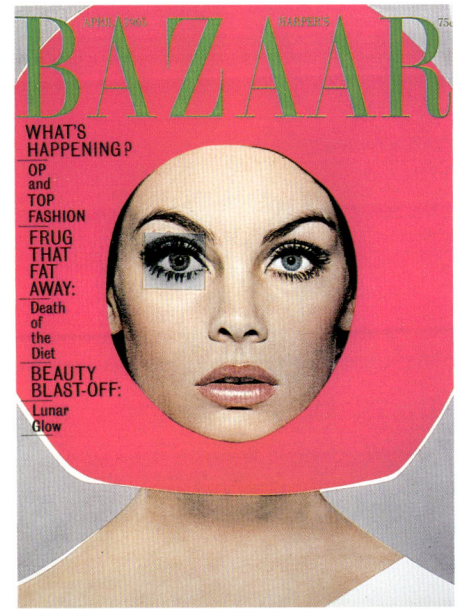

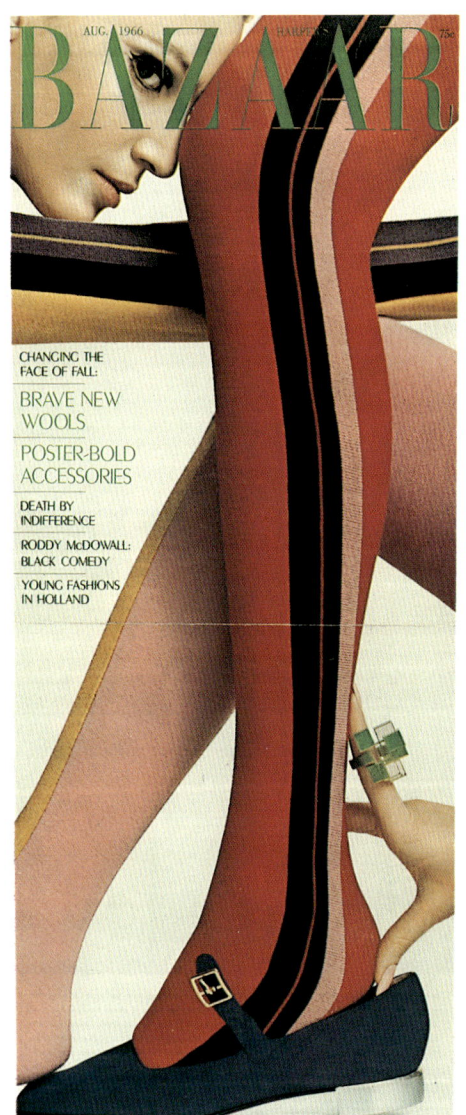

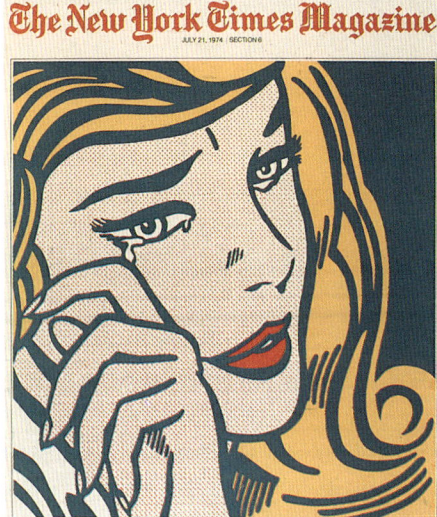

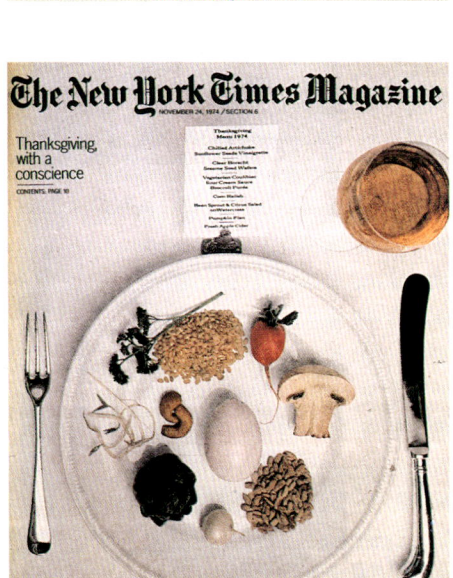

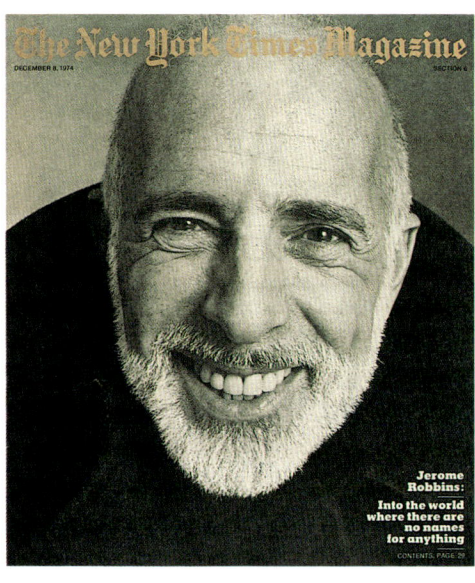

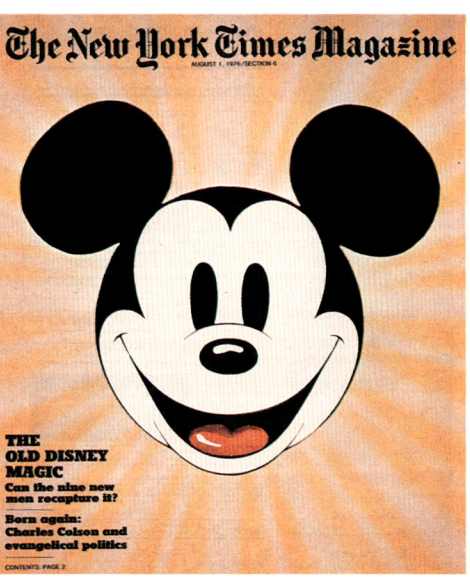

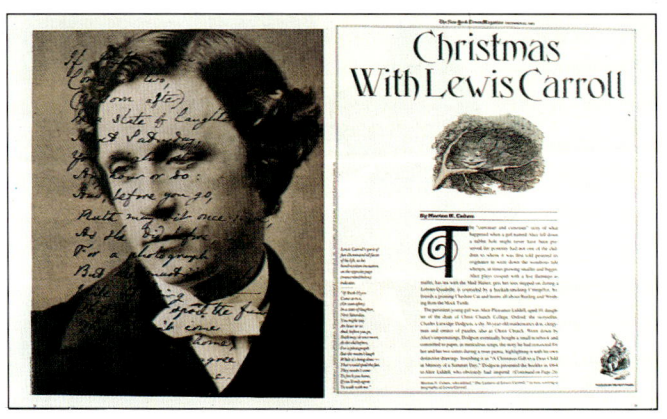

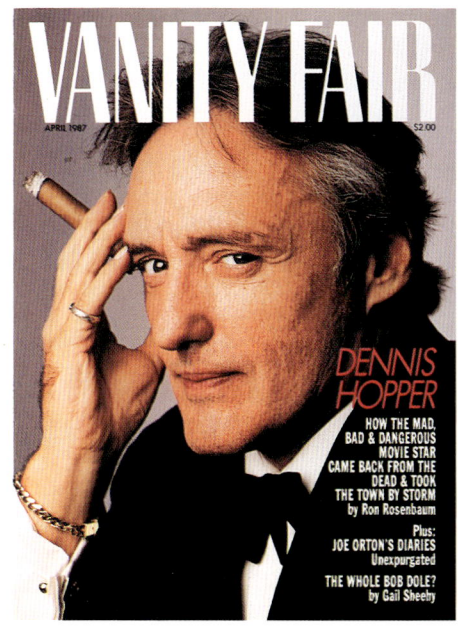

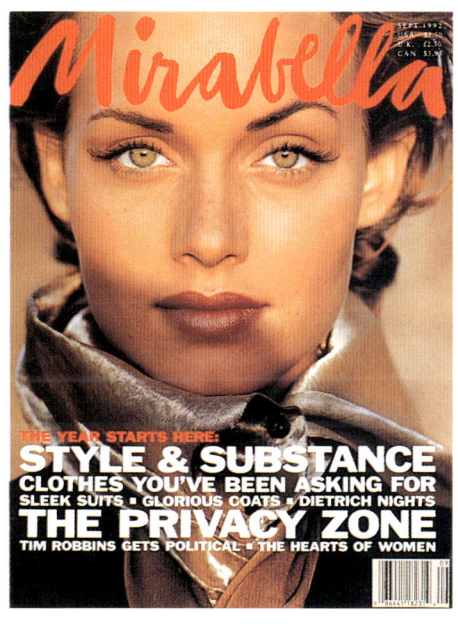

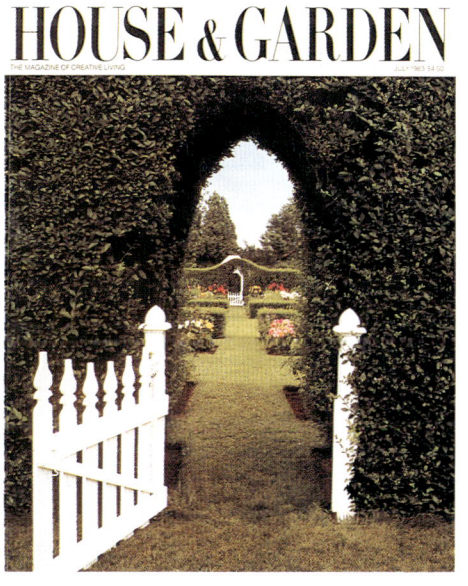

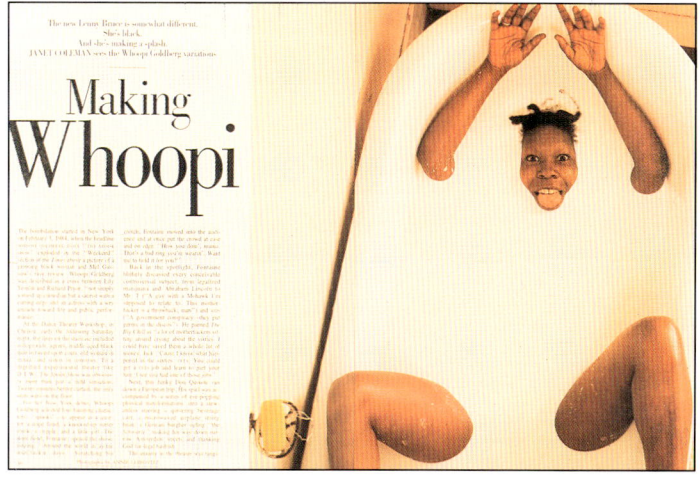

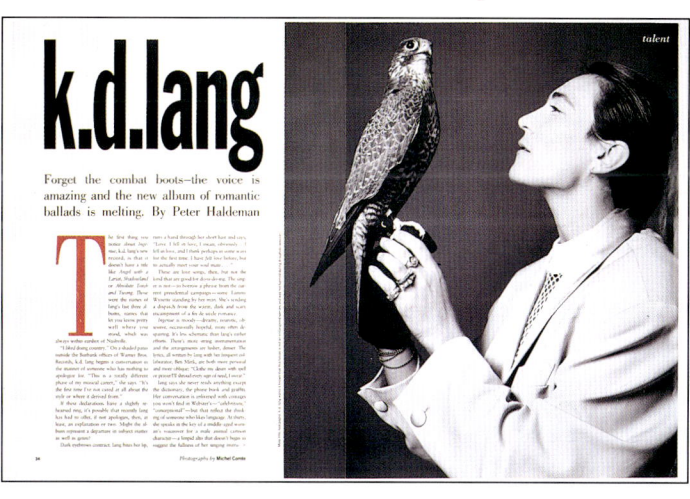

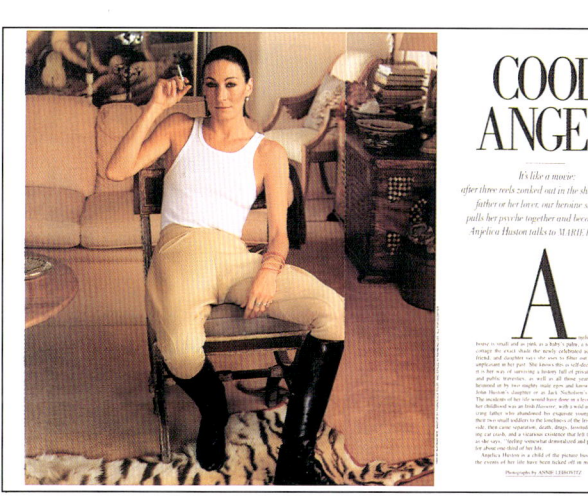

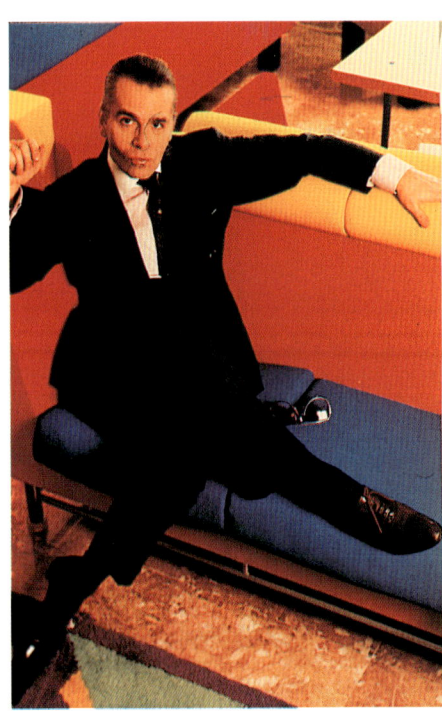

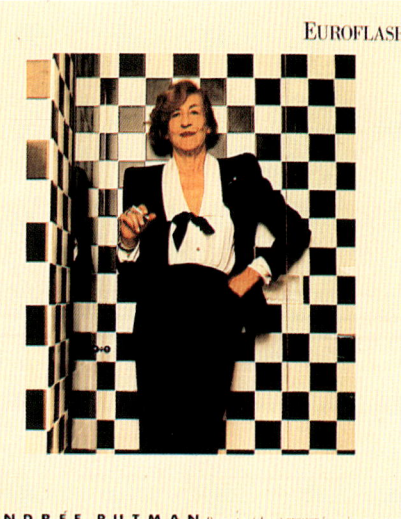

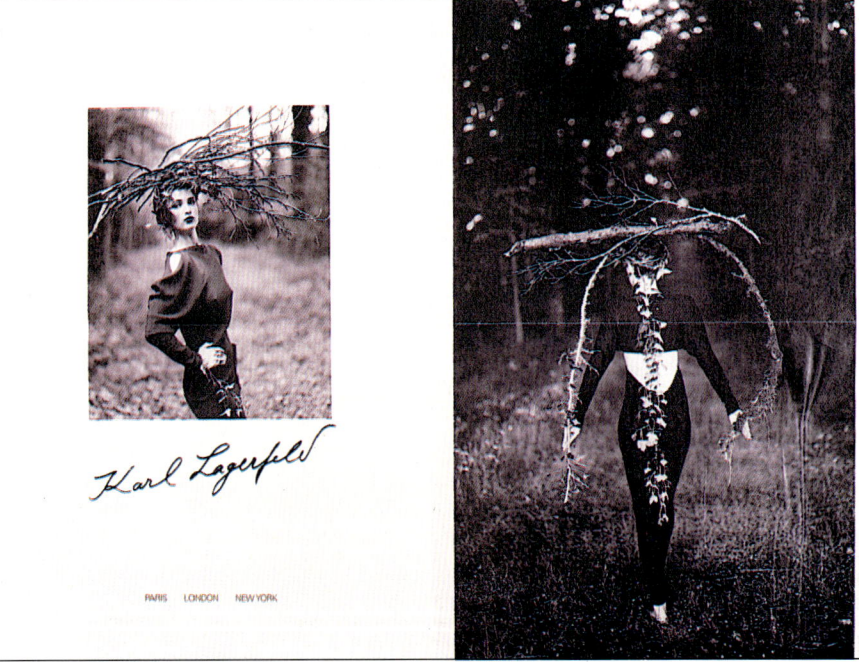

1962-71: Art Director with Bea Feitler, under Marvin Israel of *Harpers Bazaar.*

1972-74: Art Director on the Revlon Account at Scali, McCabe and Sloves, NYC.

1974-82: Art Director of the *New York Times Magazine.*

1981: Film Title Design for *My Dinner With Andre.*

1982-1983: Editorial Design Director of *House and Garden* Magazine.

1983-1987: Design Director of *Vanity Fair* Magazine.

1988-1989: Creative Director of *Vogue* Magazine.

1989-1991: Creative Director of *HG.*

1991: Established the Ruth Ansel Design Studio. Clients include; Gucci International Spring Collection, Fashion Advertising Campaign.

1992: Designed the following books: Avedon's *Alice in Wonderland; The Tiffany Touch;* Peter Beard's *The End of the Game; The White Oak Dance Project;* and DIFFA's *A Demand Performance.*

1993: Fall Fashion Catalogue for Carolyn Roehm; Judge for the Type Directors Club Design Competiton.

1994: Judge for the 10th Annual International Center of Photography Infinity Awards.

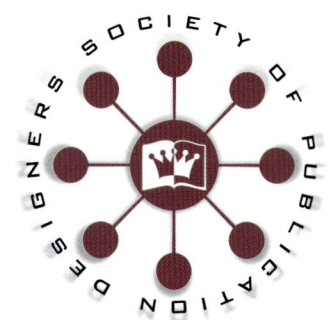

SOCIETY OF PUBLICATION DESIGNERS

COVERS
FRONT
PAGE

ANNUAL REPORTS

CONSUMER

CORPORATE

SUNDAY SUPPLEMENTS

TRADE

NEWSPAPERS

PUBLICATION Rolling Stone
AWARD Gold
ART DIRECTOR Fred Woodward
DESIGNER Fred Woodward
PHOTOGRAPHER Andrew MacPherson
PHOTO EDITOR Laurie Kratochvil
PUBLISHER Wenner Media
CATEGORY Cover
DATE March 4, 1993

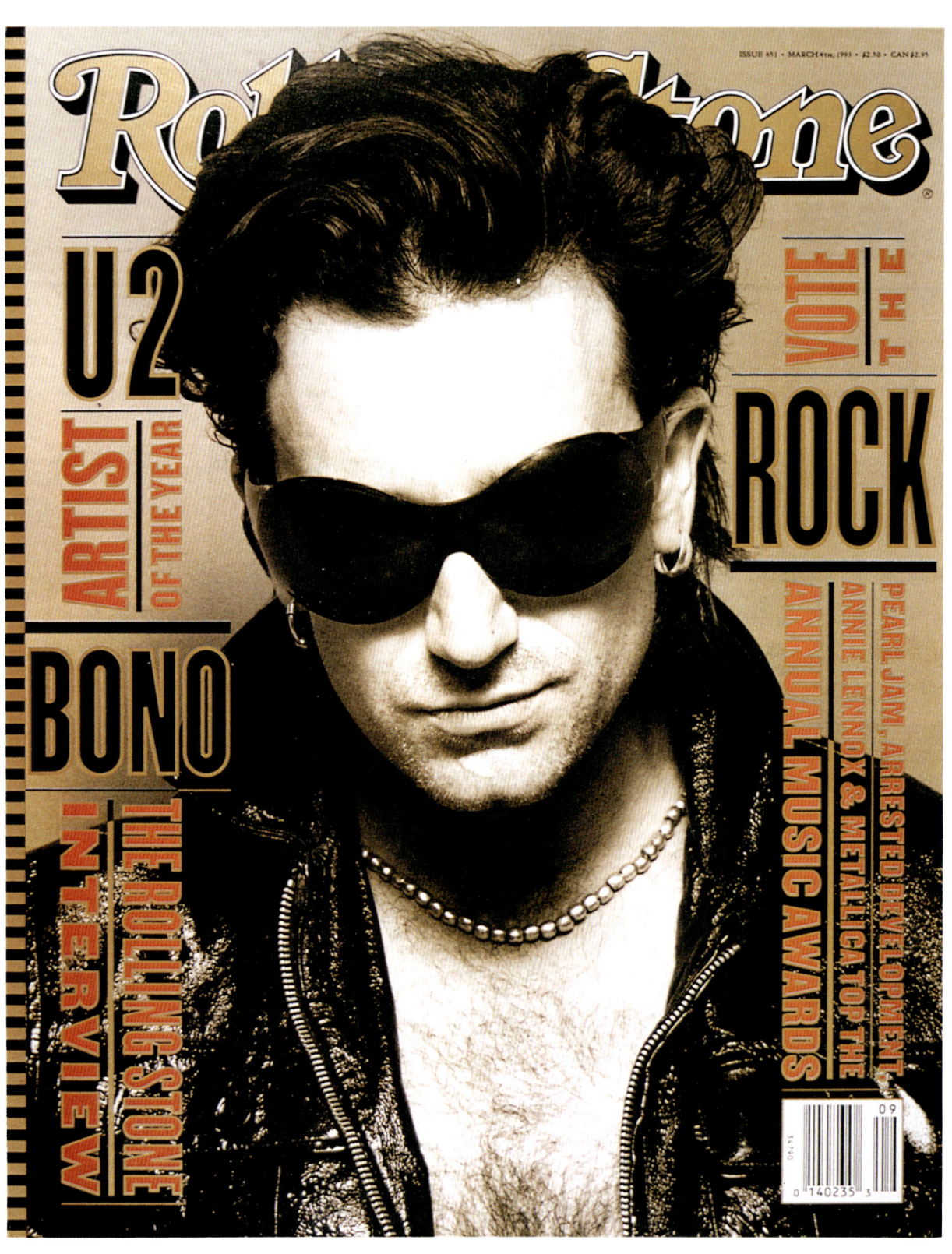

PUBLICATION	Rolling Stone
AWARD	Gold
ART DIRECTOR	Fred Woodward
DESIGNER	Fred Woodward
PHOTOGRAPHER	Patrick Demarchelier
PHOTO EDITOR	Laurie Kratochvil
PUBLISHER	Wenner Media
CATEGORY	Cover
DATE	September 16, 1993

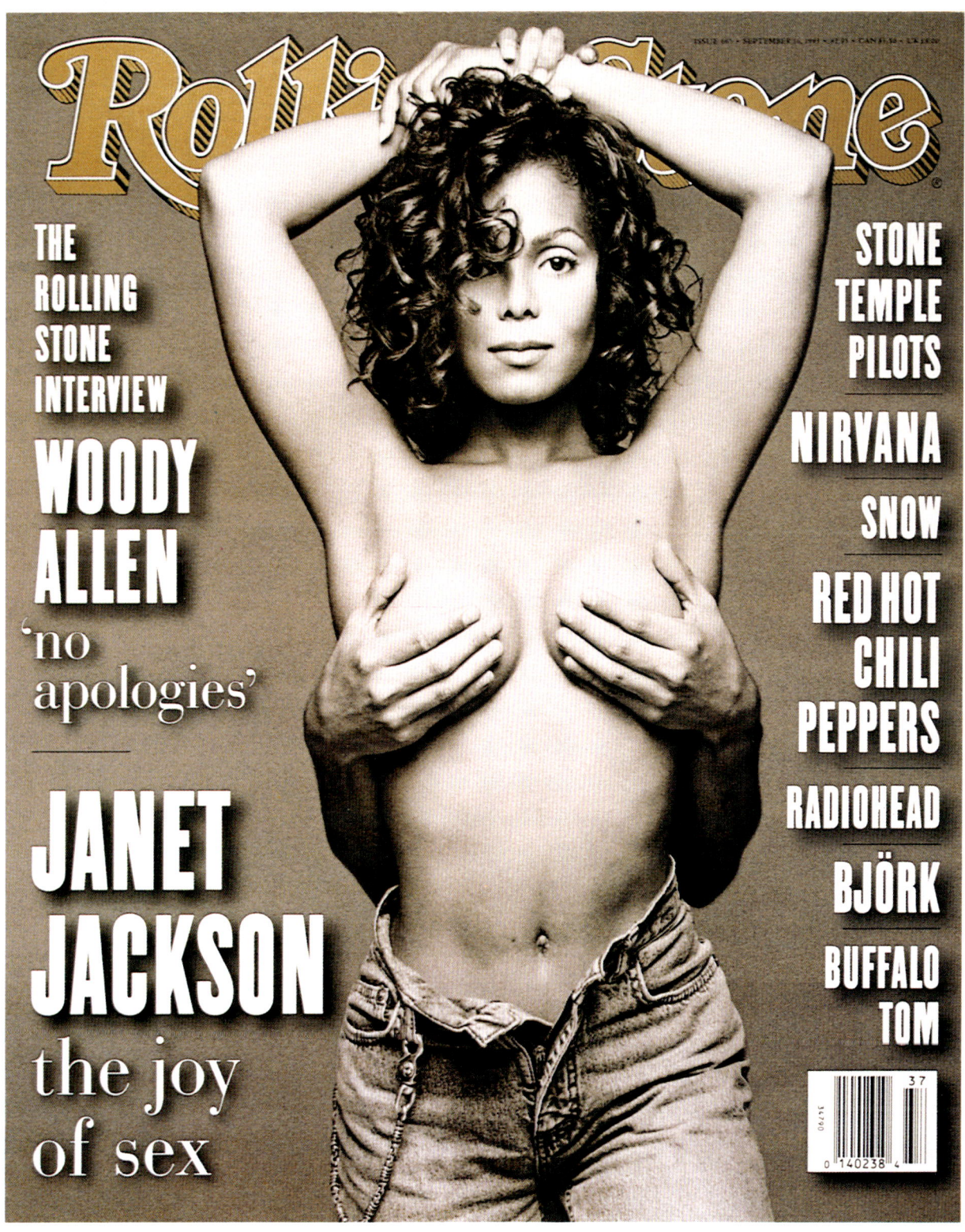

PUBLICATION   Travel & Leisure
AWARD   Gold
DESIGN DIRECTOR   Lloyd Ziff
DESIGNER   Lloyd Ziff
PHOTOGRAPHER   Philip Quirk
PHOTO EDITOR   Hazel Hammond
PUBLISHER   American Express Publishing
CATEGORY   Cover
DATE   March 1993

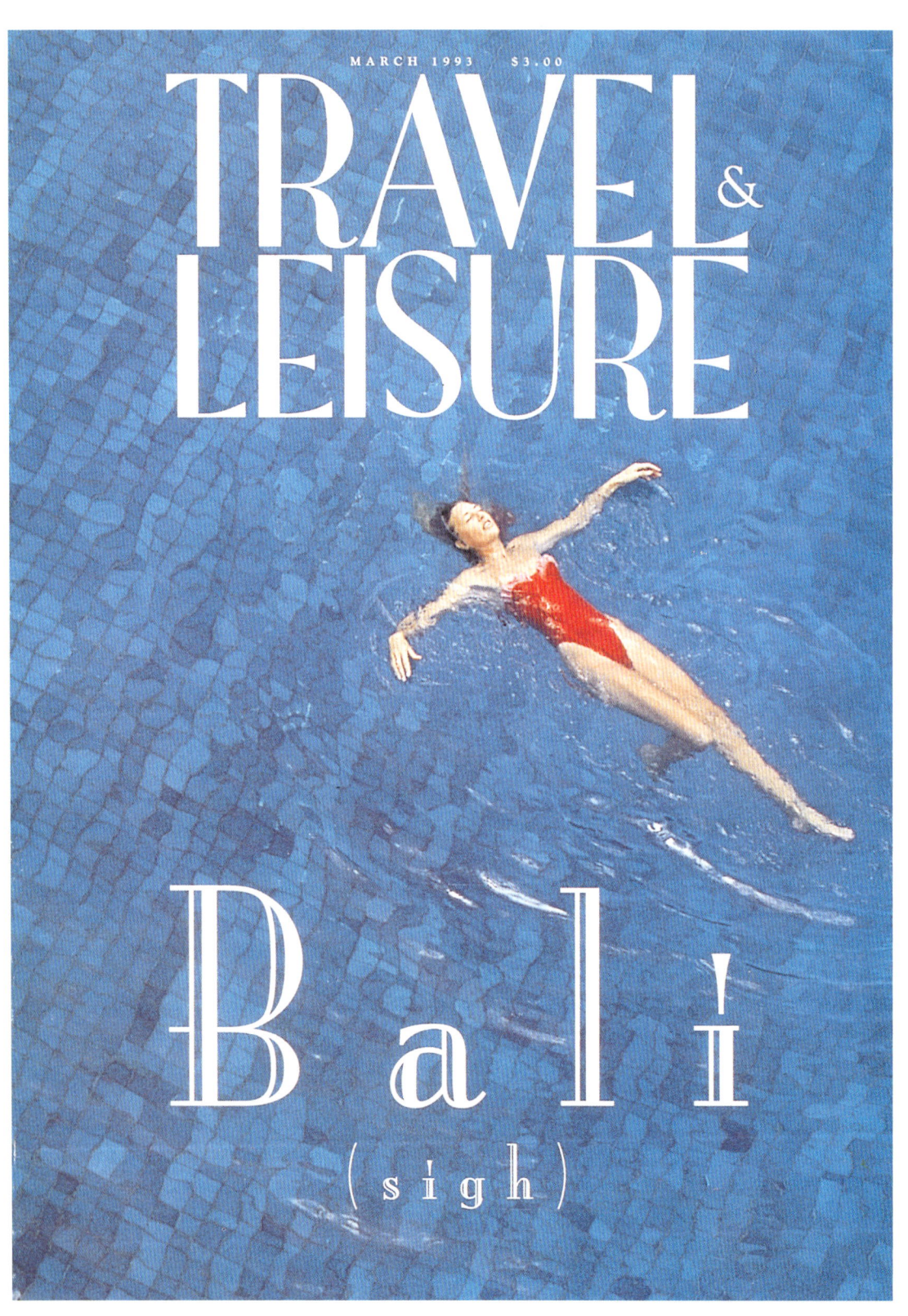

MARCH 1993 $3.00

TRAVEL & LEISURE

Bali
(sigh)

PUBLICATION	Vibe
AWARD	Gold
DESIGN DIRECTOR	Gary Koepke
ART DIRECTOR	Richard Baker
DESIGNER	Gary Koepke
PHOTOGRAPHER	Dan Winters
PHOTO EDITOR	George Pitts
PUBLISHER	Time Inc. Ventures
STUDIO	Koepke International Ltd.
CATEGORY	Cover
DATE	October 1993

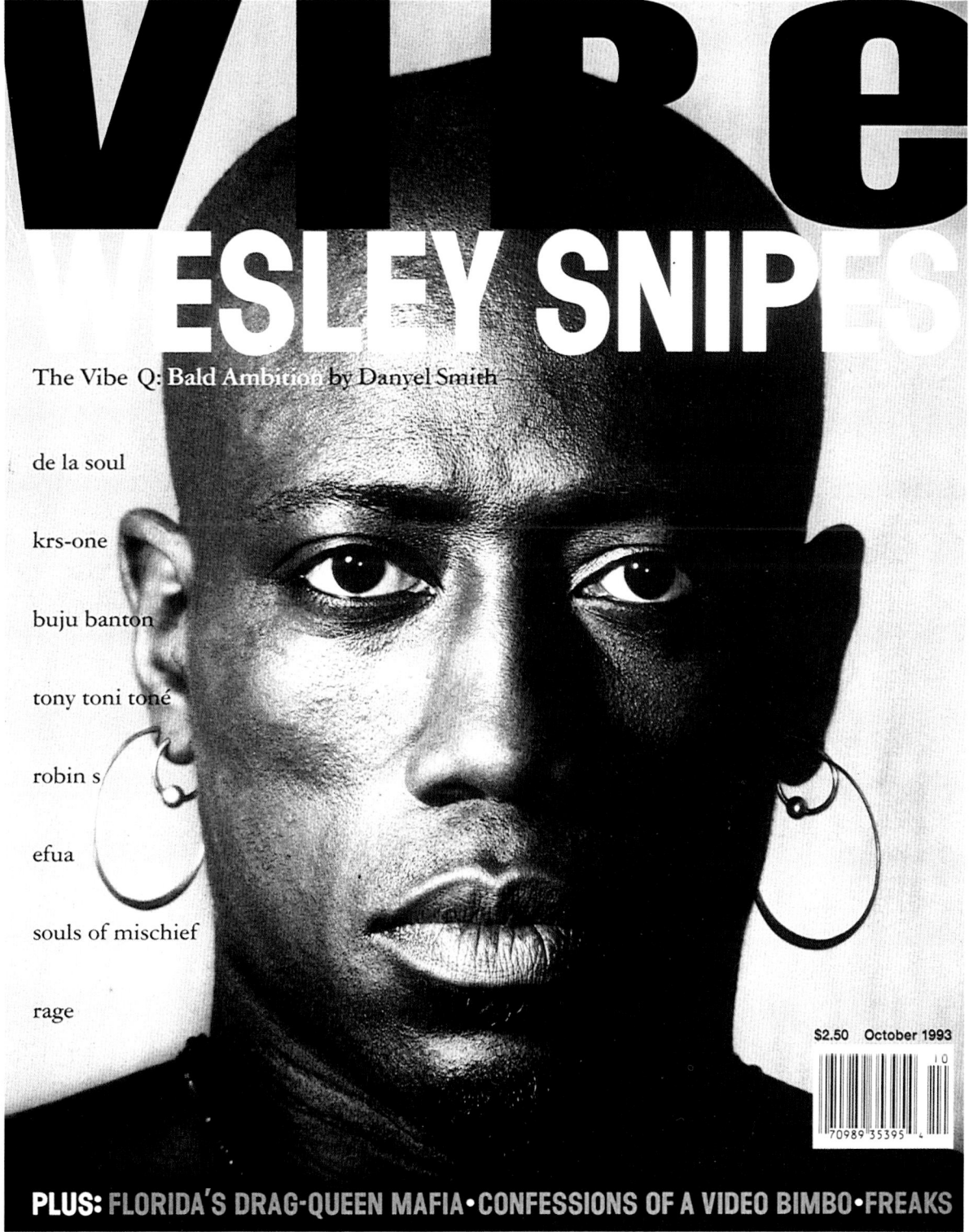

VIBe

WESLEY SNIPES

The Vibe Q: Bald Ambition by Danyel Smith

de la soul

krs-one

buju banton

tony toni toné

robin s

efua

souls of mischief

rage

$2.50   October 1993

70989 35395

PLUS: FLORIDA'S DRAG-QUEEN MAFIA•CONFESSIONS OF A VIDEO BIMBO•FREAKS

PUBLICATION	Entertainment Weekly
AWARD	Silver
DESIGN DIRECTOR	Michael Grossman
ART DIRECTOR	Mark Michaelson
DESIGNER	Michael Grossman
PHOTOGRAPHER	Alastair Train
PHOTO EDITORS	Mary Dunn, Doris Brautigan
PUBLISHER	Time Inc.
CATEGORY	Cover
DATE	January 8, 1993

PUBLICATION	Entertainment Weekly
AWARD	Silver
DESIGN DIRECTOR	Michael Grossman
ART DIRECTOR	Mark Michaelson
DESIGNER	Mark Michaelson
PHOTOGRAPHER	Jeffrey Thurnher
PHOTO EDITORS	Mary Dunn, Doris Brautigan
PUBLISHER	Time Inc.
CATEGORY	Cover
DATE	August 20, 1993

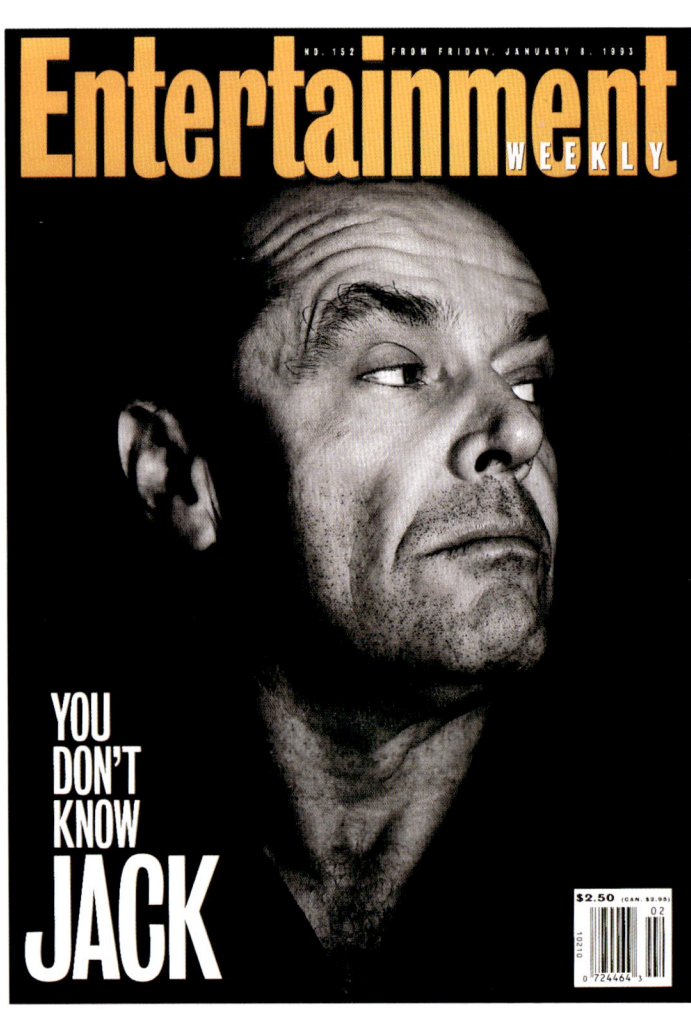

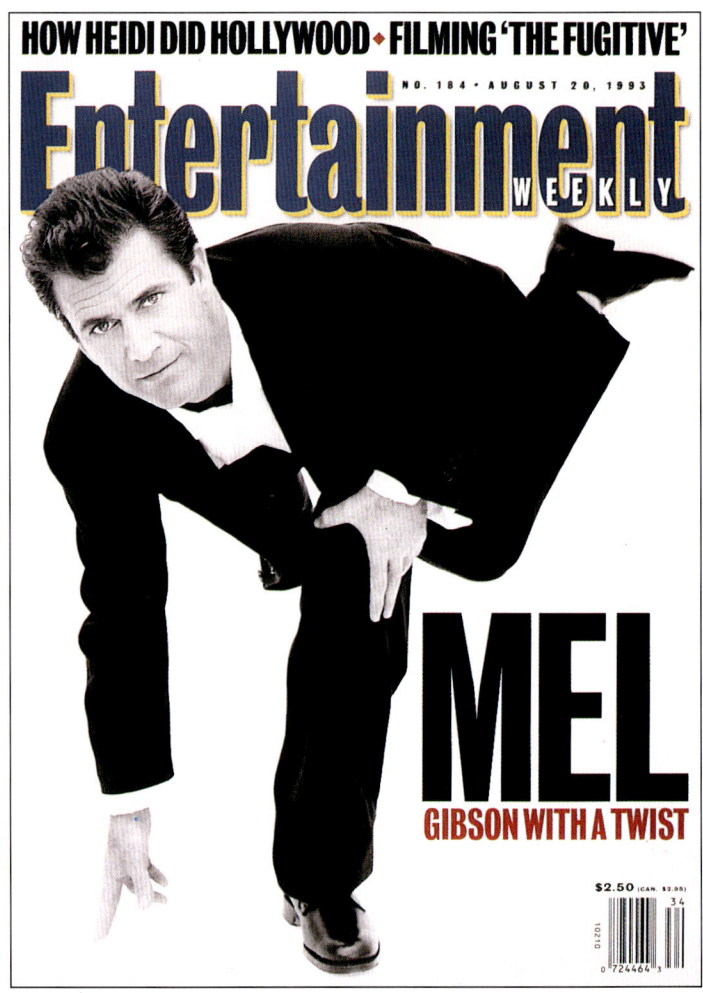

PUBLICATION	American Photo
AWARD	Silver
ART DIRECTOR	Mark Gartland
DESIGNER	Patricia Marroquin
PHOTOGRAPHER	Helmut Newton
PUBLISHER	Hachette Filipacchi Magazines, Inc.
CATEGORY	Cover
DATE	November/December 1993

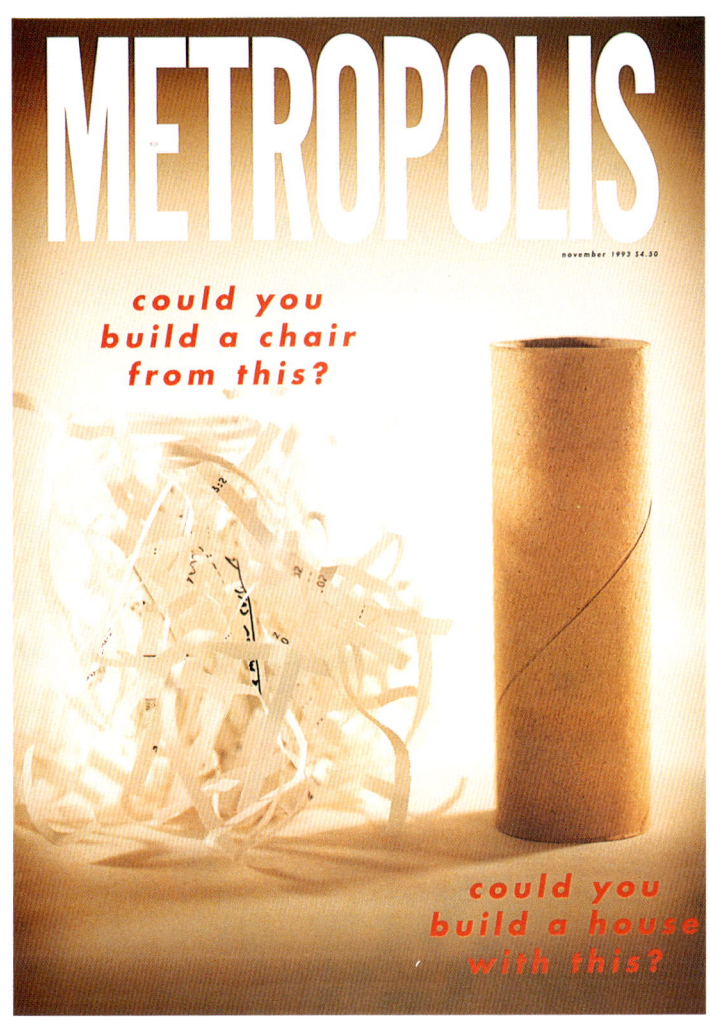

PUBLICATION   Metropolis
AWARD   Silver
ART DIRECTORS   Carl Lehmann-Haupt, Nancy Cohen
DESIGNERS   Carl Lehmann-Haupt, Nancy Cohen
PHOTOGRAPHER   Ilisa Katz
PUBLISHER   Bellerophon Publications
CATEGORY   Cover
DATE   November 1993

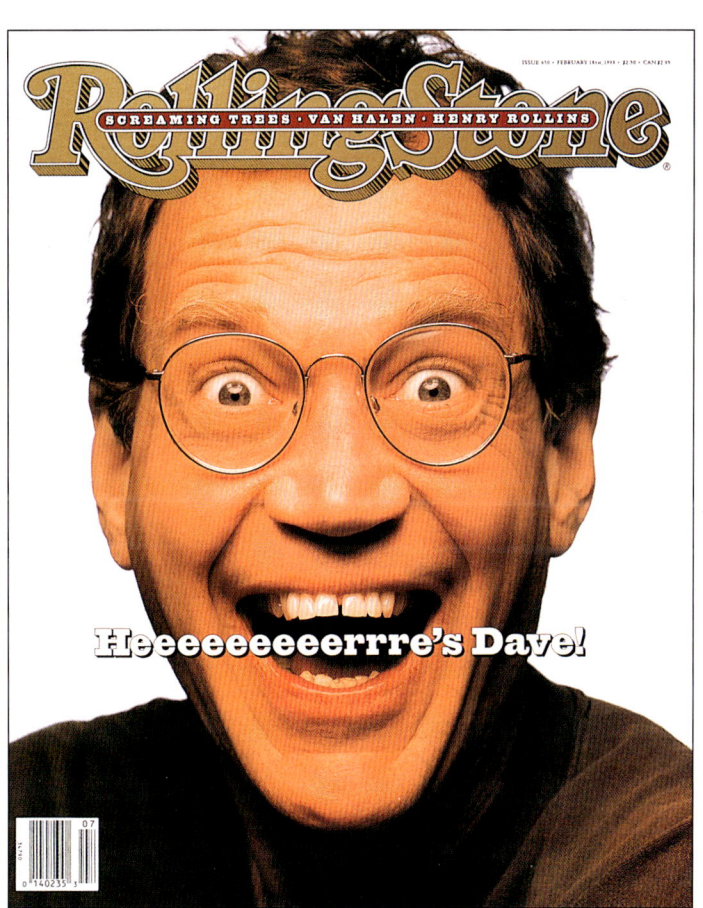

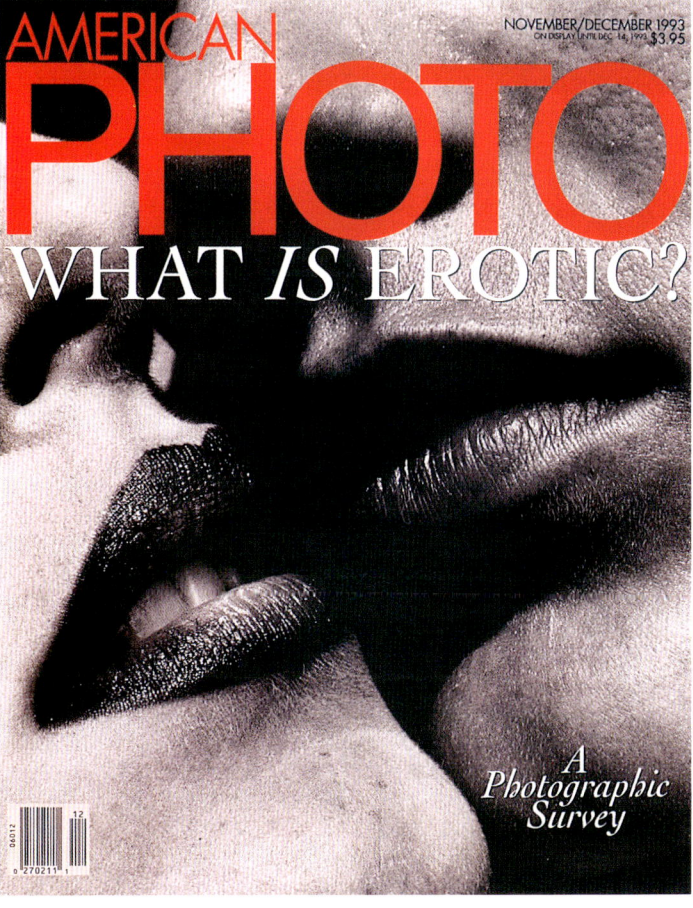

PUBLICATION   Rolling Stone
AWARD   Silver
ART DIRECTOR   Fred Woodward
DESIGNER   Fred Woodward
PHOTOGRAPHER   Mark Seliger
PHOTO EDITOR   Laurie Kratochvil
PUBLISHER   Wenner Media
CATEGORY   Cover
DATE   February 18, 1993

PUBLICATION   Anchorage Daily News - Impulse
AWARD   Silver
ART DIRECTOR   Galie Jean-Louis
DESIGNER   Galie Jean-Louis
ILLUSTRATOR   Amy Guip
PHOTOGRAPHERS   Frank Ockenfels 3, The Douglas Brothers
PUBLISHER   Anchorage Daily News
CATEGORY   Newspapers/Front Page
DATE   Dec. 4, '93/April 10, '93/Nov. 27, '93/Dec. 11, '93

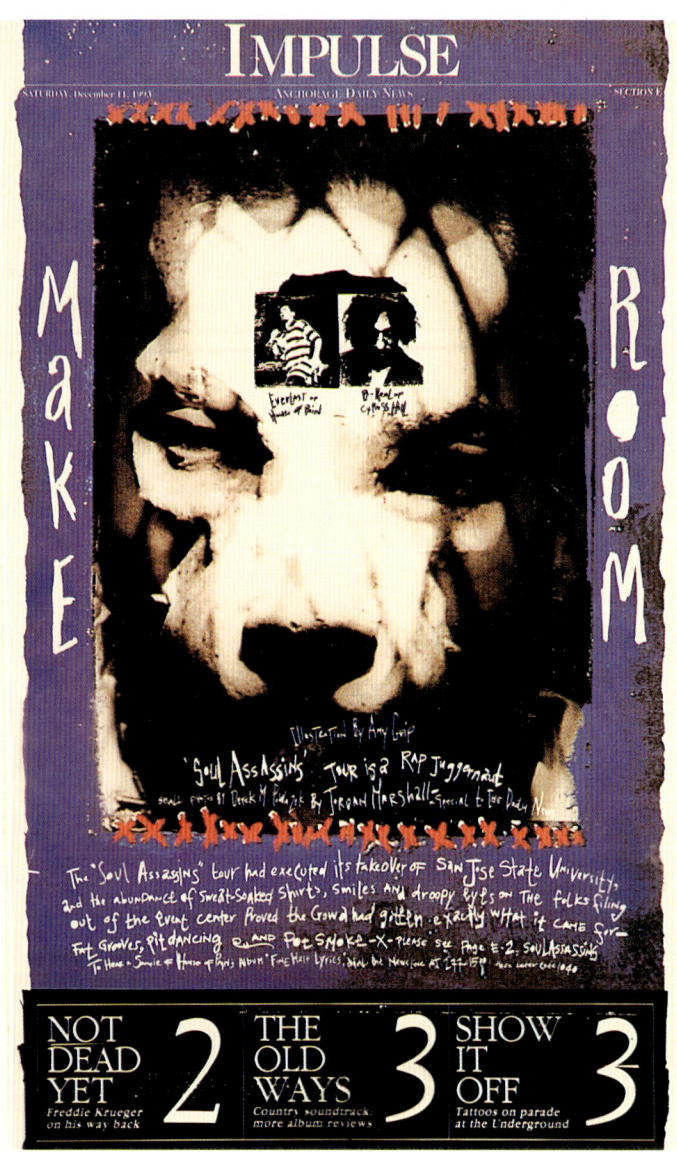

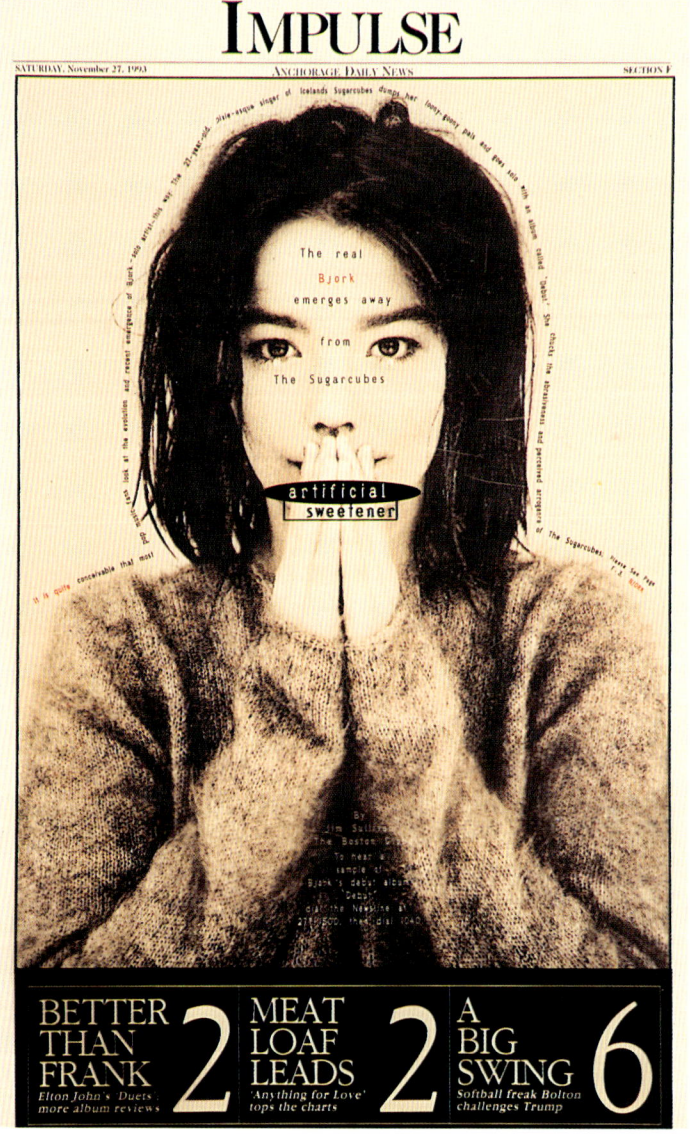

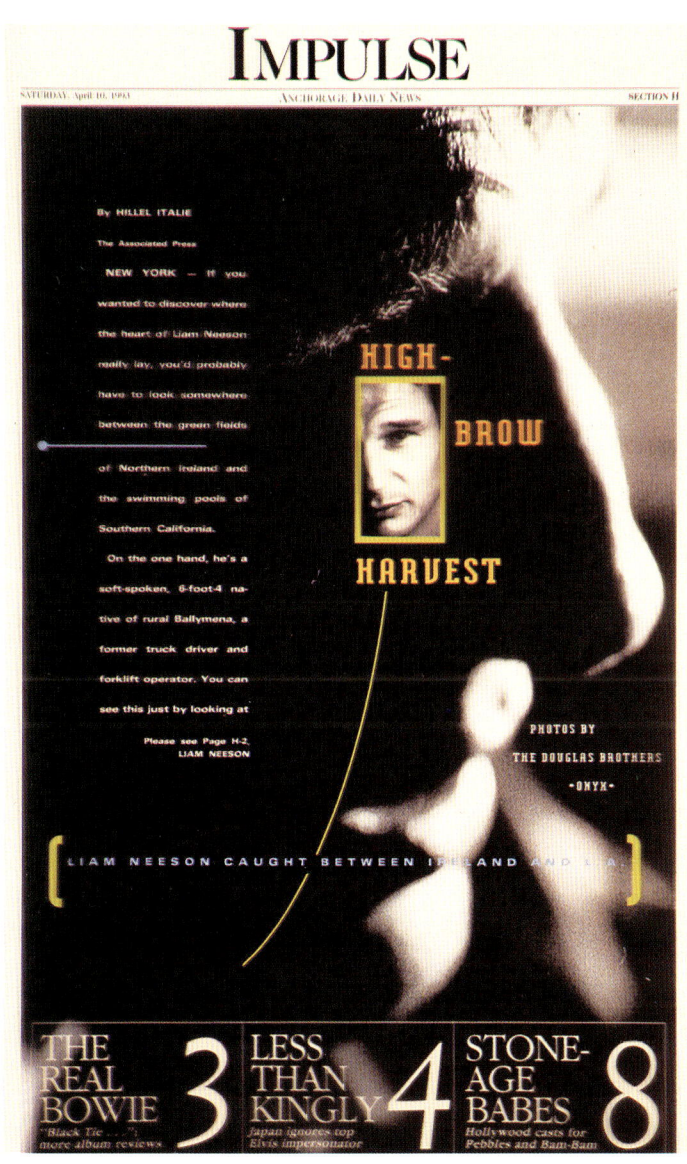

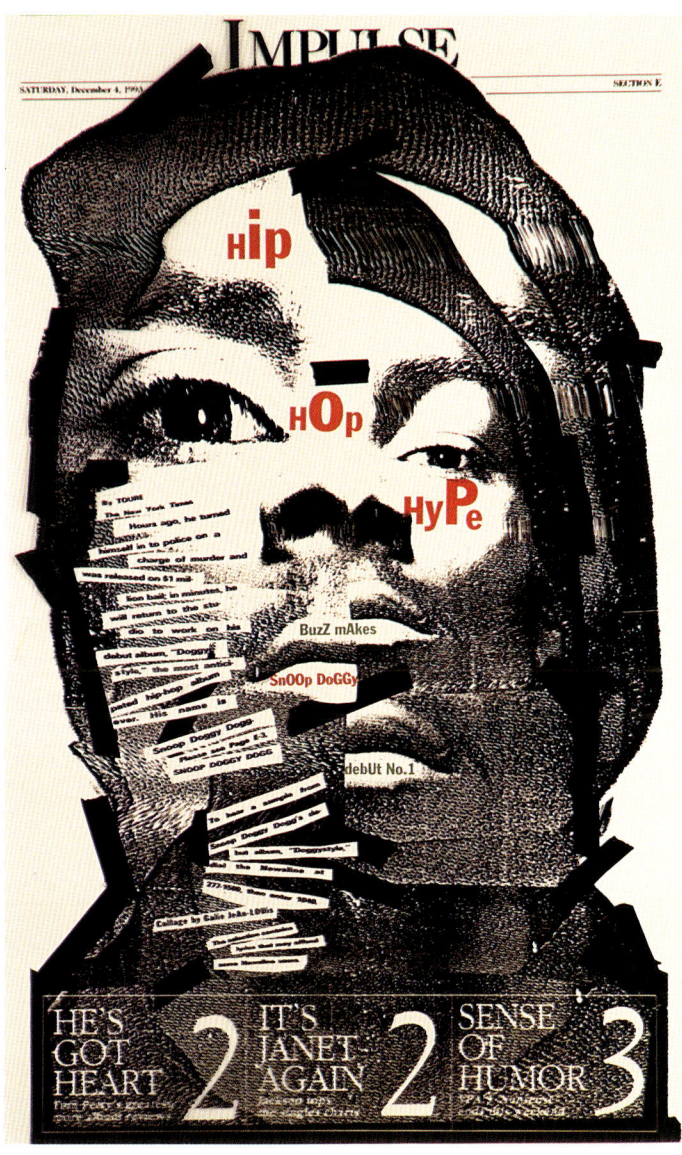

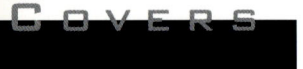

PUBLICATION Invention & Technology
AWARD Merit
ART DIRECTOR Peter Morance
DESIGNER Peter Morance
PHOTOGRAPHER National Archives
PHOTO EDITOR Jane Colihan
PUBLISHER American Heritage
CATEGORY Cover
DATE Summer 1993

PUBLICATION Condé Nast Traveler
AWARD Merit
DESIGN DIRECTOR Diana LaGuardia
ART DIRECTOR Christin Gangi
DESIGNER Rockwell Harwood
PHOTOGRAPHER Macduff Everton
PHOTO EDITOR Kathleen Klech
PUBLISHER The Condé Nast Publications Inc.
CATEGORY Cover
DATE September 1993

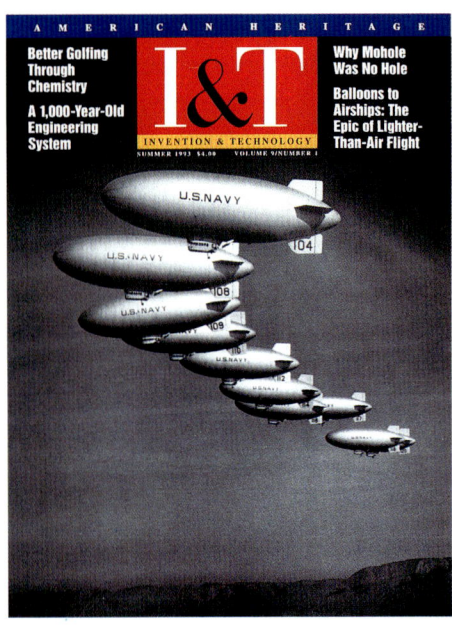

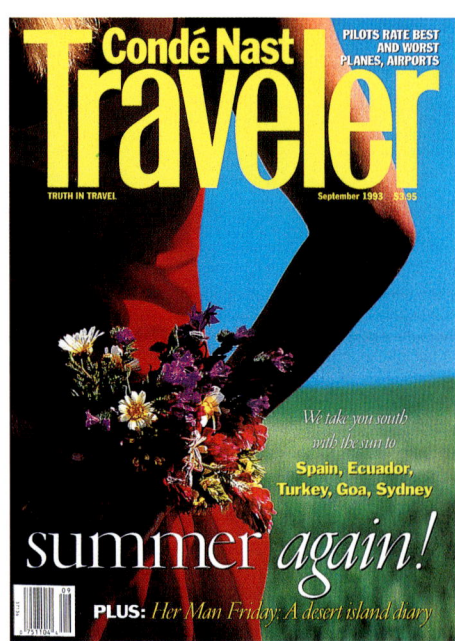

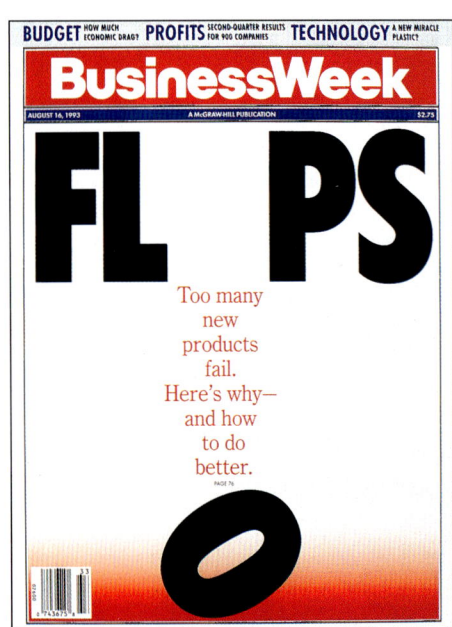

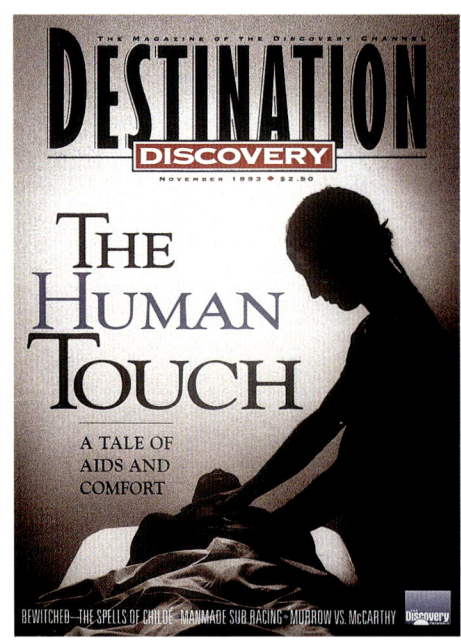

PUBLICATION Business Week
AWARD Merit
ART DIRECTOR Malcolm Frouman
DESIGNER Cynthia Friedman
PUBLISHER McGraw-Hill Publications
CATEGORY Cover
DATE August 16, 1993

PUBLICATION Destination Discovery
AWARD Merit
ART DIRECTOR John Lyle Sanford
PHOTOGRAPHER Richard Robinson
PUBLISHER Discovery Communications Inc.
CATEGORY Cover
DATE November 1993

PUBLICATION	Departures
AWARD	Merit
ART DIRECTOR	Bernard Scharf
PHOTOGRAPHER	Chris Rainier
PUBLISHER	American Express Publishing
CATEGORY	Cover
DATE	February/March 1993

PUBLICATION	Fast Company
AWARD	Merit
DESIGN DIRECTORS	John Schmitz, Roger Black
ILLUSTRATOR	Jim McMullan
PUBLISHER	Fast Company Ltd., Partnership
STUDIO	Roger Black, Inc.
CATEGORY	Cover
DATE	November 1993

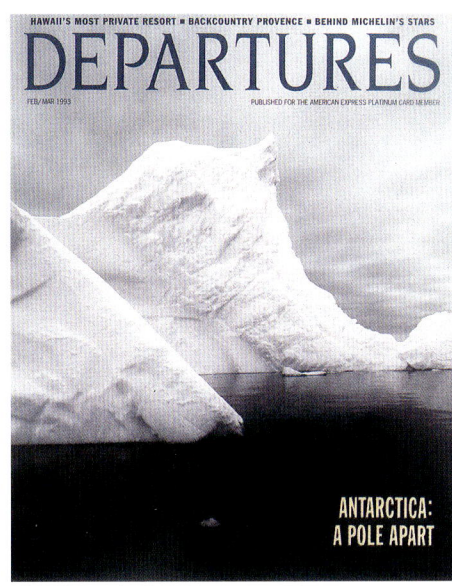

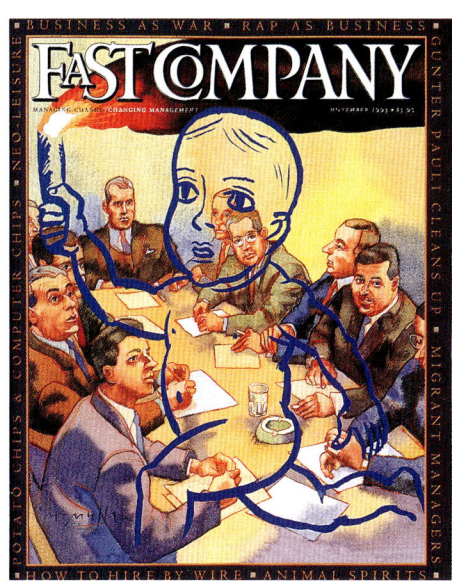

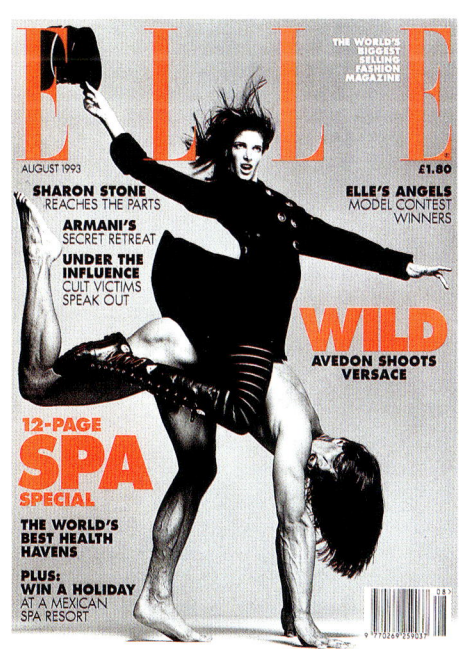

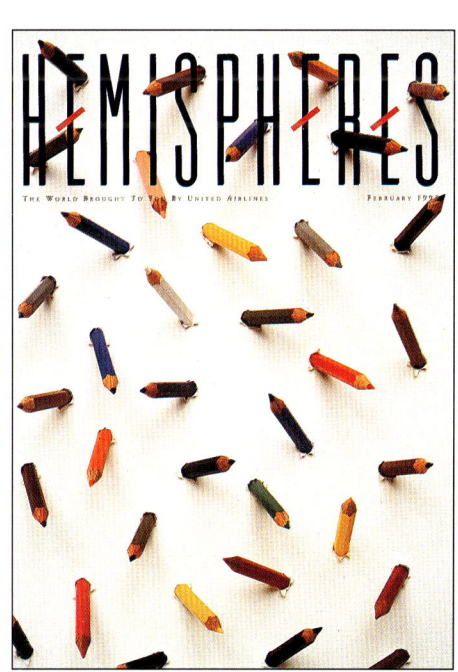

PUBLICATION	British Elle
AWARD	Merit
DESIGN DIRECTOR	Cath Caldwell
DESIGNER	Cath Caldwell
PHOTOGRAPHER	Richard Avedon
PHOTO EDITOR	June Stanier
PUBLISHER	Hachette/EMAP (UK)
CATEGORY	Cover
DATE	August 1993

PUBLICATION	Hemispheres
AWARD	Merit
ART DIRECTORS	Jaimey Easler, Greg Hausler
ILLUSTRATOR	Pierre Mendell
PUBLISHER	Pace Communications
CATEGORY	Cover
DATE	February 1993

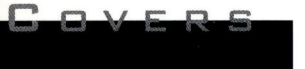

PUBLICATION	Life
AWARD	Merit
DESIGN DIRECTOR	Tom Bentkowski
ART DIRECTOR	Nora Sheehan
DESIGNER	Nora Sheehan
PHOTOGRAPHER	William Albert Allard
PUBLISHER	Time Inc.
CATEGORY	Cover
DATE	April 5, 1993

PUBLICATION	Men's Journal
AWARD	Merit
DESIGN DIRECTOR	Matthew Drace
DESIGNER	Matthew Drace
PHOTOGRAPHER	George H.H. Huey
PUBLISHER	Wenner Media
CATEGORY	Cover
DATE	May/June 1993

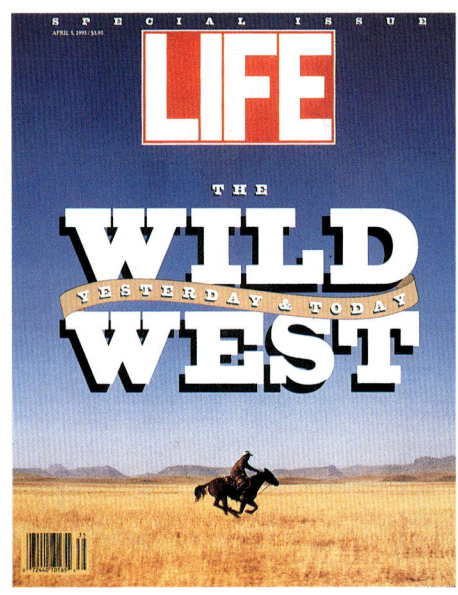

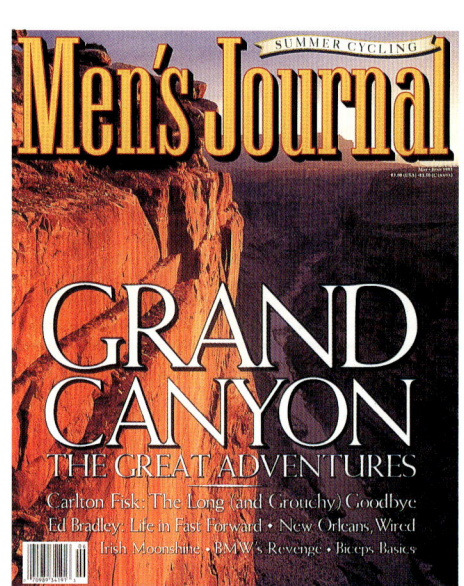

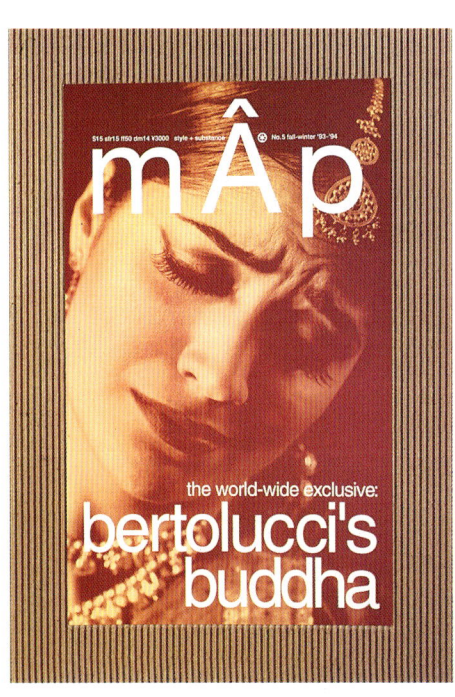

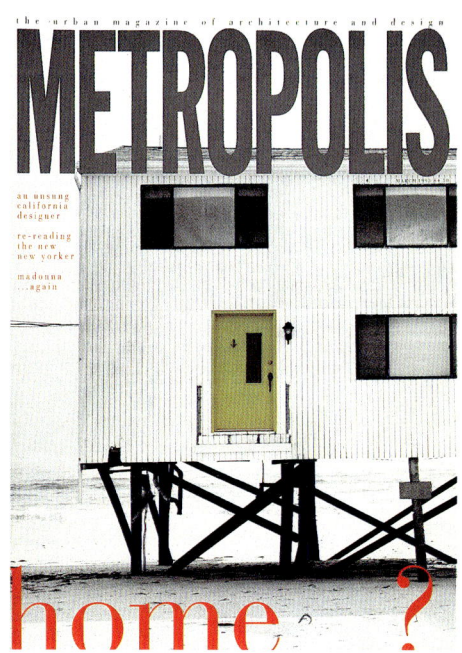

PUBLICATION	Mâp
AWARD	Merit
DESIGN DIRECTOR	Robert Bergman-Ungar
DESIGNER	Guan Liong The
PHOTOGRAPHER	David Seidner
PUBLISHER	Mâp Publications Inc.
CATEGORY	Cover
DATE	December 12, 1993

PUBLICATION	Metropolis
AWARD	Merit
ART DIRECTORS	Carl Lehmann-Haupt, Nancy Cohen
DESIGNERS	Carl Lehmann-Haupt, Nancy Cohen
PHOTOGRAPHER	Mara Kurtz
PUBLISHER	Bellerophon Publications, Inc.
CATEGORY	Cover
DATE	March 1993

PUBLICATION	Metropolis
AWARD	Merit
ART DIRECTORS	Carl Lehmann-Haupt, Nancy Cohen
DESIGNERS	Carl Lehmann-Haupt, Nancy Cohen
PHOTOGRAPHER	Kristine Larsen
PUBLISHER	Bellerophon Publications, Inc.
CATEGORY	Cover
DATE	September 1993

PUBLICATION	Newsweek
AWARD	Merit
ART DIRECTORS	Patricia Bradbury, Peter Comitini
DESIGNER	Mark Inglis
PHOTOGRAPHER	U.S. Navy/Underwood Photo
PUBLISHER	Newsweek, Inc.
CATEGORY	Cover
DATE	January 11, 1993

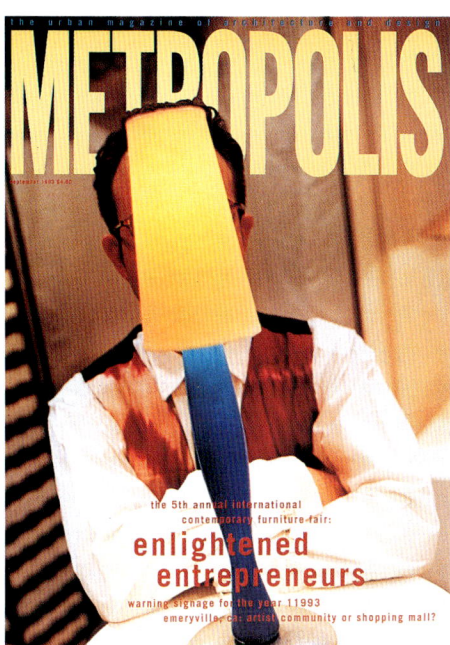

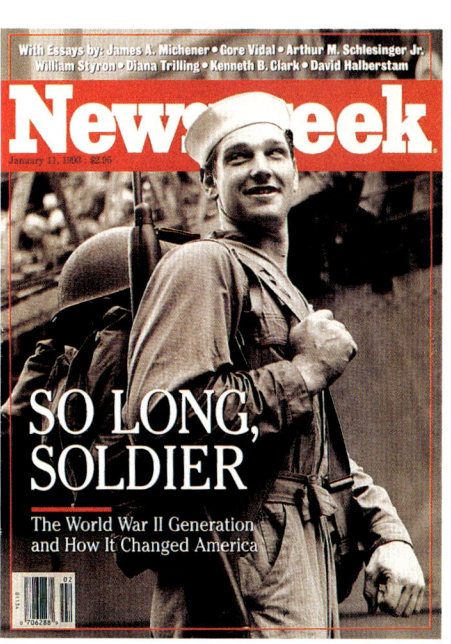

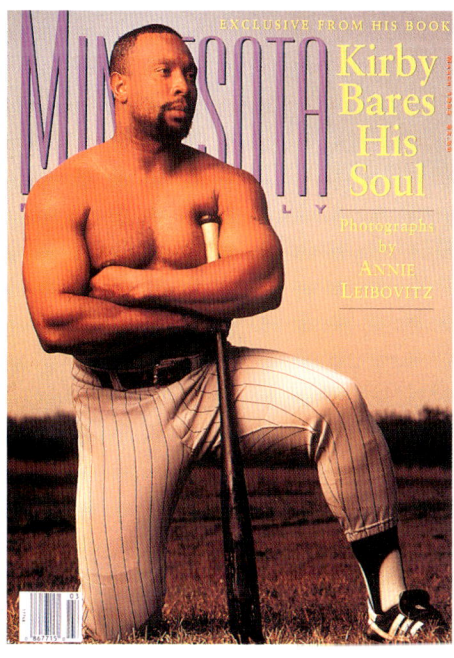

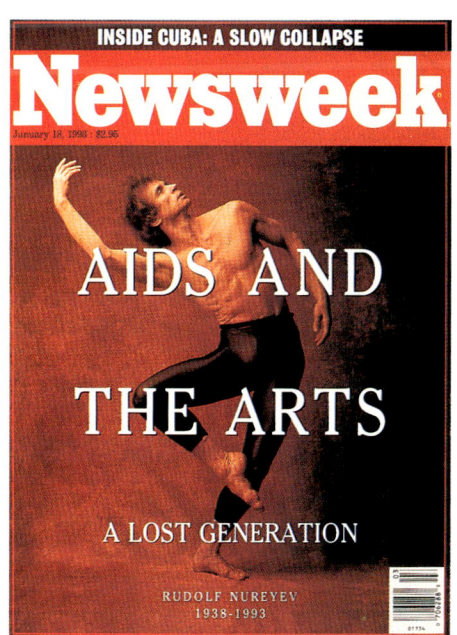

PUBLICATION	Minnesota Monthly
AWARD	Merit
ART DIRECTOR	Mark Shafer
DESIGNERS	Mark Shafer, Brian Donahue
PHOTOGRAPHER	Annie Leibovitz
PUBLISHER	Minnesota Monthly Publications
CATEGORY	Cover
DATE	March 1993

PUBLICATION	Newsweek
AWARD	Merit
ART DIRECTORS	Patricia Bradbury, Peter Comitini
DESIGNER	Mark Inglis
PHOTOGRAPHER	Snowdon/Camera Press/Globe
PUBLISHER	Newsweek, Inc.
CATEGORY	Cover
DATE	January 18, 1993

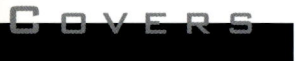

PUBLICATION   Rolling Stone
AWARD   Merit
ART DIRECTOR   Fred Woodward
DESIGNER   Fred Woodward
PHOTOGRAPHER   Albert Watson
PHOTO EDITOR   Laurie Kratochvil
PUBLISHER   Wenner Media
CATEGORY   Cover
DATE   April 29, 1993

PUBLICATION   Rolling Stone
AWARD   Merit
ART DIRECTOR   Fred Woodward
DESIGNER   Fred Woodward
PHOTOGRAPHER   Mark Seliger
PHOTO EDITOR   Laurie Kratochvil
PUBLISHER   Wenner Media
CATEGORY   Cover
DATE   May 13, 1993

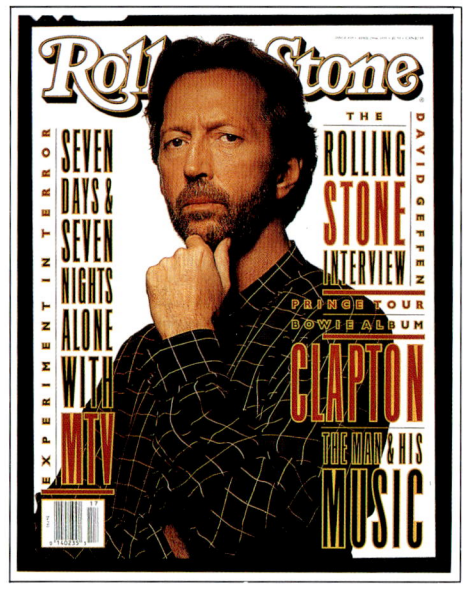

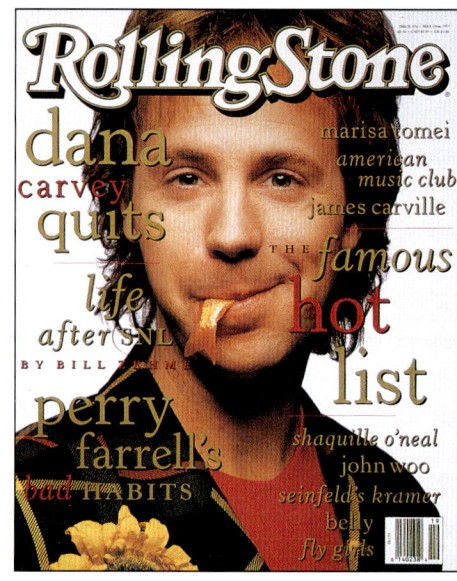

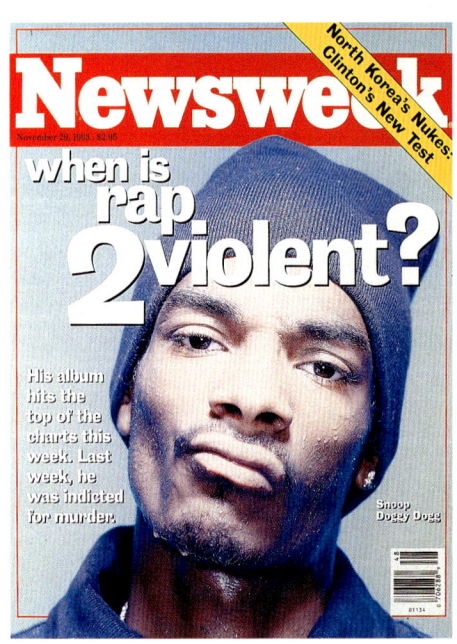

PUBLICATION   Newsweek
AWARD   Merit
ART DIRECTORS   Patricia Bradbury, Peter Comitini
PHOTOGRAPHER   Dan Winters
PUBLISHER   Newsweek, Inc.
CATEGORY   Cover
DATE   November 29, 1993

PUBLICATION   Rolling Stone
AWARD   Merit
ART DIRECTOR   Fred Woodward
DESIGNER   Fred Woodward
PHOTOGRAPHER   Mark Seliger
PHOTO EDITOR   Laurie Kratochvil
PUBLISHER   Wenner Media
CATEGORY   Cover
DATE   July 8-22, 1993

PUBLICATION San Francisco Focus
AWARD Merit
ART DIRECTOR Mark Ulriksen
DESIGNER Mark Ulriksen
PHOTOGRAPHER Andrew Eccles
PUBLISHER KQED, Inc.
CATEGORY Cover
DATE December 1993

PUBLICATION Time
AWARD Merit
DESIGN DIRECTOR Arthur Hochstein
ART DIRECTOR Rudolph C. Hoglund
PHOTOGRAPHER Archive Photo - Lambert Studios
PUBLISHER Time Inc.
CATEGORY Cover
DATE November 22, 1993

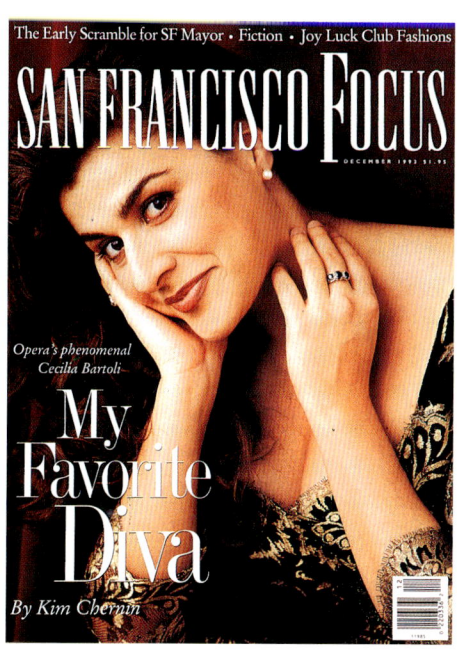

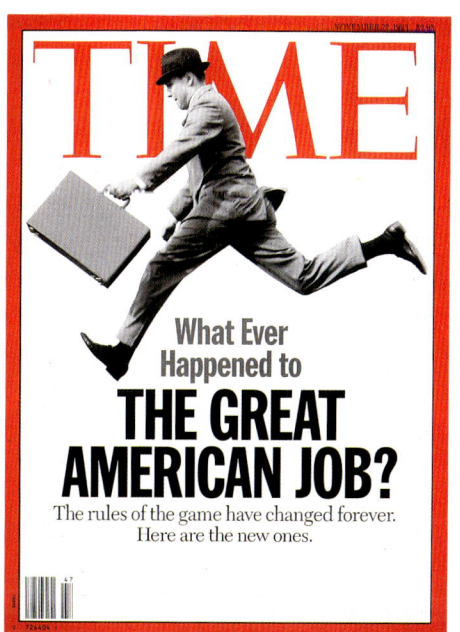

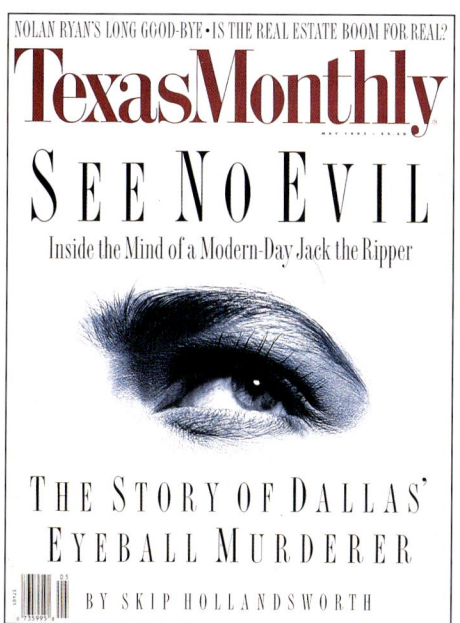

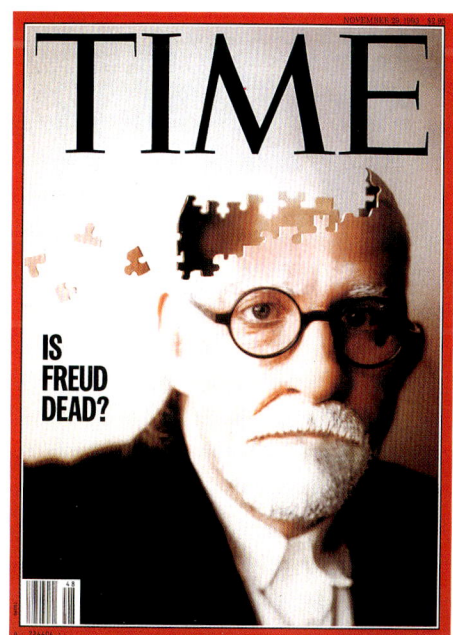

PUBLICATION Texas Monthly
AWARD Merit
DESIGN DIRECTOR D.J. Stout
DESIGNER D.J. Stout
PHOTOGRAPHER Geof Kern
PHOTO EDITOR D.J. Stout
PUBLISHER Texas Monthly
CATEGORY Cover
DATE May 1993

PUBLICATION Time
AWARD Merit
DESIGN DIRECTOR Arthur Hochstein
ART DIRECTOR Rudolph C. Hoglund
ILLUSTRATOR Matt Mahurin
PUBLISHER Time Inc.
CATEGORY Cover
DATE November 29, 1993

PUBLICATION Travel & Leisure
AWARD Merit
DESIGN DIRECTOR Lloyd Ziff
DESIGNER Lloyd Ziff
PHOTOGRAPHER Geof Kern
PHOTO EDITOR Hazel Hammond
PUBLISHER American Express
Publishing
CATEGORY Cover
DATE May 1993

PUBLICATION Travel & Leisure
AWARD Merit
DESIGN DIRECTOR Lloyd Ziff
DESIGNER Lloyd Ziff
PHOTOGRAPHER Bob Krist
PHOTO EDITOR Hazel Hammond
PUBLISHER American Express
Publishing
CATEGORY Cover
DATE August 1993

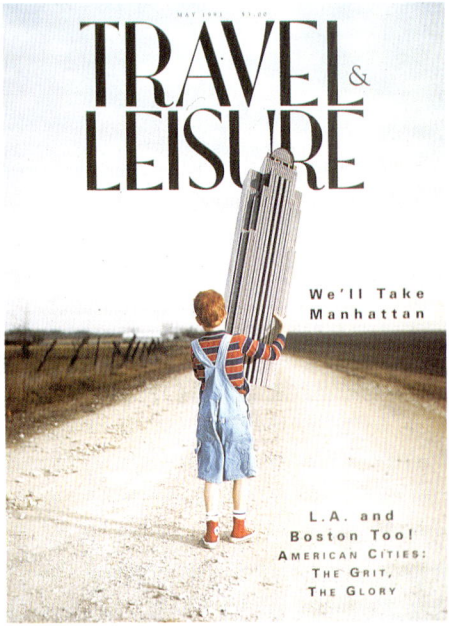

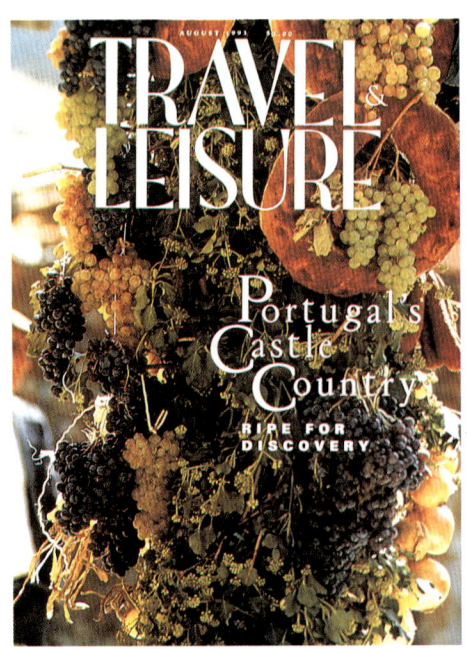

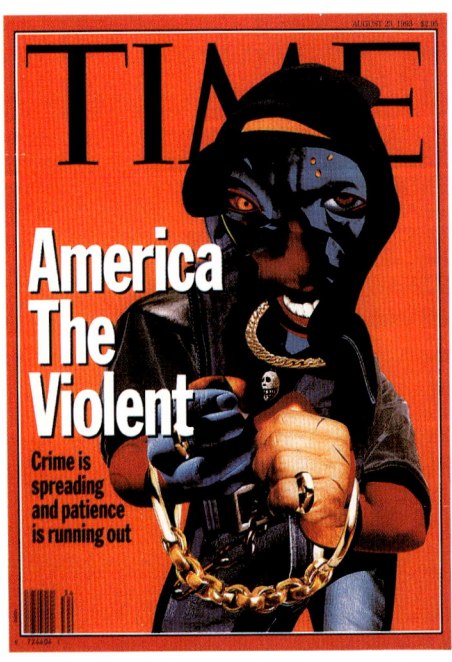

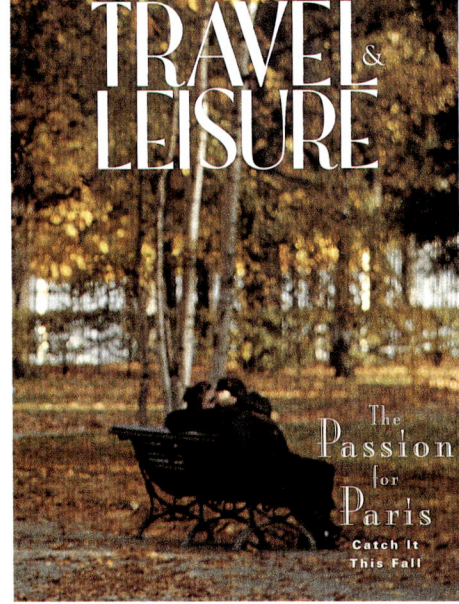

PUBLICATION Time
AWARD Merit
DESIGN DIRECTOR Arthur Hochstein
ART DIRECTOR Rudolph C. Hoglund
ILLUSTRATOR Edmund Guy
PUBLISHER Time Inc.
CATEGORY Cover
DATE August 23, 1993

PUBLICATION Travel & Leisure
AWARD Merit
DESIGN DIRECTOR Lloyd Ziff
DESIGNER Lloyd Ziff
PHOTOGRAPHER Hugues Colson
PHOTO EDITOR Hazel Hammond
PUBLISHER American Express Publishing
CATEGORY Cover
DATE September 1993

PUBLICATION Vibe
AWARD Merit
DESIGN DIRECTOR Gary Koepke
ART DIRECTOR Richard Baker
DESIGNER Gary Koepke
PHOTOGRAPHER Christian Witkins
PHOTO EDITOR George Pitts
PUBLISHER Time Inc. Ventures
STUDIO Koepke International, Ltd.
CATEGORY Cover
DATE November 1993

PUBLICATION Vibe
AWARD Merit
DESIGN DIRECTOR Gary Koepke
ART DIRECTOR Richard Baker
DESIGNER Gary Koepke
PHOTOGRAPHER Dan Winters
PHOTO EDITOR George Pitts
PUBLISHER Time Inc. Ventures
STUDIO Koepke International, Ltd.
CATEGORY Cover
DATE September 1993

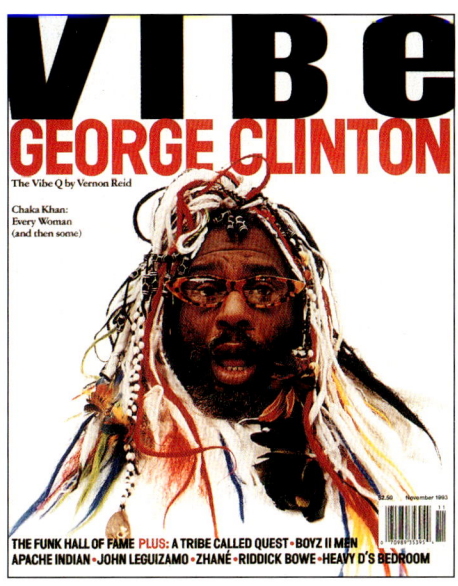

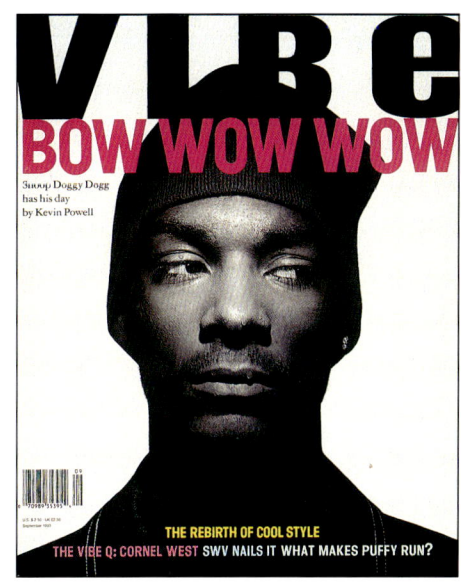

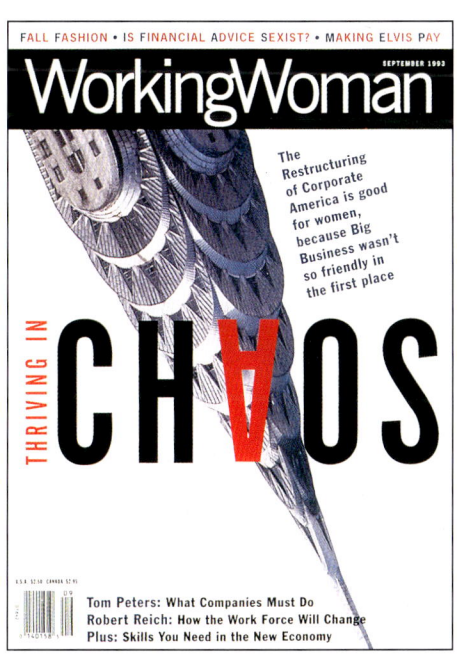

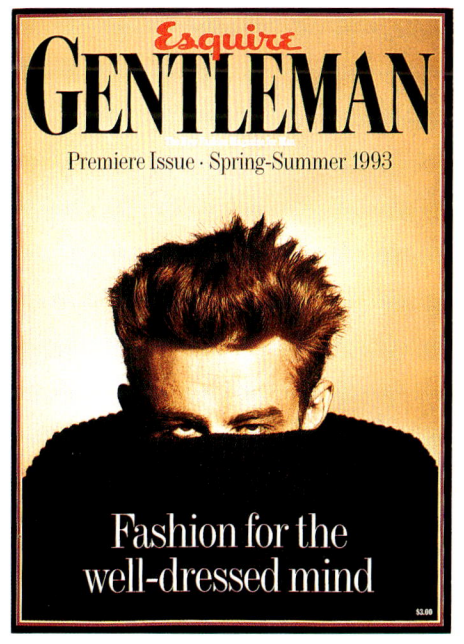

PUBLICATION Working Woman
AWARD Merit
DESIGN DIRECTOR Paula Scher
ART DIRECTOR Paula Scher
DESIGNER Paula Scher
PHOTOGRAPHER Brian Hennessy / FPG
PUBLISHER Working Woman Inc.
CATEGORY Cover
DATE September 1993

PUBLICATION Esquire Gentleman
AWARD Merit
CREATIVE DIRECTOR Roger Black
ART DIRECTOR Maryjane Fahey
DESIGNER Roger Black
PUBLISHER The Hearst Corporation
STUDIO Roger Black, Inc.
CATEGORY Cover
DATE Spring/Summer 1993

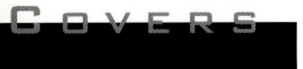

PUBLICATION	Marketing Computers
AWARD	Merit
DESIGN DIRECTOR	Carole Erger-Fass
ART DIRECTOR	Blake Taylor
PHOTOGRAPHER	Frank Micelotta
PHOTO EDITOR	Sabine Meyer
PUBLISHER	BPI, Inc.
CATEGORY	Cover
DATE	May 1993

PUBLICATION	Graphis
AWARD	Merit
DESIGN DIRECTOR	B. Martin Pedersen
ART DIRECTORS	B. Martin Pedersen, Randell Pearson
DESIGNER	B. Martin Pedersen
PHOTOGRAPHER	David Stewart
STUDIO	Pedersen Design Group, Inc.
CATEGORY	Cover
DATE	February 1993

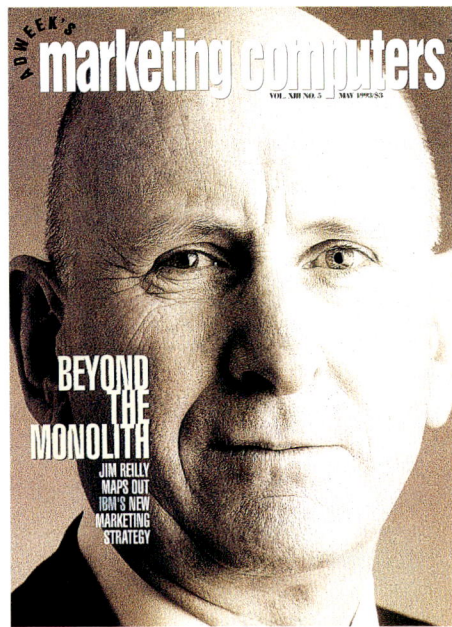

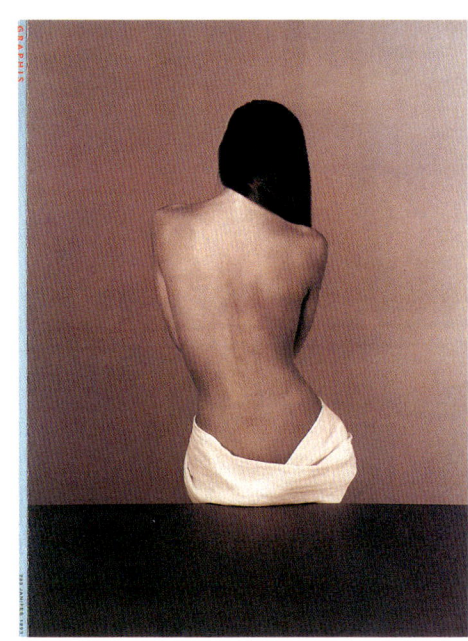

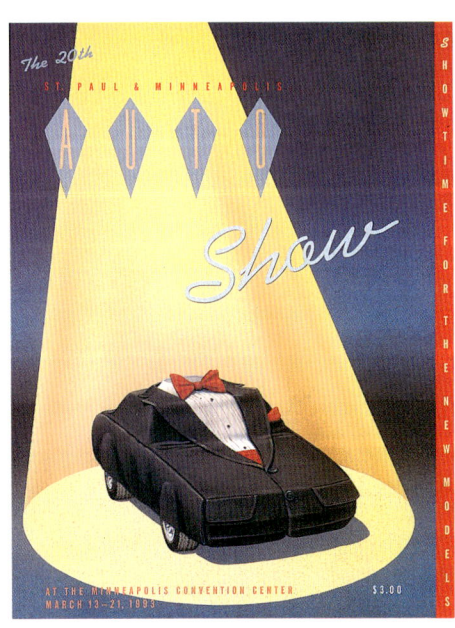

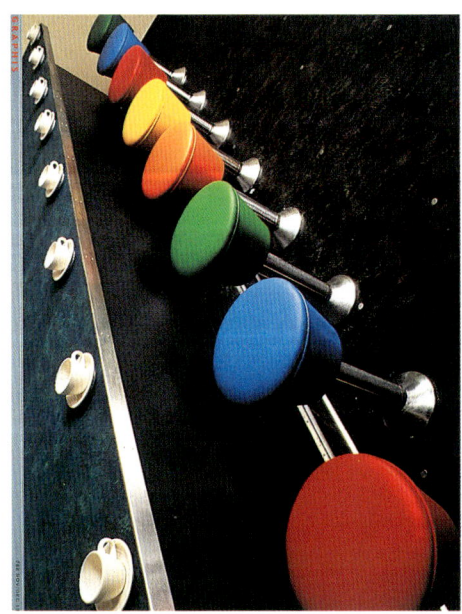

PUBLICATION	Auto Show
AWARD	Merit
ART DIRECTOR	Lynn Phelps
DESIGNER	Lynn Phelps
ILLUSTRATOR	Steve Pietzsch
PUBLISHER	Star Tribune
CATEGORY	Cover
DATE	March 1993

PUBLICATION	Graphis
AWARD	Merit
DESIGN DIRECTOR	B. Martin Pedersen
ART DIRECTORS	Greg Simpson, Randell Pearson
DESIGNER	B. Martin Pedersen
PHOTOGRAPHER	Devon T.C. Worman
STUDIO	Pedersen Design Group, Inc.
CATEGORY	Cover
DATE	December 1993

PUBLICATION Footwear News
AWARD Merit
DESIGN DIRECTOR Elizabeth Slott
DESIGNER Elizabeth Slott
PHOTOGRAPHER Andreas Bleckmann
PUBLISHER Fairchild Publications
CATEGORY Cover
DATE April 15, 1993

PUBLICATION Number
AWARD Merit
DESIGN DIRECTOR Bruce Crocker
DESIGNERS Bruce Crocker, Lee Busch
PHOTOGRAPHER Joe Viesti
PHOTO EDITOR Bruce Crocker
PUBLISHER Boston Acoustics
STUDIO Crocker Inc.
CATEGORY Cover
DATE October 1, 1993

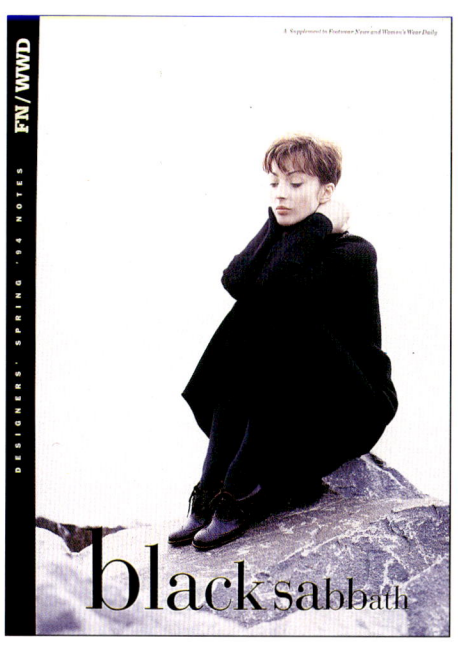

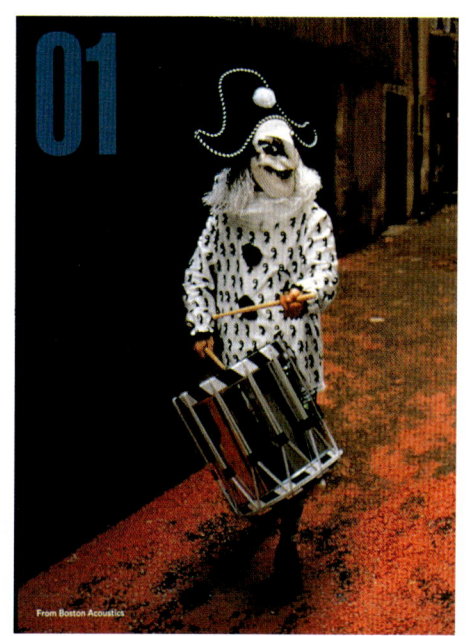

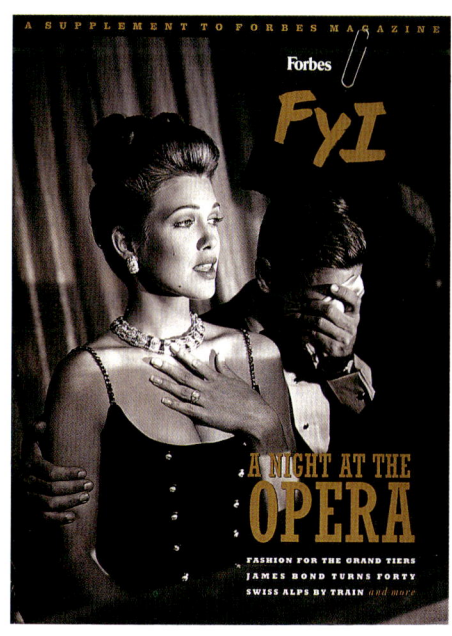

PUBLICATION Forbes FYI
AWARD Merit
ART DIRECTOR Alexander Isley
DESIGNER Lynette Cortez
PHOTOGRAPHER J. Michael Myers
STUDIO Alexander Isley Design
CATEGORY Cover
DATE November 22, 1993

PUBLICATION	Upper & Lower Case
AWARD	Merit
ART DIRECTORS	Woody Pirtle, John Klotnia
DESIGNERS	John Klotnia, Ivette Montes de Oca
PUBLISHER	International Typeface Corporation
STUDIO	Pentagram Design, NYC
CATEGORY	Cover
DATE	December 1993

PUBLICATION	Team Leader
AWARD	Merit
DESIGN DIRECTOR	Doug Gottlieb
DESIGNER	Doug Gottlieb
PHOTOGRAPHER	Timothy Reagan
PUBLISHER	Fairchild Publications
CATEGORY	Cover
DATE	July 19, 1993

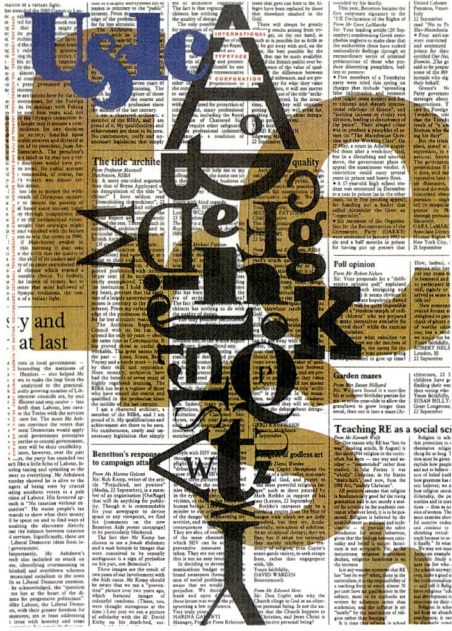

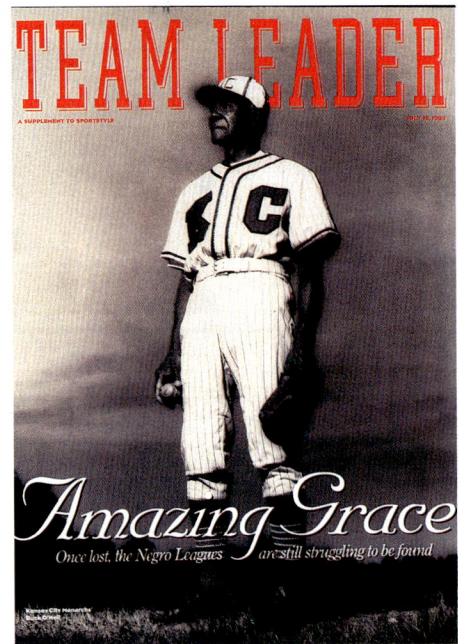

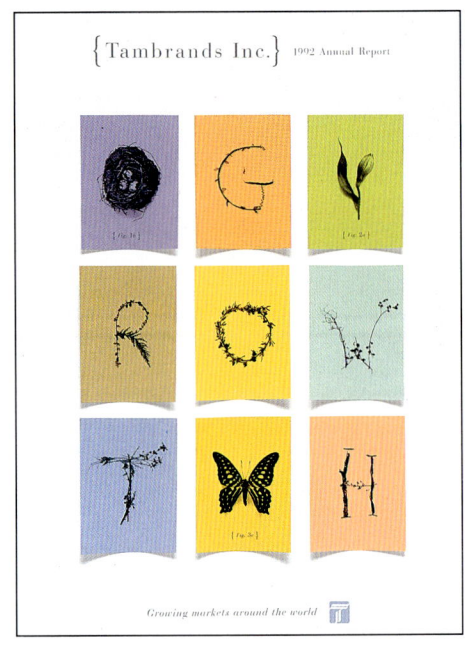

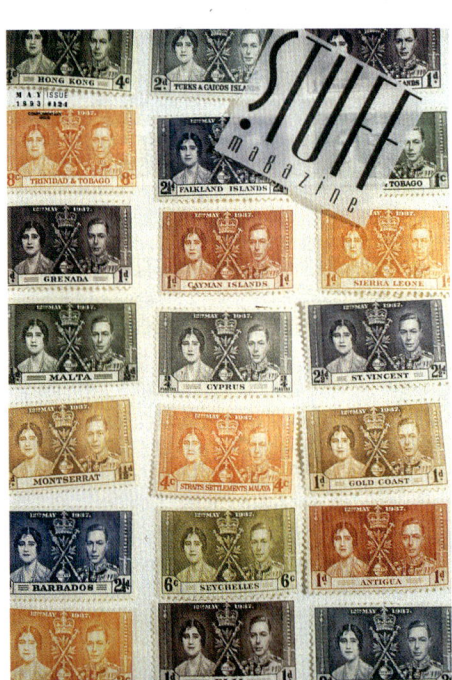

PUBLICATION	Tambrands Inc., 1992 Annual Report
AWARD	Merit
CREATIVE DIRECTOR	Kent Hunter
DESIGNER	Steven Fabrizio
PHOTOGRAPHERS	Alan Abrams, Francesca Lacagnina, John Riley, Mark Jenkinson
STUDIO	Frankfurt Balkind Partners
CATEGORY	Cover
DATE	March 1993

PUBLICATION	Stuff
AWARD	Merit
DESIGN DIRECTOR	Tyler Smith
DESIGNER	Tyler Smith
PHOTOGRAPHER	Michael Warren
STUDIO	Tyler Smith
CATEGORY	Cover
DATE	May 1993

PUBLICATION   Regional Review
AWARD   Merit
DESIGN DIRECTOR   Ronn Campisi
ILLUSTRATOR   Seth Jaben
STUDIO   Ronn Campisi Design
CATEGORY   Cover
DATE   Spring 1993

PUBLICATION   The New York Times/
               Travel
AWARD   Merit
DESIGN DIRECTOR   Tom Bodkin
ART DIRECTOR   Genevieve Williams
ILLUSTRATOR   Patrick Blackwell
PUBLISHER   The New York Times
CATEGORY   Newspapers/Front Page
DATE   February 7, 1993

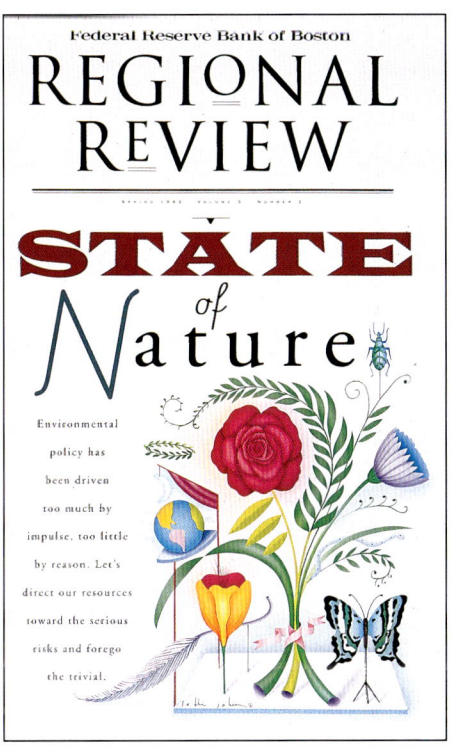

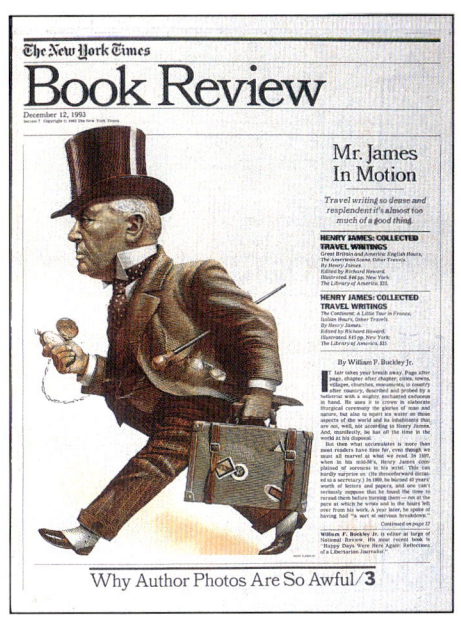

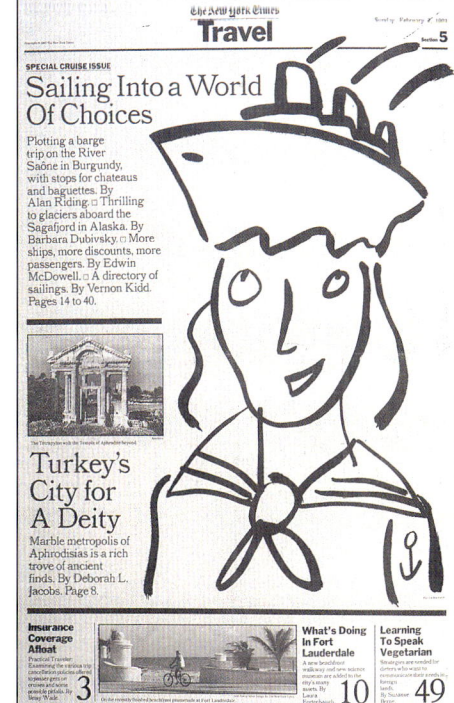

PUBLICATION   The New York Times/
               Book Review
AWARD   Merit
ART DIRECTOR   Steve Heller
ILLUSTRATOR   Mark Summers
PUBLISHER   The New York Times
CATEGORY   Cover
DATE   December 12, 1993

62

PUBLICATION	The New York Times/ Summer Arts
AWARD	Merit
ART DIRECTOR	Linda Brewer
ILLUSTRATOR	Jeffrey Fisher
PUBLISHER	The New York Times
CATEGORY	Cover
DATE	May 16, 1993

63

PUBLICATION	The New York Times/ Summer Times
AWARD	Merit
ART DIRECTOR	Nancy Kent
ILLUSTRATOR	Ed Koren
PUBLISHER	The New York Times
CATEGORY	Cover
DATE	June 13, 1993

64

PUBLICATION	The New York Times/ Travel
AWARD	Merit
ART DIRECTOR	Nicki Kalish
ILLUSTRATOR	Terry Allen
PUBLISHER	The New York Times
CATEGORY	Newspapers/Front Page
DATE	November 21, 1993

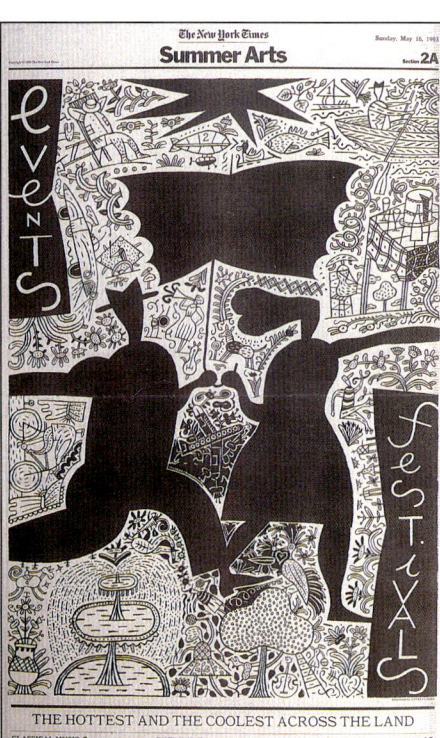

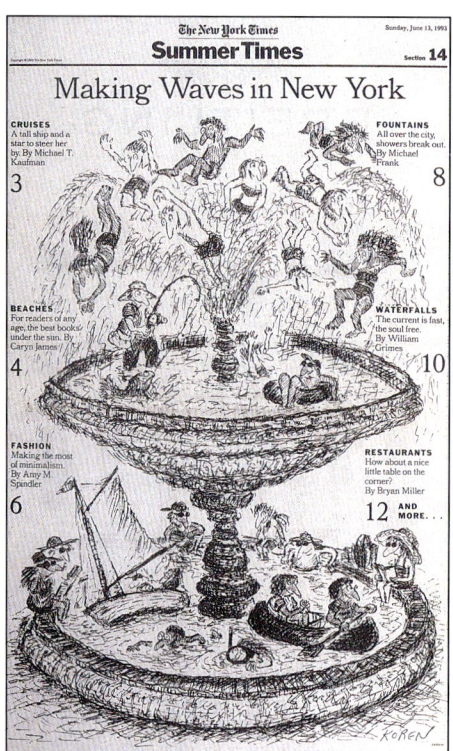

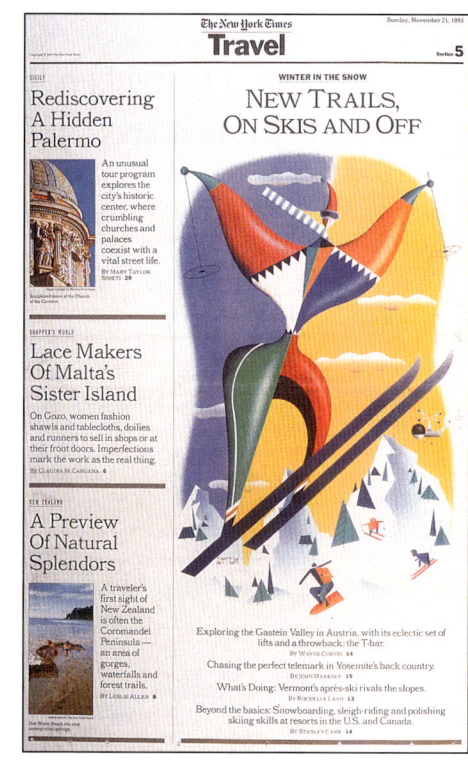

PUBLICATION The New York Times
             Magazine
AWARD   Merit
ART DIRECTOR Janet Froelich
DESIGNER   Paula Scher
PUBLISHER   The New York Times
CATEGORY   Cover
DATE   November 28, 1993

PUBLICATION The New York Times
             Magazine
AWARD   Merit
ART DIRECTOR Janet Froelich
PHOTOGRAPHER Brad Guice
PHOTO EDITOR Kathy Ryan
PUBLISHER   The New York Times
CATEGORY   Cover
DATE   November 14, 1993

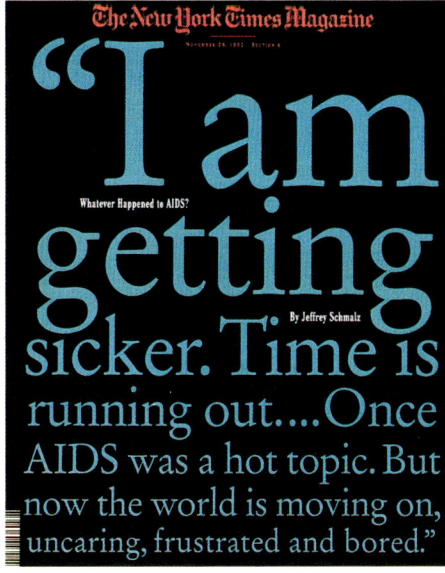

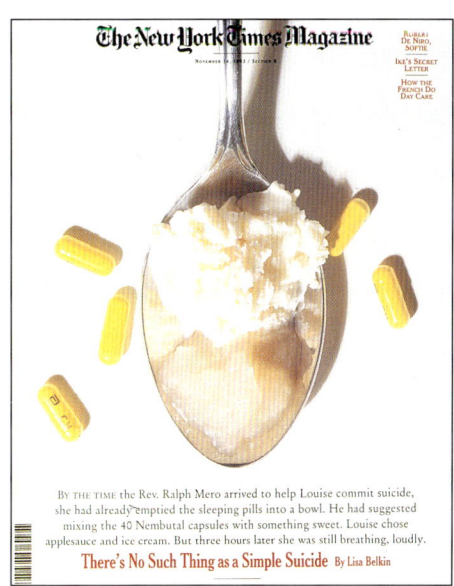

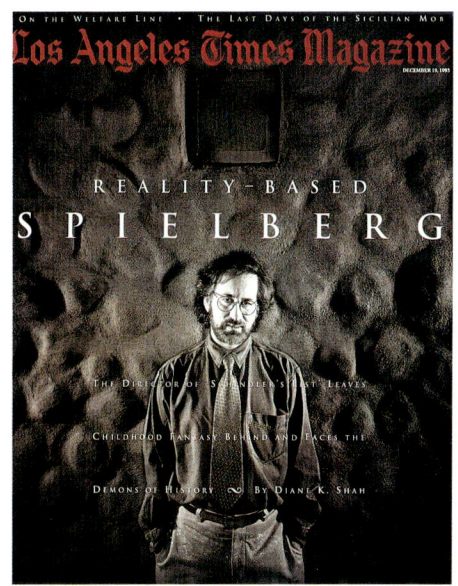

PUBLICATION The Los Angeles Times Magazine
AWARD   Merit
ART DIRECTOR Nancy Duckworth
DESIGNER   Nancy Duckworth
PHOTOGRAPHER Dan Winters
PHOTO EDITOR Lisa Thackaberry
PUBLISHER   Times Mirror
CATEGORY   Cover
DATE   December 19, 1993

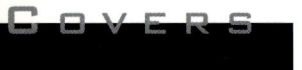

PUBLICATION   The Boston Globe/Travel
AWARD   Merit
DESIGNER   Neil C. Pinchin
ILLUSTRATOR   Neil C. Pinchin
PUBLISHER   The Boston Globe
CATEGORY   Newspapers/Front Page
DATE   October 10, 1993

PUBLICATION   The Village Voice
AWARD   Merit
DESIGN DIRECTOR   Robert Newman
ART DIRECTORS   Florian Bachleda,
Jesse Reyes
PUBLISHER   VV Publishing Corporation
CATEGORY   Newspapers/Front Page
DATE   December 14, 1993

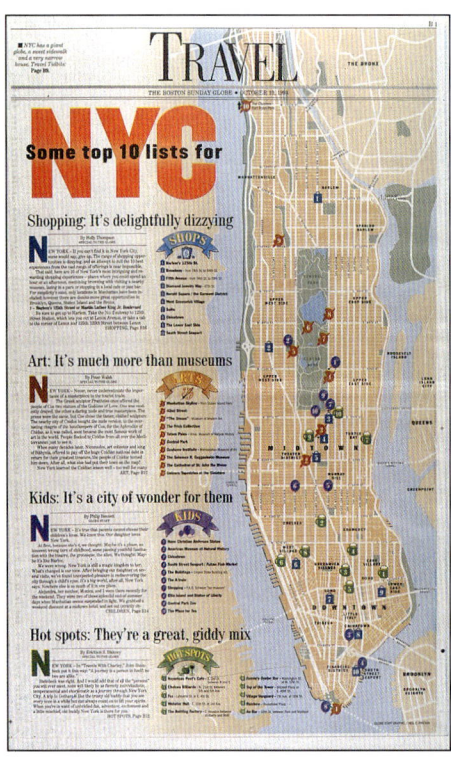

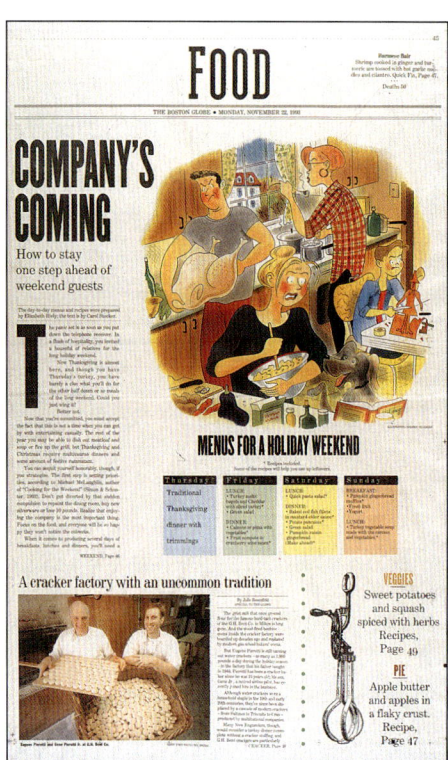

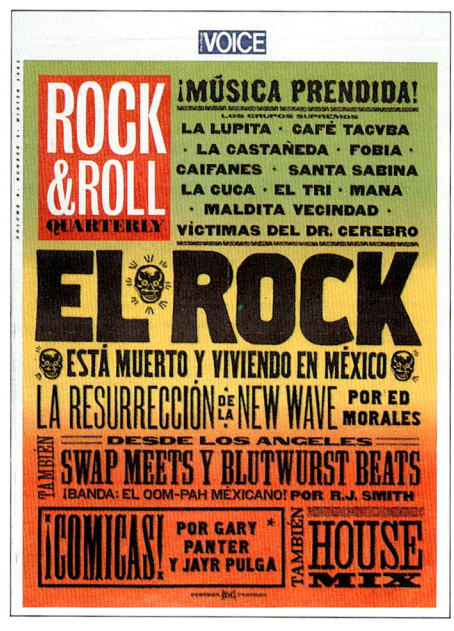

PUBLICATION   The Boston Globe/Food
AWARD   Merit
ART DIRECTOR   Rena Sokolow
DESIGNER   Rena Sokolow
ILLUSTRATOR   Maurice Vellekoop
PHOTOGRAPHER   Bill Greene
PUBLISHER   The Boston Globe
CATEGORY   Newspapers/Front Page
DATE   December 22, 1993

PUBLICATION   The Village Voice
AWARD   Merit
DESIGN DIRECTOR   Robert Newman
ART DIRECTORS   Florian Bachleda, Jennifer Gilman
ILLUSTRATOR   Stephen Kroninger
PUBLISHER   VV Publishing Co.
CATEGORY   Newspapers/Front Page
DATE   October 12, 1993

PUBLICATION   The Village Voice
AWARD   Merit
DESIGN DIRECTOR   Robert Newman
ART DIRECTOR   Florian Bachleda
ILLUSTRATOR   Steve Brodnor
PUBLISHER   VV Publishing Co.
CATEGORY   Newspapers/Front Page
DATE   September 28, 1993

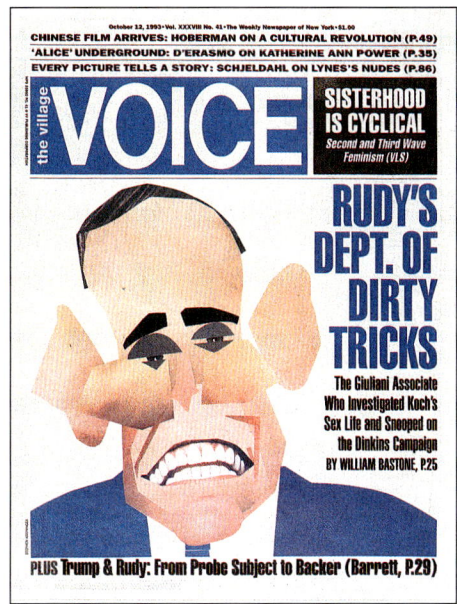

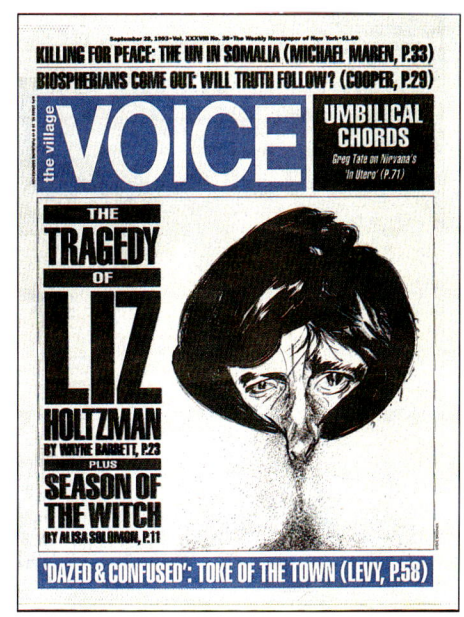

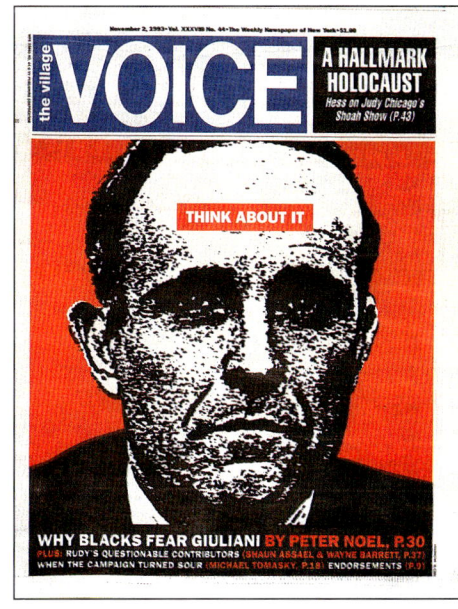

PUBLICATION   The Village Voice
AWARD   Merit
DESIGN DIRECTOR   Robert Newman
ART DIRECTOR   Jennifer Gilman
PHOTOGRAPHER   Fred W. McDarrah
PUBLISHER   VV Publishing Co.
CATEGORY   Newspapers/Front Page
DATE   November 2, 1993

PUBLICATION   The Village Voice
AWARD   Merit
DESIGN DIRECTOR   Robert Newman
PUBLISHER   VV Publishing Co.
CATEGORY   Newspapers/Front Page
DATE   August 3, 1993

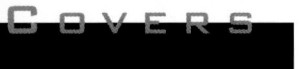

PUBLICATION The Wall Street Journal Reports
AWARD Merit
DESIGN DIRECTOR Greg Leeds
DESIGNER Greg Leeds
ILLUSTRATOR Steve Lyons
PUBLISHER Dow Jones & Co., Inc.
CATEGORY Newspapers/Front Page
DATE November 15, 1993

PUBLICATION The Wall Street Journal Reports
AWARD Merit
DESIGN DIRECTOR Greg Leeds
DESIGNER Greg Leeds
ILLUSTRATOR Raul Colon
PUBLISHER Dow Jones & Co., Inc.
CATEGORY Newspapers/Front Page
DATE January 20, 1993

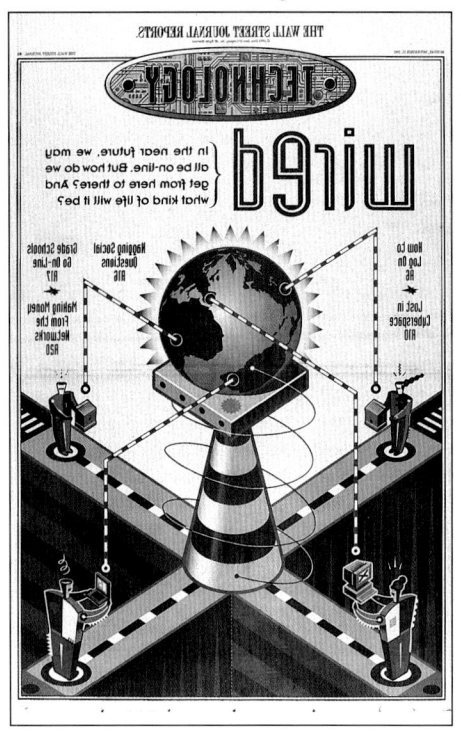

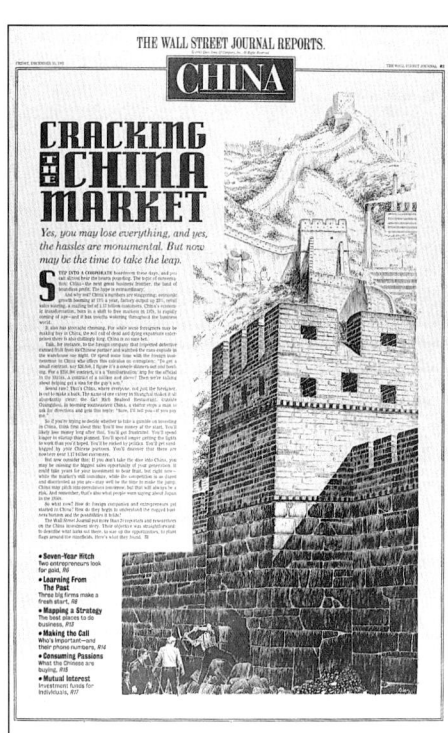

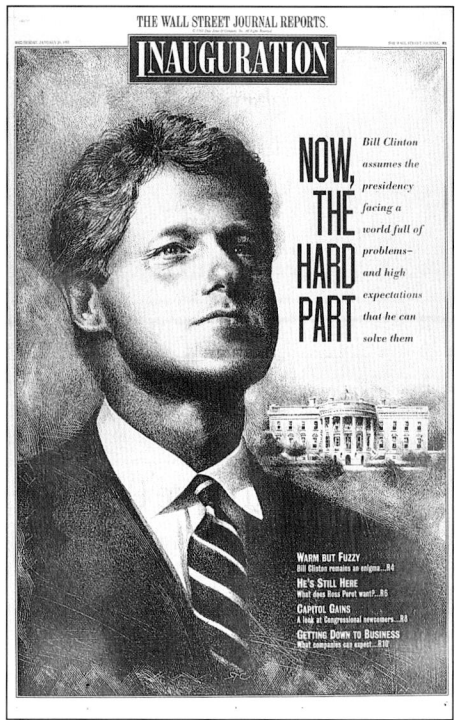

PUBLICATION The Wall Street Journal Reports
AWARD Merit
DESIGN DIRECTOR Greg Leeds
DESIGNER Greg Leeds
ILLUSTRATOR Chris Bing
PUBLISHER Dow Jones & Co., Inc.
CATEGORY Newspapers/Front Page
DATE December 10, 1993

PUBLICATION	The New York Times/Styles
AWARD	Merit
ART DIRECTOR	Michael Valenti
PHOTOGRAPHERS	Naum Kazhdan, Corina Lecca
PUBLISHER	The New York Times
CATEGORY	Newspapers/Front Page
DATE	November 14, 1993

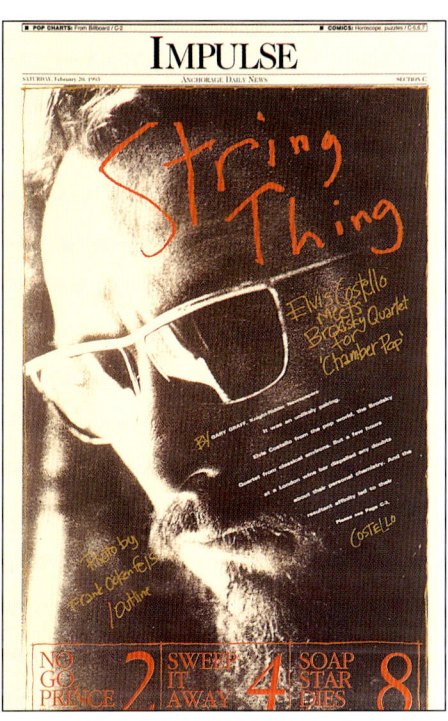

PUBLICATION	Anchorage Daily News - Impulse
AWARD	Merit
DESIGN DIRECTOR	Galie Jean-Louis
DESIGNER	Galie Jean-Louis
PHOTOGRAPHER	Frank Ockenfels 3
PUBLISHER	Anchorage Daily News
CATEGORY	Newspapers/Front Page
DATE	February 20, 1993

PUBLICATION	The Wall Street Journal Reports
AWARD	Merit
DESIGN DIRECTOR	Greg Leeds
DESIGNER	Greg Leeds
ILLUSTRATOR	Chris Bing
PUBLISHER	Dow Jones & Co., Inc.
CATEGORY	Newspapers/Front Page
DATE	October 15, 1993

PUBLICATION	The Wall Street Journal Reports
AWARD	Merit
DESIGN DIRECTOR	Greg Leeds
DESIGNER	Greg Leeds
ILLUSTRATOR	David Suter
PUBLISHER	Dow Jones & Co., Inc.
CATEGORY	Newspapers/Front Page
DATE	June 21, 1993

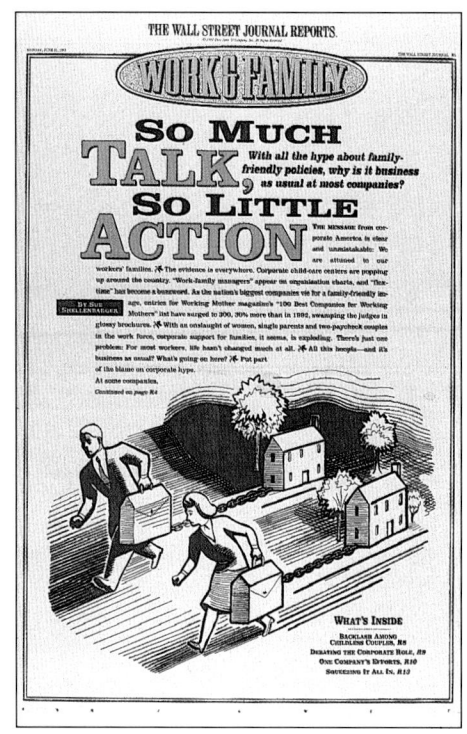

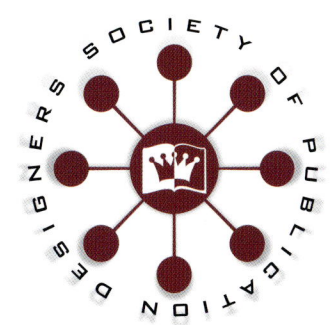

DESIGN
ENTIRE
ISSUE
REDESIGN
SINGLE PAGE
SPREAD
STORY
INFORMATION GRAPHICS

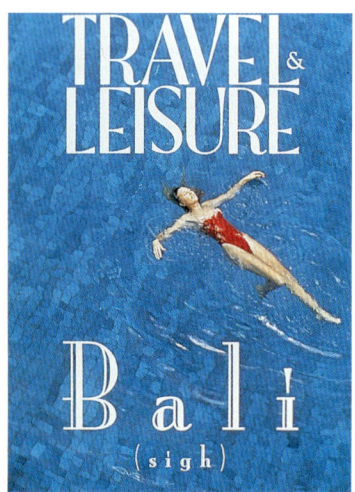

PUBLICATION	Sculpture Review
AWARD	Merit
DESIGN DIRECTOR	Michael Schubert
ART DIRECTOR	Sylvia de Martino
DESIGNER	Lisa Gabbay
PHOTO EDITOR	David Finn
STUDIO	Ruder Finn Design
CATEGORY	Design/Redesign
DATE	1993 (No. 1, 2, & 3)

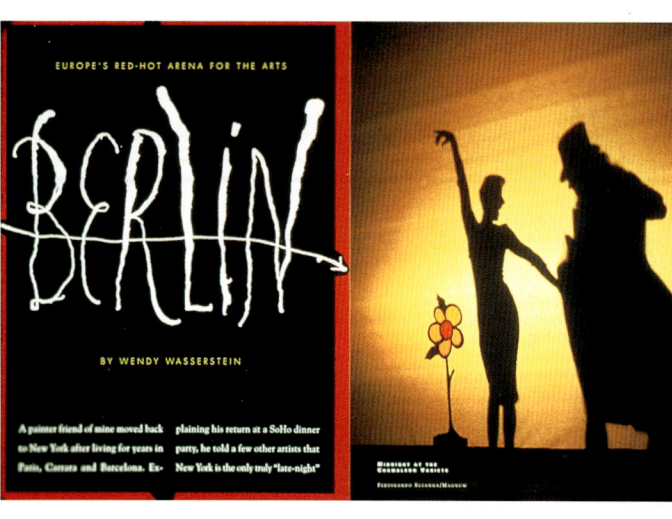

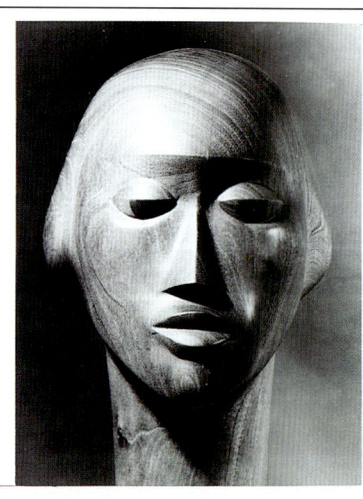

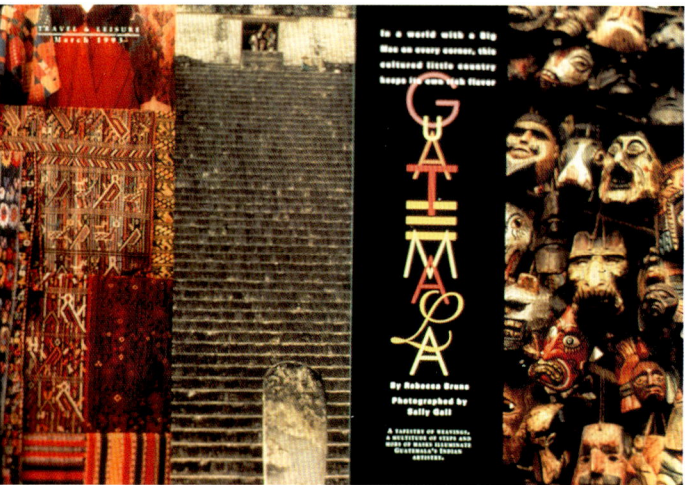

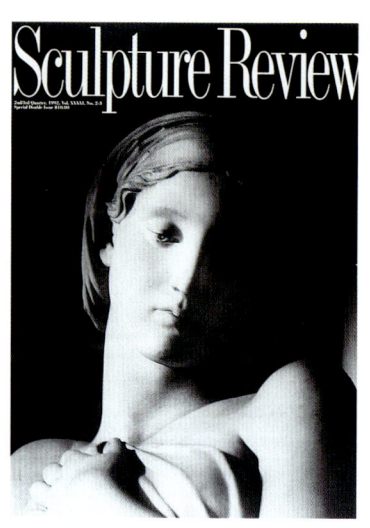

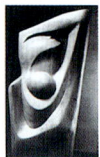

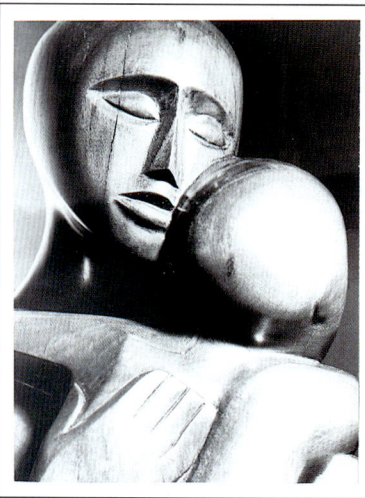

PUBLICATION	Travel & Leisure
AWARD	Merit
DESIGN DIRECTOR	Lloyd Ziff
DESIGNER	Lloyd Ziff
ILLUSTRATORS	Mick Haggerty, Philip Quirk
PHOTOGRAPHERS	Ferdinando Scianna / Magnum, Sally Gall
PHOTO EDITOR	Hazel Hammond
PUBLISHER	American Express Publishing
CATEGORY	Design/Redesign
DATE	February/March 1993

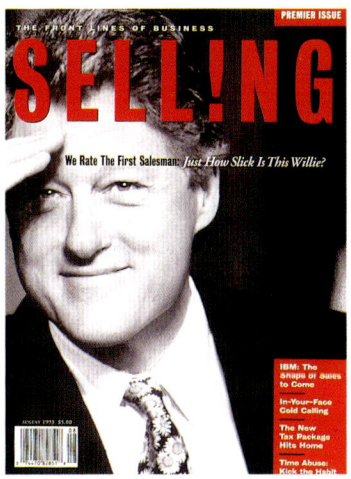

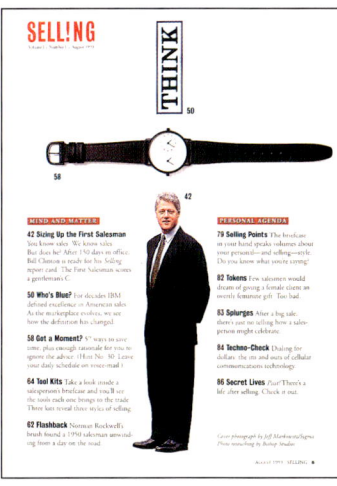

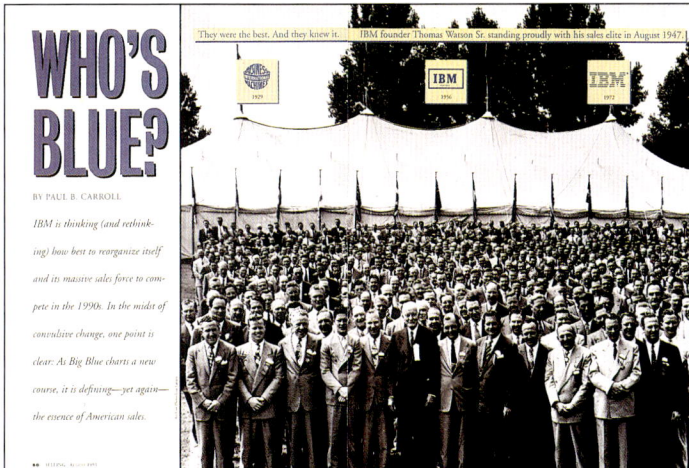

PUBLICATION	Selling
AWARD	Merit
DESIGN DIRECTORS	Walter Bernard, Milton Glaser
ART DIRECTOR	Teresa Fernandes
DESIGNERS	Walter Bernard, Milton Glaser, Nancy Eising, Teresa Fernandes, Sharon Okamoto, Frank Baseman
PHOTO EDITOR	Jim Franco
PUBLISHER	Capital Cities / ABC, Inc.
STUDIO	WBMG, Inc.
CATEGORY	Design/Redesign
DATE	August 1993

PUBLICATION	Theatre Crafts International
AWARD	Merit
ART DIRECTOR	Joanne Hixson
ILLUSTRATOR	Ruth Carter
PHOTOGRAPHERS	Ebey Roberts, David Lee/ Warner Brothers, Joseph Lederer
PUBLISHER	Entertainment Technology Communications Group
CATEGORY	Design/Redesign
DATE	February 1993

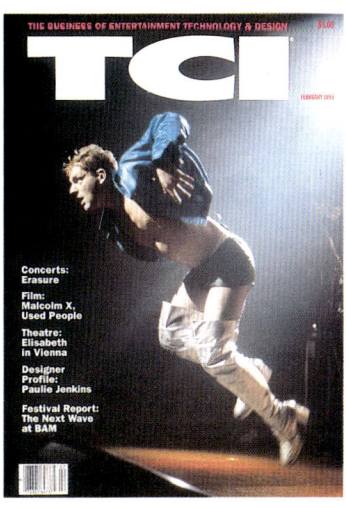

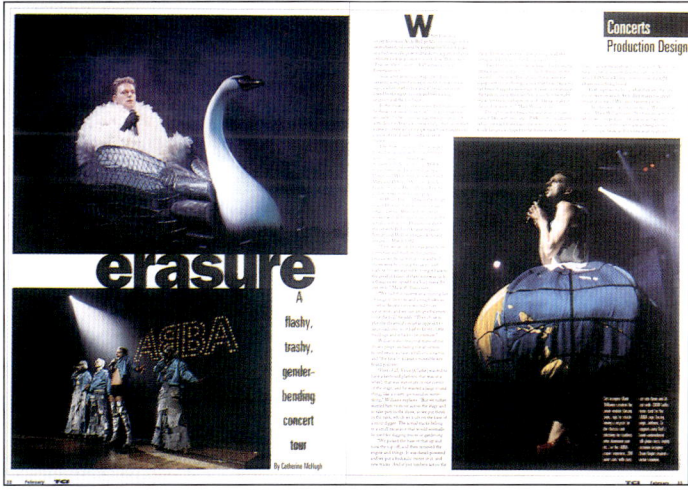

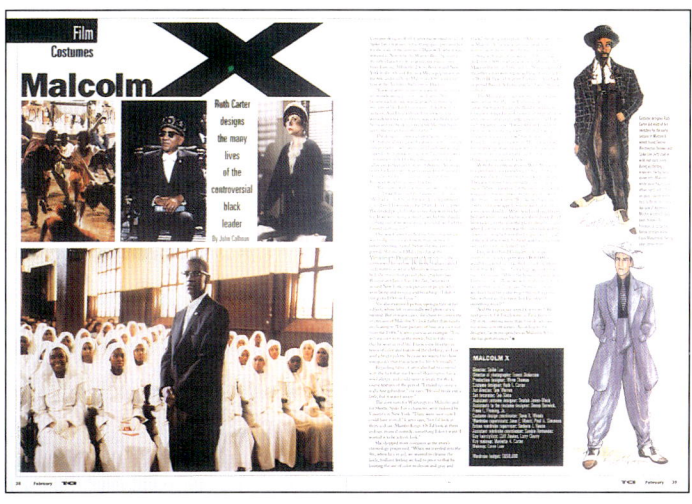

PUBLICATION	FrancoFile
AWARD	Merit
DESIGN DIRECTOR	Iris A. Brown
DESIGNER	Iris A. Brown
PUBLISHER	Food and Wines from France, Inc.
STUDIO	Iris A. Brown Design
CATEGORY	Design/Redesign
DATE	May 1993/September 1993

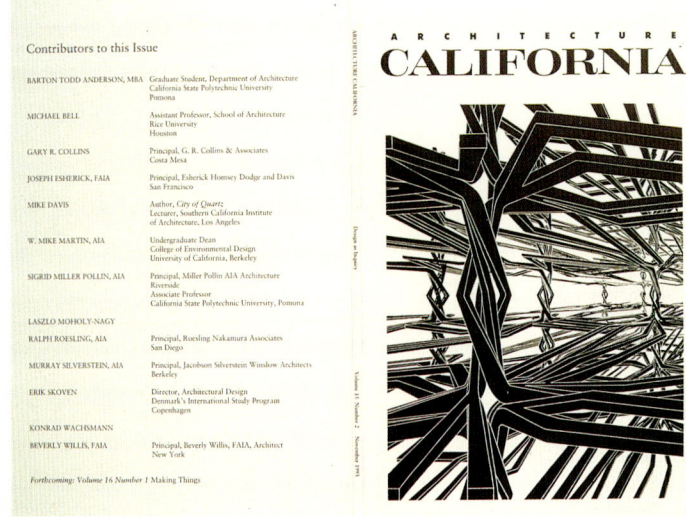

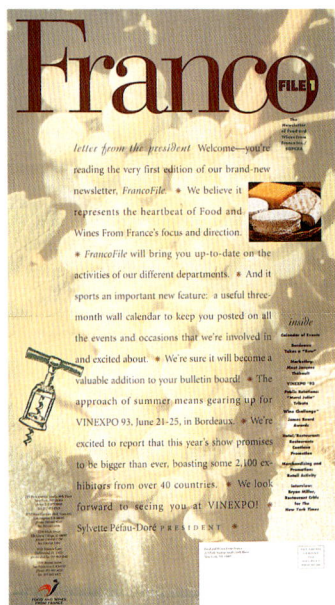

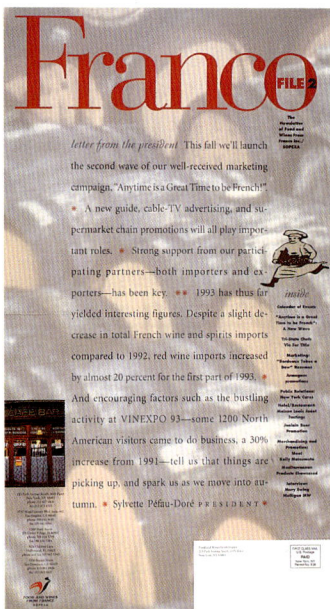

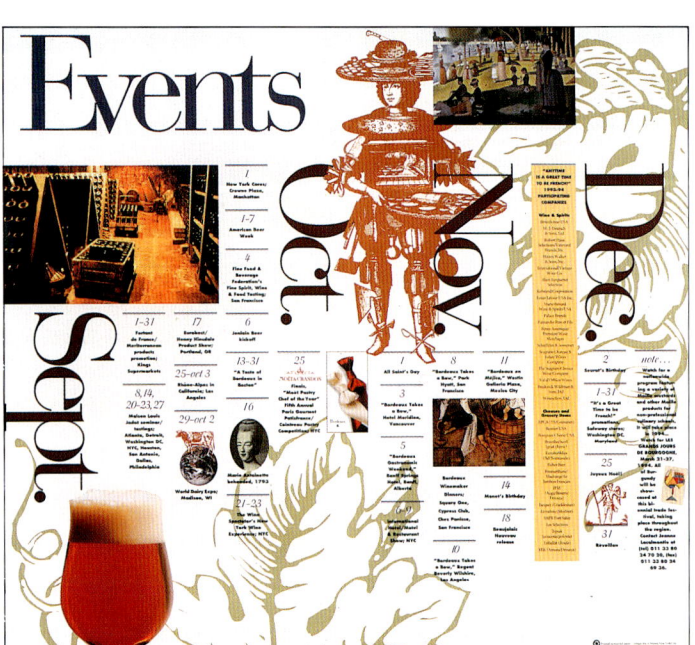

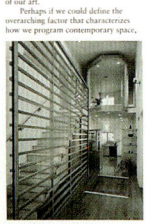
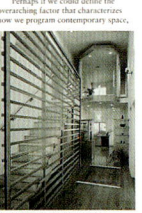
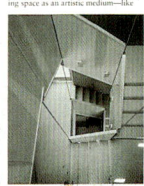

Gifts of Impurities

Sigrid Miller Pollin, AIA

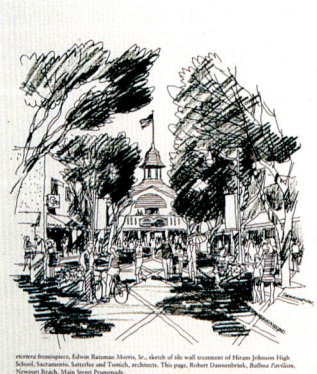

California Sketches

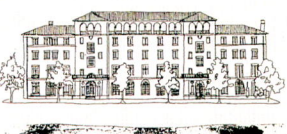
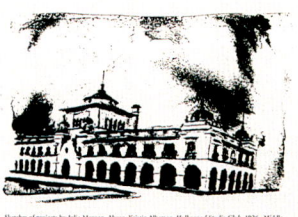

PUBLICATION	Architecture California
AWARD	Merit
DESIGN DIRECTOR	Michael Dunlavey
DESIGNER	Kevin Yee
STUDIO	The Dunlavey Studio, Inc.
CATEGORY	Design/Redesign
DATE	November 6, 1993

PUBLICATION	Family Life
AWARD	Merit
ART DIRECTOR	Don Morris
DESIGNERS	Don Morris, Laura Eisman, James Reyman
PHOTO EDITOR	Jane Clark
PUBLISHER	Wenner Media
CATEGORY	Design/Entire Issue
DATE	September/October 1993

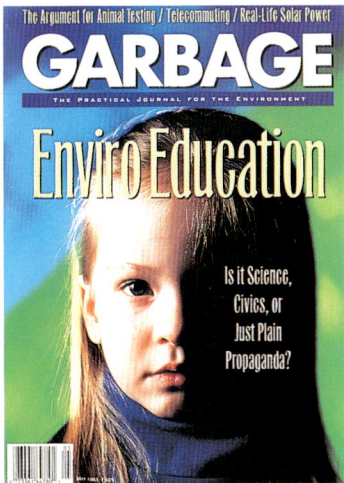

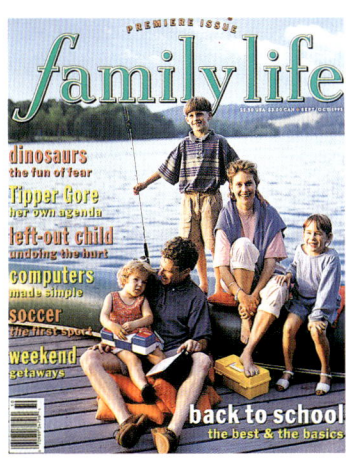

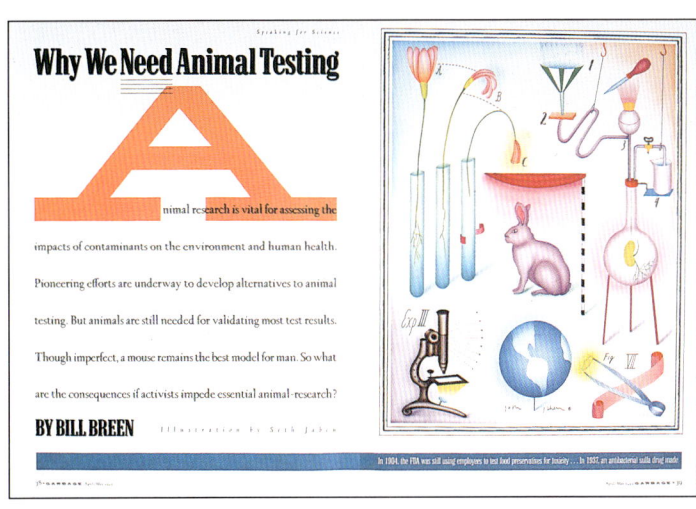

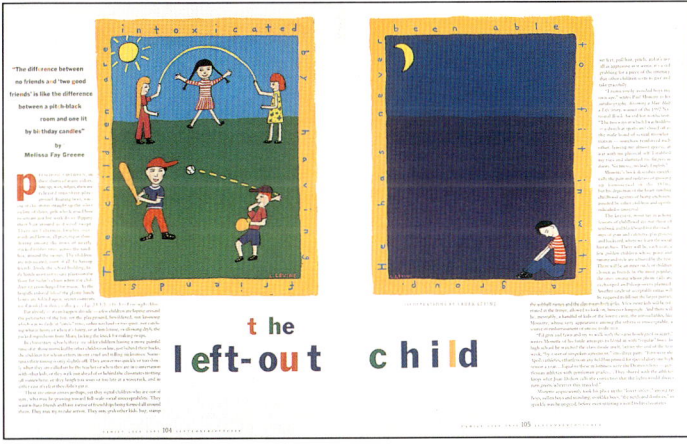

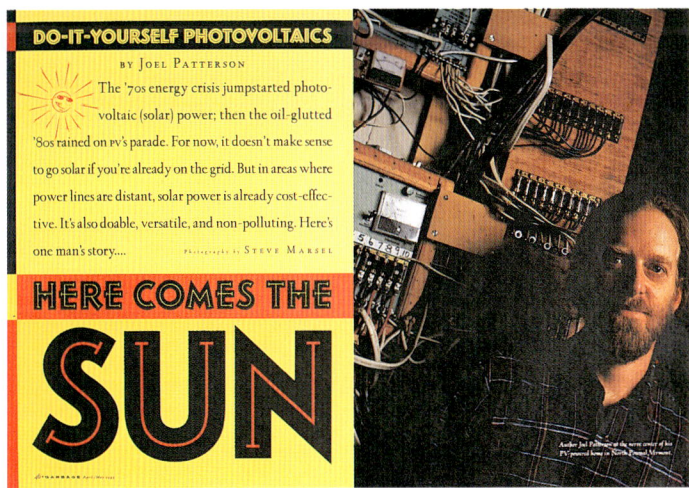

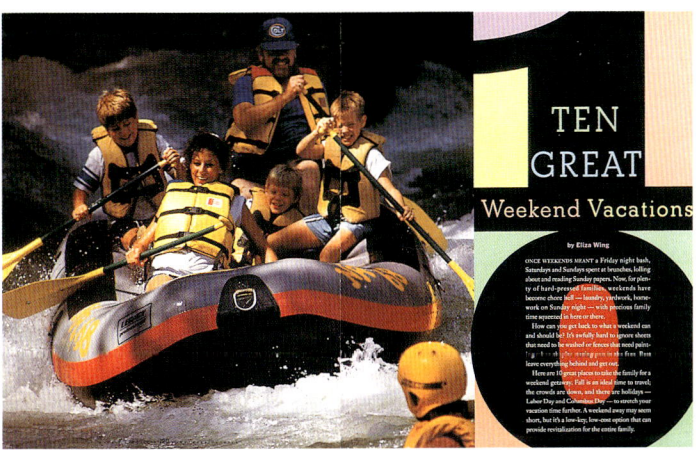

PUBLICATION	Garbage
AWARD	Merit
DESIGN DIRECTOR	Patrick Mitchell
DESIGNER	Patrick Mitchell
ILLUSTRATORS	Seth Jaben, Terry Allen
PHOTOGRAPHERS	Steve Marsel, Christopher Harting
PUBLISHER	Dovetale Publishers
CATEGORY	Design/Entire Issue
DATE	May 1993

PUBLICATION   Garbage
AWARD   Merit
DESIGN DIRECTOR   Patrick Mitchell
DESIGNER   Patrick Mitchell
ILLUSTRATORS   Dan Yaccarino, Jeff Jackson, Gary Tanhauser
PHOTOGRAPHERS   Chris Harting, Jonnie Miles
PUBLISHER   Dovetale Publishers
CATEGORY   Design/Entire Issue
DATE   July 1993

PUBLICATION   Garbage
AWARD   Merit
DESIGN DIRECTOR   Patrick Mitchell
DESIGNER   Patrick Mitchell
ILLUSTRATOR   Gary Tanhauser
PHOTOGRAPHERS   Christine Alicino, Neal Farris
PUBLISHER   Dovetale Publishers
CATEGORY   Design/Entire Issue
DATE   December/January 1993

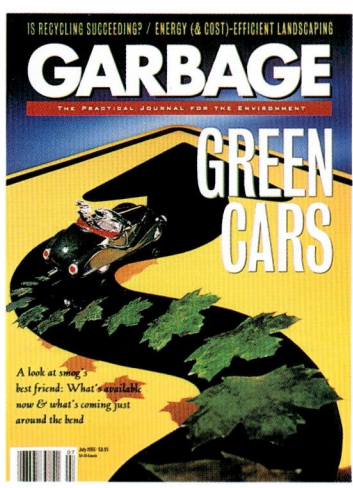

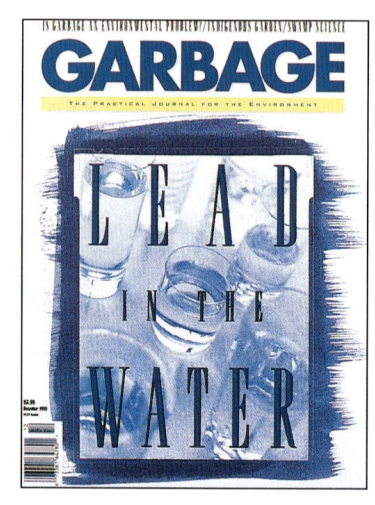

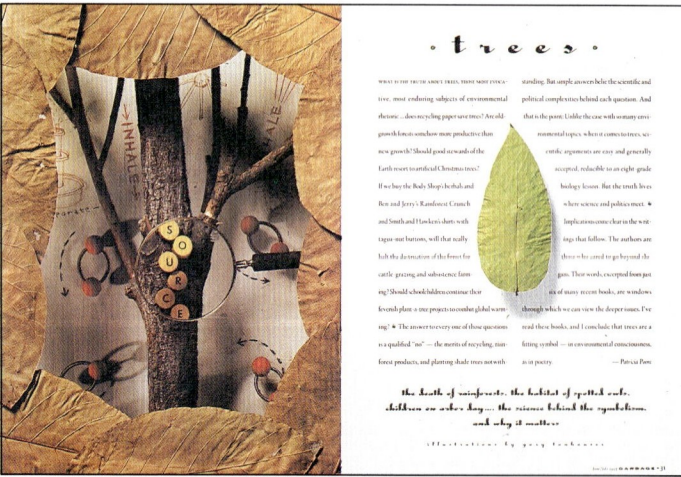

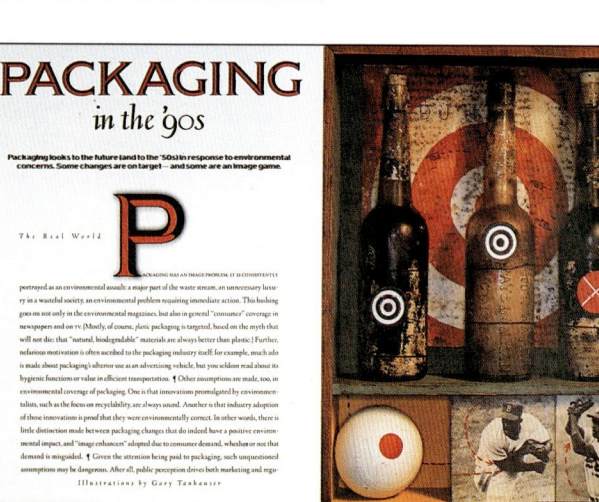

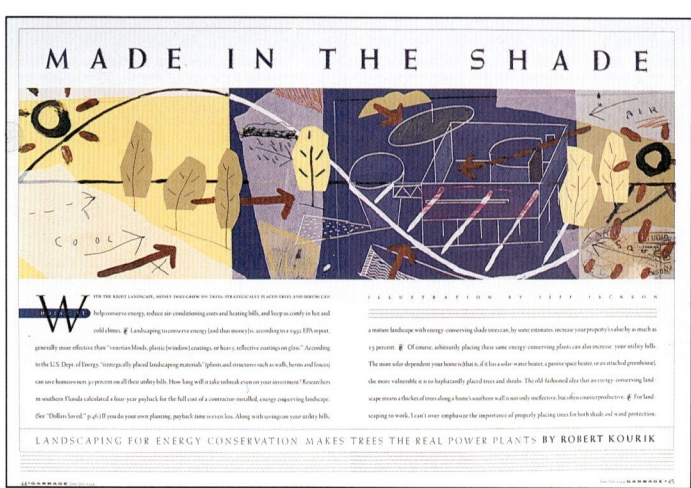

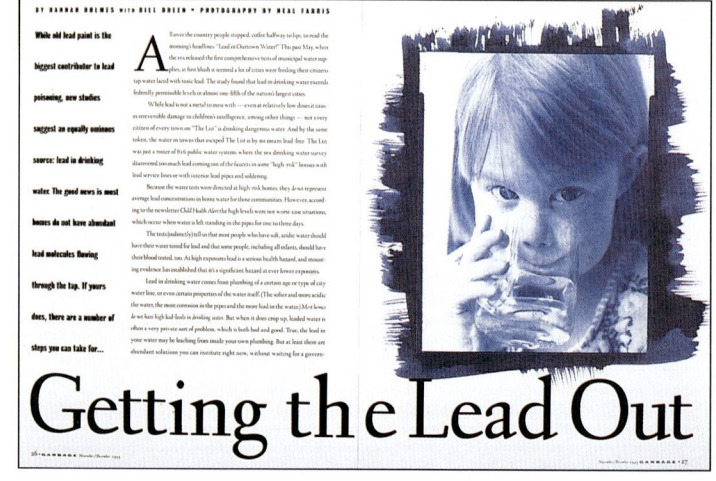

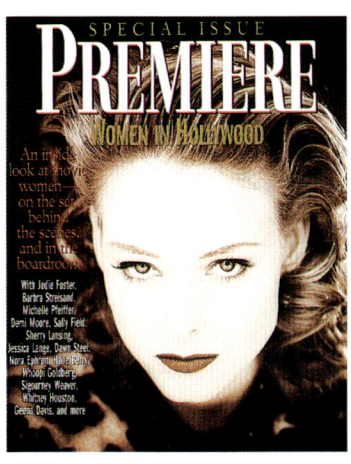

PUBLICATION   Travel & Leisure
AWARD   Merit
DESIGN DIRECTOR   Lloyd Ziff
DESIGNER   Lloyd Ziff
ILLUSTRATOR   Mick Haggerty
PHOTOGRAPHERS   Geof Kern, Langdon Clay, Timothy Hursley,
 Sally Gall
PHOTO EDITOR   Hazel Hammond
PUBLISHER   American Express Publishing
CATEGORY   Design/Entire Issue
DATE   May 1993

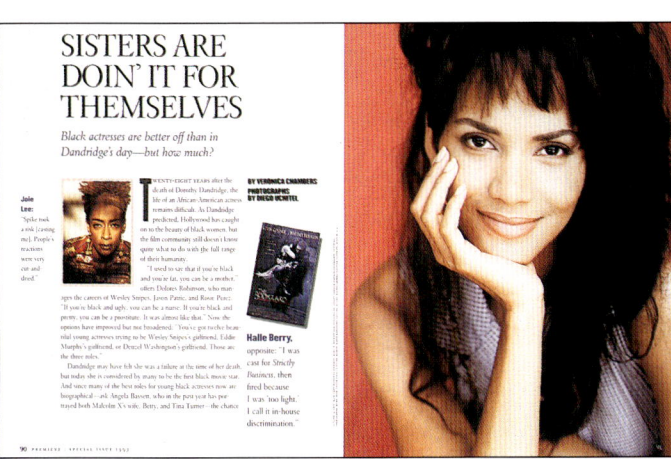

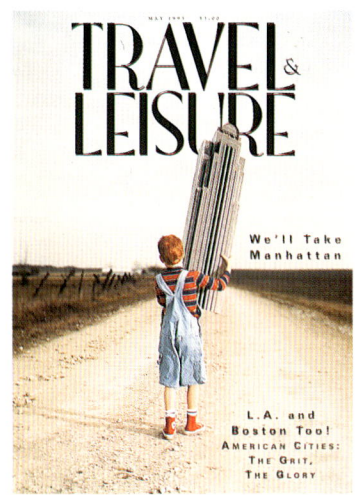

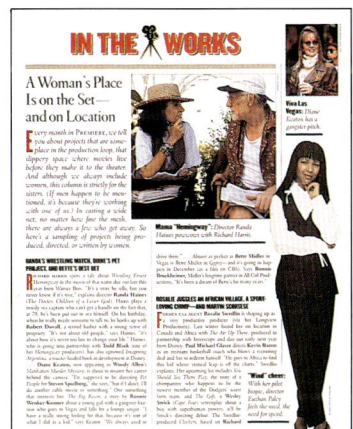

PUBLICATION   Premiere
AWARD   Merit
DESIGN DIRECTOR   John Schmitz
ART DIRECTOR   Mariana Ochs
DESIGNER   Jennifer Altemus
PHOTOGRAPHERS   Steve Sands/Outline, John Farmer,
 Blake Little/Visages, Diego Uchitel
PHOTO EDITOR   Charlie Holland
PUBLISHER   K III Magazines
STUDIO   Roger Black, Inc.
CATEGORY   Design/Entire Issue
DATE   Summer 1993

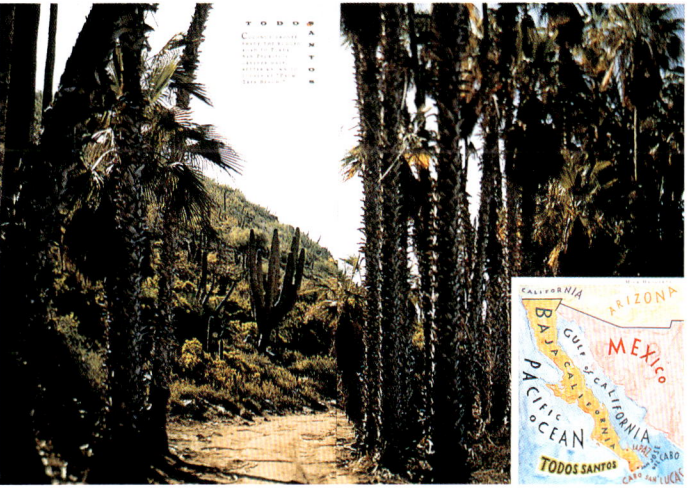

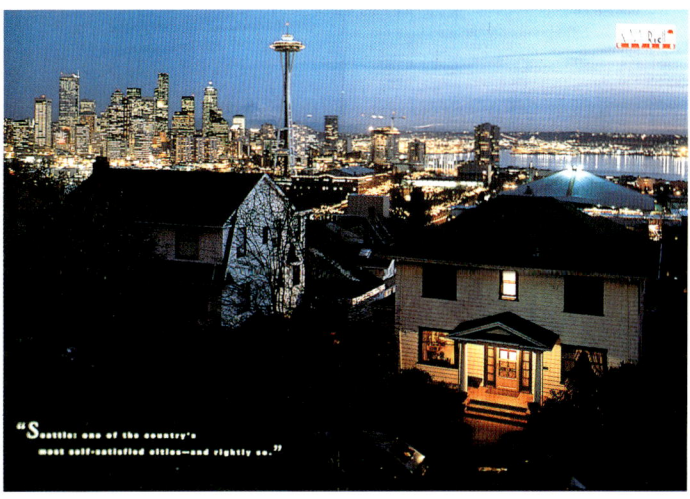

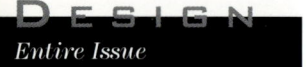

PUBLICATION	Vibe
AWARD	Merit
DESIGN DIRECTOR	Gary Koepke
ART DIRECTOR	Richard Baker
DESIGNERS	Gary Koepke, Richard Baker
PHOTOGRAPHERS	Dan Winters, Mario Castellanos, Ruven Afanador
PHOTO EDITOR	George Pitts
PUBLISHER	Time Inc. Ventures
STUDIO	Koepke International, Ltd.
CATEGORY	Design/Entire Issue
DATE	September 1993

PUBLICATION	Vibe
AWARD	Merit
DESIGN DIRECTOR	Gary Koepke
ART DIRECTOR	Richard Baker
DESIGNERS	Richard Baker, Gary Koepke
PHOTOGRAPHERS	Christian Witkins, Dana Lixenberg
PHOTO EDITOR	George Pitts
PUBLISHER	Time Inc. Ventures
STUDIO	Koepke International, Ltd.
CATEGORY	Design/Entire Issue
DATE	November 1993

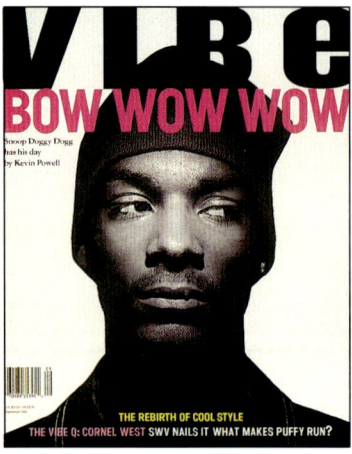
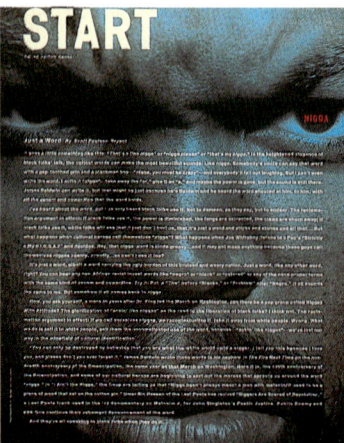
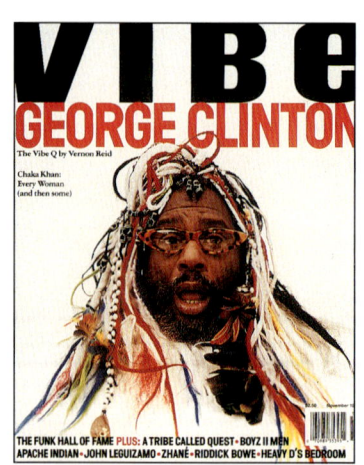

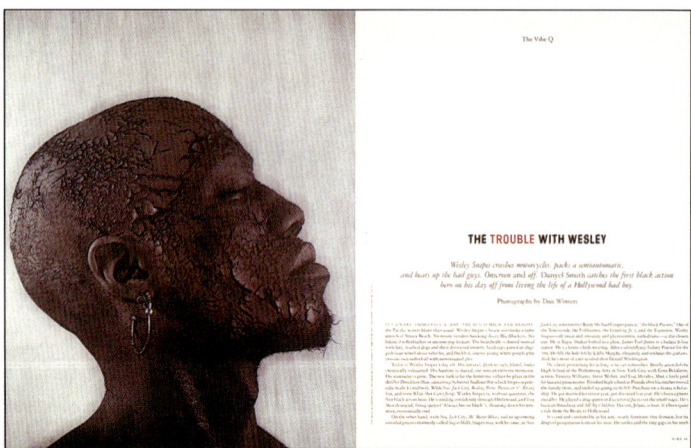

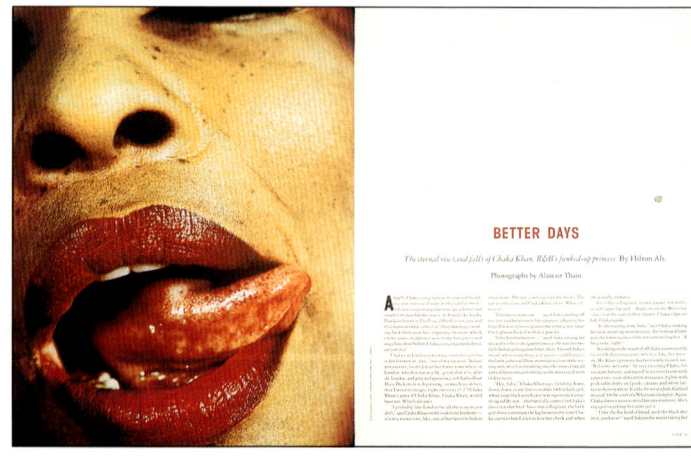

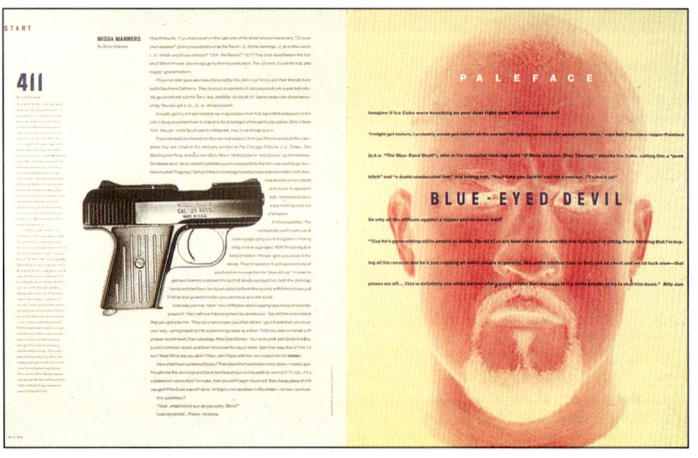
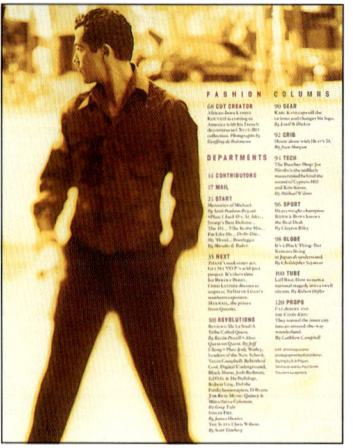
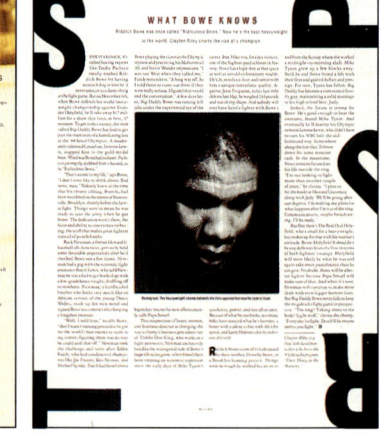

56

PUBLICATION American Photo
AWARD Merit
ART DIRECTOR Mark Gartland
DESIGNER Patricia Marroquin
PHOTOGRAPHER Robert Mapplethorpe
PUBLISHER Hachette Filipacchi Magazines, Inc.
CATEGORY Design/Entire Issue
DATE March/April 1993

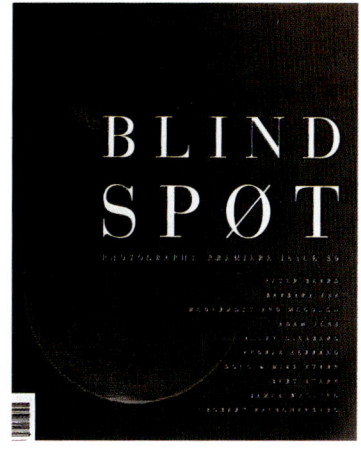

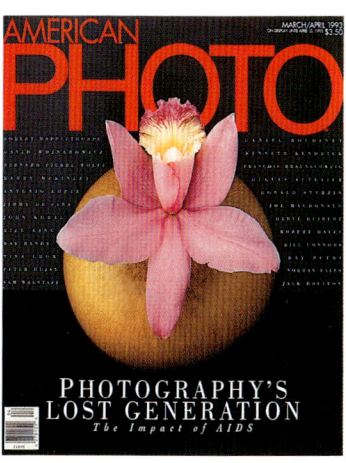

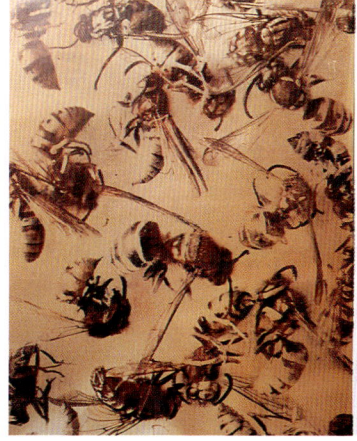

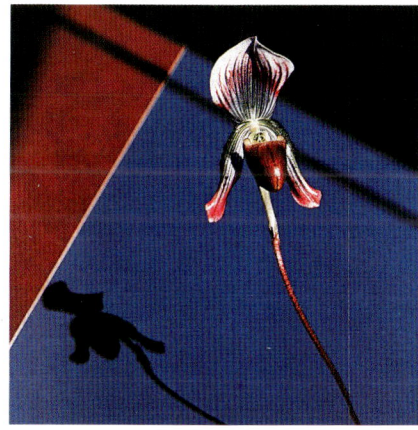

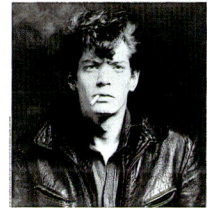

for

ROBERT MAPPLETHORPE

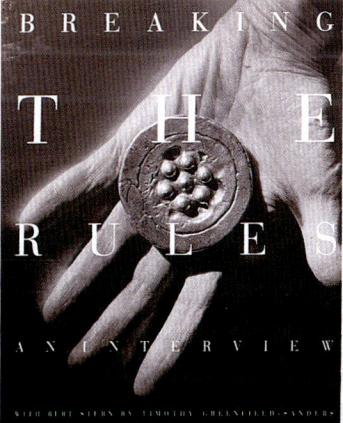

BILL KING

JOHN KOBAL

PETER HUJAR

ROBERT MAPPLETHORPE

BERNARD PIERRE WOLFF

SAM WAGSTAFF

PHOTOGRAPHY'S

TINA CHOW

ANTONIO LOPEZ

DAVID WOJNAROWICZ

BARRY MCKINLEY

JIMMY DE SANA

WAY BANDY

LOST GENERATION

NORMAN EALES

JOE MACDONALD

JACK BOULTON

FRANÇOIS BRAUNSCHWEIG

HUGUES AUTEXIER

DANIEL BOUDINET

DONALD STERZIN

KEN KENDRICK

RAY PETRI

HERVÉ GUIBERT

ROBERT HAYES

BILL CONNORS

PUBLICATION Blindspot
AWARD Merit
DESIGN DIRECTOR Robert Bergman-Ungar
ART DIRECTOR Robert Bergman-Ungar
DESIGNER Guan Liong The
PHOTO EDITOR Robert Bergman-Ungar
PUBLISHER Blindspot Photography, Inc.
CATEGORY Design/Entire Issue
DATE September 15, 1993

PUBLICATION	Das Papier (Switzerland)
AWARD	Merit
DESIGN DIRECTOR	Robert Bergman-Ungar
ART DIRECTOR	Robert Bergman-Ungar
DESIGNER	Guan Liong The
ILLUSTRATOR	Robert Bergman-Ungar
PHOTOGRAPHERS	Max Bee, Daniel Schwartz, Adrian Fritchi, Daniel Valance
PUBLISHER	Mâp Publications, Inc.
CATEGORY	Design/Entire Issue
DATE	May 12, 1993

PUBLICATION	The New Yorker
AWARD	Merit
DESIGN DIRECTORS	Caroline Mailhot, Wynn Dan
ILLUSTRATORS	Mike Reagan, Owen Smith
PUBLISHER	The Condé Nast Publications Inc.
CATEGORY	Design/Entire Issue
DATE	December 6, 1993

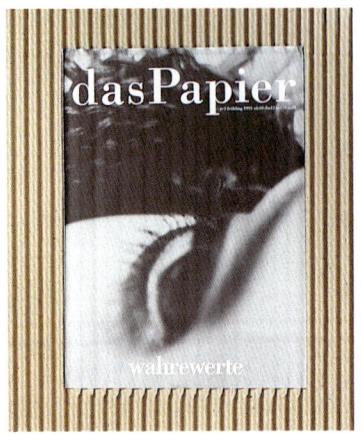

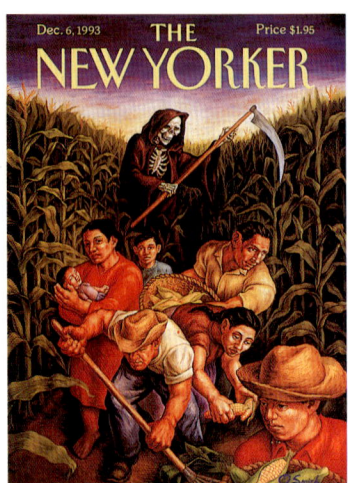

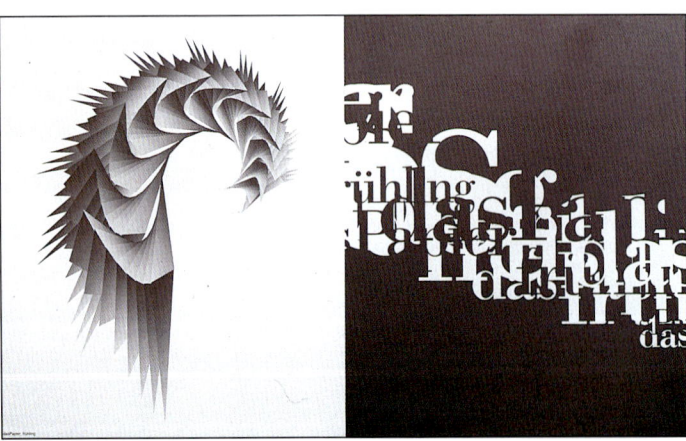

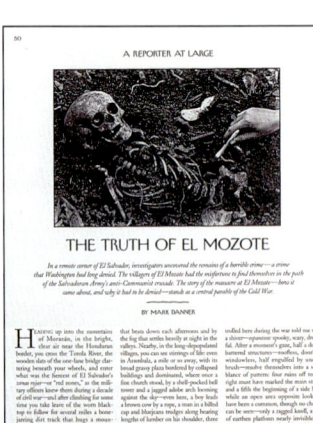

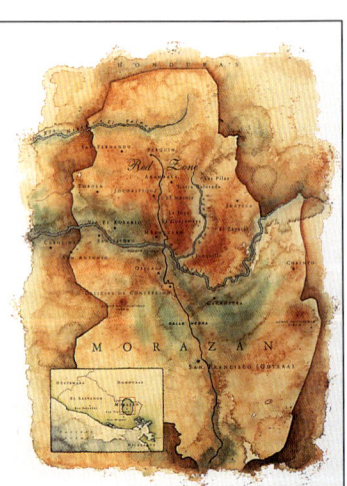

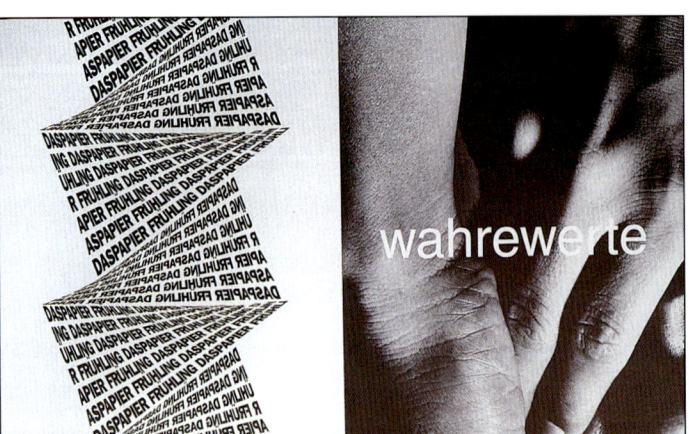

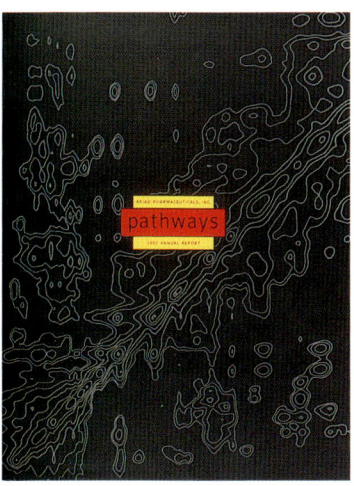

PUBLICATION   Adobe Systems Incorporated
              1992 Annual Report
AWARD   Merit
CREATIVE DIRECTOR   Aubrey Balkind
DESIGNER   Kin Yuen
ILLUSTRATORS Henrik Drescher, Pamela Hobbs
PHOTOGRAPHERS Jeffrey Newbury, Jock McDonald, Julie Powell
STUDIO   Frankfurt Balkind Partners
CATEGORY   Design/Entire Issue
DATE   March 1993

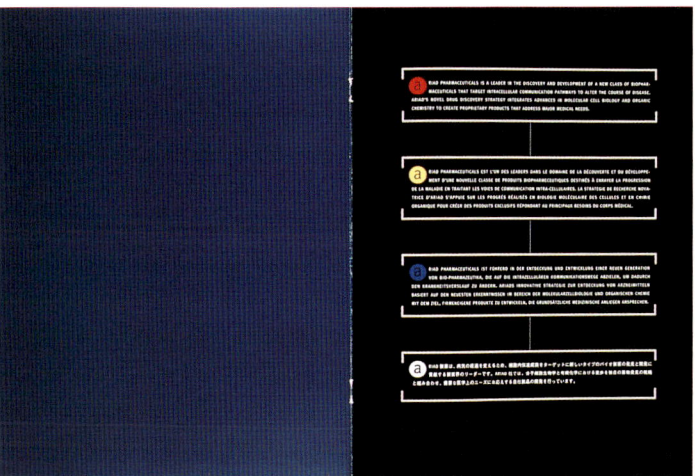

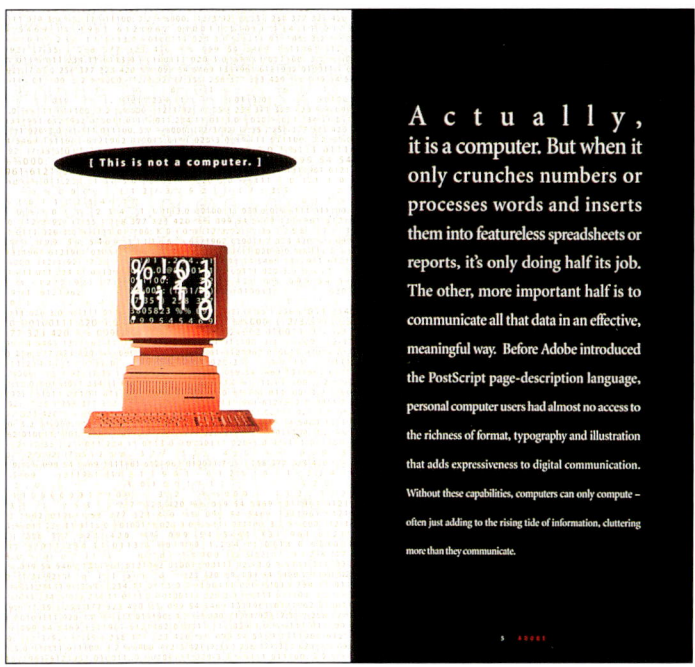

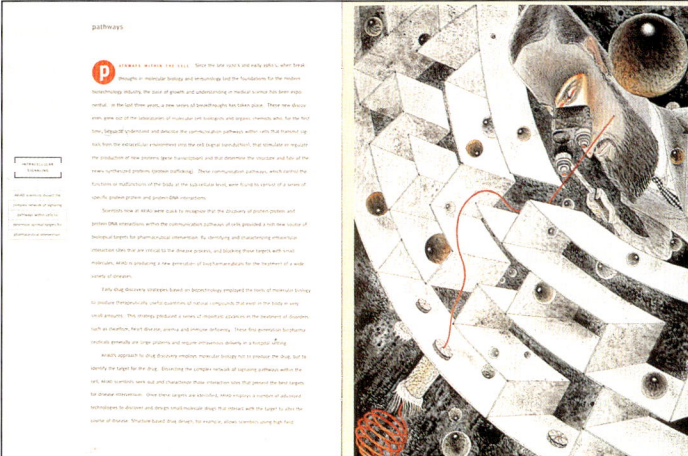

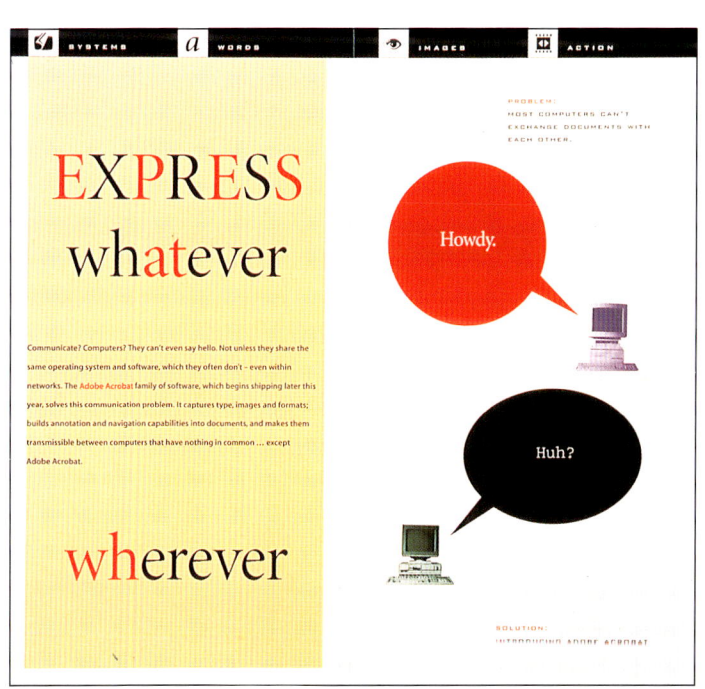

PUBLICATION   Ariad Pharmaceuticals 1992 Annual Report
AWARD   Merit
DESIGN DIRECTORS Susan Hochbaum, Woody Pirtle
ART DIRECTORS   Susan Hochbaum, Woody Pirtle
DESIGNERS   Susan Hochbaum, Woody Pirtle
ILLUSTRATORS   Jack Unruh, Barbara Kelley
CLIENT   Ariad Pharmaceuticals, Inc.
STUDIO   Pentagram Design
CATEGORY   Design/Entire Issue
DATE   May 1993

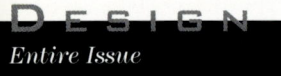

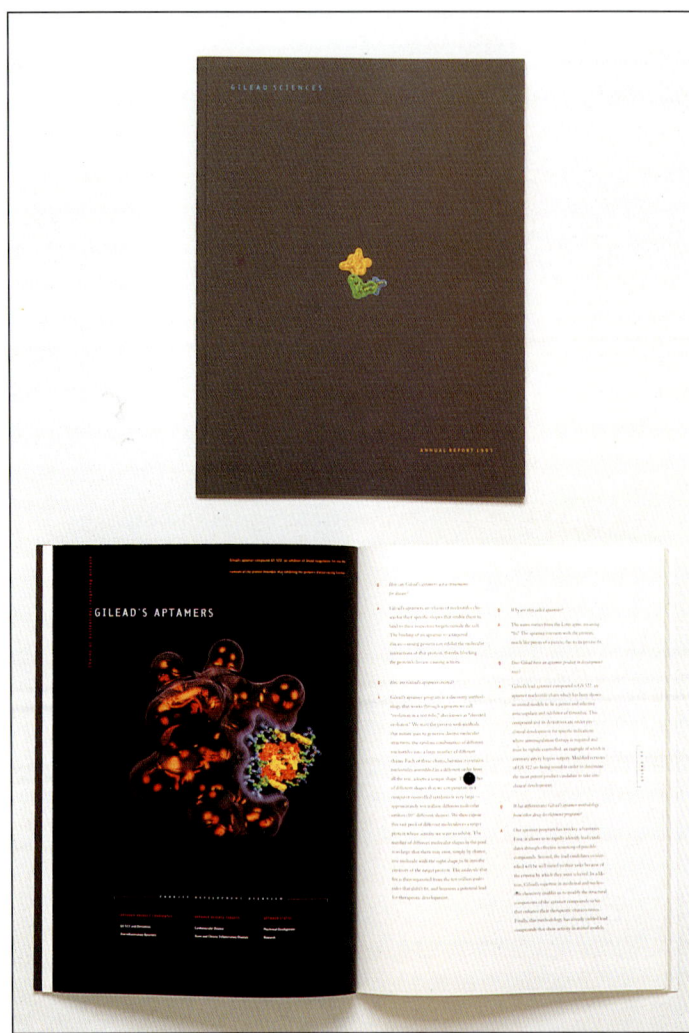

PUBLICATION   Gilead Sciences 1993 Annual Report
AWARD   Merit
DESIGN DIRECTOR   Bill Cahan
ART DIRECTOR   Bill Cahan
DESIGNER   David Gilmour
ILLUSTRATOR   Doug Struthers
STUDIO   Cahan & Associates
CATEGORY   Design/Entire Issue

PUBLICATION   Celestial Seasonings 1992
AWARD   Merit
DESIGN DIRECTOR   Lowell Williams
ART DIRECTOR   Lowell Williams
DESIGNERS   Melinda Maniscalco, Matt Magana
PHOTOGRAPHERS   Thomas Arledge, Kirk Anyx
STUDIO   Pentagram Design
CATEGORY   Design/Entire Issue
DATE   December 1993

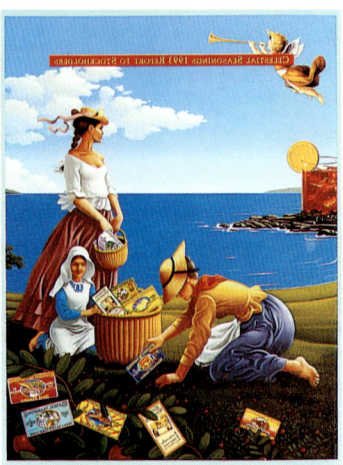

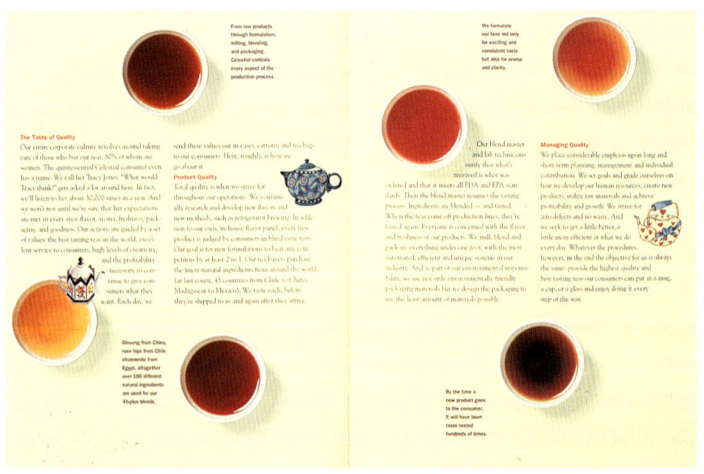

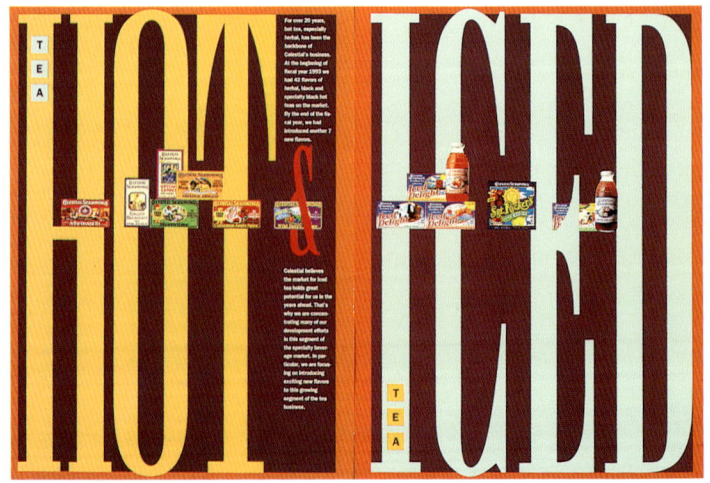

PUBLICATION	Chips & Technologies, Inc. 1993 Annual Report
AWARD	Merit
DESIGN DIRECTOR	Bill Cahan
ART DIRECTOR	Bill Cahan
DESIGNER	Guthrie Dolin
PHOTOGRAPHER	David Magnusson
STUDIO	Cahan & Associates
CATEGORY	Design/Entire Issue
DATE	1993

PUBLICATION	COR Therapeutics, Inc. 1992 Annual Report
AWARD	Merit
DESIGN DIRECTOR	Bill Cahan
ART DIRECTOR	Bill Cahan
DESIGNER	Jean Orlebeke
PHOTOGRAPHERS	Jeffrey Newbury, Stan Muselick, David Scharf, Walter Lopez, Larry Bercolo, Jock McDonald
STUDIO	Cahan & Associates
CATEGORY	Design/Entire Issue
DATE	1993

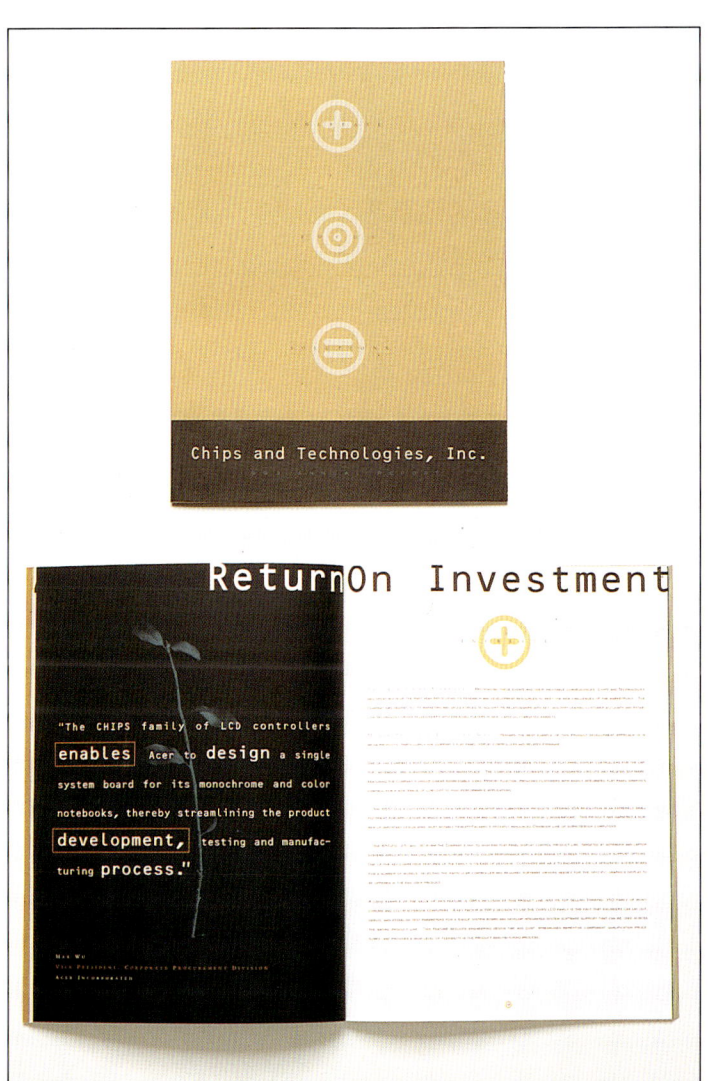

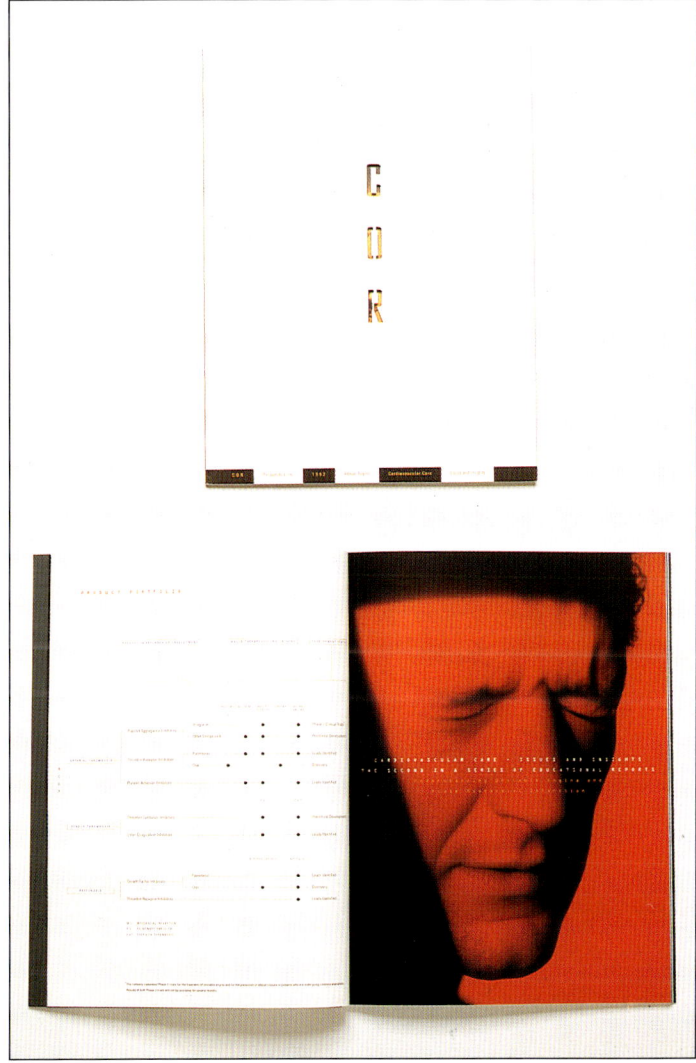

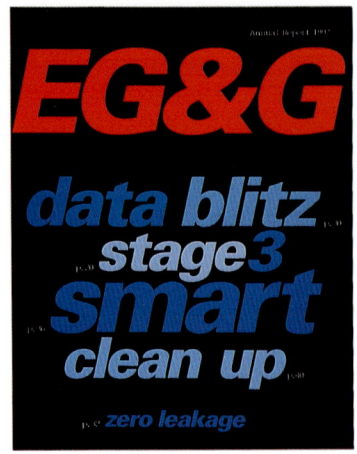

PUBLICATION   E. I. du Pont de Nemours and Company 1992
              Annual Report
AWARD   Merit
CREATIVE DIRECTOR   Aubrey Balkind
DESIGNER   Kin Yuen
ILLUSTRATOR   Holland
PHOTOGRAPHER   Greg Weiner
STUDIO   Frankfurt Balkind Partners
CATEGORY   Design/Entire Issue
DATE   March 1993

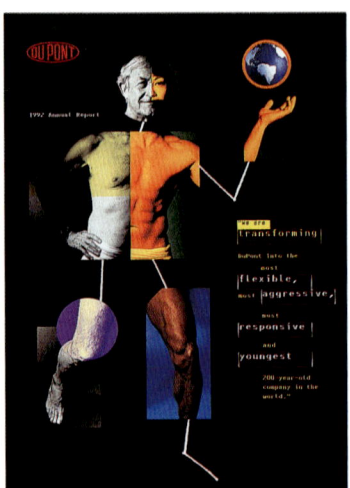

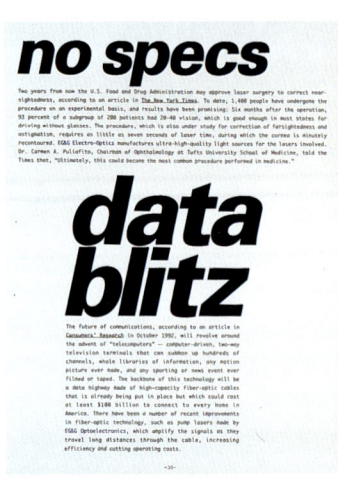

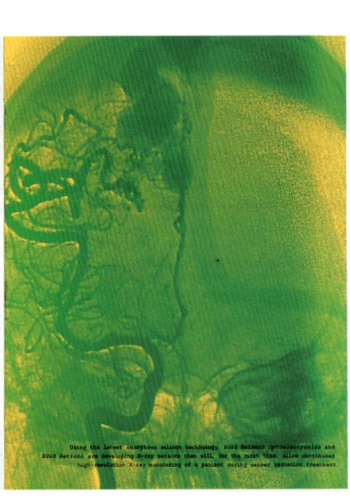

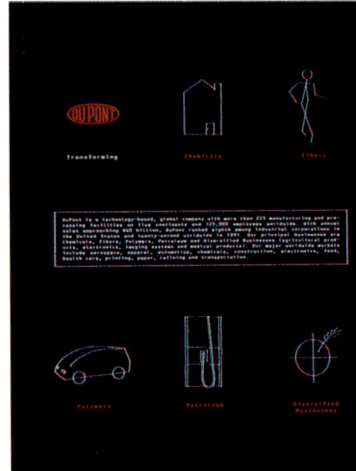

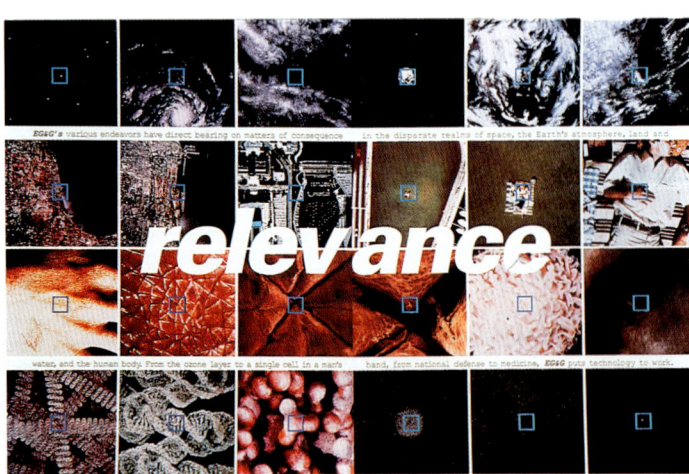

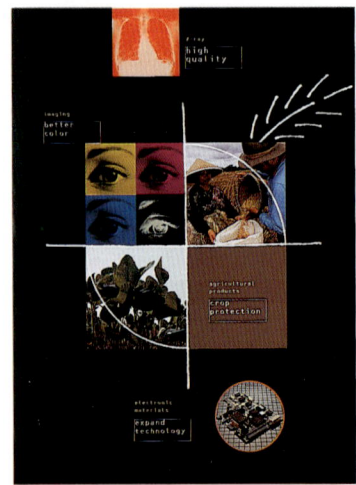

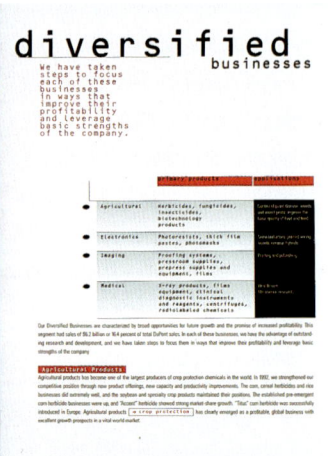

PUBLICATION   EG&G. Inc., 1992 Annual Report
AWARD   Merit
CREATIVE DIRECTOR   Aubrey Balkind
DESIGNERS   Andreas Combuchen, Hans Neubert
PHOTOGRAPHER   Arnold Newman
STUDIO   Frankfurt Balkind Partners
CATEGORY   Design/Entire Issue
DATE   March 1993

PUBLICATION	Inside King World Annual Report 1993
AWARD	Merit
DESIGN DIRECTOR	Leslie Segal
ART DIRECTOR	Victor Rivera
DESIGNER	Daniel Koh
CLIENT	King World
STUDIO	Addison Design
CATEGORY	Design/Entire Issue
DATE	December 31, 1993

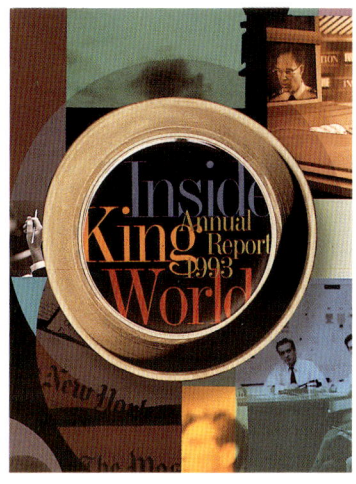

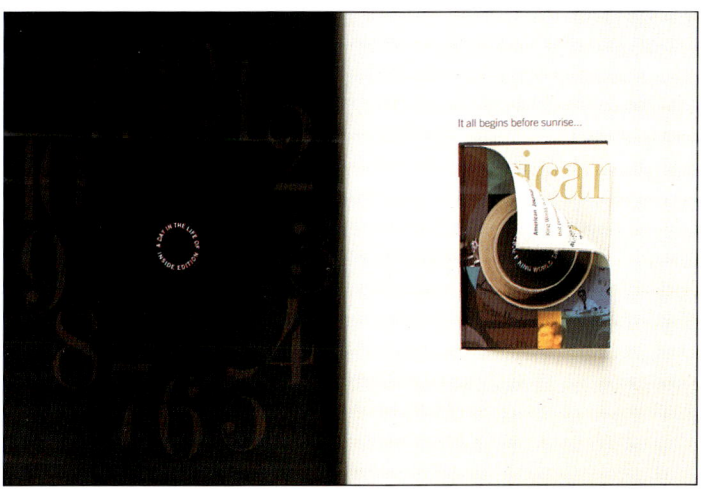

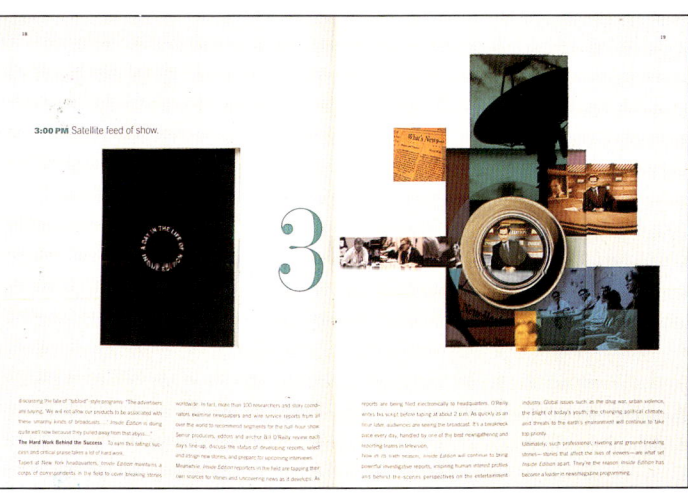

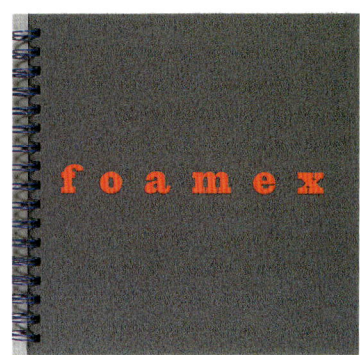

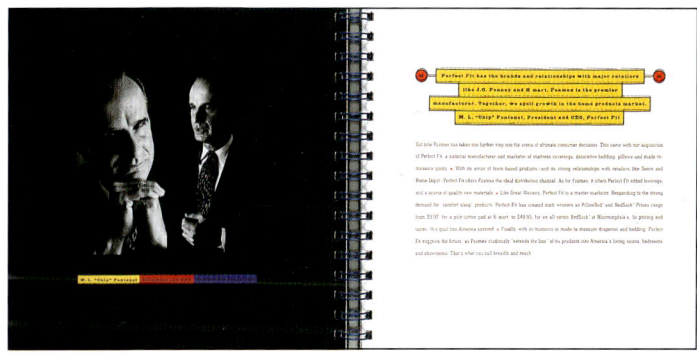

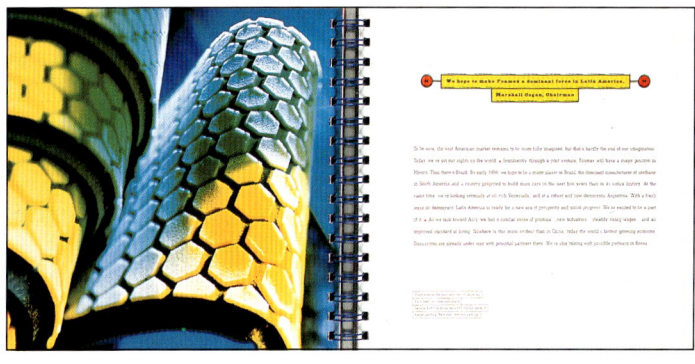

PUBLICATION	Foamex
AWARD	Merit
DESIGN DIRECTORS	Peter Harrison, Susan Hochbaum
ART DIRECTORS	Peter Harrison, Susan Hochbaum
DESIGNERS	Susan Hochbaum, Kevin Lauterbach
PHOTOGRAPHERS	John Madere, Kenji Toma
PUBLISHER	'21' International Holdings
STUDIO	Pentagram Design
CATEGORY	Design/Entire Issue
DATE	November 1993

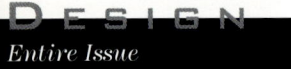

PUBLICATION	The Limited, Inc. 1992 Annual Report
AWARD	Merit
CREATIVE DIRECTOR	Aubrey Balkind
DESIGNER	Robert Wong
CLIENT	The Limited
STUDIO	Frankfurt Balkind Partners
CATEGORY	Design/Entire Issue
DATE	March 1993

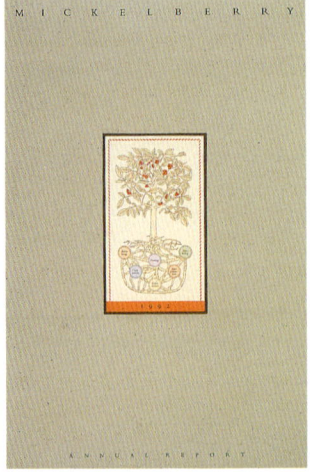

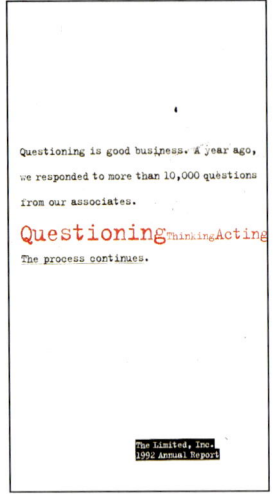

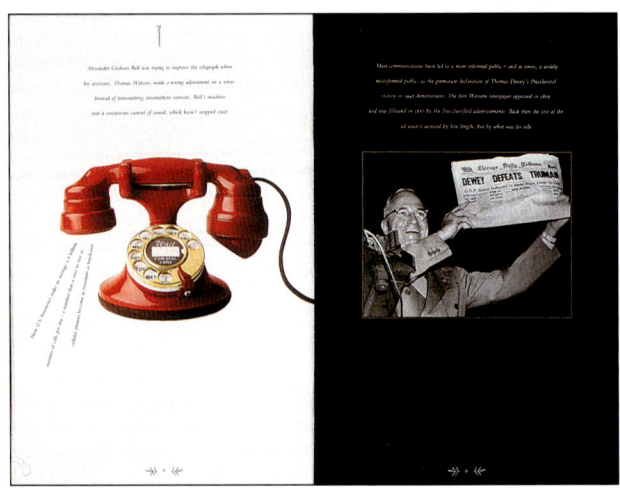

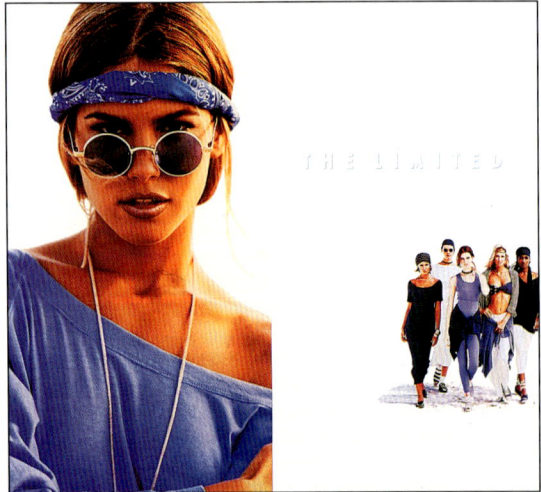

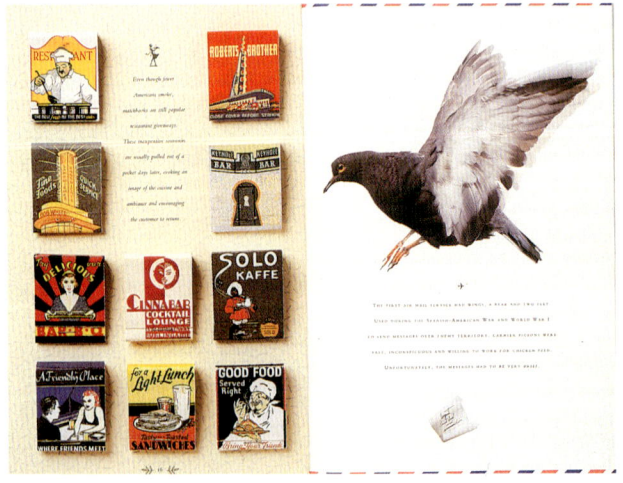

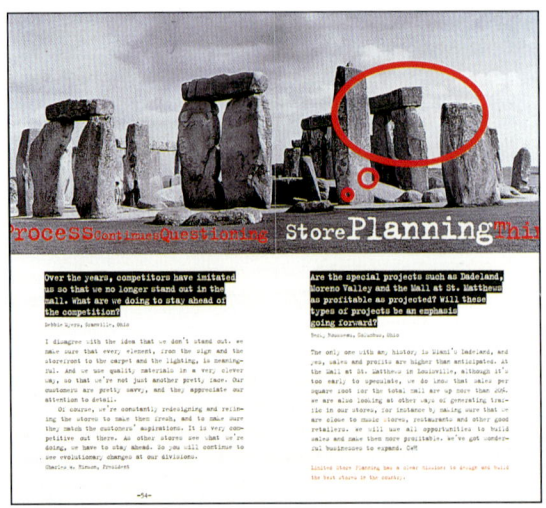

PUBLICATION	Mickelberry 1992 Annual Report
AWARD	Merit
DESIGN DIRECTOR	Peter Harrison
ART DIRECTOR	Peter Harrison
DESIGNERS	Peter Harrison, Christina Freyss
PHOTOGRAPHER	William Whitehurst
CLIENT	Mickelberry Corporation
STUDIO	Pentagram Design
CATEGORY	Design/Entire Issue
DATE	April 1993

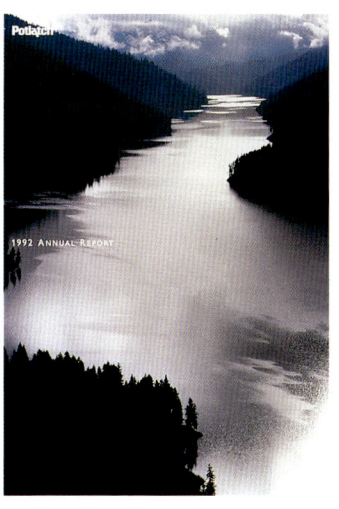

PUBLICATION The Progressive Corporation
             1992 Annual Report
AWARD   Merit
DESIGN DIRECTORS Mark Schwartz, Joyce Nesnadny
ART DIRECTORS Mark Schwartz, Joyce Nesnadny
DESIGNERS   Joyce Nesnadny, Michelle Moehler
PHOTOGRAPHER Neil Winokur
STUDIO   Nesnadny & Schwartz
CATEGORY   Design/Entire Issue
DATE   March 15, 1993

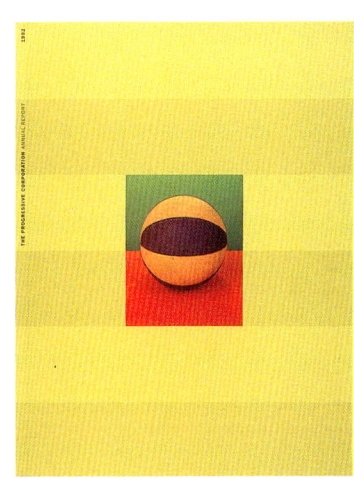

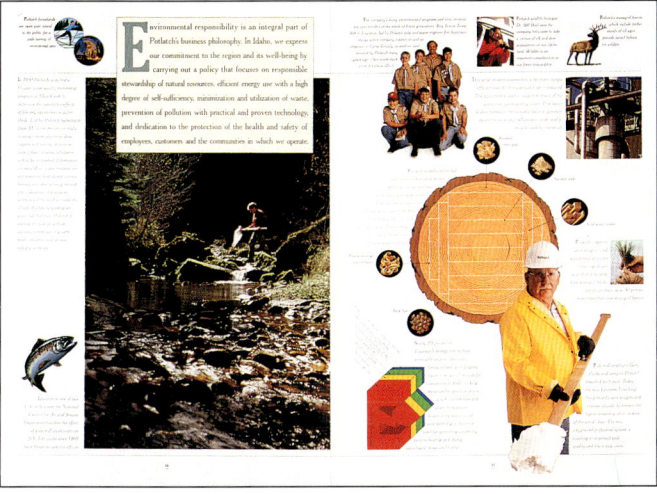

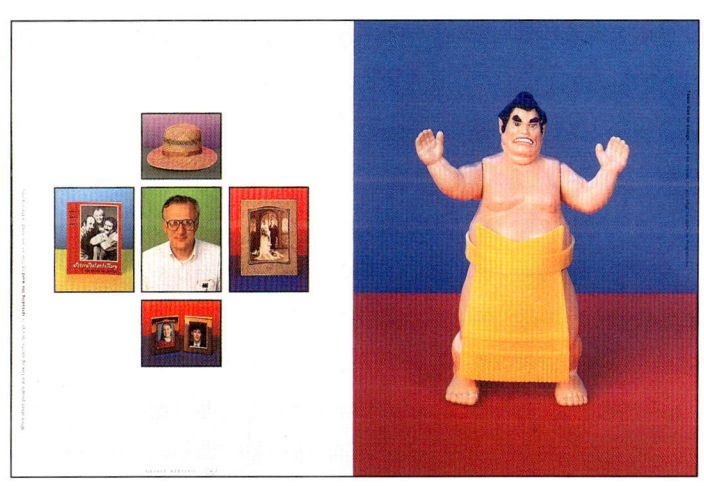

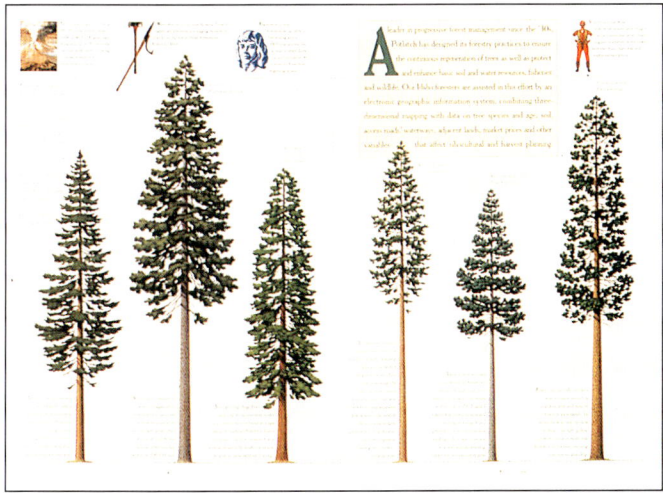

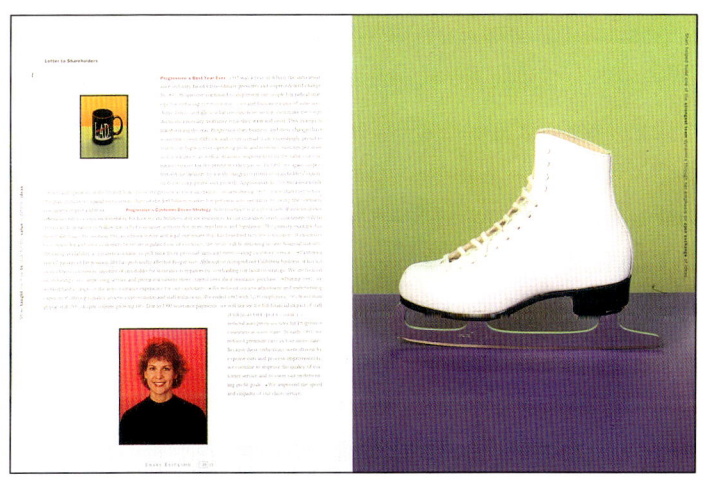

PUBLICATION Potlatch 1992 Annual Report
AWARD   Merit
DESIGN DIRECTOR Kit Hinrichs
ART DIRECTOR Kit Hinrichs
DESIGNERS   Belle How, Amy Chan
ILLUSTRATORS Justin Carroll, Will Nelson, Kathy O'Brien,
             Dave Stevenson
PHOTOGRAPHERS Tom Tracy, Bob Esparza, Barry Robinson
CLIENT   Potlatch Corporation
STUDIO   Pentagram Design
CATEGORY   Design/Entire Issue
DATE   March 9, 1993

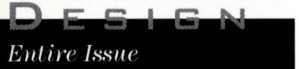

PUBLICATION   QVC Network, Inc. 1992 Annual Report
AWARD   Merit
CREATIVE DIRECTOR   Aubrey Balkind
DESIGN DIRECTOR   Kent Hunter
DESIGNERS   Andreas Combüchen, Matt Rollins
PHOTOGRAPHERS   Jose Picayo, Julie Powell
CLIENT   QVC Network, Inc.
STUDIO   Frankfurt Balkind Partners
CATEGORY   Design/Entire Issue
DATE   June 1993

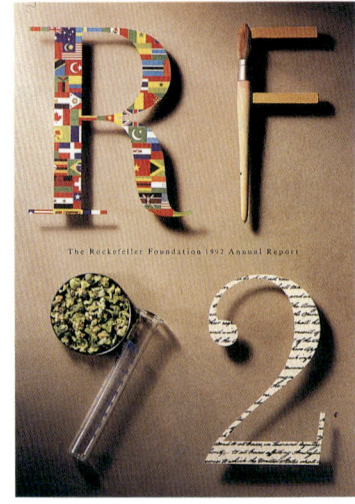

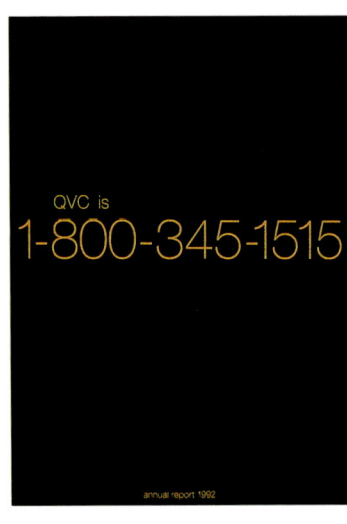

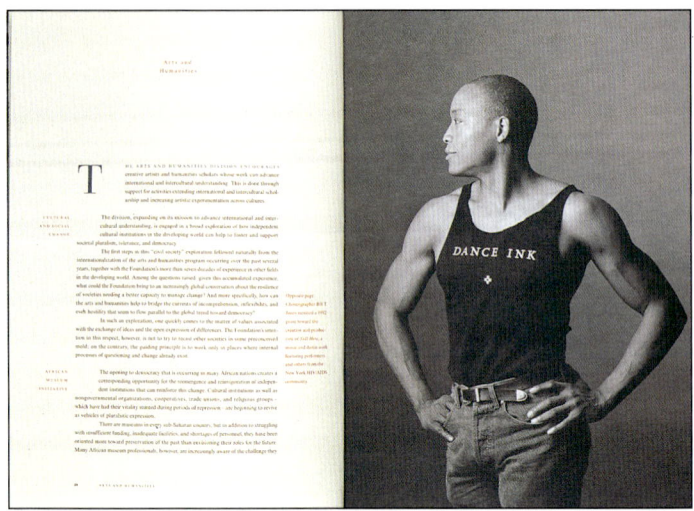

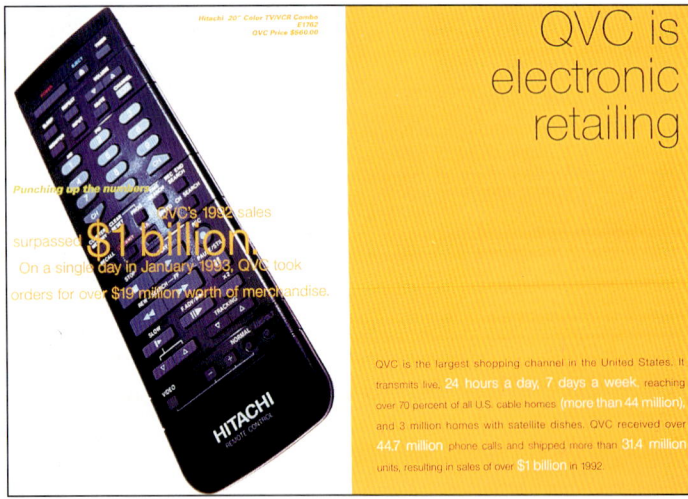

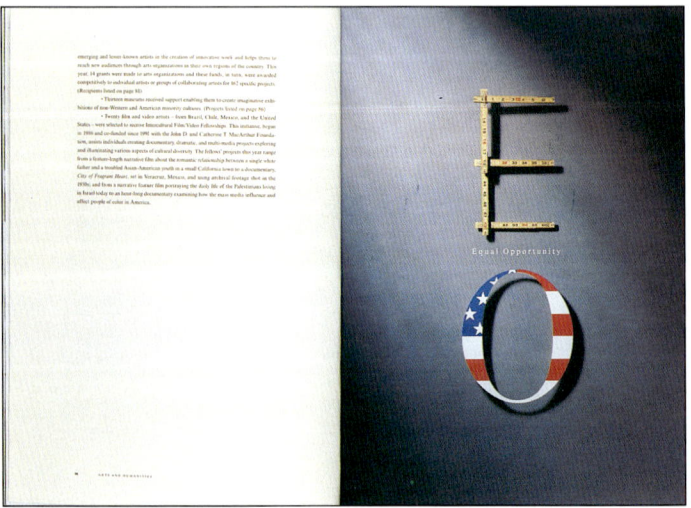

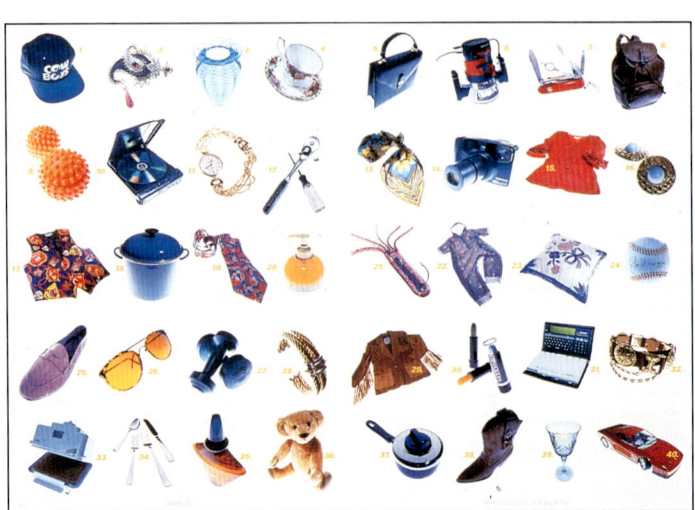

PUBLICATION   Rockefeller Foundation 1992 Annual Report
AWARD   Merit
DESIGN DIRECTORS   Woody Pirtle, John Klotnia
ART DIRECTORS   Woody Pirtle, John Klotnia
DESIGNERS   Woody Pirtle, John Klotnia
CLIENT   Rockefeller Foundation
STUDIO   Pentagram Design
CATEGORY   Design/Entire Issue
DATE   April 1993

PUBLICATION	The Seagram Ltd. 1993 Annual Report
AWARD	Merit
CREATIVE DIRECTOR	Aubrey Balkind, Danny Abelson, Kent Hunter
DESIGNERS	Benjamin Bailey, Matt Rollins
PHOTOGRAPHER	James L. Robinson
CLIENT	The Seagram Co., Ltd.
STUDIO	Frankfurt Balkind Partners
CATEGORY	Design/Entire Issue
DATE	April 1993

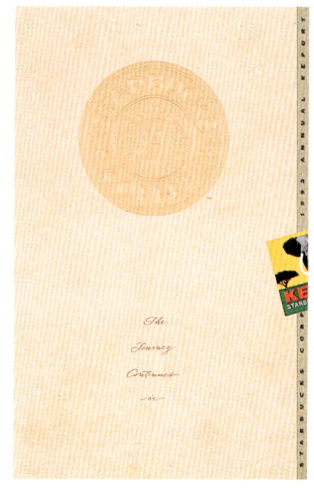

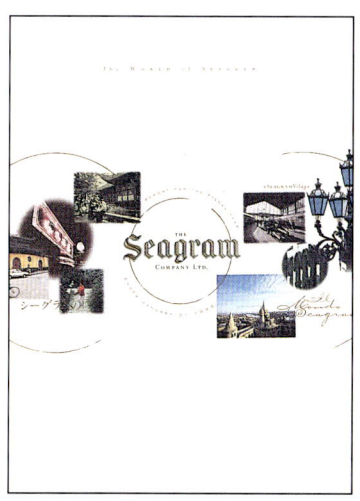

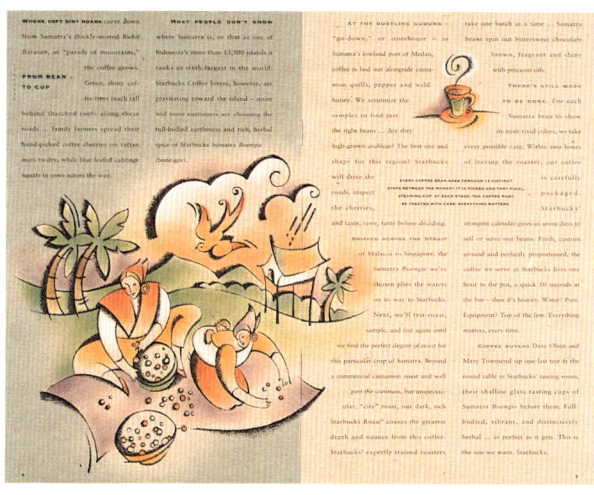

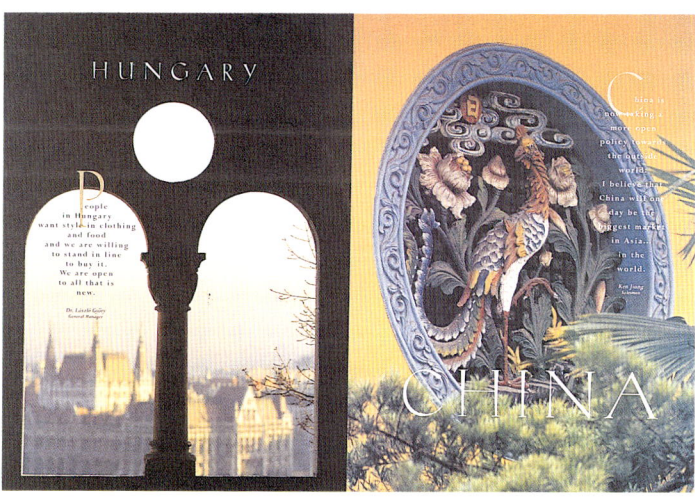

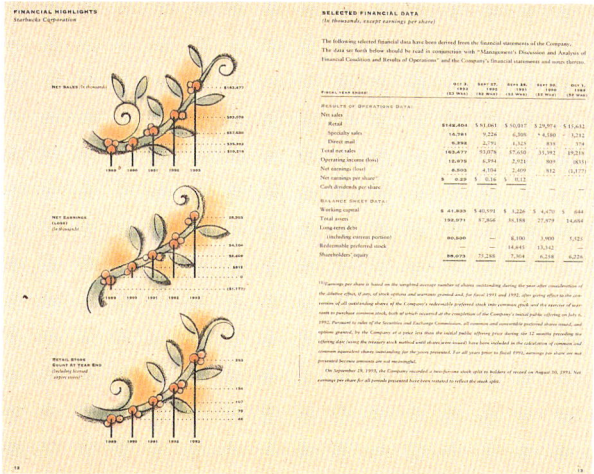

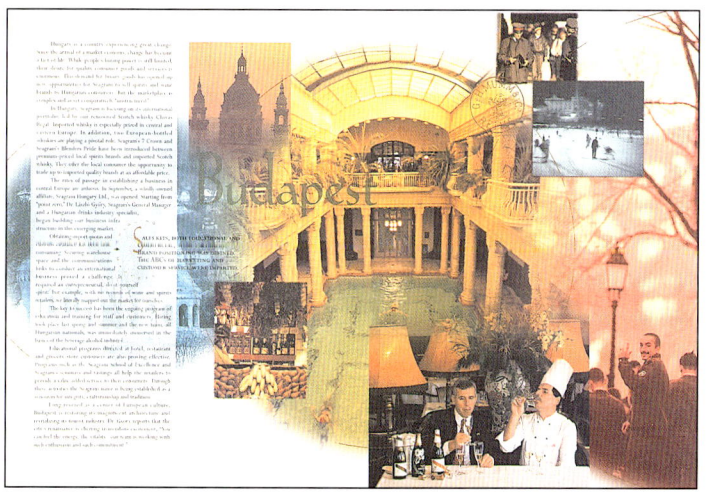

PUBLICATION	Starbucks Coffee Company 1993 Annual Report
AWARD	Merit
ART DIRECTOR	Jack Anderson
DESIGNERS	Bruce Branson-Meyer, Mary Hutchison, Jack Anderson, Julie Tanagi-Lock
ILLUSTRATOR	Julia LaPine
CLIENT	Starbucks Coffee Company
STUDIO	Hornall Anderson Design Works
CATEGORY	Design/Entire Issue
DATE	January 1994

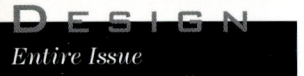

PUBLICATION	Trident Microsystems 1993 Annual Report
AWARD	Merit
DESIGN DIRECTOR	Bill Cahan
ART DIRECTOR	Bill Cahan
DESIGNER	Sharrie Brooks
CLIENT	Trident Microsystems
STUDIO	Cahan & Associates
CATEGORY	Design/Entire Issue

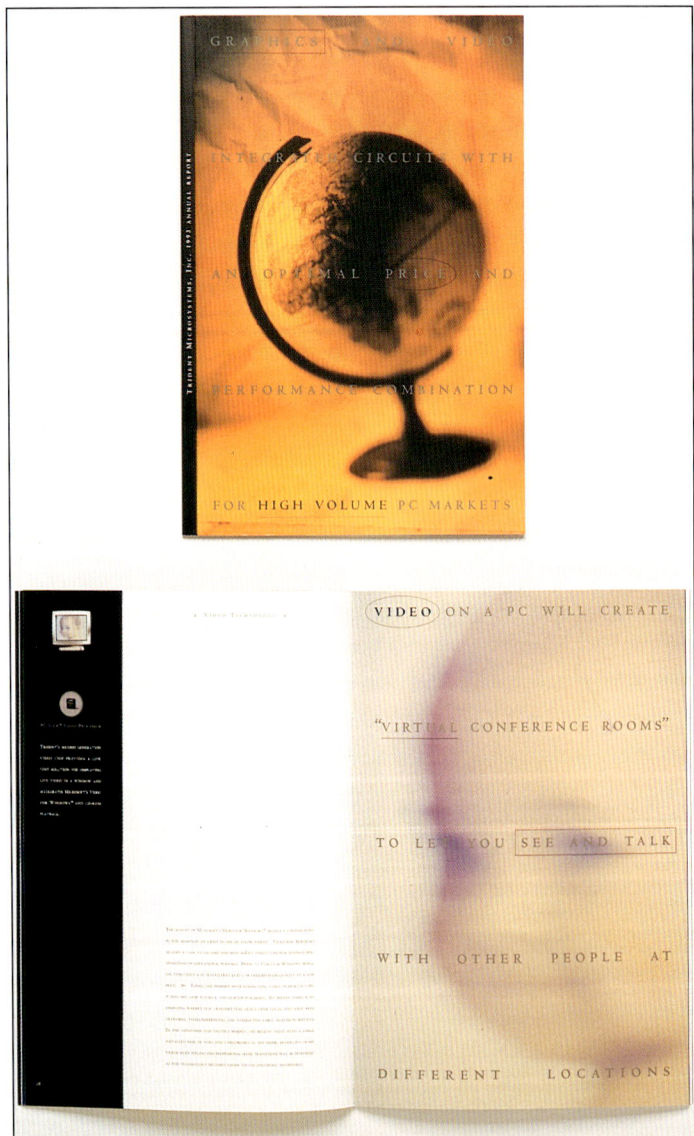

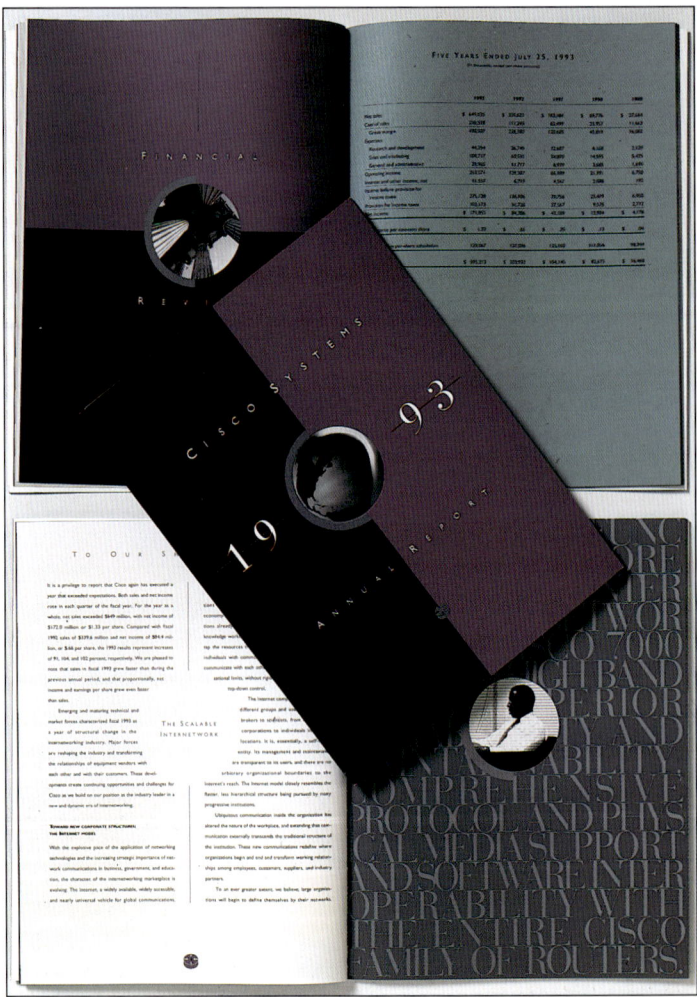

PUBLICATION	Cisco Systems Annual Report 1993
AWARD	Merit
DESIGN DIRECTOR	Peggy Burke
ART DIRECTOR	Peggy Burke
DESIGNERS	Andy Harding, Peggy Burke
PHOTOGRAPHER	Geoffrey Nelson
CLIENT	Cisco Systems
STUDIO	1185 Design
CATEGORY	Design/Entire Issue
DATE	October 1, 1993

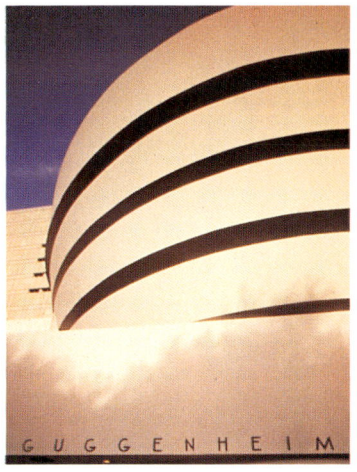

PUBLICATION   Guggenheim Magazine
AWARD   Merit
DESIGN DIRECTOR   Massimo Vignelli
DESIGNERS   Massimo Vignelli, Dani Piderman
ILLUSTRATORS   Dani Piderman, Roy Lichtenstein,
    Frank O. Gehry Associates,
    James Rosenquist, Claes Oldenburg
PHOTOGRAPHER   Allende Salazar
PUBLISHER   Guggenheim Museum Publications
STUDIO   Vignelli Associates
CATEGORY   Design/Entire Issue
DATE   Fall 1993

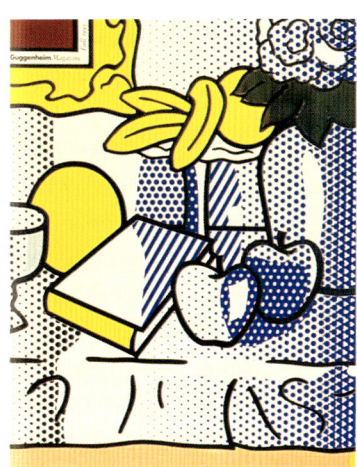

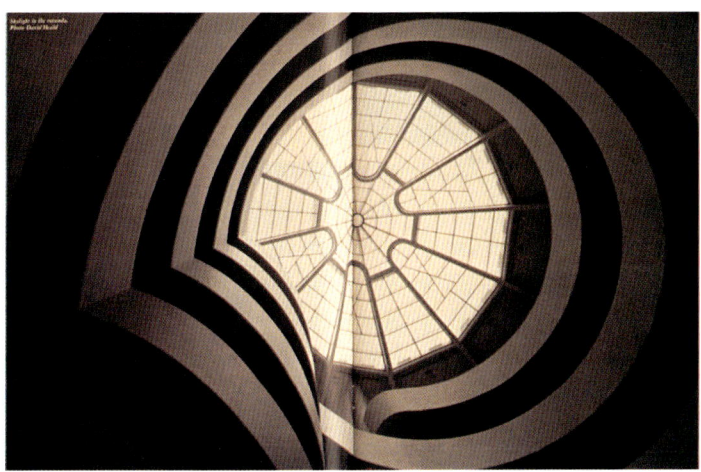

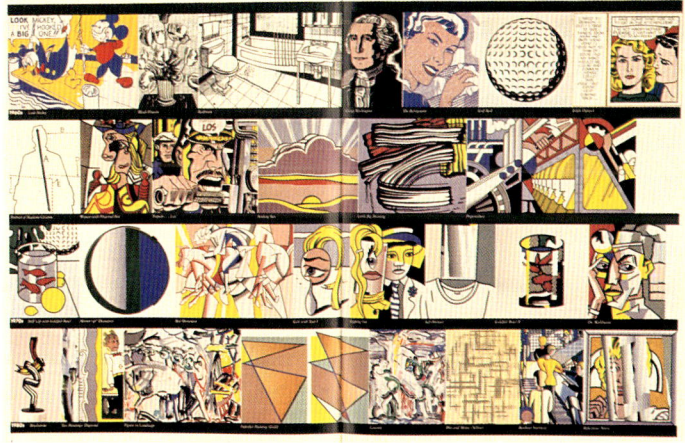

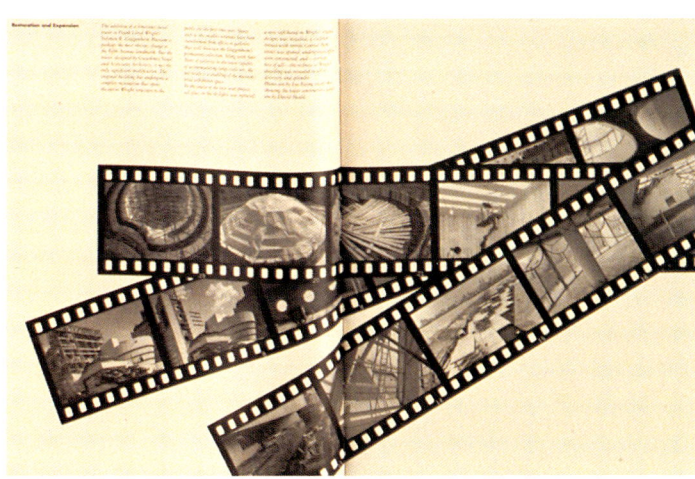

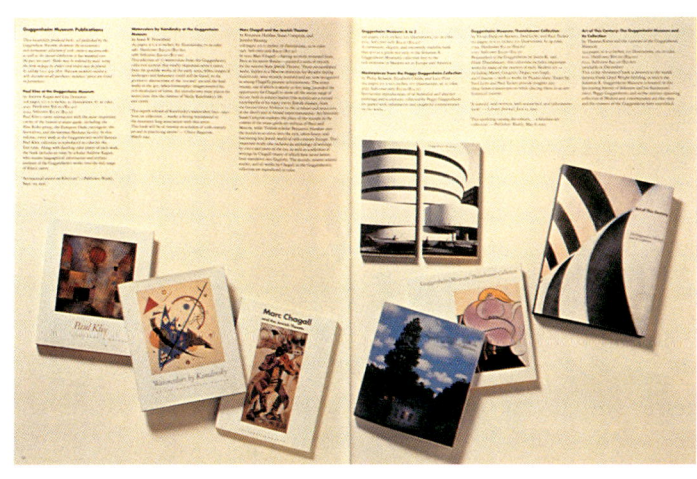

PUBLICATION   Guggenheim Magazine
AWARD   Merit
DESIGN DIRECTOR   Massimo Vignelli
DESIGNERS   Massimo Vignelli, Dani Piderman
PHOTOGRAPHERS   Lee Ewing, David Heald
PUBLISHER   Guggenheim Museum Publications
STUDIO   Vignelli Associates
CATEGORY   Design/Entire Issue
DATE   June 1993

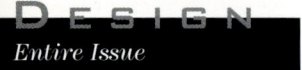

PUBLICATION	Simpson NEO		PUBLICATION	Number
AWARD	Merit		AWARD	Merit
DESIGN DIRECTOR	Woody Pirtle		DESIGN DIRECTOR	Bruce Crocker
DESIGNERS	Woody Pirtle, John Klotnia		DESIGNERS	Bruce Crocker, Lee Busch
CLIENT	Simpson Paper Company		PHOTO EDITOR	Bruce Crocker
STUDIO	Pentagram Design		CLIENT	Boston Acoustics
CATEGORY	Design/Entire Issue		STUDIO	Crocker, Inc.
DATE	September 1993		CATEGORY	Design/Entire Issue
			DATE	October 1, 1993

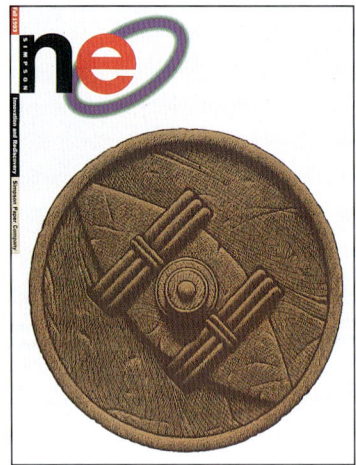

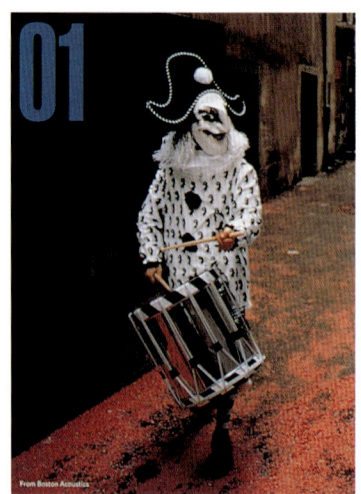

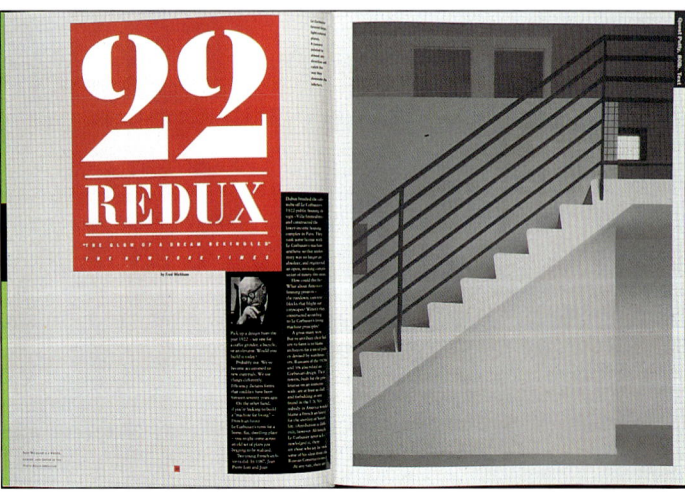

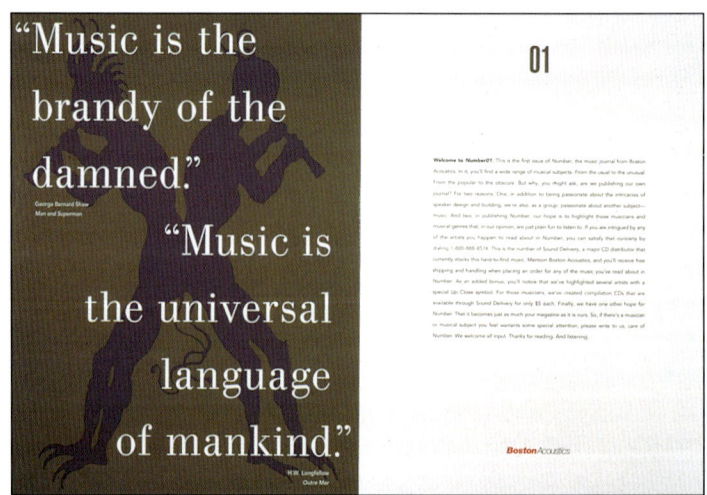

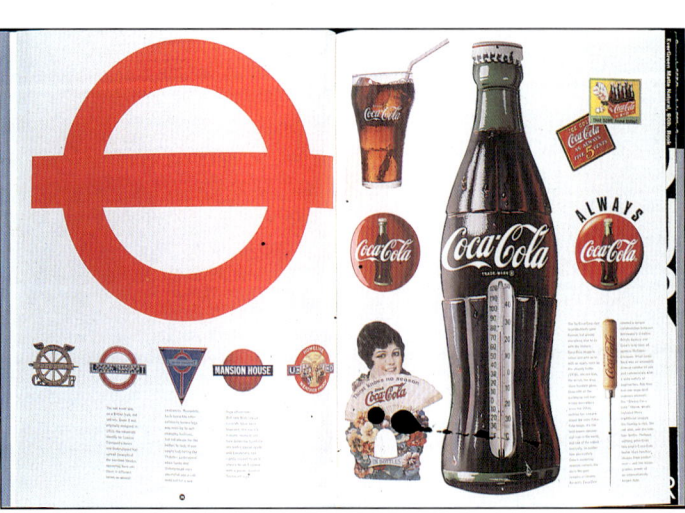

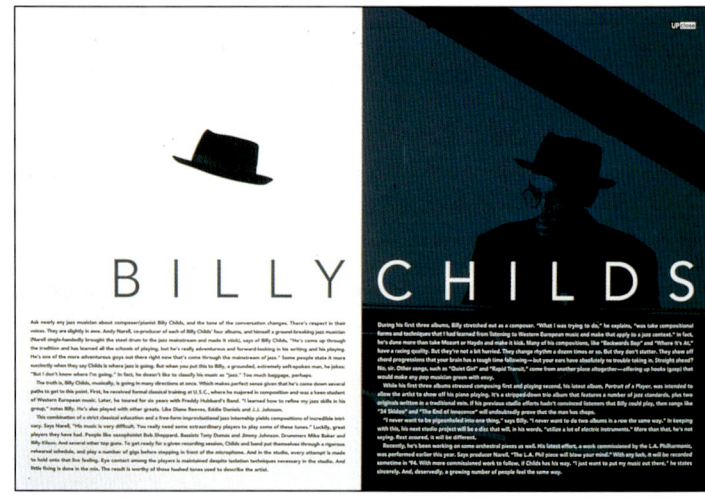

PUBLICATION   Skald
AWARD   Merit
DESIGN DIRECTOR   Kit Hinrichs
ART DIRECTOR   Kit Hinrichs
DESIGNER   Jackie Foshaug
ILLUSTRATORS   Dave Stevenson, Magellan Geographix,
Rodica Prato
PHOTOGRAPHERS   Barry Robinson, Harvey Lloyd
STUDIO   Pentagram Design
CATEGORY   Design/Entire Issue
DATE   March 1993

PUBLICATION   Oracle Corporation
AWARD   Merit
DESIGN DIRECTOR   Robert Kastigar
ART DIRECTOR   Earl Gee
DESIGNERS   Earl Gee, Fani Chung
ILLUSTRATORS   Jamie Hogan, David Wilcox, Philippe Weisbecker,
Darrel Kolosta, Steve Campbell, Greg Wenzel
PHOTOGRAPHERS   Henrik Kam, Geoffrey Nelson
CLIENT   Oracle Corporation
STUDIO   Earl Gee Design
CATEGORY   Design/Entire Issue
DATE   December 15, 1993

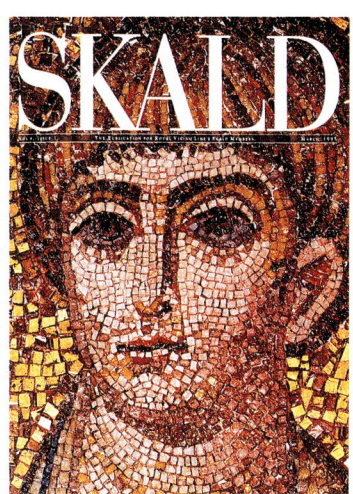

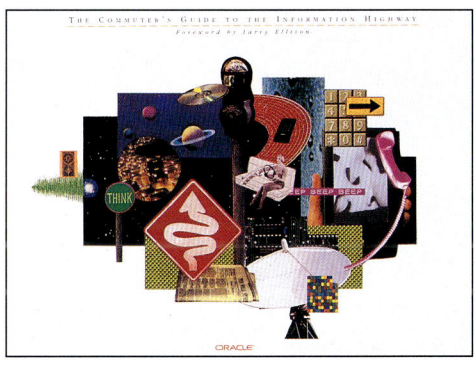

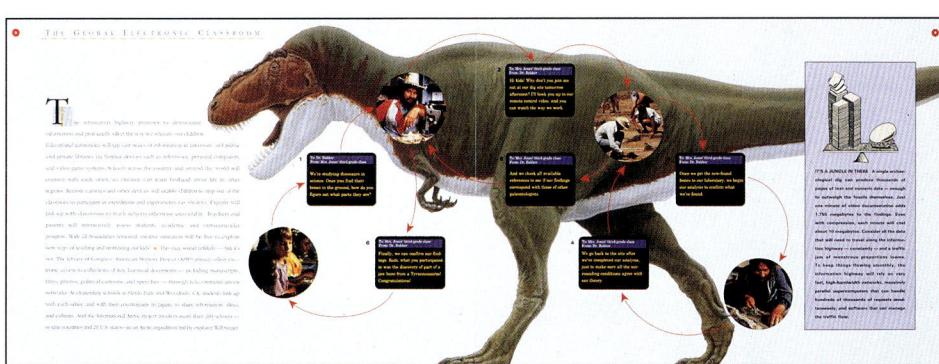

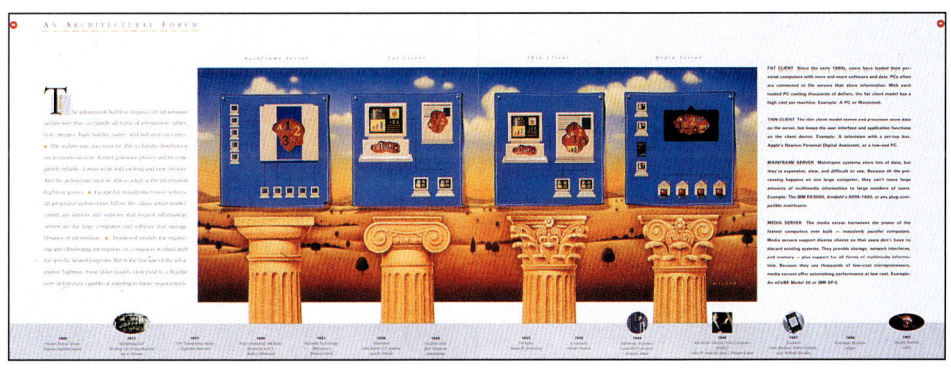

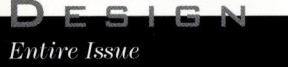

PUBLICATION   Subjective Reasoning
AWARD   Merit
ART DIRECTORS   Michael Gericke, Paula Scher, William Drenttel
DESIGNERS   Michael Gericke, Sharon Harel, Donna Ching
ILLUSTRATOR   Hammond Incorporated
PHOTOGRAPHERS   Christopher Morris Morris, Black Star
CLIENT   Champion International
CATEGORY   Design/Entire Issue
DATE   June 1, 1993

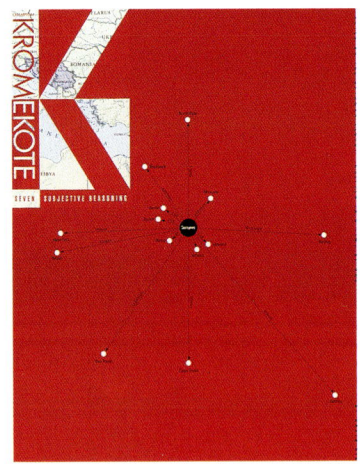

PUBLICATION   Magnet Design & Communications
AWARD   Merit
DESIGN DIRECTOR   Gregory Johnson
DESIGNER   M. Page Miller
ILLUSTRATORS   M. Page Miller, Claudy Mejia
PHOTOGRAPHERS   Debi Fox, Ken Wyner
PHOTO EDITOR   M. Page Miller
STUDIO   Magnet Design & Communications, Inc.
CATEGORY   Design/Entire Issue
DATE   December 15, 1993

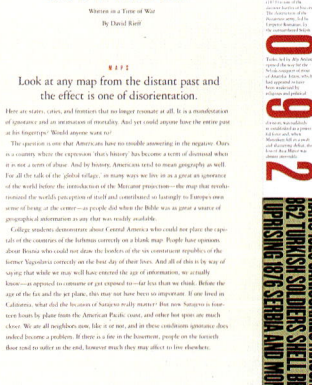

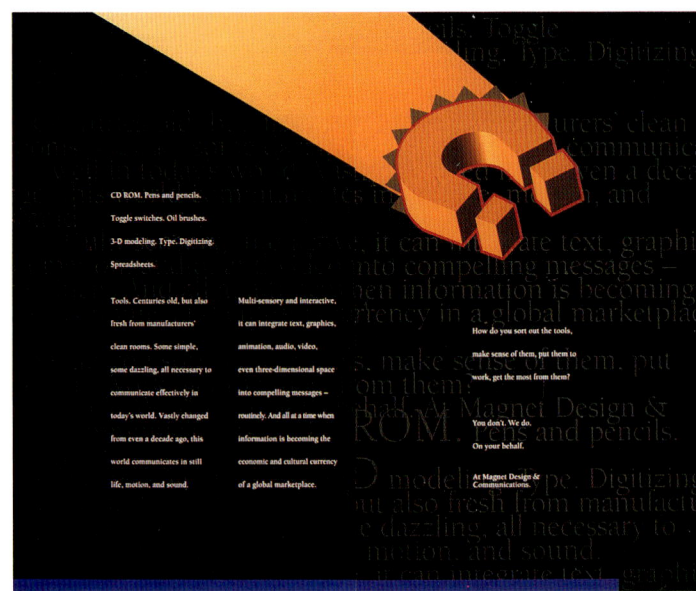

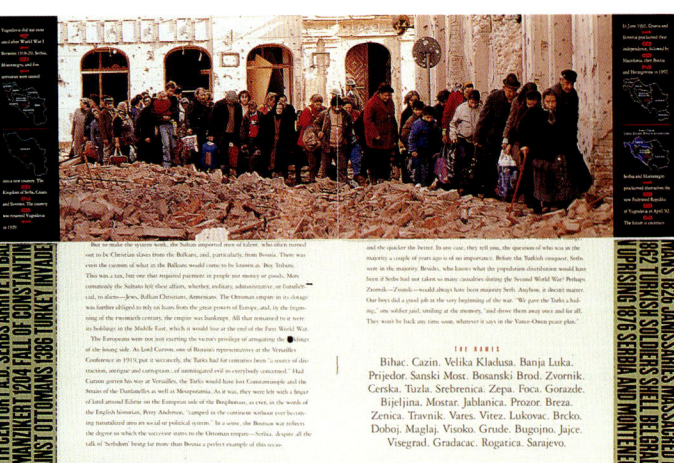

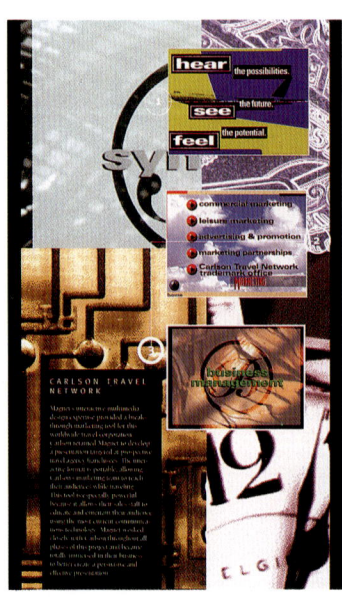

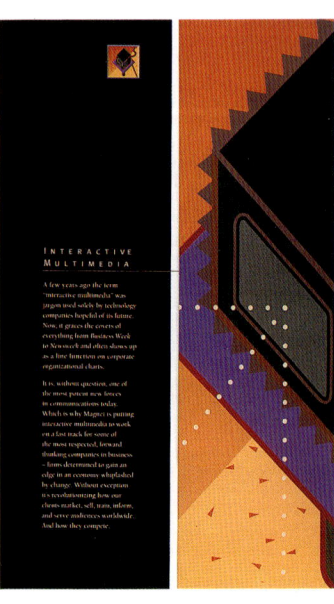

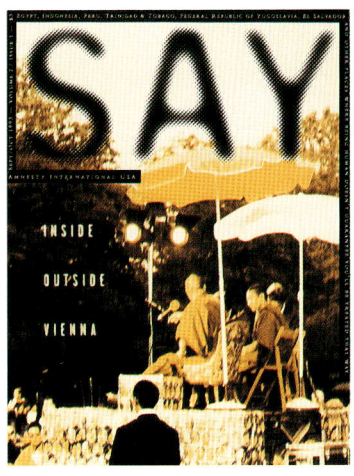

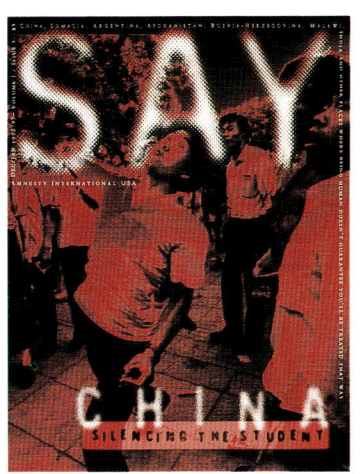

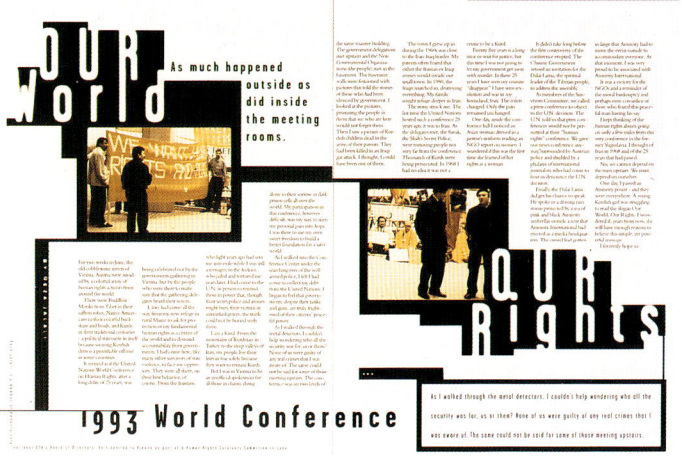

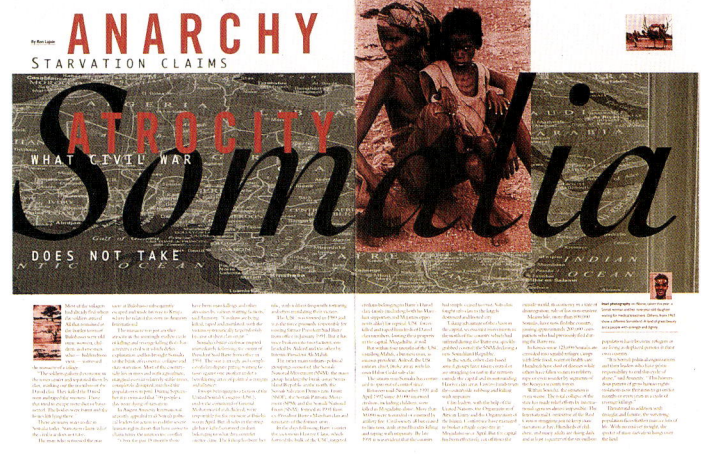

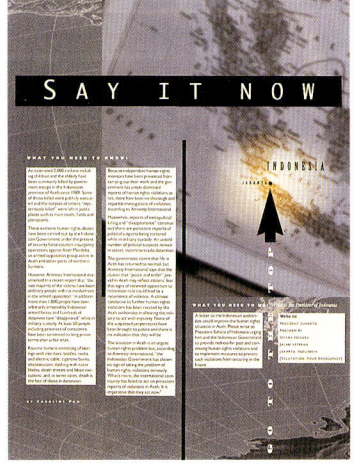

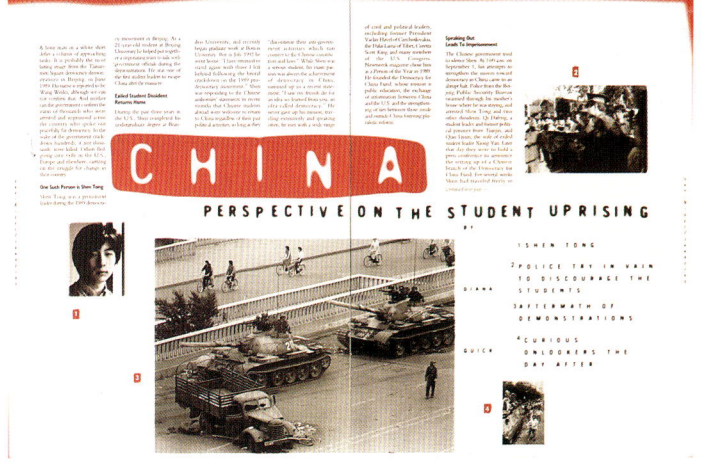

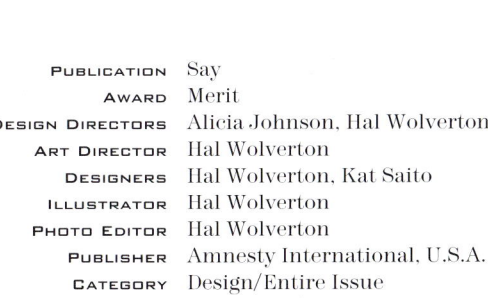

PUBLICATION   Say
AWARD   Merit
DESIGN DIRECTORS Alicia Johnson, Hal Wolverton
ART DIRECTOR   Hal Wolverton
DESIGNERS   Hal Wolverton, Kat Saito
ILLUSTRATOR   Hal Wolverton
PHOTO EDITOR   Hal Wolverton
PUBLISHER   Amnesty International, U.S.A.
CATEGORY   Design/Entire Issue
DATE   September/October 1993

PUBLICATION   Say
AWARD   Merit
DESIGN DIRECTORS Alicia Johnson, Hal Wolverton
ART DIRECTOR   Hal Wolverton
DESIGNERS   Hal Wolverton, Jerome Schiller
PHOTO EDITOR   Hal Wolverton
PUBLISHER   Amnesty International, U.S.A.
CATEGORY   Design/Entire Issue
DATE   December 1992/January 1993

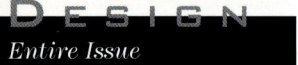

PUBLICATION	Say
AWARD	Merit
DESIGN DIRECTORS	Alicia Johnson, Hal Wolverton
ART DIRECTOR	Hal Wolverton
DESIGNERS	Hal Wolverton, Kat Saito
PHOTOGRAPHER	Robbie McClaran
PHOTO EDITOR	Hal Wolverton
PUBLISHER	Amnesty International, U.S.A.
CATEGORY	Design/Entire Issue
DATE	November/December 1993

PUBLICATION	Say
AWARD	Merit
DESIGN DIRECTORS	Alicia Johnson, Hal Wolverton
ART DIRECTOR	Hal Wolverton
DESIGNER	Hal Wolverton
PHOTO EDITOR	Hal Wolverton
PUBLISHER	Amnesty International, U.S.A.
CATEGORY	Design/Entire Issue
DATE	June/July 1993

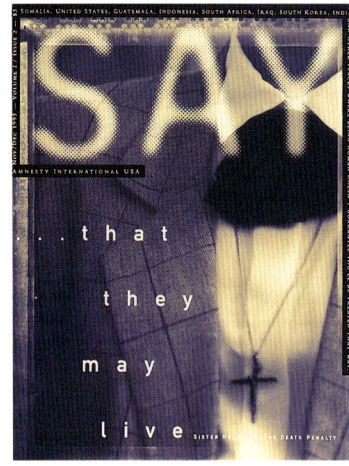

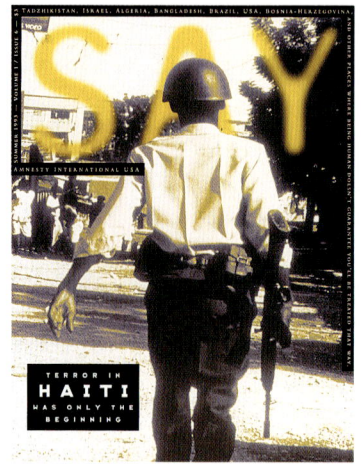

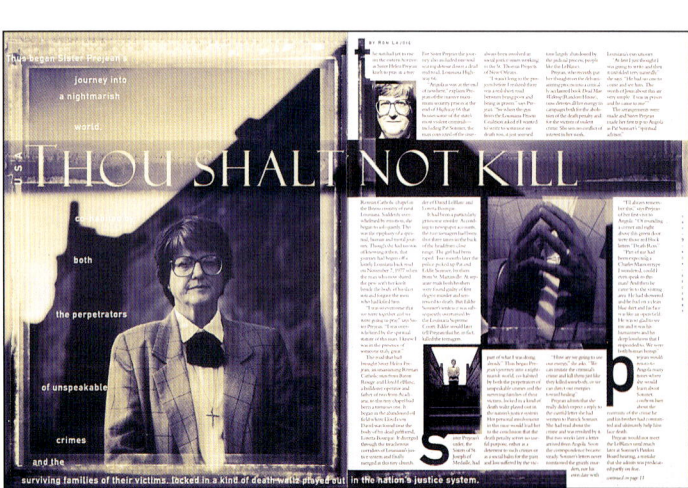

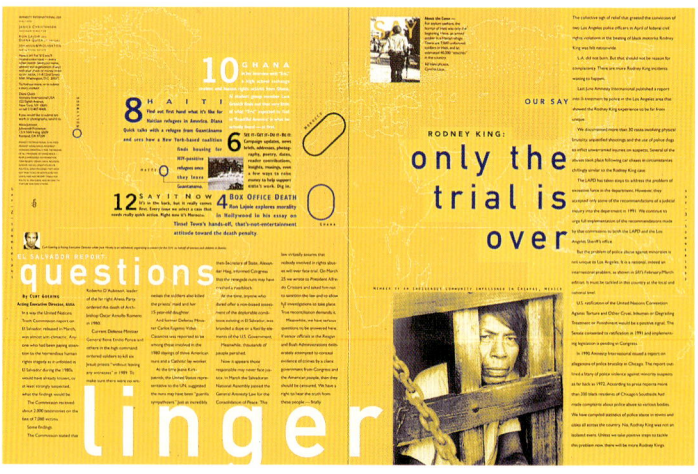

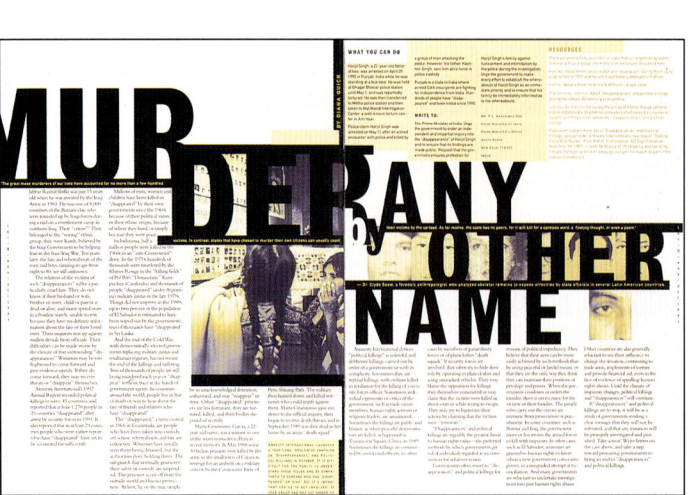

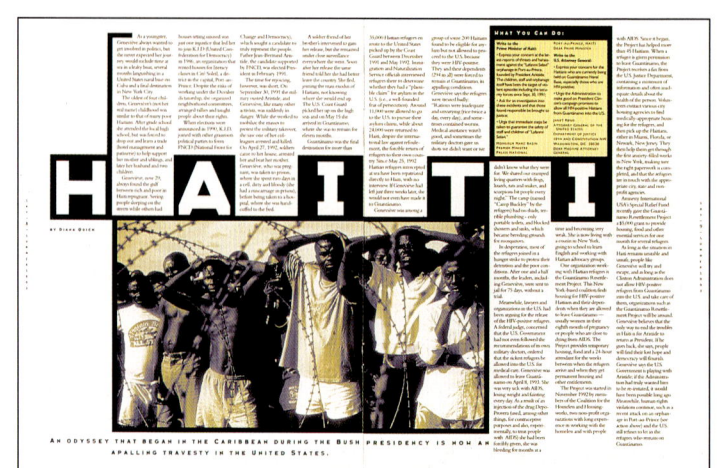

PUBLICATION	Hemispheres
AWARD	Merit
ART DIRECTORS	Jaimey Easler, Greg Hausler
ILLUSTRATORS	Heather Cooper, Colorado Historical Society
PHOTOGRAPHERS	Lee Marmon, Ernest Schwiebert
PHOTO EDITOR	Audrey Simpson
PUBLISHER	Pace Communications
CATEGORY	Design/Entire Issue
DATE	November 1993

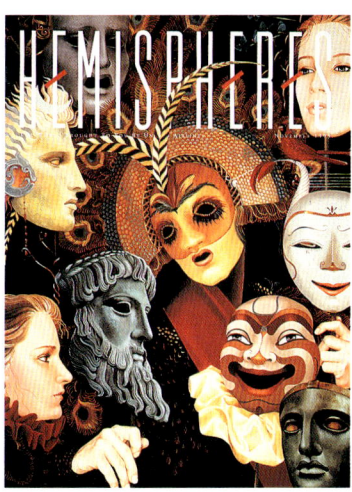

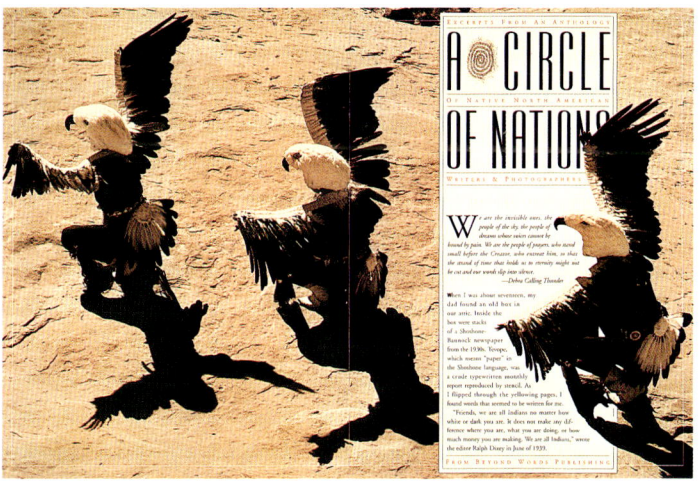

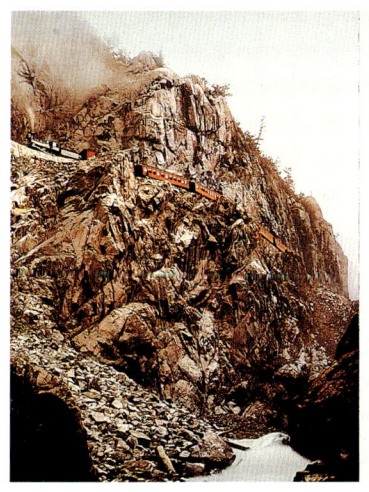
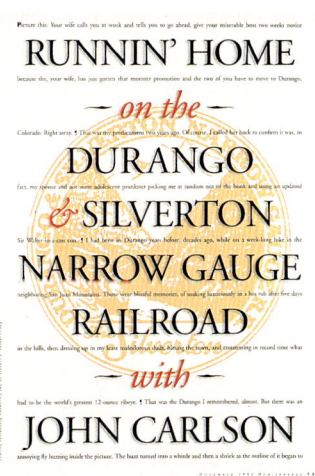

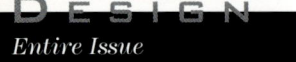

PUBLICATION	The Boston Globe Magazine/Your Home
AWARD	Merit
ART DIRECTOR	Jacqueline Berthet
DESIGNER	Cynthia Hoffman
PHOTOGRAPHERS	Nancy Hill, Suki Coughlin, Eric Roth, Yunghi Kim
PUBLISHER	The Boston Globe
CATEGORY	Design/Entire Issue
DATE	September 26, 1993

PUBLICATION	The Los Angeles Times Magazine
AWARD	Merit
ART DIRECTOR	Nancy Duckworth
DESIGNERS	Steven Banks, Carol Wakano, John D'Angona, Nancy Duckworth
PHOTO EDITOR	Lisa Thackaberry
PUBLISHER	Times Mirror
CATEGORY	Design/Entire Issue
DATE	December 19, 1993

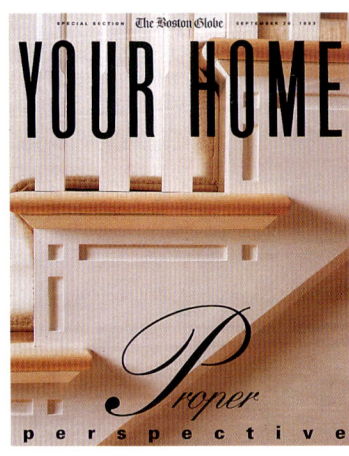

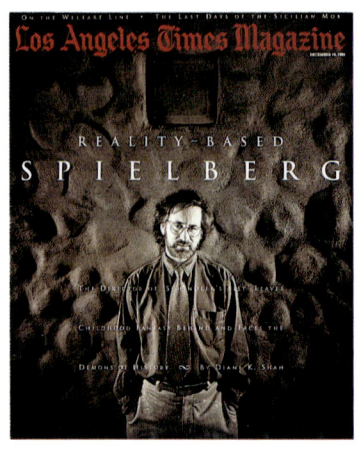

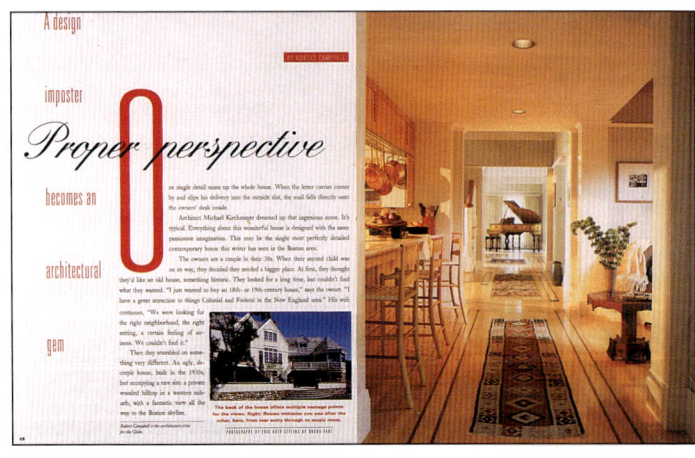

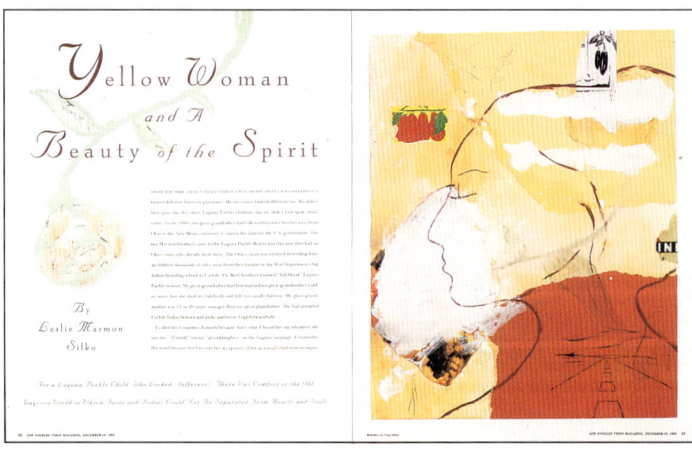

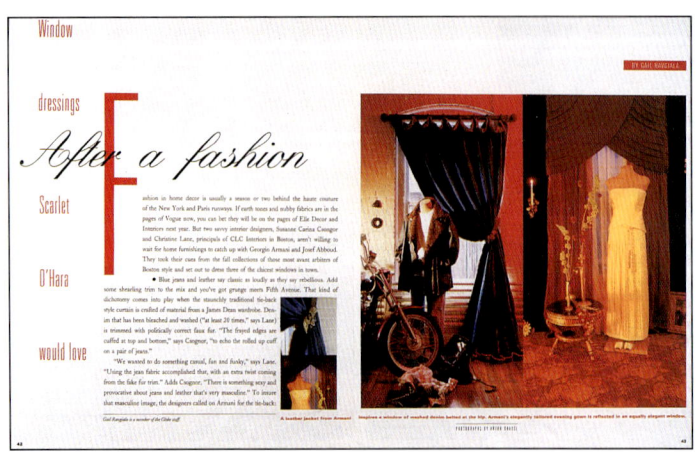

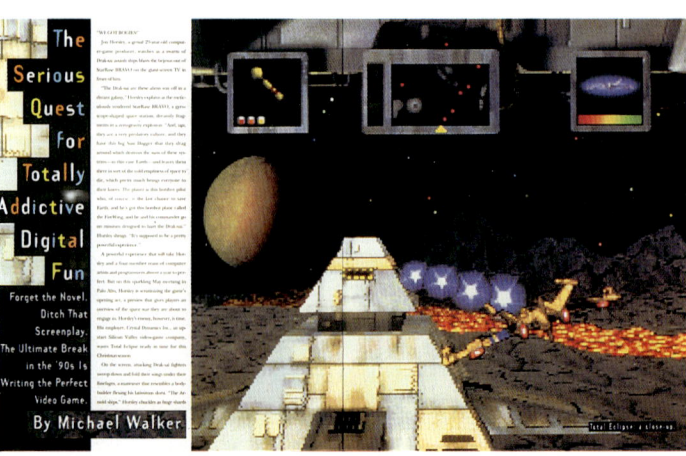

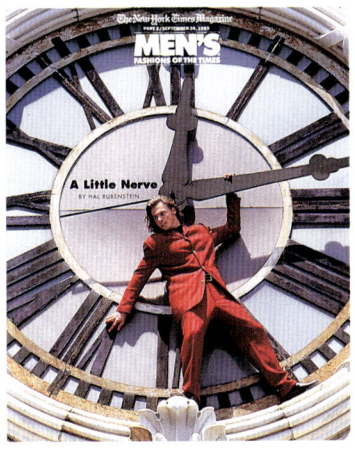

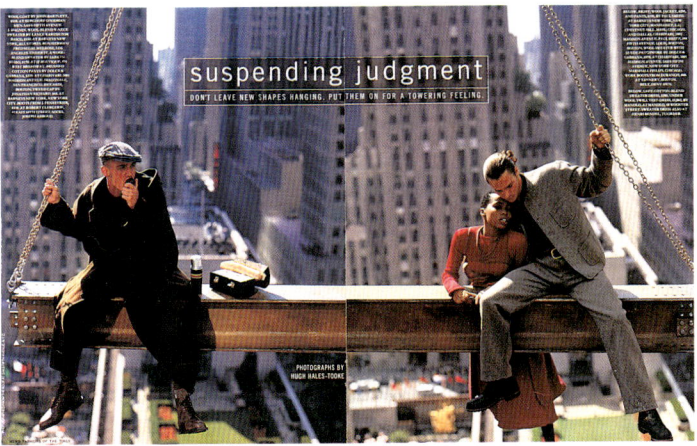

suspending judgment
DON'T LEAVE NEW SHAPES HANGING. PUT THEM ON FOR A TOWERING FEELING.

PHOTOGRAPHS BY HUGH HALES-TOOKE

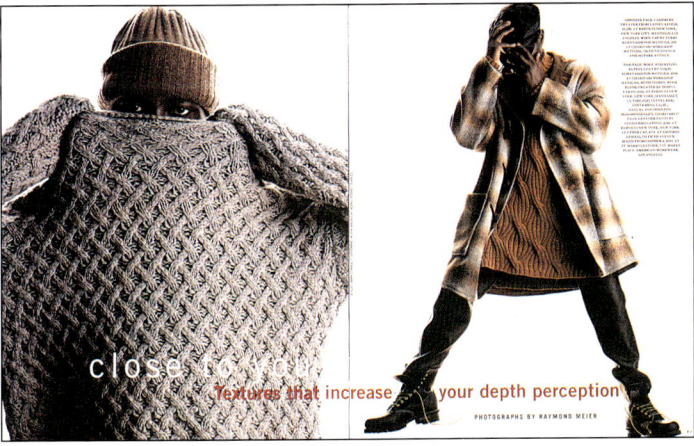

close to you
Textures that increase your depth perception

PHOTOGRAPHS BY RAYMOND MEIER

PUBLICATION   The New York Times Magazine/
              Men's Fashions of the Times
AWARD   Merit
ART DIRECTORS Janet Froelich, Gina Davis
PHOTOGRAPHERS Hugh Hales-Tooke, Raymond Meier,
              Guzman, Randall Mesdon, Aldo Rossi
PUBLISHER   The New York Times
CATEGORY   Design/Entire Issue
DATE   September 26, 1993

PUBLICATION   The Boston Globe Magazine
AWARD   Merit
DESIGN DIRECTOR Lucy Bartholomay
DESIGNER   Lucy Bartholomay
ILLUSTRATOR   Leslie Cober-Gentry
PHOTOGRAPHER   Tom Herde
PHOTO EDITOR   Lucy Bartholomay
PUBLISHER   The Boston Globe
CATEGORY   Design/Entire Issue
DATE   September 12, 1993

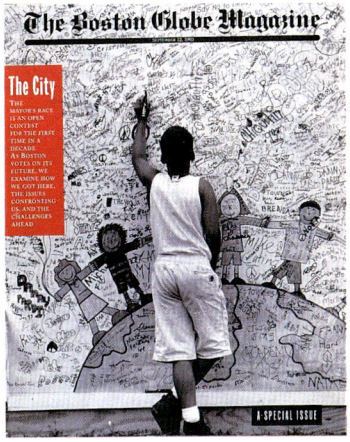

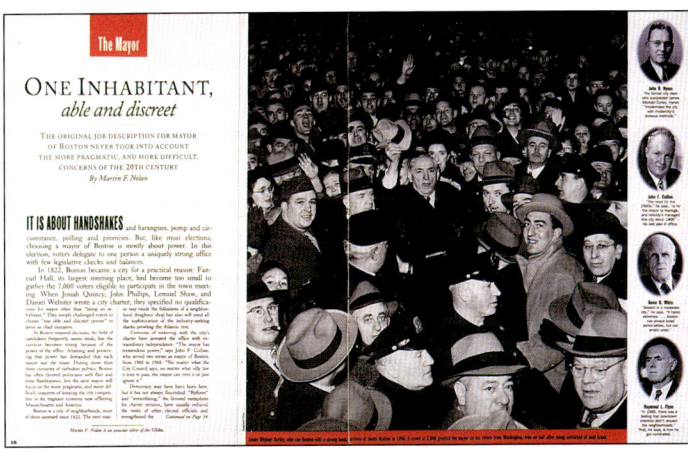

ONE INHABITANT, able and discreet

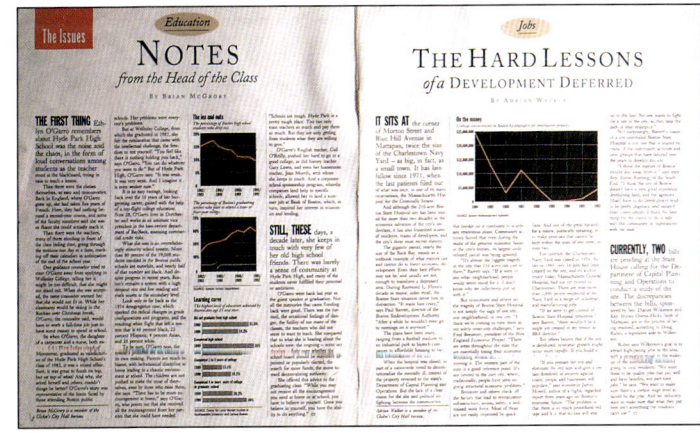

PUBLICATION	The Boston Globe/Your Home
AWARD	Merit
ART DIRECTOR	Aldona Charlton
DESIGNER	Aldona Charlton
PUBLISHER	The Boston Globe
CATEGORY	Design/Entire Issue
DATE	March 7, 1993

PUBLICATION	The Boston Globe/Adventures in Travel
AWARD	Merit
ART DIRECTOR	Rena Sokolow
DESIGNER	Rena Sokolow
PUBLISHER	The Boston Globe
CATEGORY	Design/Entire Issue
DATE	March 28, 1993

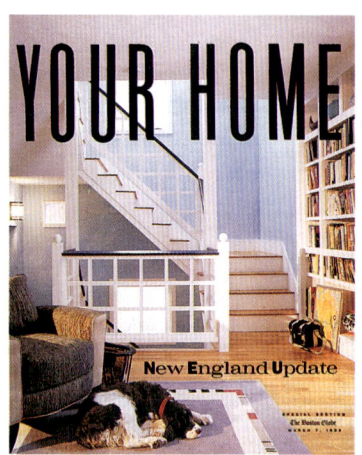

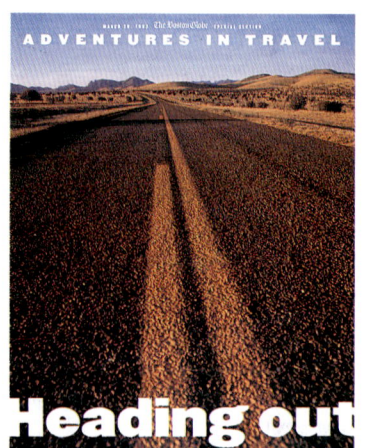

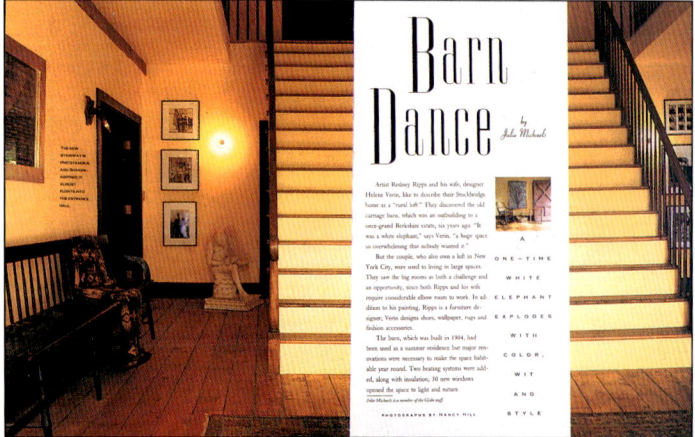

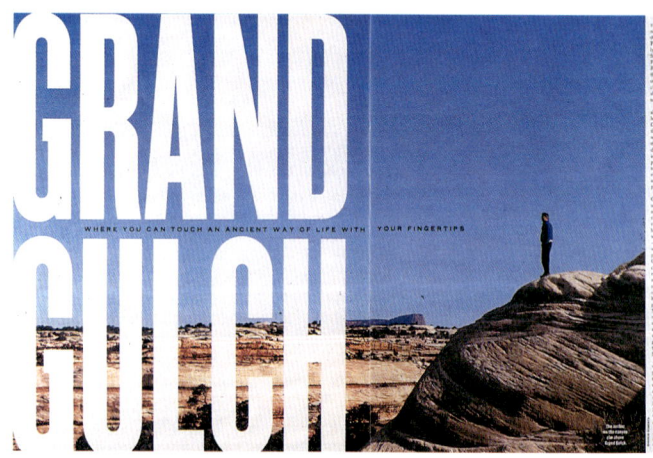
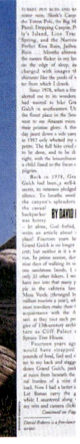

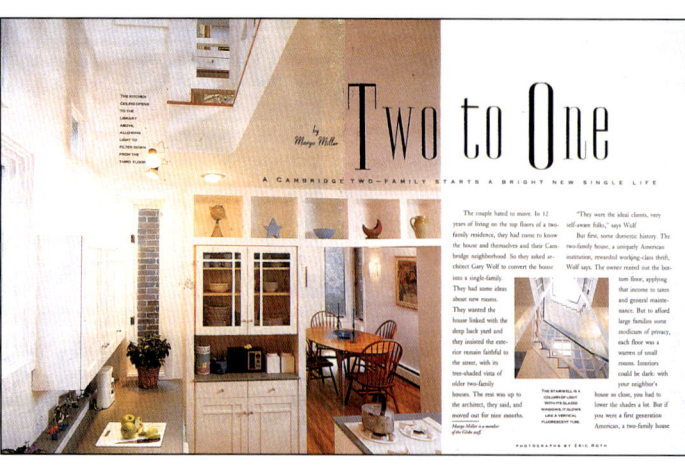

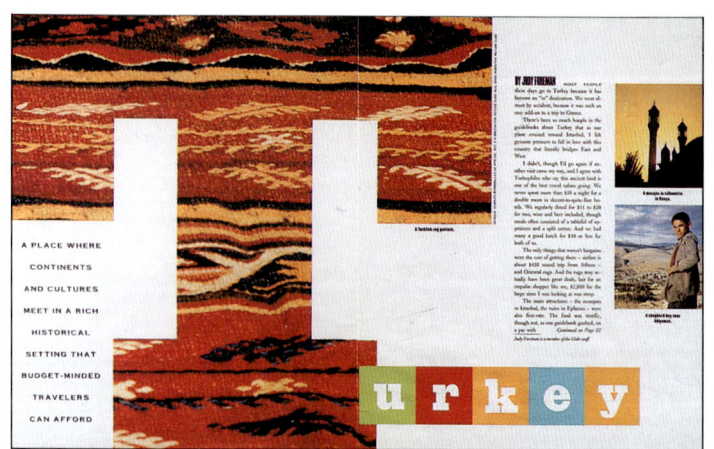

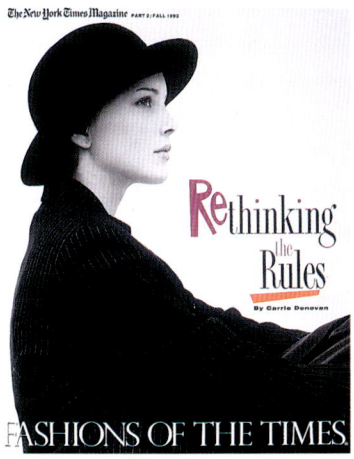

PUBLICATION The New York Times Magazine/
                Men's Fashions of the Times
AWARD Merit
ART DIRECTORS Janet Froelich, Gina Davis
PHOTOGRAPHERS Lois Greenfield, Diego Uchitel, Randall Mesden,
                Norman Watson
PUBLISHER The New York Times
CATEGORY Design/Entire Issue
DATE March 28, 1993

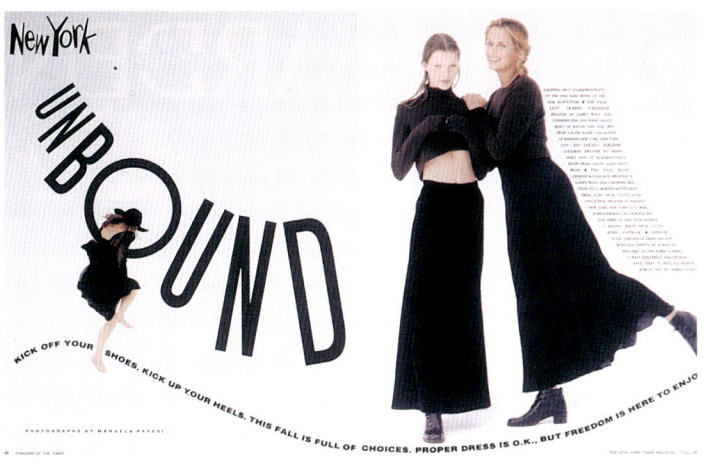

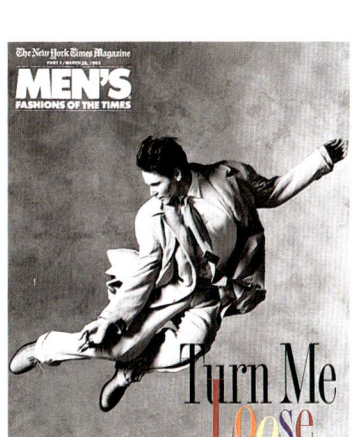

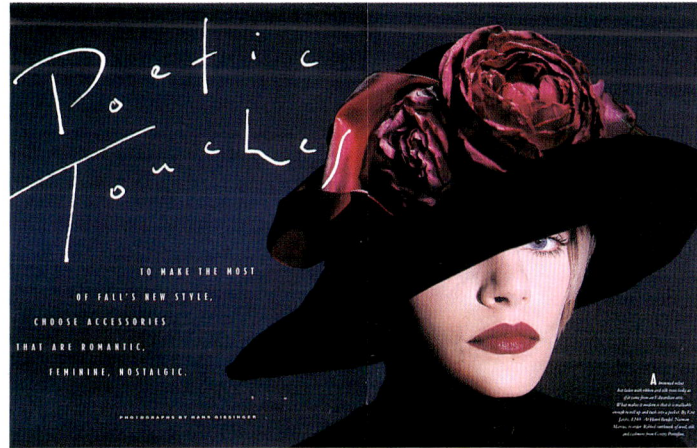

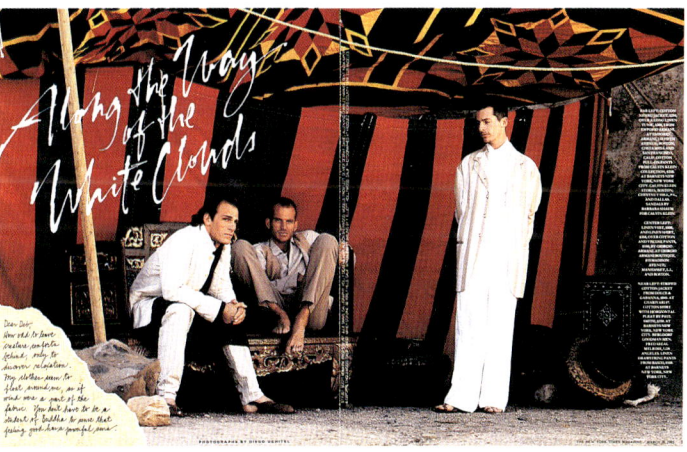

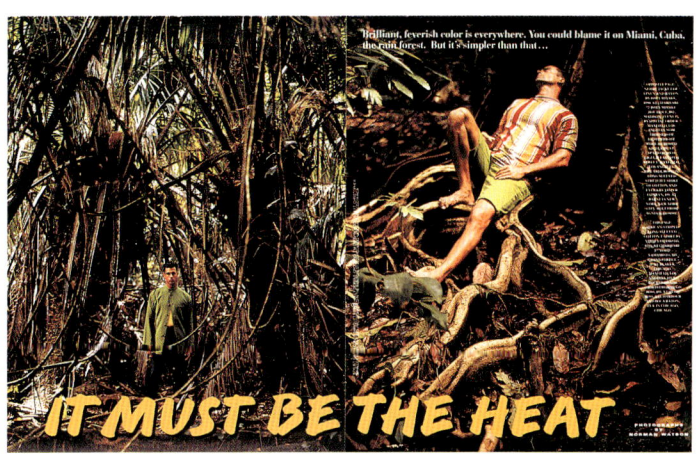

PUBLICATION The New York Times /Fashions of the Times
AWARD Merit
ART DIRECTOR Tuan Dao
PHOTOGRAPHER John Huba
PUBLISHER The New York Times
CATEGORY Design/Entire Issue
DATE Fall 1993

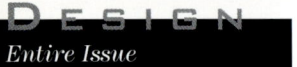

PUBLICATION	The Los Angeles Times Magazine
AWARD	Merit
ART DIRECTOR	Nancy Duckworth
DESIGNERS	Steven Banks, Carol Wakano, John D'Angona, Nancy Duckworth
PHOTO EDITOR	Lisa Thackaberry
PUBLISHER	Times Mirror
CATEGORY	Design/Entire Issue
DATE	August 29, 1993

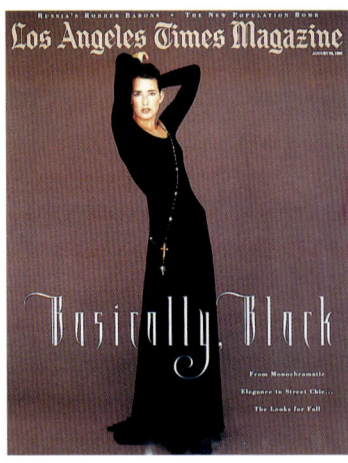

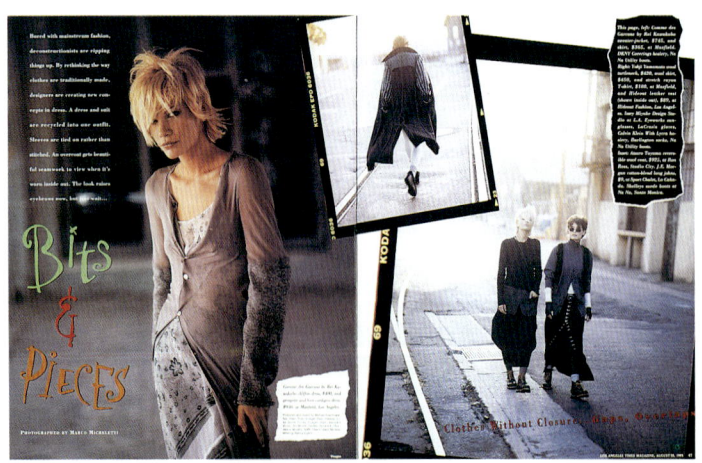

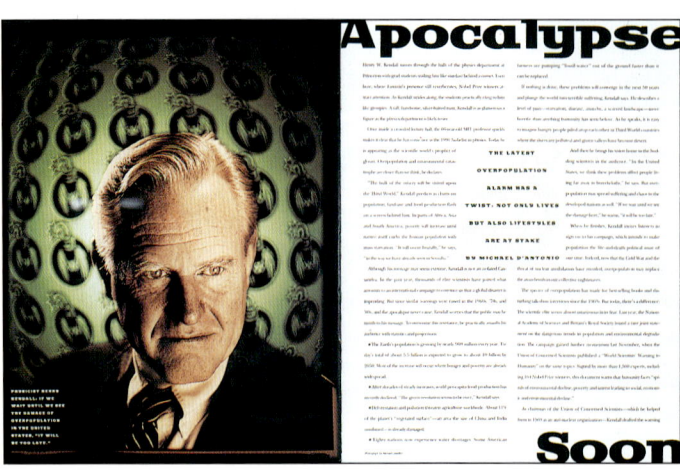

PUBLICATION   Graphis

AWARD   Merit

DESIGN DIRECTOR   B. Martin Pedersen

ART DIRECTORS   B. Martin Pedersen, Randell Pearson

DESIGNER   B. Martin Pedersen

STUDIO   Pedersen Design Group, Inc.

CATEGORY   Design/Entire Issue

DATE   June 1993

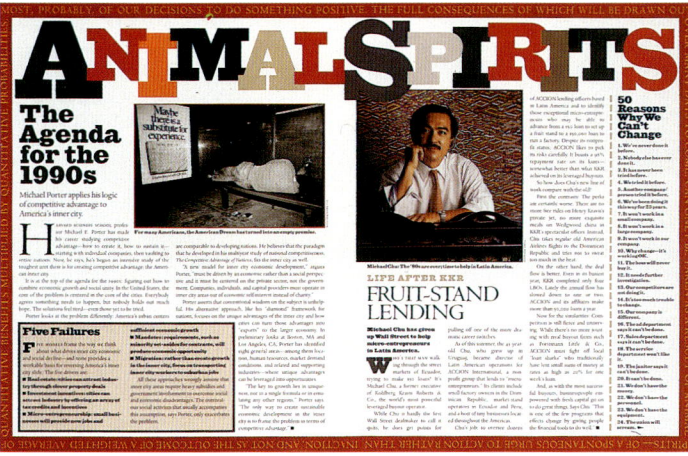

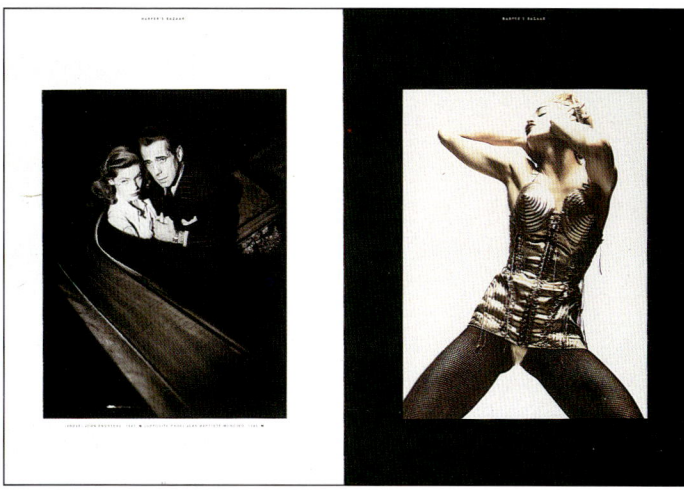

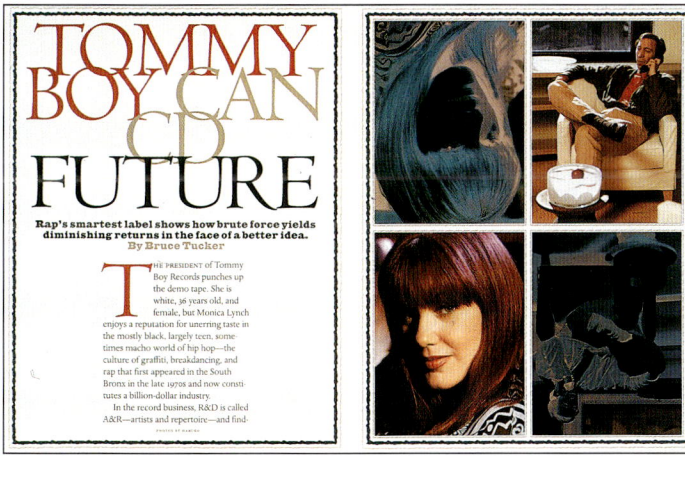

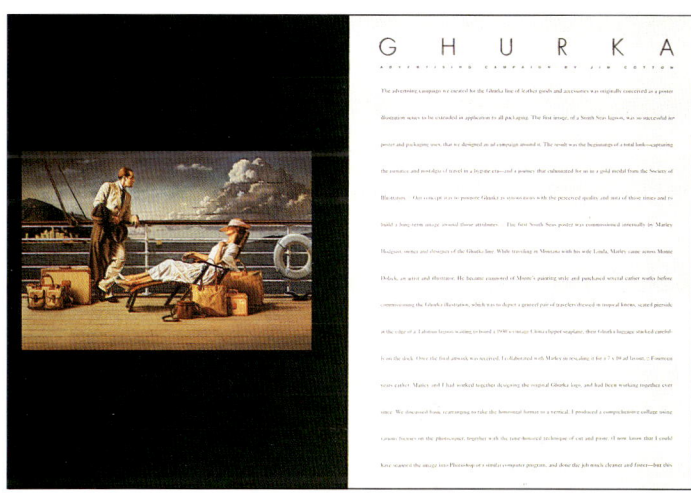

PUBLICATION   Fast Company

AWARD   Merit

DESIGN DIRECTORS   John Schmitz, Roger Black

DESIGNERS   John Schmitz, Roger Black, Jennifer Altemus

PHOTOGRAPHERS   Haruko, Eli Reed/Magnum, Tony Rinaldo

PUBLISHER   Fast Company Limited Partnership

STUDIO   Roger Black, Inc.

CATEGORY   Design/Entire Issue

DATE   November 1993

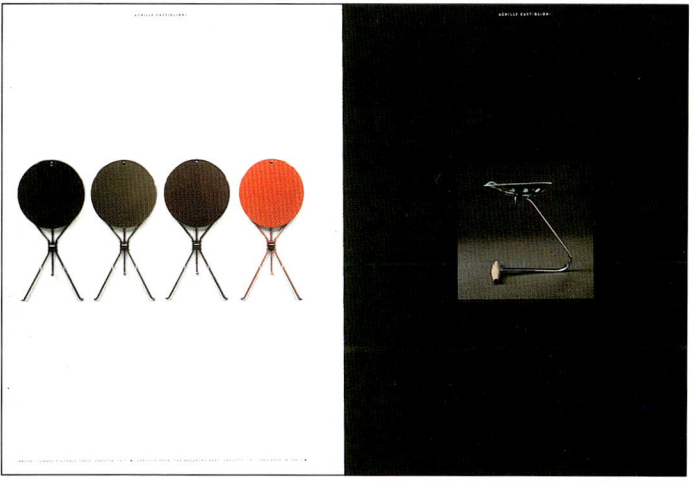

PUBLICATION	Lax
AWARD	Merit
DESIGN DIRECTOR	Mark Sackett
ART DIRECTORS	Mark Sackett, Brad Benedict
DESIGNERS	Mark Sackett, Wayne Sakamoto
ILLUSTRATORS	Mark Sackett, Wayne Sakamoto, Dave Willardson
PUBLISHER	L.A.X. Magazine
STUDIO	Sackett Design Associates
CATEGORY	Design/Entire Issue
DATE	January 1, 1993

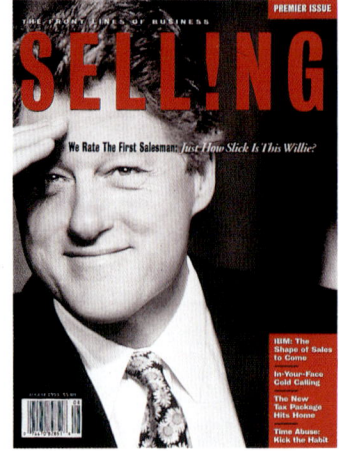

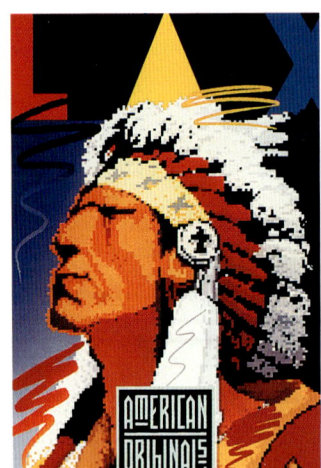

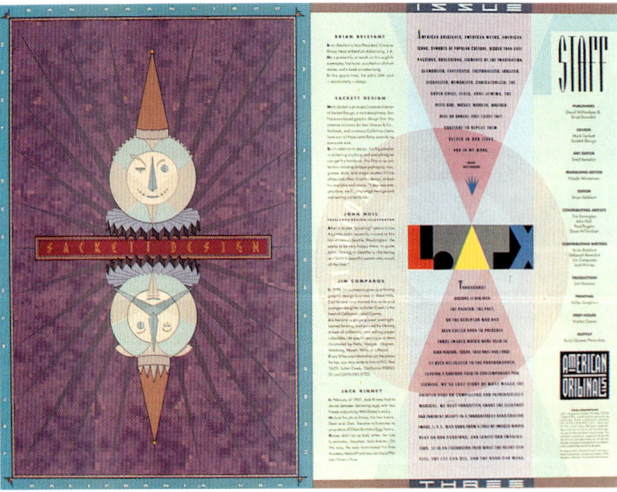

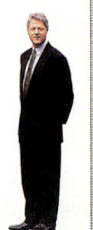

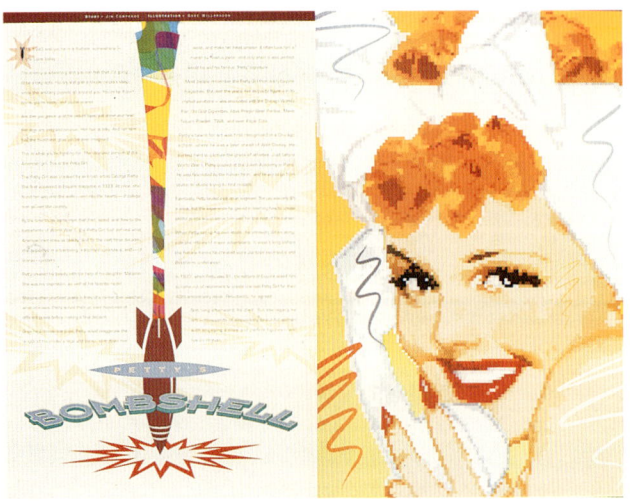

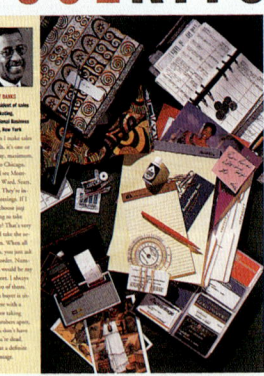

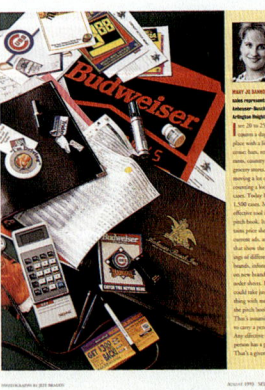

PUBLICATION	Selling
AWARD	Merit
DESIGN DIRECTORS	Walter Bernard, Milton Glaser
ART DIRECTOR	Teresa Fernandes
DESIGNERS	Teresa Fernandes, Nancy Eising, Walter Bernard, Milton Glaser, Sharon Okamoto, Frank Baseman
ILLUSTRATOR	Michael Klein
PHOTOGRAPHERS	Cynthia Johnson/ Gamma Liaison, Monica Stevenson, Jeff Brady
PHOTO EDITOR	Jim Franco
PUBLISHER	Capital Cities/ABC, Inc. Publishing Group
STUDIO	WBMG, Inc.
CATEGORY	Design/Entire Issue
DATE	August 1993

PUBLICATION	Selling
AWARD	Merit
DESIGN DIRECTOR	Teresa Fernandes
DESIGNERS	Teresa Fernandes, Robin Terra
PHOTOGRAPHERS	Craig Daniels, William Duke, Villard Books
PHOTO EDITOR	Jim Franco
PUBLISHER	Capital Cities/ABC, Inc. Publishing Group
CATEGORY	Design/Entire Issue
DATE	September 1993

PUBLICATION	Upper & Lower Case
AWARD	Merit
ART DIRECTOR	Paul Davis
DESIGNERS	Lisa Mazur, Chalkley Calderwood, Haruetai Muodtong
PUBLISHER	International Typeface Corporation
STUDIO	Paul Davis Studio
CATEGORY	Design/Entire Issue
DATE	May 1993

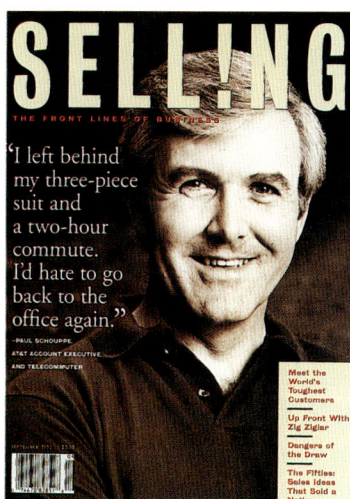

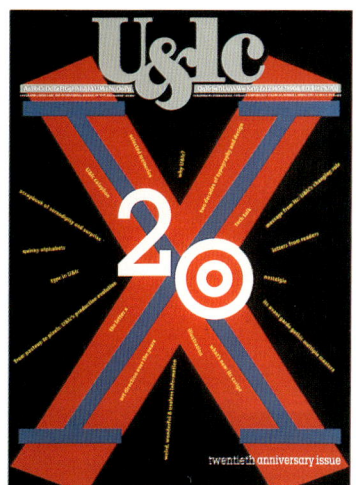

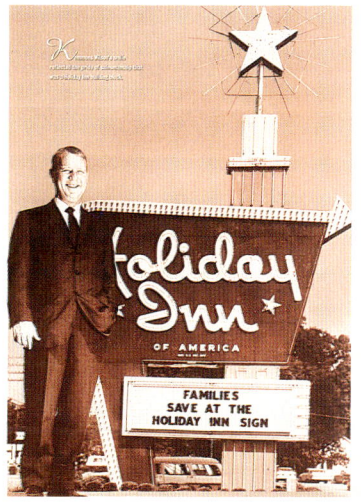

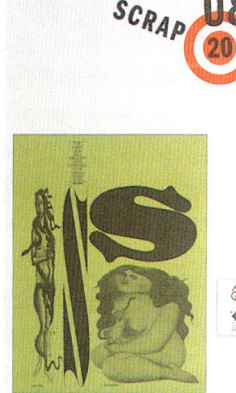

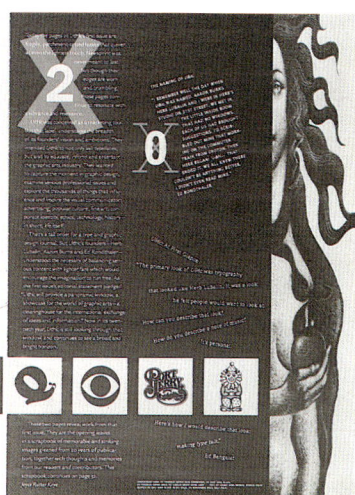

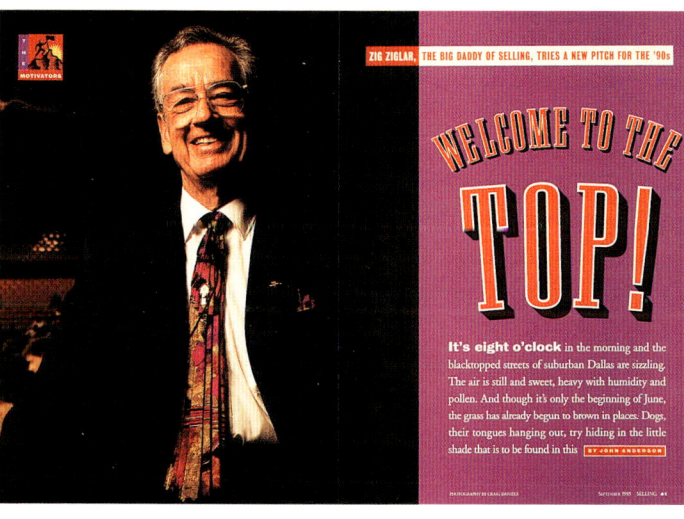

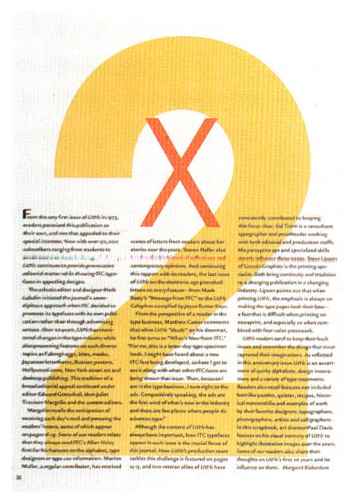

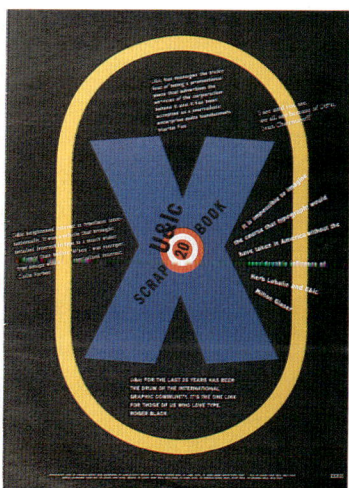

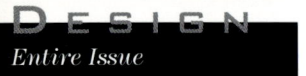

PUBLICATION	Corning
AWARD	Merit
DESIGN DIRECTOR	Susan Slover
ART DIRECTOR	Sonia Biancalani
DESIGNER	Sonia Biancalani
CLIENT	Corning Incorporated/Environmental Division
STUDIO	Susan Slover Design
CATEGORY	Design/Entire Issue
DATE	June/July 1993

PUBLICATION	Corning
AWARD	Merit
DESIGN DIRECTOR	Susan Slover
ART DIRECTOR	Sonia Biancalani
DESIGNER	Sonia Biancalani
CLIENT	Corning Incorporated/Environmental Division
STUDIO	Susan Slover Design
CATEGORY	Design/Entire Issue
DATE	October/November 1993

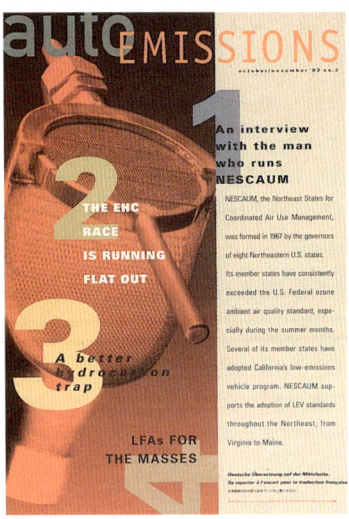

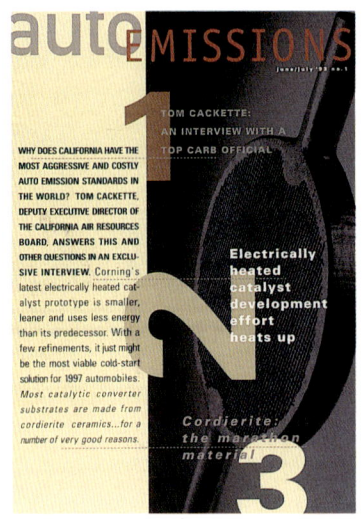

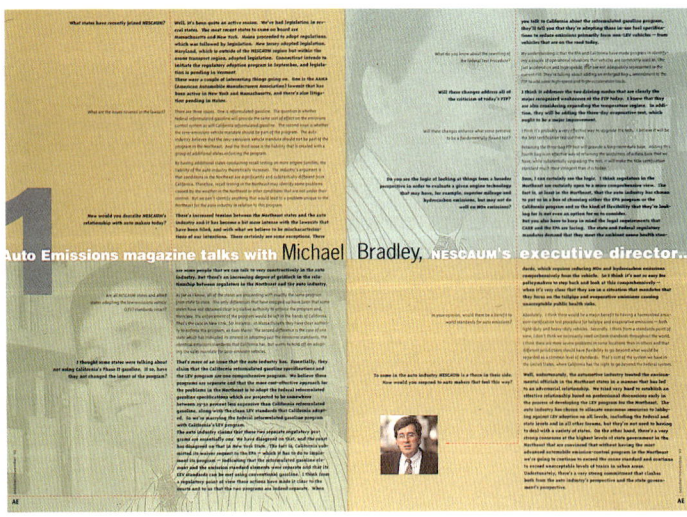

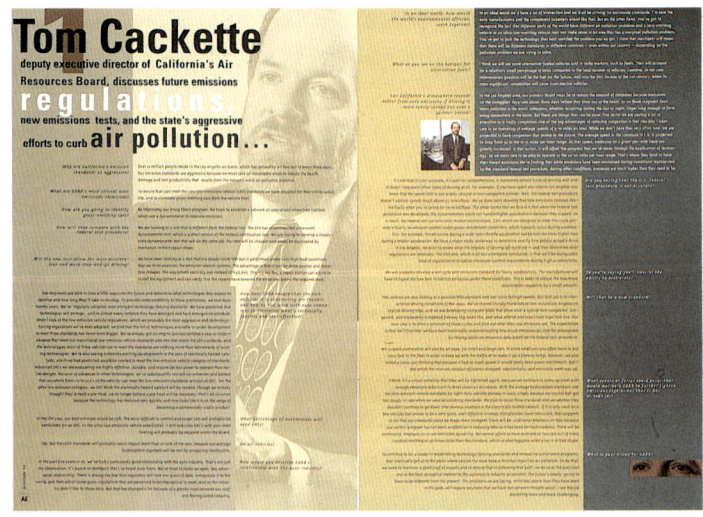

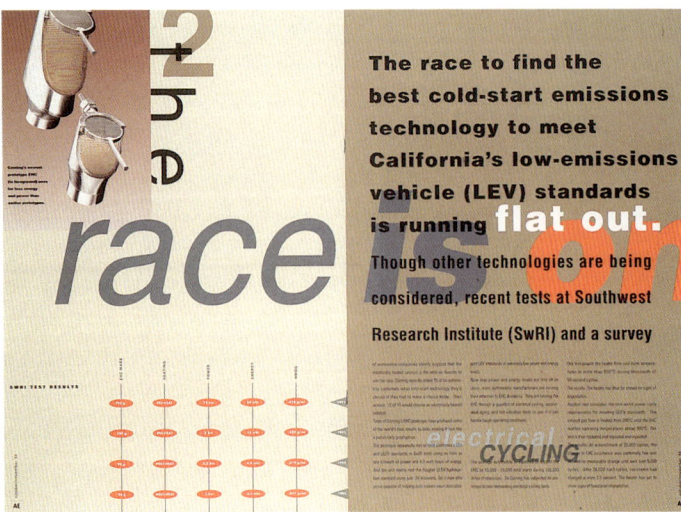

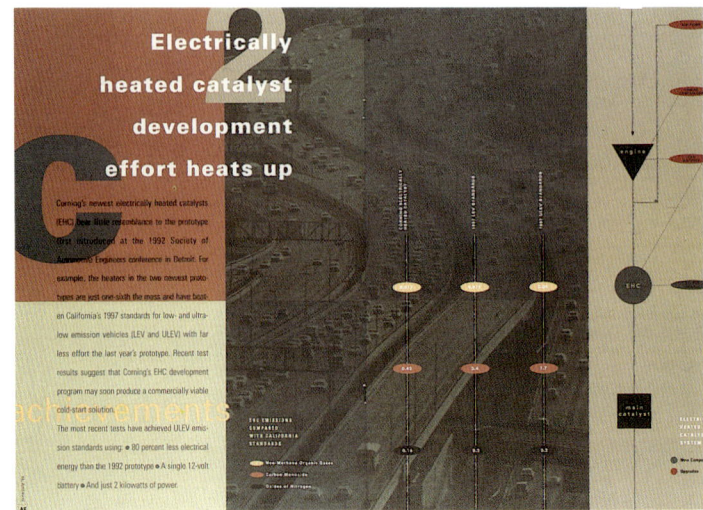

PUBLICATION	America's Agenda
AWARD	Merit
DESIGN DIRECTOR	Ellen Jacob
ART DIRECTOR	Maxine Davidowitz
ILLUSTRATOR	Mick Wiggins
PHOTOGRAPHERS	Will Van Overbeek, Rick Maiman/Sygma, Brad Trent/Outline
PUBLISHER	Scholastic, Inc.
CATEGORY	Design/Entire Issue
DATE	Spring 1993

PUBLICATION	Blueprint
AWARD	Merit
ART DIRECTOR	John Belknap
ILLUSTRATOR	Ted Benoit
PHOTOGRAPHERS	Chris Barker, Jannes Linder, Fabrizo Petri
PUBLISHER	Wordsearch Ltd.
CATEGORY	Design/Entire Issue
DATE	December 1993

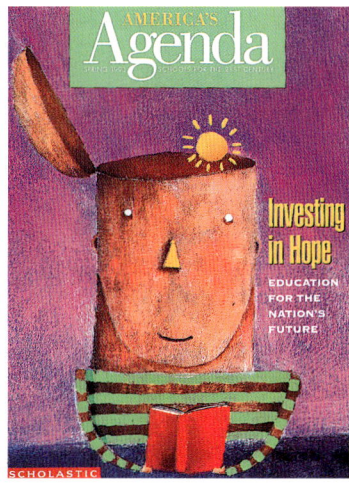

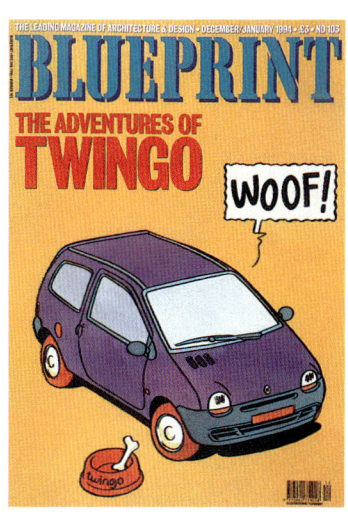

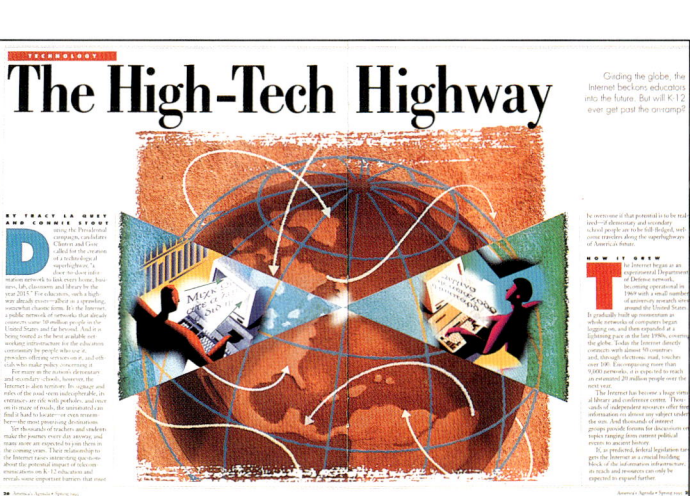

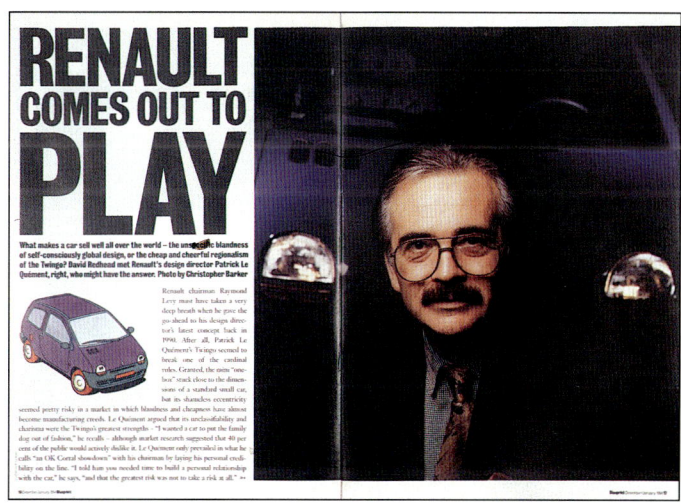

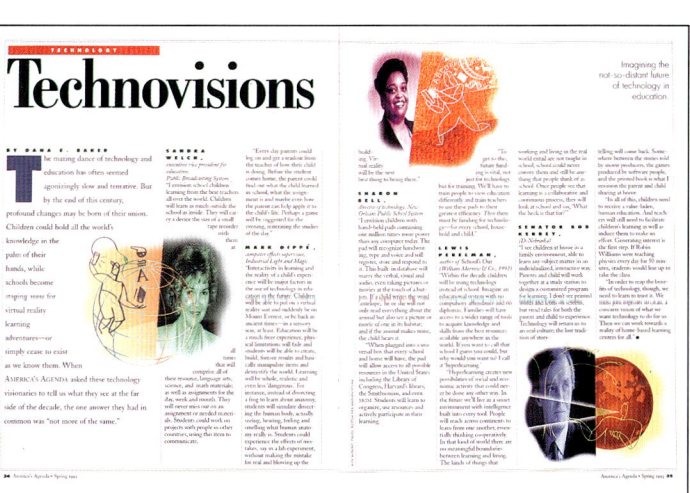

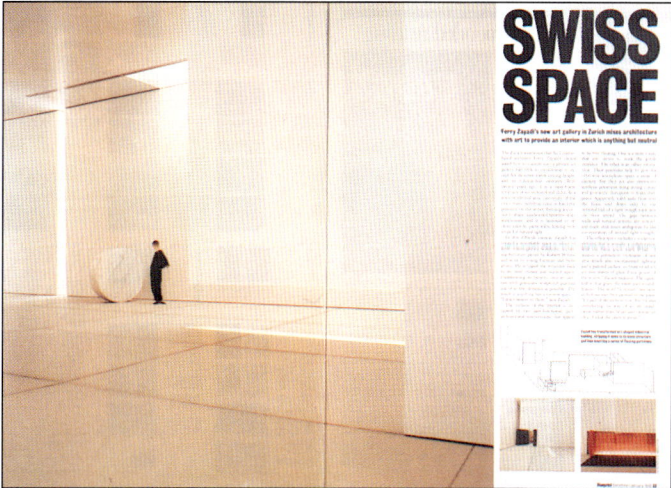

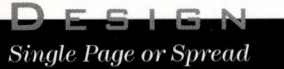

PUBLICATION	Metropolis
AWARD	Silver
ART DIRECTORS	Carl Lehmann-Haupt, Nancy Cohen
DESIGNERS	Carl Lehmann-Haupt, Nancy Cohen
PHOTOGRAPHER	Ilene S. Hoffman
PUBLISHER	Bellerophon Publications
CATEGORY	Design/Single Page or Spread
DATE	June 1993

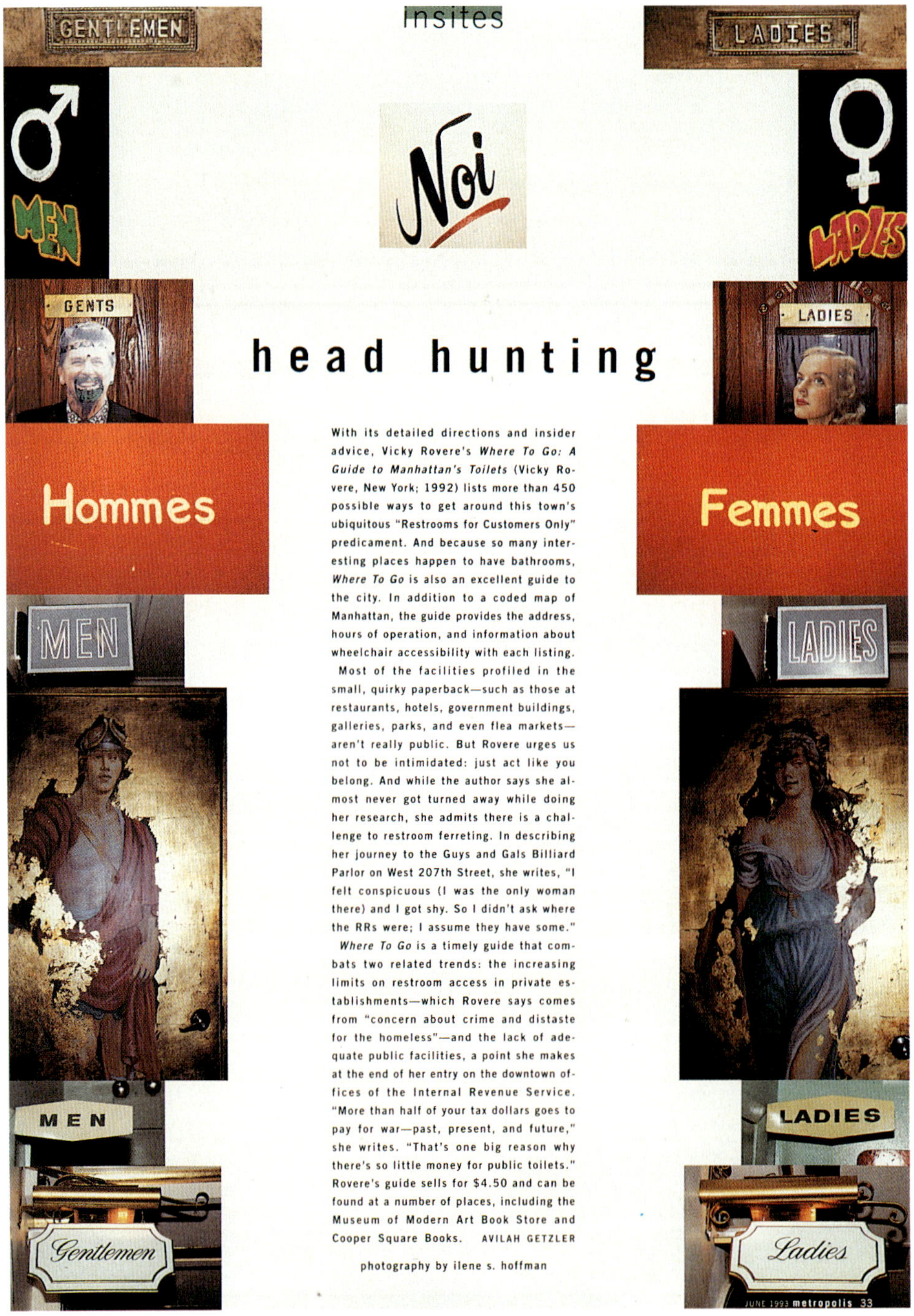

insites

Noi

head hunting

GENTLEMEN

GENTS

Hommes

MEN

MEN

Gentlemen

LADIES

LADIES

Femmes

LADIES

LADIES

Ladies

With its detailed directions and insider advice, Vicky Rovere's *Where To Go: A Guide to Manhattan's Toilets* (Vicky Rovere, New York; 1992) lists more than 450 possible ways to get around this town's ubiquitous "Restrooms for Customers Only" predicament. And because so many interesting places happen to have bathrooms, *Where To Go* is also an excellent guide to the city. In addition to a coded map of Manhattan, the guide provides the address, hours of operation, and information about wheelchair accessibility with each listing.

Most of the facilities profiled in the small, quirky paperback—such as those at restaurants, hotels, government buildings, galleries, parks, and even flea markets—aren't really public. But Rovere urges us not to be intimidated: just act like you belong. And while the author says she almost never got turned away while doing her research, she admits there is a challenge to restroom ferreting. In describing her journey to the Guys and Gals Billiard Parlor on West 207th Street, she writes, "I felt conspicuous (I was the only woman there) and I got shy. So I didn't ask where the RRs were; I assume they have some."

Where To Go is a timely guide that combats two related trends: the increasing limits on restroom access in private establishments—which Rovere says comes from "concern about crime and distaste for the homeless"—and the lack of adequate public facilities, a point she makes at the end of her entry on the downtown offices of the Internal Revenue Service. "More than half of your tax dollars goes to pay for war—past, present, and future," she writes. "That's one big reason why there's so little money for public toilets." Rovere's guide sells for $4.50 and can be found at a number of places, including the Museum of Modern Art Book Store and Cooper Square Books. AVILAH GETZLER

photography by ilene s. hoffman

PUBLICATION Rolling Stone
AWARD Silver
ART DIRECTOR Fred Woodward
DESIGNERS Fred Woodward, Gail Anderson
ILLUSTRATOR Al Hirschfeld
PUBLISHER Wenner Media
CATEGORY Design/Single Page or Spread
DATE February 18, 1993

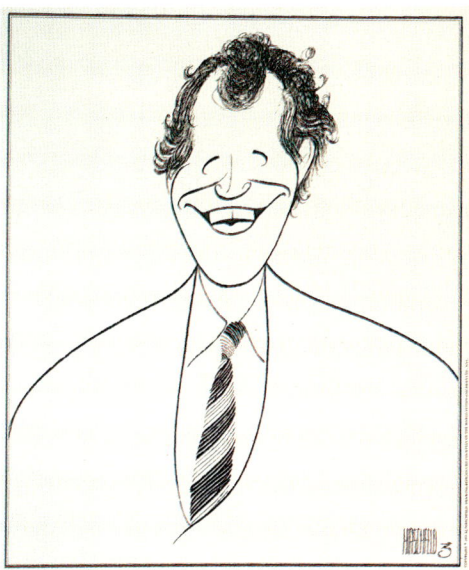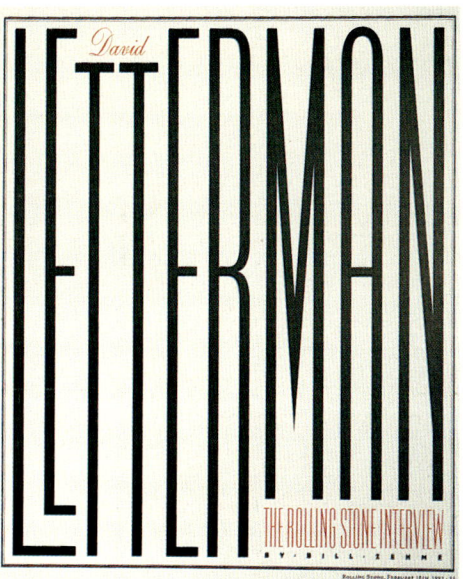

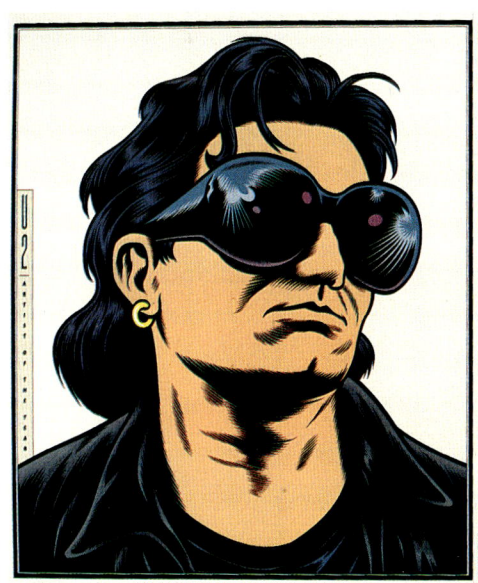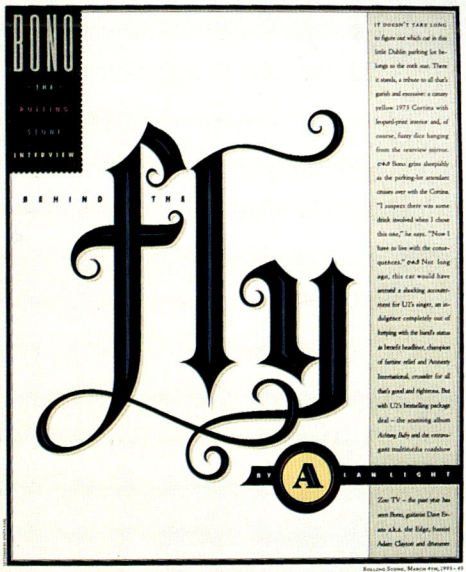

PUBLICATION Rolling Stone
AWARD Silver
ART DIRECTOR Fred Woodward
DESIGNER Debra Bishop
ILLUSTRATOR Charles Burns
PUBLISHER Wenner Media
CATEGORY Design/Single Page or Spread
DATE March 4, 1993

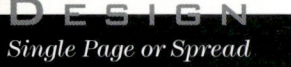

PUBLICATION	Vibe
AWARD	Silver
DESIGN DIRECTOR	Gary Koepke
ART DIRECTOR	Richard Baker
DESIGNER	Gary Koepke
PHOTOGRAPHER	Dan Winters
PHOTO EDITOR	George Pitts
PUBLISHER	Time Inc. Ventures
STUDIO	Koepke International, Ltd
CATEGORY	Design/Single Page or Spread
DATE	September 1993

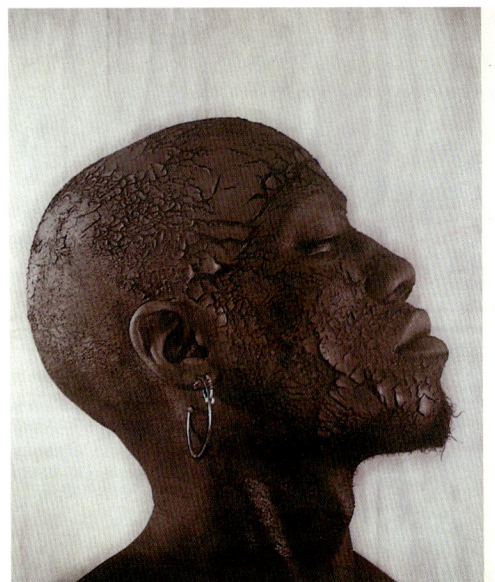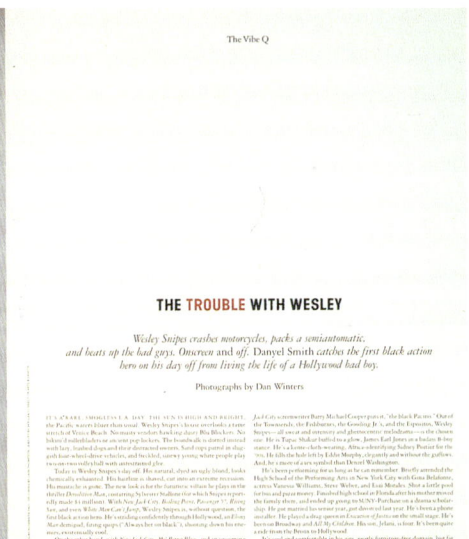

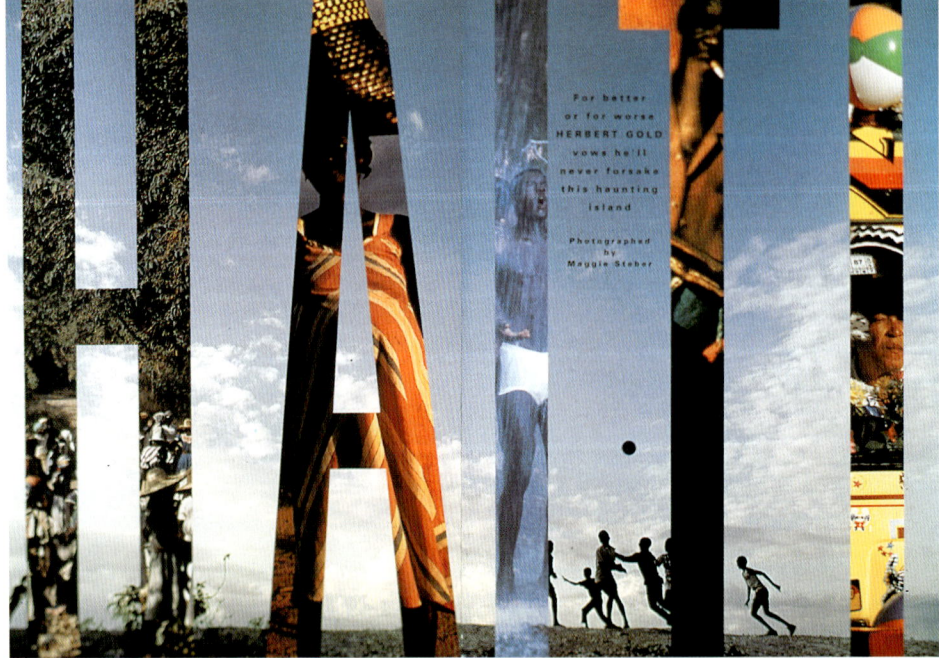

PUBLICATION	Travel & Leisure
AWARD	Silver
DESIGN DIRECTOR	Lloyd Ziff
DESIGNER	Lloyd Ziff
PHOTOGRAPHER	Maggie Steber
PHOTO EDITOR	Hazel Hammond
PUBLISHER	American Express Publishing
CATEGORY	Design/Single Page or Spread
DATE	June 1993

PUBLICATION Rolling Stone
AWARD Silver
ART DIRECTOR Fred Woodward
DESIGNER Debra Bishop
PHOTOGRAPHER Doug Rosa
PHOTO EDITOR Denise Sfraga
PUBLISHER Wenner Media
CATEGORY Design/Single Page or Spread
DATE May 13, 1993

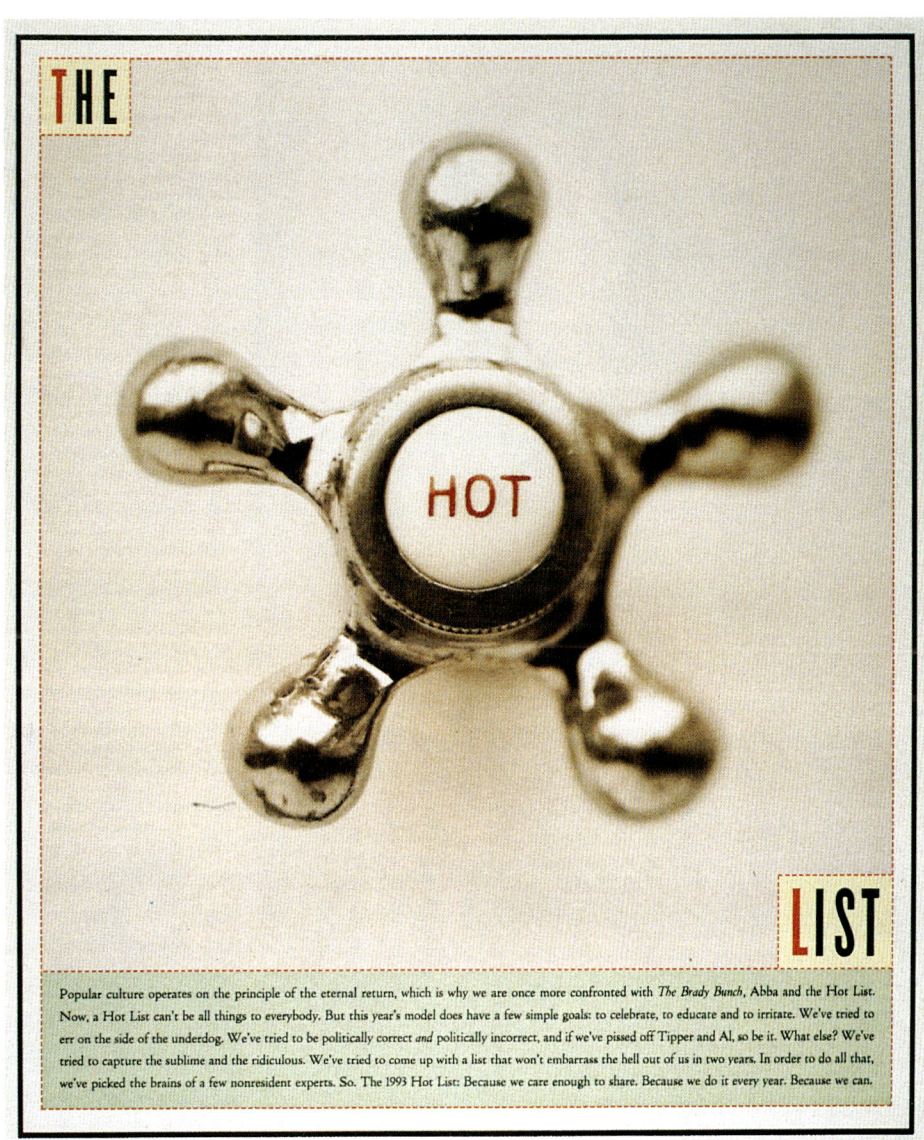

THE

HOT

LIST

Popular culture operates on the principle of the eternal return, which is why we are once more confronted with *The Brady Bunch*, Abba and the Hot List. Now, a Hot List can't be all things to everybody. But this year's model does have a few simple goals: to celebrate, to educate and to irritate. We've tried to err on the side of the underdog. We've tried to be politically correct *and* politically incorrect, and if we've pissed off Tipper and Al, so be it. What else? We've tried to capture the sublime and the ridiculous. We've tried to come up with a list that won't embarrass the hell out of us in two years. In order to do all that, we've picked the brains of a few nonresident experts. So. The 1993 Hot List: Because we care enough to share. Because we do it every year. Because we can.

ROLLING STONE, MAY 13TH, 1993 · 61

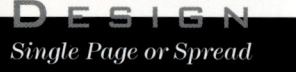
PUBLICATION	10 Percent
AWARD	Merit
DESIGN DIRECTOR	Paul Martinez
DESIGNER	Paul Martinez
PHOTOGRAPHER	Barry Muniz
PHOTO EDITOR	Barry Muniz
PUBLISHER	Browning Grace Communications
STUDIO	The Movement
CATEGORY	Design/Single Page or Spread
DATE	July 1, 1993

PUBLICATION	Discover
AWARD	Merit
ART DIRECTOR	David Armario
DESIGNER	James Lambertus
ILLUSTRATOR	Anita Kunz
PUBLISHER	Disney Magazine Publishing, Inc.
CATEGORY	Design/Single Page or Spread
DATE	September 1993

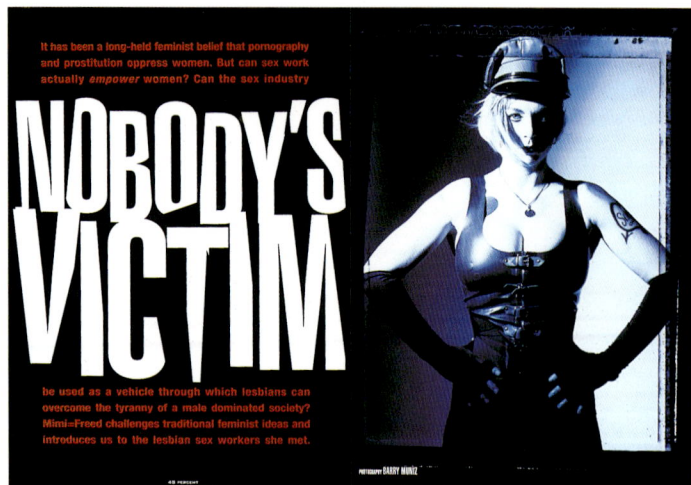

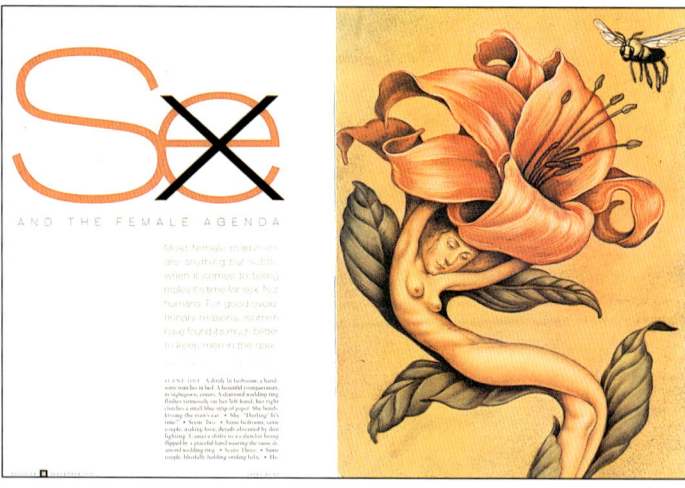

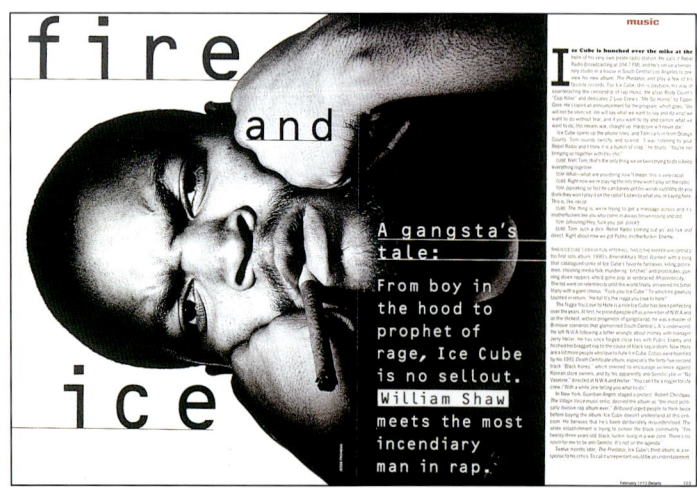

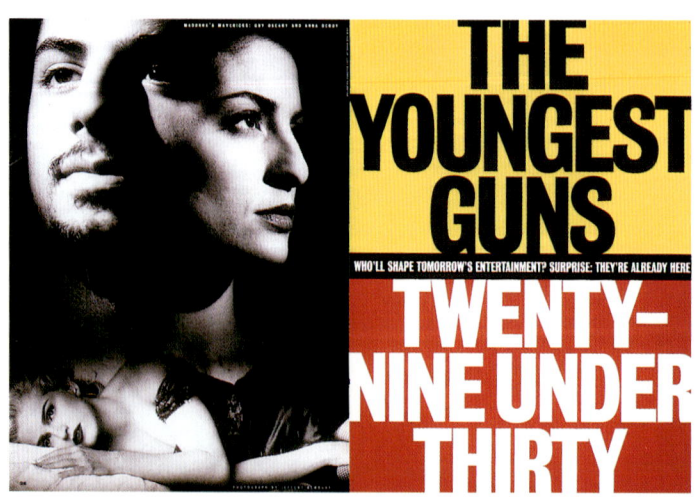

PUBLICATION	Details
AWARD	Merit
ART DIRECTOR	B.W. Honeycutt
DESIGNER	Markus Kiersztan
PHOTOGRAPHER	Jesse Frohman
PHOTO EDITOR	Greg Pond
PUBLISHER	The Condé Nast Publications Inc.
CATEGORY	Design/Single Page or Spread
DATE	February 1993

PUBLICATION	Entertainment Weekly
AWARD	Merit
DESIGN DIRECTOR	Michael Grossman
DESIGNER	Miriam Campiz
PHOTOGRAPHER	Jeffery Newbury
PHOTO EDITORS	Mary Dunn, Ramiro Fernandez
PUBLISHER	Time Inc.
CATEGORY	Design/Single Page or Spread
DATE	February 26, 1993

PUBLICATION   Entertainment Weekly
AWARD   Merit
DESIGN DIRECTOR   Michael Grossman
DESIGNER   Jill Armus
PHOTOGRAPHER   Andrew Brusso
PHOTO EDITORS   Mary Dunn, Doris Brautigan
PUBLISHER   Time Inc.
CATEGORY   Design/Single Page or Spread
DATE   October 1, 1993

PUBLICATION   Life
AWARD   Merit
DESIGN DIRECTOR   Tom Bentkowski
DESIGNER   Jean Andreuzzi
PHOTOGRAPHER   Gilles Saussier
PHOTO EDITOR   David Friend
PUBLISHER   Time Inc.
CATEGORY   Design/Single Page or Spread
DATE   November 1993

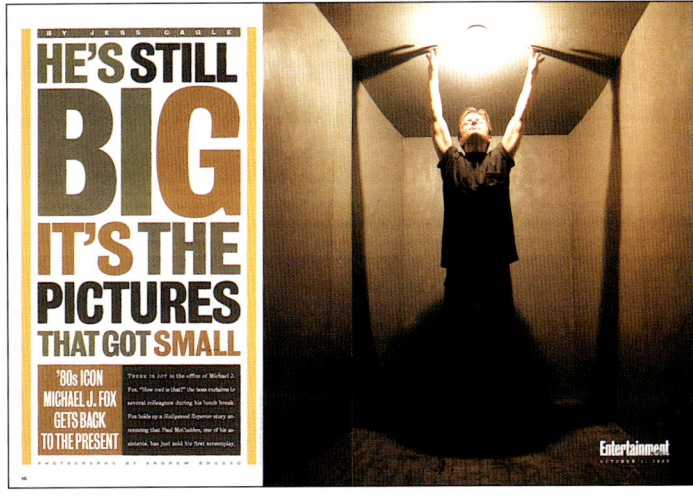

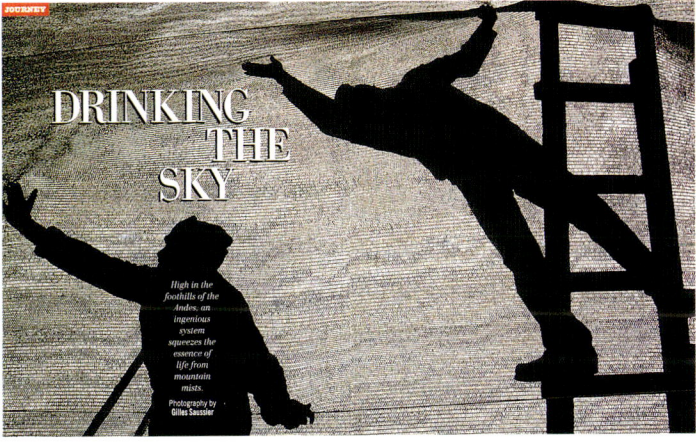

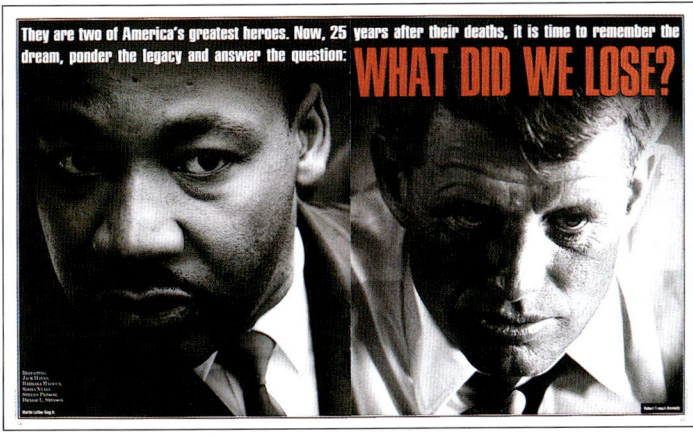

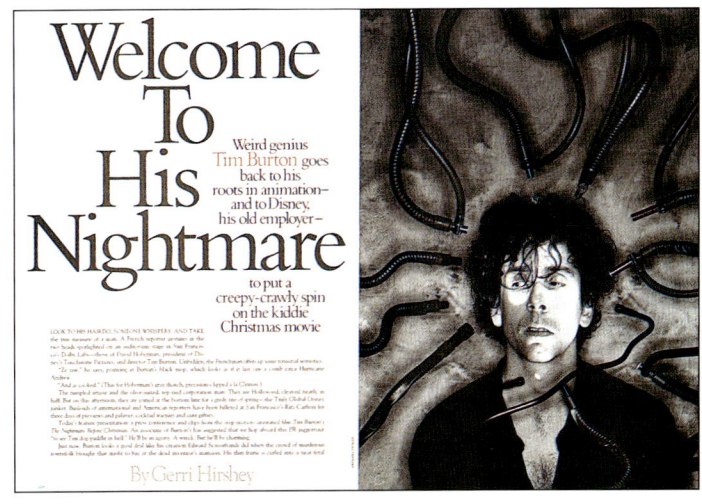

PUBLICATION   Life
AWARD   Merit
DESIGN DIRECTOR   Tom Bentkowski
DESIGNER   Nora Sheehan
PHOTOGRAPHERS   Ivan Massar, Cornell Capa
PHOTO EDITOR   David Friend
PUBLISHER   Time Inc.
CATEGORY   Design/Single Page or Spread
DATE   April 1993

PUBLICATION   GQ
AWARD   Merit
CREATIVE DIRECTOR   Robert Priest
DESIGNER   Laura Harrigan
PHOTOGRAPHER   Gregory Heisler
PHOTO EDITOR   Karen Frank
PUBLISHER   The Condé Nast Publications Inc.
CATEGORY   Design/Single Page or Spread
DATE   November 1993

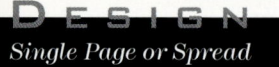
PUBLICATION   Premiere
AWARD   Merit
ART DIRECTOR   John Korpics
DESIGNER   John Korpics
PHOTOGRAPHER   Firooz Zahedi
PHOTO EDITOR   Charlie Holland
PUBLISHER   K-III Magazines
CATEGORY   Design/Single Page or Spread
DATE   November 1993

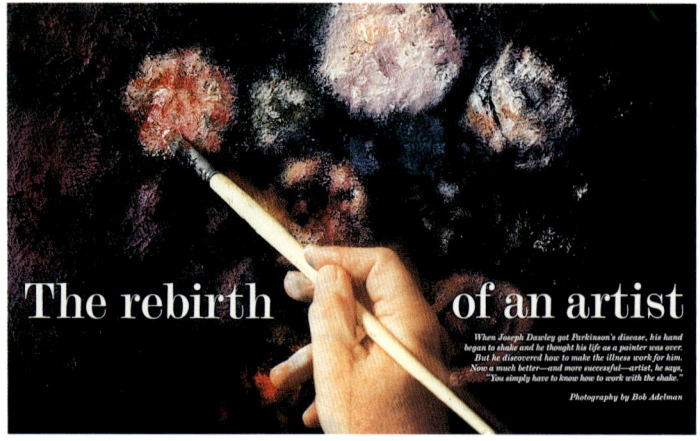

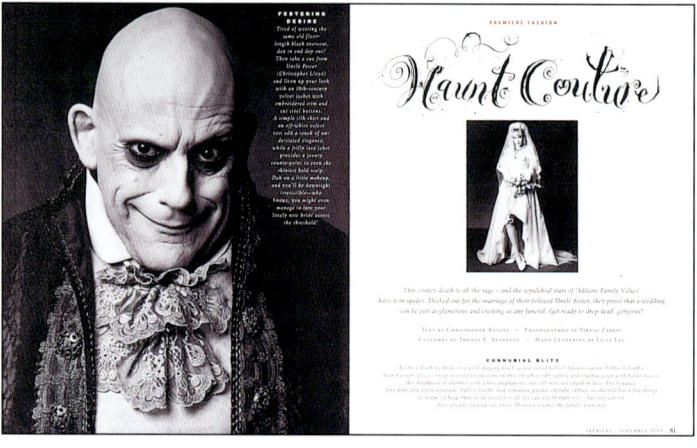

PUBLICATION   Life
AWARD   Merit
DESIGN DIRECTOR   Tom Bentkowski
DESIGNER   Dean Abatemarco
PHOTOGRAPHER   Bob Adelman
PHOTO EDITOR   David Friend
PUBLISHER   Time Inc.
CATEGORY   Design/Single Page or Spread
DATE   June 1993

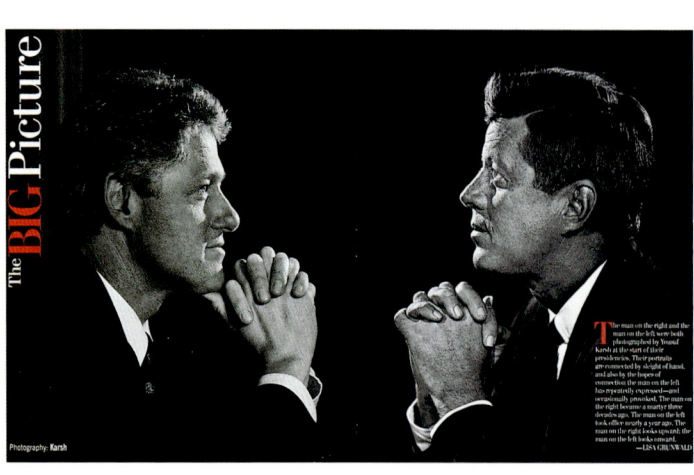

PUBLICATION   Life
AWARD   Merit
DESIGN DIRECTOR   Tom Bentkowski
DESIGNER   Marti Golon
PHOTOGRAPHER   Josef Karsh
PHOTO EDITOR   David Friend
PUBLISHER   Time Inc.
CATEGORY   Design/Single Page or Spread
DATE   December 1993

PUBLICATION   Premiere
AWARD   Merit
ART DIRECTOR   John Korpics
DESIGNER   John Korpics
PHOTOGRAPHER   Firouz Zahedi
PHOTO EDITOR   Charlie Holland
PUBLISHER   K-III Magazines
CATEGORY   Design/Single Page or Spread
DATE   September 1993

PUBLICATION	Rolling Stone
AWARD	Merit
ART DIRECTOR	Fred Woodward
DESIGNER	Debra Bishop
PHOTOGRAPHER	Herb Ritts
PHOTO EDITOR	Laurie Kratochvil
PUBLISHER	Wenner Media
CATEGORY	Design/Single Page or Spread
DATE	April 29, 1993

PUBLICATION	Rolling Stone
AWARD	Merit
ART DIRECTOR	Fred Woodward
DESIGNER	Gail Anderson
PHOTOGRAPHER	Matt Mahurin
PHOTO EDITOR	Laurie Kratochvil
PUBLISHER	Wenner Media
CATEGORY	Design/Single Page or Spread
DATE	May 27, 1993

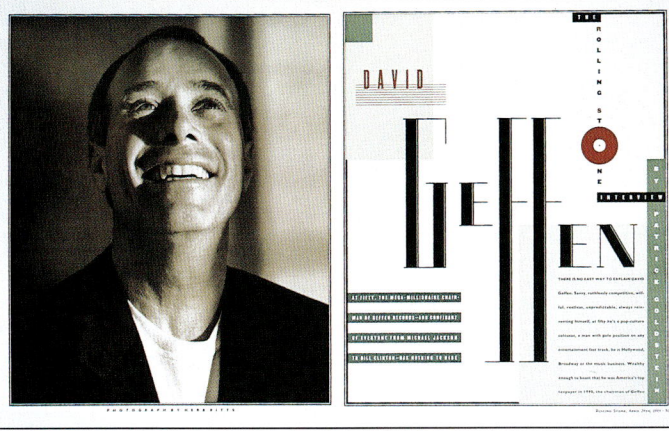
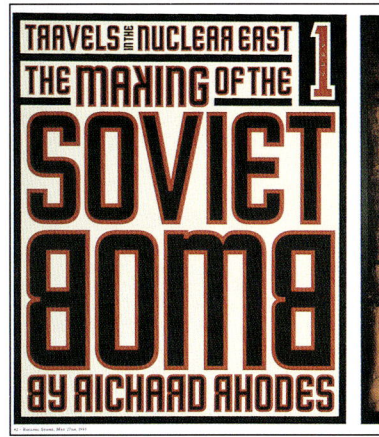
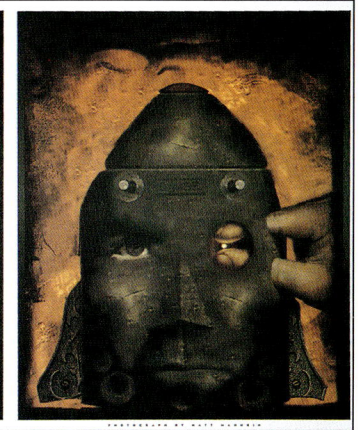

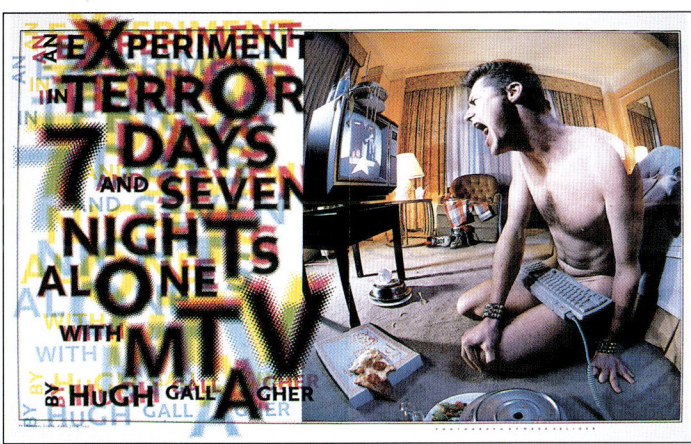
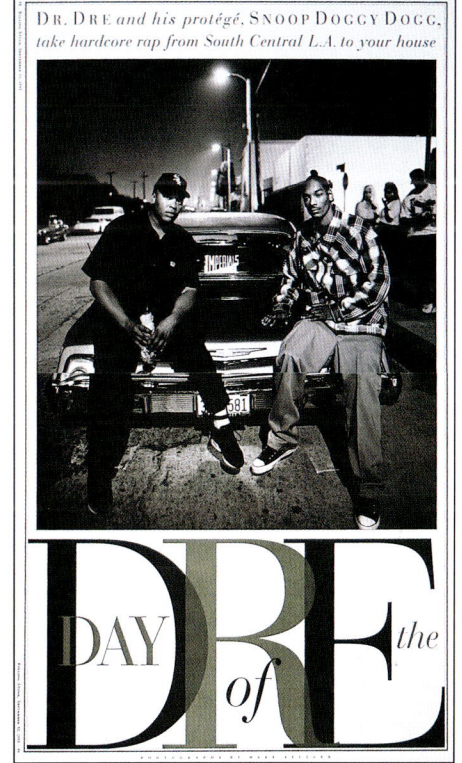

PUBLICATION	Rolling Stone
AWARD	Merit
DESIGN DIRECTOR	Fred Woodward
ART DIRECTOR	Fred Woodward
DESIGNER	Angela Skouras
PHOTOGRAPHER	Mark Seliger
PHOTO EDITOR	Laurie Kratochvil
PUBLISHER	Wenner Media
CATEGORY	Design/Single Page or Spread
DATE	April 29, 1993

PUBLICATION	Rolling Stone
AWARD	Merit
ART DIRECTOR	Fred Woodward
DESIGNER	Geraldine Hessler
PHOTOGRAPHER	Mark Seliger
PHOTO EDITOR	Laurie Kratochvil
PUBLISHER	Wenner Media
CATEGORY	Design/Single Page or Spread
DATE	September 30, 1993

PUBLICATION	Sports Illustrated
AWARD	Merit
DESIGN DIRECTOR	Steven Hoffman
DESIGNER	F. Darrin Perry
ILLUSTRATOR	Matt Groening
PUBLISHER	Time Inc.
CATEGORY	Design/Single Page or Spread
DATE	December 27, 1993 - January 3, 1994

PUBLICATION	Sports Illustrated
AWARD	Merit
DESIGN DIRECTOR	Steven Hoffman
DESIGNER	Steven Hoffman
PHOTOGRAPHER	Simon Bruty
PHOTO EDITOR	Heinz Kluetmeier
PUBLISHER	Time Inc.
CATEGORY	Design/Single Page or Spread
DATE	October 18, 1993

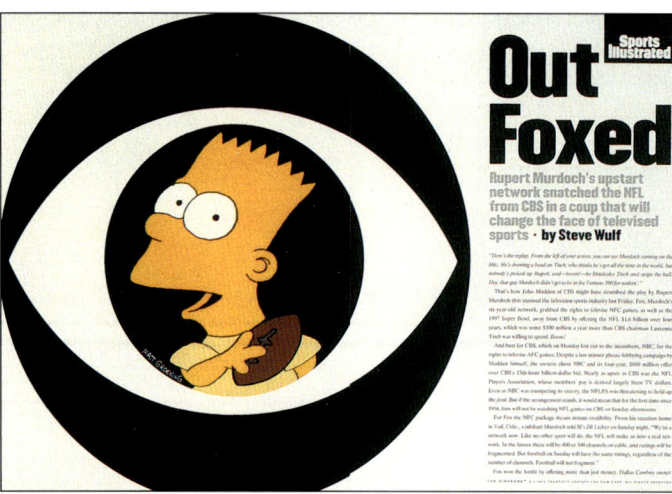

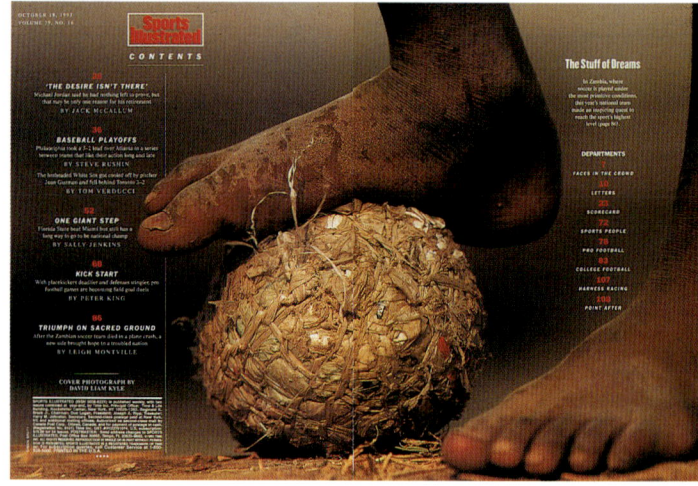

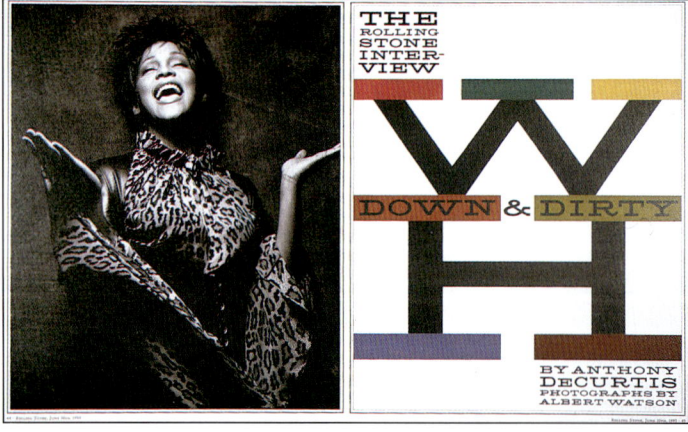

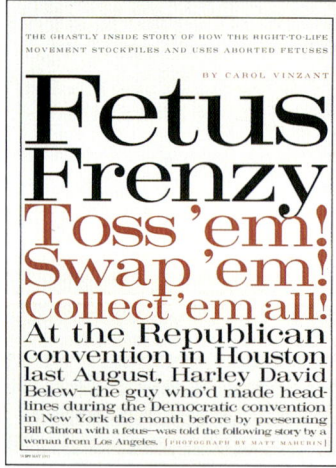

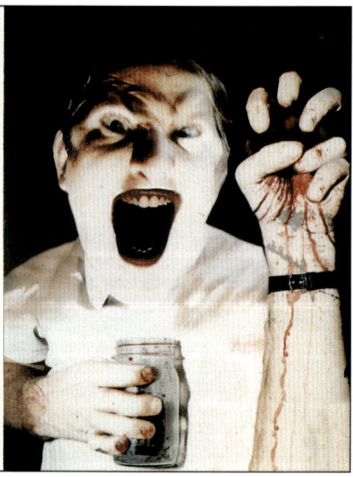

PUBLICATION	Rolling Stone
AWARD	Merit
ART DIRECTOR	Fred Woodward
DESIGNER	Fred Woodward
PHOTOGRAPHER	Albert Watson
PHOTO EDITOR	Laurie Kratochvil
PUBLISHER	Wenner Media
CATEGORY	Design/Single Page or Spread
DATE	June 10, 1993

PUBLICATION	Spy
AWARD	Merit
ART DIRECTOR	Christiaan Kuypers
DESIGNERS	Christiaan Kuypers, Daniel Carter
PHOTOGRAPHER	Matt Mahurin
PUBLISHER	Spy Corporation
CATEGORY	Design/Single Page or Spread
DATE	May 1993

PUBLICATION	Rolling Stone
AWARD	Merit
ART DIRECTOR	Fred Woodward
DESIGNERS	Fred Woodward, Gail Anderson
ILLUSTRATOR	Skip Liepke
PUBLISHER	Wenner Media
CATEGORY	Design/Single Page or Spread
DATE	April 29, 1993

PUBLICATION	Rolling Stone
AWARD	Merit
ART DIRECTOR	Fred Woodward
DESIGNER	Debra Bishop
PHOTOGRAPHER	Kurt Markus
PHOTO EDITOR	Laurie Kratochvil
PUBLISHER	Wenner Media
CATEGORY	Design/Single Page or Spread
DATE	April 1, 1993

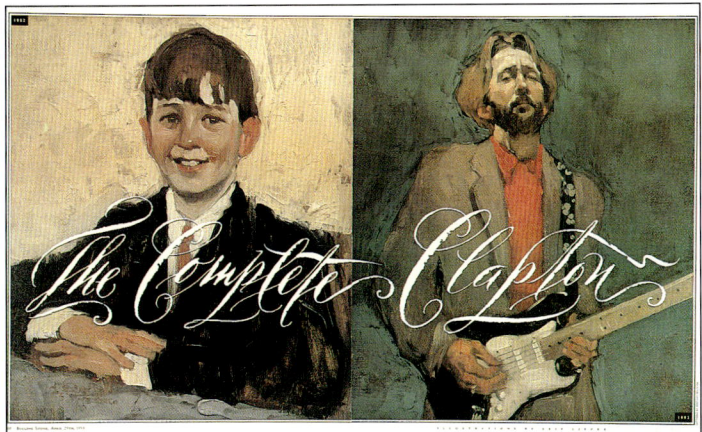

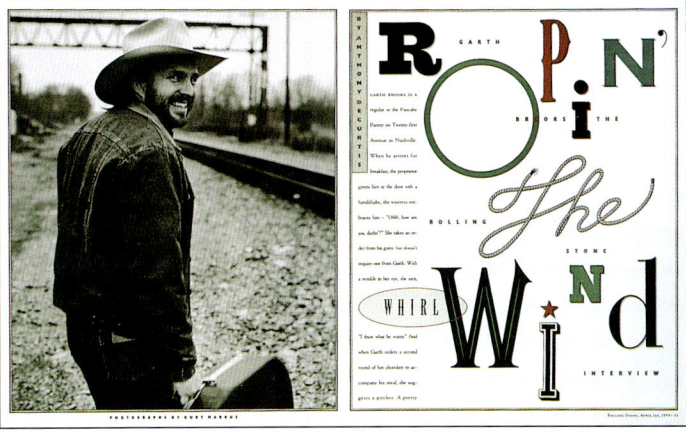

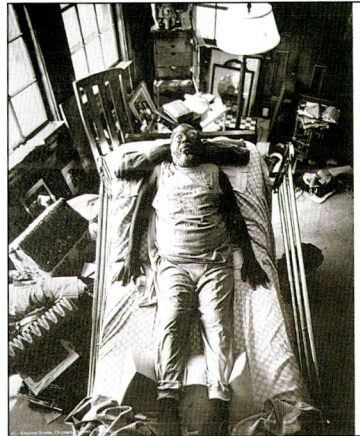

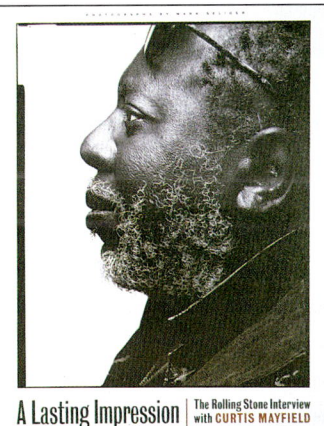

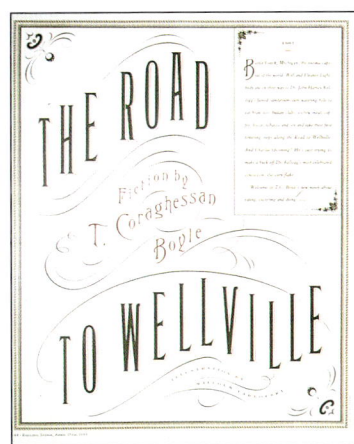

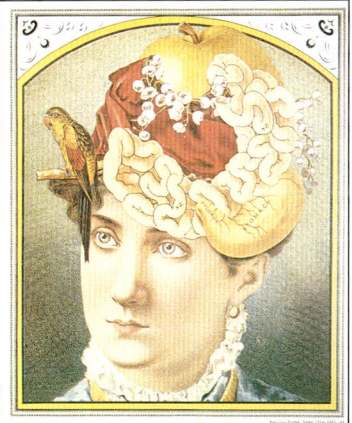

PUBLICATION	Rolling Stone
AWARD	Merit
ART DIRECTOR	Fred Woodward
DESIGNERS	Gail Anderson, Fred Woodward
PHOTOGRAPHER	Mark Seliger
PHOTO EDITOR	Laurie Kratochvil
PUBLISHER	Wenner Media
CATEGORY	Design/Single Page or Spread
DATE	October 28, 1993

PUBLICATION	Rolling Stone
AWARD	Merit
ART DIRECTOR	Fred Woodward
DESIGNER	Catherine Gilmore-Barnes
ILLUSTRATOR	Malcolm Tarlofsky
PUBLISHER	Wenner Media
CATEGORY	Design/Single Page or Spread
DATE	April 15, 1993

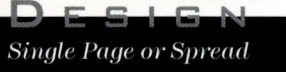

PUBLICATION	Working Woman
AWARD	Merit
ART DIRECTOR	Jolene Cuyler
DESIGNER	Lisa Goldenberg
ILLUSTRATOR	Anita Kunz
PUBLISHER	Lang Communications
CATEGORY	Design/Single Page or Spread
DATE	February 1993

PUBLICATION	Rolling Stone
AWARD	Merit
ART DIRECTOR	Fred Woodward
DESIGNER	Angela Skouras
PHOTOGRAPHER	Frank Ockenfels 3
PHOTO EDITOR	Laurie Kratochvil
PUBLISHER	Wenner Media
CATEGORY	Design/Single Page or Spread
DATE	March 18, 1993

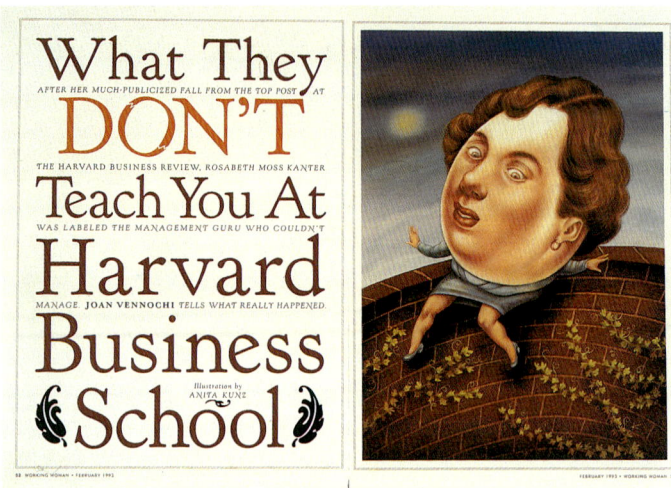

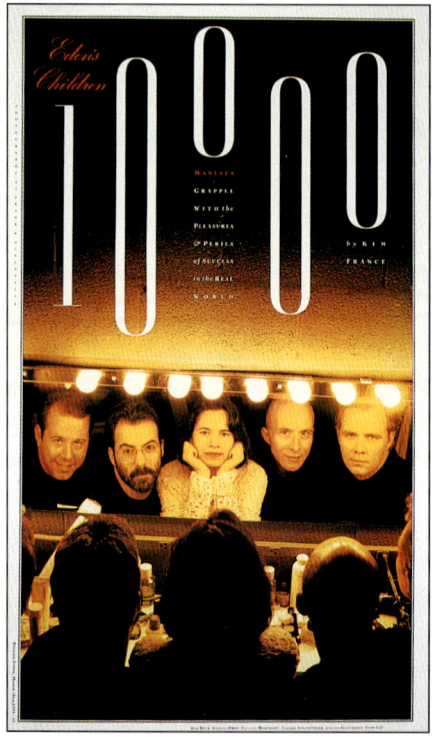

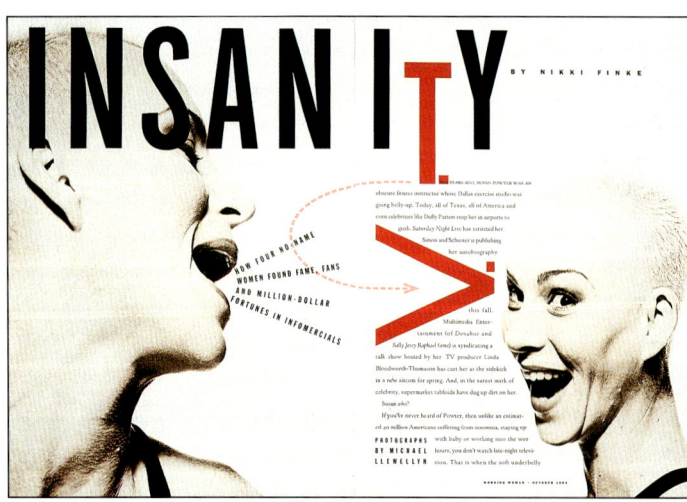

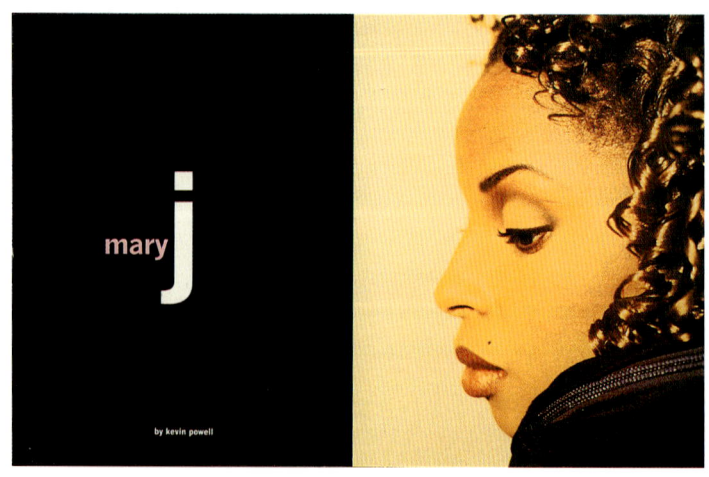

PUBLICATION	Working Woman
AWARD	Merit
ART DIRECTOR	Jolene Cuyler
PHOTOGRAPHER	Michael Llewellyn
PHOTO EDITOR	Clare Lissaman
PUBLISHER	Lang Communications
CATEGORY	Design/Single Page or Spread
DATE	October 1993

PUBLICATION	YSB
AWARD	Merit
DESIGN DIRECTOR	Fo Wilson
ART DIRECTORS	Fo Wilson, Elizabeth Rodriguez
DESIGNER	Elizabeth Rodriguez
PHOTOGRAPHER	Accelerator
PUBLISHER	Paige Publications
CATEGORY	Design/Single Page or Spread
DATE	March 1993

PUBLICATION Caring
AWARD Merit
DESIGN DIRECTOR Mark Geer
ART DIRECTOR Mark Geer
DESIGNER Mark Geer
ILLUSTRATOR Dave Calver
STUDIO Geer Design, Inc.
CATEGORY Design/Single Page or Spread
DATE May 1, 1993

PUBLICATION Pacifica
AWARD Merit
DESIGN DIRECTOR Kunio Hayashi
DESIGNERS Kunio Hayashi, Kevin Wilson
ILLUSTRATOR Ralph Kagehiro
PHOTOGRAPHER Kenichi Otake
PUBLISHER Media Five Limited
CATEGORY Design/Single Page or Spread
DATE December 1, 1993

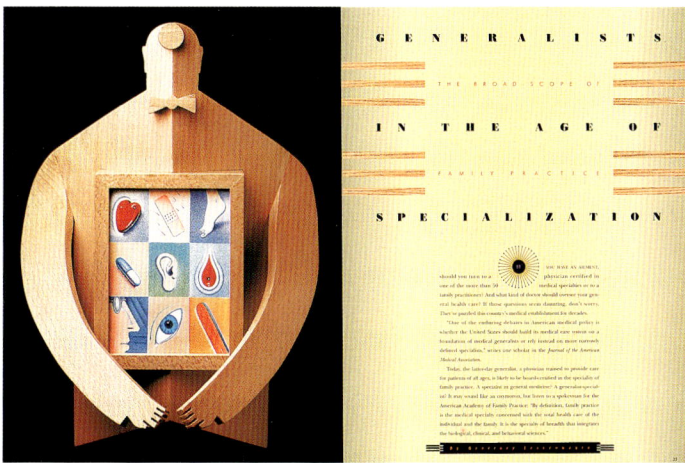

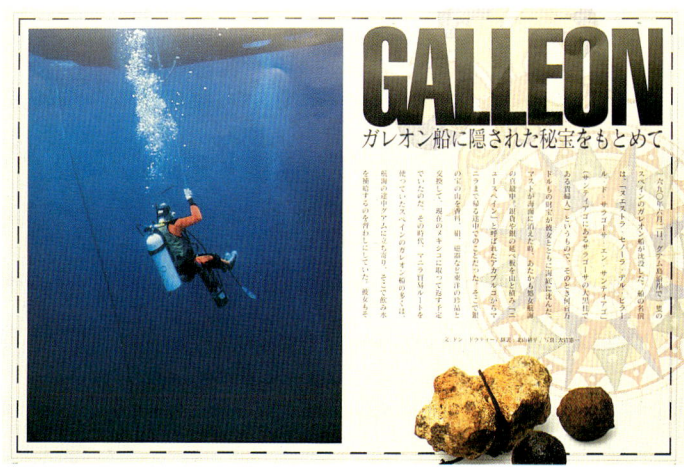

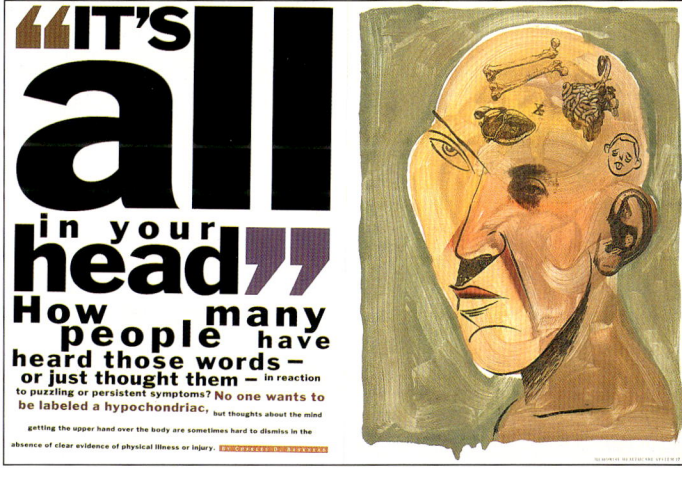

PUBLICATION Caring
AWARD Merit
DESIGN DIRECTOR Mark Geer
ART DIRECTOR Mark Geer
DESIGNER Mark Geer
ILLUSTRATOR John Kleber
STUDIO Geer Design, Inc.
CATEGORY Design/Single Page or Spread
DATE September 1, 1993

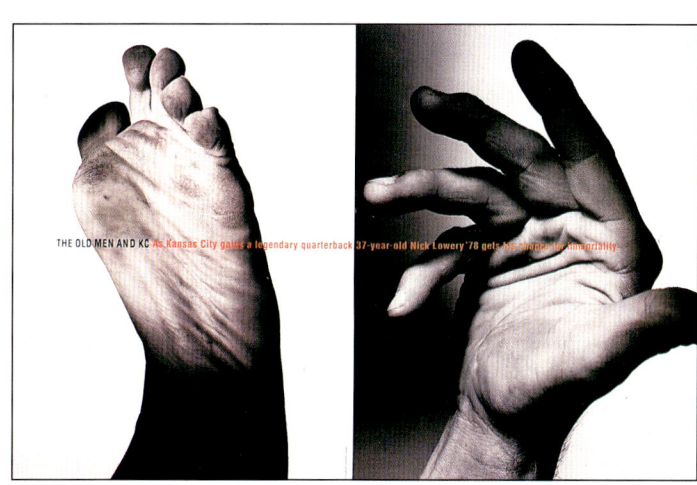

PUBLICATION Dartmouth Alumni Magazine
AWARD Merit
DESIGN DIRECTOR Scott Menchin
ART DIRECTOR Scott Menchin
PHOTOGRAPHER Ken Shung
STUDIO Scott Menchin Design
CATEGORY Design/Single Page or Spread
DATE Winter 1993

PUBLICATION	Profiles		PUBLICATION	Traces
AWARD	Merit		AWARD	Merit
DESIGN DIRECTOR	John Sizing		DESIGN DIRECTOR	R. Lloyd Brooks, Julie Larsen Maher
ART DIRECTOR	John T. Perry, III		ART DIRECTOR	R. Lloyd Brooks
PUBLISHER	Marblehead Communications, Inc.		DESIGNER	R. Lloyd Brooks, Julie Larsen Maher
CATEGORY	Design/Single Page or Spread		ILLUSTRATOR	Kin Hubbard
DATE	May 1993		PHOTOGRAPHER	Kim Heacox
			PHOTO EDITOR	Kent Calder, Deborah A. Behler
			STUDIO	Dean Johnson Design
			CLIENT	Indiana Historical Society
			CATEGORY	Design/Single Page or Spread
			DATE	Fall 1993

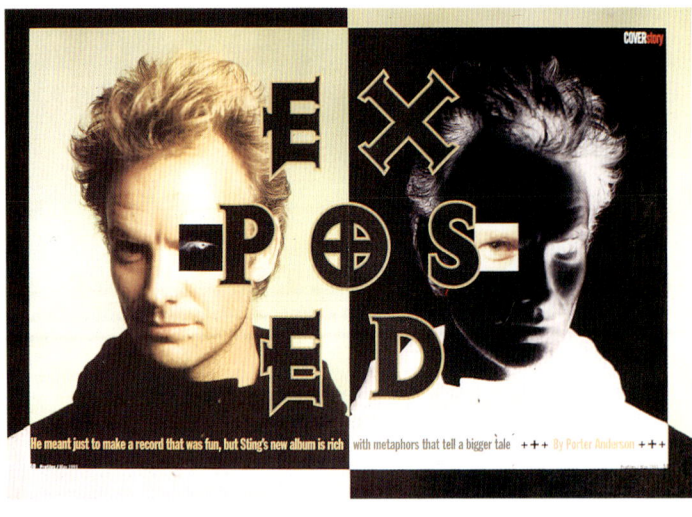

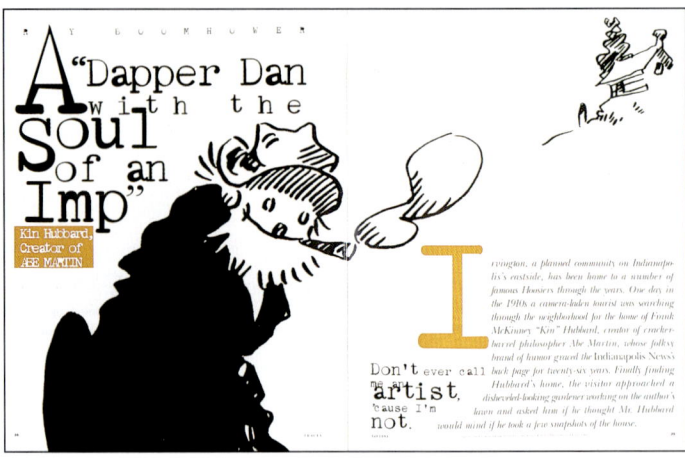

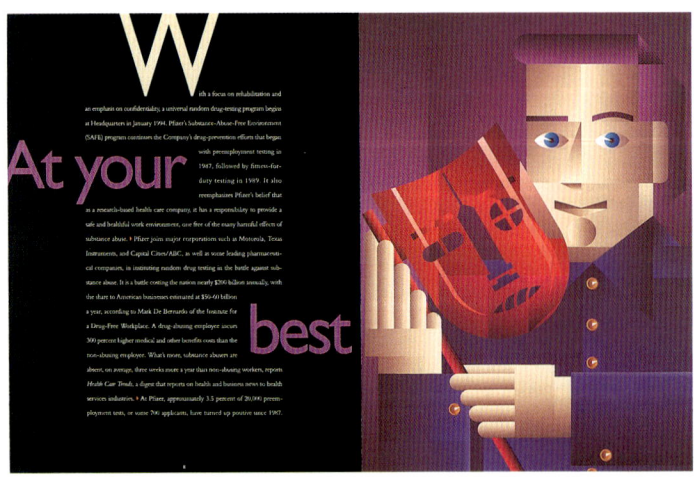

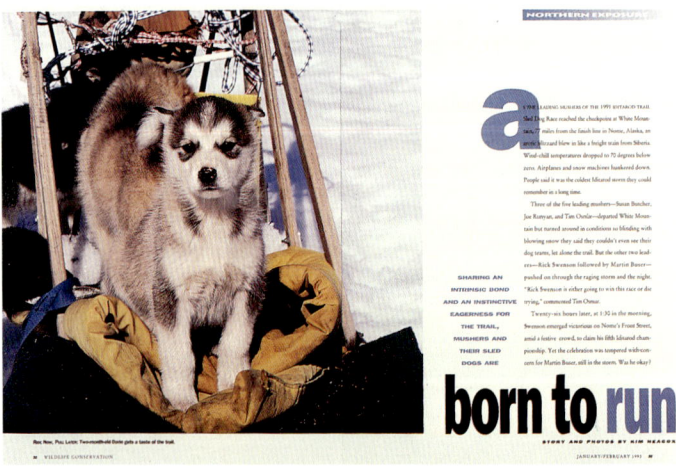

PUBLICATION	Scene		PUBLICATION	Wildlife Conservation
AWARD	Merit		AWARD	Merit
DESIGN DIRECTOR	Theo Fels		DESIGN DIRECTOR	Julie Larsen Maher
ART DIRECTORS	David Barnett, Theo Fels		DESIGNER	Julie Larsen Maher
DESIGNER	Theo Fels		PHOTOGRAPHER	Kim Heacox
ILLUSTRATOR	Don Arday		PHOTO EDITOR	Deborah A. Behler
STUDIO	The Barnett Group		PUBLISHER	Wildlife Conservation Society
CLIENT	Pfizer Inc.		CATEGORY	Design/Single Page or Spread
CATEGORY	Design/Single Page or Spread		DATE	January/February 1993
DATE	November 1993			

PUBLICATION	World
AWARD	Merit
DESIGN DIRECTOR	Donna Bonavita
DESIGNER	Donna Bonavita
ILLUSTRATOR	Michael Rocco Pinciotti
PHOTOGRAPHER	George Ross
STUDIO	KPMG
CATEGORY	Design/Single Page or Spread
DATE	Number 2, 1993

PUBLICATION	World Tour
AWARD	Merit
DESIGN DIRECTOR	Gary Koepke
DESIGNERS	Gary Koepke, Diddo Ramm
ILLUSTRATOR	Phillip Guston
PHOTO EDITOR	Sebastian Buffa
PUBLISHER	Dun & Bradstreet Software
STUDIO	Koepke International, LTD.
CATEGORY	Design/Single Page or Spread
DATE	July - September 1993

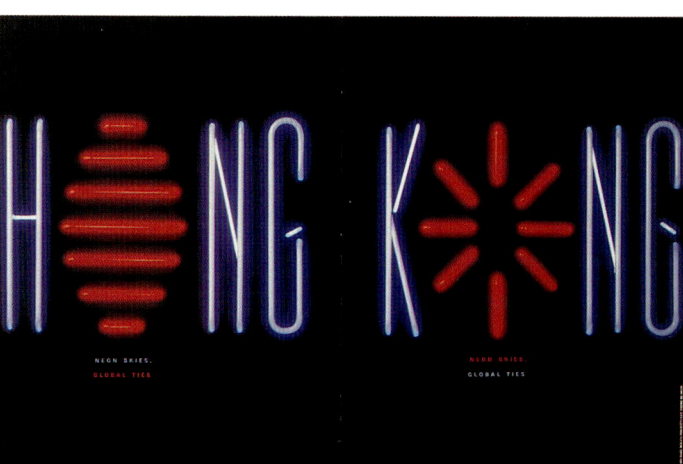

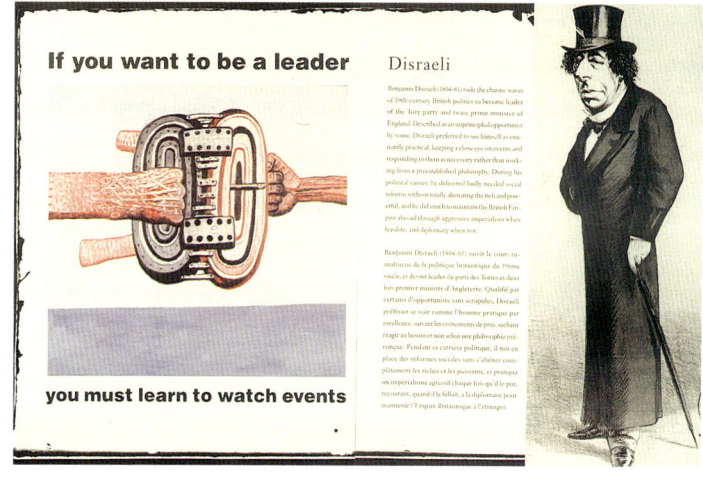

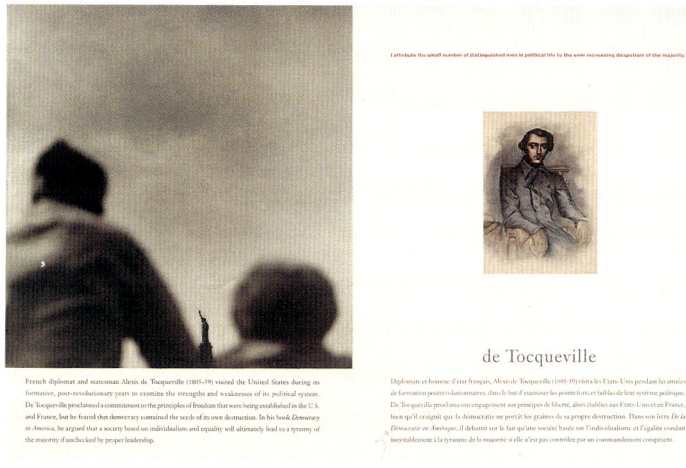

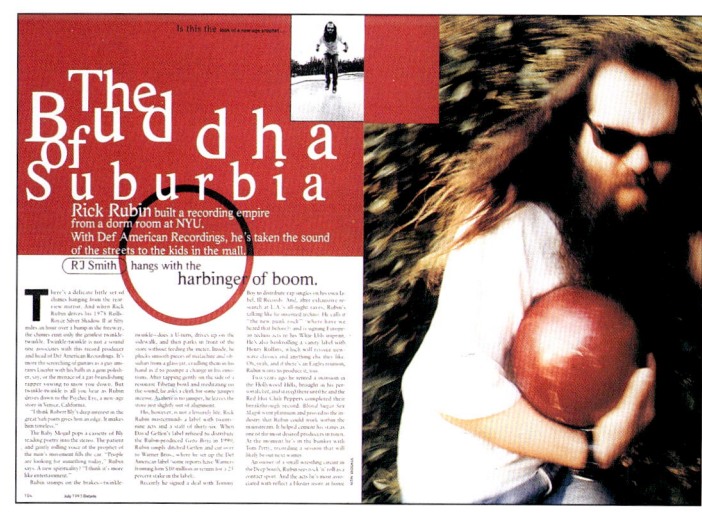

PUBLICATION	World Tour
AWARD	Merit
DESIGN DIRECTOR	Gary Koepke
DESIGNERS	Gary Koepke, Diddo Ramm
PHOTOGRAPHER	Dan Winters
PHOTO EDITOR	Sebastian Buffa
PUBLISHER	Dun & Bradstreet Software
STUDIO	Koepke International, LTD.
CATEGORY	Design/Single Page or Spread
DATE	July - September 1993

PUBLICATION	Details
AWARD	Merit
ART DIRECTOR	B.W. Honeycutt
DESIGNER	Markus Kiersztan
PHOTOGRAPHER	Nitin Vadukul
PUBLISHER	The Condé Nast Publications Inc.
CATEGORY	Design/Single Page or Spread

PUBLICATION	The Boston Globe/Food
AWARD	Merit
ART DIRECTOR	Sue Dawson
ILLUSTRATOR	Mary Lynn Blasutta
PHOTOGRAPHER	Lane Turner
PUBLISHER	The Boston Globe Publishing Co.
CATEGORY	Design/Single Page or Spread
DATE	February 10, 1993

PUBLICATION	The Boston Globe/ Health Science
AWARD	Merit
DESIGN DIRECTOR	Cynthia Daniels
DESIGNER	Cynthia Daniels
PUBLISHER	The Boston Globe Publishing Co.
CATEGORY	Design/Single Page or Spread
DATE	June 7, 1993

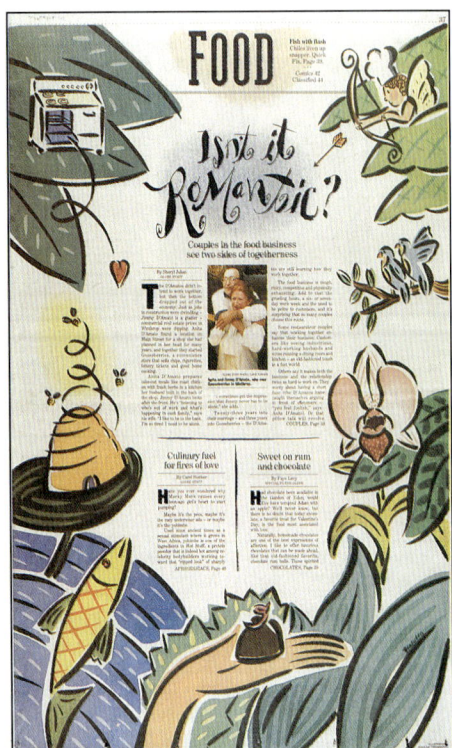

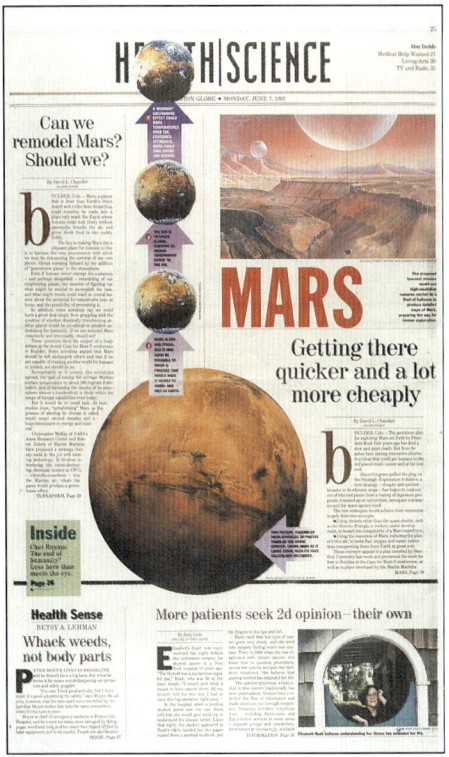

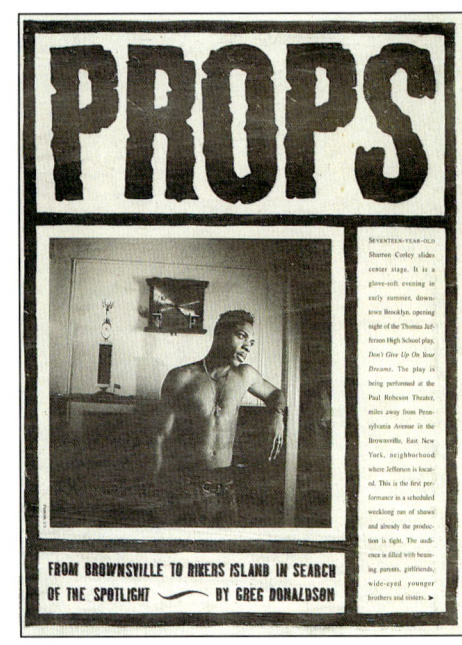

PUBLICATION	The Village Voice
AWARD	Merit
DESIGN DIRECTOR	Robert Newman
ART DIRECTOR	Florian Bachleda
PHOTOGRAPHER	C.T. Wemple
PHOTO EDITOR	Tom McGovern
PUBLISHER	VV Publishing Co.
CATEGORY	Design/Single Page or Spread
DATE	November 9, 1993

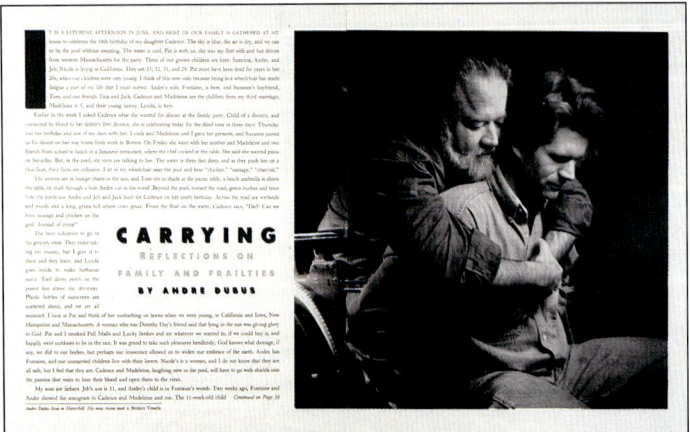

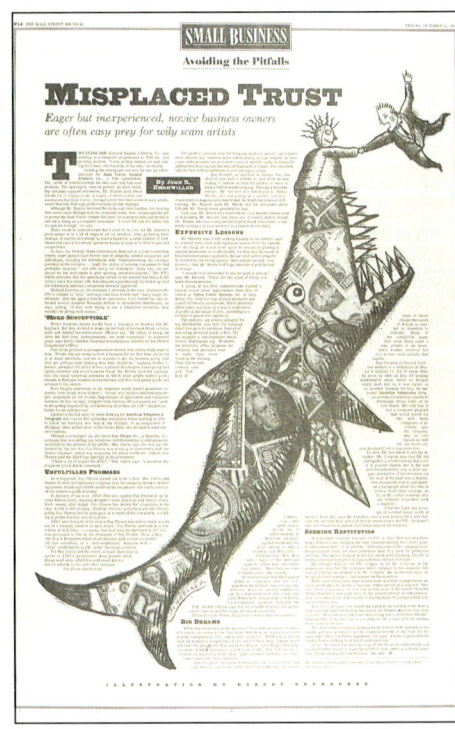

PUBLICATION	The Boston Globe Magazine
AWARD	Merit
DESIGN DIRECTOR	Lucy Bartholomay
DESIGNER	Lucy Bartholomay
ILLUSTRATOR	Lucy Bartholomay
PUBLISHER	The Boston Globe
CATEGORY	Design/Single Page or Spread
DATE	December 26, 1993

PUBLICATION	The Wall Street Journal Reports
AWARD	Merit
DESIGN DIRECTOR	Greg Leeds
DESIGNER	Greg Leeds
ILLUSTRATOR	Robert Neubecker
PUBLISHER	Dow Jones & Co., Inc.
CATEGORY	Design/Single Page or Spread
DATE	October 15, 1993

PUBLICATION	The Washington Times
AWARD	Merit
DESIGN DIRECTOR	Joseph W. Scopin
ART DIRECTOR	John Kascht
DESIGNER	John Kascht
PHOTO EDITOR	Glen Stubbe
PUBLISHER	The Washington Times Corp.
CATEGORY	Design/Single Page or Spread
DATE	September 12, 1993

PUBLICATION	The Washington Times
AWARD	Merit
DESIGN DIRECTOR	Joseph W. Scopin
ART DIRECTOR	John Kascht
DESIGNER	John Kascht
PHOTOGRAPHER	Kenneth Lambert
PHOTO EDITOR	Glen Stubbe
PUBLISHER	The Washington Times Corp.
CATEGORY	Design/Single Page or Spread
DATE	July 11, 1993

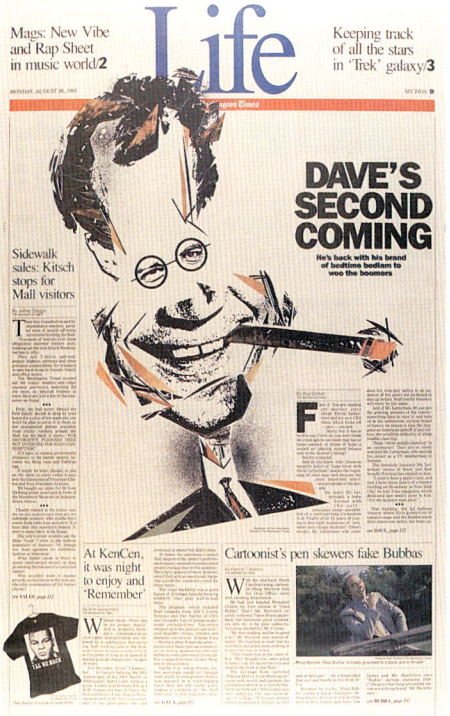

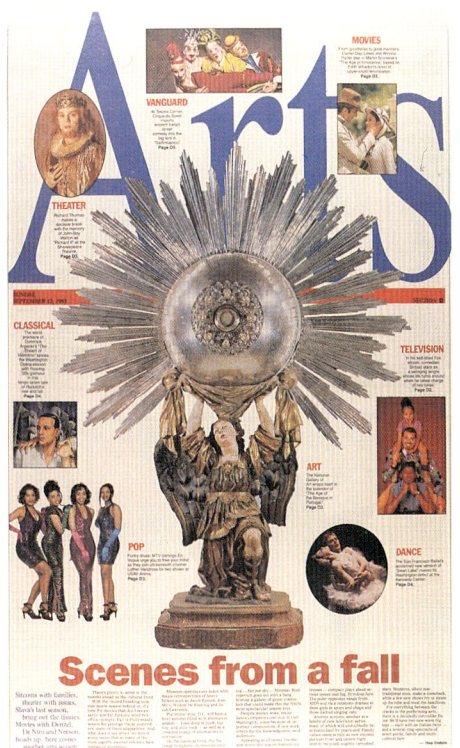

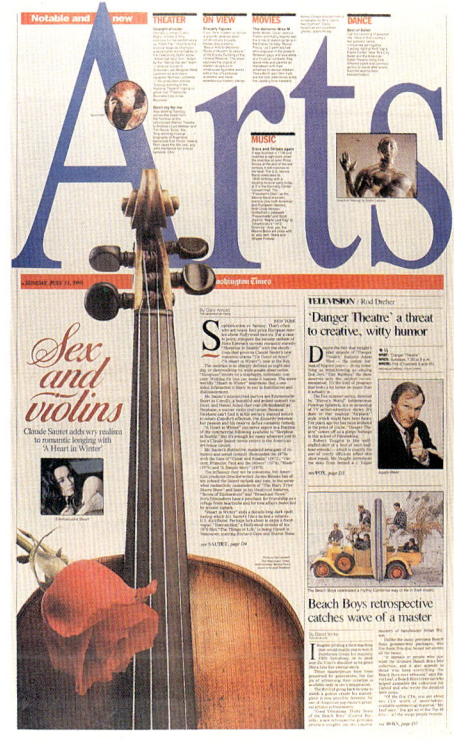

PUBLICATION	The Washington Times
AWARD	Merit
DESIGN DIRECTOR	Joseph W. Scopin
ART DIRECTOR	Dolores Motichka
DESIGNER	Dolores Motichka
ILLUSTRATOR	Don Asmussen
PHOTOGRAPHERS	Ruth Fremson, Bert Goulait
PHOTO EDITOR	Glen Stubbe
PUBLISHER	The Washington Times Corp.
CATEGORY	Design/Single Page or Spread
DATE	August 30, 1993

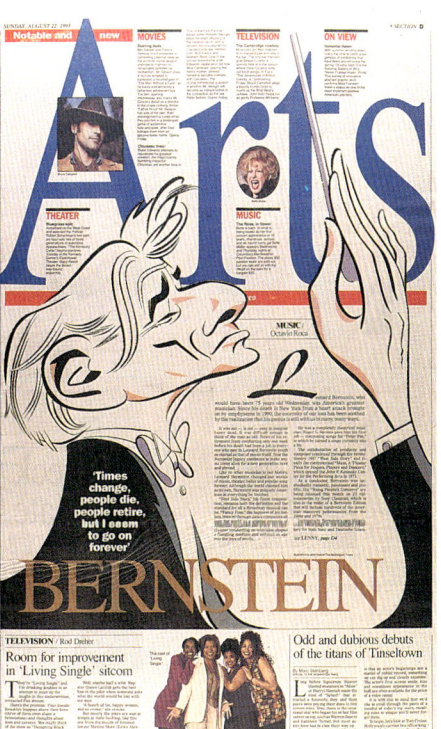

PUBLICATION	The Washington Times
AWARD	Merit
DESIGN DIRECTOR	Joseph W. Scopin
ART DIRECTOR	John Kascht
DESIGNER	John Kascht
ILLUSTRATOR	John Kascht
PHOTO EDITOR	Glen Stubbe
PUBLISHER	The Washington Times Corp.
CATEGORY	Design/Single Page or Spread
DATE	August 22, 1993

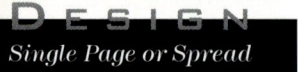

PUBLICATION	The Boston Globe/Arts Etc.
AWARD	Merit
ART DIRECTOR	Sue Dawson
PUBLISHER	The Boston Globe
CATEGORY	Design/Single Page or Spread
DATE	April 11, 1993

PUBLICATION	The Boston Globe
AWARD	Merit
ART DIRECTOR	Rena Sokolow
DESIGNER	Rena Sokolow
ILLUSTRATOR	Scott Menchin
PUBLISHER	The Boston Globe
CATEGORY	Design/Single Page or Spread
DATE	October 3, 1993

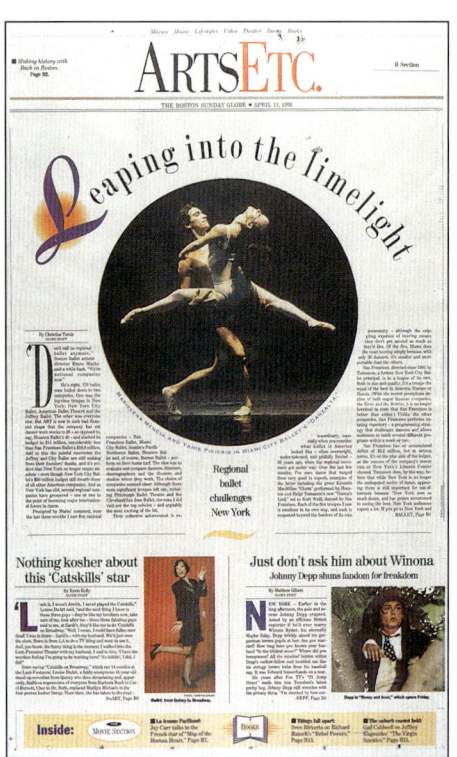

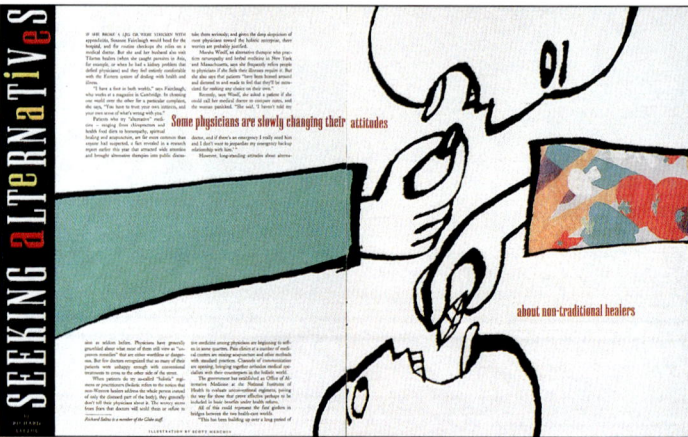

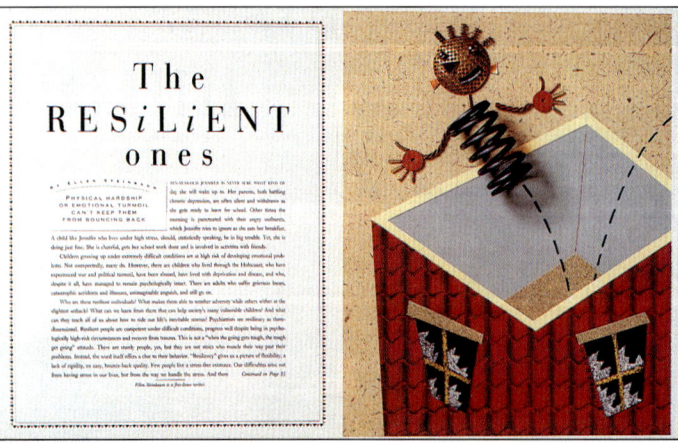

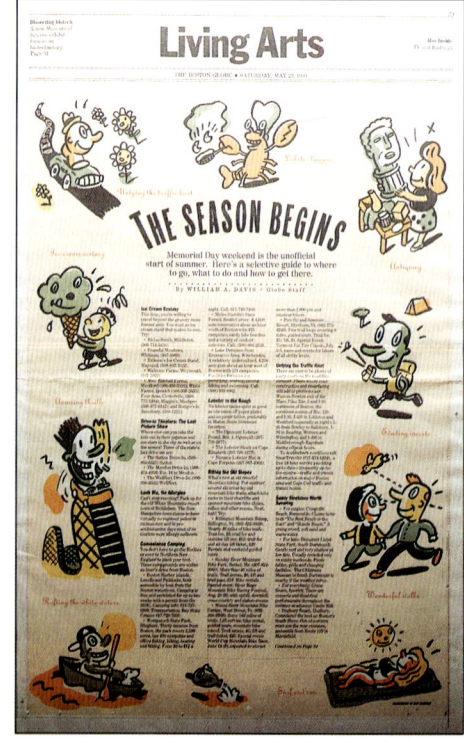

PUBLICATION	The Boston Globe
AWARD	Merit
ART DIRECTOR	Cynthia Hoffman
DESIGNER	Cynthia Hoffman
ILLUSTRATOR	Steven Guarnaccia
PUBLISHER	The Boston Globe
CATEGORY	Design/Single Page or Spread
DATE	April 25, 1993

PUBLICATION	The Boston Globe
AWARD	Merit
ART DIRECTOR	Jane Simon
DESIGNER	Jane Simon
ILLUSTRATOR	Gary Baseman
PUBLISHER	The Boston Globe
CATEGORY	Design/Single Page or Spread
DATE	May 29, 1993

PUBLICATION	The Washington Times
AWARD	Merit
DESIGN DIRECTOR	Joseph W. Scopin
ART DIRECTOR	Dolores Motichka
DESIGNER	Dolores Motichka
ILLUSTRATOR	Dolores Motichka
PHOTOGRAPHER	Glen Stubbe
PHOTO EDITOR	Glen Stubbe
PUBLISHER	The Washington Times Corp.
CATEGORY	Design/Single Page or Spread
DATE	February 11, 1993

PUBLICATION	The Washington Times
AWARD	Merit
DESIGN DIRECTOR	Joseph W. Scopin
ART DIRECTOR	John Kascht
DESIGNER	John Kascht
ILLUSTRATOR	John Kascht
PHOTO EDITOR	Glen Stubbe
PUBLISHER	The Washington Times Corp.
CATEGORY	Design/Single Page or Spread
DATE	November 28, 1993

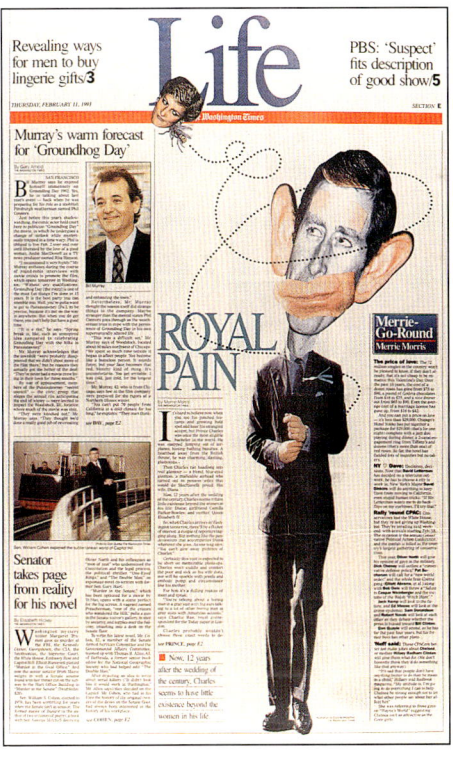

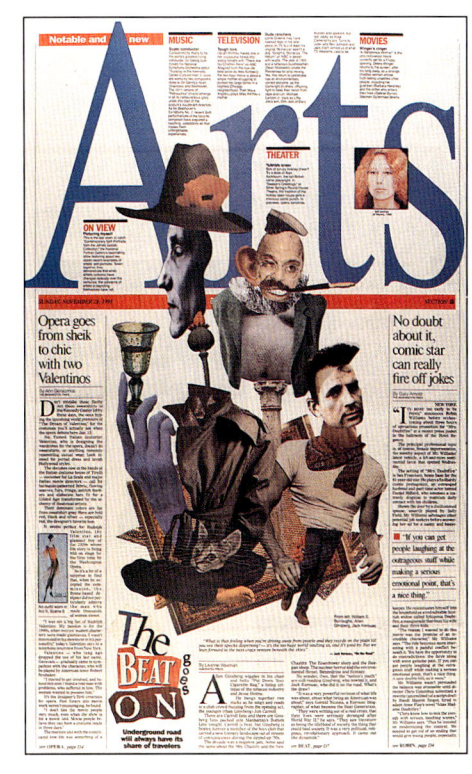

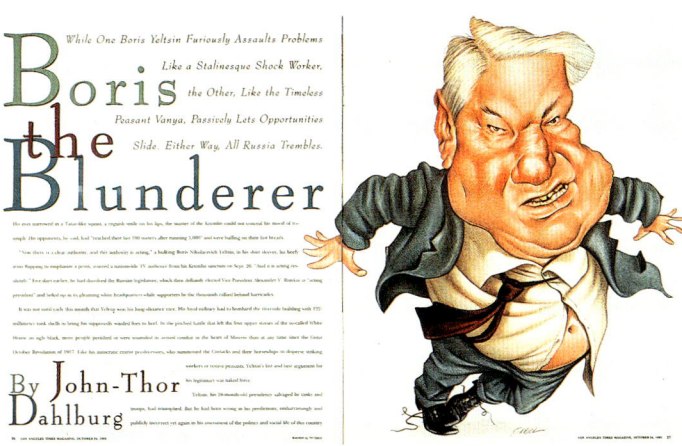

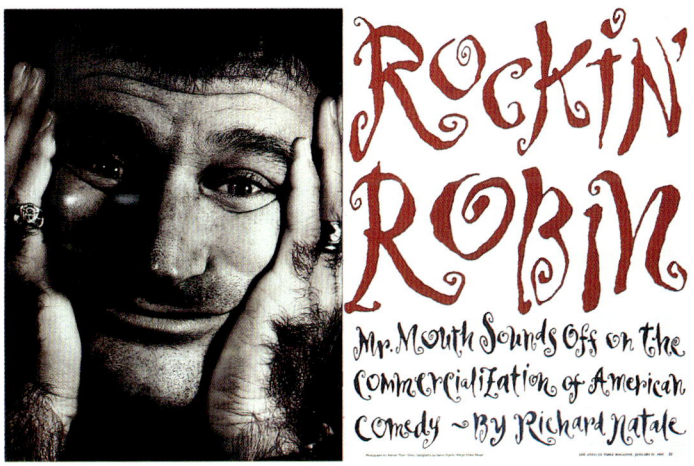

PUBLICATION	The Los Angeles Times Magazine
AWARD	Merit
ART DIRECTOR	Nancy Duckworth
DESIGNER	Steven Banks
ILLUSTRATOR	Tim Gabor
PUBLISHER	Times Mirror
CATEGORY	Design/Single Page or Spread
DATE	October 24, 1993

PUBLICATION	The Los Angeles Times Magazine
AWARD	Merit
ART DIRECTORS	Nancy Duckworth, Steven Banks
ILLUSTRATOR	Nancy Ogami
PHOTOGRAPHER	Alastair Train
PHOTO EDITOR	Lisa Thackaberry
PUBLISHER	Times Mirror
CATEGORY	Design/Single Page or Spread
DATE	January 31, 1993

PUBLICATION	The New York Times Magazine
AWARD	Merit
ART DIRECTOR	Janet Froelich
DESIGNER	Kathi Rota
ILLUSTRATOR	Amy Guip
PUBLISHER	The New York Times
CATEGORY	Design/Single Page or Spread
DATE	May 23, 1993

PUBLICATION	The Los Angeles Times Magazine
AWARD	Merit
ART DIRECTOR	Nancy Duckworth
DESIGNER	Nancy Duckworth
ILLUSTRATOR	Christian Clayton
PUBLISHER	Times Mirror
CATEGORY	Design/Single Page or Spread
DATE	April 25, 1993

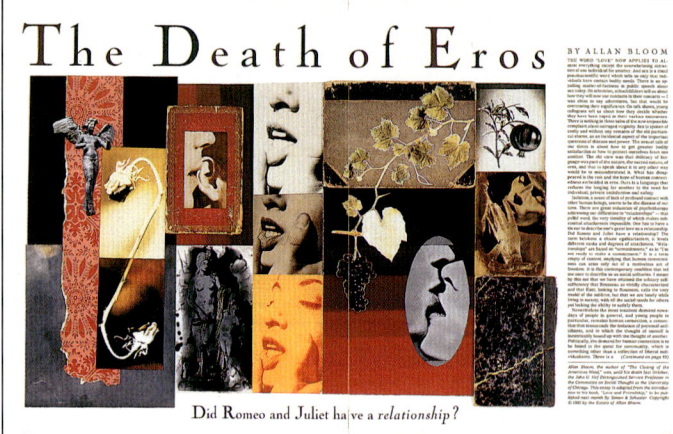

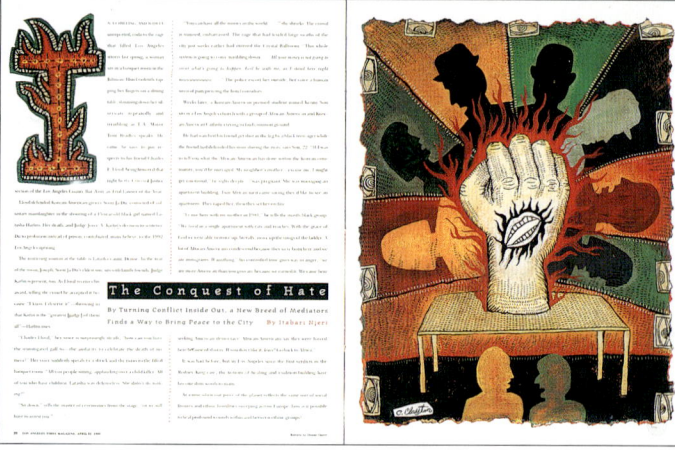

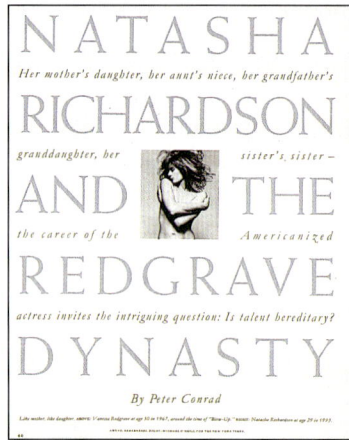

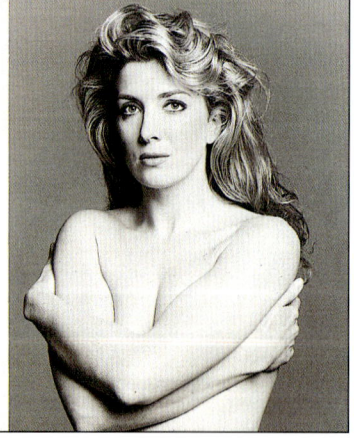

PUBLICATION	The New York Times Magazine
AWARD	Merit
ART DIRECTOR	Janet Froelich
DESIGNER	Petra Mercker
PHOTOGRAPHER	Michael O'Neill
PHOTO EDITOR	Kathy Ryan
PUBLISHER	The New York Times
CATEGORY	Design/Single Page or Spread
DATE	June 6, 1993

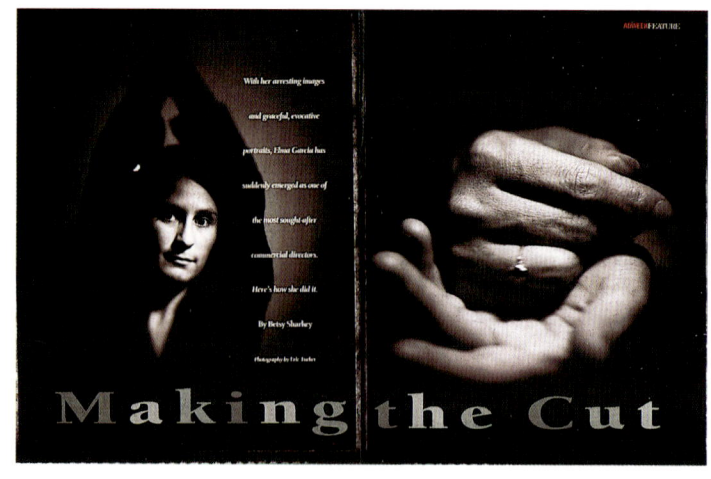

PUBLICATION	Adweek
AWARD	Merit
DESIGN DIRECTOR	Carole Erger-Fass
ART DIRECTOR	Blake Taylor
PHOTOGRAPHER	Eric Tucker
PHOTO EDITOR	Sabine Meyer
PUBLISHER	BPI, Inc.
CATEGORY	Design/Single Page or Spread
DATE	November 22, 1993

PUBLICATION	The Washington Post Magazine
AWARD	Merit
ART DIRECTOR	Kelly Doe
DESIGNER	Kelly Doe
ILLUSTRATOR	Lane Smith
PUBLISHER	The Washington Post
CATEGORY	Design/Single Page or Spread
DATE	May 30, 1993

PUBLICATION	The Washington Post Magazine
AWARD	Merit
ART DIRECTOR	Richard Baker
DESIGNER	Richard Baker
PHOTOGRAPHER	Sam Shere
PHOTO EDITOR	Deborah Needleman
PUBLISHER	The Washington Post
CATEGORY	Design/Single Page or Spread
DATE	January 17, 1993

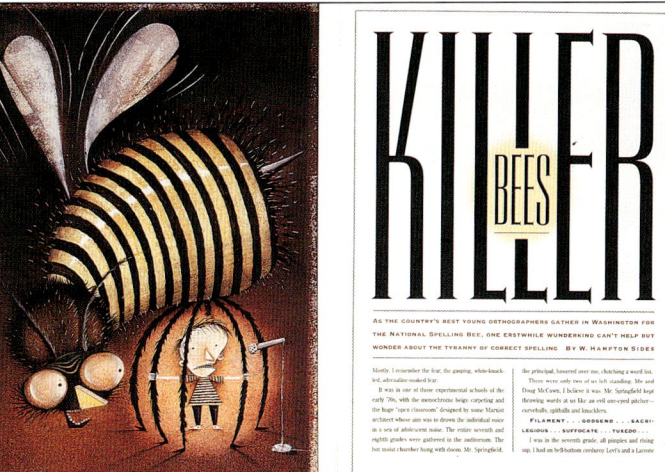

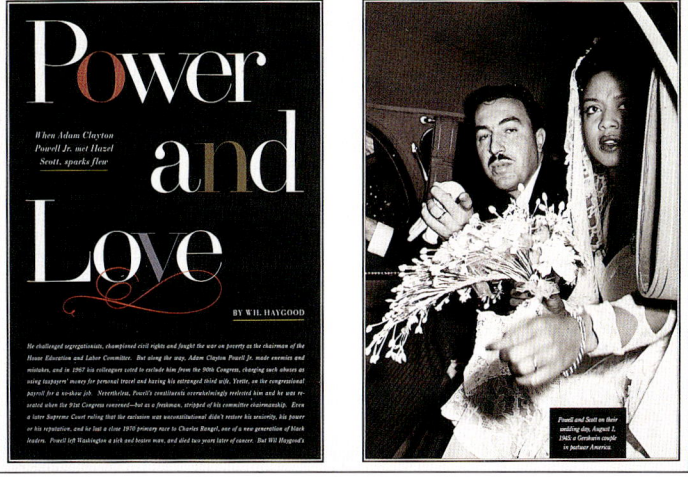

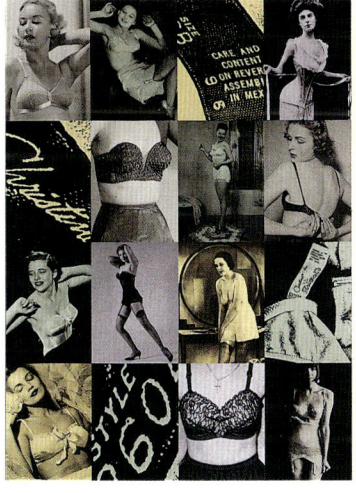

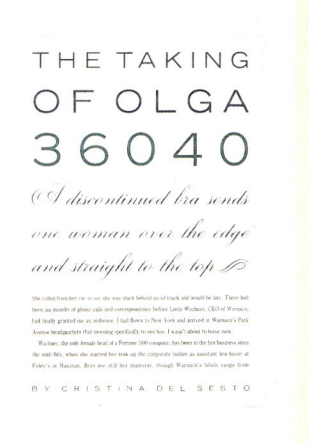

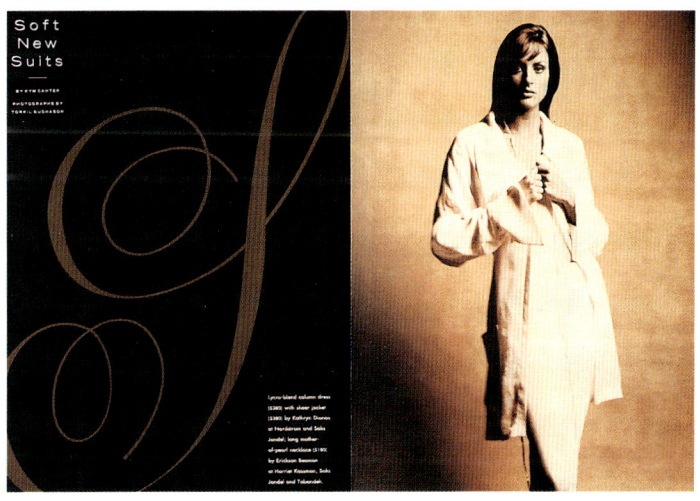

PUBLICATION	The Washington Post Magazine
AWARD	Merit
ART DIRECTOR	Richard Baker
DESIGNER	Kelly Doe
PHOTO EDITOR	Deborah Needleman
PUBLISHER	The Washington Post
CATEGORY	Design/Single Page or Spread
DATE	March 7, 1993

PUBLICATION	The Washington Post Magazine
AWARD	Merit
ART DIRECTOR	Kelly Doe
DESIGNER	Kelly Doe
ILLUSTRATOR	Lane Smith
PUBLISHER	The Washington Post
CATEGORY	Design/Single Page or Spread
DATE	May 30, 1993

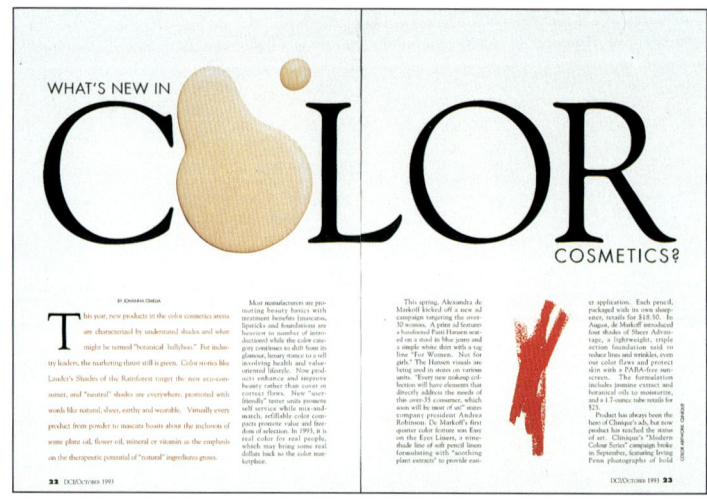

PUBLICATION   Graphis
AWARD   Merit
DESIGN DIRECTOR   B. Martin Pedersen
ART DIRECTORS   B. Martin Pedersen, Randell Pearson
DESIGNER   B. Martin Pedersen
PHOTOGRAPHER   Poul Ib Henriksen
STUDIO   Pedersen Design Group, Inc.
CATEGORY   Design/Single Page or Spread
DATE   August 1993

PUBLICATION   Drugs & Cosmetic Industry
AWARD   Merit
ART DIRECTOR   Irasema Rivera
DESIGNER   Irasema Rivera
PHOTOGRAPHER   Clinique
PUBLISHER   Advanstar Communications, Inc.
CATEGORY   Design/Single Page or Spread
DATE   October 15, 1993

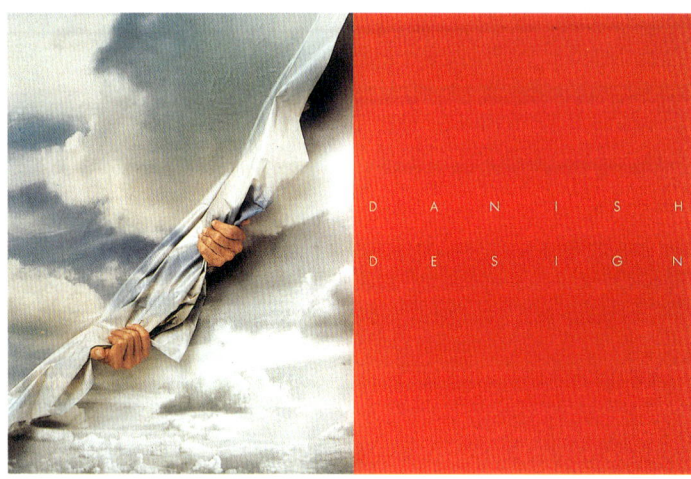

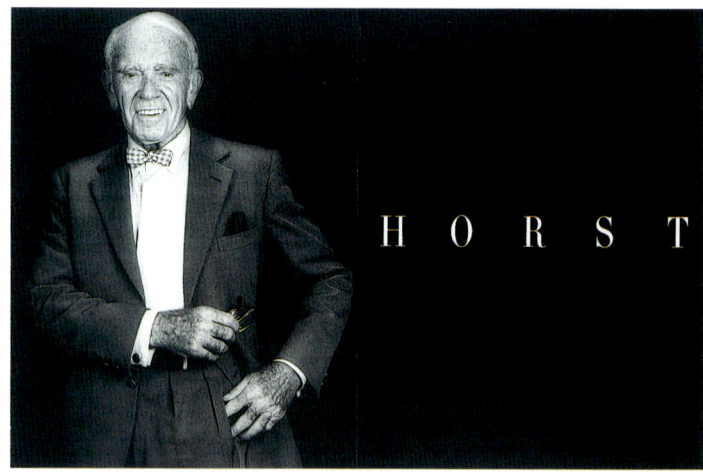

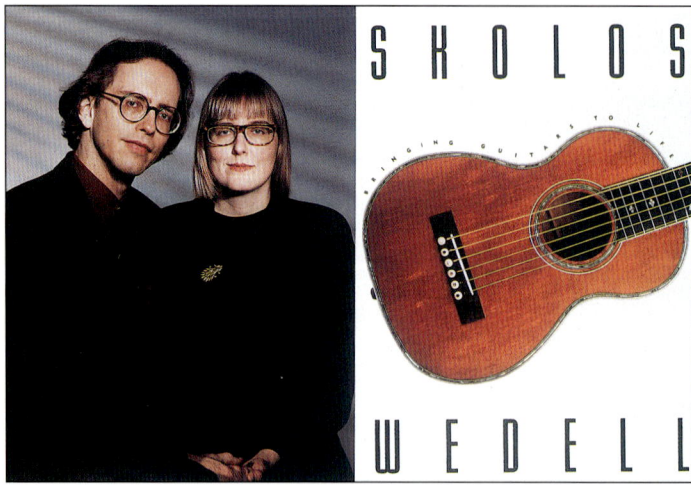

PUBLICATION   Graphis
AWARD   Merit
DESIGN DIRECTOR   B. Martin Pedersen
ART DIRECTORS   B. Martin Pedersen, Randell Pearson
DESIGNER   B. Martin Pedersen
STUDIO   Pedersen Design Group, Inc.
CATEGORY   Design/Single Page or Spread
DATE   April 1993

PUBLICATION   Graphis
AWARD   Merit
DESIGN DIRECTOR   B. Martin Pedersen
ART DIRECTORS   B. Martin Pedersen, Randell Pearson,
  Greg Simpson
DESIGNER   B. Martin Pedersen
PHOTOGRAPHER   Robert Mappelthorpe
STUDIO   Pedersen Design Group, Inc.
CATEGORY   Design/Single Page or Spread
DATE   October 1993

PUBLICATION   Adweek
AWARD   Merit
DESIGN DIRECTOR Carole Erger-Fass
ART DIRECTOR   Blake Taylor
PHOTOGRAPHER   Frank Veronsky
PHOTO EDITOR   Sabine Meyer
PUBLISHER   BPI, Inc.
CATEGORY   Design/Single Page or Spread
DATE   July 12, 1993

PUBLICATION   Number
AWARD   Merit
DESIGN DIRECTOR Bruce Crocker
DESIGNERS   Bruce Crocker, Lee Busch
PHOTOGRAPHER   Nick White
PHOTO EDITOR   Bruce Crocker
PUBLISHER   Boston Acoustics
CATEGORY   Design/Single Page or Spread
DATE   October 1, 1993

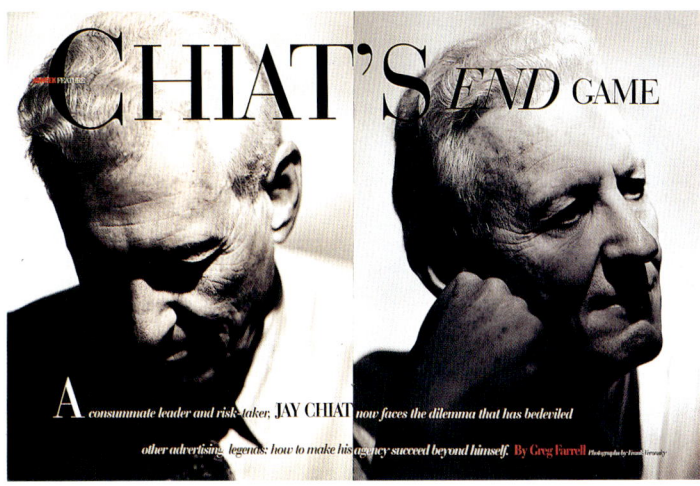

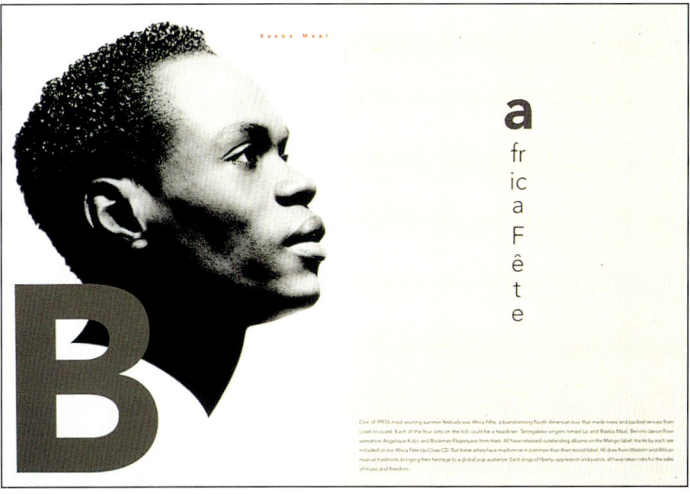

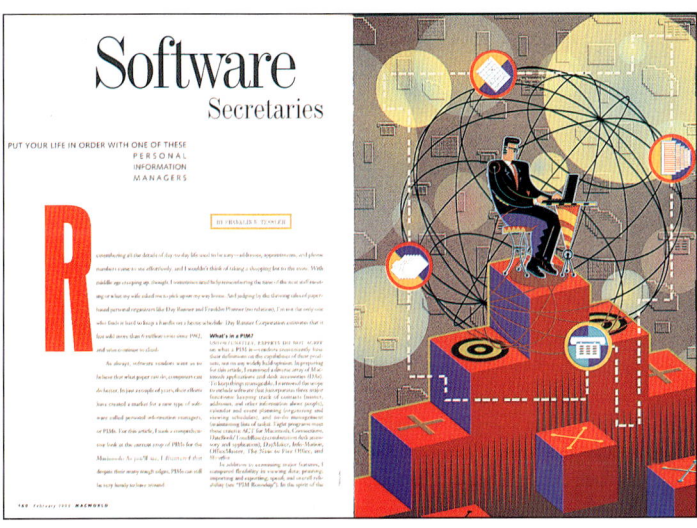

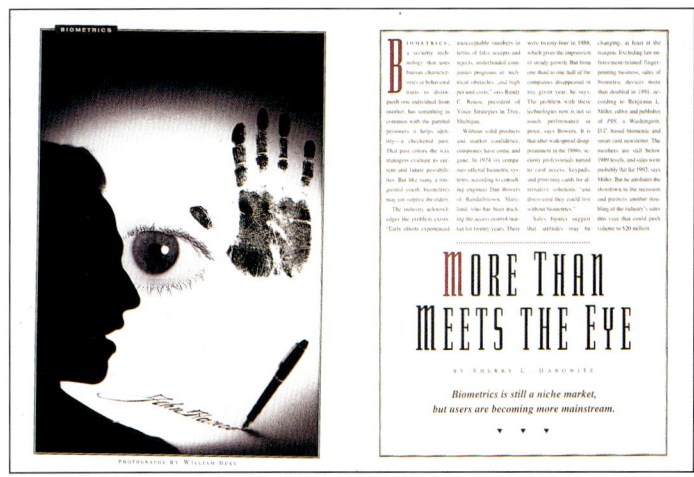

PUBLICATION   MacWorld
AWARD   Merit
DESIGN DIRECTOR Dennis Mcleod
ART DIRECTOR   Kent Tayenaka
DESIGNER   Tim Johnson
ILLUSTRATOR   Steve Lyons
PUBLISHER   Macworld Communications
CATEGORY   Design/Single Page or Spread
DATE   February 1993

PUBLICATION   Security Management
AWARD   Merit
ART DIRECTOR   Roy Comiskey
DESIGNER   Roy Comiskey
PHOTOGRAPHER   William Duke
PUBLISHER   American Society for Industrial Security
CATEGORY   Design/Single Page or Spread
DATE   February 1993

PUBLICATION	Upper & Lower Case
AWARD	Merit
ART DIRECTOR	Paul Davis
DESIGNERS	Lisa Mazur, Chalkley Calderwood
PUBLISHER	International Typeface Corporation
STUDIO	Paul Davis Studio
CATEGORY	Design/Single Page or Spread
DATE	May 1993

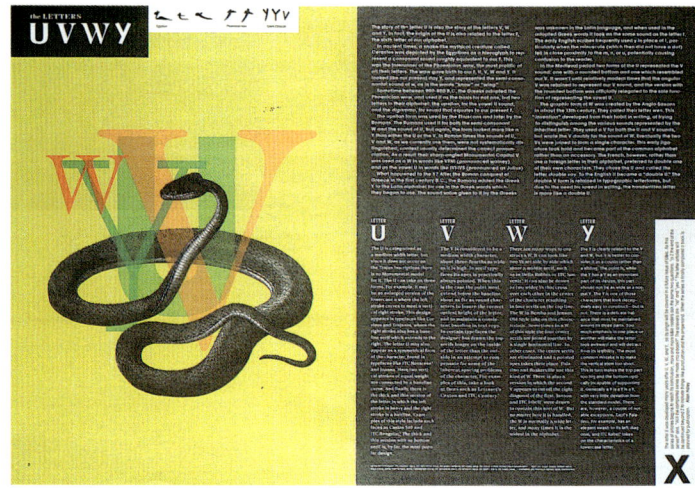

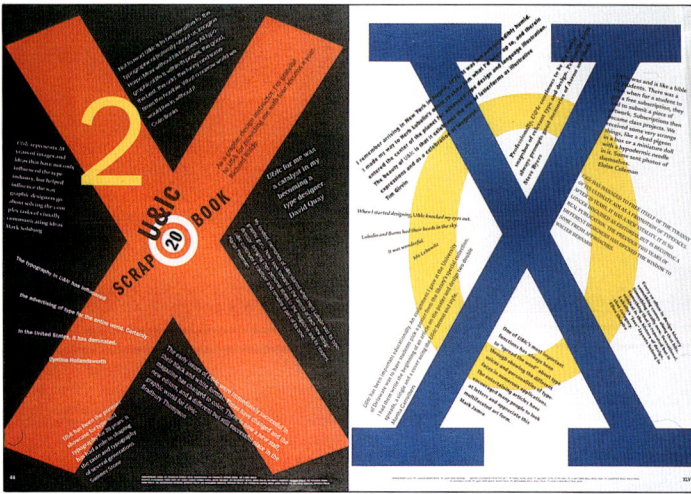

PUBLICATION	Upper & Lower Case
AWARD	Merit
ART DIRECTOR	Paul Davis
DESIGNER	Lisa Mazur
PUBLISHER	International Typeface Corporation
STUDIO	Paul Davis Studio
CATEGORY	Design/Single Page or Spread
DATE	January 1993

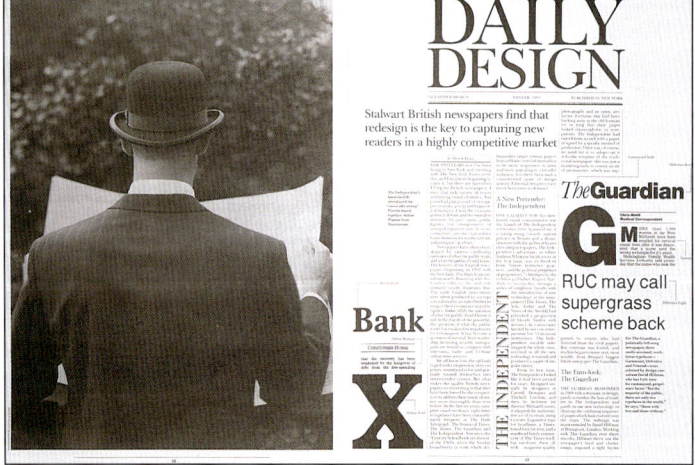

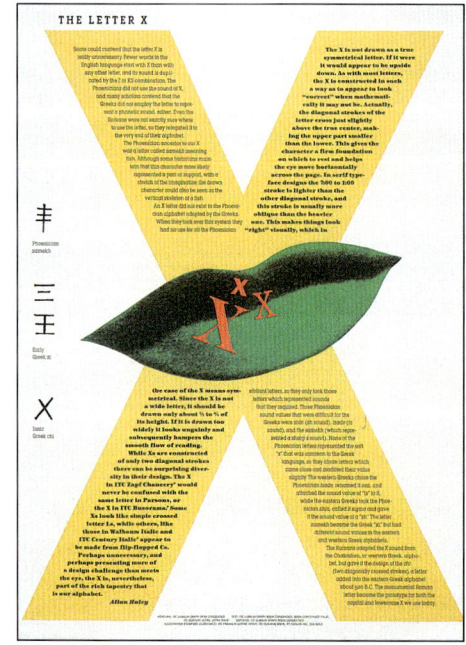

PUBLICATION	Upper & Lower Case
AWARD	Merit
ART DIRECTORS	Woody Pirtle, John Klotnia
DESIGNERS	John Klotnia, Ivette Montes de Oca
PHOTOGRAPHER	Gentl & Hyers
PUBLISHER	International Typeface Corporation
STUDIO	Paul Davis Studio
CATEGORY	Design/Single Page or Spread
DATE	December 1993

PUBLICATION	Upper & Lower Case
AWARD	Merit
ART DIRECTOR	Paul Davis
DESIGNER	Lisa Mazur
PUBLISHER	International Typeface Corporation
STUDIO	Paul Davis Studio
CATEGORY	Design/Single Page or Spread
DATE	May 1993

PUBLICATION	Life
AWARD	Silver
DESIGN DIRECTOR	Tom Bentkowski
DESIGNER	Nora Sheehan
PHOTOGRAPHERS	Ivan Massar, Cornell Capa
PHOTO EDITOR	David Friend
PUBLISHER	Time Inc.
CATEGORY	Design/Story
DATE	April 1993

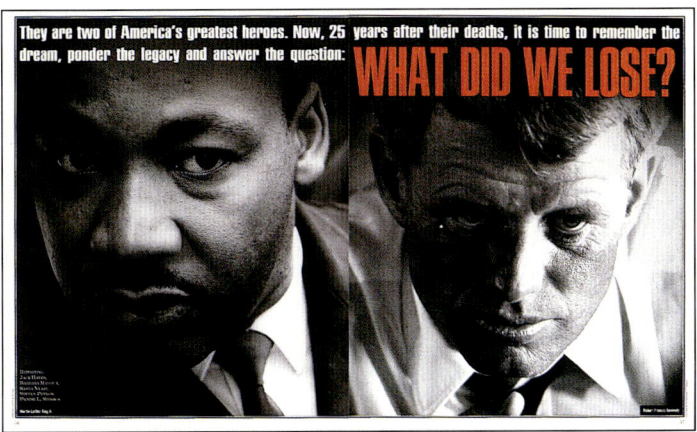

They are two of America's greatest heroes. Now, 25 years after their deaths, it is time to remember the dream, ponder the legacy and answer the question: WHAT DID WE LOSE?

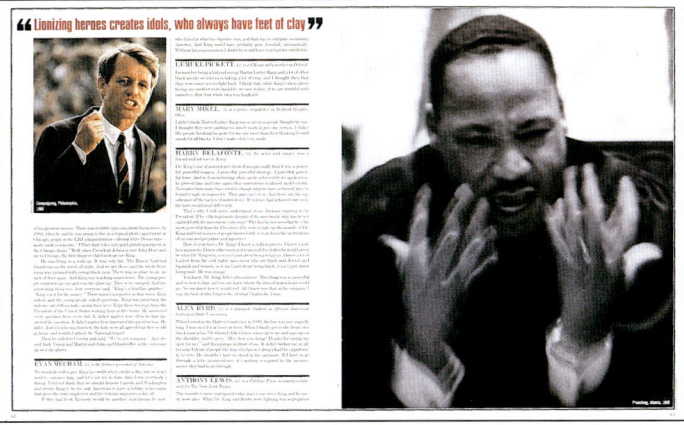

❝ Lionizing heroes creates idols, who always have feet of clay ❞

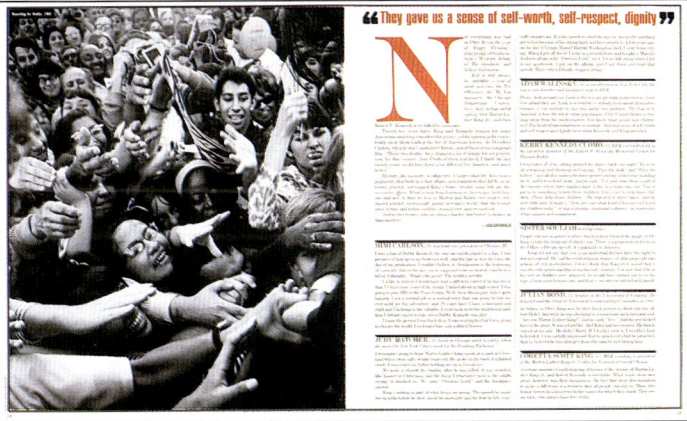

❝ They gave us a sense of self-worth, self-respect, dignity ❞

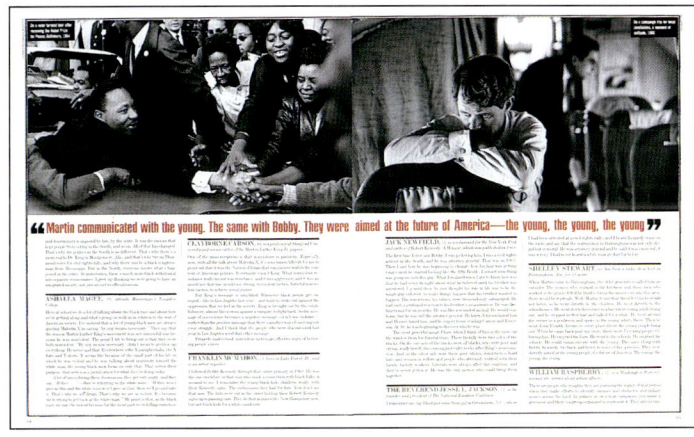

❝ Martin communicated with the young. The same with Bobby. They were aimed at the future of America—the young, the young, the young ❞

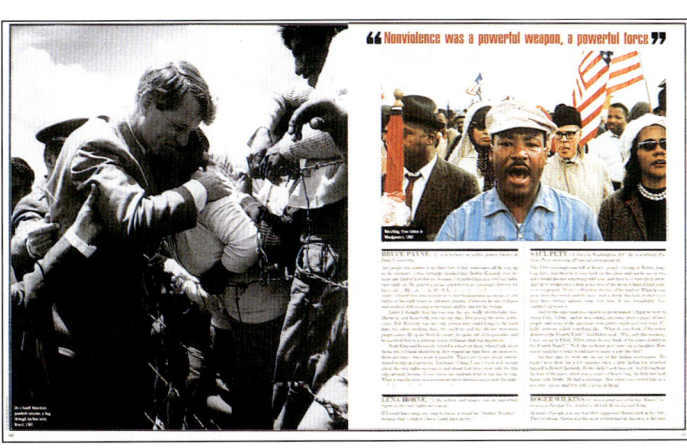

❝ Nonviolence was a powerful weapon, a powerful force ❞

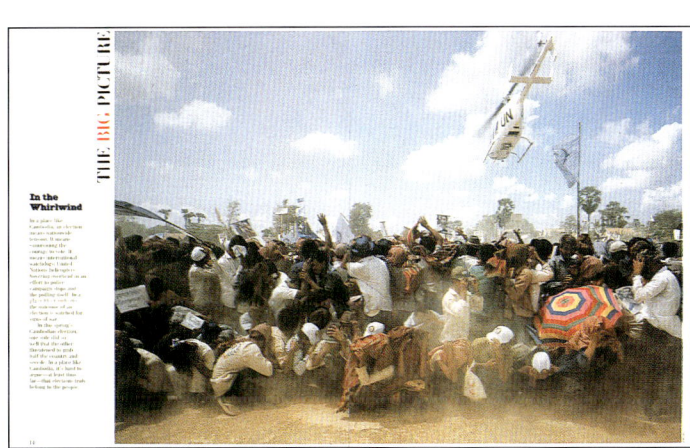

THE BIG PICTURE

In the Whirlwind

PUBLICATION	The Boston Globe Magazine
AWARD	Merit
ART DIRECTOR	Catherine Aldrich
DESIGNER	Catherine Aldrich
PHOTOGRAPHER	Hornick / Rivlin
PUBLISHER	The Boston Globe
CATEGORY	Design/Story
DATE	January 21, 1993

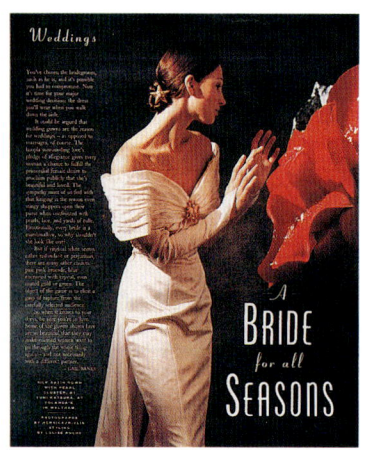

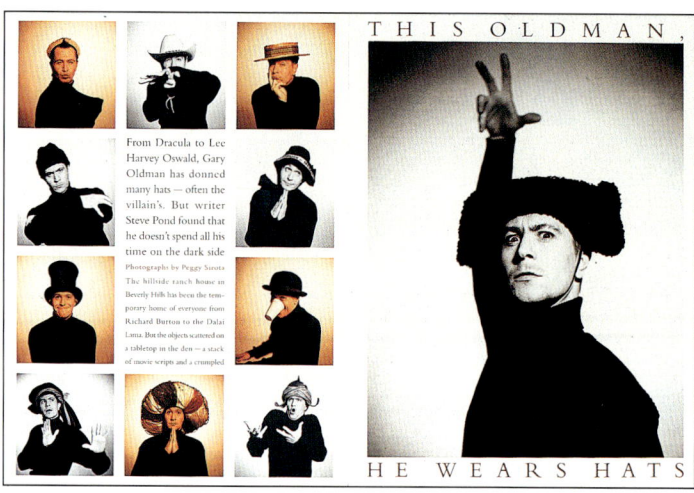

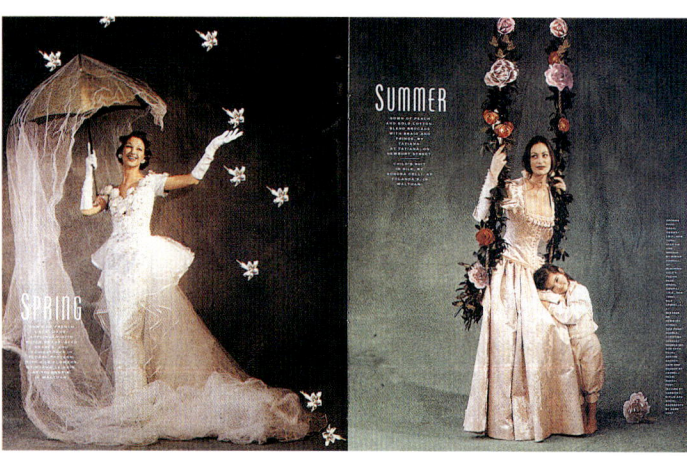

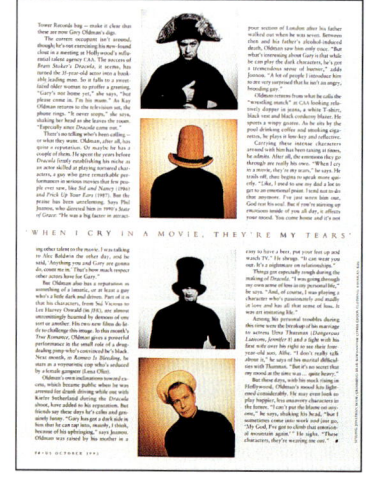

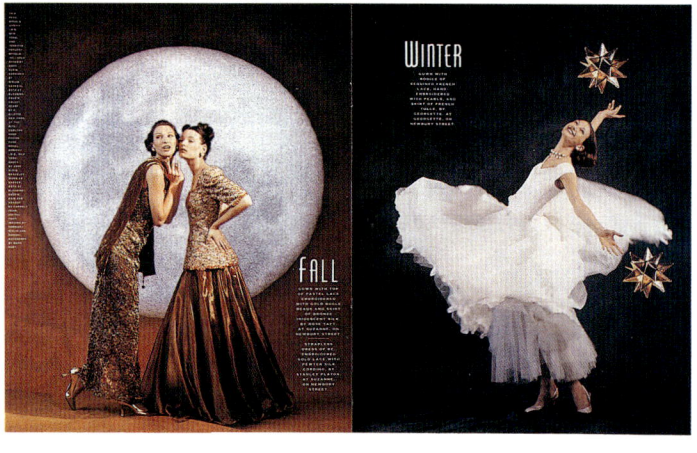

PUBLICATION	US
AWARD	Merit
ART DIRECTOR	Diddo Ramm
DESIGNER	Diddo Ramm
PHOTOGRAPHER	Peggy Sirota
PHOTO EDITOR	Jennifer Crandall
PUBLISHER	Wenner Media
CATEGORY	Design/Story
DATE	October 1993

PUBLICATION	Condé Nast Traveler
AWARD	Merit
DESIGN DIRECTOR	Diana LaGuardia
ART DIRECTOR	Christin Gangi
DESIGNER	Rockwell Harwood
PHOTOGRAPHER	Joseph Hunwick
PHOTO EDITOR	Kathleen Klech
PUBLISHER	The Condé Nast Publications Inc.
CATEGORY	Design/Story
DATE	October 1993

PUBLICATION	Condé Nast Traveler
AWARD	Merit
DESIGN DIRECTOR	Diana LaGuardia
ART DIRECTOR	Christin Gangi
DESIGNER	Steve Orr
PHOTOGRAPHER	Hakan Ludwigsson
PHOTO EDITOR	Kathleen Klech
PUBLISHER	The Condé Nast Publications Inc.
CATEGORY	Design/Story
DATE	November 1993

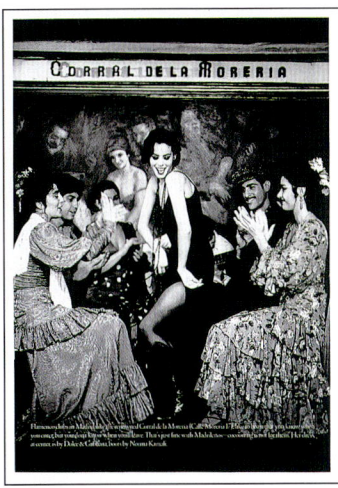
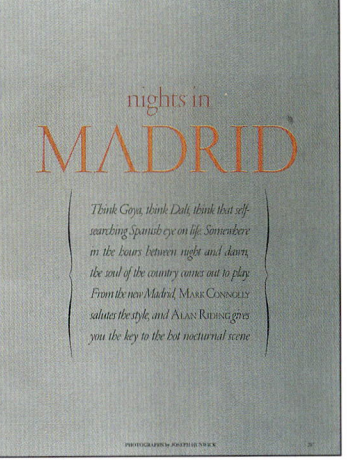
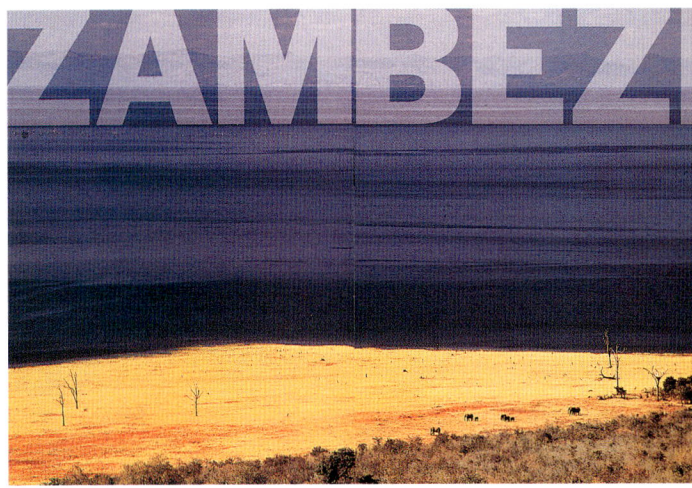

nights in
MADRID

Think Goya, think Dalí, think that self-searching Spanish eye on life. Somewhere in the hours between night and dawn, the soul of the country comes out to play. From the new Madrid, MARK CONNOLLY salutes the style, and ALAIN RIDING gives you the key to the hot nocturnal scene

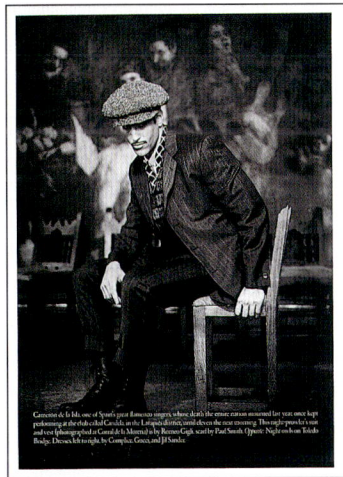
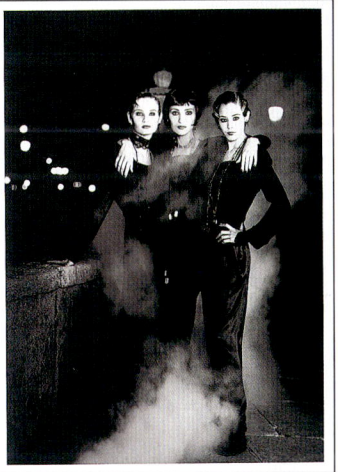

Zimbabwe's mighty river snakes along a remote and fragile wilderness. Are these its final days? GRAHAM BOYNTON canoes through an Eden in peril

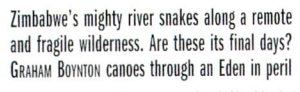
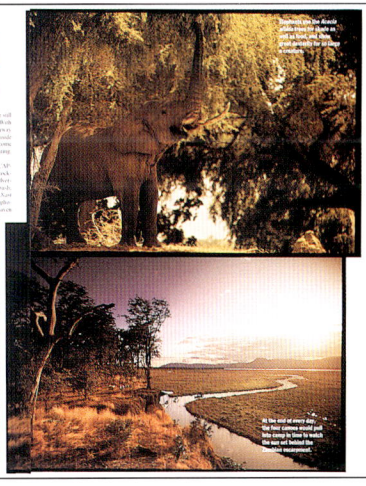

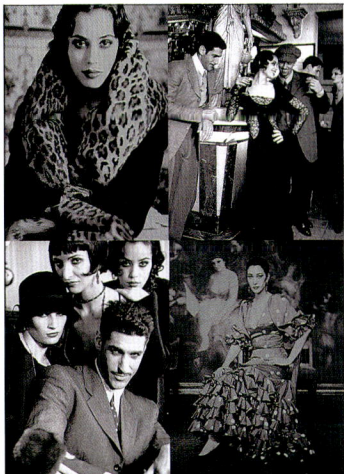
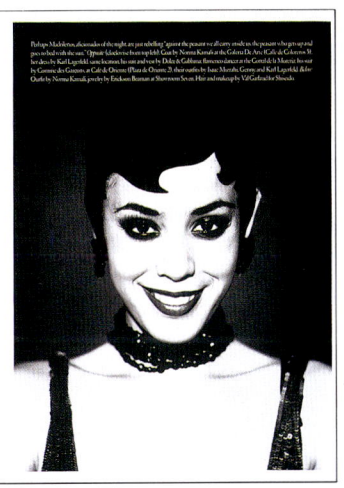
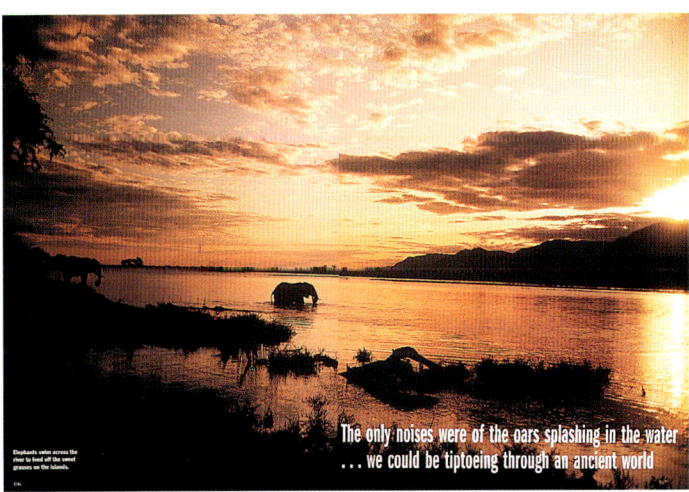

The only noises were of the oars splashing in the water
...we could be tiptoeing through an ancient world

PUBLICATION	Discover
AWARD	Merit
ART DIRECTOR	David Armario
DESIGNER	James Lambertus
PHOTOGRAPHER	Dan Winters
PHOTO EDITOR	John Barker
PUBLISHER	Disney Magazine Publishing, Inc.
CATEGORY	Design/Story
DATE	November 1993

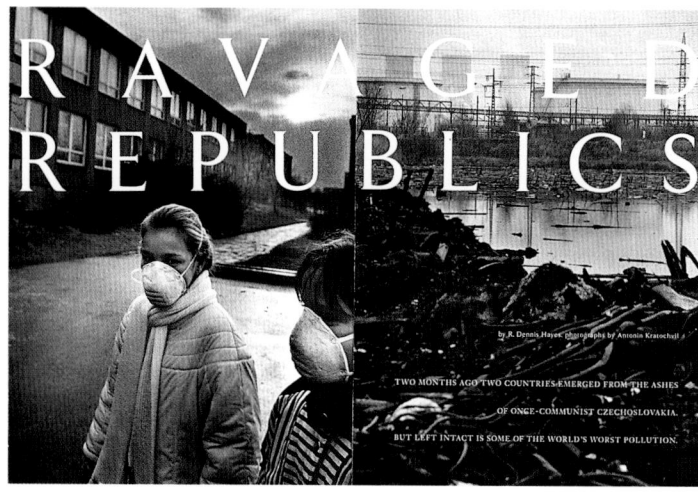

RAVAGED REPUBLICS

by R. Dennis Hayes, photographs by Antonin Kratochvil

TWO MONTHS AGO TWO COUNTRIES EMERGED FROM THE ASHES
OF ONCE-COMMUNIST CZECHOSLOVAKIA.
BUT LEFT INTACT IS SOME OF THE WORLD'S WORST POLLUTION.

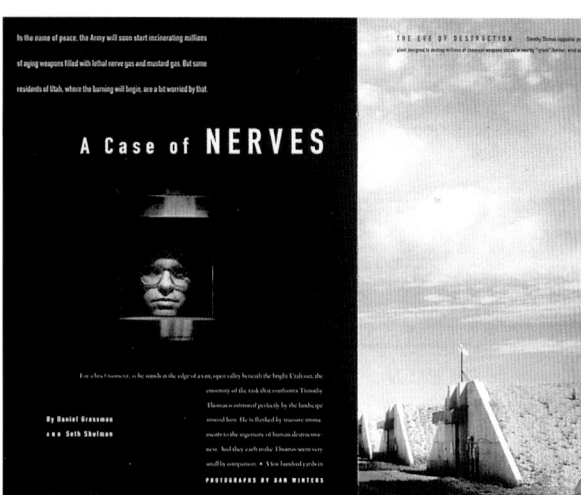

A Case of NERVES

By Daniel Grossman and Seth Shulman

PHOTOGRAPHS BY DAN WINTERS

In the name of peace, the Army will soon start incinerating millions of aging weapons filled with lethal nerve gas and mustard gas. But some residents of Utah, where the burning will begin, are a bit worried by that.

THE EVE OF DESTRUCTION

For a brief moment, as he stands at the edge of a vast, open valley beneath the bright Utah sun, the enormity of the task that confronts Timothy Thomas is mirrored perfectly by the landscape around here. He is flanked by massive storage mounds to the rigorous of human destruction now. And they can't strike Thomas seems very smaller by comparison.

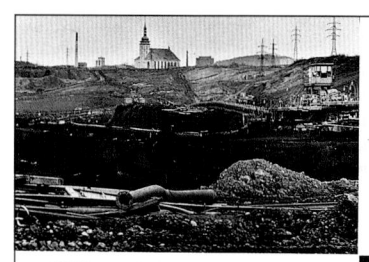

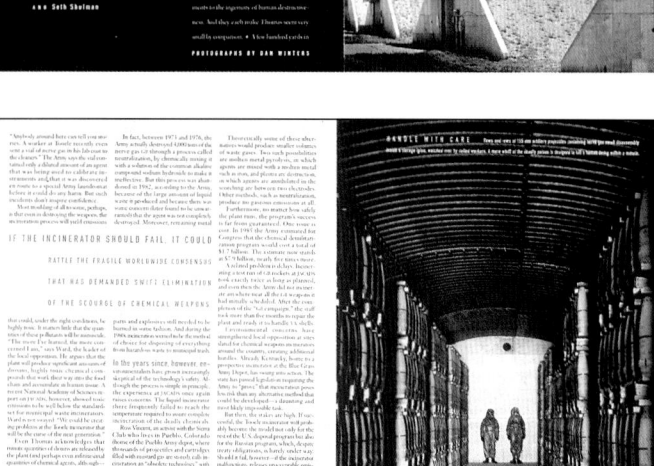

HANDLE WITH CARE

IF THE INCINERATOR SHOULD FAIL. IT COULD

RATTLE THE FRAGILE WORLDWIDE CONSENSUS

THAT HAS DEMANDED SWIFT ELIMINATION

OF THE SCOURGE OF CHEMICAL WEAPONS

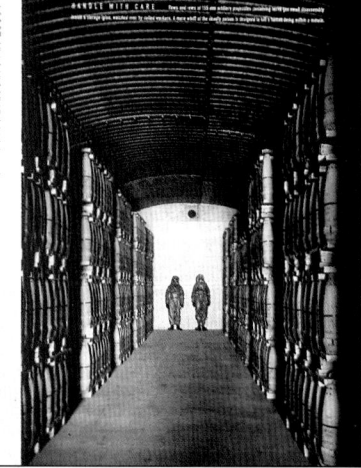

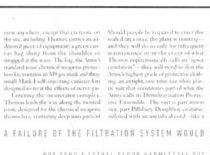

MOON SUIT

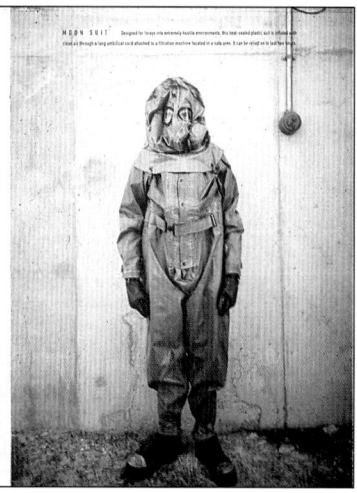

A FAILURE OF THE FILTRATION SYSTEM WOULD

NOT SEND A LETHAL CLOUD HARMLESSLY OUT

TO SEA. THE CITY OF TOOELE (POPULATION

13,887) IS ONLY 17 MILES FROM THE PLANT

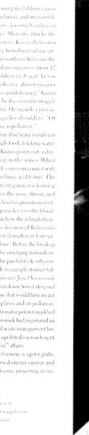

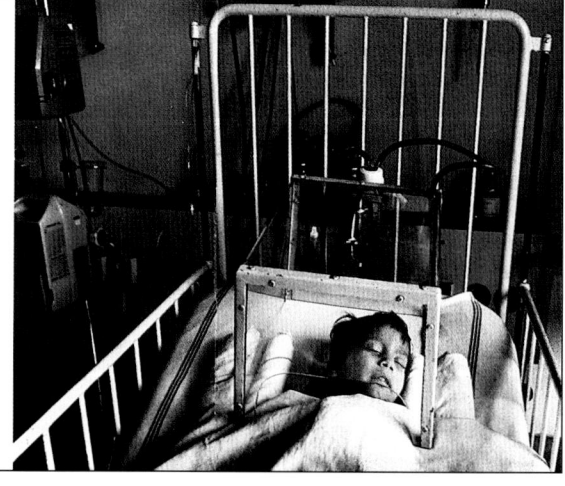

PUBLICATION	Discover
AWARD	Merit
ART DIRECTOR	David Armario
DESIGNERS	James Lambertus, David Armario
PHOTOGRAPHER	Antonin Kratochvil
PHOTO EDITORS	John Barker, Dawn Morishige
PUBLISHER	Disney Magazine Publishing, Inc.
CATEGORY	Design/Story
DATE	March 1993

PUBLICATION	Discover
AWARD	Merit
ART DIRECTOR	David Armario
DESIGNER	David Armario
PHOTOGRAPHER	Dan Winters
PHOTO EDITOR	John Barker
PUBLISHER	Disney Magazine Publishing, Inc.
CATEGORY	Design/Story
DATE	April 1993

PUBLICATION	Entertainment Weekly
AWARD	Merit
DESIGN DIRECTOR	Michael Grossman
ART DIRECTOR	Arlene Lappen
DESIGNER	Arlene Lappen
PHOTO EDITOR	Mary Dunn
PUBLISHER	Time Inc.
CATEGORY	Design/Story
DATE	October 22, 1993

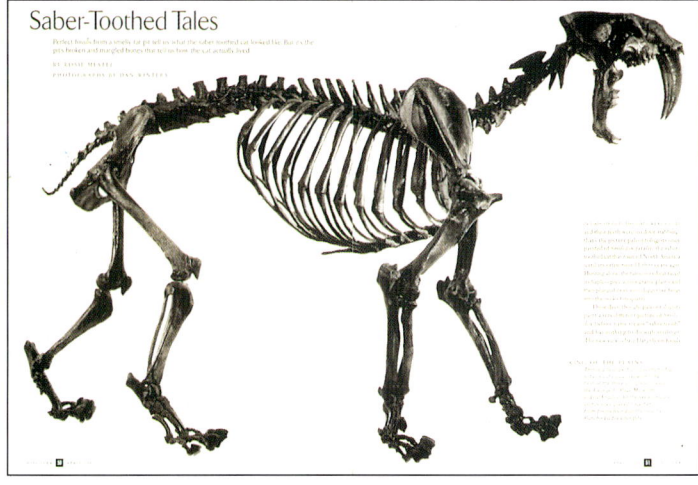

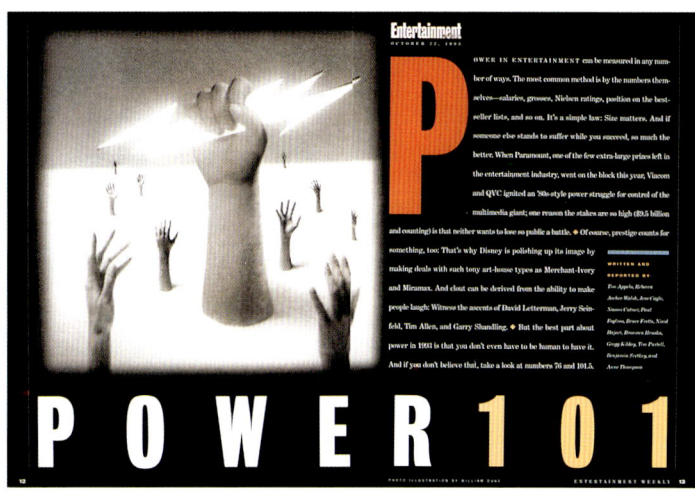

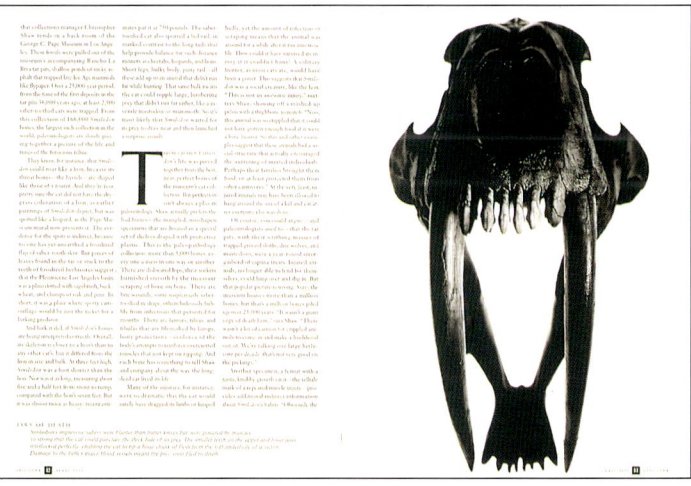

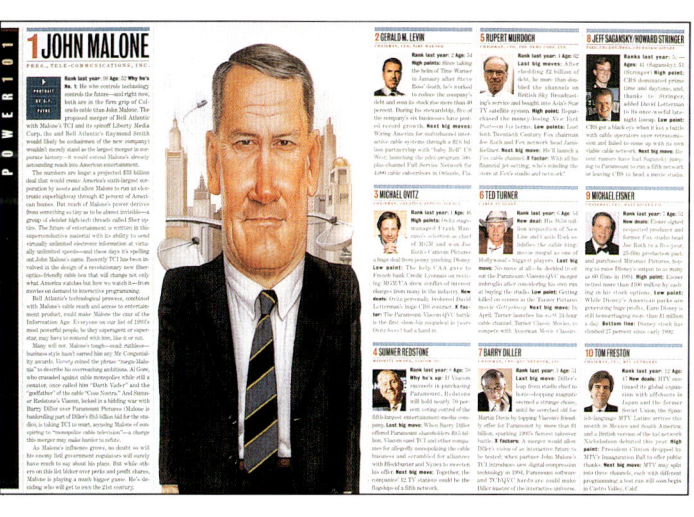

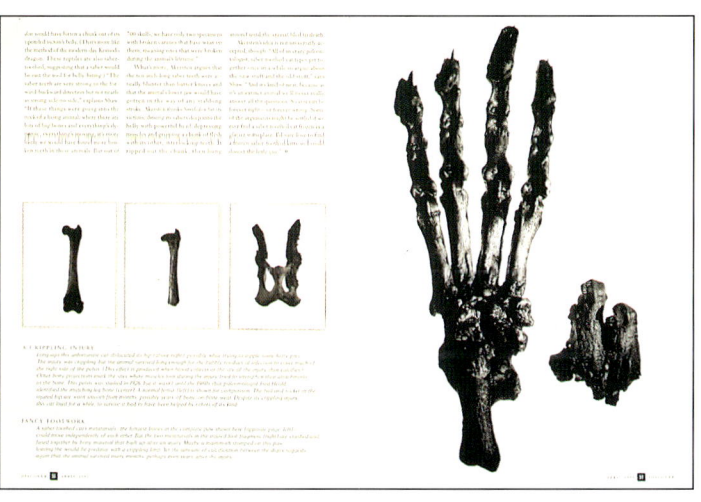

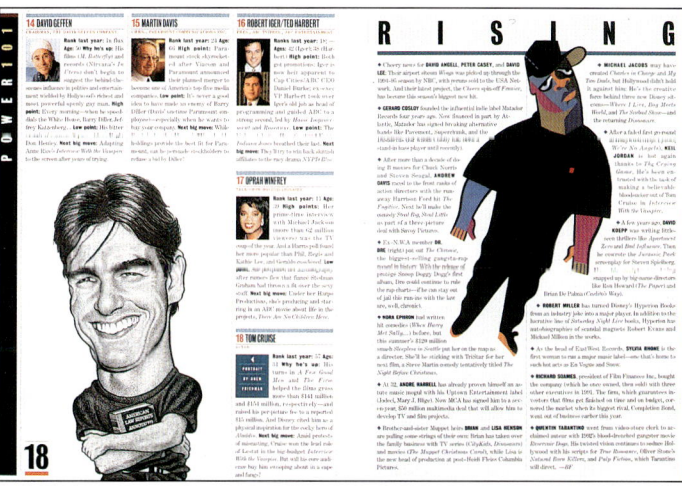

PUBLICATION	Entertainment Weekly
AWARD	Merit
DESIGN DIRECTOR	Michael Grossman
ART DIRECTOR	Mark Michaelson
DESIGNERS	Mark Michaelson, Miriam Campiz
PHOTO EDITORS	Mary Dunn, Doris Brautigan, Ramiro Fernandez
PUBLISHER	Time Inc.
CATEGORY	Design/Story
DATE	March 5, 1993

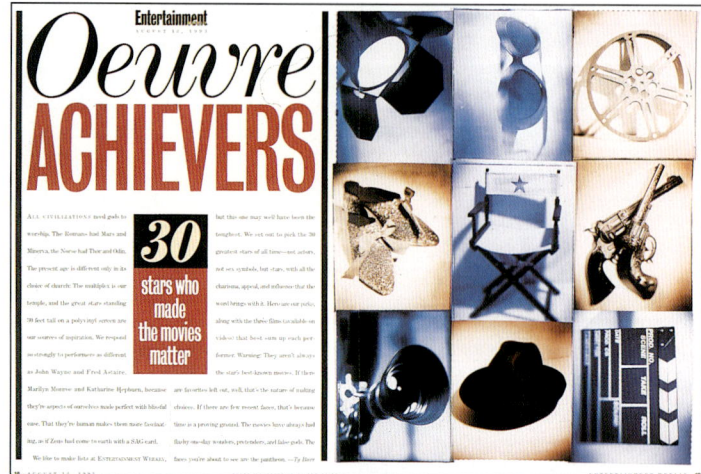

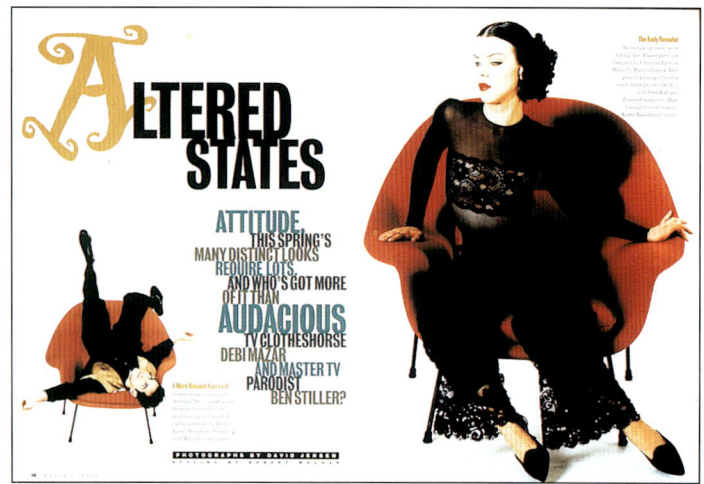

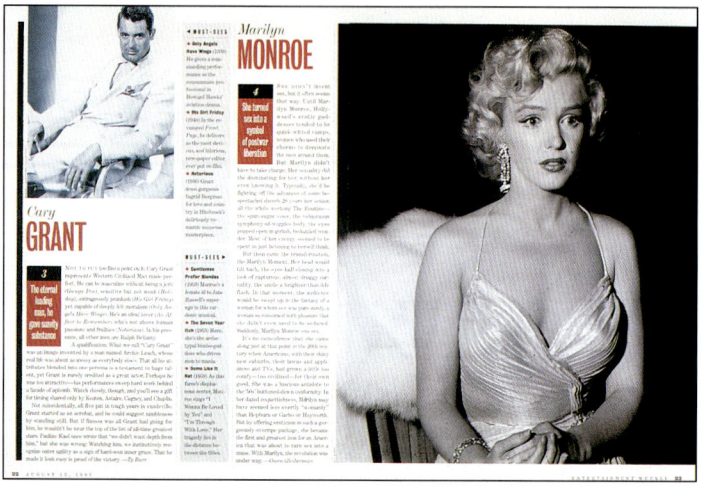

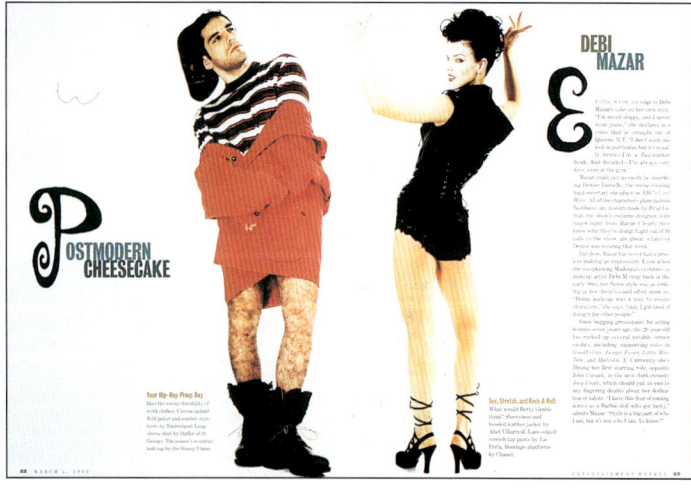

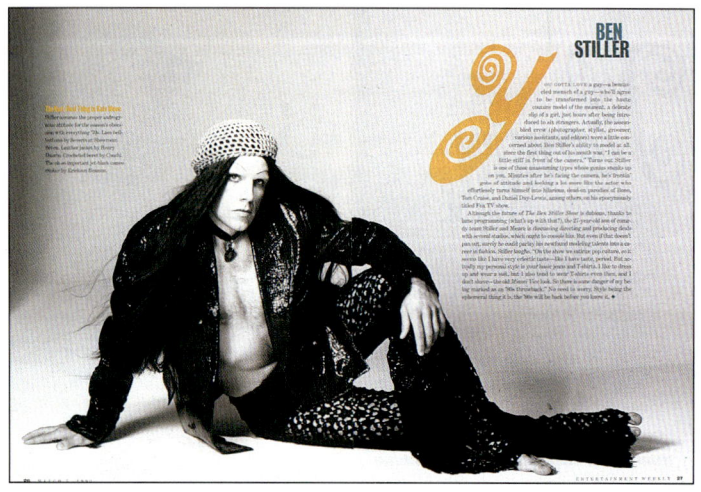

PUBLICATION	Entertainment Weekly
AWARD	Merit
DESIGN DIRECTOR	Michael Grossman
DESIGNER	Jill Armus
PHOTOGRAPHER	Tom Tavee
PHOTO EDITORS	Mary Dunn, Alice Babcock
PUBLISHER	Time Inc.
CATEGORY	Design/Story
DATE	August 13, 1993

PUBLICATION	Esquire
AWARD	Merit
ART DIRECTOR	Rhonda Rubinstein
DESIGNERS	Rhonda Rubinstein, David O'Connor
PHOTOGRAPHERS	David Barry, Rob Kinmoth, J.B. Diederich,
	Marion Efflinger, John Goodman, John Chiasson
PHOTO EDITOR	Betsy Horan
PUBLISHER	The Hearst Corporation
CATEGORY	Design/Story
DATE	July 1993

PUBLICATION	Esquire
AWARD	Merit
ART DIRECTOR	Rhonda Rubinstein
DESIGNER	Rhonda Rubinstein
ILLUSTRATOR	Robert Goldstrom
PUBLISHER	The Hearst Corporation
CATEGORY	Design/Story
DATE	May 1993

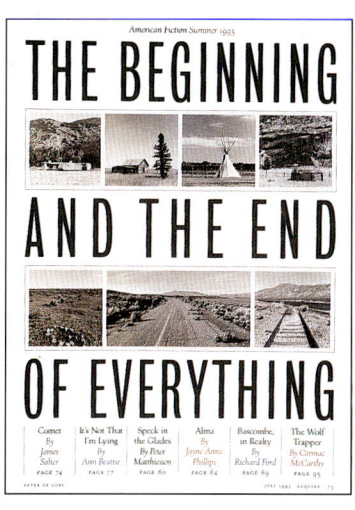

THE BEGINNING AND THE END OF EVERYTHING

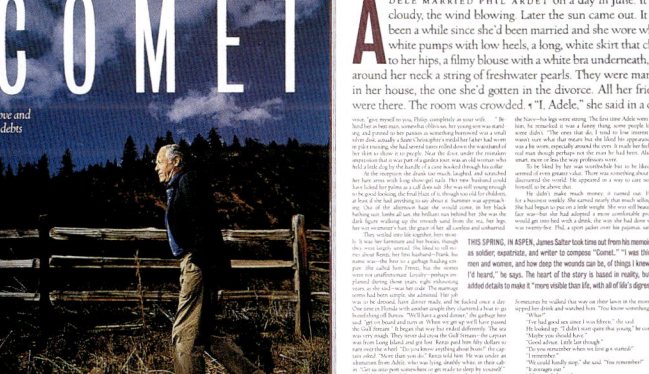

COMET

By James Salter

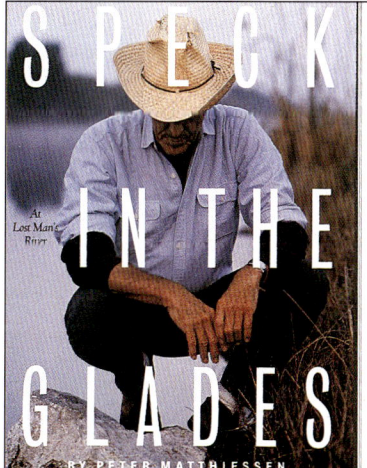

SPECK IN THE GLADES

By Peter Matthiessen

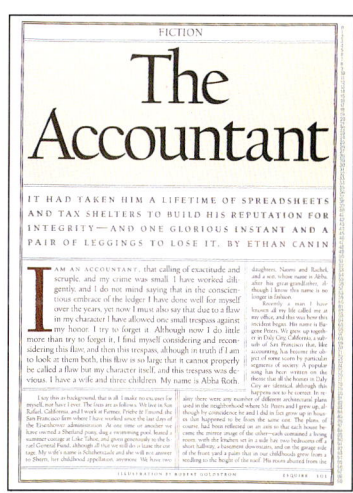

The Accountant

IT HAD TAKEN HIM A LIFETIME OF SPREADSHEETS AND TAX SHELTERS TO BUILD HIS REPUTATION FOR INTEGRITY—AND ONE GLORIOUS INSTANT AND A PAIR OF LEGGINGS TO LOSE IT. BY ETHAN CANIN

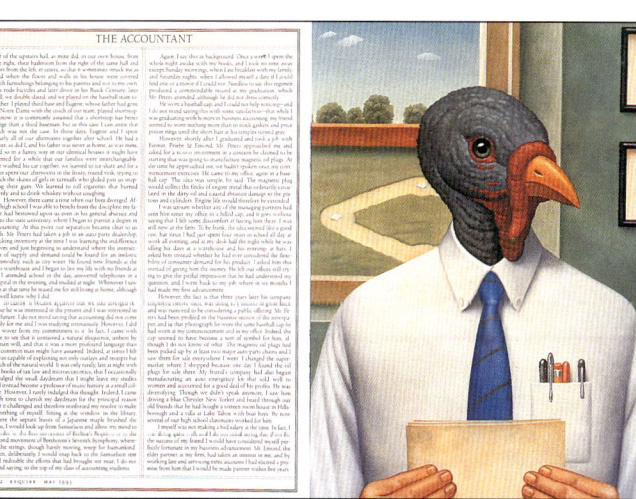

THE ACCOUNTANT

PUBLICATION	Esquire
AWARD	Merit
DESIGN DIRECTOR	Roger Black
DESIGNER	Roger Black
PHOTO EDITOR	Betsy Horan
PUBLISHER	The Hearst Corporation
CATEGORY	Design/Story
DATE	December 1993

PUBLICATION	GQ
AWARD	Merit
CREATIVE DIRECTOR	Robert Priest
DESIGNER	Laura Harrigan
PHOTOGRAPHER	Mark Weiss
PHOTO EDITOR	Karen Frank
PUBLISHER	The Condé Nast Publications Inc.
CATEGORY	Design/Story
DATE	December 1993

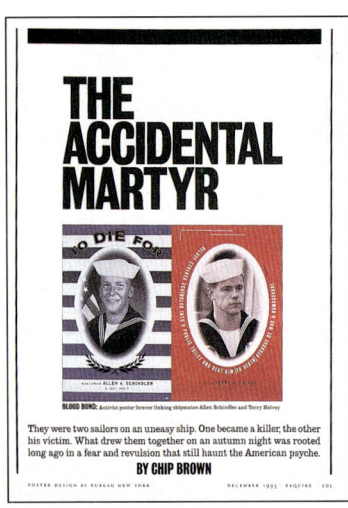

THE ACCIDENTAL MARTYR

BLOOD BOND: *Activist poster forever linking shipmates Allen Schindler and Terry Helvey.*

They were two sailors on an uneasy ship. One became a killer, the other his victim. What drew them together on an autumn night was rooted long ago in a fear and revulsion that still haunt the American psyche.

BY CHIP BROWN

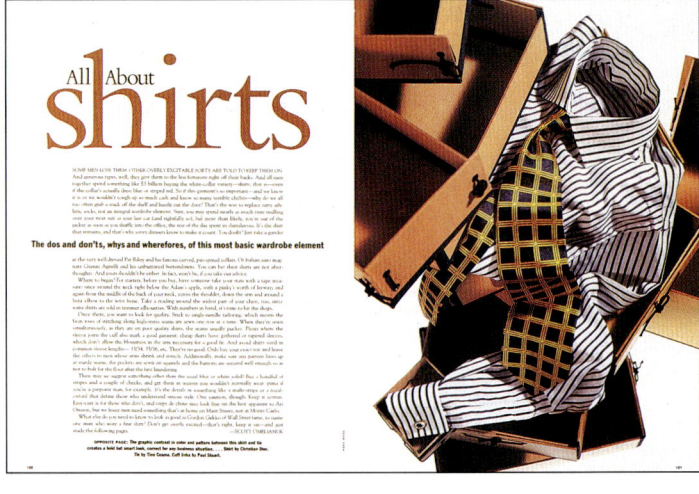

All About shirts

The dos and don'ts, whys and wherefores, of this most basic wardrobe element

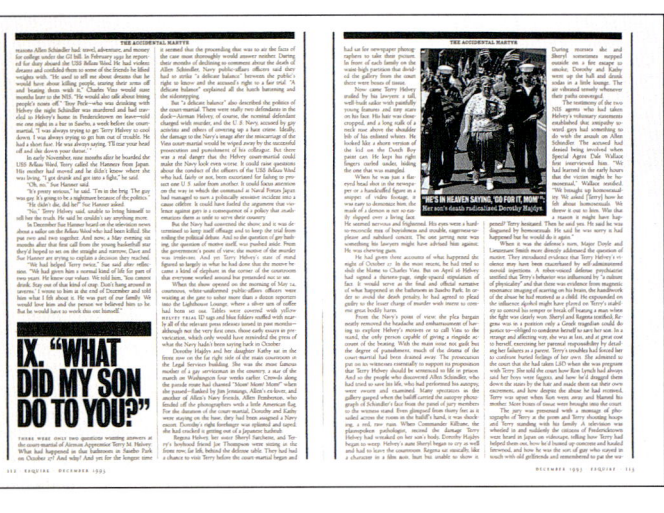

patterns

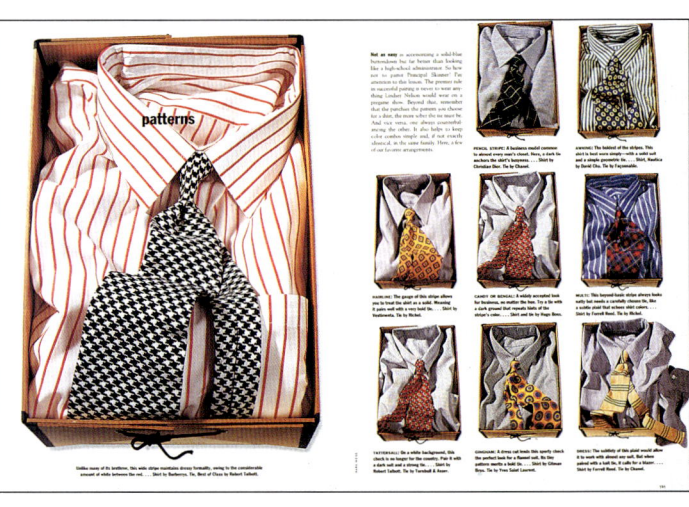

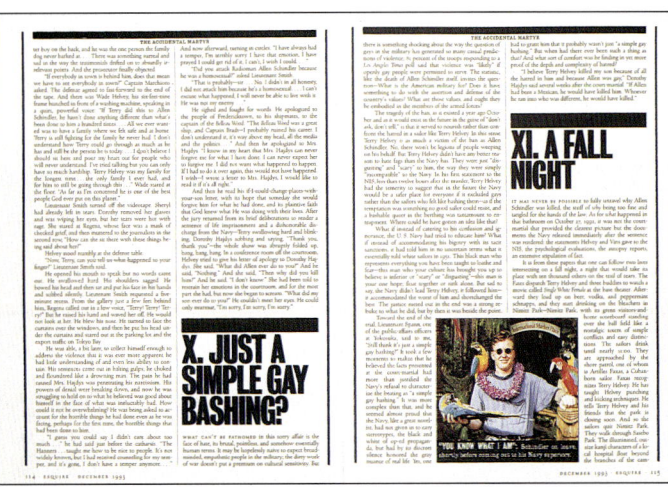

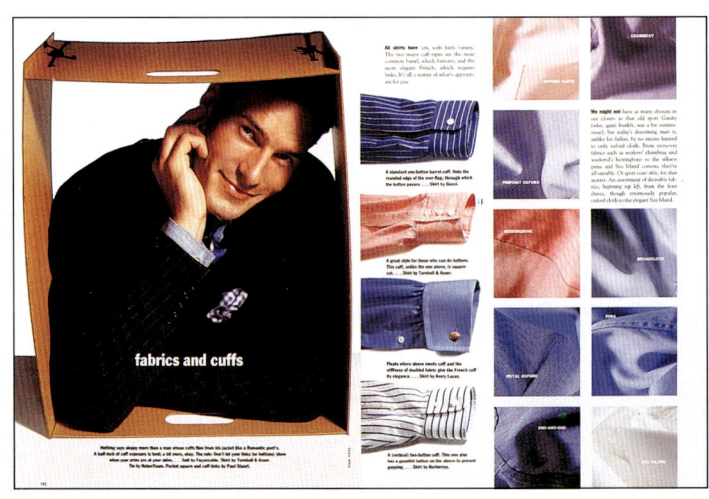

fabrics and cuffs

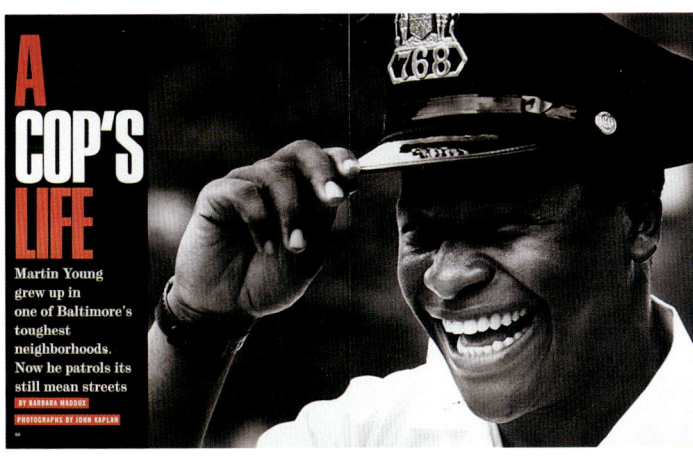

A COP'S LIFE

Martin Young
grew up in
one of Baltimore's
toughest
neighborhoods.
Now he patrols its
still mean streets

BY BARBARA MADDUX

PHOTOGRAPHS BY JOHN KAPLAN

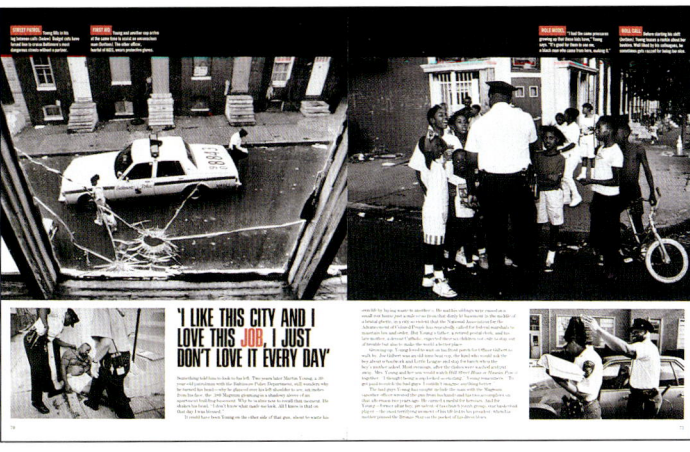

'I LIKE THIS CITY AND I LOVE THIS JOB, I JUST DON'T LOVE IT EVERY DAY'

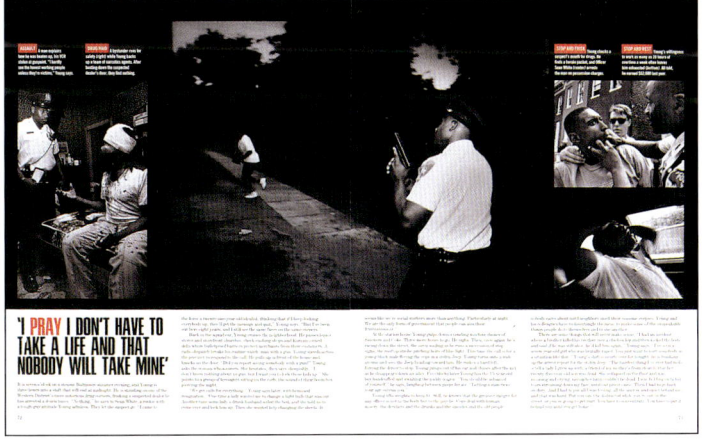

'I PRAY I DON'T HAVE TO TAKE A LIFE AND THAT NOBODY WILL TAKE MINE'

PUBLICATION   Life
AWARD   Merit
DESIGN DIRECTOR Tom Bentkowski
DESIGNER   Marti Golon
PHOTOGRAPHER   John Kaplan
PHOTO EDITOR   David Friend
PUBLISHER   Time Inc.
CATEGORY   Design/Story
DATE   February 1993

PUBLICATION   Life
AWARD   Merit
DESIGN DIRECTOR Tom Bentkowski
DESIGNER   Mimi Park
PHOTOGRAPHER   Christopher Morris
PHOTO EDITOR   David Friend
PUBLISHER   Time Inc.
CATEGORY   Design/Story
DATE   October 1993

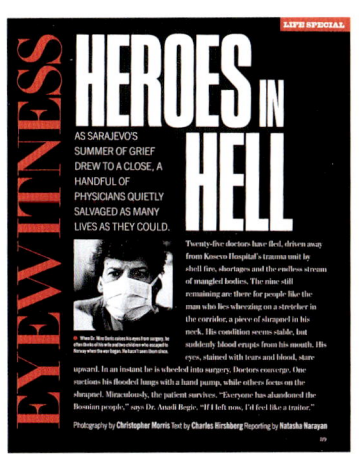

EYEWITNESS

LIFE SPECIAL

HEROES IN HELL

AS SARAJEVO'S SUMMER OF GRIEF DREW TO A CLOSE, A HANDFUL OF PHYSICIANS QUIETLY SALVAGED AS MANY LIVES AS THEY COULD.

Photography by Christopher Morris Text by Charles Hirshberg Reporting by Natasha Narayan

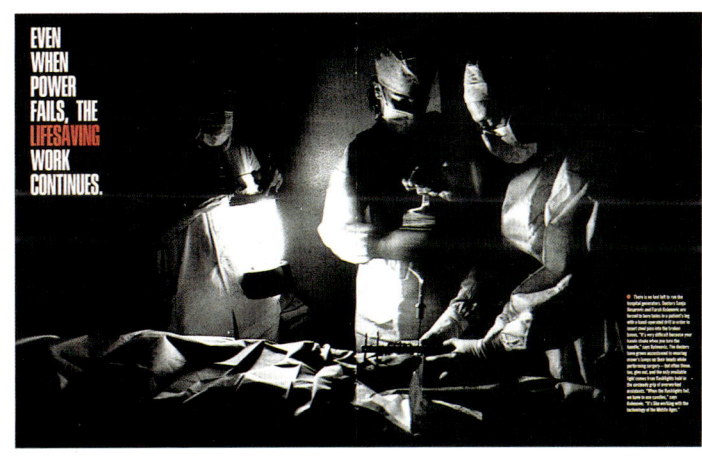

EVEN WHEN POWER FAILS, THE LIFESAVING WORK CONTINUES.

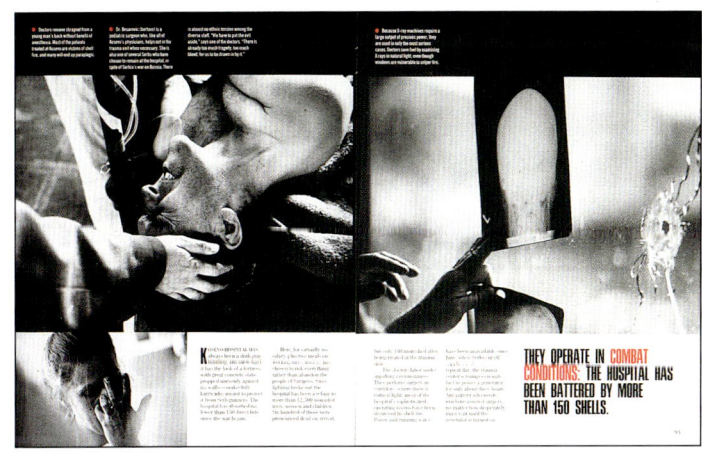

THEY OPERATE IN COMBAT CONDITIONS: THE HOSPITAL HAS BEEN BATTERED BY MORE THAN 150 SHELLS.

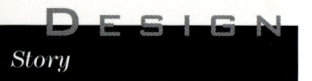

PUBLICATION	Life
AWARD	Merit
DESIGN DIRECTOR	Tom Bentowski
DESIGNER	Mimi Park
PHOTOGRAPHER	Jeanne Moutoussamy
PUBLISHER	Time Inc.
CATEGORY	Design/Story
DATE	November 1993

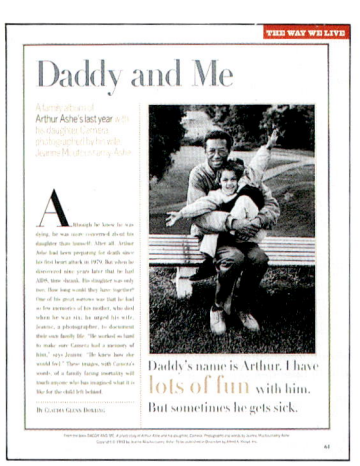

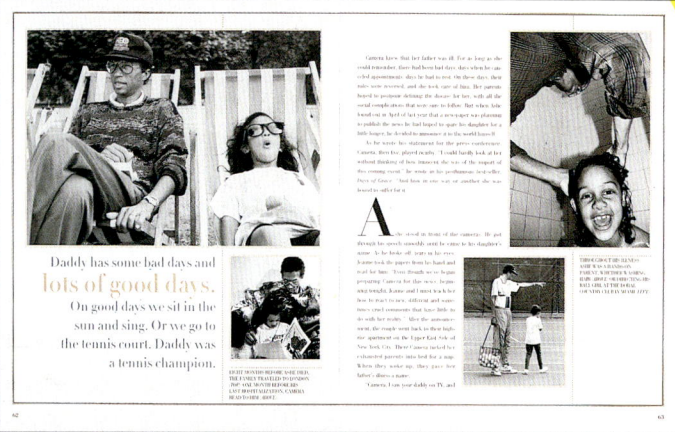

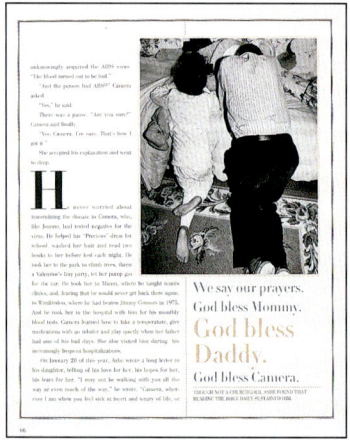

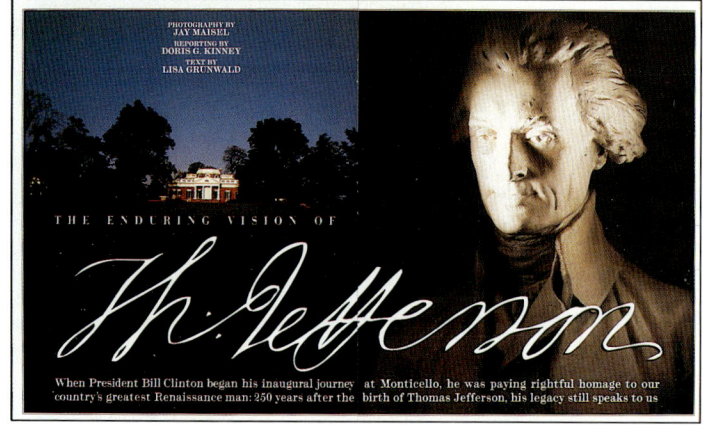

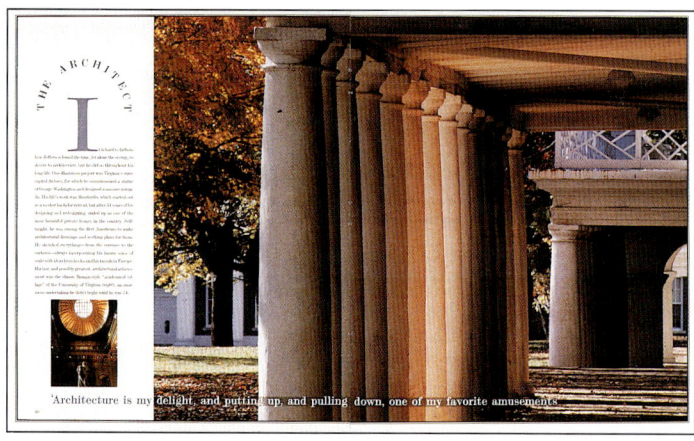

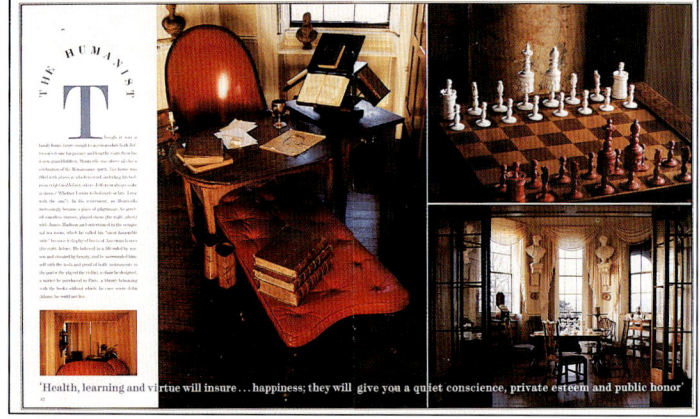

PUBLICATION	Life
AWARD	Merit
DESIGN DIRECTOR	Tom Bentkowski
DESIGNER	Marti Golon
PHOTOGRAPHER	Jay Maisel
PHOTO EDITOR	David Friend
PUBLISHER	Time Inc.
CATEGORY	Design/Story
DATE	May 1993

PUBLICATION   Life
AWARD   Merit
DESIGN DIRECTOR   Tom Bentkowski
DESIGNER   Marti Golon
PHOTOGRAPHER   Geoffrey Clifford
PHOTO EDITOR   David Friend
PUBLISHER   Time Inc.
CATEGORY   Design/Story
DATE   December 1993

PUBLICATION   Life
AWARD   Merit
DESIGN DIRECTOR   Tom Bentkowski
DESIGNER   Charles Pates
PHOTOGRAPHER   John Kaplan
PHOTO EDITOR   David Friend
PUBLISHER   Time Inc.
CATEGORY   Design/Story
DATE   May 1993

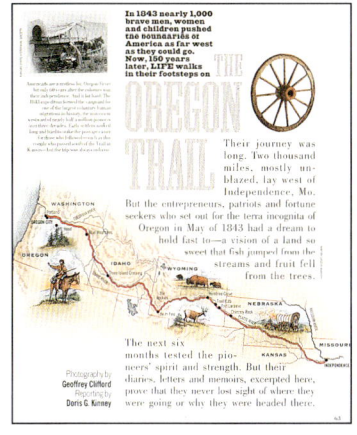

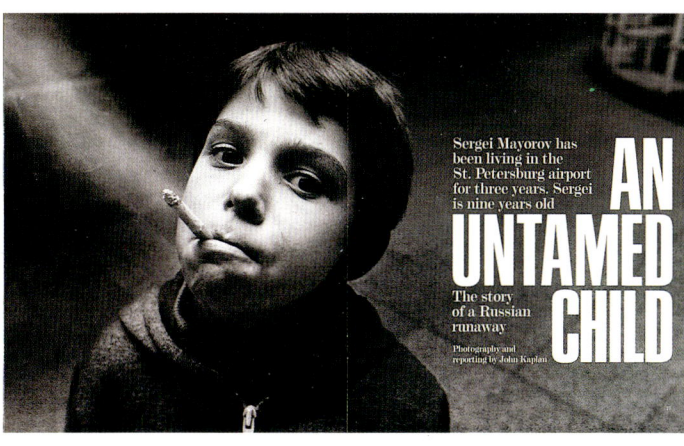

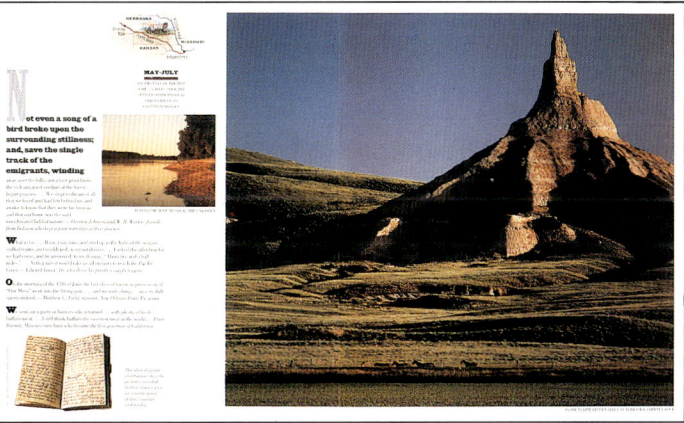

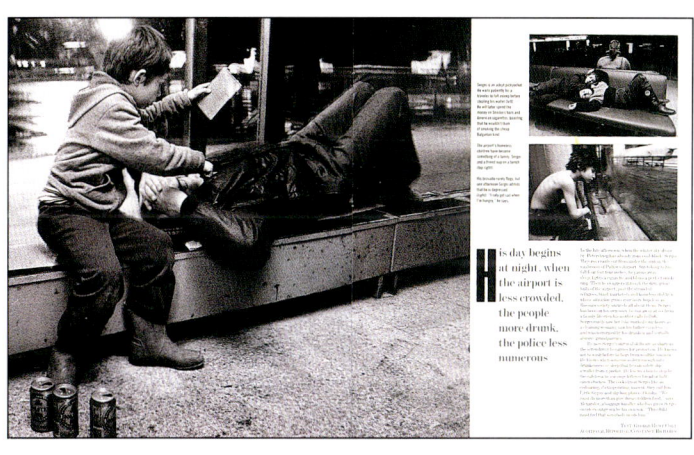

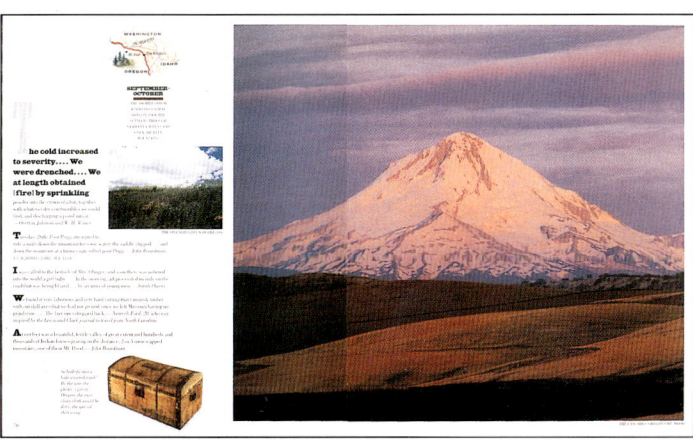

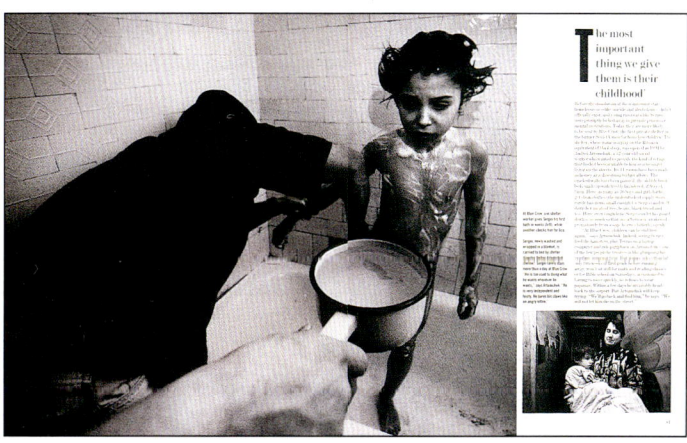

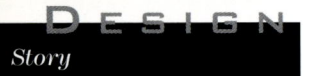

PUBLICATION	Life		PUBLICATION	Life
AWARD	Merit		AWARD	Merit
DESIGN DIRECTOR	Tom Bentkowski		DESIGN DIRECTOR	Tom Bentkowski
DESIGNER	Jean Andreuzzi		DESIGNER	Dean Abatemareo
PHOTOGRAPHER	William Neill		PHOTOGRAPHER	Henry Horenstein
PHOTO EDITOR	David Friend		PHOTO EDITOR	David Friend
PUBLISHER	Time Inc.		PUBLISHER	Time Inc.
CATEGORY	Design/Story		CATEGORY	Design/Story
DATE	October 1993		DATE	June 1993

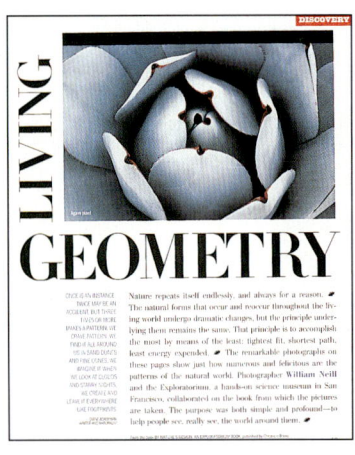

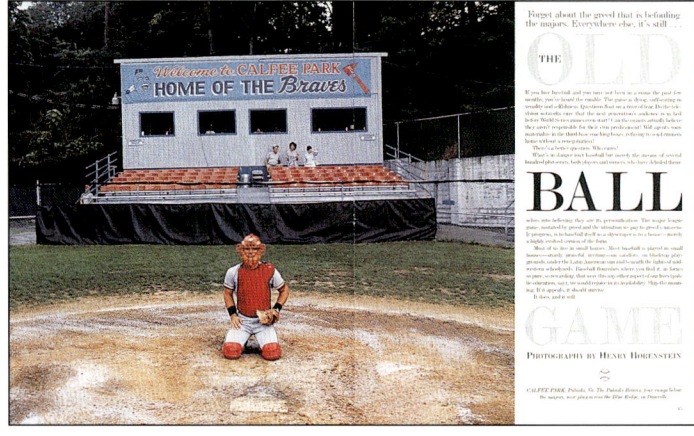

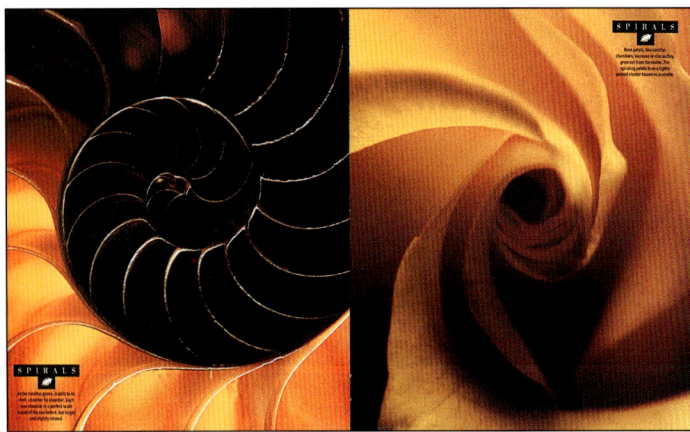

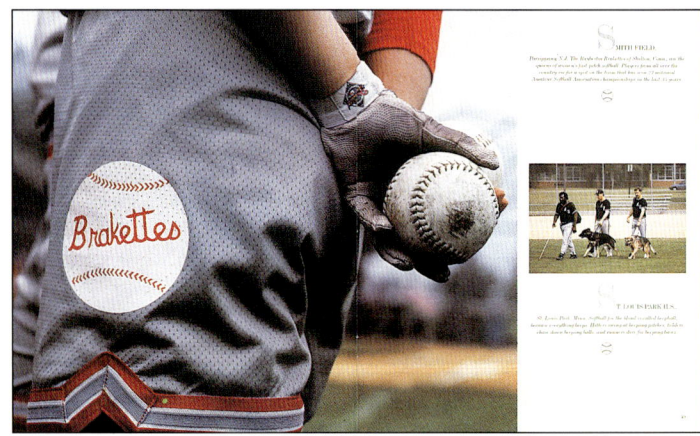

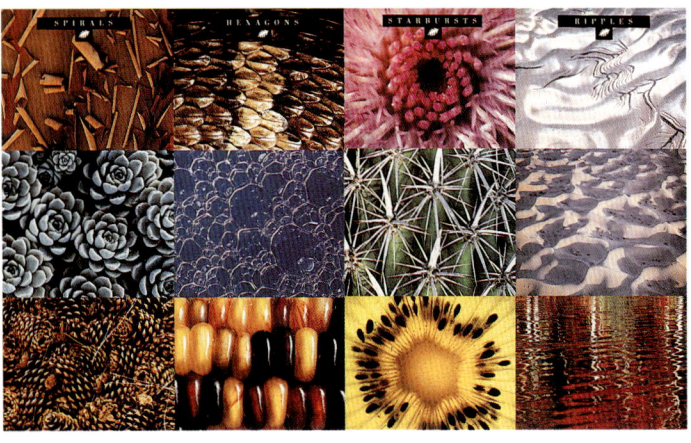

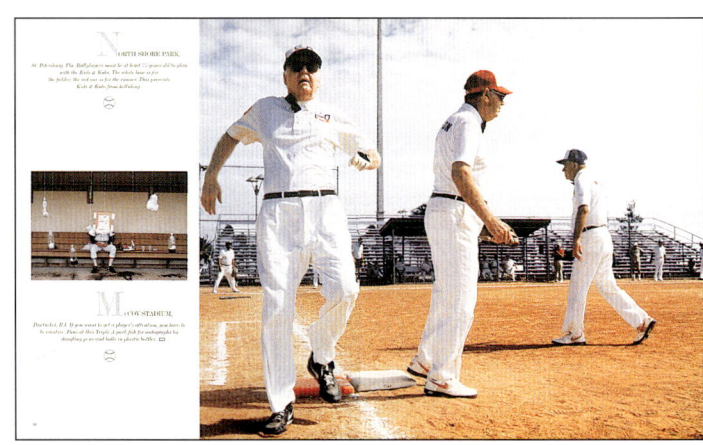

PUBLICATION   Vibe
AWARD   Merit
DESIGN DIRECTOR   Gary Koepke
ART DIRECTOR   Richard Baker
DESIGNER   Gary Koepke
PHOTOGRAPHER   Darryl Turner
PHOTO EDITOR   George Pitts
PUBLISHER   Time Inc. Ventures
STUDIO   Koepke International, Ltd.
CATEGORY   Design/Story
DATE   October 1993

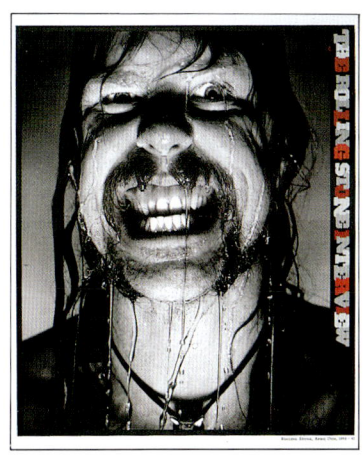

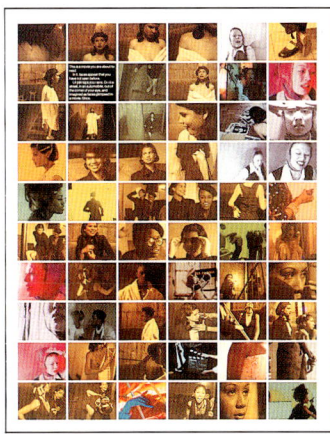
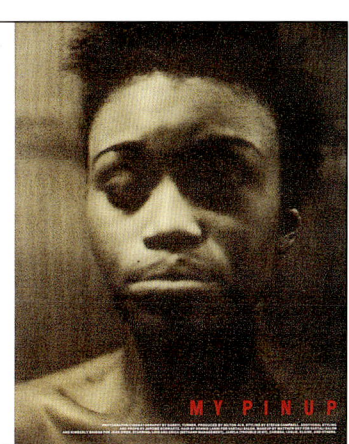

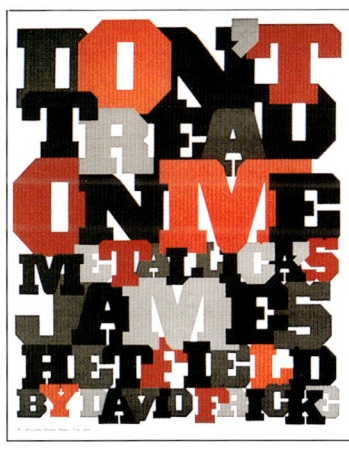
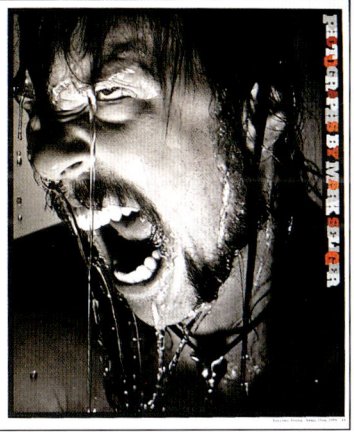

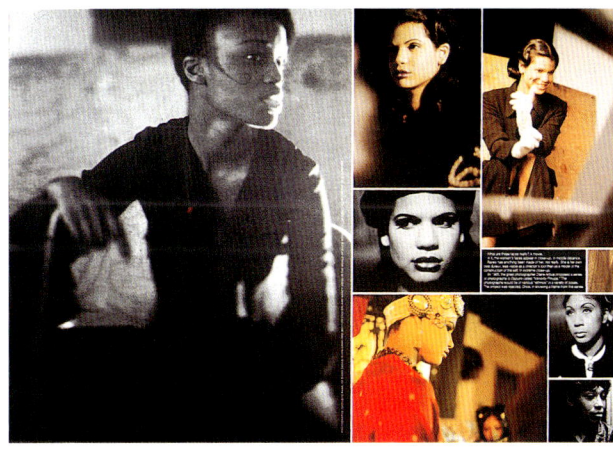

PUBLICATION   Rolling Stone
AWARD   Merit
ART DIRECTOR   Fred Woodward
DESIGNERS   Fred Woodward, Gail Anderson
PHOTOGRAPHER   Mark Seliger
PHOTO EDITOR   Laurie Kratochvil
PUBLISHER   Wenner Media
CATEGORY   Design/Story
DATE   April 15, 1993

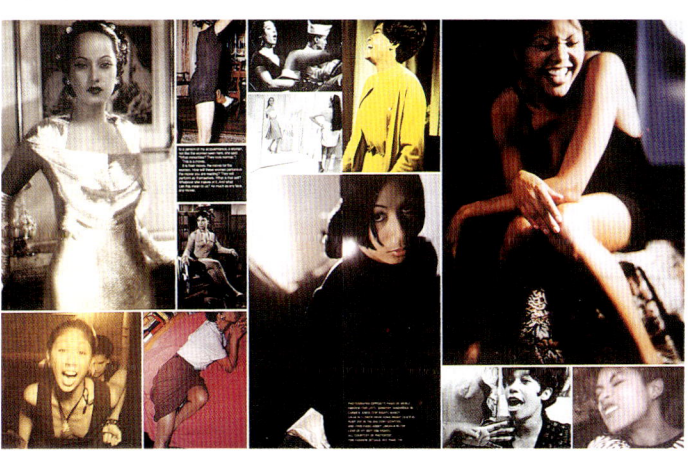

PUBLICATION	Texas Monthly
AWARD	Merit
DESIGN DIRECTOR	D.J. Stout
DESIGNER	D.J. Stout
PHOTOGRAPHER	Courtesy of Movie Still Archives
PHOTO EDITOR	D.J. Stout
PUBLISHER	Texas Monthly
CATEGORY	Design/Story
DATE	October 1993

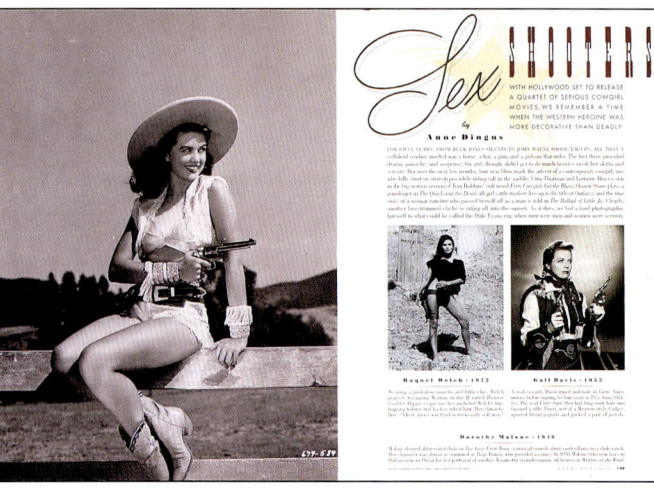

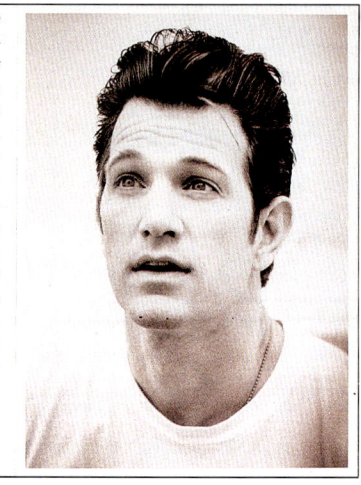

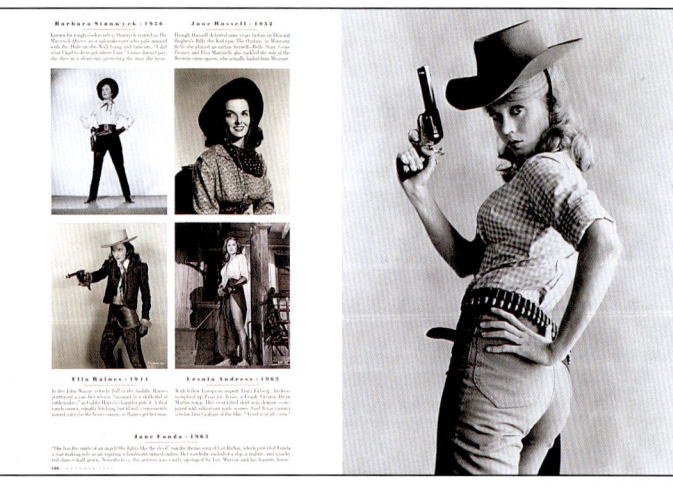

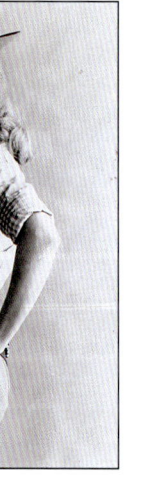

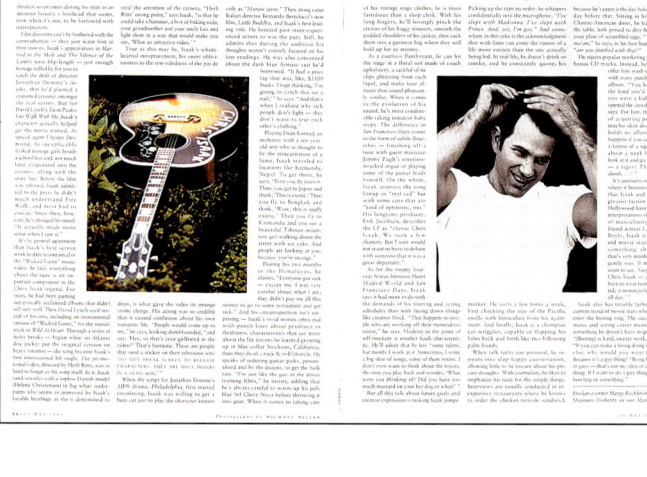

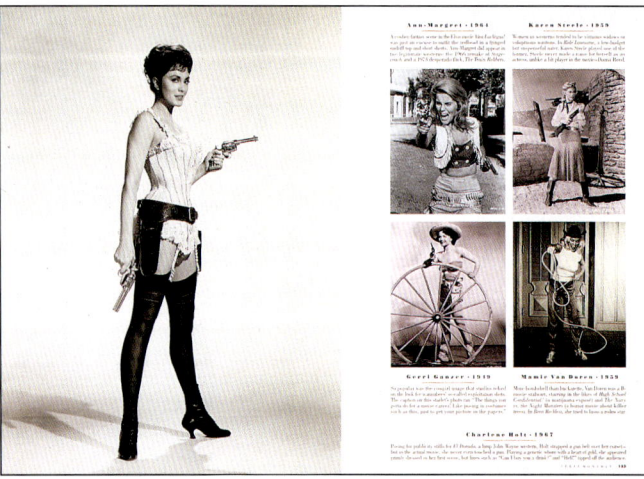

PUBLICATION	US
AWARD	Merit
ART DIRECTOR	Pamela Berry
DESIGNER	Pamela Berry
PHOTOGRAPHER	Michael Miller
PHOTO EDITOR	Jennifer Crandall
PUBLISHER	Wenner Media
CATEGORY	Design/Story
DATE	May 1993

PUBLICATION	Allure
AWARD	Merit
DESIGN DIRECTOR	Shawn Young
ART DIRECTOR	Shawn Young
DESIGNER	Shawn Young
PHOTOGRAPHER	Michael Thompson
PHOTO EDITOR	Judy White
PUBLISHER	The Condé Nast Publications Inc.
CATEGORY	Design/Story
DATE	November 1993

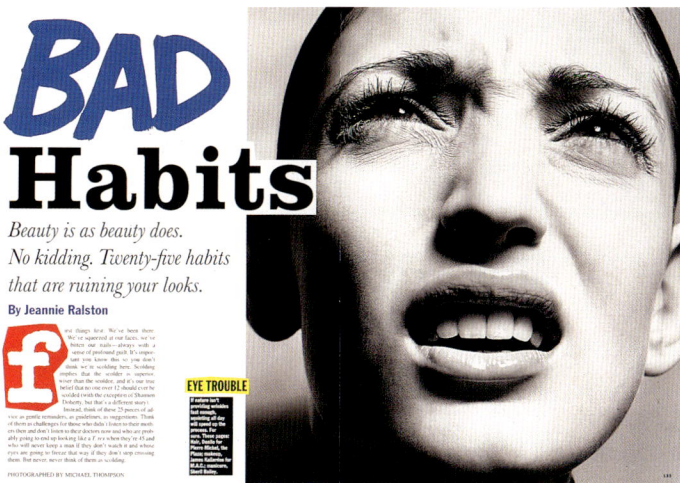

BAD Habits

Beauty is as beauty does.
No kidding. Twenty-five habits
that are ruining your looks.

By Jeannie Ralston

PHOTOGRAPHED BY MICHAEL THOMPSON

EYE TROUBLE

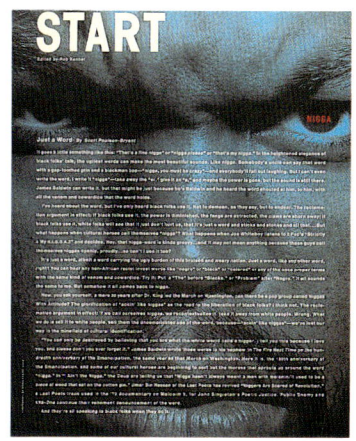

START

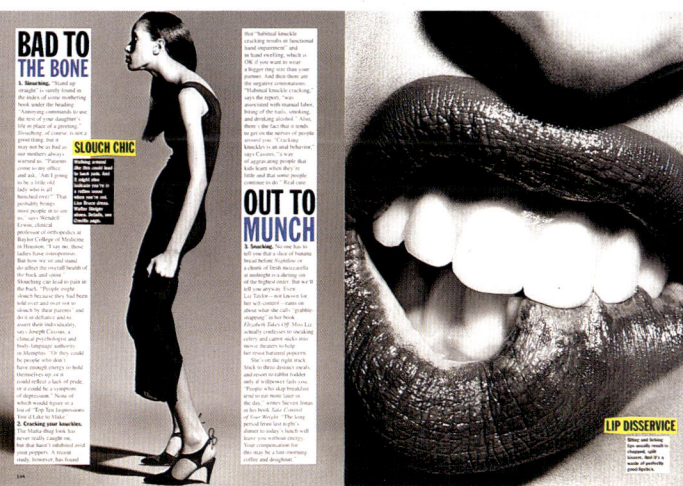

BAD TO THE BONE

SLOUCH CHIC

OUT TO MUNCH

LIP DISSERVICE

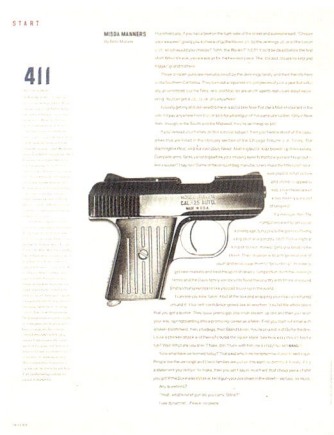

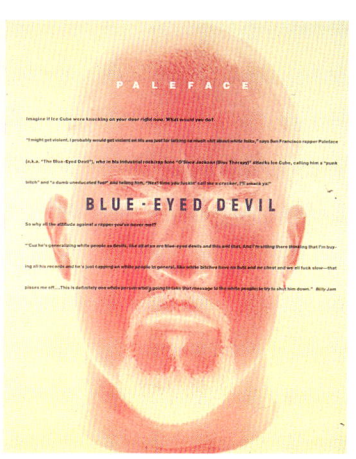

START

411

PALEFACE

BLUE-EYED DEVIL

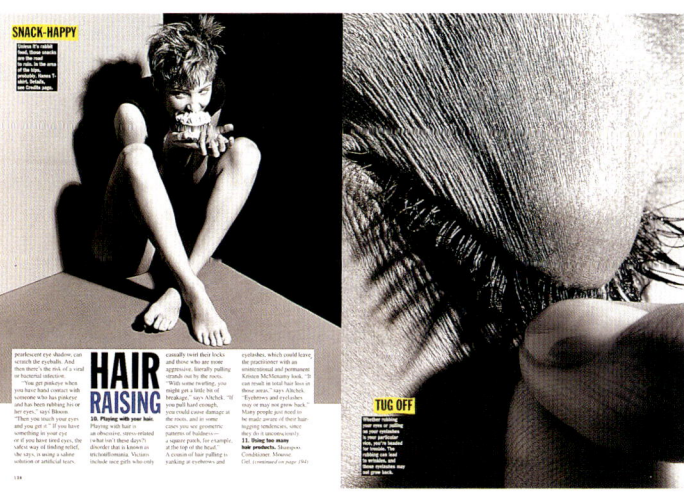

SNACK-HAPPY

HAIR RAISING

TUG OFF

PUBLICATION	Vibe
AWARD	Merit
DESIGN DIRECTOR	Gary Koepke
ART DIRECTOR	Richard Baker
DESIGNER	Richard Baker
PHOTOGRAPHERS	Mario Castellanos, Howard Rosenberg
PHOTO EDITOR	George Pitts
PUBLISHER	Time Inc. Ventures
STUDIO	Koepke International, Ltd.
CATEGORY	Design/Story
DATE	September 1993

PUBLICATION	Working Woman
AWARD	Merit
ART DIRECTOR	Jolene Cuyler
DESIGNER	Lisa Goldenberg
ILLUSTRATOR	Robert Pryor
PUBLISHER	Lang Communications
CATEGORY	Design/Story
DATE	June 1993

PUBLICATION	Elle
AWARD	Merit
ART DIRECTOR	Nora Sheehan
PHOTOGRAPHER	Serge Lutens
PUBLISHER	Hachette Filipacchi Magazines, Inc.
CATEGORY	Design/Story
DATE	December 1993

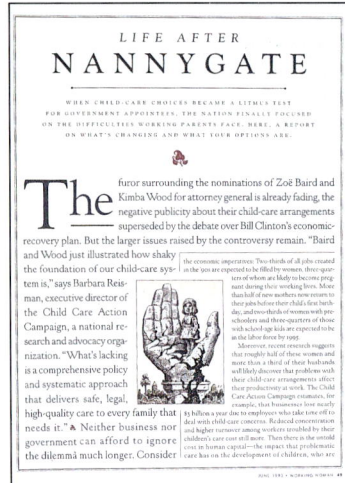

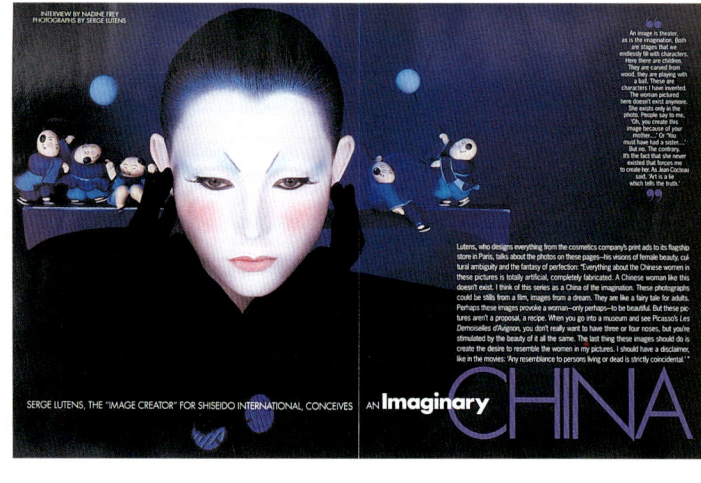

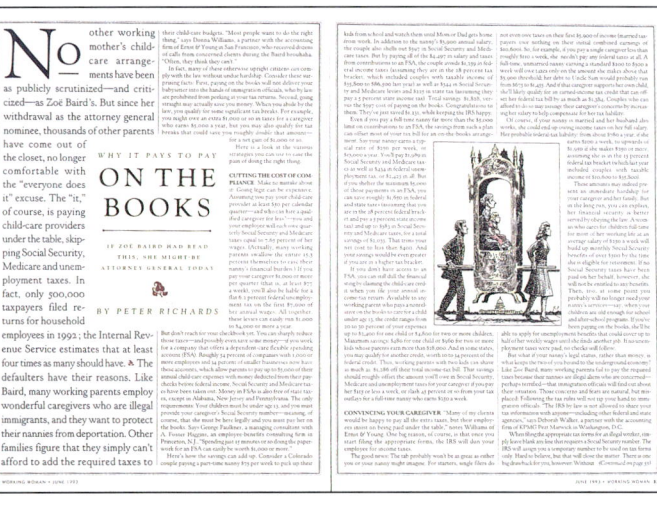

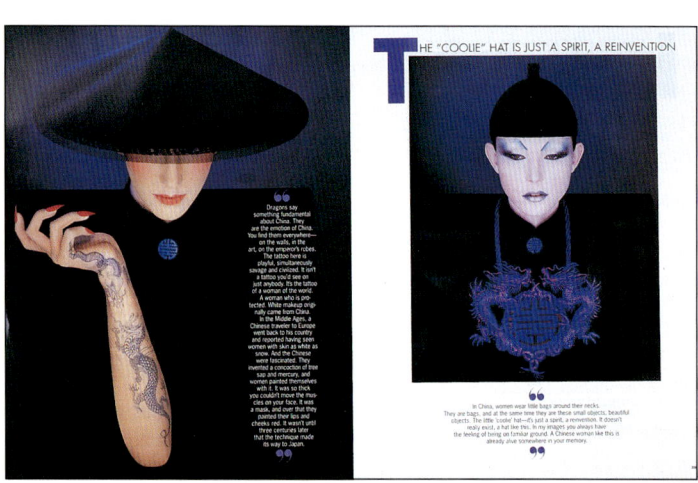

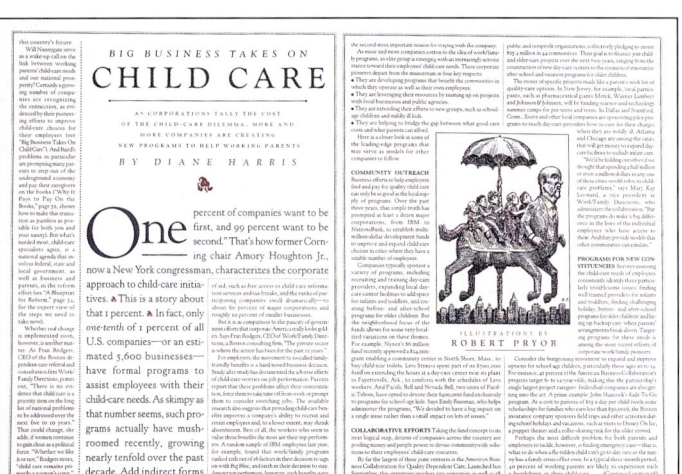

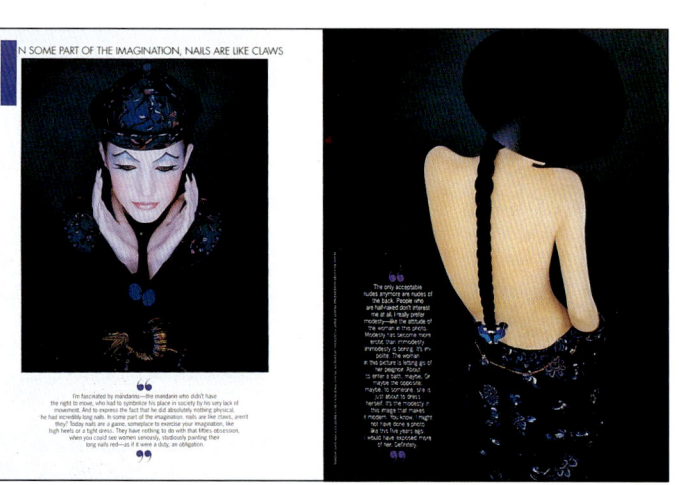

PUBLICATION Bride's & Your New Home
AWARD Merit
ART DIRECTOR Phyllis Richmond Cox
DESIGNER Phyllis Richmond Cox
PHOTOGRAPHER Grant Peterson
PUBLISHER The Condé Nast Publications Inc.
CATEGORY Design/Story
DATE June/July 1993

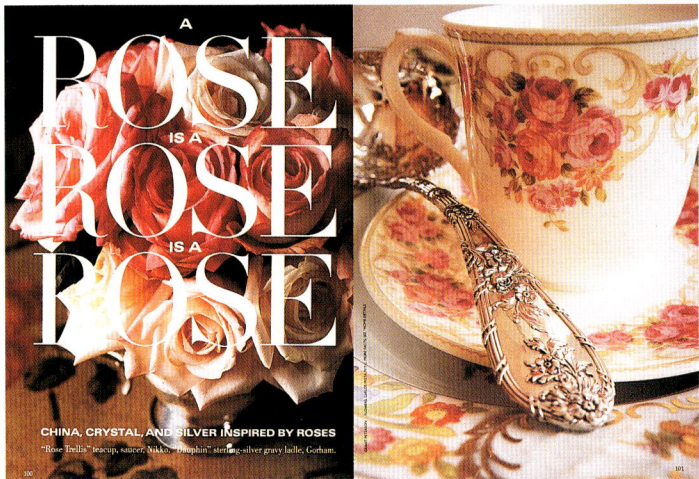

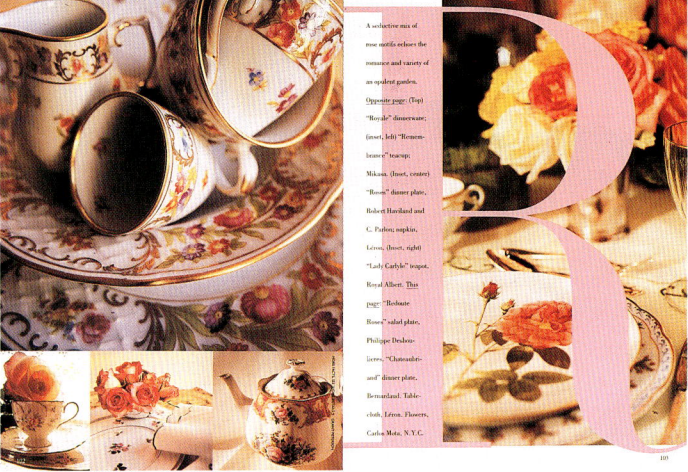

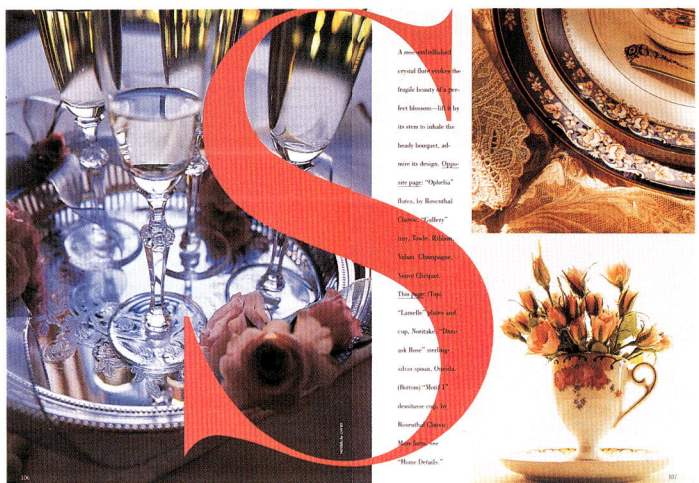

PUBLICATION	United Airline's Hemispheres
AWARD	Merit
DESIGN DIRECTOR	Kit Hinrichs
ART DIRECTOR	Jaimey Easler
DESIGNER	Jackie Foshaug
ILLUSTRATOR	Eiko Ishioka
PHOTOGRAPHER	David Seidner
CLIENT	United Airlines
STUDIO	Pentagram Design Group
CATEGORY	Design/Story
DATE	December 1993

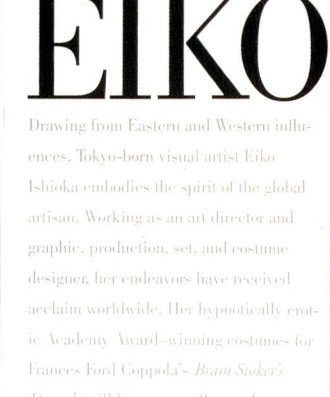

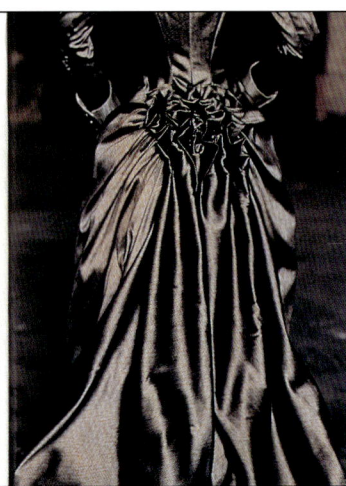

EIKO

Drawing from Eastern and Western influences, Tokyo-born visual artist Eiko Ishioka embodies the spirit of the global artisan. Working as an art director and graphic, production, set, and costume designer, her endeavors have received acclaim worldwide. Her hypnotically erotic Academy Award–winning costumes for Frances Ford Coppola's *Bram Stoker's Dracula* will haunt as well as seduce you.

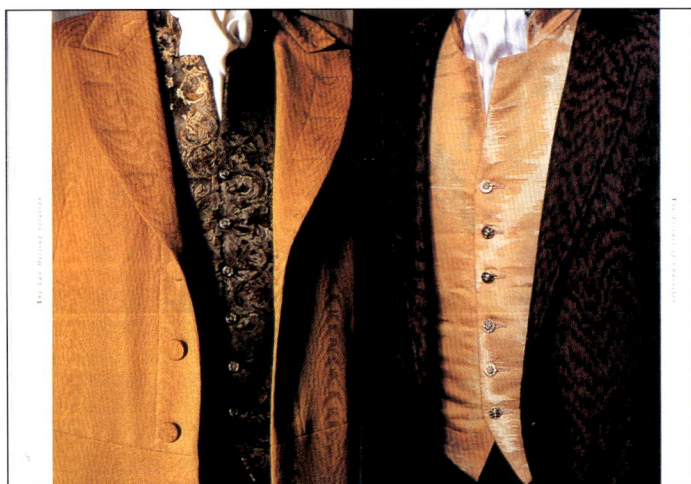

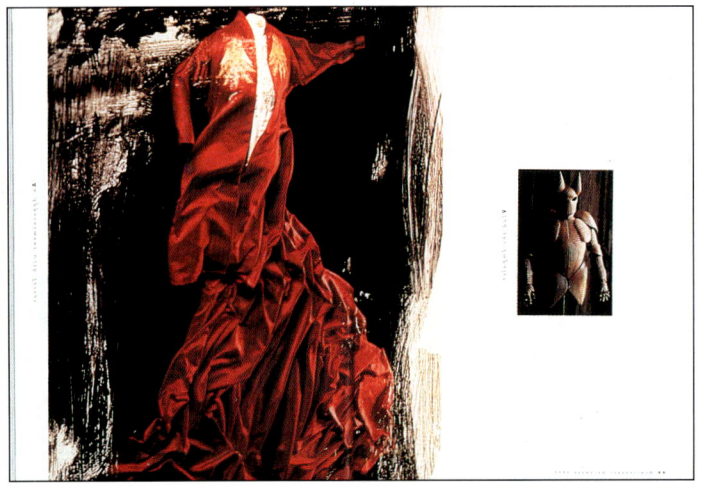

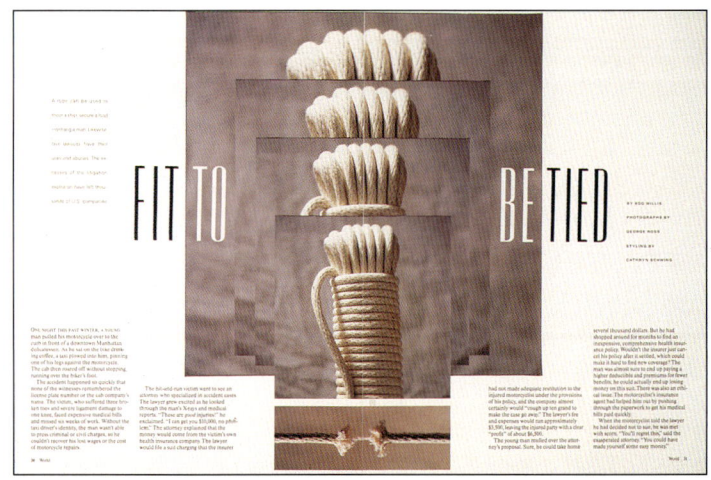

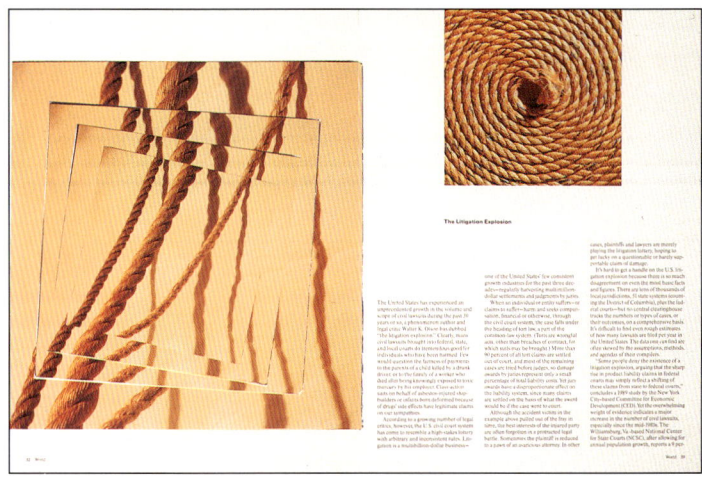

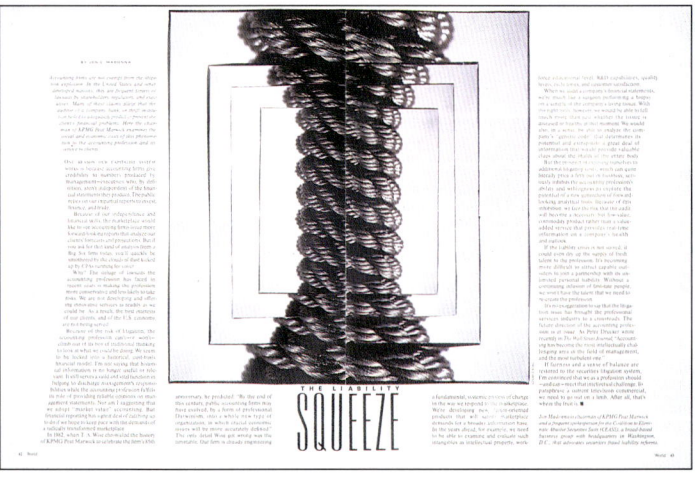

PUBLICATION	World
AWARD	Merit
ART DIRECTOR	Donna Bonavita
DESIGNER	Donna Bonavita
PHOTOGRAPHER	George Ross
PUBLISHER	KPMG
STUDIO	KPMG
CATEGORY	Design/Story
DATE	May 1993

PUBLICATION World Tour
AWARD Merit
CREATIVE DIRECTOR Gary Koepke
DESIGNERS Diddo Ramm, Gary Koepke
PHOTOGRAPHER Vernon Beiber
PHOTO EDITOR Sabastian Buffa
PUBLISHER Dun & Bradstreet Software
STUDIO Koepke International, LTD.
CATEGORY Design/Story
DATE July - September 1993

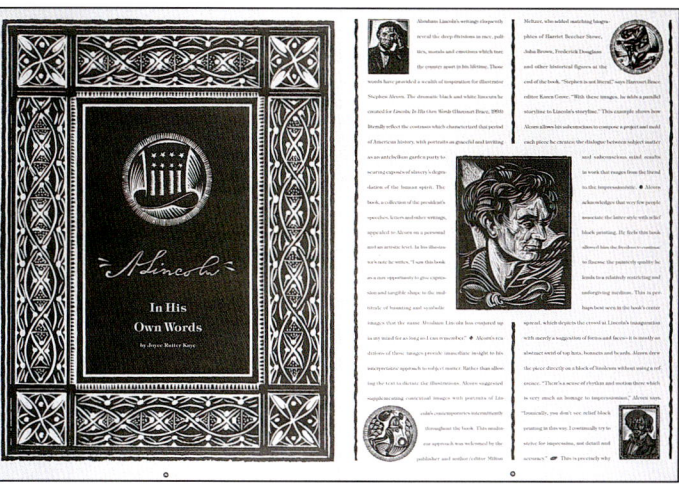

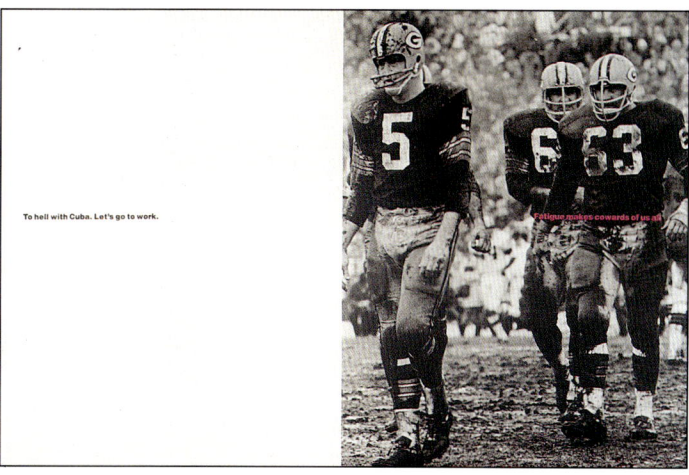

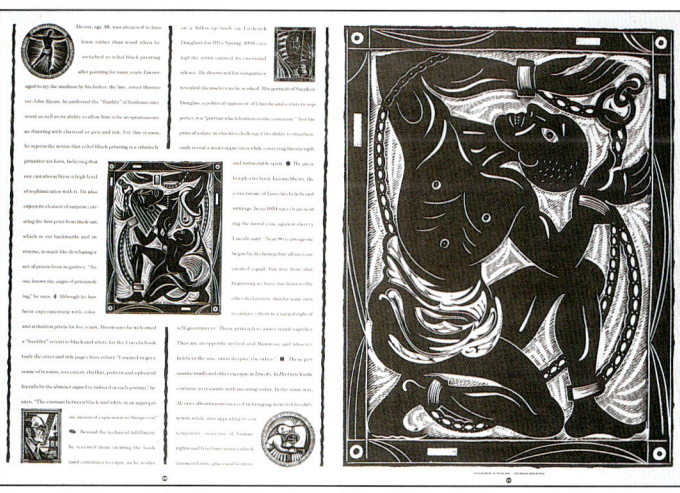

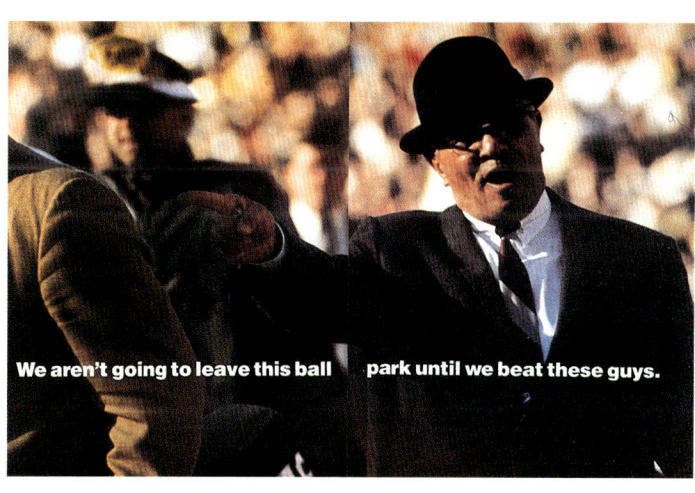

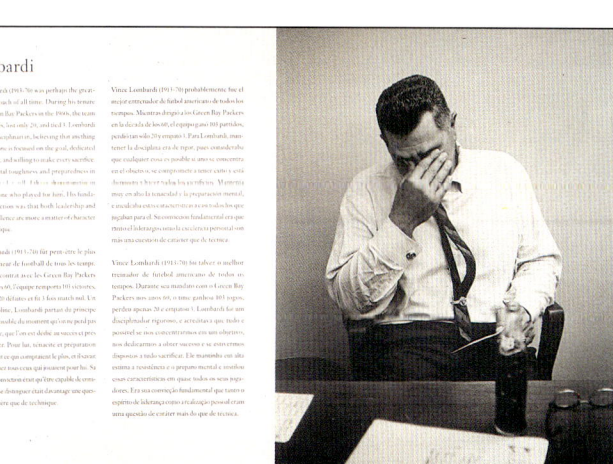

PUBLICATION Upper & Lower Case
AWARD Merit
ART DIRECTORS Woody Pirtle, John Klotnia
DESIGNERS John Klotnia, Ivette Montes de Oca
ILLUSTRATOR Stephen Alcorn
PUBLISHER International Typeface Corporation
STUDIO Pentagram Design Group
CATEGORY Design/Story
DATE September 1993

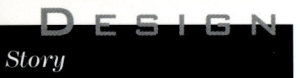
PUBLICATION	The New York Times Magazine
AWARD	Merit
ART DIRECTOR	Janet Froelich
DESIGNER	Gina Davis
PHOTOGRAPHER	Ellen Binder
PHOTO EDITOR	Kathy Ryan
PUBLISHER	The New York Times
CATEGORY	Design/Story
DATE	October 31, 1993

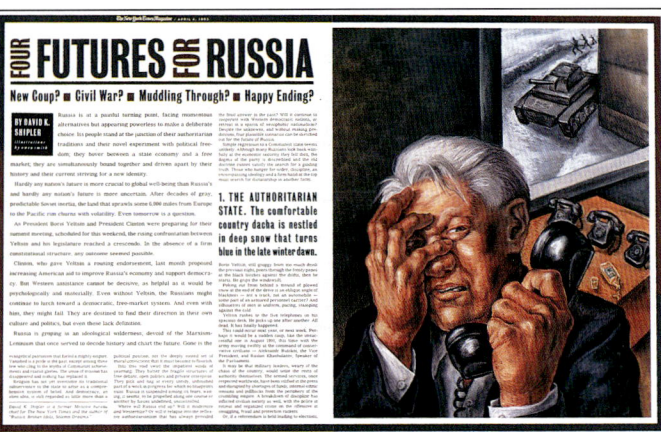

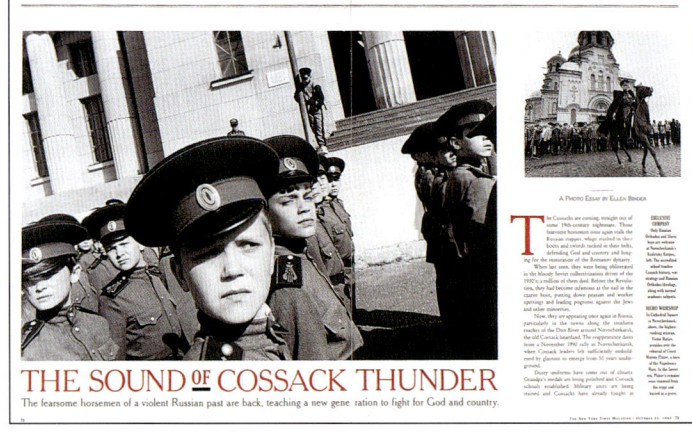

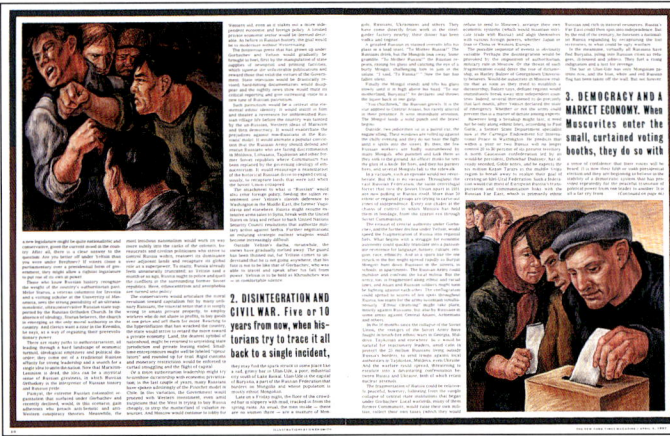

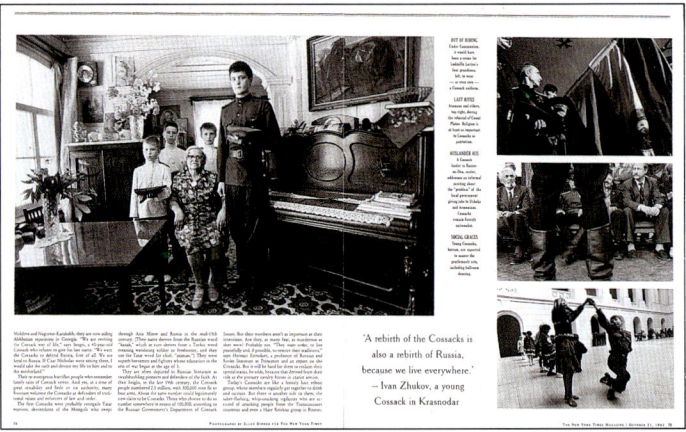

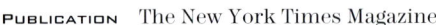

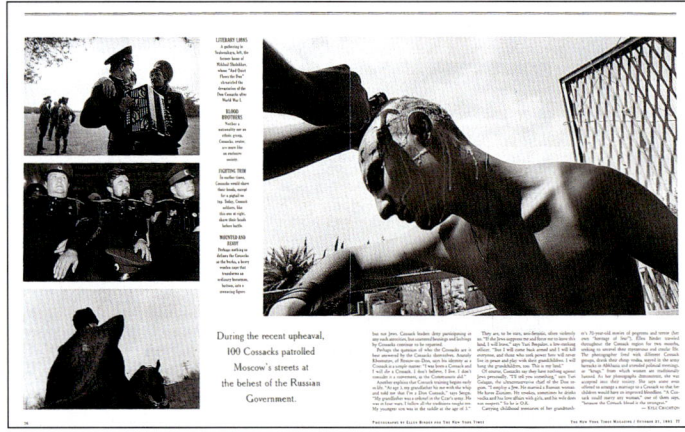

PUBLICATION	The New York Times Magazine
AWARD	Merit
ART DIRECTOR	Janet Froelich
DESIGNERS	Janet Froelich, Kayo Der Serkissian
ILLUSTRATOR	Owen Smith
PUBLISHER	The New York Times
CATEGORY	Design/Story
DATE	April 4, 1993

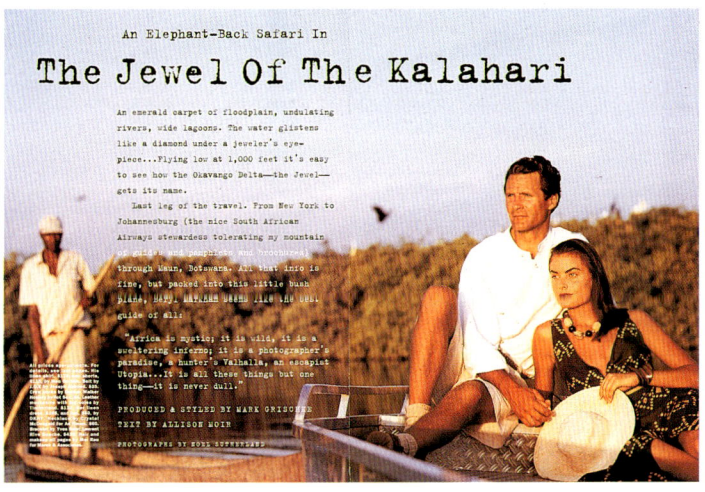

An Elephant-Back Safari In

The Jewel Of The Kalahari

An emerald carpet of floodplain, undulating rivers, wide lagoons. The water glistens like a diamond under a jeweler's eyepiece...Flying low at 1,000 feet it's easy to see how the Okavango Delta—the Jewel—gets its name.

Last leg of the travel. From New York to Johannesburg (the nice South African Airways stewardess tolerating my mountain of luggage was horrified to see a mongoose peek out), through Maun, Botswana. And that into is fine, but packed into this little bush plane, baby, mayhem seems like the real guide of all!

"Africa is mystic; it is wild, it is a sweltering inferno; it is a photographer's paradise, a hunter's Valhalla, an escapist Utopia...It is all these things but one thing—it is never dull."

PRODUCED & STYLED BY MARK GRISCHKE
TEXT BY ALLISON MOIR
PHOTOGRAPHS BY NOEL SUTHERLAND

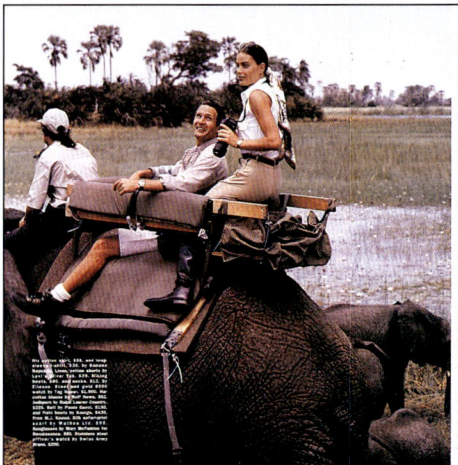

"Up, Abu, Up!"

We saddle up at dawn, two riders and a mahout per elephant. Quite a procession we are—three adult "ellies" with six babies straggling behind. Splashing in single file thru swamp, floodplain, tiptoeing, as elephants do (if you can believe it), down trodden game paths. Elvis we're not: the five tons of elephant beneath me can swat at a less-than-swift 3 m.p.h.

Riding big Abu is surprisingly similar to riding a horse. A very big horse. "Stretch do-o-o-own, Abu!" the mahout yell, and this incredible beast lies down on his stomach, offering his "knee" for me to step on. (Amazing! I'd always thought African elephants couldn't be trained.) I scramble up and straddle the howdah, J. climbs up, then our mahout gets on Abu's neck, his legs hidden by the massive, flapping ears, and commands, "Up, Abu, Up!" Abu's front legs straighten, and we cling to the howdah, stuck at 45 degrees until this puissant pachyderm levels like standing up. "Up, Abu, Up!"...

Higher than an elephant's eye, I look down on a young male giraffe, his tawny face cradled by the waxy, tender mopane leaves that he's nibbling. Cocking his head quizzically, he eyes our oncoming procession less than ten yards from his picnic spot.

This is really a "Stealth Safari." On the back of an elephant we blend with the wildlife. Our smell is masked by the elephant—and hooch!—and no noisy, smoke-spewing engine to send animals running. We're part of the herd, part of the African landscape...

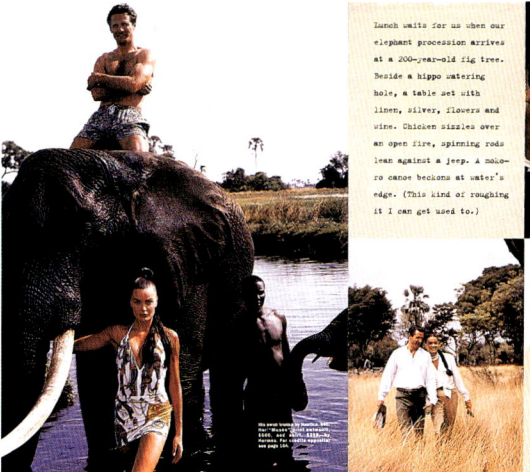

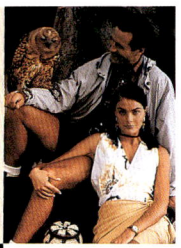

Lunch waits for us when our elephant procession arrives at a 200-year-old fig tree. Beside a hippo watering hole, a table set with linen, silver, flowers and wine. Chicken sizzles over an open fire, spinning rods lean against a jeep. A mokoro canoe beckons at water's edge. (This kind of roughing it I can get used to.)

We spend the afternoon, blissfully hot and lazy, fishing for bream and catfish, photographing yawning hippos, climbing the aged fig, and mastering the pole-driven mokoro. And what of our redoubtable ellies and mahouts? Asleep, shaded from the unforgiving midday sun.

PUBLICATION	Forbes FYI
AWARD	Merit
ART DIRECTOR	Alexander Isley
DESIGNER	Lynette Cortez
PHOTOGRAPHER	Noel Sutherland
PUBLISHER	Forbes, Inc.
STUDIO	Alex Isley Design
CATEGORY	Design/Story
DATE	March 15, 1993

PUBLICATION	Upper & Lower Case
AWARD	Merit
ART DIRECTORS	Woody Pirtle, John Klotnia
DESIGNERS	John Klotnia, Ivette Montes de Oca
PHOTOGRAPHER	John Paul Gidress
PUBLISHER	International Typeface Corporation
STUDIO	Pentagram Design Group
CATEGORY	Design/Story
DATE	September 1993

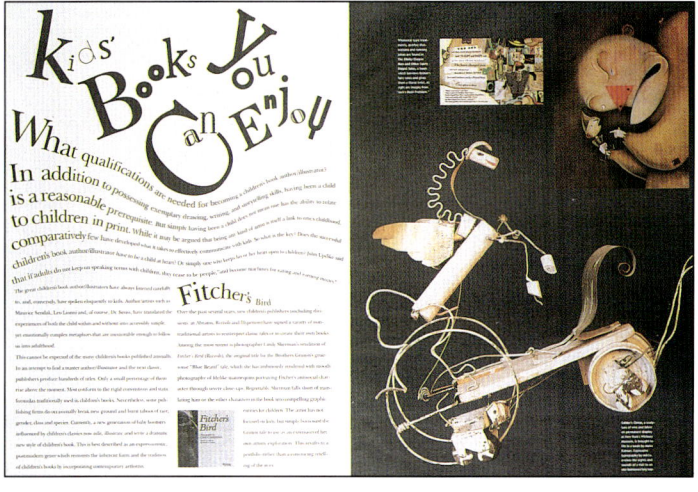

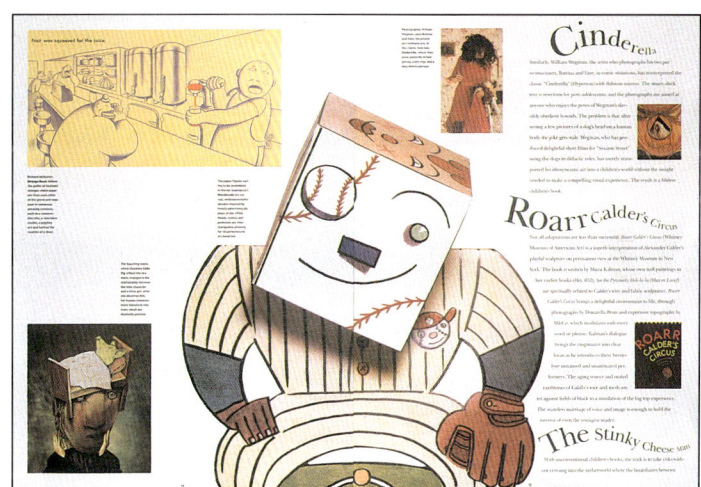

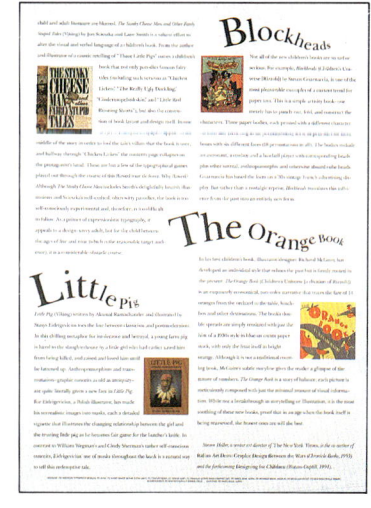

PUBLICATION	Discover
AWARD	Silver
ART DIRECTOR	David Armario
DESIGNER	James Lambertus
ILLUSTRATOR	Alan Cober
PHOTO EDITOR	John Barker
PUBLISHER	Disney Magazine Publishing, Inc.
CATEGORY	Information Graphics
DATE	April 1993

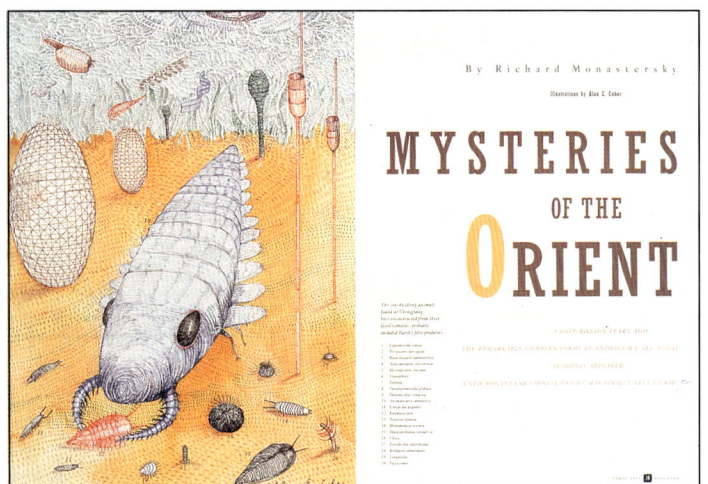

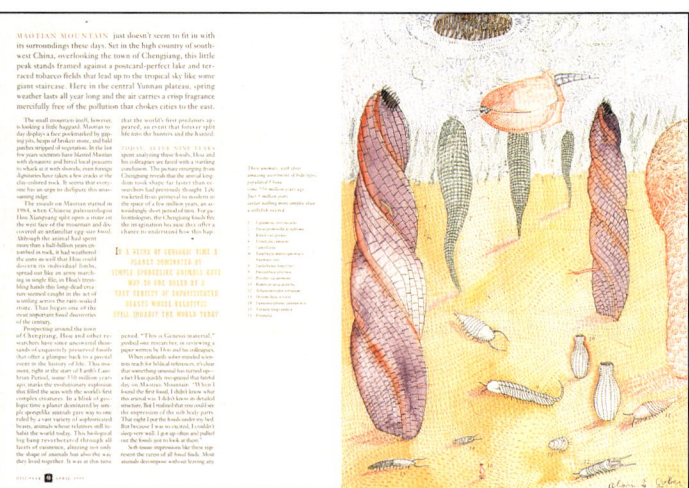

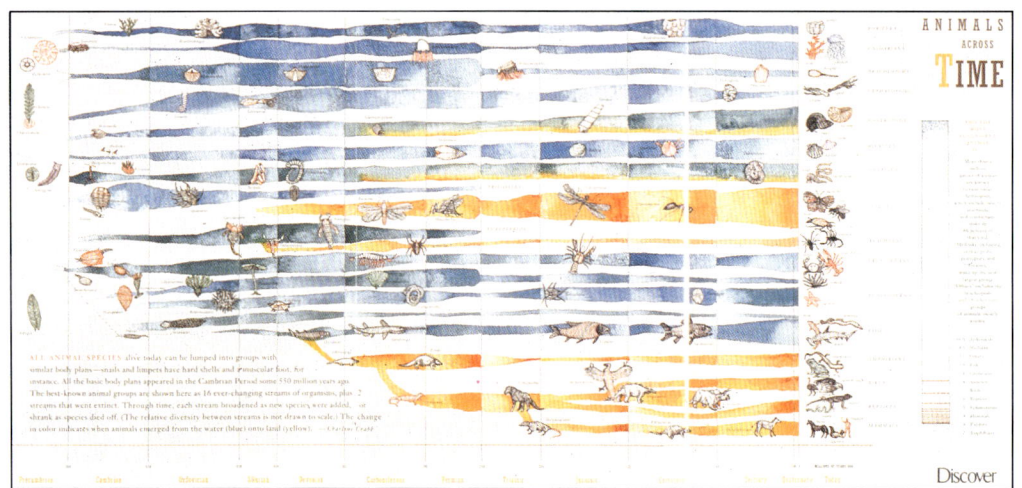

PUBLICATION	Condé Nast Traveler
AWARD	Merit
DESIGN DIRECTOR	Diana La Guardia
ART DIRECTOR	Christin Gangi
DESIGNER	John Grimwade
PUBLISHER	The Condé Nast Publications Inc.
CATEGORY	Information Graphics
DATE	May 1993

PUBLICATION	Condé Nast Traveler
AWARD	Merit
DESIGN DIRECTOR	Diana La Guardia
ART DIRECTOR	Christin Gangi
DESIGNER	John Grimwade
PUBLISHER	The Condé Nast Publications Inc.
CATEGORY	Information Graphics
DATE	December 1993

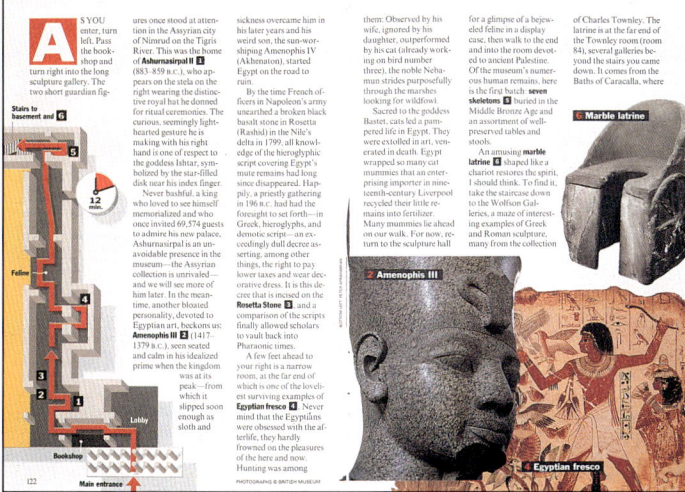

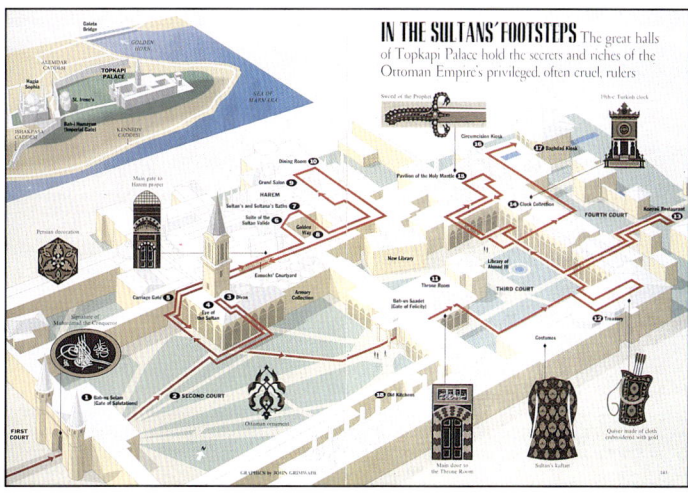

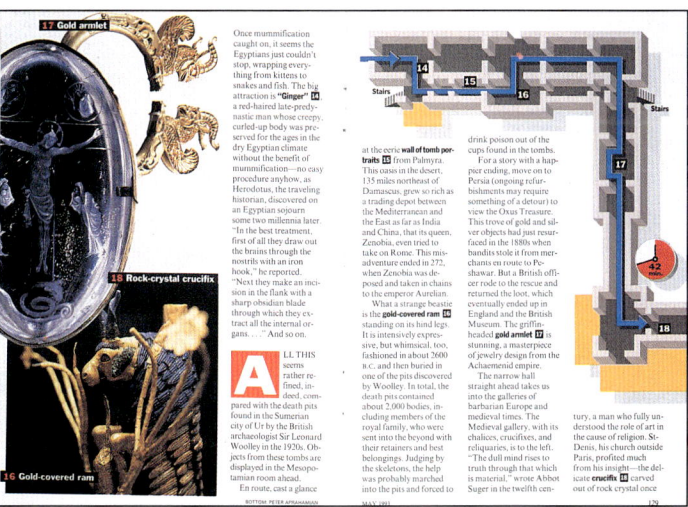

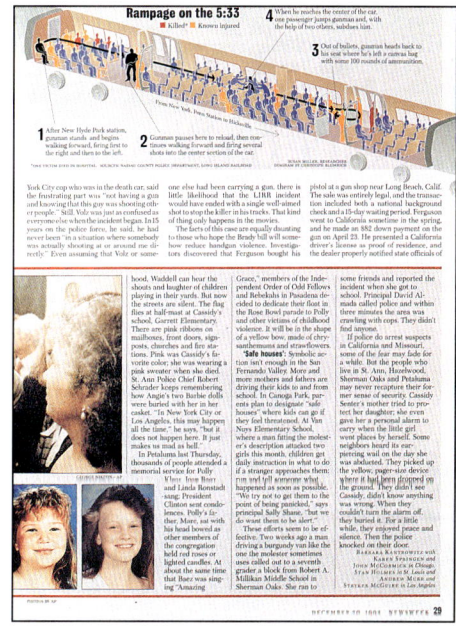

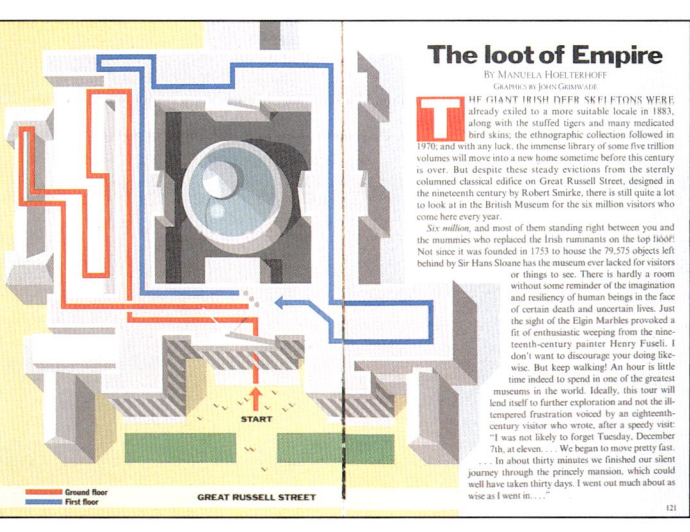

PUBLICATION	Newsweek
AWARD	Merit
ART DIRECTORS	Patricia Bradbury, Bonnie Scranton
ILLUSTRATOR	Christoph Blumrich
PUBLISHER	Newsweek, Inc.
CATEGORY	Information Graphics
DATE	December 20, 1993

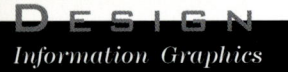

PUBLICATION Kids Discover
AWARD Merit
ART DIRECTORS Will Hopkins, Mary K. Baumann
ILLUSTRATOR Acme Design Co.
PUBLISHER Kids Discover
STUDIO Hopkins/Baumann
CATEGORY Information Graphics
DATE October 1993

PUBLICATION Details
AWARD Merit
ART DIRECTOR B.W. Honeycutt
DESIGNER Brian Kobberger
ILLUSTRATOR Nigel Holmes
PUBLISHER The Condé Nast Publications Inc.
CATEGORY Information Graphics
DATE June 1993

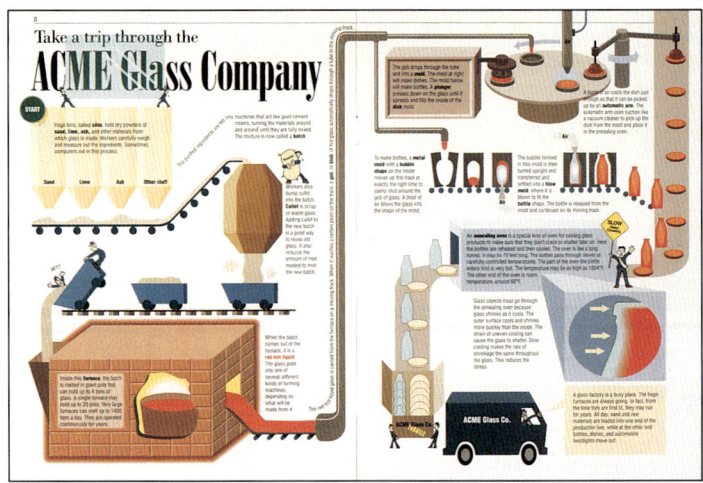

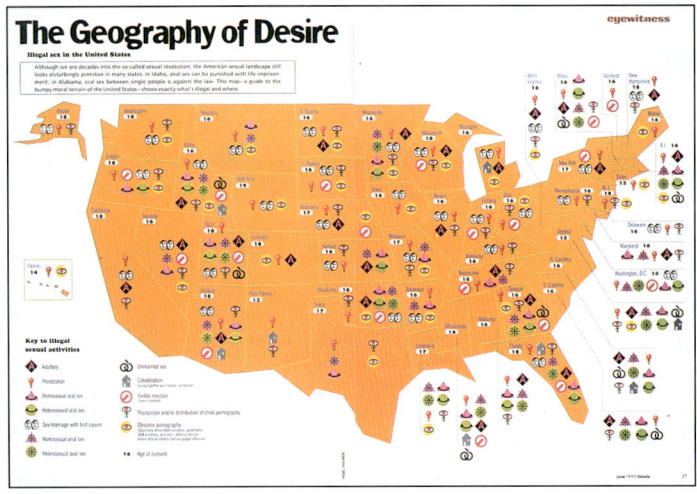

PUBLICATION Kids Discover
AWARD Merit
ART DIRECTORS Will Hopkins, Mary K. Baumann
ILLUSTRATOR Acme Design Co.
PUBLISHER Kids Discover
STUDIO Hopkins/Baumann
CATEGORY Information Graphics
DATE January 1993

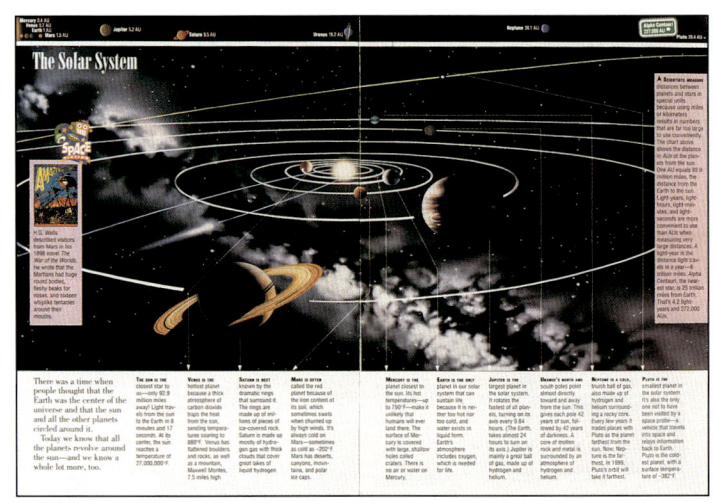

PUBLICATION	Discover
AWARD	Merit
ART DIRECTOR	David Armario
DESIGNERS	James Lambertus, David Armario
ILLUSTRATOR	Philip Anderson
PUBLISHER	Disney Magazine Publishing, Inc.
CATEGORY	Information Graphics
DATE	August 1993

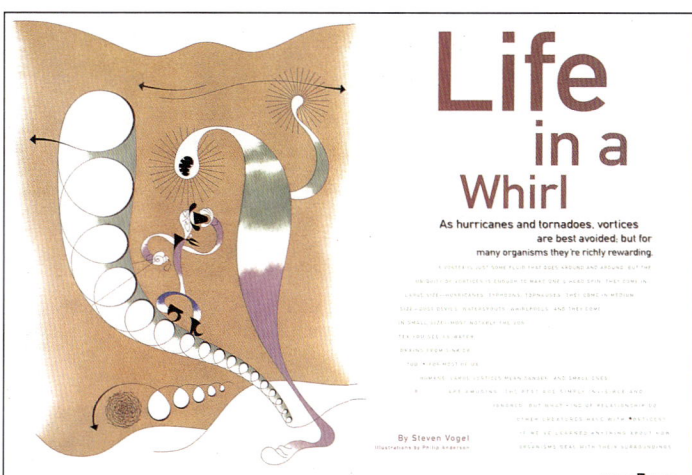

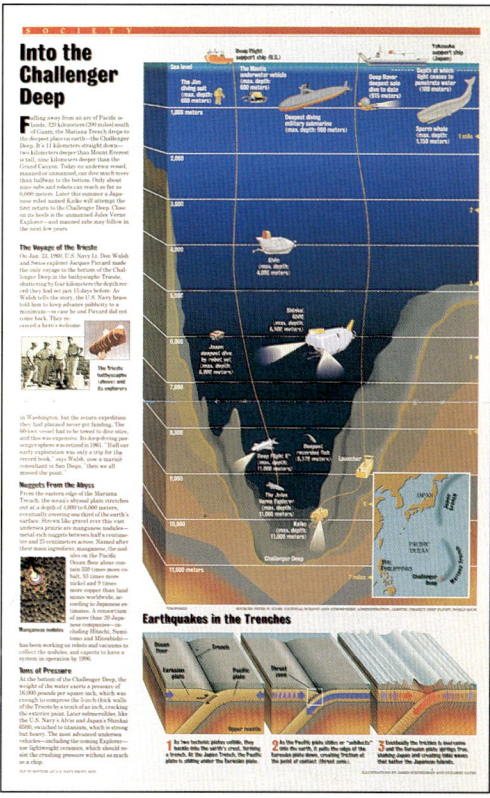

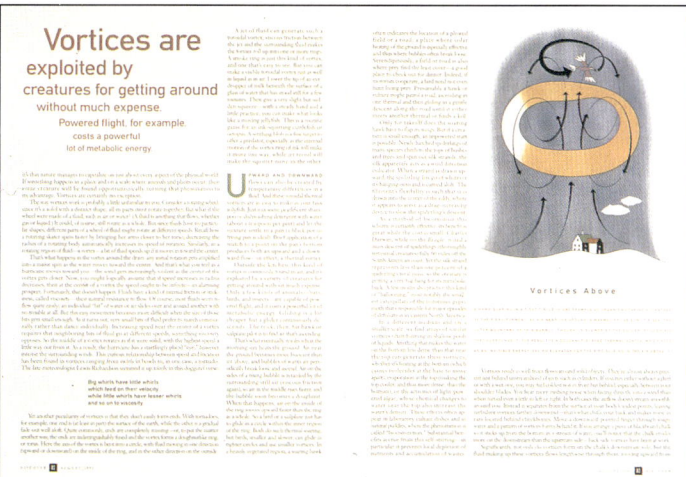

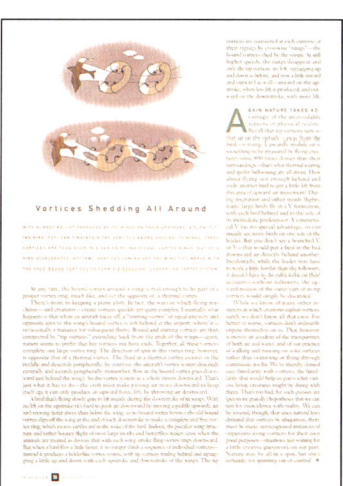

PUBLICATION	Newsweek
AWARD	Merit
ART DIRECTOR	Patricia Bradbury
DESIGNERS	Jim McManus, Meredith Hamilton
ILLUSTRATORS	Jared Schneidman, Guilbert Gates
PUBLISHER	Newsweek, Inc.
CATEGORY	Information Graphics
DATE	July 5, 1993

PUBLICATION	Blood: Bearer of Life and Death
AWARD	Merit
ART DIRECTOR	Rodney C. Williams
DESIGNER	Leon Lawrence III
ILLUSTRATOR	Tim Phelps, CMI, FAMI
CLIENT	Howard Hughes Medical Institute
CATEGORY	Information Graphics
DATE	November 1993

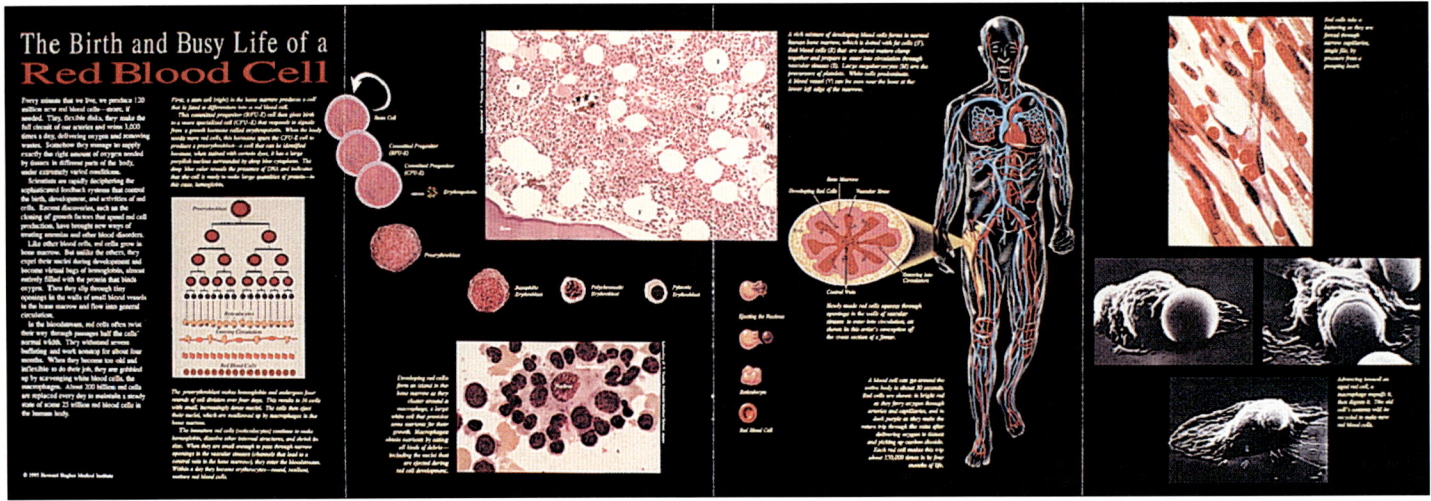

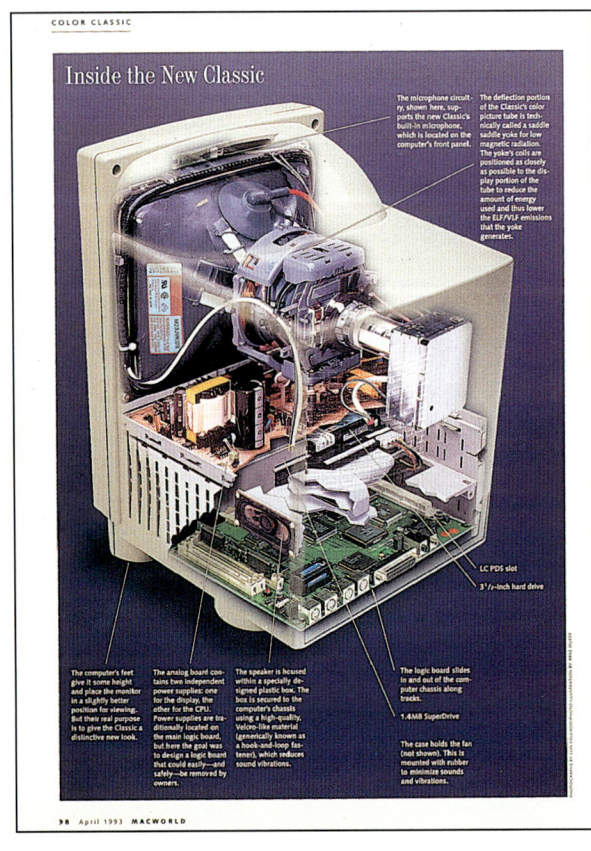

PUBLICATION	MacWorld
AWARD	Merit
DESIGN DIRECTOR	Dennis McLod
DESIGNER	Arne Hurty
ILLUSTRATOR	Arne Hurty
PHOTOGRAPHER	Luis Delgado
PUBLISHER	Macworld Communications, Inc.
CATEGORY	Information Graphics
DATE	April 1993

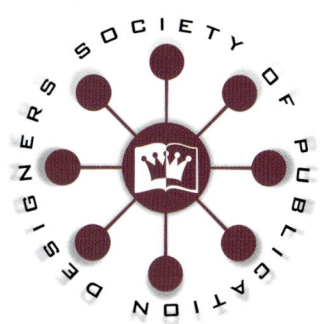

ILLUS
TRATION
STORY
SINGLE PAGE
SPREAD

PUBLICATION   GQ
AWARD   Gold
CREATIVE DIRECTOR   Robert Priest
DESIGNER   Robert Priest
ILLUSTRATOR   C. F. Payne
PUBLISHER   The Condé Nast Publications Inc.
CATEGORY   Illustration/Single Page or Spread
DATE   April 1993

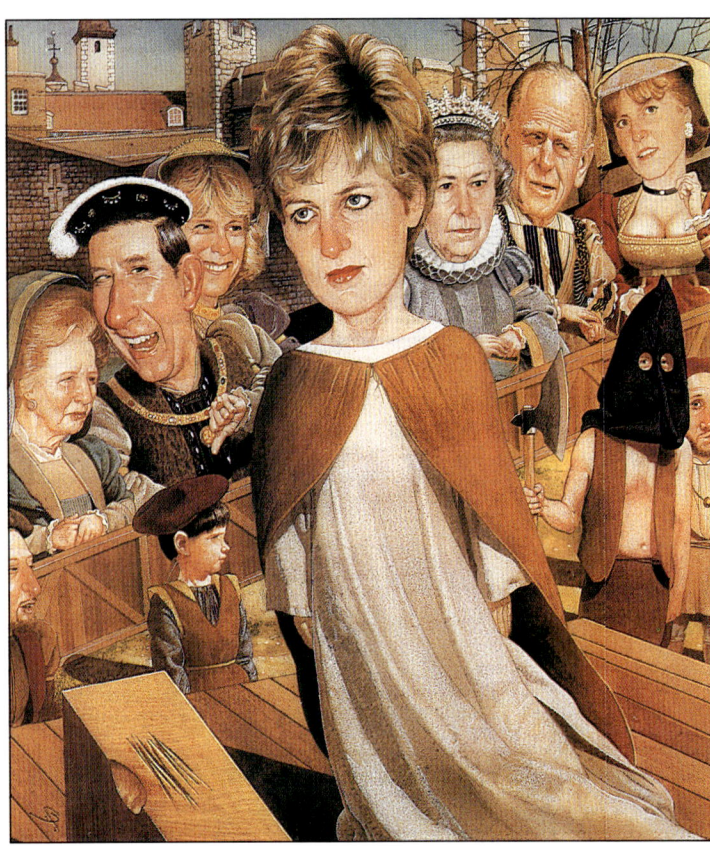

Noblesse Besieged

Right now he's as woeful as Lear, but there are plenty of reasons to keep Charles in charge

By John Mortimer

A chap's dreams are troubled by his ancestors, particularly when they are noisy, autocratic and impatient with one's sincere desire to do, on the whole and as far as one decently can, the right thing. The distinguished forebears of Prince Charles Philip Arthur George, heir to the throne of England, seem to throng his bedroom by night, and it's worth recalling their names. They include not only Queen Victoria but both kings Harold, the William of Normandy who fought the Battle of Hastings, Catherine *and* Peter the Great of Russia, Charlemagne, Frederick Barbarossa, the Byzantine emperors Michael VIII and Andronicus Palaeologus, King Zygmunt I of Poland and Gedimin of Lithuania, the Viking king Sven Forkbeard and Frederick the Great, the emperor Charles V, Pope Nicholas III and El Cid. The prince is also one of the nearest living relations of George Washington and descends from Vlad Dracul, vaivode of Wallachia (the father of the original Dracula), and possibly from Genghis Khan.

As Charles lies in his bed at Sandringham with his five pounds ready for the church collection, and his paint box prepared for a harmless afternoon sketching the Norfolk countryside, the hoarse voices of blood-stained ancestors are, perhaps, urging him to pronounce sentences of death or exile, to lock the editors of tabloid newspapers in damp dungeons for the remainder of their natural lives, to send his other enemies to their

PUBLICATION   Rolling Stone
AWARD   Silver
ART DIRECTOR   Fred Woodward
DESIGNERS   Fred Woodward, Gail Anderson
ILLUSTRATOR   Skip Liepke
PUBLISHER   Wenner Media
CATEGORY   Illustration/Single Page or Spread
DATE   April 29, 1993

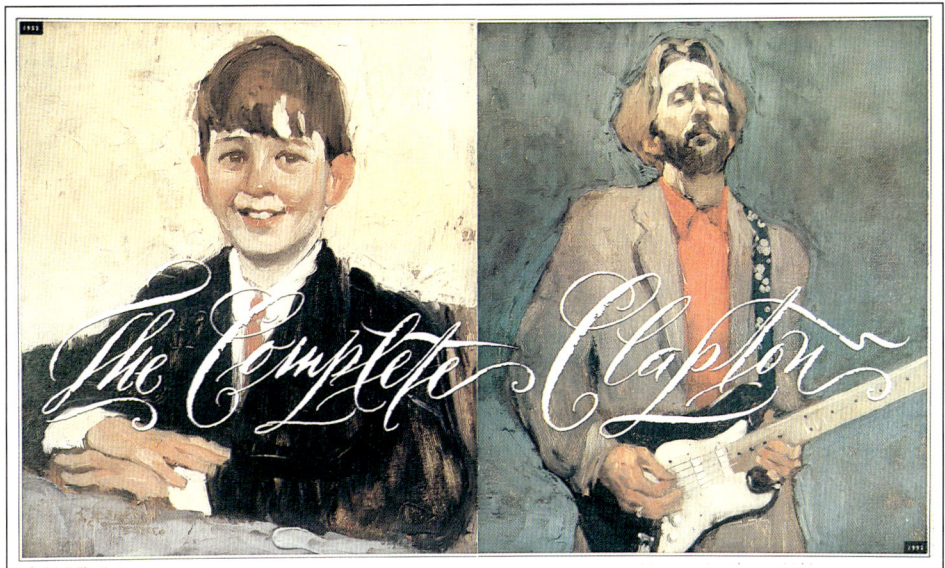

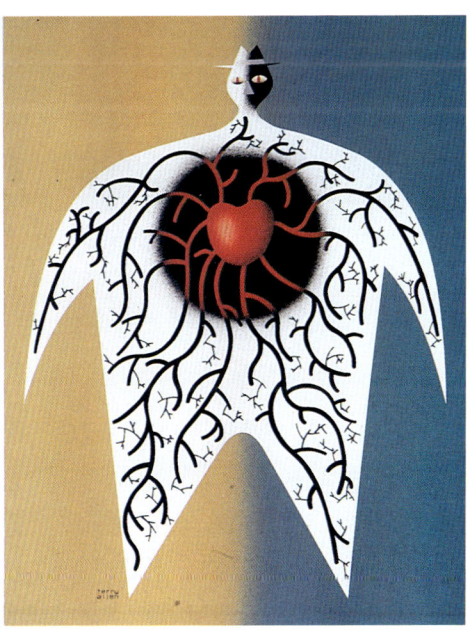

PUBLICATION   Stanford Medicine
AWARD   Silver
ART DIRECTOR   David Armario
DESIGNER   David Armario
ILLUSTRATOR   Terry Allen
PUBLISHER   Stanford University
CATEGORY   Illustration/Single Page or Spread
DATE   Fall 1993

PUBLICATION   The Boston Globe Magazine
AWARD   Silver
ART DIRECTOR   Lucy Bartholomay
DESIGNER   Lucy Bartholomay
ILLUSTRATOR   Scott Menchin
PUBLISHER   The Boston Globe
CATEGORY   Illustration/Single Page or Spread
DATE   March 14, 1993

What's the matter with men?

Violent behavior, emotional distance, and higher rates of drug addiction among men can't be explained by hormones. The problem, experts say, is cultural beliefs about masculinity—everything packed into the phrase "a real man." [BY ANITA DIAMANT]

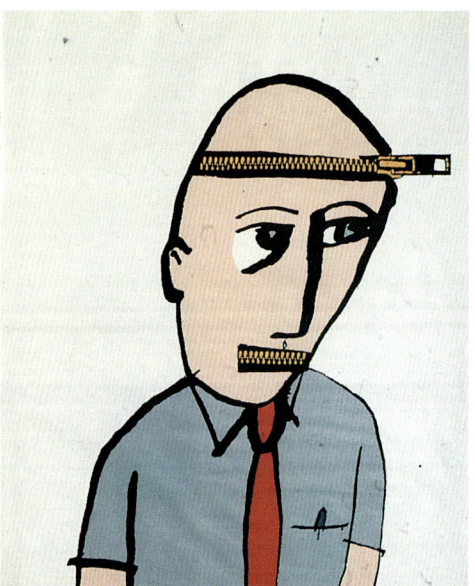

Last August, at the American Psychological Association's annual conference in Washington, D.C., nearly 500 therapists, researchers, and graduate students attended a symposium called "Toward a New Psychology of Men." The audience, most of it male, heard the leading lights in the field discuss the perplexing, even alarming, state of the male psyche.

Every year men commit suicide, die in car accidents, and drink themselves to death at much higher rates than women. Thousands beat, stalk, or kill the women they claim to love. Men who provide for their families and who support gender equality under the law are assailed by complaints that they seem incapable of real intimacy, spontaneous acts of housework, or any understanding of why Anita Hill found it hard to rock the boat in which Clarence Thomas held the tiller.

Experts on the podium roundly dispatched the idea that violent behavior, emotional distance, or higher rates of drug addic-

Anita Diamant writes a column for this magazine.

tion and drowning among men could be explained by hormones. According to them, the answer to the question "What's the matter with men?" is not biological maleness but cultural beliefs about masculinity – everything packed into the phrase "a real man."

Before and after the speakers' presentations, a corps of friendly, earnest men circulated orange index cards, seeking support for formation of a new division of the American Psychological Association devoted to "the psychological study of men and masculinity." (At least 700 members, 1 percent of the organization's membership, must sign cards in order for a new field of study to attain formal recognition.)

Ron Levant, a Brookline psychologist and coauthor of *Between Father and Child*, is leading the drive to make the psychology of men the APA's 50th division. He expects to have the requisite number of cards in hand by the 1993 conference, which will be held this summer in Toronto. *Continued on Page 33*

14 ILLUSTRATION BY SCOTT MENCHIN

TOW **Z** ONE

Q. How can a man who doesn't even own a car get towed twice in one day?
A. Easy. He lives in Boston.

By Paul Hemp

I was reading the other day about the unforgiving electronic parking meters recently installed in Cambridge, the ones with flashing digital displays that indicate not only that your time has expired but precisely how long you've been illegally parked.

Such municipal ingenuity brought to mind the time two years ago when I was towed twice in 12 hours from parking spaces on Beacon Hill. An unusual feat – and I don't even own a car.

Indeed, if there's a guaranteed cure for the urge to go bargain-hunting on the Auto Mile, it's that sickening feeling you get from seeing, twice in 12 hours, an empty space by the curb where your car once was.

Don't get me wrong. I love to drive. I love cars. If anyone can direct me to a rust-free, three-on-the-tree 1967 Dodge Dart convertible, I'll abandon my vow to steer clear of car ownership while living in Boston.

But you'll have to admit, there's something nice about never having to remember what the odometer read at your last oil change. Never having to wonder about that funny noise – or are you just imagining it? – when you downshift. Never having to take out a second mortgage to pay your auto insurance premium.

And never – or at least rarely – having to deal with Boston drivers. In fact, during those infrequent times when I am behind the wheel, I have a tactic to counter their rudeness. When someone blasts his horn or shouts an expletive, I wave cheerfully as the car whizzes past. The befuddled driver, head cranked over shoulder, wonders: "Do I know that guy?" With luck, the fellow will lie awake, trying to figure out who I was.

But it's not just Boston that's to blame for my aversion to auto ownership. When I moved to Vermont some years back, to work for a newspaper there, my car problems seemed to multiply. I bought a used Volkswagen Super Beetle, with that trusty engine over the rear wheels, designed for good traction on slippery winter roads. The first day that it snowed, I bought studded tires and went hurtling around town, only to come around a bend and skid into a car stretched broadside across the road. The driver? The wife of the man who had sold me the tires.

Perhaps my worst luck came the February night I went to cover a town meeting in tiny Baltimore, Vermont. On the way, I ran out of gas. After hitchhiking to a service station, I returned to find I

had locked my keys in the car. I called the police, they jimmied open my door, and I raced off across snowy back roads to catch the end of the session. On arrival, I discovered I'd made a mistake: The meeting was in fact scheduled for the following night. Only a trifle irritated, I headed home, took an icy corner too fast, and barreled up and over a snowbank.

But I stray from my tale.

I live on Beacon Hill. And everyone knows that parking places there are as rare as a Winnebago in Back Bay. But as a neighborhood resident, I have always felt somewhat savvy about local parking practices. When a friend loaned me her car to do some errands, I figured I'd find someplace to park for the night.

I got home around 7:30 in the evening and found a spot at the corner of Pinckney and West Cedar streets. Okay, so a sign said: No Stopping Any Time. But my car blocked nothing but a mailbox. Directly across the street, another vehicle was parked in the identical corner spot. And certainly no one would be checking for violations at this late hour.

I went for a run along the Charles. On the way back, I spotted a rare visitors' parking place, vacant, right in front of my apartment. Better safe than sorry, I thought, so I went to fetch the keys to move the car, which was just around the corner.

When I returned, a motorcycle cop was surveying the space where the car had been. Yes, it had been towed, only five minutes before. And what about the car across the street? "They took down the sign," he said, "so we can't tow that car."

Oh.

I went home and called the Boston Transportation Department tow lot on Frontage Road, just off the expressway in South Boston. I didn't have the license number of my friend's car, but a friendly clerk checked the model and color on his computer and reported that it had just been brought in. He also gave me directions to the lot and explained the tow fees.

Don't let anyone kid you: Despite the hassle, getting towed in Boston is a bargain compared to most cities, almost better than paying for a space in some high-priced garage. It's just $12 for the tow fee, plus $3 an hour storage for the first five hours. The maximum combined fee for the first 24 hours is $27 – and they take Visa and Mastercard. But those initial *Continued on Page 33*

Paul Hemp is a member of the Globe staff.

14 ILLUSTRATION BY HANOCH ERNESTO PIVEN

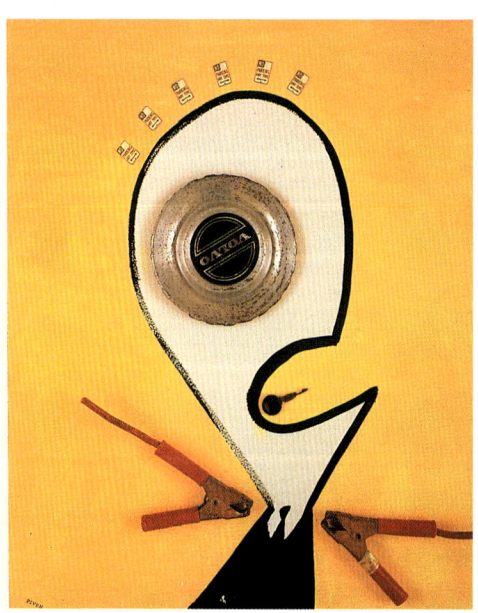

PUBLICATION   The Boston Globe Magazine
AWARD   Silver
ART DIRECTOR   Lucy Bartholomay
DESIGNER   Lucy Bartholomay
ILLUSTRATOR   Hanoch Piven
PUBLISHER   The Boston Globe
CATEGORY   Illustration/Single Page or Spread
DATE   May 23, 1993

PUBLICATION   Discover
AWARD   Merit
ART DIRECTOR   David Armario
DESIGNER   James Lambertus
ILLUSTRATOR   Janet Wooley
PUBLISHER   Disney Magazine Publishing, Inc.
CATEGORY   Illustration/Single Page or Spread
DATE   September 1993

PUBLICATION   Entertainment Weekly
AWARD   Merit
DESIGN DIRECTOR   Michael Grossman
ART DIRECTOR   Arlene Lappen
ILLUSTRATOR   Hanoch Piven
PUBLISHER   Time Inc.
CATEGORY   Illustration/Single Page or Spread
DATE   April 2, 1993

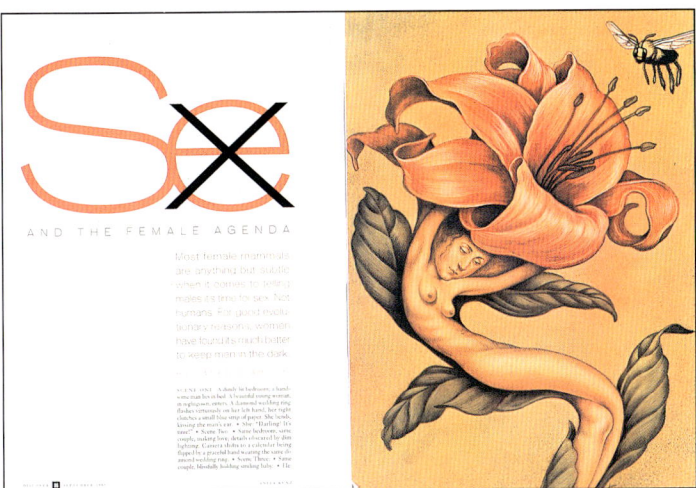

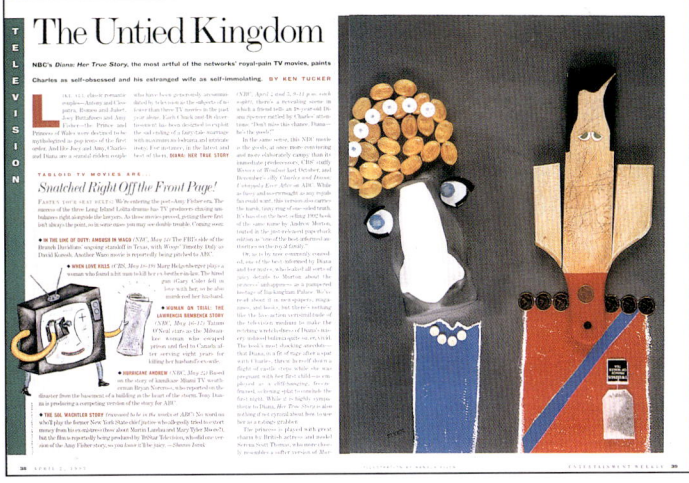

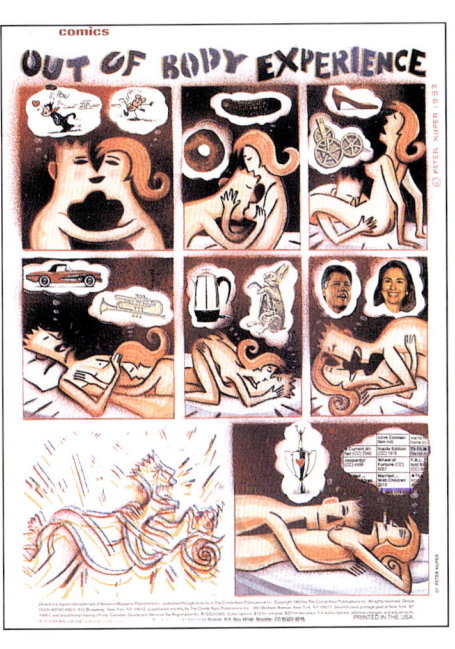

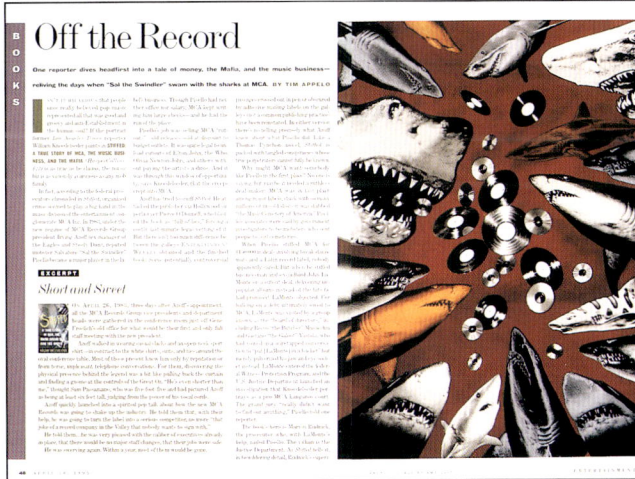

PUBLICATION   Details
AWARD   Merit
ART DIRECTOR   B.W. Honeycutt
ILLUSTRATOR   Peter Kuper
PUBLISHER   The Condé Nast Publications Inc.
CATEGORY   Illustration/Single Page or Spread
DATE   June 1993

PUBLICATION   Entertainment Weekly
AWARD   Merit
DESIGN DIRECTOR   Michael Grossman
ART DIRECTORS   Mark Michaelson, Arlene Lappen
DESIGNER   Michael Picon
ILLUSTRATOR   Amy Guip
PUBLISHER   Time Inc.
CATEGORY   Illustration/Single Page or Spread
DATE   April 30, 1993

PUBLICATION   Entertainment Weekly
AWARD   Merit
CREATIVE DIRECTOR Michael Grossman
ART DIRECTOR   Mark Michaelson
DESIGNER   Mark Michaelson
ILLUSTRATOR   Stepen Kroninger
PUBLISHER   Time Inc.
CATEGORY   Illustration/Single Page or Spread
DATE   January 29, 1993

PUBLICATION   Kiplinger's Personal Finance
AWARD   Merit
DESIGN DIRECTOR Timothy Cain
ART DIRECTOR   Timothy Cain
DESIGNER   Greg Breeding
ILLUSTRATOR   C.F. Payne
CLIENT   Kiplinger Washington Editors
CATEGORY   Illustration/Single Page or Spread
DATE   May 1993

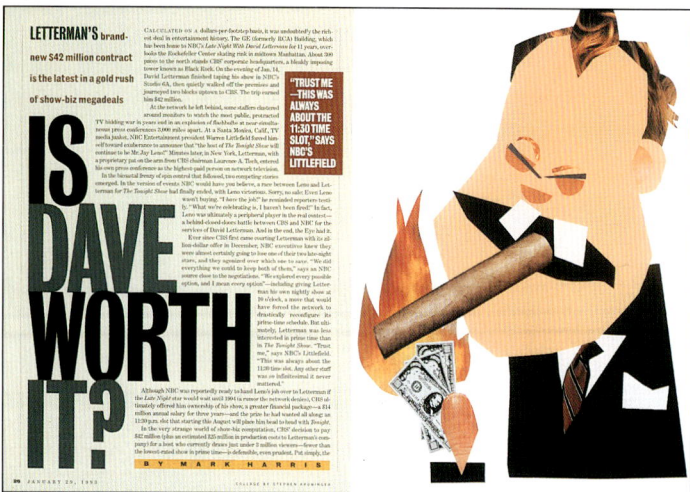

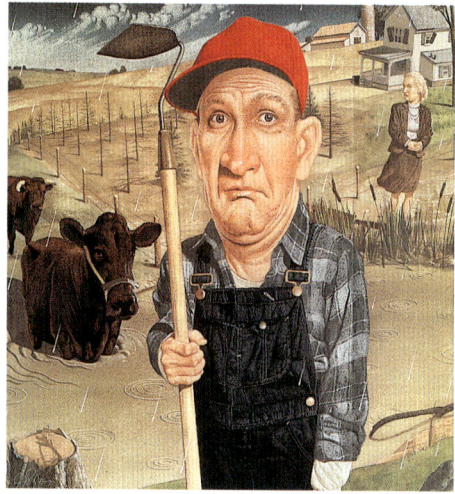

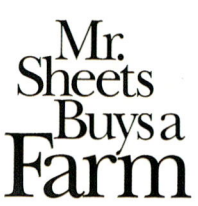

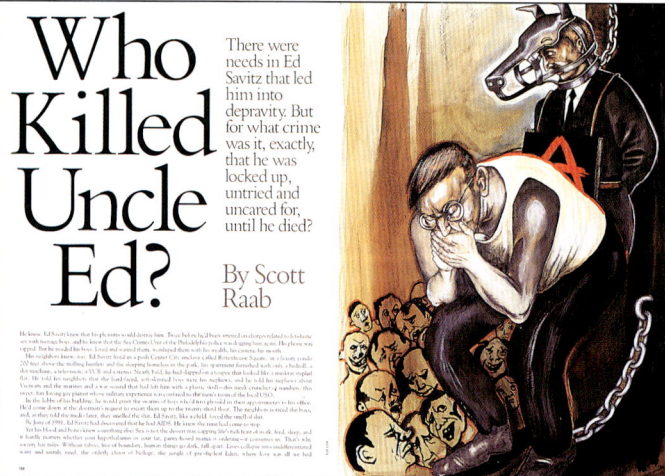

PUBLICATION   GQ
AWARD   Merit
CREATIVE DIRECTOR Robert Priest
DESIGNER   Robert Priest
ILLUSTRATOR   Sue Coe
PUBLISHER   The Condé Nast Publications Inc.
CATEGORY   Illustration/Single Page or Spread
DATE   June 1993

PUBLICATION   Omni
AWARD   Merit
ART DIRECTOR   Dwayne Flinchum
DESIGNER   Suzette Ruys
ILLUSTRATOR   Joel Peter Johnson
PUBLISHER   General Media Publishing
CATEGORY   Illustration/Single Page or Spread
DATE   May 1993

PUBLICATION   Men's Journal
AWARD   Merit
DESIGN DIRECTOR   Matthew Drace
ART DIRECTOR   Matthew Drace
DESIGNER   Giovanni C. Russo
ILLUSTRATOR   C.F. Payne
PUBLISHER   Wenner Media
CATEGORY   Illustration/Single Page or Spread
DATE   May/June 1993

PUBLICATION   Men's Journal
AWARD   Merit
DESIGN DIRECTOR   Giovanni C. Russo
ART DIRECTOR   Matthew Drace
DESIGNER   Giovanni C. Russo
ILLUSTRATOR   Brad Holland
PUBLISHER   Wenner Media
CATEGORY   Illustration/Single Page or Spread
DATE   March/April 1993

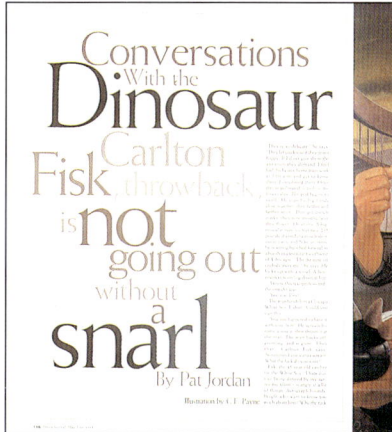
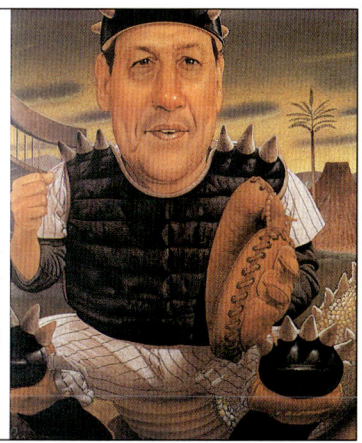

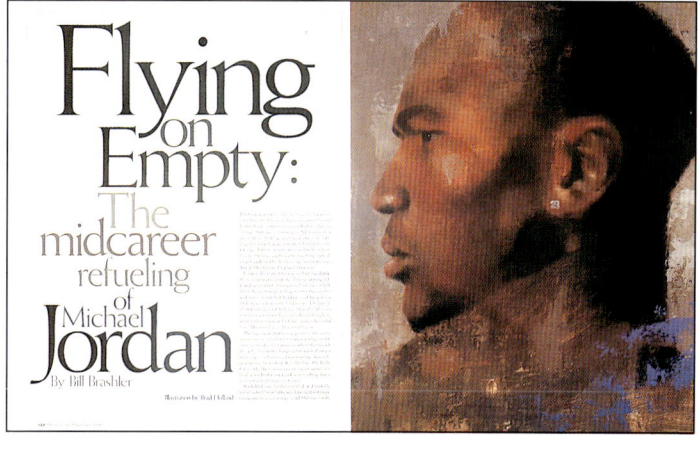

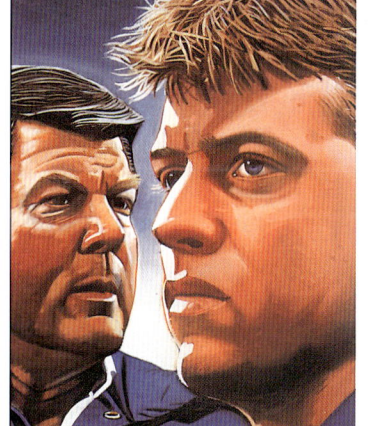
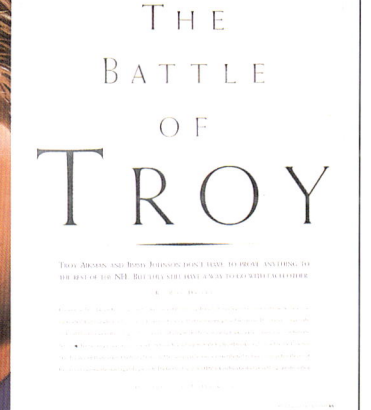

PUBLICATION   Men's Journal
AWARD   Merit
ART DIRECTOR   Matthew Drace
DESIGNER   Giovanni C. Russo
ILLUSTRATOR   Julian Allen
PUBLISHER   Wenner Media
CATEGORY   Illustration/Single Page or Spread
DATE   October 1993

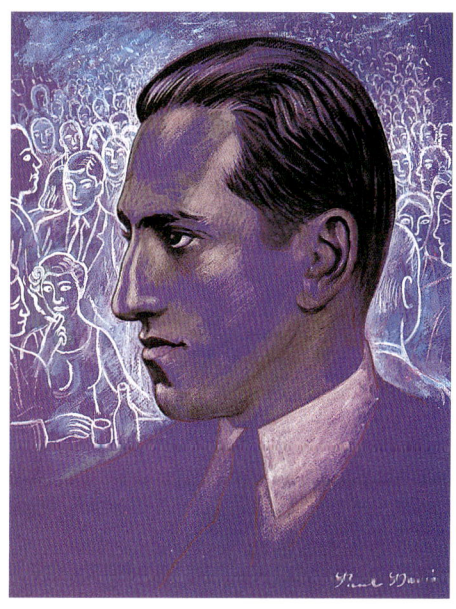

PUBLICATION   The New Yorker
AWARD   Merit
ART DIRECTOR   Christine Curry
ILLUSTRATOR   Paul Davis
PUBLISHER   The Condé Nast Publications Inc.
CATEGORY   Illustration/Single Page or Spread
DATE   May 31 1993

PUBLICATION	Playboy	**PUBLICATION**	Premiere
AWARD	Merit	**AWARD**	Merit
ART DIRECTOR	Tom Staebler	**ART DIRECTOR**	John Korpics
DESIGNER	Kerig Pope	**DESIGNER**	John Korpics
ILLUSTRATOR	Janet Wooley	**ILLUSTRATOR**	Gary Kelley
PUBLISHER	Playboy	**PUBLISHER**	K-III Magazines
CATEGORY	Illustration/Single Page or Spread	**CATEGORY**	Illustration/Single Page or Spread
DATE	October 1, 1993	**DATE**	May 1993

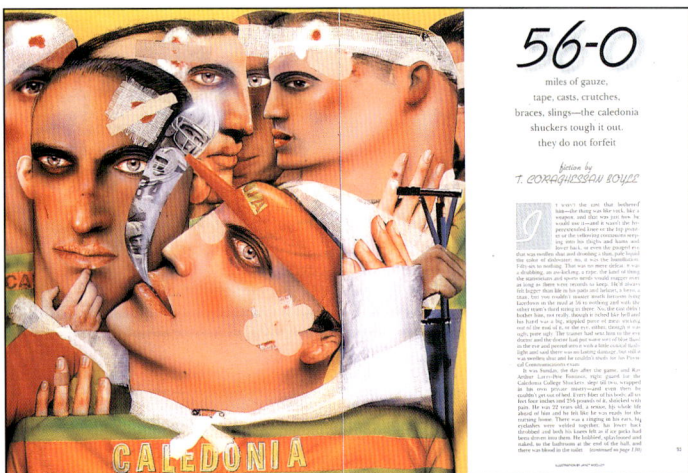

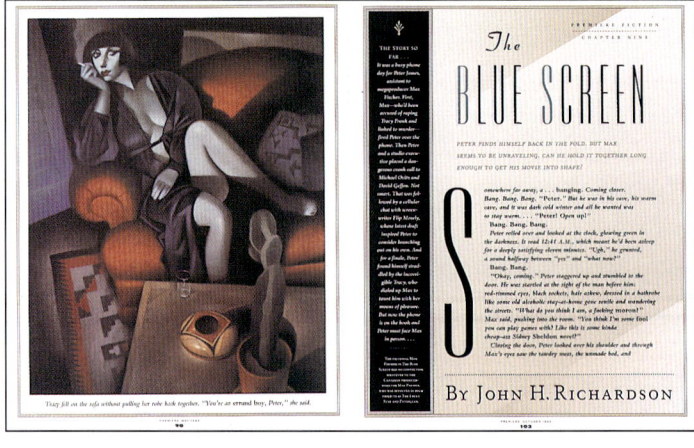

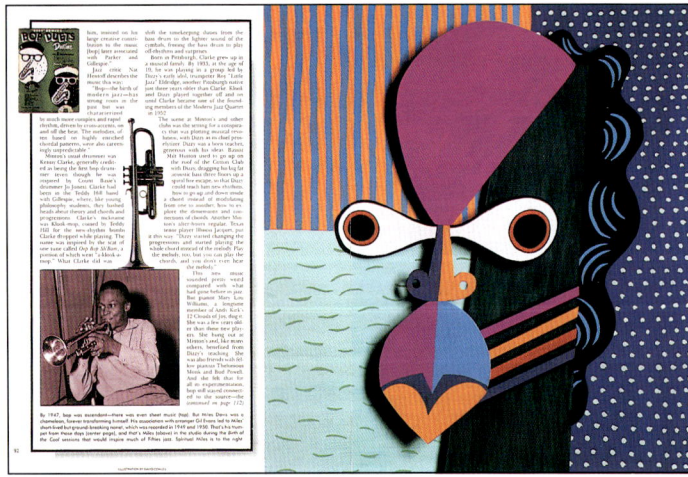

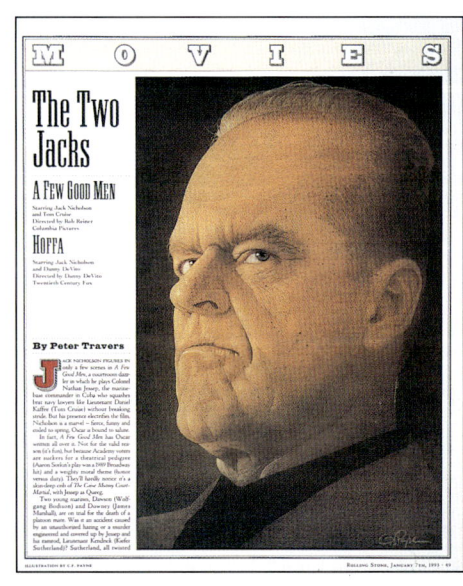

PUBLICATION	Playboy
AWARD	Merit
ART DIRECTOR	Tom Staebler
DESIGNER	Kristin Korjenek
ILLUSTRATOR	David Cowles
PUBLISHER	Playboy
CATEGORY	Illustration/Single Page or Spread
DATE	February 1, 1993

PUBLICATION	Rolling Stone
AWARD	Merit
ART DIRECTOR	Fred Woodward
ILLUSTRATOR	C.F. Payne
PUBLISHER	Wenner Media
CATEGORY	Illustration/Single Page or Spread
DATE	January 7, 1993

PUBLICATION Rolling Stone
AWARD Merit
ART DIRECTOR Fred Woodward
DESIGNERS Fred Woodward, Gail Anderson
ILLUSTRATOR Al Hirschfeld
PUBLISHER Wenner Media
CATEGORY Illustration/Single Page or Spread
DATE February 18, 1993

PUBLICATION Rolling Stone
AWARD Merit
ART DIRECTOR Fred Woodward
DESIGNER Catherine Gilmore-Barnes
ILLUSTRATOR Malcolm Tarlofsky
PUBLISHER Wenner Media
CATEGORY Illustration/Single Page or Spread
DATE April 15, 1993

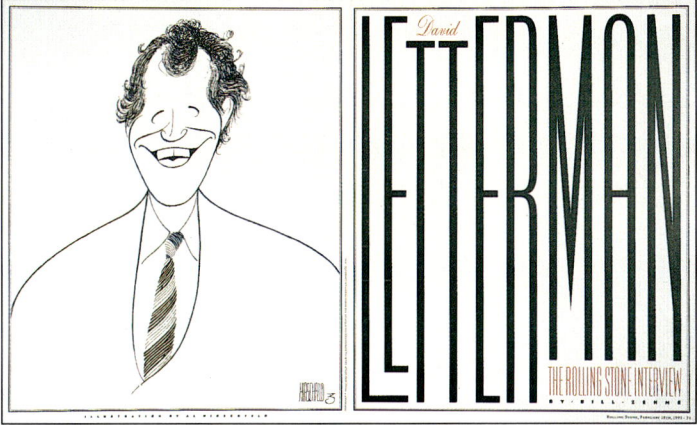

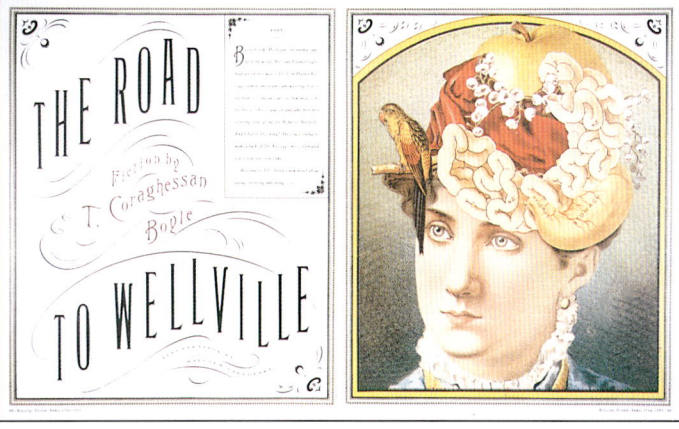

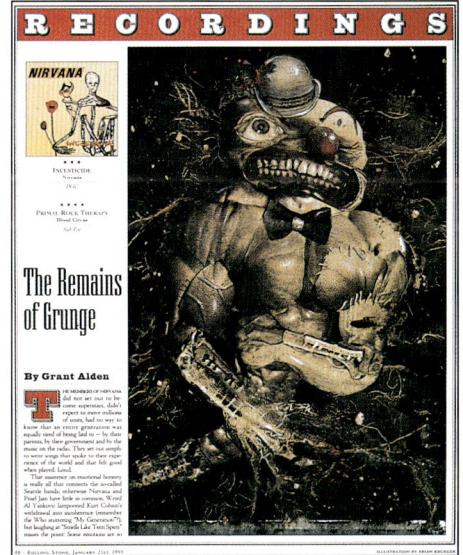

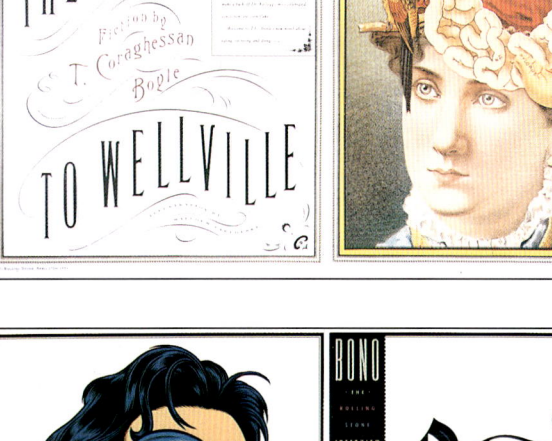

PUBLICATION Rolling Stone
AWARD Merit
ART DIRECTOR Fred Woodward
ILLUSTRATOR Brian Krueger
PUBLISHER Wenner Media
CATEGORY Illustration/Single Page or Spread
DATE January 21, 1993

PUBLICATION Rolling Stone
AWARD Merit
ART DIRECTOR Fred Woodward
DESIGNER Debra Bishop
ILLUSTRATOR Charles Burns
PUBLISHER Wenner Media
CATEGORY Illustration/Single Page or Spread
DATE March 4, 1993

PUBLICATION	San Francisco Focus
AWARD	Merit
ART DIRECTOR	Mark Ulriksen
DESIGNER	Andrew Danish
ILLUSTRATOR	Henrik Drescher
PUBLISHER	KQED, Inc.
CATEGORY	Illustration/Single Page or Spread
DATE	April 1993

PUBLICATION	Rolling Stone
AWARD	Merit
ART DIRECTOR	Fred Woodward
ILLUSTRATOR	Philip Burke
PUBLISHER	Wenner Media
CATEGORY	Illustration/Single Page or Spread
DATE	July 8-22, 1993

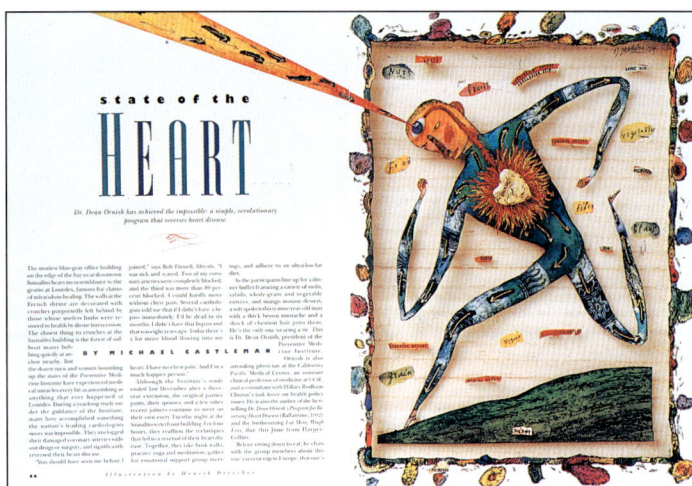

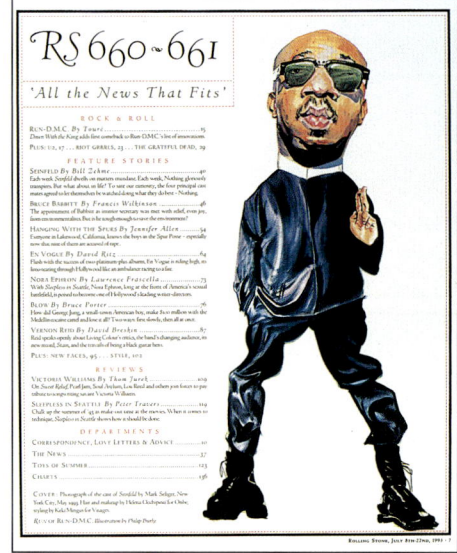

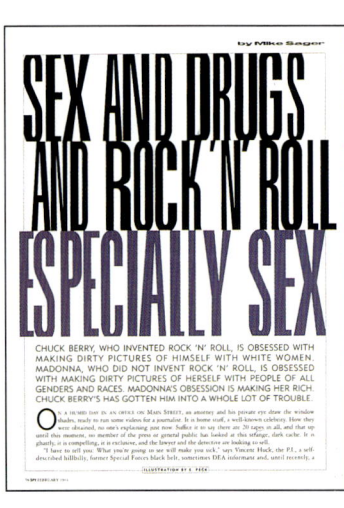

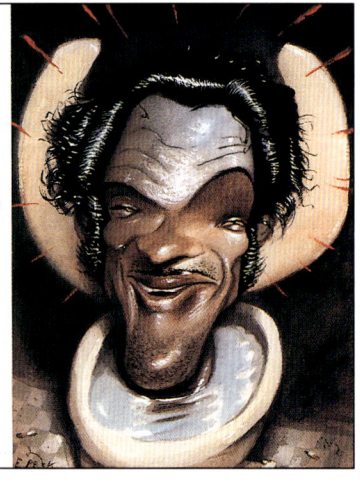

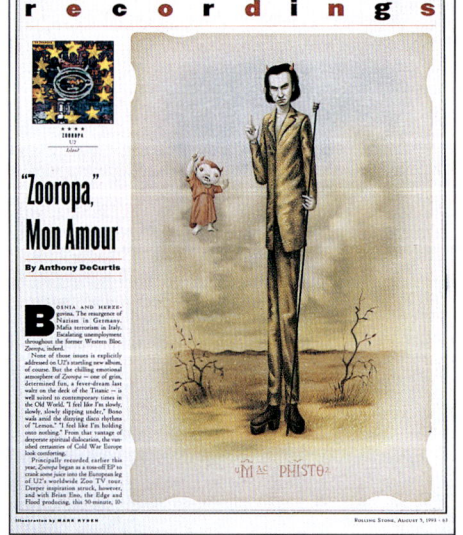

PUBLICATION	Spy
AWARD	Merit
ART DIRECTOR	Christiaan Kuypers
DESIGNERS	Christiaan Kuypers, Daniel Carter
ILLUSTRATOR	Everett Peck
PUBLISHER	Spy Corporation
CATEGORY	Illustration/Single Page or Spread
DATE	February 1993

PUBLICATION	Rolling Stone
AWARD	Merit
ART DIRECTOR	Fred Woodward
ILLUSTRATOR	Mark Ryden
PUBLISHER	Wenner Media
CATEGORY	Illustration/Single Page or Spread
DATE	August 5, 1993

PUBLICATION	Time
AWARD	Merit
ART DIRECTOR	Rudolph C. Hoglund
DESIGNER	Kenneth Smith
ILLUSTRATOR	Hanoch Piven
PUBLISHER	Time Inc.
CATEGORY	Illustration/Single Page or Spread
DATE	October 11, 1993

PUBLICATION	Time
AWARD	Merit
ART DIRECTOR	Rudolph C. Hoglund
DESIGNER	Betsy Brecht
ILLUSTRATOR	Mark Fredrickson
PUBLISHER	Time Inc.
CATEGORY	Illustration/Single Page or Spread
DATE	July 12, 1993

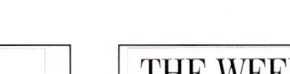

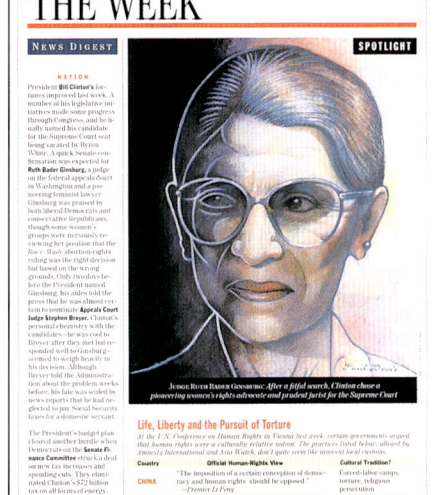

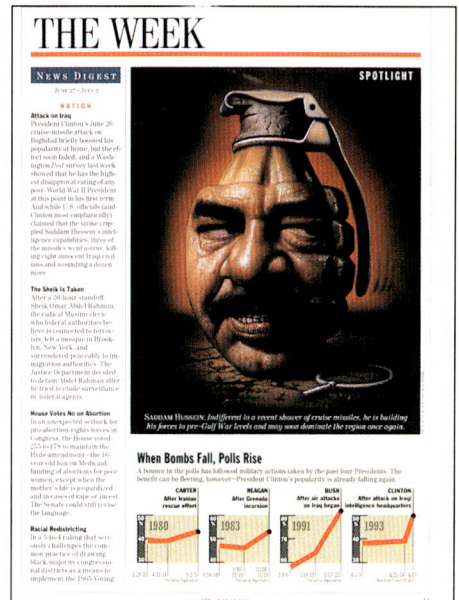

PUBLICATION	Time
AWARD	Merit
ART DIRECTOR	Rudolph C. Hoglund
DESIGNER	Kenneth Smith
ILLUSTRATOR	Paul Davis
PUBLISHER	Time Inc.
CATEGORY	Illustration/Single Page or Spread
DATE	June 28, 1993

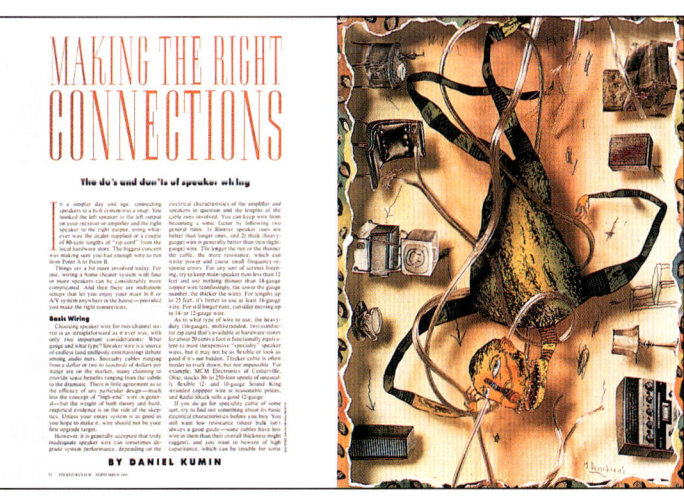

PUBLICATION	Stereo Review
AWARD	Merit
DESIGN DIRECTOR	Sue Llewellyn
DESIGNER	Mindy Oswald
ILLUSTRATOR	Henrik Drescher
PUBLISHER	Hachette Filipacchi Magazines, Inc.
CATEGORY	Illustration/Single Page or Spread
DATE	September 1993

PUBLICATION   Time International
AWARD   Merit
ART DIRECTOR   Rudolph C. Hoglund
DESIGNER   Kenneth Smith
ILLUSTRATOR   Andrea Ventura
PUBLISHER   Time Inc.
CATEGORY   Illustration/Single Page or Spread
DATE   May 31, 1993

PUBLICATION   Time
AWARD   Merit
ART DIRECTOR   Rudolph C. Hoglund
DESIGNER   Kenneth Smith
ILLUSTRATOR   Philip Burke
PUBLISHER   Time Inc.
CATEGORY   Illustration/Single Page or Spread
DATE   November 29, 1993

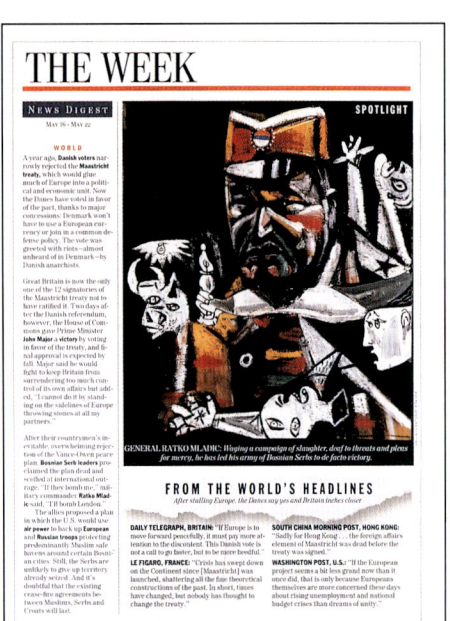

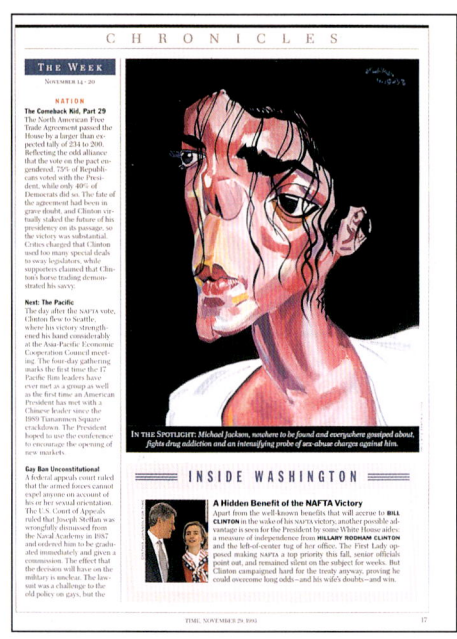

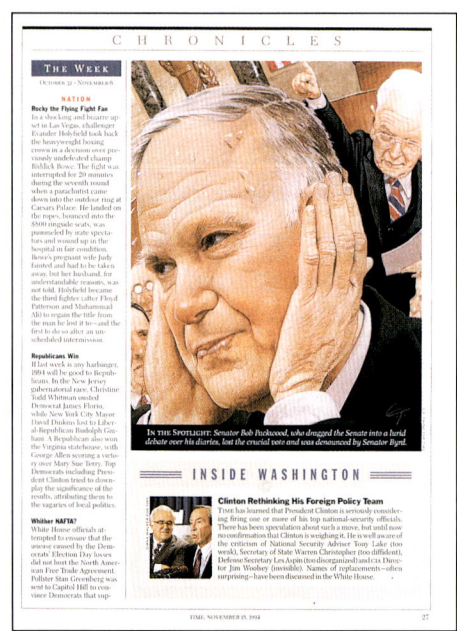

PUBLICATION   Time
AWARD   Merit
ART DIRECTOR   Rudolph C. Hoglund
DESIGNER   Kenneth Smith
ILLUSTRATOR   C.F. Payne
PUBLISHER   Time Inc.
CATEGORY   Illustration/Single Page or Spread
DATE   November 15, 1993

PUBLICATION	Word Perfect
AWARD	Merit
DESIGN DIRECTOR	Ron Stucki
ART DIRECTOR	Don Lambson
DESIGNER	Don Lambson
ILLUSTRATOR	Janet Wooley
PUBLISHER	Word Perfect Corporation
CATEGORY	Illustration/Single Page or Spread
DATE	May 1993

PUBLICATION	Yankee
AWARD	Merit
ART DIRECTOR	J. Porter
ILLUSTRATOR	C.F. Payne
PUBLISHER	Yankee Publishing, Inc.
CATEGORY	Illustration/Single Page or Spread
DATE	February 1993

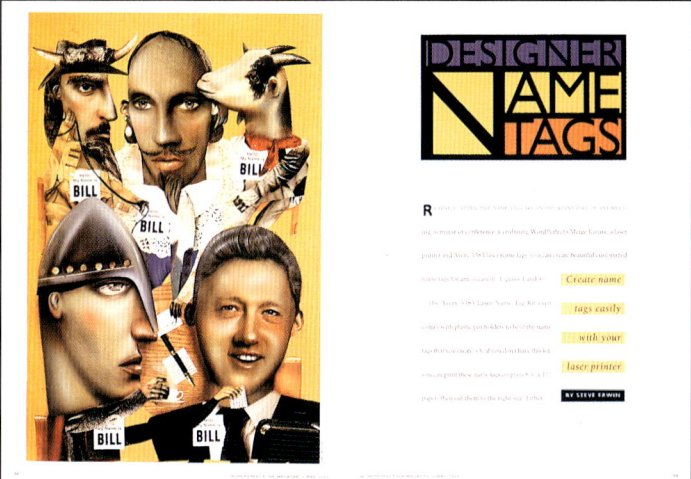

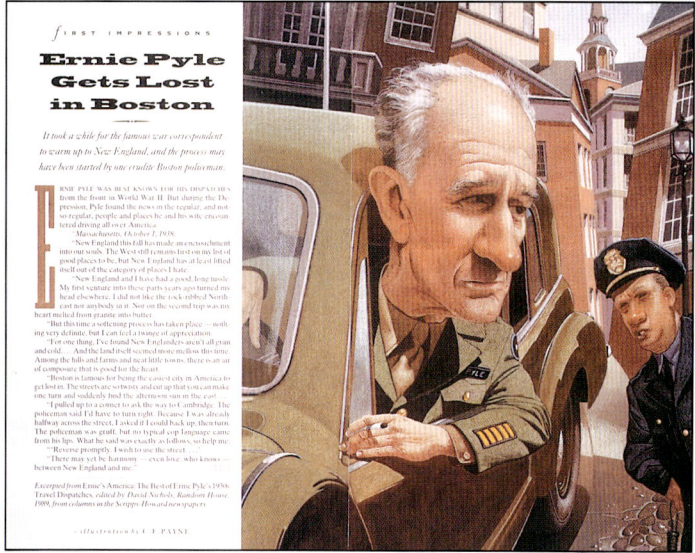

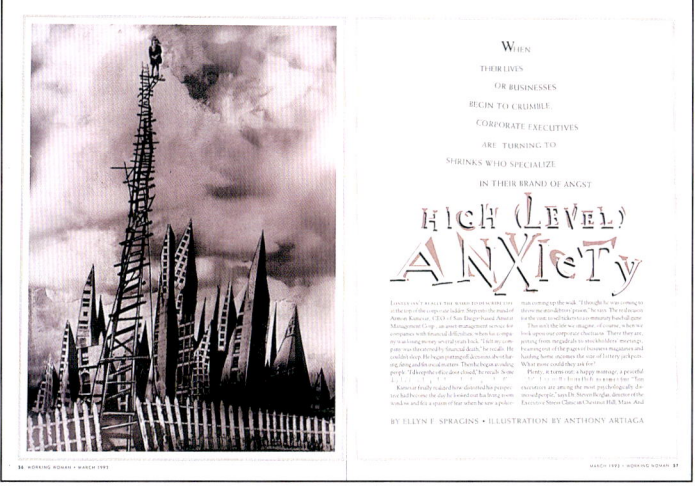

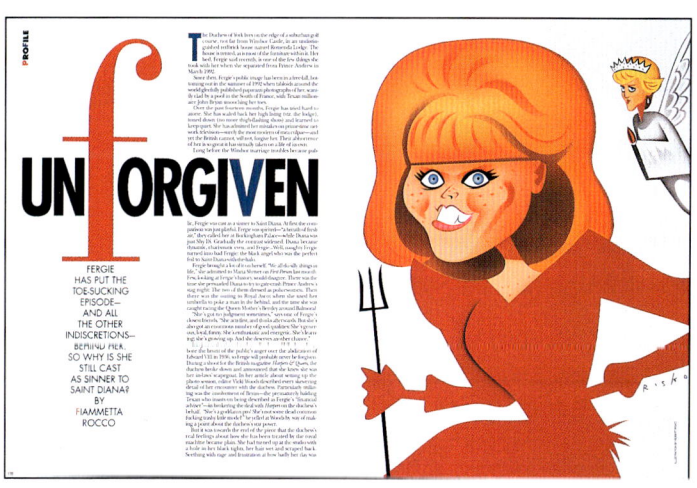

PUBLICATION	Working Woman
AWARD	Merit
ART DIRECTOR	Jolene Cuyler
DESIGNER	Gigi Fava
ILLUSTRATOR	Anthony Artiaca
PHOTO EDITOR	Clare Lissaman
PUBLISHER	Lang Communications
CATEGORY	Illustration/Single Page or Spread
DATE	March 1993

PUBLICATION	Elle
AWARD	Merit
ART DIRECTOR	Nora Sheehan
DESIGNER	Nora Sheehan
ILLUSTRATOR	Robert Risko
PUBLISHER	Hachette Filipacchi Magazines, Inc.
CATEGORY	Illustration/Single Page or Spread
DATE	November 1993

PUBLICATION	Smart Money
AWARD	Merit
ART DIRECTOR	Joseph Dizney
DESIGNER	Joseph Dizney
ILLUSTRATOR	Jeffrey Fisher
PUBLISHER	Dow Jones/Hearst Corporation
CATEGORY	Illustration/Single Page or Spread
DATE	April 1993

PUBLICATION	Profiles
AWARD	Merit
DESIGN DIRECTOR	John Sizing
ILLUSTRATOR	Gary Tanhauser
PUBLISHER	Marblehead Communications, Inc.
CATEGORY	Illustration/Single Page or Spread
DATE	April 1993

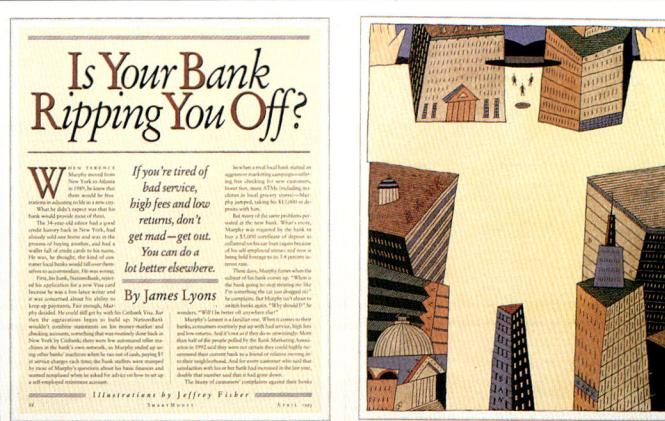

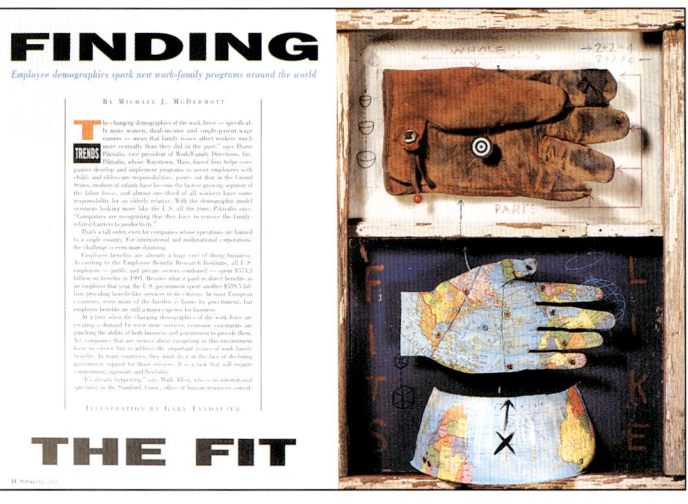

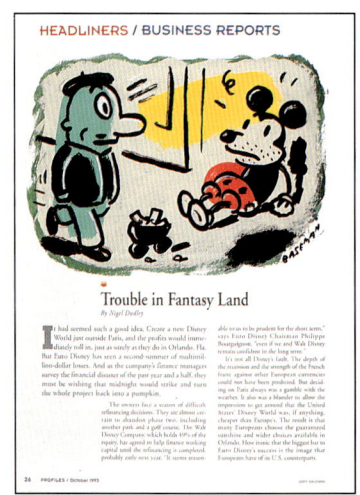

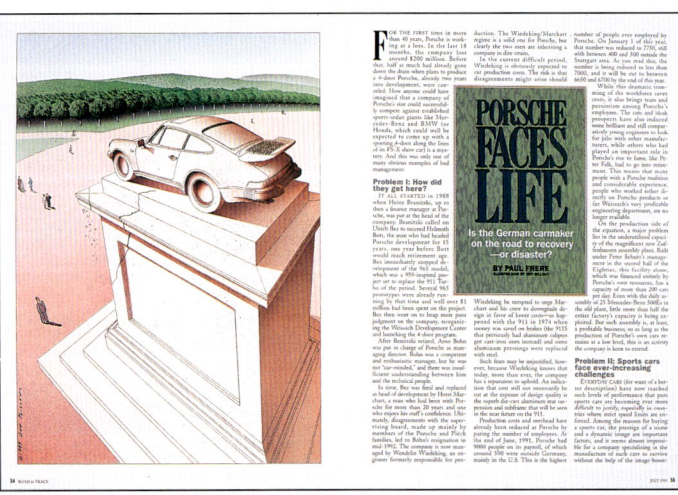

PUBLICATION	Profiles
AWARD	Merit
DESIGN DIRECTOR	John Sizing
ILLUSTRATOR	Gary Baseman
PUBLISHER	Marblehead Communications, Inc.
CATEGORY	Illustration/Single Page or Spread
DATE	October 1993

PUBLICATION	Road & Track
AWARD	Merit
ART DIRECTOR	Richard M. Baron
DESIGNER	Richard M. Baron
ILLUSTRATOR	Guy Billout
PUBLISHER	Hachette Filipacchi Magazines, Inc.
CATEGORY	Illustration/Single Page or Spread
DATE	July 1993

PUBLICATION	Overture
AWARD	Merit
ART DIRECTOR	Carla Frank
DESIGNER	Carla Frank
ILLUSTRATOR	Rip Kastaris
STUDIO	Carla Frank Design
CATEGORY	Illustration/Single Page or Spread
DATE	September/October 1993

PUBLICATION	Stanford Medicine
AWARD	Merit
ART DIRECTOR	David Armario
DESIGNER	David Armario
ILLUSTRATOR	Brian Cronin
PUBLISHER	Stanford University
STUDIO	Armario Design
CATEGORY	Illustration/Single Page or Spread
DATE	Summer 1993

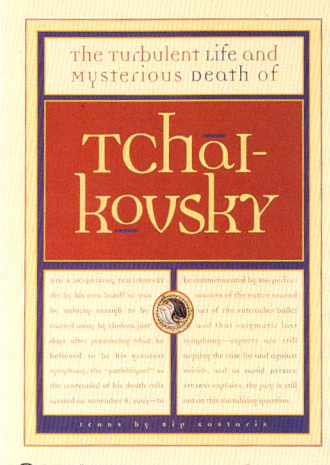
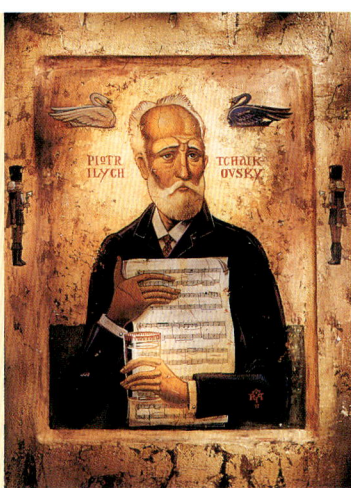

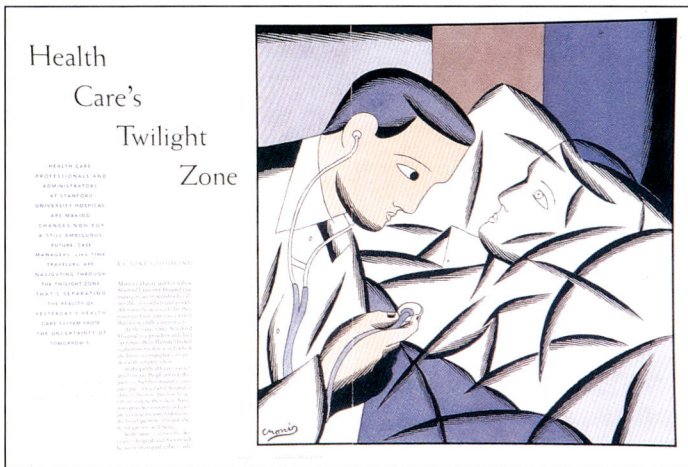

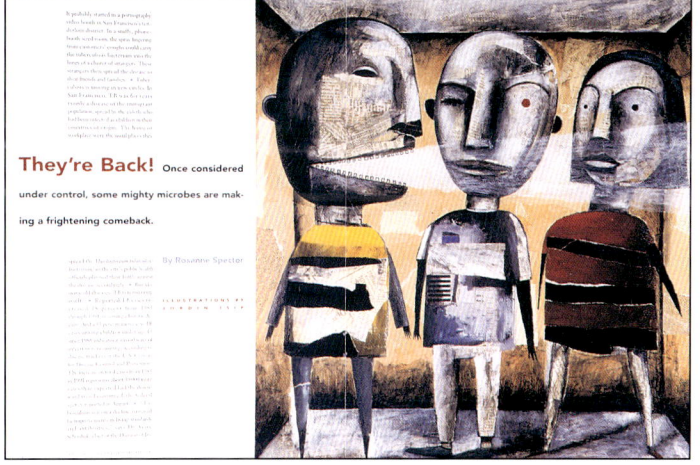

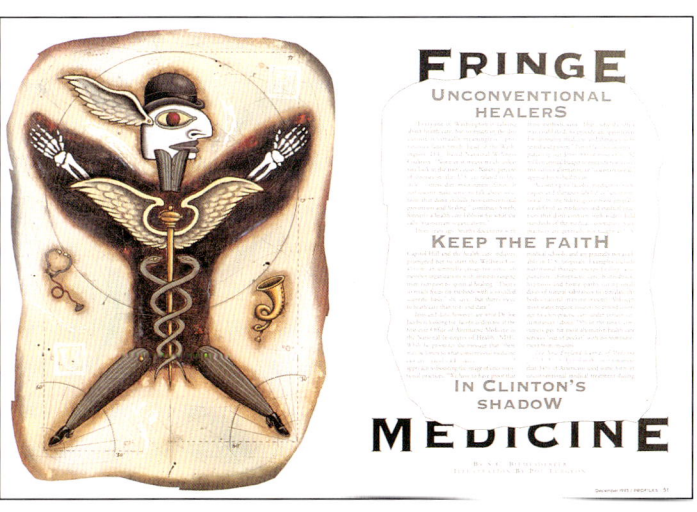

PUBLICATION	Stanford Medicine
AWARD	Merit
ART DIRECTOR	David Armario
DESIGNER	David Armario
ILLUSTRATOR	Jordin Isip
PUBLISHER	Stanford University
STUDIO	Armario Design
CATEGORY	Illustration/Single Page or Spread
DATE	Fall 1993

PUBLICATION	Profiles
AWARD	Merit
DESIGN DIRECTOR	John Sizing
ART DIRECTOR	Joe J. Polevy
ILLUSTRATOR	Pol Turgeon
PUBLISHER	Marblehead Communications, Inc.
CATEGORY	Illustration/Single Page or Spread
DATE	December 1993

PUBLICATION The Wall Street Journal Reports
AWARD Merit
DESIGN DIRECTOR Greg Leeds
DESIGNER Greg Leeds
ILLUSTRATOR Robert Neubecker
PUBLISHER Dow Jones & Co., Inc.
CATEGORY Illustration/Single Page or Spread
DATE October 15, 1993

PUBLICATION The Wall Street Journal Reports
AWARD Merit
DESIGN DIRECTOR Greg Leeds
ART DIRECTOR Nick Klein
DESIGNER Nick Klein
ILLUSTRATOR Brian Cronin
PUBLISHER Dow Jones & Co., Inc.
CATEGORY Illustration/Single Page or Spread
DATE November 15, 1993

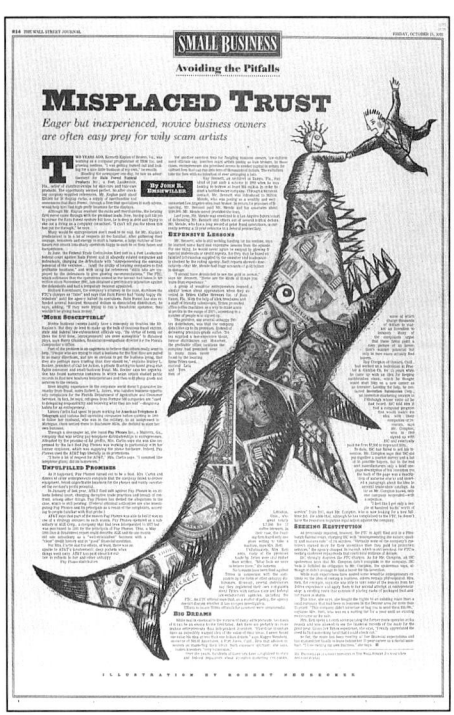

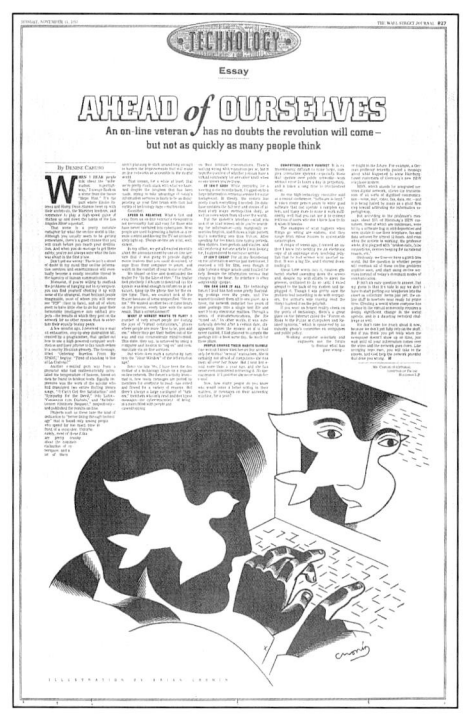

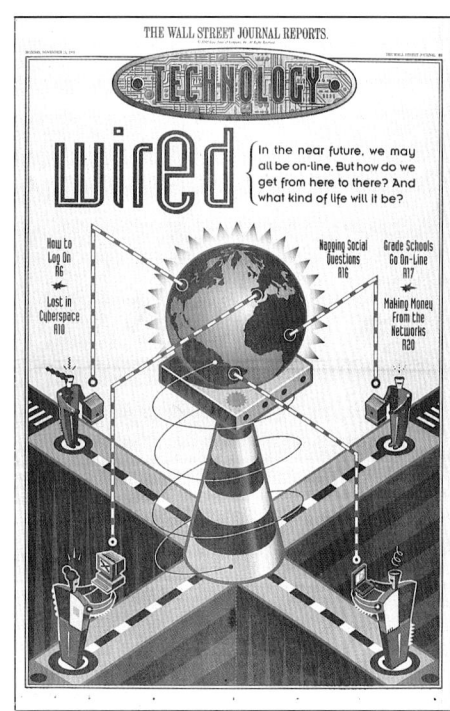

PUBLICATION The Wall Street Journal Reports
AWARD Merit
DESIGN DIRECTOR Greg Leeds
DESIGNER Greg Leeds
ILLUSTRATOR Steve Lyons
PUBLISHER Dow Jones & Co., Inc.
CATEGORY Illustration/Single Page or Spread
DATE November 15, 1993

PUBLICATION   The Village Voice
AWARD   Merit
DESIGN DIRECTOR   Robert Newman
ART DIRECTOR   Florian Bachleda
ILLUSTRATOR   Jordin Isip
PUBLISHER   VV Publishing Corporation
CATEGORY   Illustration/Single Page or Spread
DATE   July 20, 1993

PUBLICATION   The New York Times Magazine
AWARD   Merit
ART DIRECTOR   Janet Froelich
DESIGNER   Kathi Rota
ILLUSTRATOR   Anita Kunz
PUBLISHER   The New York Times
CATEGORY   Illustration/Single Page or Spread
DATE   May 23, 1993

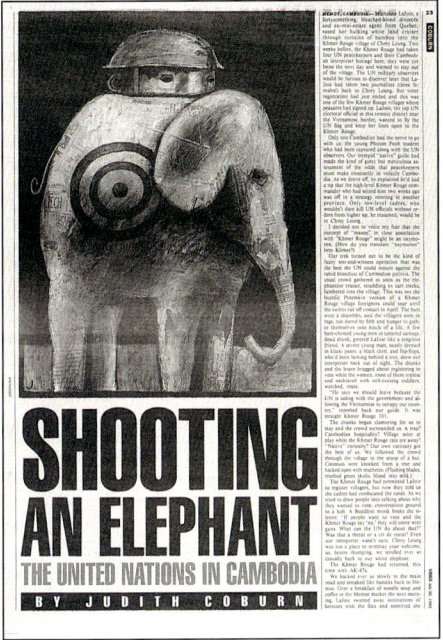

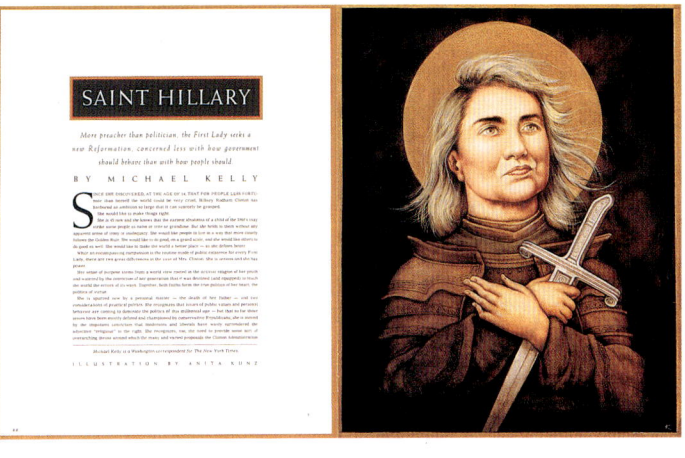

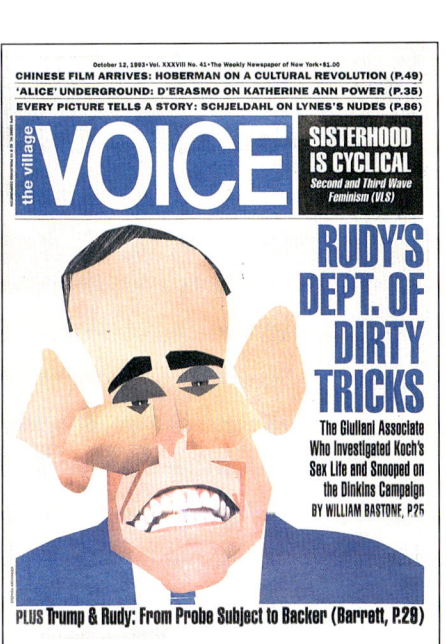

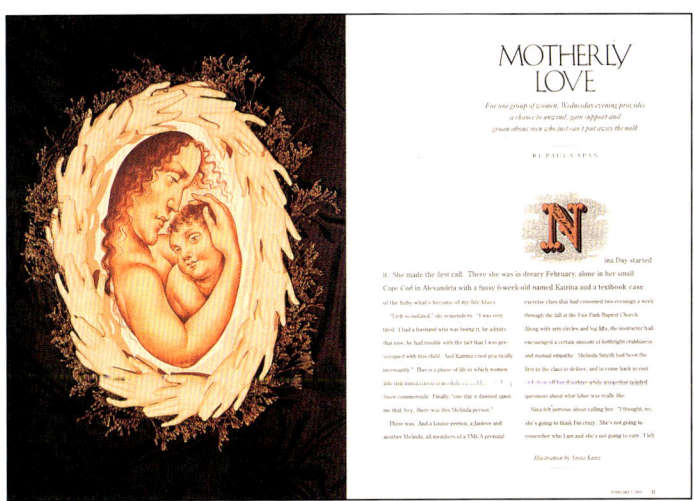

PUBLICATION   The Village Voice
AWARD   Merit
DESIGN DIRECTOR   Robert Newman
ART DIRECTORS   Florian Bachleda, Jennifer Gilman
ILLUSTRATOR   Stephen Kroninger
PUBLISHER   VV Publishing Corporation
CATEGORY   Illustration/Single Page or Spread
DATE   October 12, 1993

PUBLICATION   The Washington Post Magazine
AWARD   Merit
ART DIRECTOR   Richard Baker
DESIGNER   Richard Baker
ILLUSTRATOR   Anita Kunz
PUBLISHER   The Washington Post
CATEGORY   Illustration/Single Page or Spread
DATE   February 7, 1993

PUBLICATION   The Washington Post Magazine
AWARD   Merit
ART DIRECTOR   Kelly Doe
DESIGNER   Kelly Doe
ILLUSTRATOR   C.F. Payne
PUBLISHER   The Washington Post
CATEGORY   Illustration/Single Page or Spread
DATE   October 17, 1993

PUBLICATION   The Washington Post Magazine
AWARD   Merit
ART DIRECTOR   Richard Baker
DESIGNER   Richard Baker
ILLUSTRATOR   J. Otto Seibold
PUBLISHER   The Washington Post
CATEGORY   Illustration/Single Page or Spread
DATE   March 21, 1993

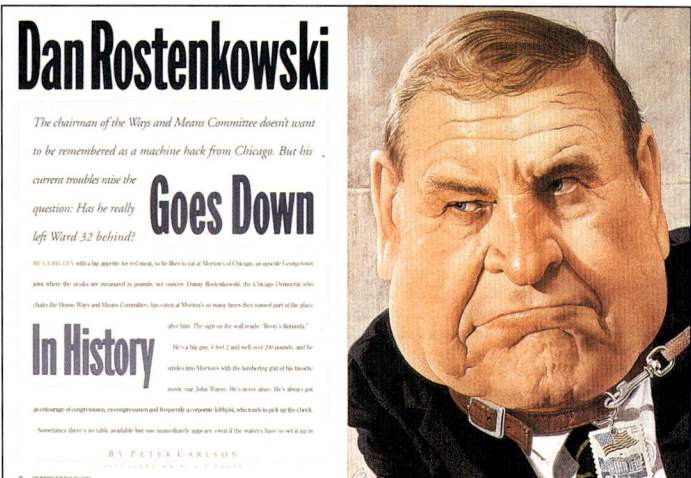

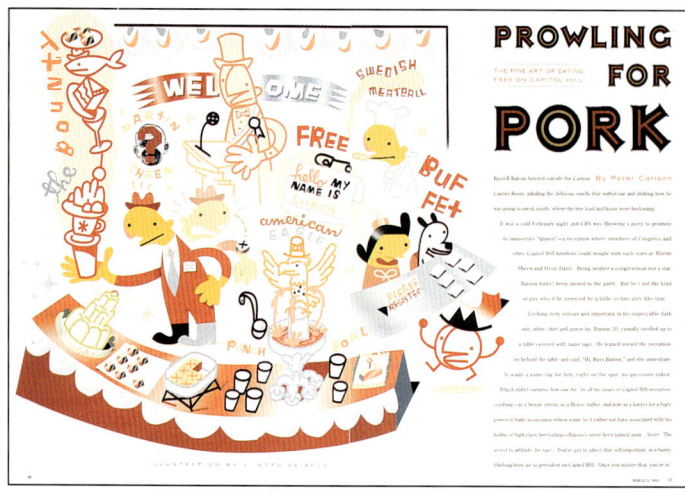

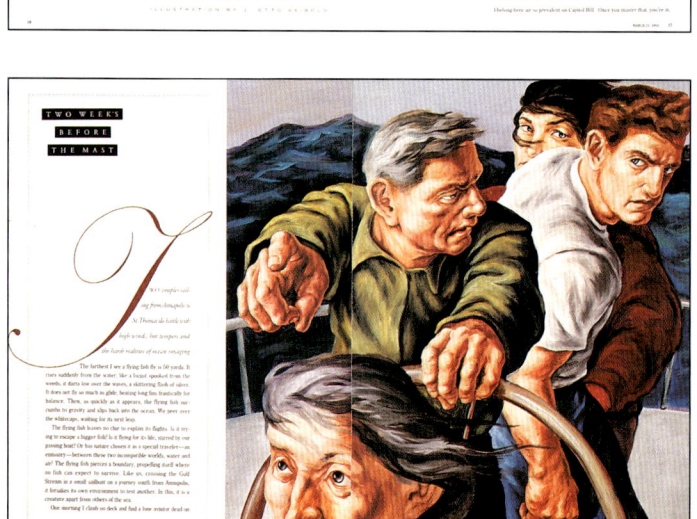

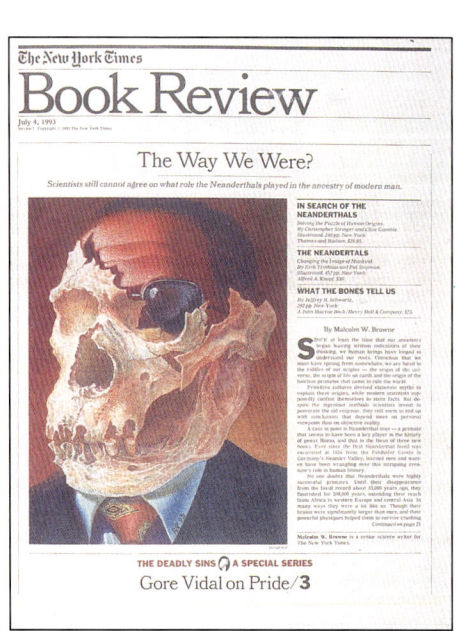

PUBLICATION   The Washington Post Magazine
AWARD   Merit
ART DIRECTOR   Kelly Doe
DESIGNER   Kelly Doe
ILLUSTRATOR   Owen Smith
PUBLISHER   The Washington Post
CATEGORY   Illustration/Single Page or Spread
DATE   May 16, 1993

PUBLICATION   The New York Times Book Review
AWARD   Merit
DESIGN DIRECTOR   Steven Heller
ILLUSTRATOR   Ray Bartkus
PUBLISHER   The New York Times
CATEGORY   Illustration/Single Page or Spread
DATE   July 4, 1993

PUBLICATION   The Philadelphia Inquirer Magazine
AWARD   Merit
DESIGN DIRECTOR   Jessica Helfand
ART DIRECTOR   Bert Fox
DESIGNER   Jessica Helfand
ILLUSTRATOR   Gregory Manchess
PUBLISHER   Philadelphia Inquirer
CATEGORY   Illustration/Single Page or Spread
DATE   June 13, 1993

PUBLICATION   The New York Times Book Review
AWARD   Merit
ART DIRECTOR   Steve Heller
ILLUSTRATOR   Henrik Drescher
PUBLISHER   The New York Times
CATEGORY   Illustration/Single Page or Spread
DATE   November 28, 1993

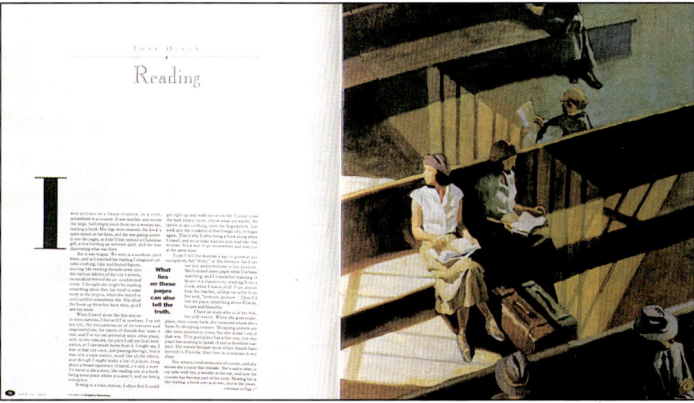

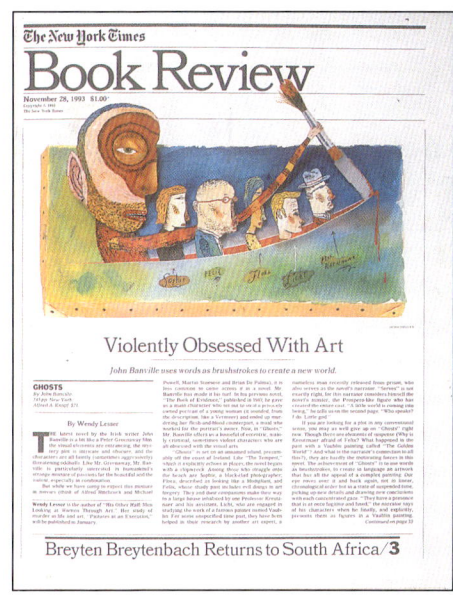

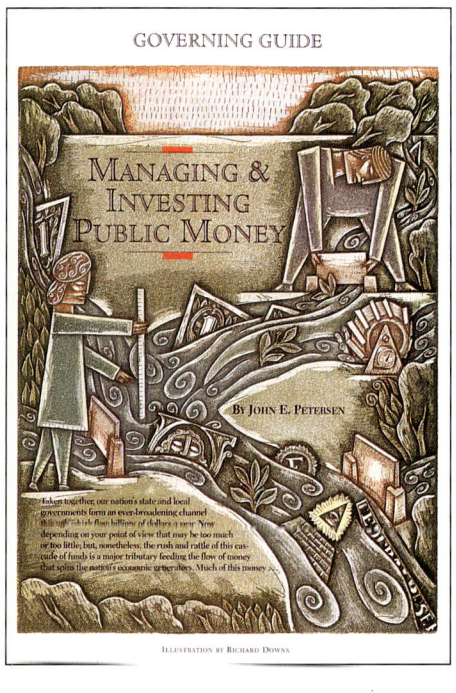

PUBLICATION   Governing
AWARD   Merit
ART DIRECTOR   Richard Steadham
DESIGNER   Richard Steadham
ILLUSTRATOR   Richard Downs
PUBLISHER   Congressional Quarterly
CATEGORY   Illustration/Single Page or Spread
DATE   March 1, 1993

PUBLICATION   In Touch
AWARD   Merit
DESIGN DIRECTOR   Bett McLean
ART DIRECTOR   Michael Miller
DESIGNER   Kimberly Hollis-Widmer
ILLUSTRATOR   Peter Sis
PUBLISHER   Whittle Communications
CATEGORY   Illustration/Single Page or Spread
DATE   Spring 1993

PUBLICATION	Macworld
AWARD	Merit
DESIGN DIRECTOR	Dennis McLeod
ART DIRECTOR	Joanne Hoffman
DESIGNER	Hae Yuon Kim
ILLUSTRATOR	Gary Tanhauser
PUBLISHER	Macworld Communications, Inc.
CATEGORY	Illustration/Single Page or Spread
DATE	February 1993

PUBLICATION	Macworld
AWARD	Merit
DESIGN DIRECTOR	Dennis McLeod
ART DIRECTOR	Kent Tayenaka
DESIGNER	Hae Yuon Kim
ILLUSTRATOR	Glen Mitsui
PUBLISHER	Macworld Communications, Inc.
CATEGORY	Illustration/Single Page or Spread
DATE	October 1993

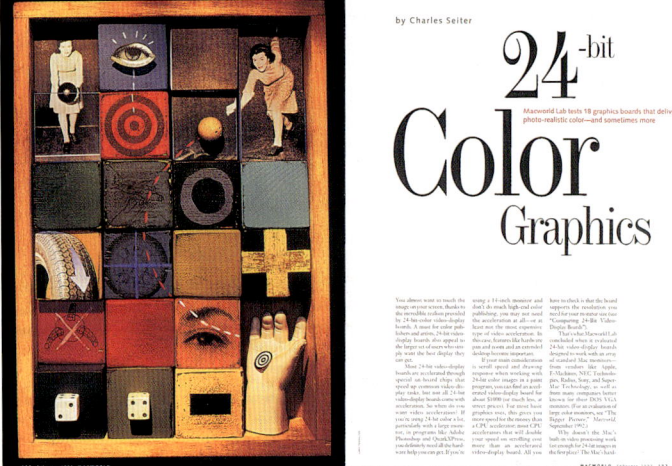

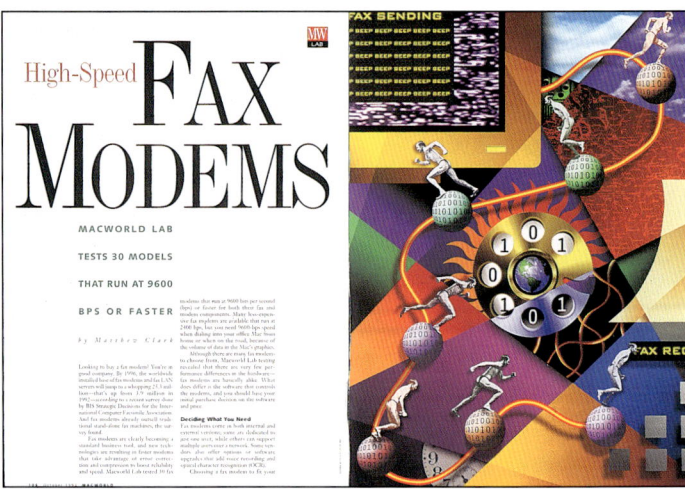

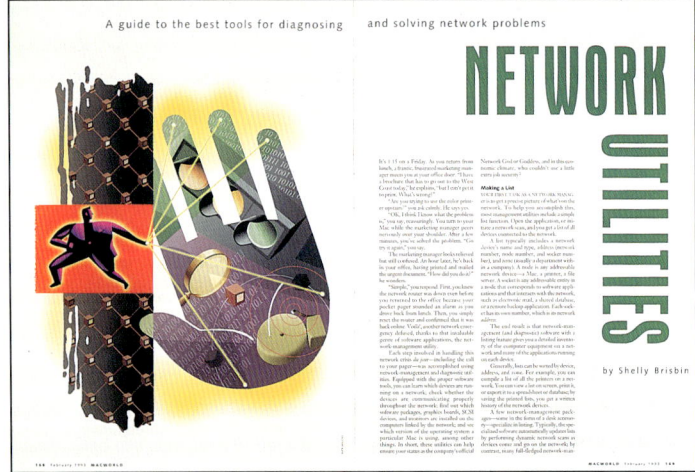

PUBLICATION	Macworld
AWARD	Merit
DESIGN DIRECTOR	Dennis McLeod
ART DIRECTOR	Joanne Hoffman
DESIGNER	Leslie Barton
ILLUSTRATOR	Mick Wiggins
PUBLISHER	Macworld Communications, Inc.
CATEGORY	Illustration/Single Page or Spread
DATE	February 1993

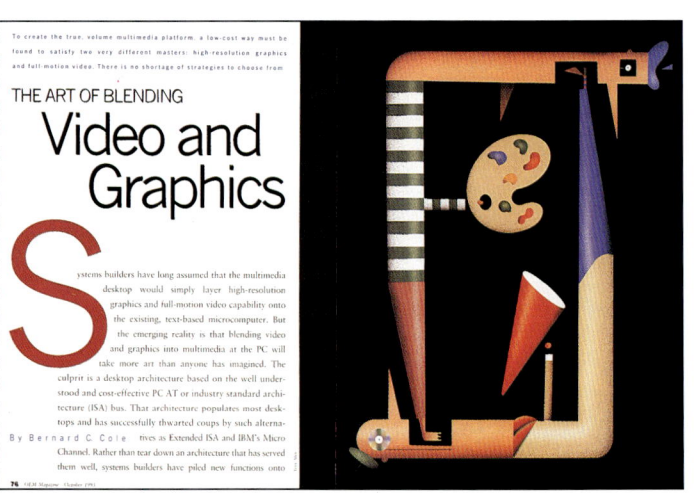

PUBLICATION	OEM Magazine
AWARD	Merit
ART DIRECTOR	Mira Ramji-Stein
DESIGNER	Mira Ramji-Stein
ILLUSTRATOR	Terry Allen
PUBLISHER	CMP Publications, Inc.
CATEGORY	Illustration/Single Page or Spread
DATE	October 1993

PUBLICATION	NewMedia
AWARD	Merit
ART DIRECTOR	Nancy Cutler
ILLUSTRATOR	Robert Pastrana
PUBLISHER	Hypermedia Communications
CATEGORY	Illustration/Single Page or Spread
DATE	September 1993

PUBLICATION	Sales & Marketing Management
AWARD	Merit
ART DIRECTOR	Charles Doherty
DESIGNER	Charles Doherty
ILLUSTRATOR	James Yang
PUBLISHER	Bill Communications
CATEGORY	Illustration/Single Page or Spread
DATE	January 1, 1993

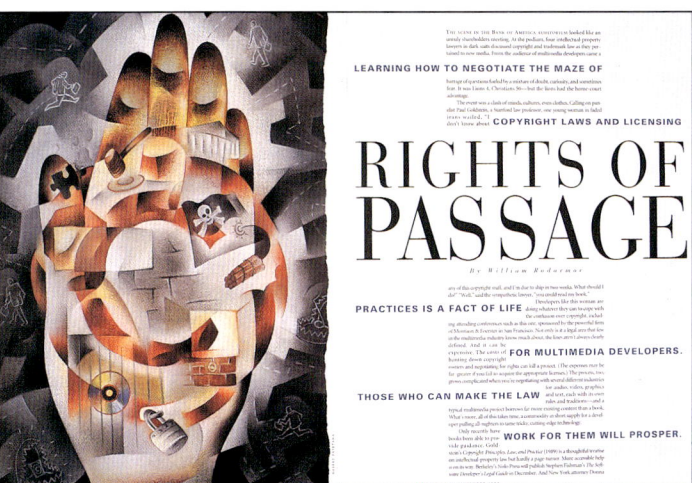

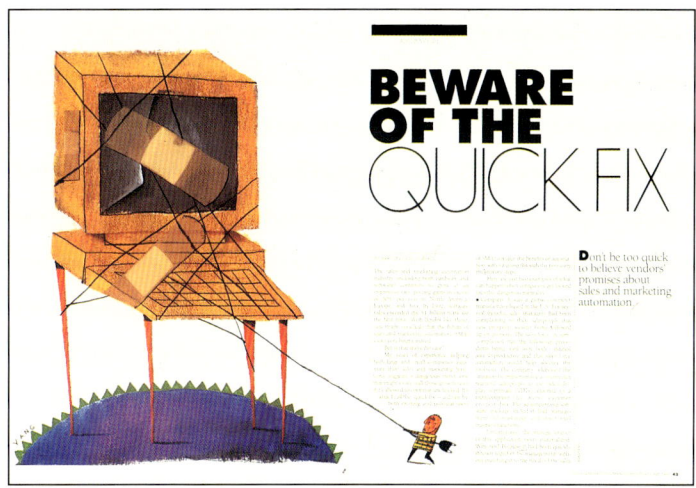

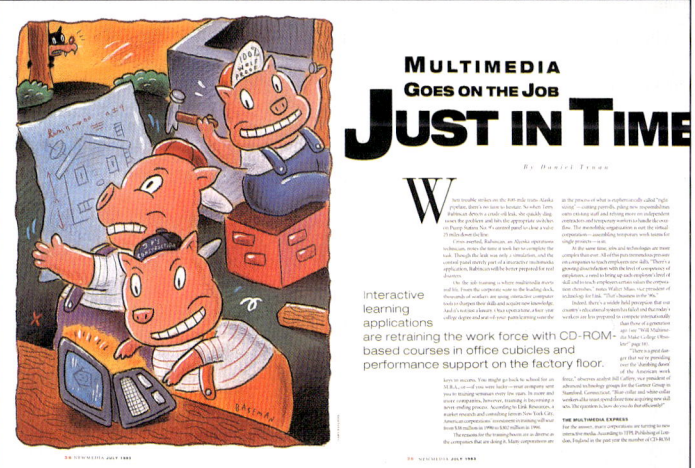

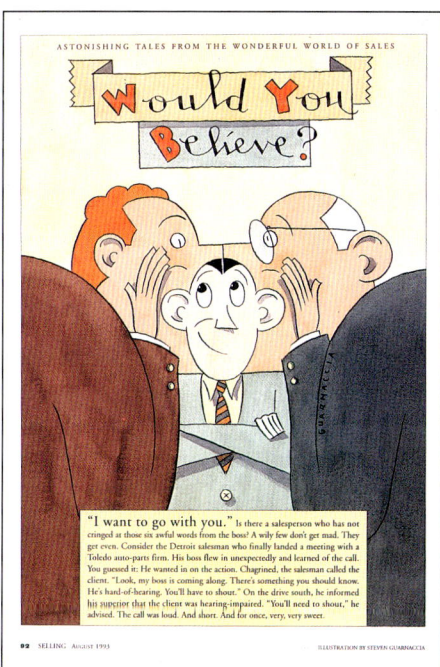

PUBLICATION	NewMedia
AWARD	Merit
ART DIRECTOR	Nancy Cutler
ILLUSTRATOR	Gary Baseman
PUBLISHER	Hypermedia Communications
CATEGORY	Illustration/Single Page or Spread
DATE	July 1993

PUBLICATION	Selling
AWARD	Merit
DESIGN DIRECTORS	Walter Bernard, Milton Glaser
ART DIRECTOR	Teresa Fernandes
DESIGNER	Teresa Fernandes
ILLUSTRATOR	Steven Guarnaccia
PUBLISHER	Capital Cities/ABC, Inc. Publishing Group
STUDIO	WBMG, Inc.
CATEGORY	Illustration/Single Page or Spread
DATE	August 1993

PUBLICATION	Discover
AWARD	Silver
ART DIRECTOR	David Armario
DESIGNERS	David Armario, James Lambertus
ILLUSTRATOR	Ralph Steadman
PUBLISHER	Disney Magazine Publishing, Inc.
CATEGORY	Illustration/Story
DATE	August 1993

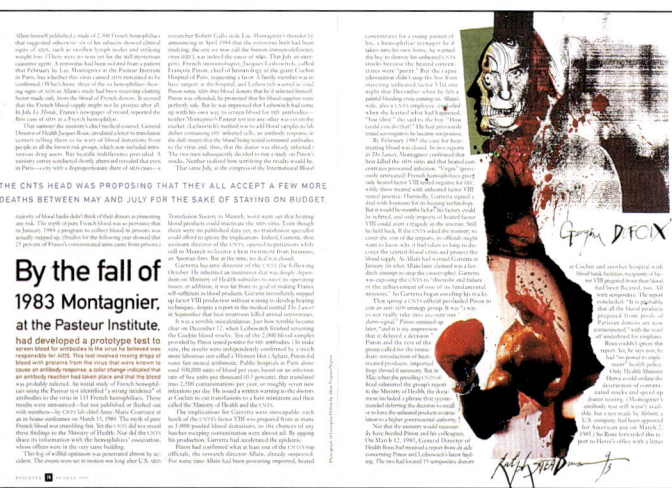

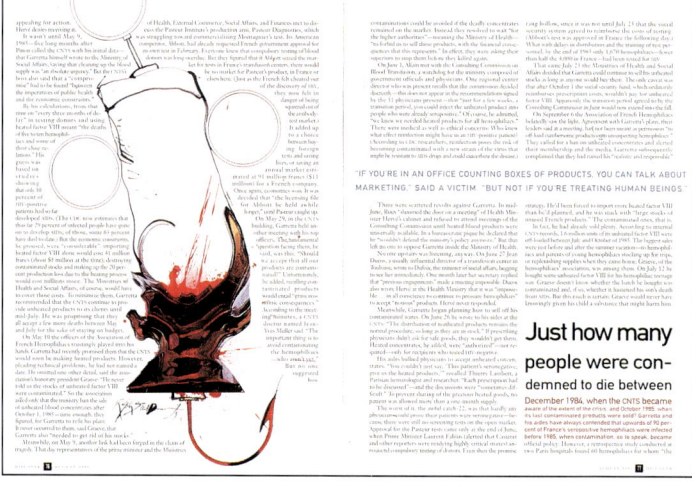

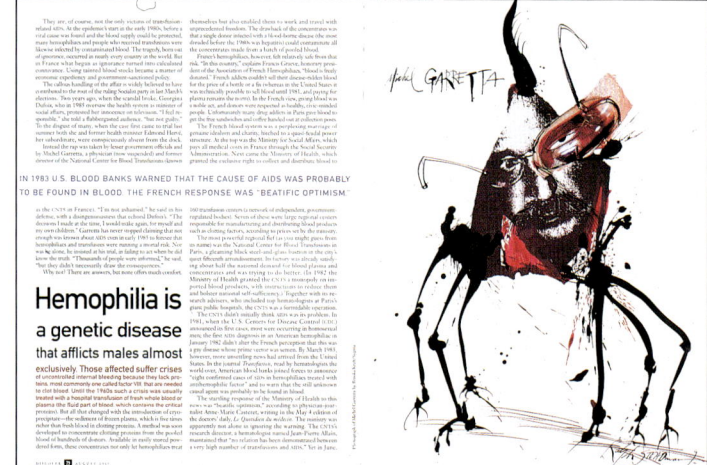

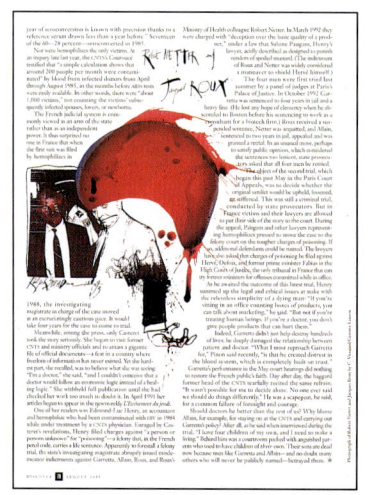

PUBLICATION   Time
AWARD   Silver
DESIGN DIRECTOR Arthur Hochstein
ART DIRECTOR   Rudolph Hoglund
DESIGNER   Paul Lussier
ILLUSTRATOR   Matt Mahurin
PUBLISHER   Time Inc.
CATEGORY   Illustration/Story
DATE   November 29, 1993

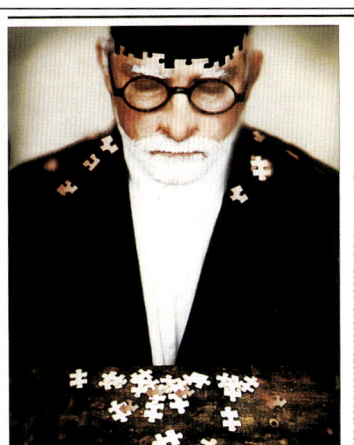

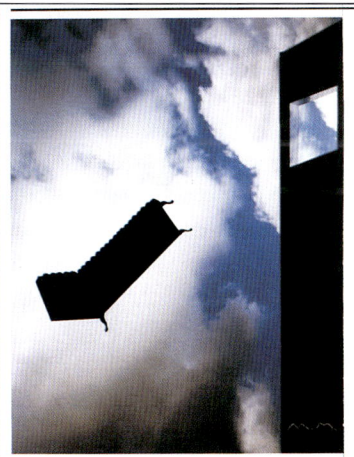

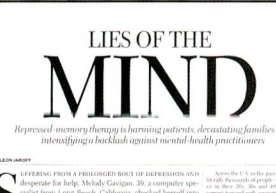

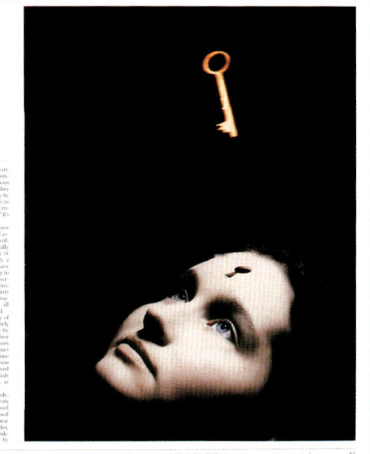

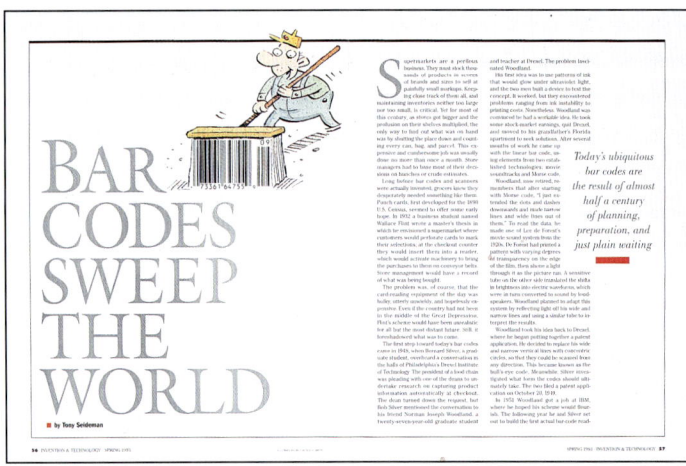

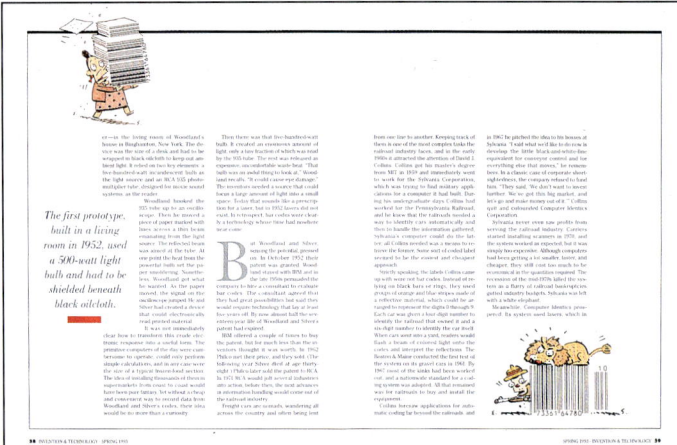

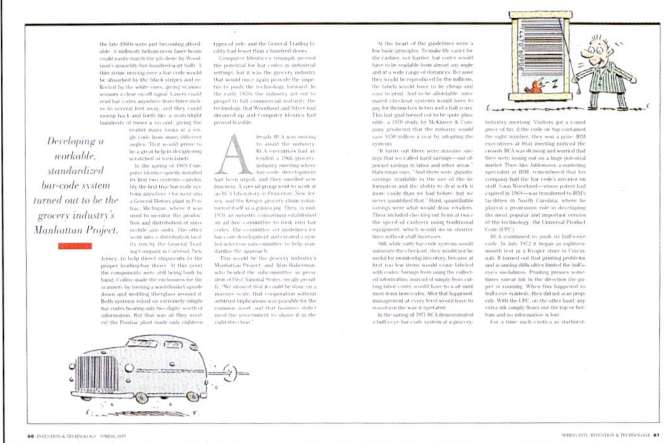

PUBLICATION	American Heritage of Invention & Technology
AWARD	Merit
ART DIRECTOR	Peter Morance
DESIGNER	Peter Morance
ILLUSTRATOR	Elwood H. Smith
PUBLISHER	American Heritage
CATEGORY	Illustration/Story
DATE	Spring 1993

PUBLICATION	Audacity
AWARD	Merit
ART DIRECTOR	Wylie Nash
DESIGNER	Wylie Nash
ILLUSTRATOR	Edward Sorel
PHOTO EDITOR	Catherine Calhoun
PUBLISHER	American Heritage
CATEGORY	Illustration/Story
DATE	Summer 1993

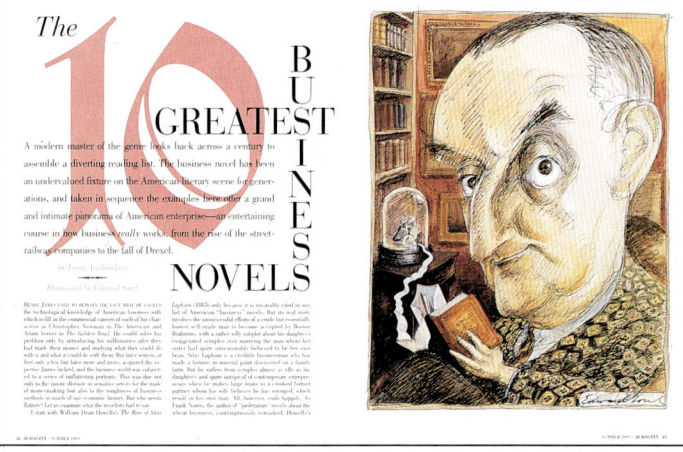

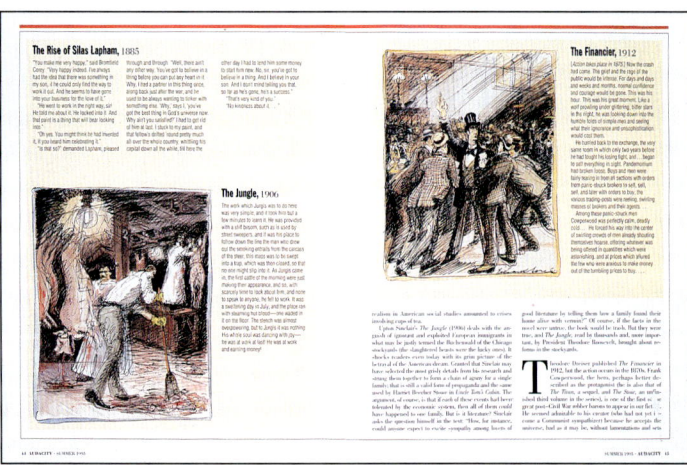

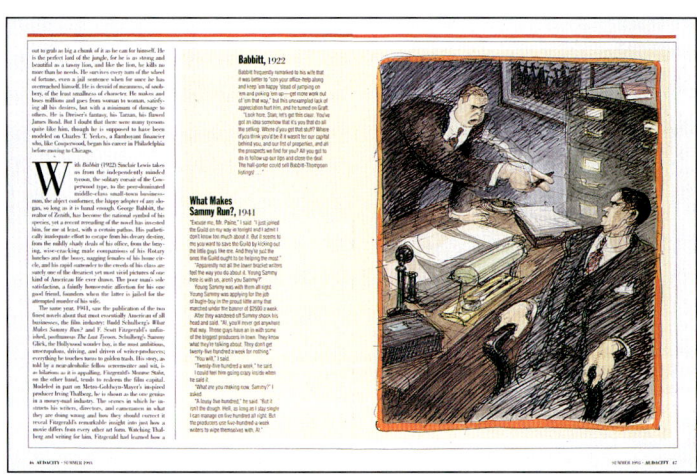

PUBLICATION	Discover
AWARD	Merit
ART DIRECTOR	David Armario
DESIGNERS	James Lambertus, David Armario
ILLUSTRATOR	Jonathon Rosen
PUBLISHER	Disney Magazine Publishing, Inc.
CATEGORY	Illustration/Story
DATE	February 1993

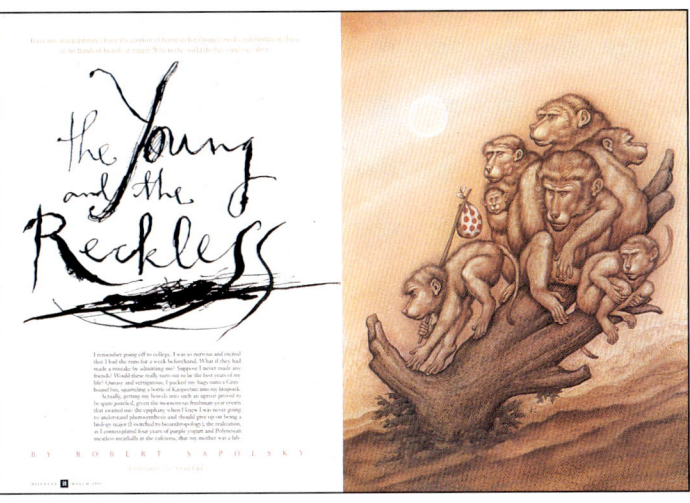

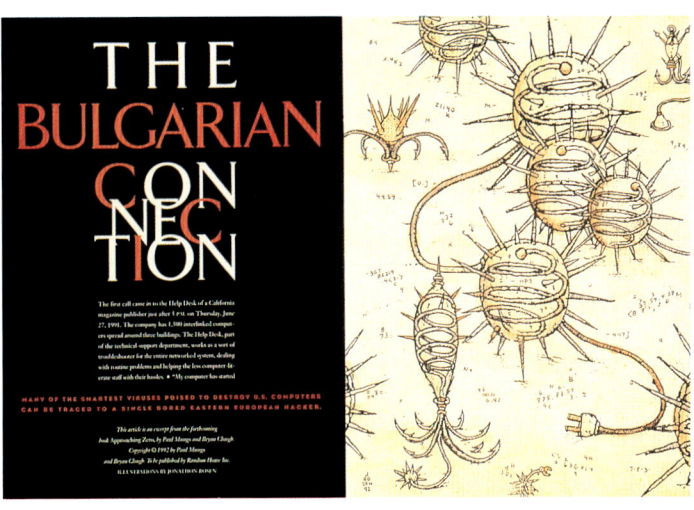

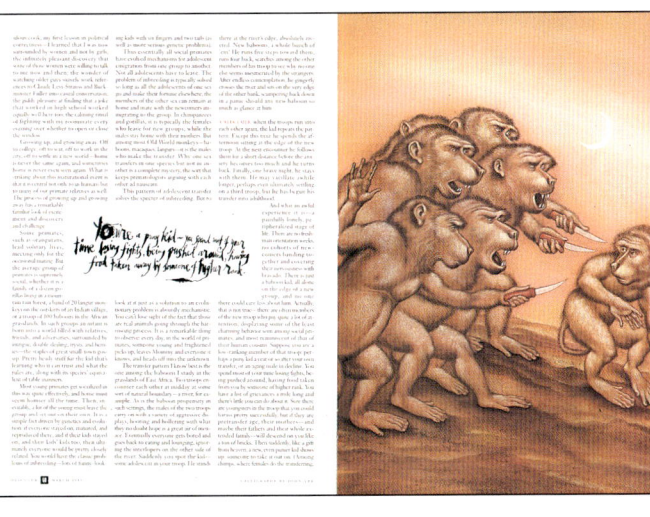

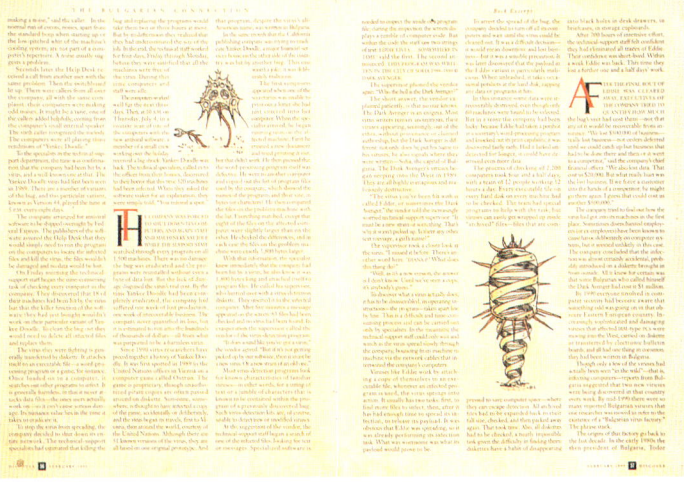

PUBLICATION	Discover
AWARD	Merit
ART DIRECTOR	David Armario
DESIGNER	David Armario
ILLUSTRATOR	Anita Kunz
PUBLISHER	Disney Magazine Publishing, Inc.
CATEGORY	Illustration/Story
DATE	March 1993

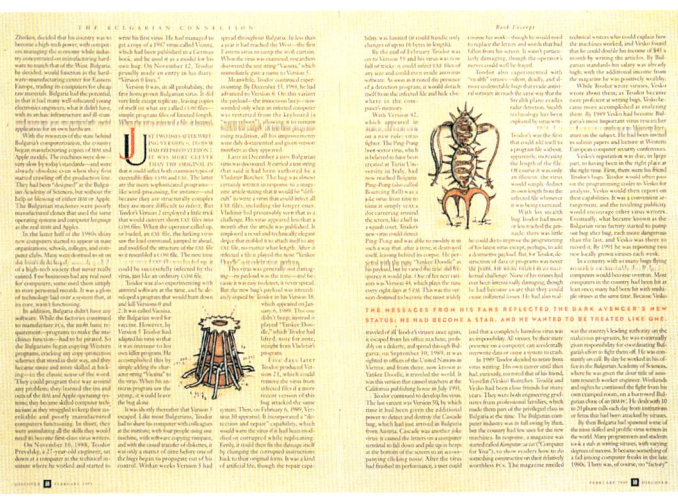

PUBLICATION	Elle Décor
AWARD	Merit
ART DIRECTOR	Jo Hay
DESIGNER	Jo Hay
ILLUSTRATORS	Andrew Zega, Bernd H. Dams
PHOTO EDITOR	Jodi Lahaye
PUBLISHER	Hachette Filipacchi Magazines, Inc.
CATEGORY	Illustration/Story
DATE	December 1993/January 1994

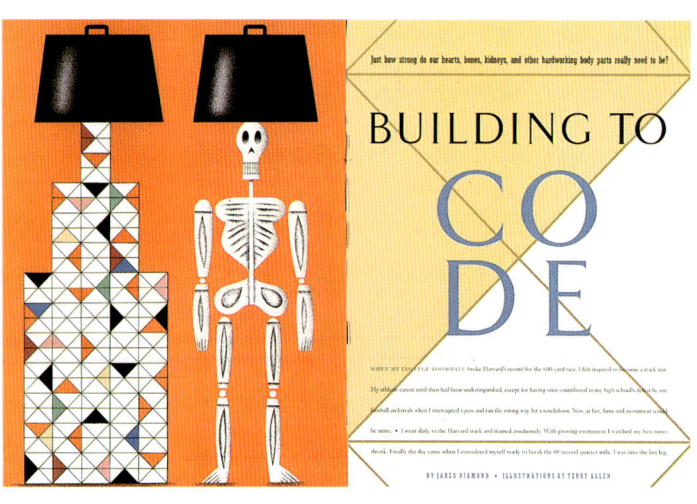

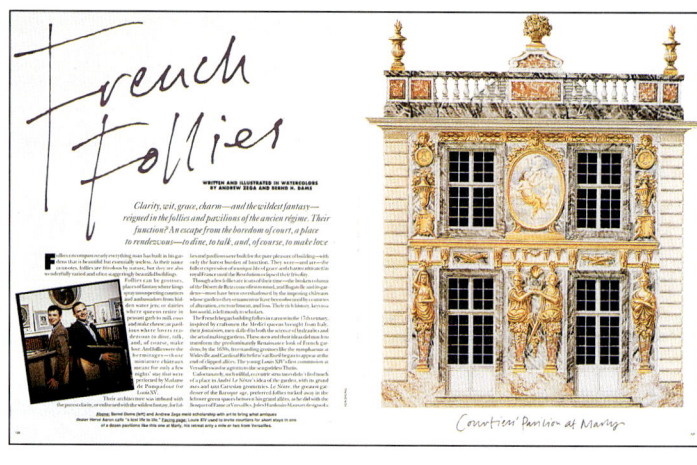

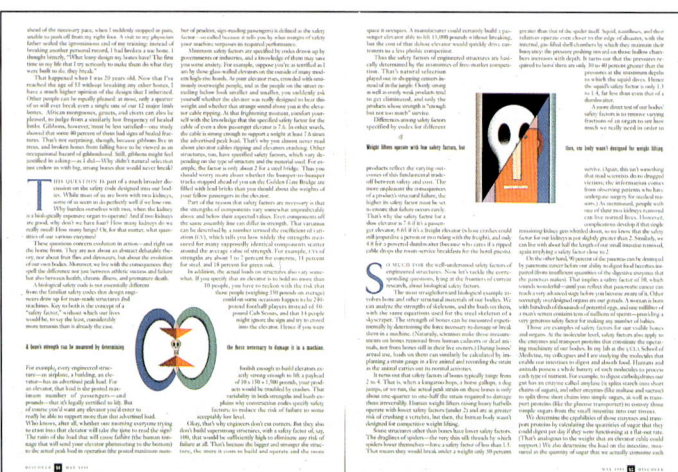

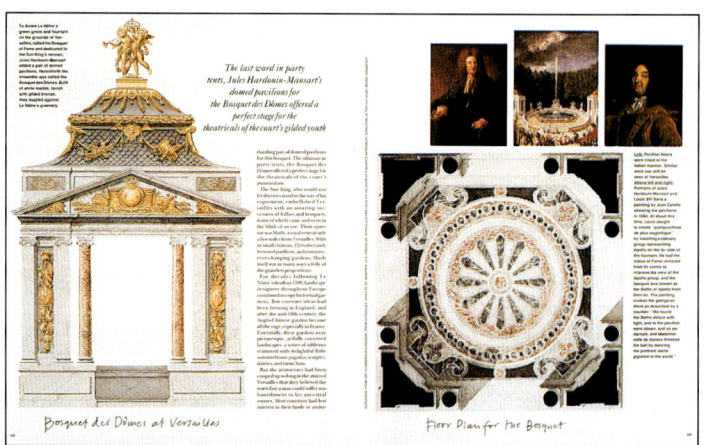

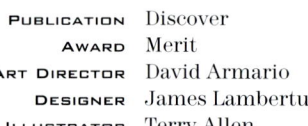

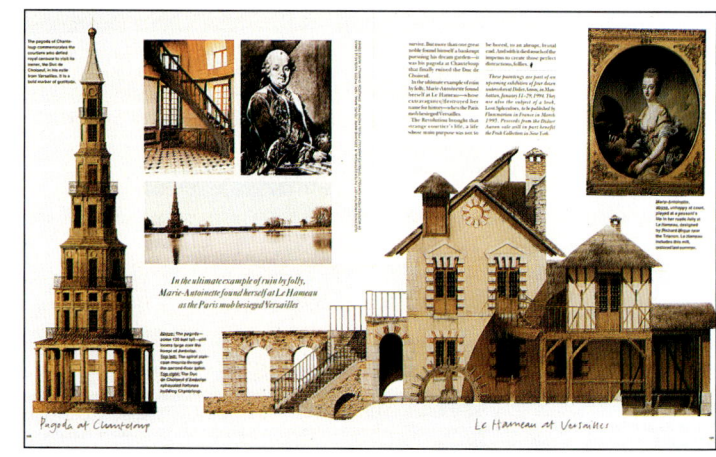

PUBLICATION	Discover
AWARD	Merit
ART DIRECTOR	David Armario
DESIGNER	James Lambertus
ILLUSTRATOR	Terry Allen
PUBLISHER	Disney Magazine Publishing, Inc.
CATEGORY	Illustration/Story
DATE	May 1993

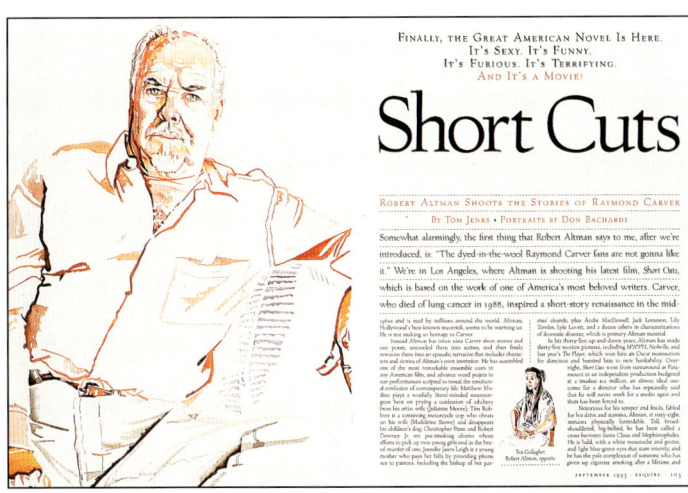

FINALLY, THE GREAT AMERICAN NOVEL IS HERE.
IT'S SEXY. IT'S FUNNY.
IT'S FURIOUS. IT'S TERRIFYING.
AND IT'S A MOVIE!

Short Cuts

ROBERT ALTMAN SHOOTS THE STORIES OF RAYMOND CARVER
BY TOM JENKS • PORTRAITS BY DON BACHARDY

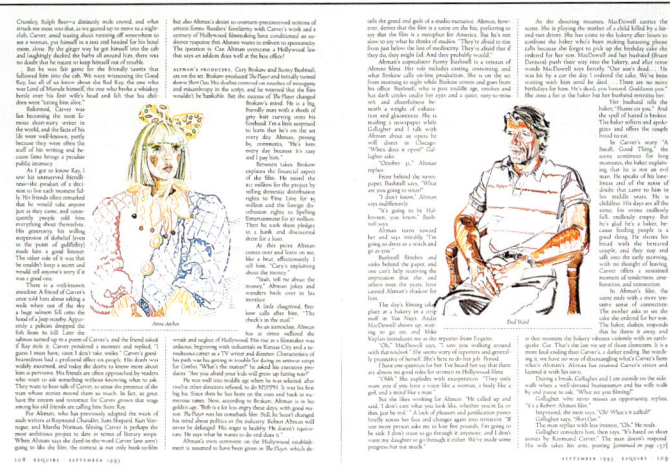

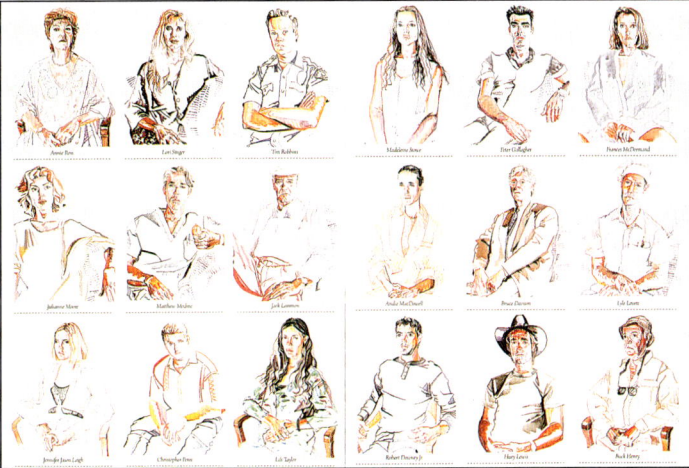

PUBLICATION Esquire
AWARD Merit
ART DIRECTOR Rhonda Rubinstein
DESIGNER David O'Connor
ILLUSTRATOR Don Bachardy
PUBLISHER The Hearst Corporation
CATEGORY Illustration/Story
DATE September 1993

PUBLICATION Family Life
AWARD Merit
ART DIRECTOR Don Morris
DESIGNERS James Reyman, Laura Eisman, Don Morris
ILLUSTRATORS Matt Mahurin, Gary Panter, Benoit
PHOTOGRAPHER Jeremy Wolff
PHOTO EDITOR Jane Clark
PUBLISHER Wenner Media
CATEGORY Illustration/Story
DATE September/October 1993

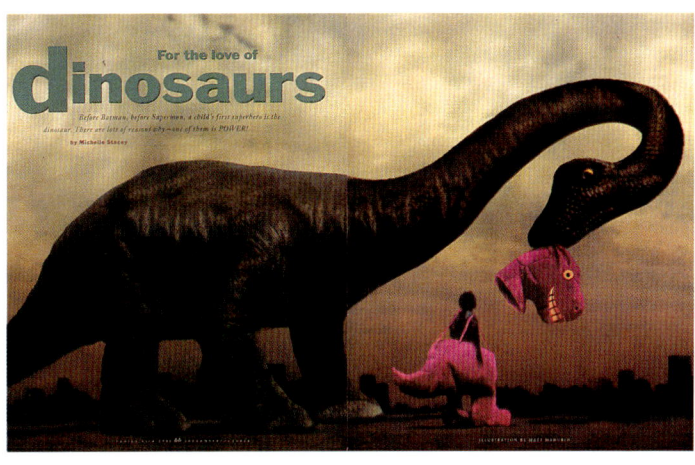

For the love of
dinosaurs

Before Batman, before Superman, a child's first superhero is the dinosaur. There are lots of reasons why—one of them is POWER!
by Michelle Stacey

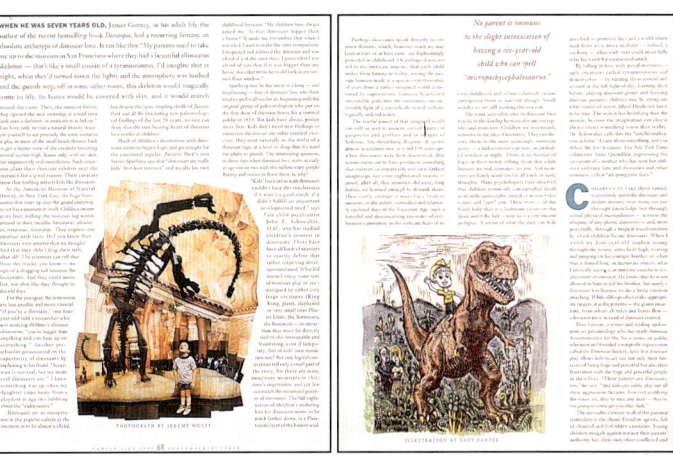

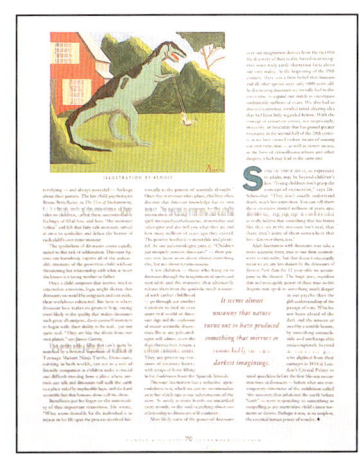

PUBLICATION Family Life
AWARD Merit
ART DIRECTOR Don Morris
DESIGNERS James Reyman, Don Morris, Laura Eisman
ILLUSTRATOR Henrik Drescher
PUBLISHER Wenner Media
CATEGORY Illustration/Story
DATE December 1993

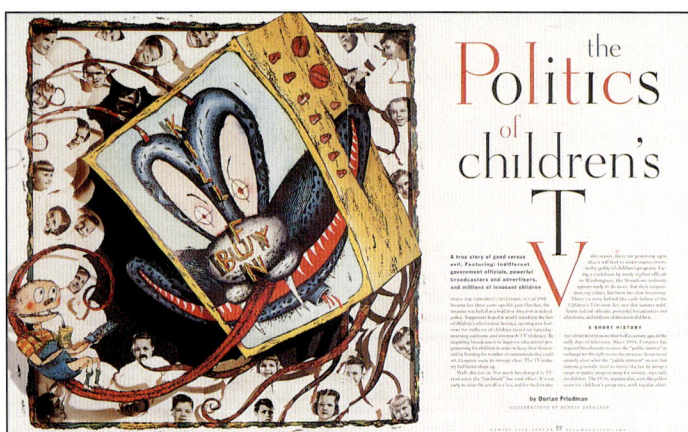

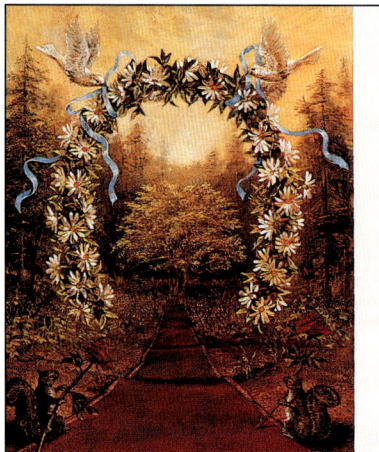

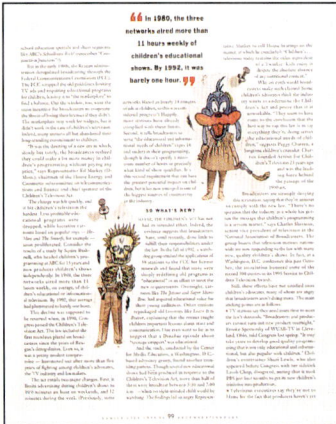

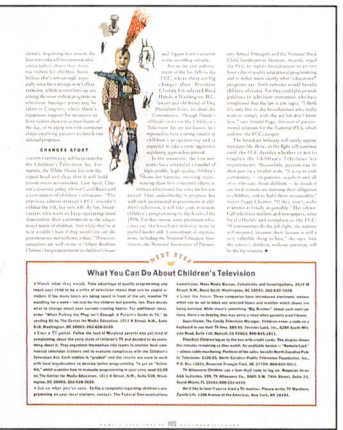

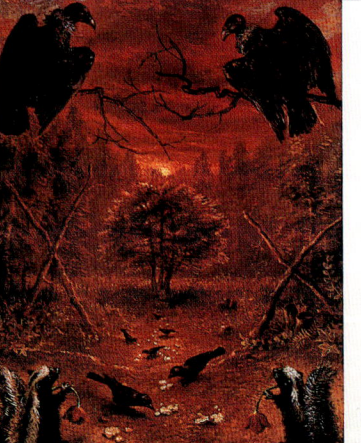

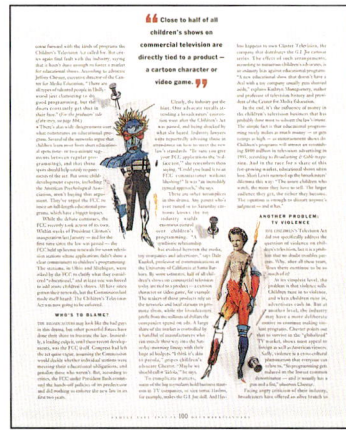

PUBLICATION Health
AWARD Merit
DESIGN DIRECTOR Jane Palecek
DESIGNER Jane Palecek
ILLUSTRATOR Thomas Woodruff
PUBLISHER Time Inc. Ventures
CATEGORY Illustration/Story
DATE September 1993

PUBLICATION	Men's Journal
AWARD	Merit
ART DIRECTOR	Matthew Drace
DESIGNER	Matthew Drace
ILLUSTRATOR	Dugald Stermer
PUBLISHER	Wenner Media
CATEGORY	Illustration/Story
DATE	March/April 1993

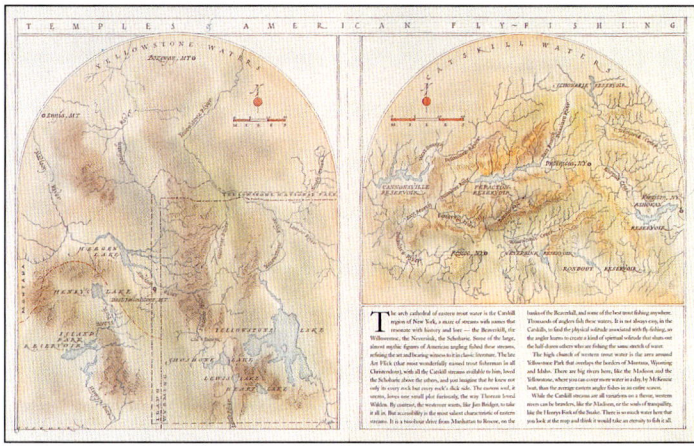

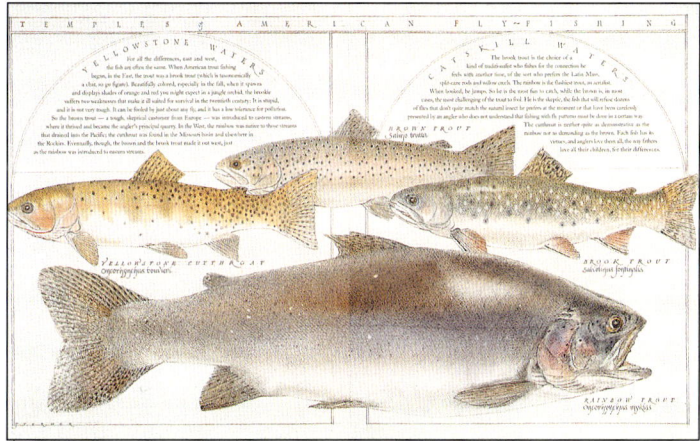

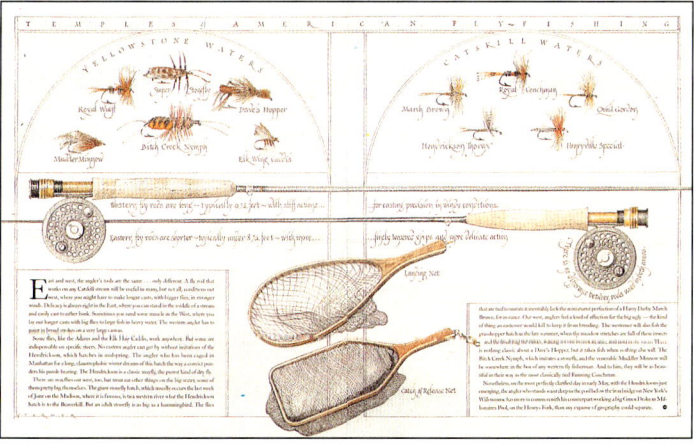

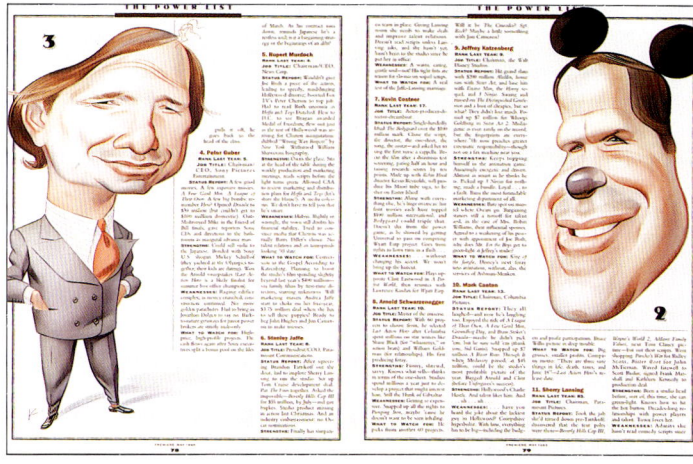

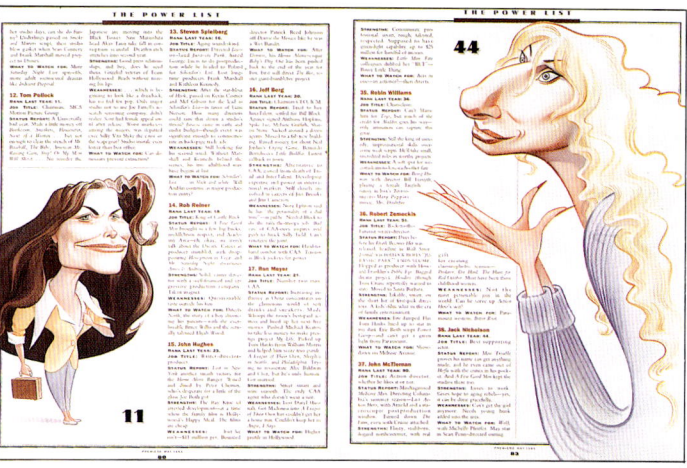

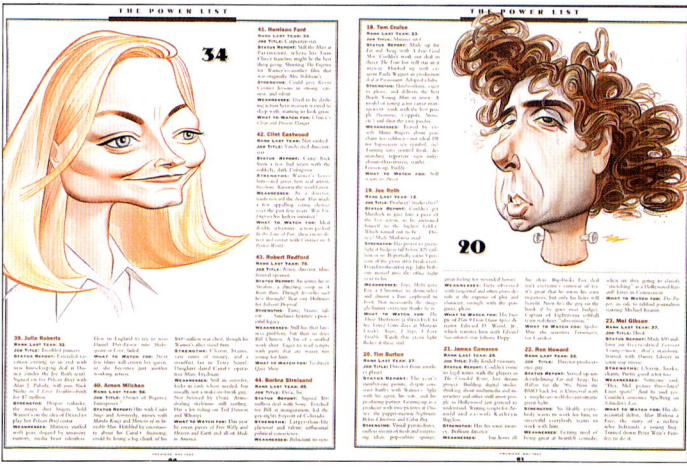

PUBLICATION	Premiere
AWARD	Merit
ART DIRECTOR	John Korpics
DESIGNER	John Korpics
ILLUSTRATOR	John Kascht
PUBLISHER	K-III Magazines
CATEGORY	Illustration/Story
DATE	May 1993

PUBLICATION	Smart Money		PUBLICATION	Sports Illustrated
AWARD	Merit		AWARD	Merit
ART DIRECTOR	Joseph Dizney		DESIGN DIRECTOR	Steven Hoffman
DESIGNER	Joseph Dizney		DESIGNER	F. Darrin Perry
ILLUSTRATOR	Brian Ajhar		ILLUSTRATOR	Brent Benger
PUBLISHER	Dow Jones/Hearst Corporation		PUBLISHER	Time, Inc.
CATEGORY	Illustration/Story		CATEGORY	Illustration/Story
DATE	August 1993		DATE	August 23, 1993

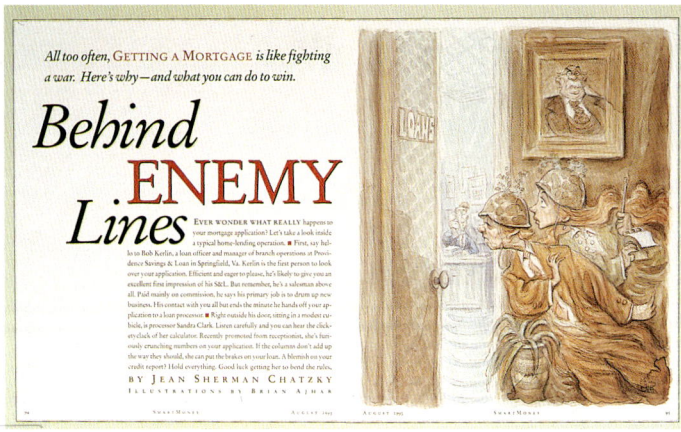

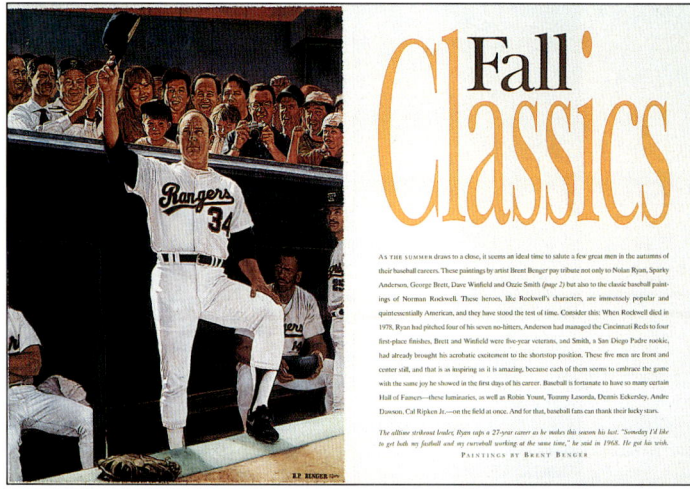

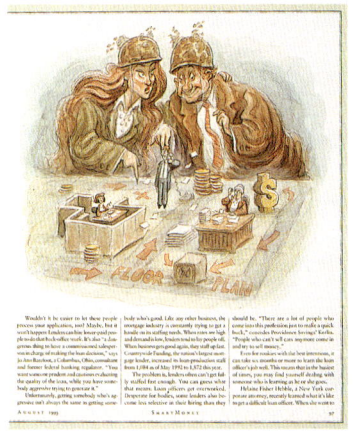

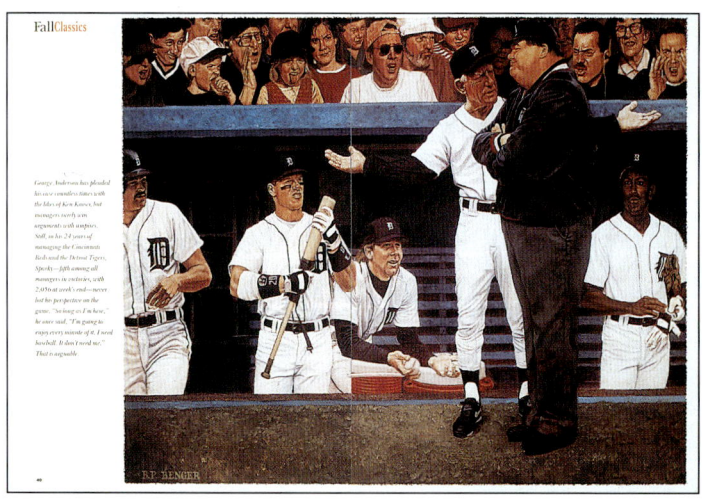

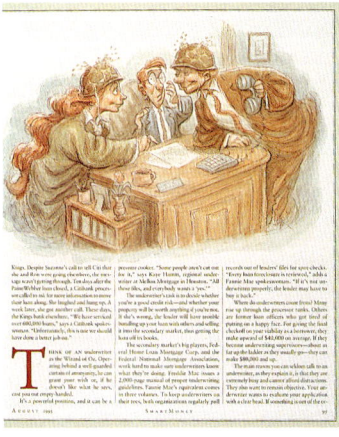

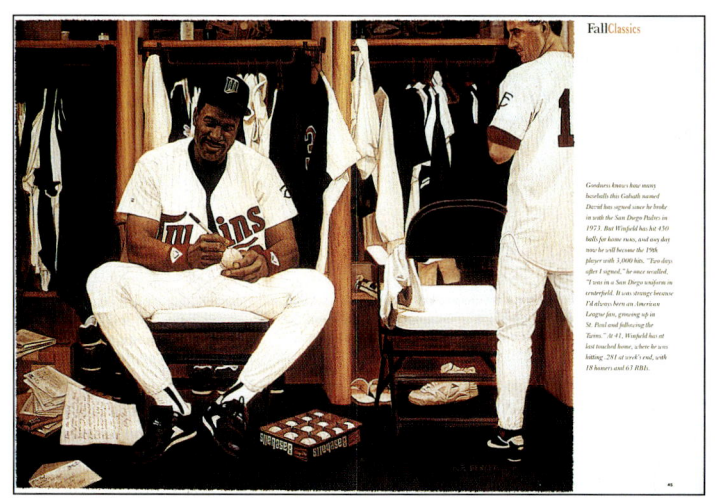

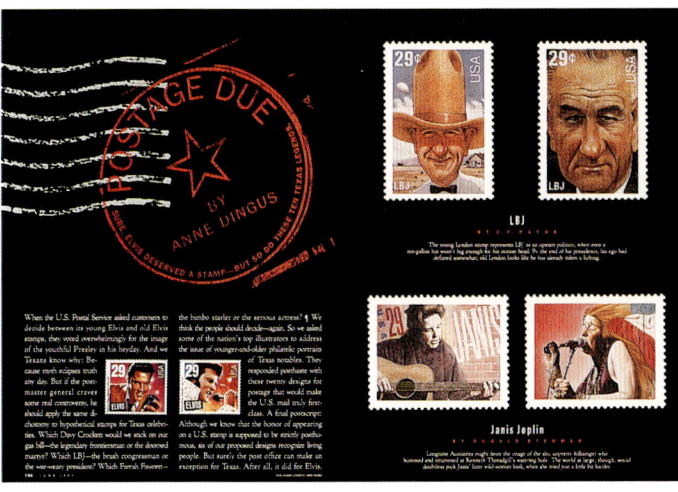

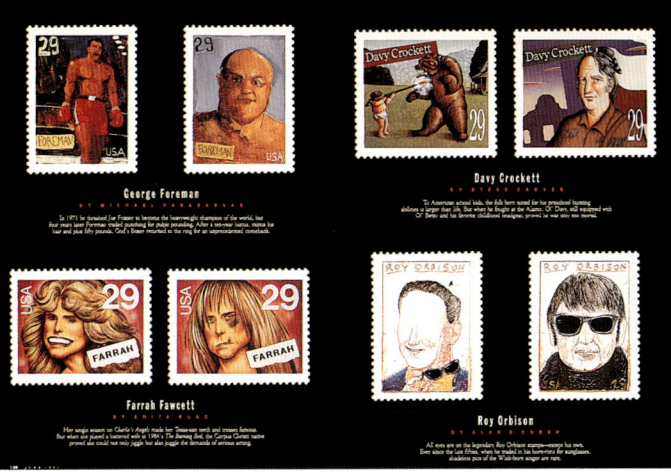

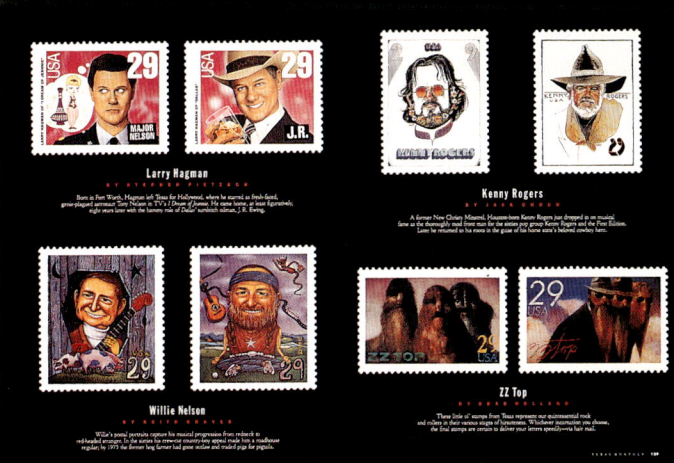

PUBLICATION   Texas Monthly
AWARD   Merit
DESIGN DIRECTOR   D.J. Stout
ART DIRECTOR   D.J. Stout
DESIGNER   D.J. Stout
ILLUSTRATORS   C.F. Payne, Dugald Stermer, Stephen Pietzsch, Keith Graves, Jack Unruh, Brad Holland, Michael Paraskevas, Anita Kunz, Steve Carver, Alan E. Cober
PHOTO EDITOR   D.J. Stout
PUBLISHER   Texas Monthly
CATEGORY   Illustration/Story
DATE   June 1993

PUBLICATION   Sports Illustrated
AWARD   Merit
DESIGN DIRECTOR   Steven Hoffman
DESIGNER   Darrin Perry
ILLUSTRATOR   Amy Guip
PUBLISHER   Time, Inc.
CATEGORY   Illustration/Story
DATE   July 19, 1993

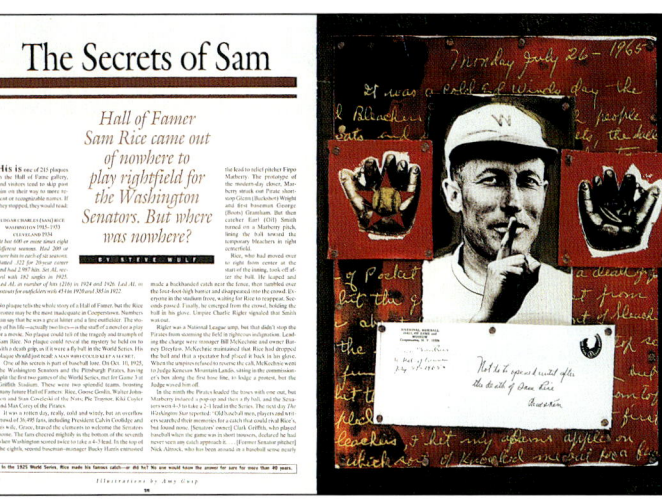

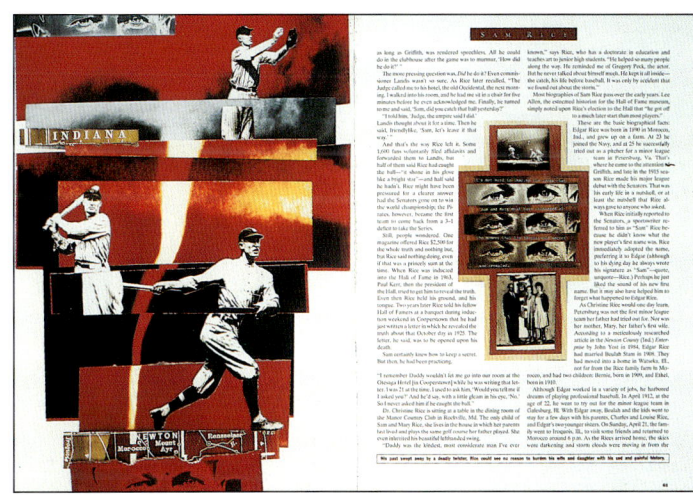

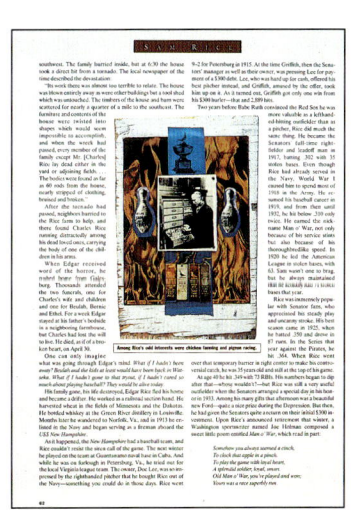

PUBLICATION	Time		**PUBLICATION**	Yankee
AWARD	Merit		**AWARD**	Merit
ART DIRECTOR	Rudolph C. Hoglund		**ART DIRECTOR**	J. Porter
DESIGNER	Christiaan Kuypers		**ILLUSTRATOR**	Jack Unruh
ILLUSTRATORS	Amy Guip, Brian Cronin, Laura Levine, Scott Menchin, Guy Billout		**PUBLISHER**	Yankee Publishing, Inc.
PUBLISHER	Time Inc.		**CATEGORY**	Illustration/Story
CATEGORY	Illustration/Story		**DATE**	May 1993
DATE	December 27, 1993			

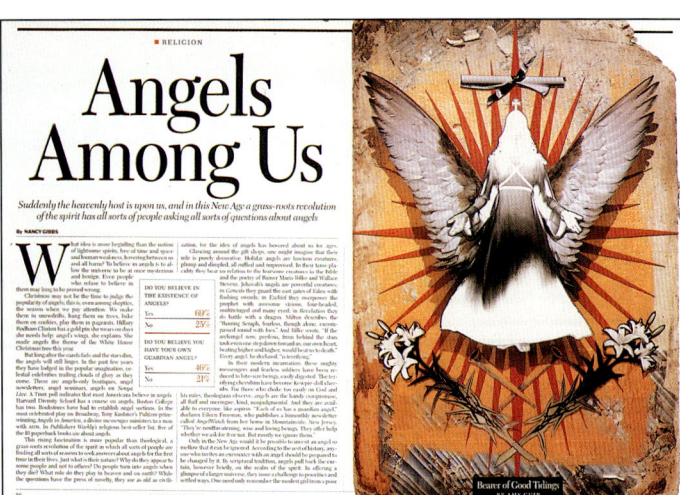

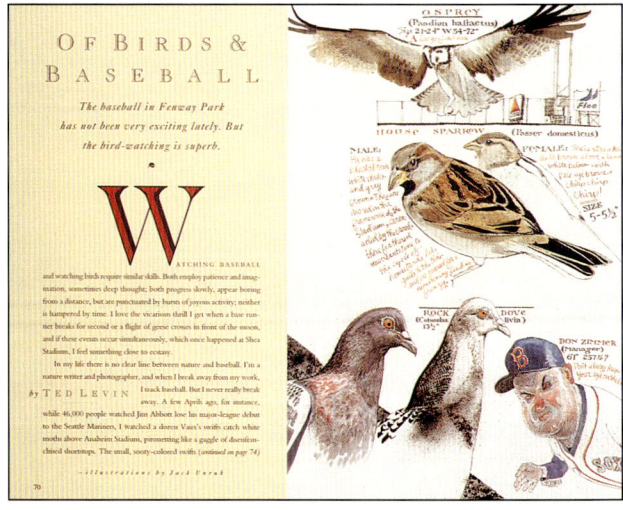

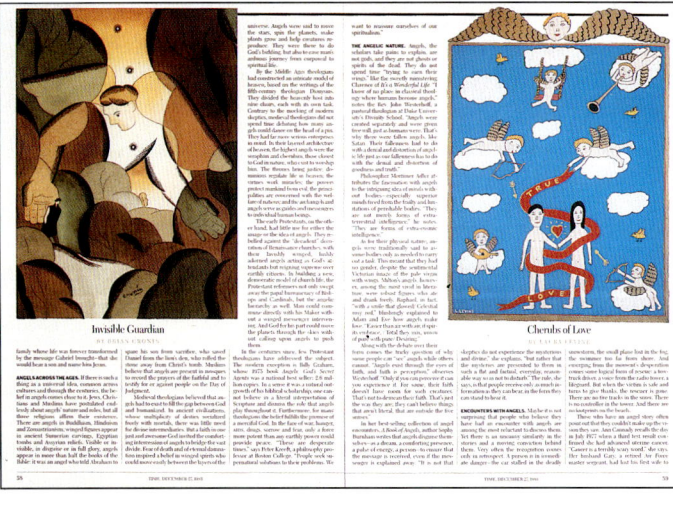

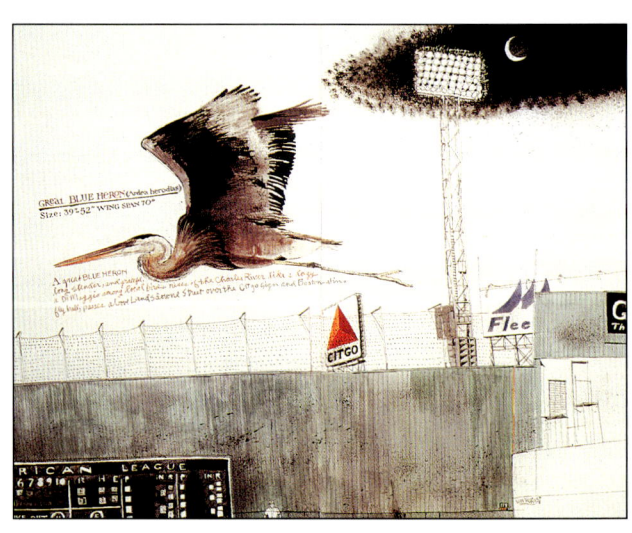

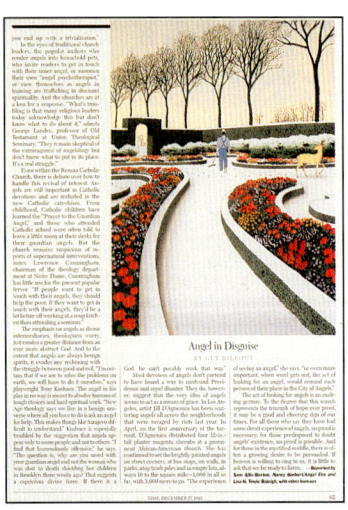

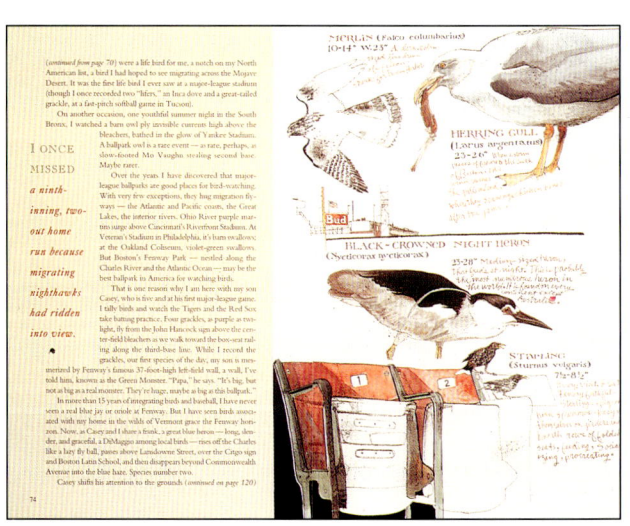

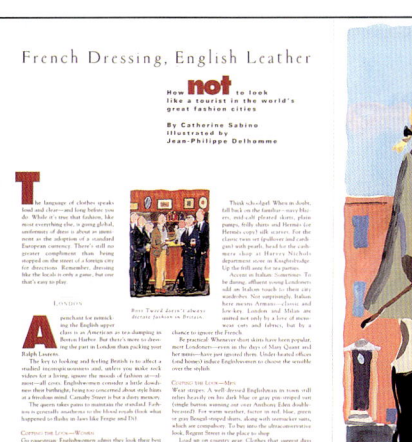

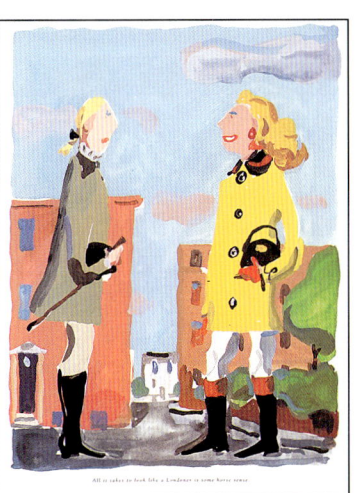

French Dressing, English Leather

How **not** to look like a tourist in the world's great fashion cities

By Catherine Sabino
Illustrated by Jean-Philippe Delhomme

The language of clothes speaks loud and clear—and long before you do. While it's true that fashion, like most everything else, is going global, uniformity of dress is about as imminent as the adoption of a standard European currency. There's still no greater compliment than being stopped on the street of a foreign city for directions. Remember, dressing like the locals is only a game, but one that's easy to play.

LONDON

A penchant for mimicking the English appreciation for class is as American as tea-dumping in Boston Harbor. But there's more to dressing the part in London than packing your Ralph Lauren.

The key to looking and feeling British is to affect a studied insouciance—and, unless you make such wishes for a living, ignore the needs of fashion at—almost—all costs. Englishwomen consider a little dowdiness their birthright, being too concerned about style hints as a frivolous mind. Canadian Street is but a dим memory. The queen takes pains to maintain the standard. Fashion is generally inoffensive to the blood royals think what happened to Bubba in Jean-like Peppie and Di).

GETTING THE LOOK—WOMEN
Go equestrian: Englishwomen adore they look their best when riding and attending hunt balls. Tweed and taffeta are their forte, and they'll wear something with a horsey insignia or gilt snaffles.

Think school-girl: When in doubt, fall back on the familiar—navy blazers, mid-calf pleated skirts, plain pumps, frilly shirts and Hermès (or Hermès copy) silk scarves. For the classic twin-set (pullover and cardigan) with pearls, head for the cashmere shop at Harvey Nichols department store in Knightsbridge. Up the frill ante for sex partner.

Accent in Italian: Sometimes, To be daring, affluent young Londoners add an Italian touch to their city wardrobes. Not surprisingly, Italian here means Armani—classic and low-key. London and Milan are united not only by a love of menswear cuts and fabrics, but by a choice to ignore the French.

Be practical: Whenever their skirts have been prominent Londoners—even in the days of Mary Quant and her minis—have just ignored them. Under-heeled offices Londoners'' induce Englishwomen to choose the sensible over the stylish.

GETTING THE LOOK—MEN
Wear stripes: A well-dressed Englishman in town will often heavily on his dark blue or gray pin-striped suit (single button, running out own Anthony Eden double-breasted). For warm weather, factor in red, blue, green or gun-Bengal striped shirts, along with seersucker suits, which are compulsory. To buy into the ultra-conservative look, Regent Street is the place to shop.

Load up on country gear: Clothes that suggest days on the grouse moor are always right for casual wear: old corduroy or cavalry twill trousers, V-necked cardigans over checked shirts, tweed jackets, suede shoes or chukka

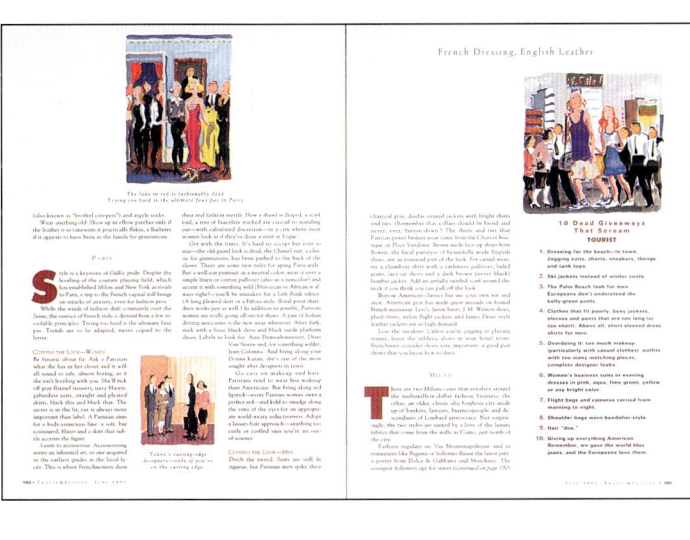

*The lady in red is fashionably chic
Trying too hard is the ultimate faux pas in Paris*

tailor known as "in-titel creepers") and argyle socks.

Wear anything old: Show up in elbow patches only if the leather is so innocent it practically flakes, a Barberry if it appears to have been in the family for generations.

PARIS

Style is a keystone of Gallic pride. Despite the beveling of the couture playing field, which has reshuffled Milan and New York as rivals to Paris, a trip to the French capital still brings on attacks of anxiety, even for fashion pros. While the winds of fashion shift constantly over the Seine, the essence of French style is derived from a few inviolable principles: Trying too hard is the ultimate faux pas. Trends are to be adapted, never copied to the letter.

GETTING THE LOOK—WOMEN
Be fussory about fit: Ask a Parisian what the loss in her closet and it will all sound so safe, almost boring, as if the tic's leveling with you. She'll tick off gray-flannel trousers, navy blazers, gabardine suits, straight and pleated skirts, black this and black that. The secret is in the fit, cut is always more important than label. A Parisian aims for a body-conscious line: a soft, but contoured, blazer and a shirt that subtly accents the figure.

Learn to accessorize: Accessorizing seems an informed art, or one acquired in the earliest grades at the local lycée. This is where Frenchwomen show

their real fashion mettle. How a shawl is draped, a scarf tied, a row of bracelets stacked are crucial to sounding out—with calculated discretion—in a city where most women look as if they've done a stint at Vogue.

Get with the times: It's hard to accept but ever so true—the old-guard look is dead; the Chanel suit, a classic for generations, has been pushed to the back of the closet. There are some rules for spring Paris style: But a well-cut pantsuit, or a neutral color, wear it over a simple linen or cotton pullover (also in a turtleneck) and accent it with something wild (Moroccan or African is always right)—you'll be mistaken for a Left Bank editor. Get long-pleated skirt or a Fifties-style, floral-print shirt dress works just as well. Or in addition to jewelry. Parisian women are really going all out for shoes. A pair of Italian driving moccasins is the new wear wherever. After dark, stick with a basic black dress and black suede platform shoes. Labels to look for: Ann Demeulemeester, Dries Van Noten and, for something wilder, Jean Colonna. And bring along your Dennis Kanat, she's one of the most sought after designers in town.

Go easy on makeup and hair: Parisians tend to wear less makeup than Americans. But bring along red lipstick—every Parisian actress owns a perfect red—and kohl to smudge along the rims of the eyes for an appropriately mid-teary seductiveness. Adopt a laissez-hair approach—anything too curly or coiffed says you're an out-of-towner.

GETTING THE LOOK—MEN
Ditch the trend: Suits are still de rigueur, but Parisian men spike their

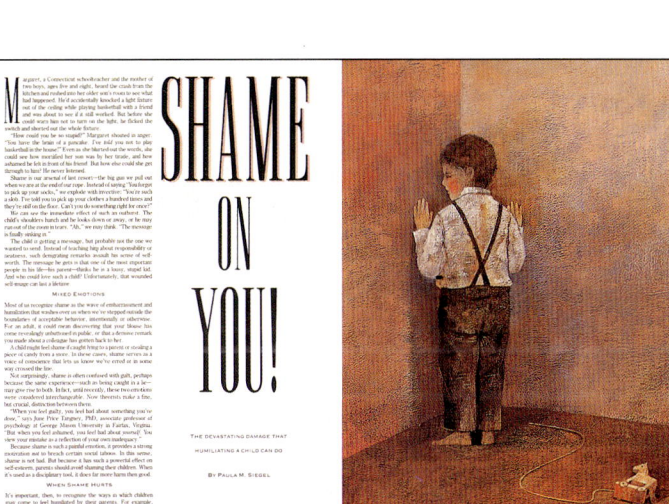

charcoal gray, double-vented jackets with bright shirts and ties. (Remember that collars should be frayed and never, ever, button-down.) The shirts and ties that Parisian power-brokers wear come from the Charvet boutique on Place Vendôme. Brown such lace-up shoes from Berott, the local purveyor of beautifully made English shoes, are an essential part of the look. For casual wear, try a chambray shirt with a cashmere pullover, faded jeans, lace-up shoes and a dark brown (never black) leather jacket. Add an artfully rumpled scarf around the neck if you think you can pull off the look.

Borrow American classics but use your own wit and style: Americans put less stock in trends over formal French menswear. Levi's, Levi's boots, J. M. Weston shoes, plaid shirts, nylon flight jackets and limes: Dean-style leather jackets are in high demand.

Live the sneakers: Unless you're jogging or playing tennis, leave the athletic shoes in your hotel room. Frenchmen consider shoes very important: a good pair shows that you know how to dress.

MILAN

There are two Milans—one that revolves around the multimillion-dollar fashion business; the other, an older, classic aha-bophemia city made up of bankers, lawyers, businesspeople and descendants of Lombard aristocracy. Not surprisingly, the two styles are united by a love of the luxury fabrics that come from the mills in Como, just north of the city.

Fashion regulars at Via Montenapoleone and at restaurants like Bagutta or Solferino flaunt the latest prêt-a-porter from Dolce & Gabbana and Moschino. The younger followers opt for street *(continued on page 152)*

10 Dead Giveaways That Scream TOURIST

1. **Dressing for the beach**—in tennis jogging suits, shorts, sneakers, thongs and tank tops.

2. **Ski jackets** instead of winter coats.

3. **The Palm Beach look** for men. Europeans don't understand the belly-green pants.

4. **Clothes that fit poorly:** boxy jackets, sleeves and pants that are too long (or too short). Above all, short-sleeved dress shirts for men.

5. **Overdoing it:** too much makeup (particularly with casual clothes), outfits with too many matching pieces, complete designer looks.

6. **Women's business suits** or evening dresses in pink, aqua, lime green, yellow or any bright color.

7. **Flight bags and cameras** carried from morning to night.

8. **Shoulder bags** worn bandolier-style.

9. **Hair "dos."**

10. **Giving up everything American.** Remember, we gave the world blue jeans, and the Europeans love them.

PUBLICATION Travel & Leisure
AWARD Merit
DESIGN DIRECTOR Lloyd Ziff
DESIGNER Lloyd Ziff
ILLUSTRATOR Jean-Philippe Delhomme
PUBLISHER American Express Publishing
CATEGORY Illustration/Story
DATE June 1993

PUBLICATION Working Mother
AWARD Merit
ART DIRECTOR Joan Ferrell
ILLUSTRATOR Wiktor Sadowski
PUBLISHER Lang Communications
CATEGORY Illustration/Story
DATE January 1993

SHAME ON YOU!

THE DEVASTATING DAMAGE THAT HUMILIATING A CHILD CAN DO

By PAULA M. SIEGEL
ILLUSTRATED BY WIKTOR SADOWSKI

Margaret, a Connecticut schoolteacher and the mother of two boys, ages five and eight, heard the crash from the kitchen and rushed into her older son's room to see what had happened. He'd accidentally knocked a light fixture out of the ceiling while playing basketball with a friend and was about to see if it still worked. But before she could warn him not to turn on the light, he flicked the switch and shorted out the whole fixture.

"How could you be so stupid?" Margaret shouted in anger.

"You have the brain of a pancake. I've told you not to play basketball in the house!" Even as she blurted out the words, she could see how mortified her son was by her tirade, and how ashamed he felt in front of his friend. But how else could she get through to him? He never listened.

Shame is our arsenal of last resort—the big gun we pull out when we are at the end of our rope. Instead of saying "You forgot to pick up your socks," we explode with invective: "You're such a slob. I've told you to pick up your clothes a hundred times and they're still on the floor. Can't you do something right for once?"

We can see the immediate effect of such an outburst. The child's shoulders hunch and he looks down or away, or he may run out of the room in tears. "Ah," we may think. "The message is finally sinking in."

The child is getting a message, but probably not the one we wanted to send. Instead of teaching him about responsibility or neatness, such denigrating remarks assault his sense of self-worth. The message he gets is that one of the most important people in his life—his parent—thinks he is a lousy, stupid kid. And who could love such a child? Unfortunately, that wounded self-image can last a lifetime.

MIXED EMOTIONS

Most of us recognize shame as the voice of embarrassment and humiliation that washes over us when we've stepped outside the boundaries of acceptable behavior, intentionally or otherwise. For an adult, it could mean discovering that your blouse has come revealingly unbuttoned in public, or that a derisive remark you made about a colleague has gotten back to her.

A child might feel shame if caught lying to a parent or stealing a piece of candy from a store. In these cases, shame serves as a voice of conscience that lets us know we've erred or in some way crossed the line.

Not surprisingly, shame is often confused with guilt, perhaps because the same experience—such as being caught in a lie—may give rise to both. In fact, until recently, these two emotions were considered interchangeable. Now theorists make a fine, but crucial, distinction between them.

"When you feel guilty, you feel bad about something you've done," says June Price Tangney, PhD, associate professor of psychology at George Mason University in Fairfax, Virginia. "But when you feel ashamed, you feel bad about yourself. You view your mistake as a reflection of your own inadequacy."

Because shame is such a painful emotion, it provides a strong motivation not to breach certain social taboos. In this sense, shame is not bad. But because it has such a powerful effect on self-esteem, parents should avoid shaming their children. When it's used as a disciplinary tool, it does far more harm than good.

WHEN SHAME HURTS

It's important, then, to recognize the ways in which children may come to feel humiliated by their parents. For example, when parents consistently "discipline" a child by making harsh,

PUBLICATION   The New York Times Magazine
AWARD   Merit
ART DIRECTOR   Janet Froelich
DESIGNER   Kathi Rota
ILLUSTRATOR   Sue Coe
PUBLISHER   The New York Times
CATEGORY   Illustration/Story
DATE   October 3, 1993

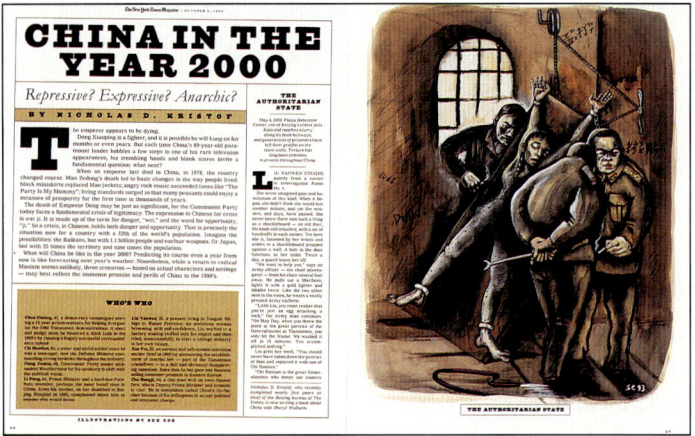

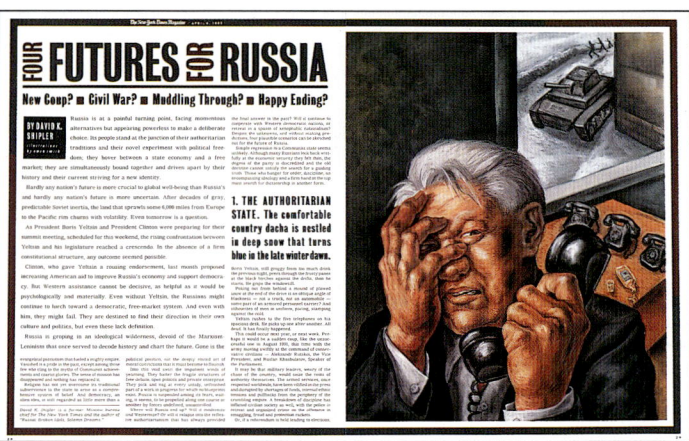

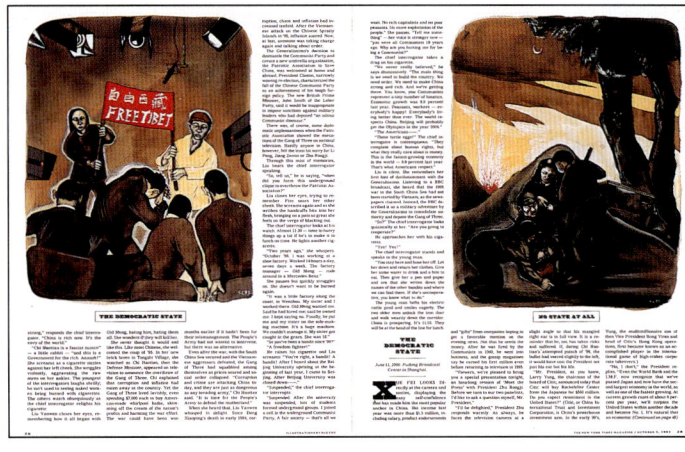

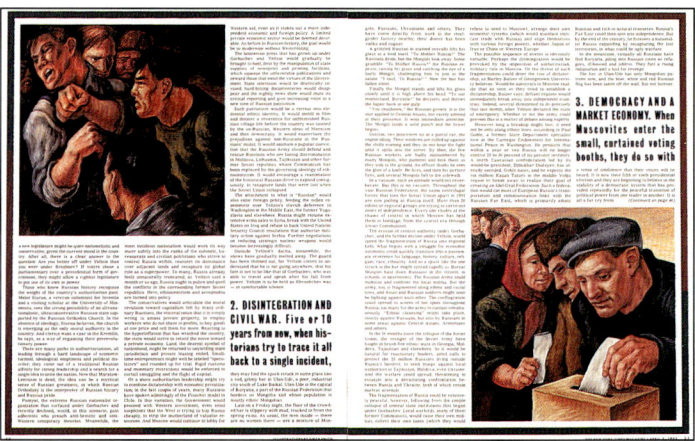

PUBLICATION   The New York Times Magazine
AWARD   Merit
ART DIRECTOR   Janet Froelich
DESIGNERS   Janet Froelich, Kayo Der Serkissian
ILLUSTRATOR   Owen Smith
PUBLISHER   The New York Times
CATEGORY   Illustration/Story
DATE   April 4, 1993

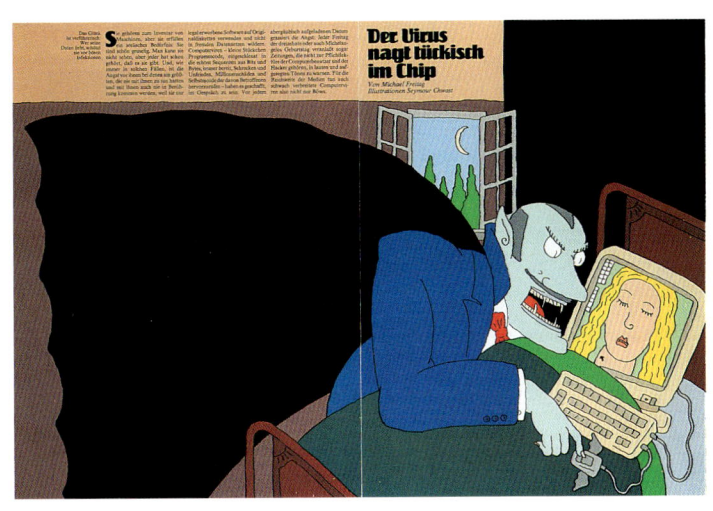

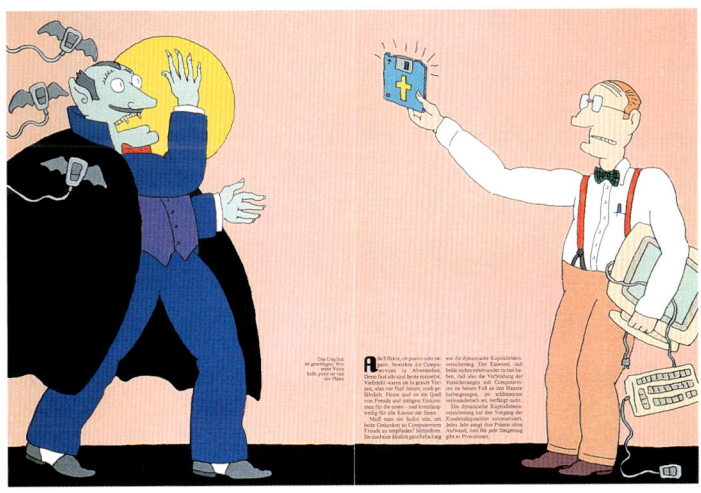

PUBLICATION   Frankfurter Allgemeine Magazin

AWARD   Merit

ART DIRECTOR   Hans-Georg Pospischil

ILLUSTRATOR   Seymour Chwast

STUDIO   The Pushpin Group, Inc.

CATEGORY   Illustration/Story

DATE   August 6, 1993

PUBLICATION	Dartmouth Alumni Magazine
AWARD	Merit
ART DIRECTORS	J. Porter, Dorisen Means
ILLUSTRATOR	Rob Day
STUDIO	J. Porter Design
CLIENT	Dartmouth College
CATEGORY	Illustration/Story
DATE	May 1993

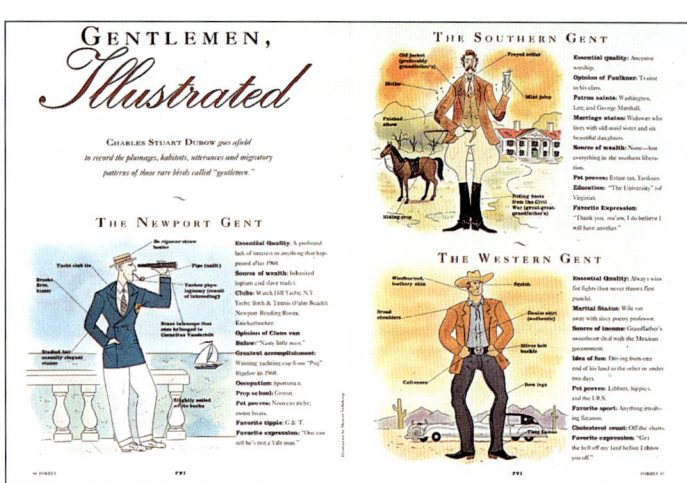

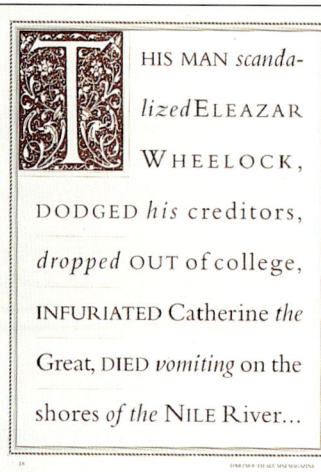

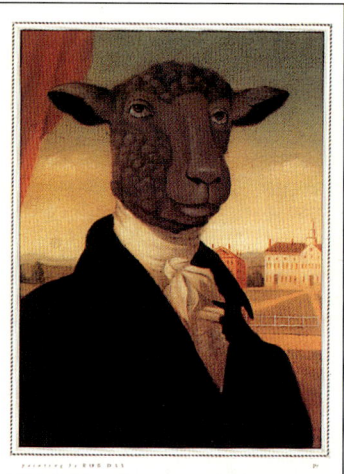

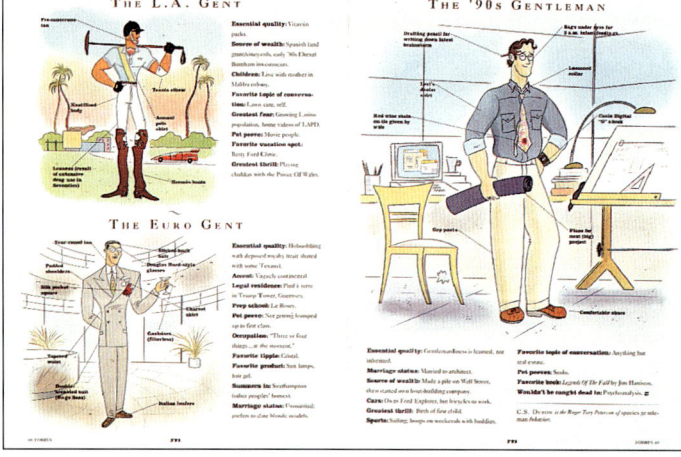

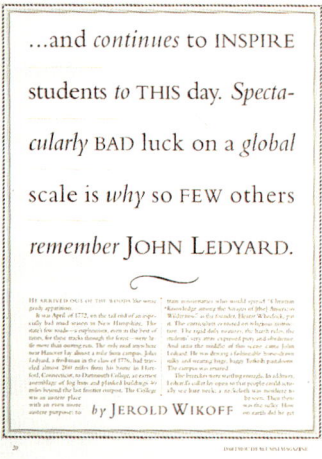

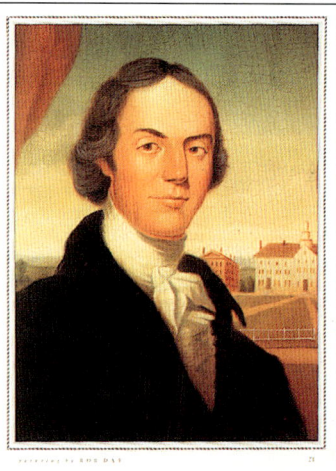

PUBLICATION	Forbes FYI
AWARD	Merit
ART DIRECTOR	Alexander Isley
DESIGNER	Lynette Cortez
ILLUSTRATOR	Maurice Vellekoop
STUDIO	Alexander Isley Design
CATEGORY	Illustration/Story
DATE	March 15, 1993

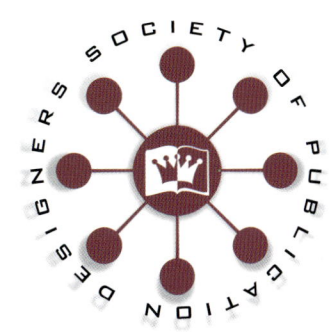
SOCIETY OF PUBLICATION DESIGNERS

PHOTO GRAPHY

PHOTOJOURNALISM

PORTRAITS

STILL LIFE

INTERIORS

TRAVEL

FASHION

BEAUTY

PUBLICATION	The New York Times Magazine
AWARD	Gold
ART DIRECTOR	Janet Froelich
DESIGNER	Nancy Harris
PHOTOGRAPHER	Matuschka
PHOTO EDITOR	Sarah Harbutt
PUBLISHER	The New York Times
CATEGORY	Photography/Photojournalism, Portraits
DATE	August 15, 1993

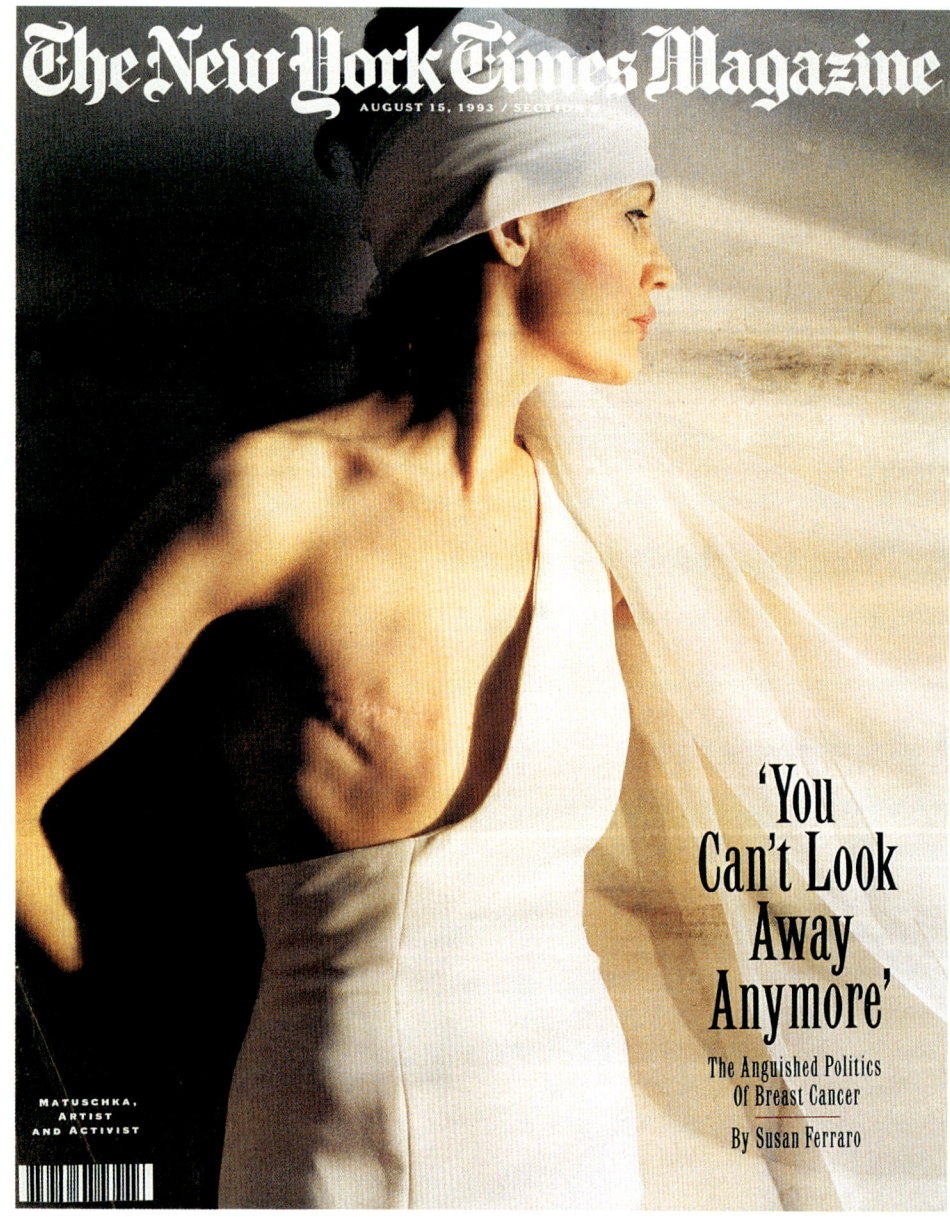

PUBLICATION	Life
AWARD	Silver
DESIGN DIRECTOR	Tom Bentkowski
DESIGNER	Jean Andreuzzi
PHOTOGRAPHER	Tim Page
PHOTO EDITORS	David Friend, Bobbi Baker Burrows
PUBLISHER	Time Inc.
CATEGORY	Photography/Photojournalism, Portraits
DATE	August 1993

THE BIG PICTURE

In the Whirlwind

In a place like Cambodia, an election means nationwide tension. It means summoning the courage to vote. It means international watchdogs: United Nations helicopters hovering overhead in an effort to police campaign stops and the polling itself. In a place like Cambodia, the outcome of an election is watched for signs of war.

In this spring's Cambodian election, one side did so well that the other threatened to grab half the country and secede. In a place like Cambodia, it's hard to argue—at least thus far—that elections truly belong to the people.

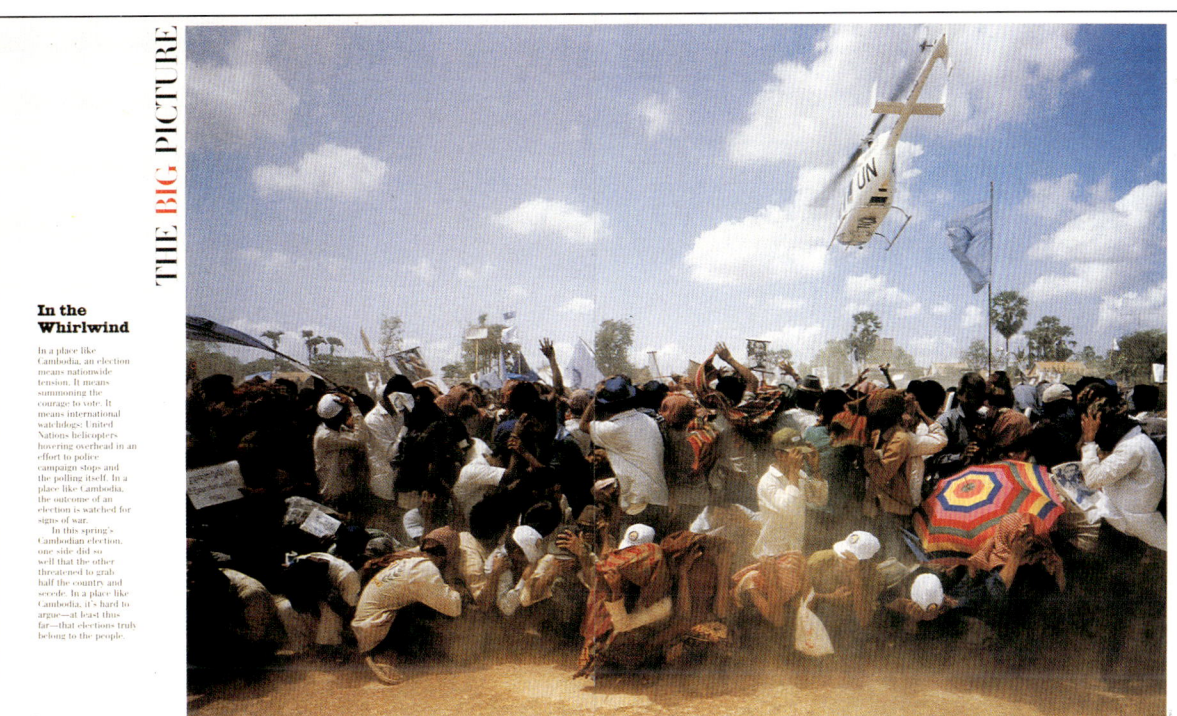

PUBLICATION	Audubon
AWARD	Merit
ART DIRECTOR	Suzanne Morin
PHOTOGRAPHER	Frans Lanting
PHOTO EDITOR	Peter Howe
PUBLISHER	National Audubon Society
CATEGORY	Photography/Photojournalism, Portraits
DATE	May/June 1993

PUBLICATION	Details
AWARD	Merit
ART DIRECTOR	B.W. Honeycutt
DESIGNER	Markus Kiersztan
PHOTOGRAPHERS	John Patrick Salisbury, Guzman
PUBLISHER	The Condé Nast Publications Inc.
CATEGORY	Photography/Photojournalism, Portraits
DATE	June 1993

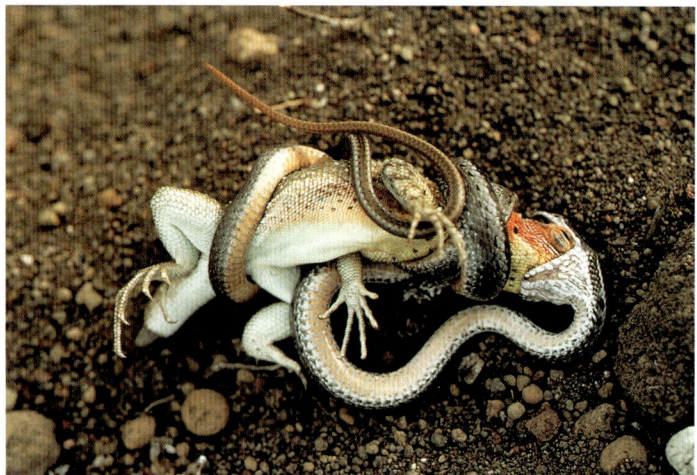

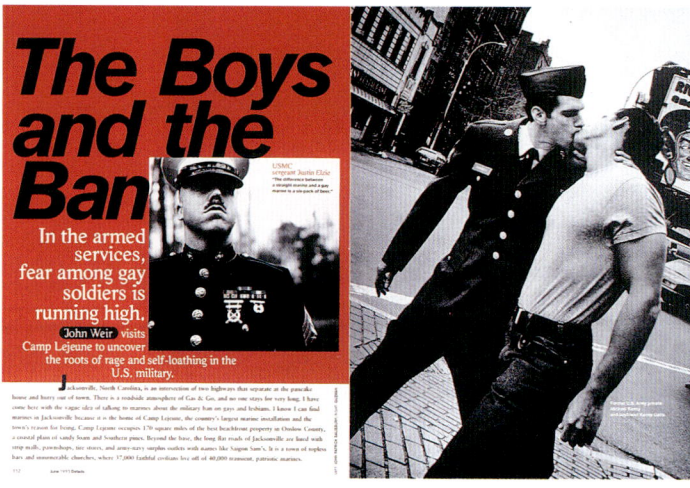

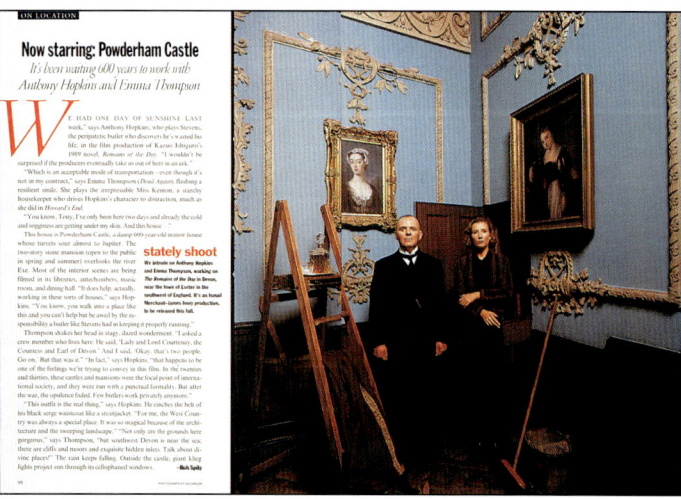

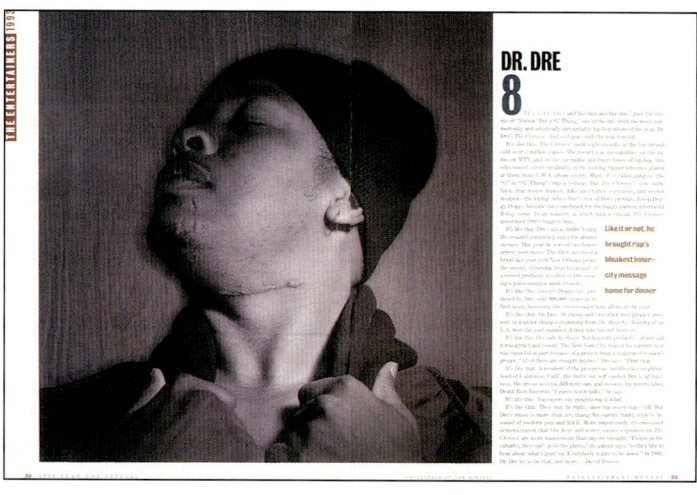

PUBLICATION	Condé Nast Traveler
AWARD	Merit
DESIGN DIRECTOR	Diana La Guardia
PHOTOGRAPHER	Lord Snowdon
PHOTO EDITOR	Kathleen Klech
PUBLISHER	The Condé Nast Publications Inc.
CATEGORY	Photography/Photojournalism, Portraits
DATE	March 1993

PUBLICATION	Entertainment Weekly
AWARD	Merit
DESIGN DIRECTOR	Michael Grossman
DESIGNER	Elizabeth Betts
PHOTOGRAPHER	Dan Winters
PHOTO EDITORS	Mary Dunn, Mark Jacobsen
PUBLISHER	Time Inc.
CATEGORY	Photography/Photojournalism, Portraits
DATE	December 31, 1993

PUBLICATION	GQ
AWARD	Merit
CREATIVE DIRECTOR	Robert Priest
DESIGN DIRECTOR	Robert Priest
DESIGNER	Laura Harrigan
PHOTOGRAPHER	Gregory Heisler
PHOTO EDITOR	Karen Frank
PUBLISHER	The Condé Nast Publications Inc.
CATEGORY	Photography/Photojournalism, Portraits
DATE	November 1993

PUBLICATION	Martha Stewart Living
AWARD	Merit
ART DIRECTOR	Gael Towey
DESIGNER	Anne Johnson
PHOTOGRAPHER	John Dugdale
PUBLISHER	Time Inc.
CATEGORY	Photography/Photojournalism, Portraits
DATE	August 1993

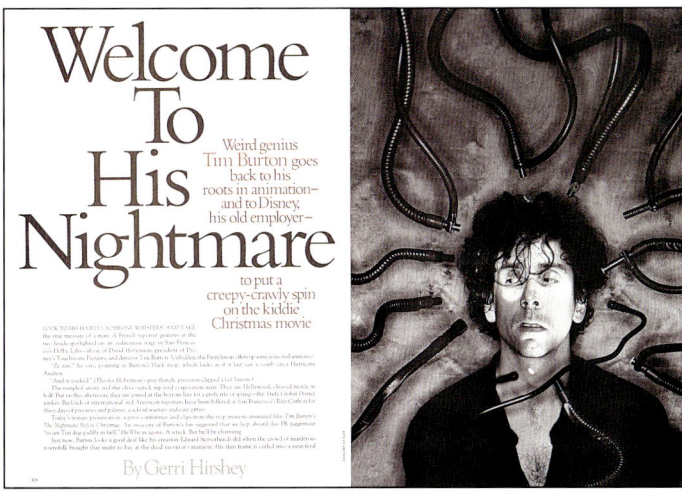

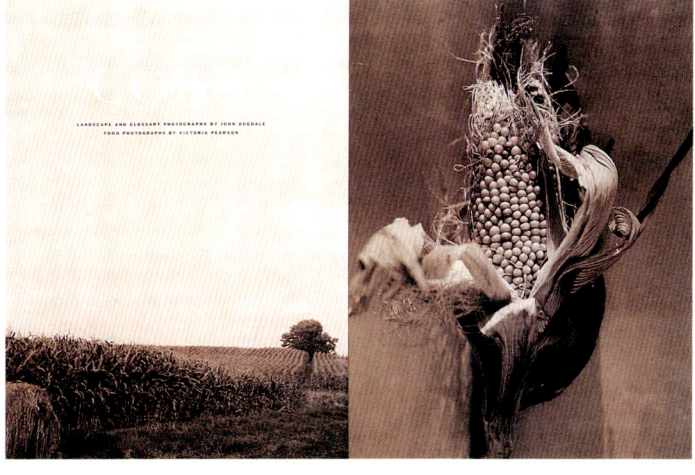

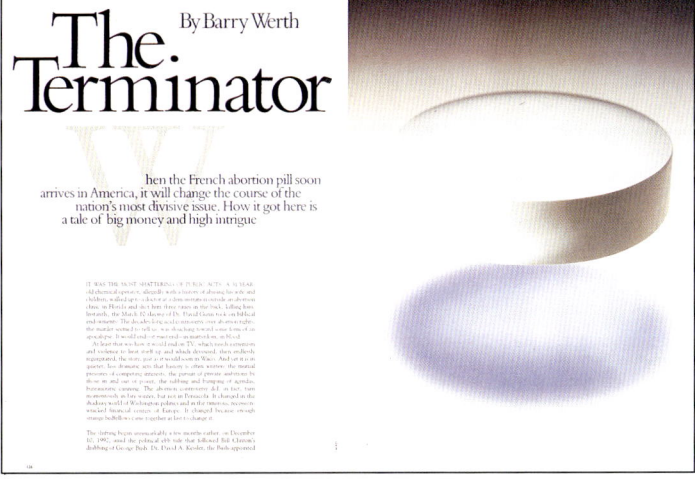

PUBLICATION	GQ
AWARD	Merit
CREATIVE DIRECTOR	Robert Priest
DESIGN DIRECTOR	Robert Priest
DESIGNER	Laura Harrigan
PHOTOGRAPHER	Hiro
PHOTO EDITOR	Karen Frank
PUBLISHER	The Condé Nast Publications Inc.
CATEGORY	Photography/Photojournalism, Portraits
DATE	July 1993

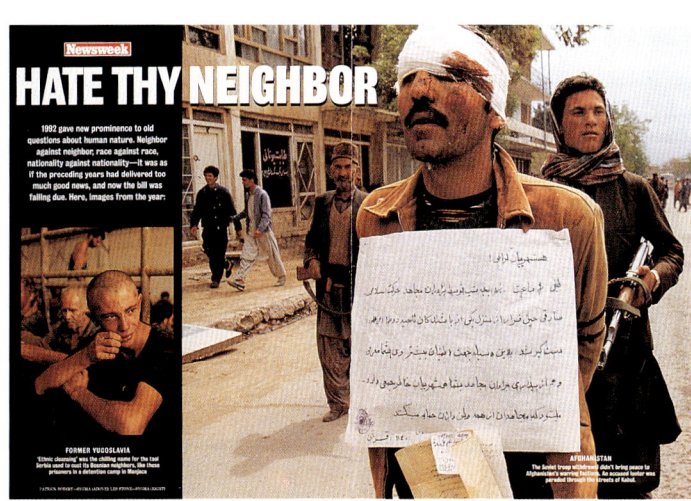

PUBLICATION	Newsweek
AWARD	Merit
ART DIRECTOR	Patricia Bradbury
DESIGNER	Doris Downes-Jewett
PHOTOGRAPHERS	Patrick Robert/Sygma, Les Stone/Sygma
PUBLISHER	Newsweek, Inc.
CATEGORY	Photography/Photojournalism, Portraits
DATE	January 4, 1993

PUBLICATION	Rolling Stone
AWARD	Merit
ART DIRECTOR	Fred Woodward
DESIGNER	Gail Anderson
PHOTOGRAPHER	Matt Mahurin
PHOTO EDITOR	Laurie Kratochvil
PUBLISHER	Wenner Media
CATEGORY	Photography/Photojournalism, Portraits
DATE	May 27, 1993

PUBLICATION	US
AWARD	Merit
ART DIRECTOR	Pamela Berry
DESIGNER	Pamela Berry
PHOTOGRAPHER	Mary Ellen Mark
PHOTO EDITOR	Jennifer Crandall
PUBLISHER	Wenner Media
CATEGORY	Photography/Photojournalism, Portraits
DATE	June 1993

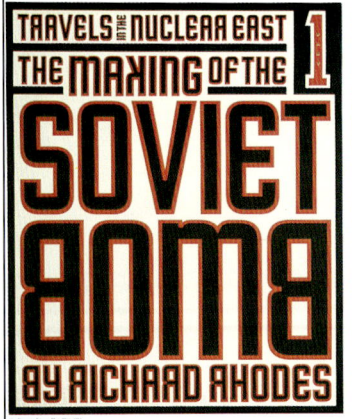
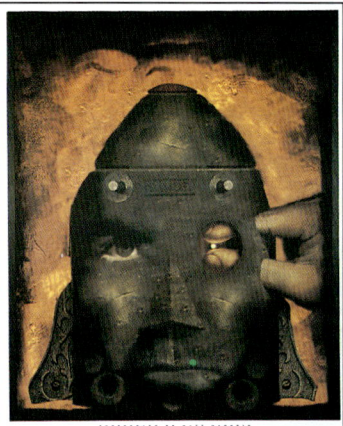
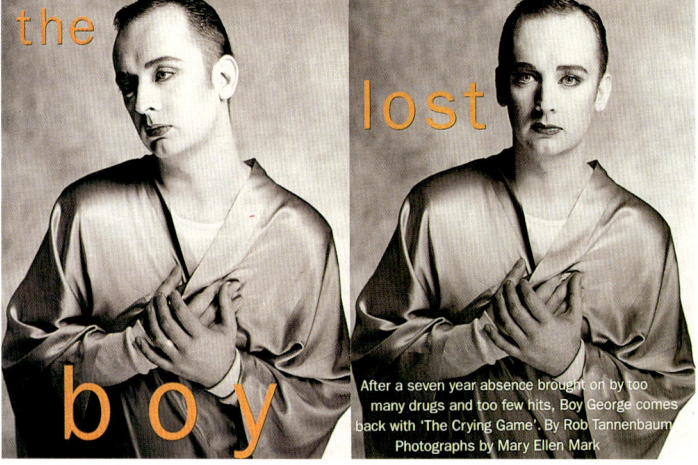

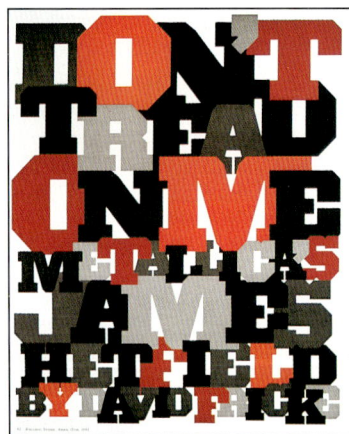
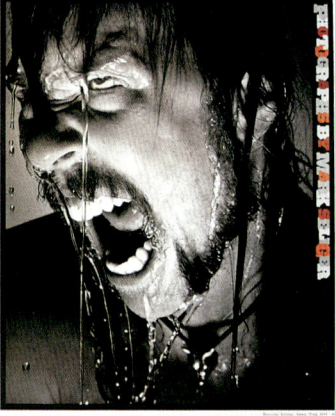

PUBLICATION	Rolling Stone
AWARD	Merit
ART DIRECTOR	Fred Woodward
DESIGNERS	Fred Woodward, Gail Anderson
PHOTOGRAPHER	Mark Seliger
PHOTO EDITOR	Laurie Kratochvil
PUBLISHER	Wenner Media
CATEGORY	Photography/Photojournalism, Portraits
DATE	April 15, 1993

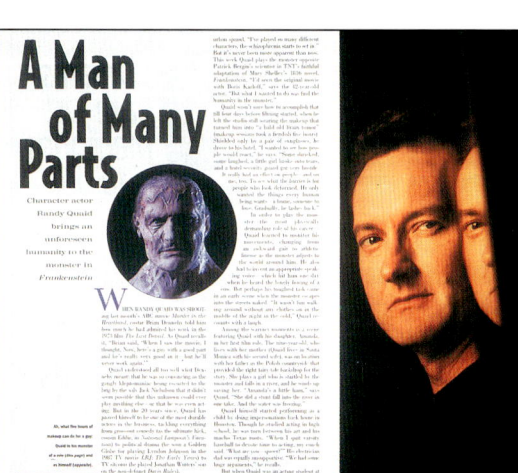

PUBLICATION	Total TV
AWARD	Merit
ART DIRECTOR	Marlene Sezni
DESIGNER	Laura Duggan
PHOTOGRAPHER	David Roth
PHOTO EDITOR	Heather Alberts
PUBLISHER	TVSM, Inc.
CATEGORY	Photography/Photojournalism, Portraits
DATE	June 1993

PUBLICATION	Sports Illustrated
AWARD	Merit
DESIGN DIRECTOR	Steven Hoffman
DESIGNER	Craig Gartner
PHOTOGRAPHER	Bill Frakes
PHOTO EDITOR	Heinz Kluetmeier
PUBLISHER	Time Inc.
CATEGORY	Photography/Photojournalism, Portraits
DATE	May 10, 1993

PUBLICATION	Sports Illustrated
AWARD	Merit
DESIGN DIRECTOR	Steven Hoffman
DESIGNER	Barbara Chilenskas
PHOTOGRAPHER	George Tiedemann
PHOTO EDITOR	Heinz Kluetmeier
PUBLISHER	Time Inc.
CATEGORY	Photography/Photojournalism, Portraits
DATE	March 29, 1993

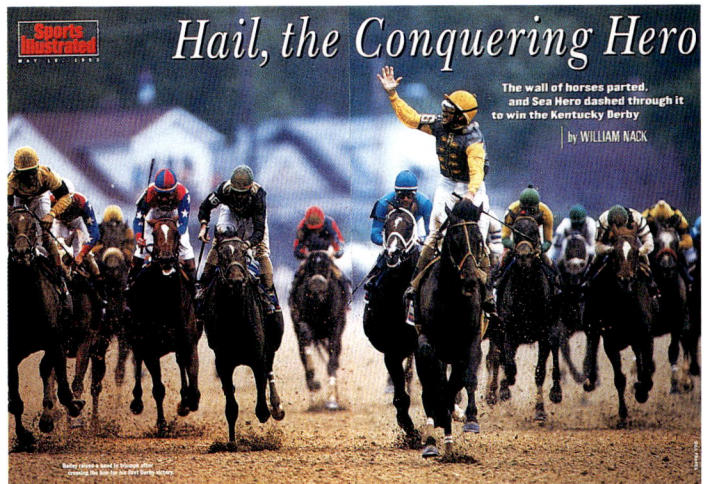

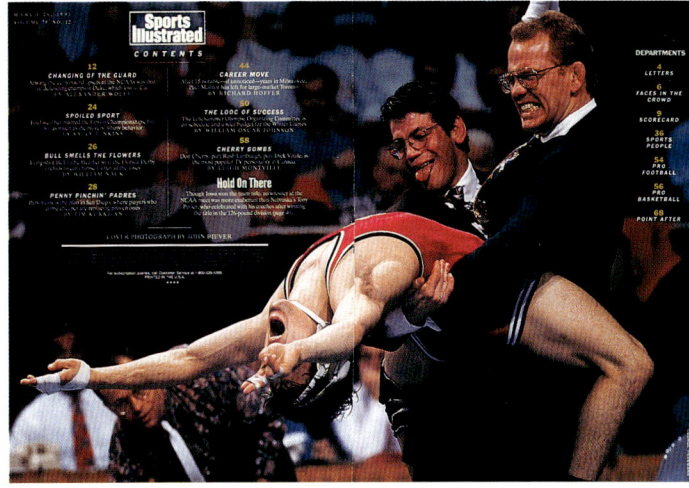

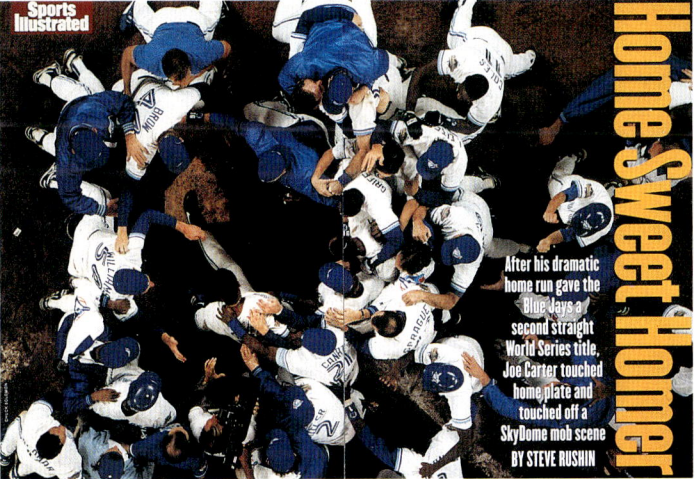

PUBLICATION	Sports Illustrated
AWARD	Merit
DESIGN DIRECTOR	Steven Hoffman
DESIGNER	Edward Truscio
PHOTOGRAPHER	Chuck Solomon
PHOTO EDITOR	Heinz Kluetmeier
PUBLISHER	Time Inc.
CATEGORY	Photography/Photojournalism, Portraits
DATE	November 1, 1993

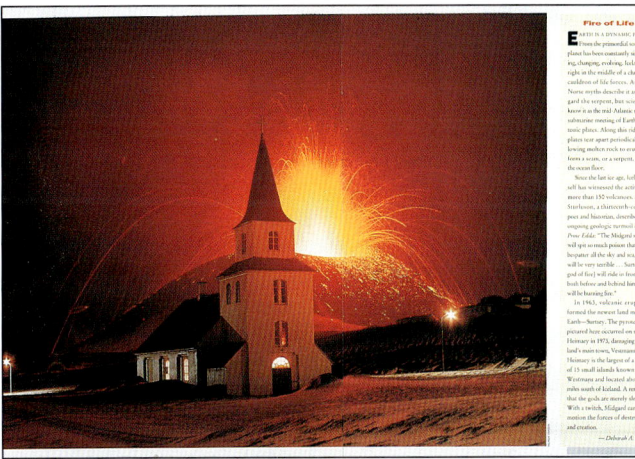

PUBLICATION	Wildlife Conservation
AWARD	Merit
DESIGN DIRECTOR	Julie Larsen Maher
ART DIRECTOR	Julie Larsen Maher
DESIGNER	Julie Larsen Maher
PHOTOGRAPHER	Sigurgeir Jonasson
PHOTO EDITOR	Julie Larsen Maher
PUBLISHER	Wildlife Conservation Society
CATEGORY	Photography/Photojournalism, Portraits
DATE	September/October 1993

PUBLICATION   The New York Times Magazine
AWARD   Merit
ART DIRECTOR   Janet Froelich
DESIGNER   Kathi Rota
PHOTOGRAPHER   Andrea Modica
PHOTO EDITOR   Kathy Ryan
PUBLISHER   The New York Times
CATEGORY   Photography/Photojournalism, Portraits
DATE   April 4, 1993

PUBLICATION   The New York Times Magazine
AWARD   Merit
ART DIRECTOR   Janet Froelich
PHOTOGRAPHER   Keith Carter
PHOTO EDITOR   Kathy Ryan
PUBLISHER   The New York Times
CATEGORY   Photography/Photojournalism, Portraits
DATE   January 31, 1993

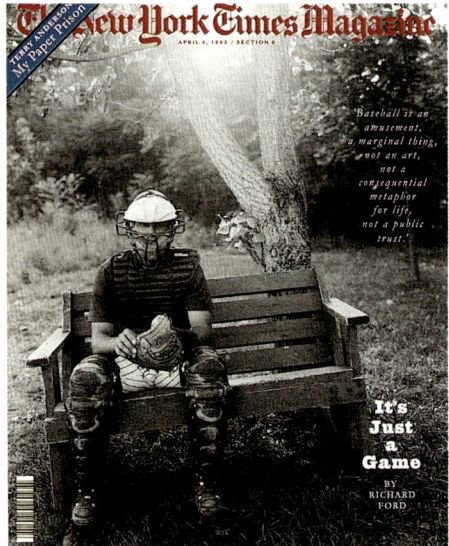

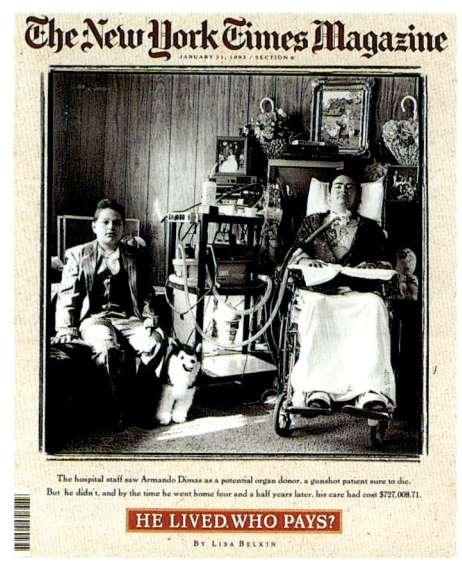

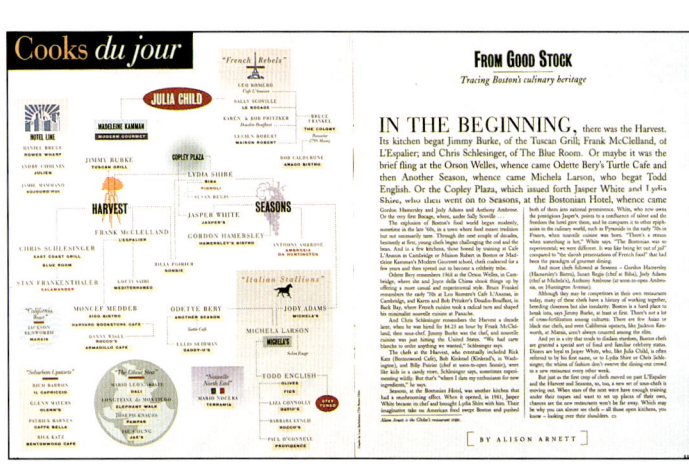

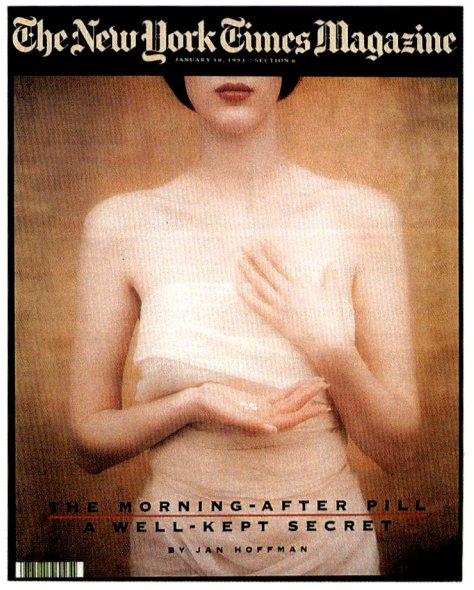

PUBLICATION   The Boston Globe Magazine
AWARD   Merit
DESIGN DIRECTOR Lucy Bartholomay
ART DIRECTOR   Lucy Bartholomay
DESIGNER   Lucy Bartholomay
PHOTOGRAPHER   Michele McDonald
PHOTO EDITOR   Lucy Bartholomay
PUBLISHER   The Boston Globe
CATEGORY   Photography/Photojournalism, Portraits
DATE   January 10, 1993

PUBLICATION   The New York Times Magazine
AWARD   Merit
ART DIRECTOR   Janet Froelich
PHOTOGRAPHER   Joyce Tenneson
PHOTO EDITOR   Kathy Ryan
PUBLISHER   The New York Times
CATEGORY   Photography/Photojournalism, Portraits
DATE   January 10, 1993

PUBLICATION	The New York Times Magazine
AWARD	Merit
ART DIRECTOR	Janet Froelich
DESIGNER	Charlene Benson
PHOTOGRAPHER	Dan Winters
PHOTO EDITOR	Kathy Ryan
PUBLISHER	The New York Times
CATEGORY	Photography/Photojournalism, Portraits
DATE	July 11, 1993

PUBLICATION	The New York Times Magazine
AWARD	Merit
ART DIRECTOR	Janet Froelich
DESIGNER	Kathi Rota
PHOTOGRAPHER	Keith Carter
PHOTO EDITOR	Keith Carter
PUBLISHER	The New York Times
CATEGORY	Photography/Photojournalism, Portraits
DATE	January 31, 1993

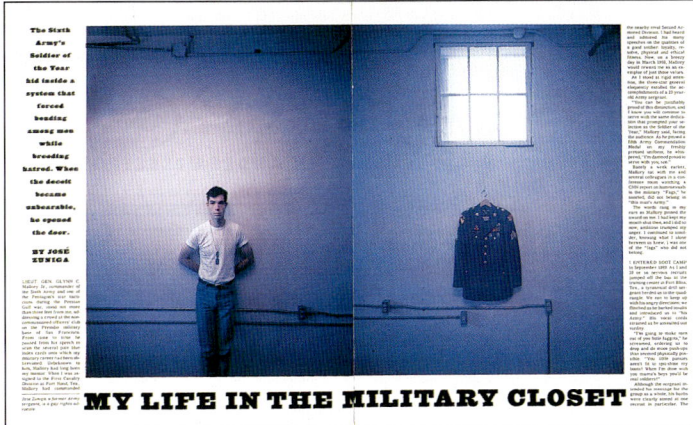

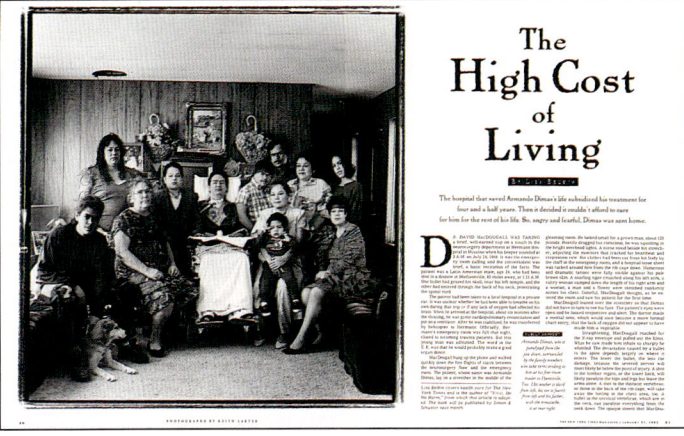

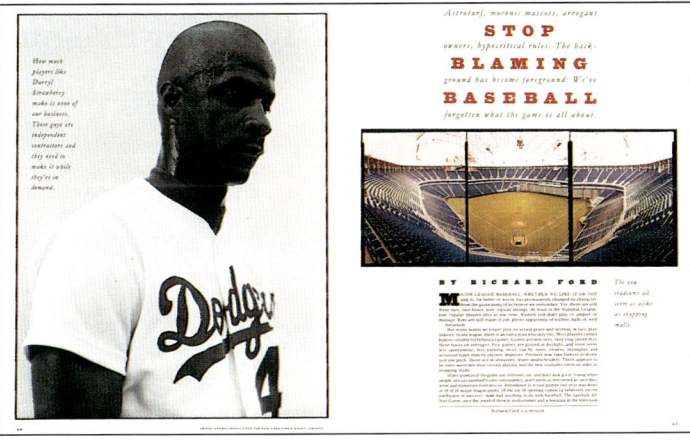

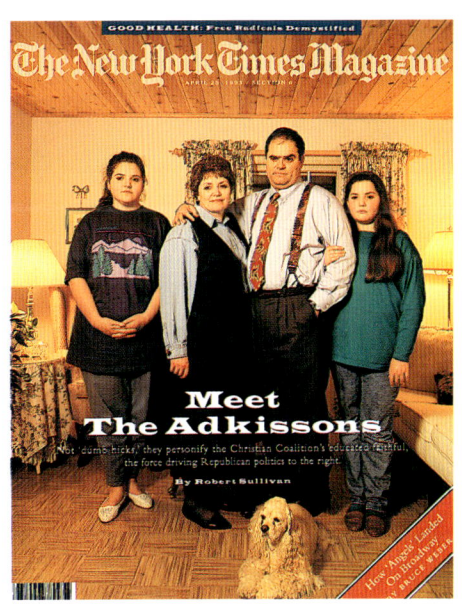

PUBLICATION	The New York Times Magazine
AWARD	Merit
ART DIRECTOR	Janet Froelich
DESIGNER	Kathi Rota
PHOTOGRAPHER	Andrea Modica
PHOTO EDITOR	Kathy Ryan
PUBLISHER	The New York Times
CATEGORY	Photography/Photojournalism, Portraits
DATE	April 4, 1993

PUBLICATION	The New York Times Magazine
AWARD	Merit
ART DIRECTOR	Janet Froelich
PHOTOGRAPHER	Robbie McClaran
PHOTO EDITOR	Kathy Ryan
PUBLISHER	The New York Times
CATEGORY	Photography/Photojournalism, Portraits
DATE	April 25, 1993

PUBLICATION	The Washington Post Magazine
AWARD	Merit
ART DIRECTOR	Kelly Doe
DESIGNER	Sandra Schneider
PHOTOGRAPHER	David Barry
PHOTO EDITOR	Deborah Needleman
PUBLISHER	The Washington Post
CATEGORY	Photography/Photojournalism, Portraits
DATE	December 19, 1993

PUBLICATION	The Washington Post Magazine
AWARD	Merit
ART DIRECTOR	Richard Baker
DESIGNER	Kelly Doe
PHOTOGRAPHER	Len Irish
PHOTO EDITOR	Deborah Needleman
PUBLISHER	The Washington Post
CATEGORY	Photography/Photojournalism, Portraits
DATE	April 11, 1993

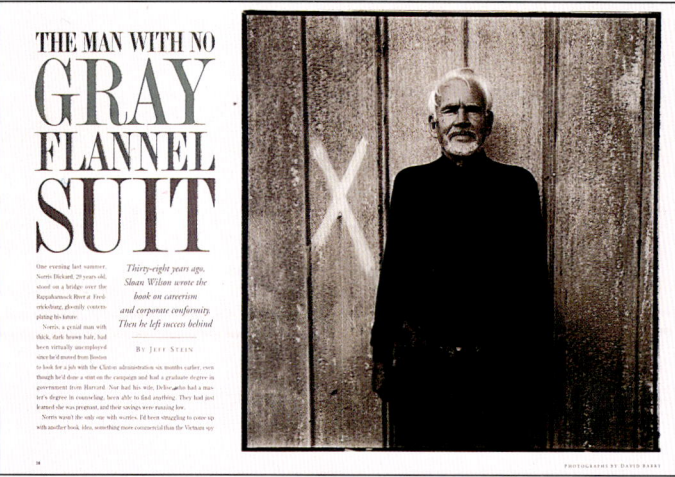

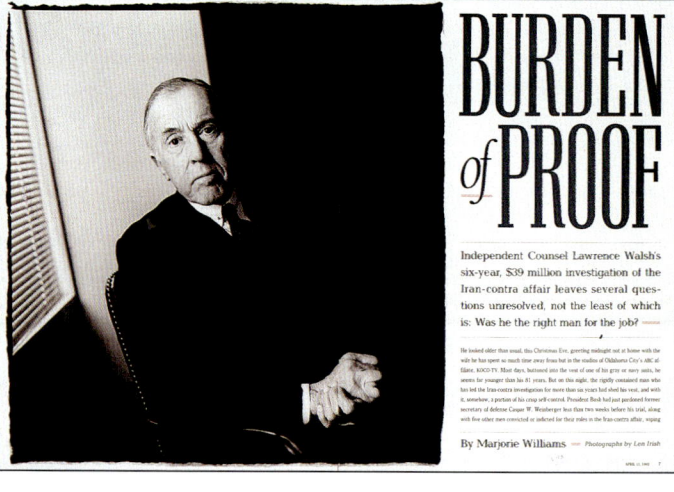

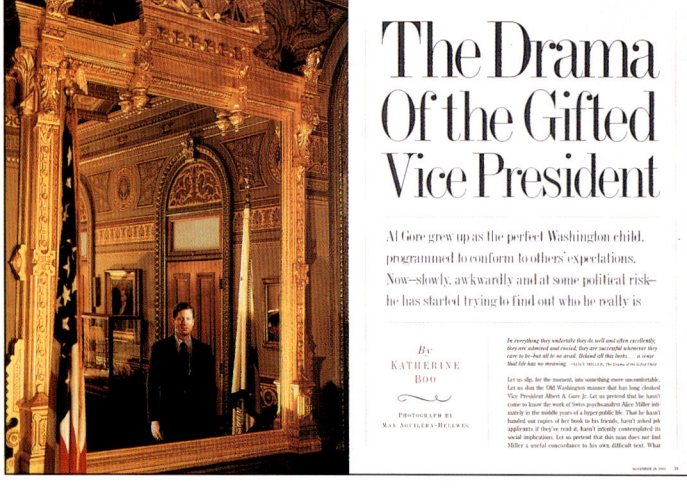

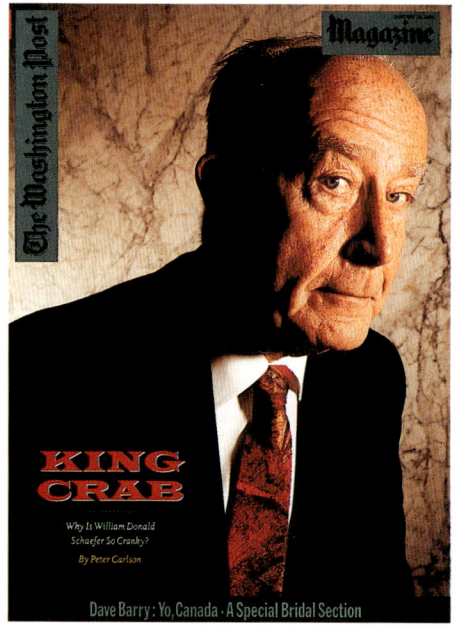

PUBLICATION	The Washington Post Magazine
AWARD	Merit
ART DIRECTOR	Kelly Doe
DESIGNER	Kelly Doe
PHOTOGRAPHER	Max Aguilera-Hellweg
PHOTO EDITOR	Deborah Needleman
PUBLISHER	The Washington Post
CATEGORY	Photography/Photojournalism, Portraits
DATE	November 28, 1993

PUBLICATION	The Washington Post Magazine
AWARD	Merit
ART DIRECTOR	Richard Baker
DESIGNER	Kelly Doe
PHOTOGRAPHER	Brian Smale
PHOTO EDITOR	Karen Tanaka
PUBLISHER	The Washington Post
CATEGORY	Photography/Photojournalism, Portraits
DATE	January 10, 1993

PUBLICATION	The Washington Post Magazine
AWARD	Merit
ART DIRECTOR	Richard Baker
DESIGNER	Kelly Doe
PHOTOGRAPHER	Chris Callis
PHOTO EDITOR	Karen Tanaka
PUBLISHER	The Washington Post
CATEGORY	Photography/Photojournalism, Portraits
DATE	February 7, 1993

PUBLICATION	The Washington Post Magazine
AWARD	Merit
ART DIRECTOR	Kelly Doe
DESIGNER	Sandra Schneider
PHOTOGRAPHER	Karen Kuehn
PHOTO EDITOR	Deborah Needleman
PUBLISHER	The Washington Post
CATEGORY	Photography/Photojournalism, Portraits
DATE	December 12, 1993

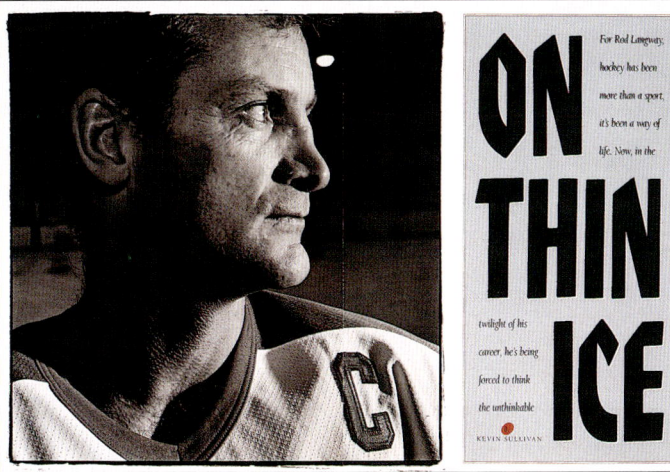

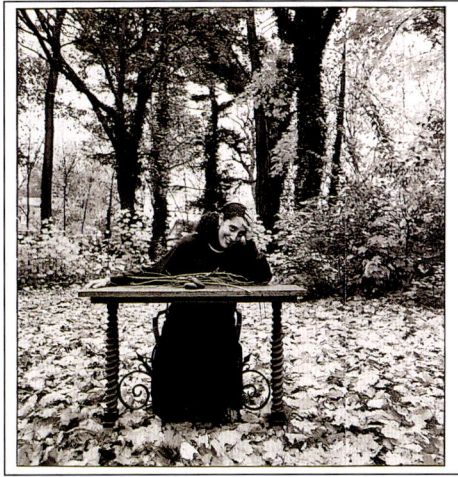

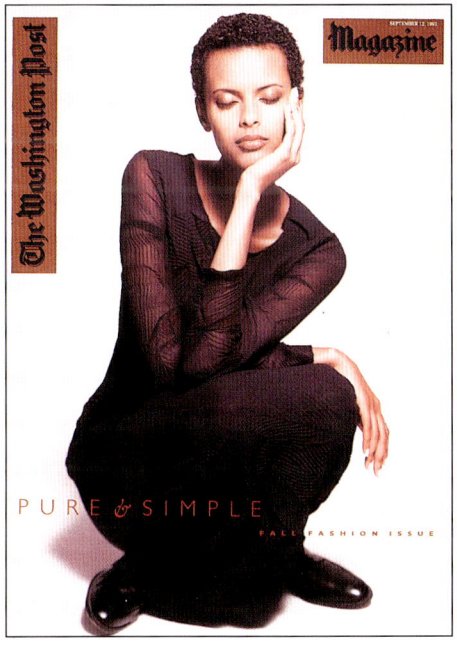

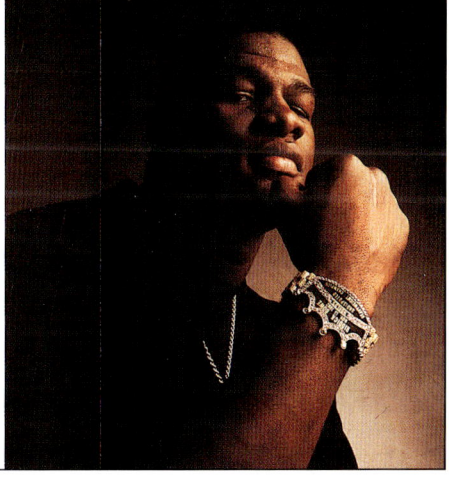

PUBLICATION	The Washington Post Magazine
AWARD	Merit
ART DIRECTOR	Kelly Doe
DESIGNER	Kelly Doe
PHOTOGRAPHER	Torkil Gudnason
PHOTO EDITOR	Deborah Needleman
PUBLISHER	The Washington Post
CATEGORY	Photography/Fashion, Beauty
DATE	September 17, 1993

PUBLICATION	The Washington Post Magazine
AWARD	Merit
ART DIRECTOR	Kelly Doe
DESIGNER	Kelly Doe
PHOTOGRAPHER	Mark Hanauer
PHOTO EDITOR	Karen Tanaka
PUBLISHER	The Washington Post
CATEGORY	Photography/Photojournalism, Portraits
DATE	July 25, 1993

PUBLICATION	Selling		PUBLICATION	Sporting Goods Dealer
AWARD	Merit		AWARD	Merit
ART DIRECTOR	Teresa Fernandes		DESIGN DIRECTOR	Ron Gabriel
DESIGNER	Teresa Fernandes		ART DIRECTOR	Ron Gabriel
PHOTOGRAPHER	Michael Levine		PHOTOGRAPHER	Timothy Reagan
PHOTO EDITOR	Jim Franco		PHOTO EDITOR	Cynthia van Roden
PUBLISHER	Capital Cities/ABC, Inc. Publishing Group		PUBLISHER	Times Mirror
CATEGORY	Photography/Photojournalism, Portraits		CATEGORY	Photography/Photojournalism, Portraits
DATE	September 1993		DATE	April 1993

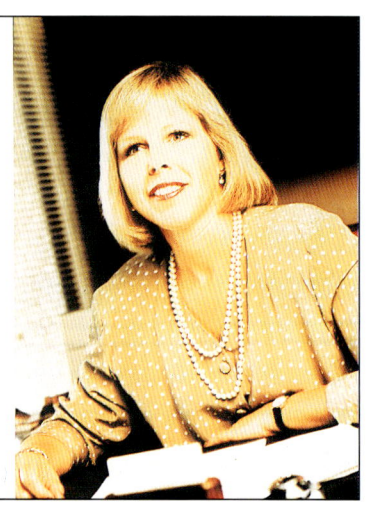

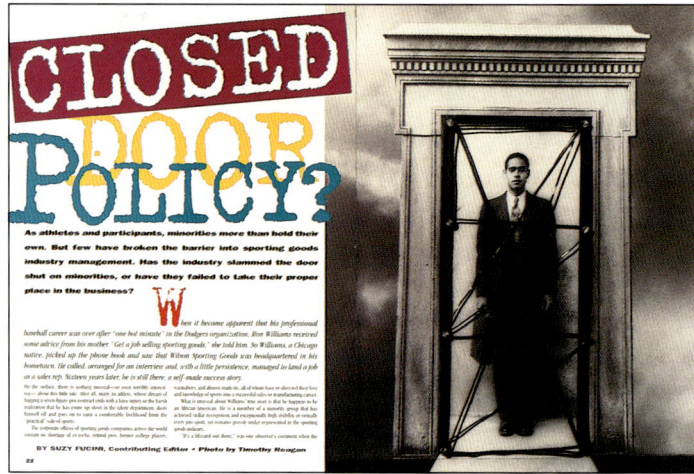

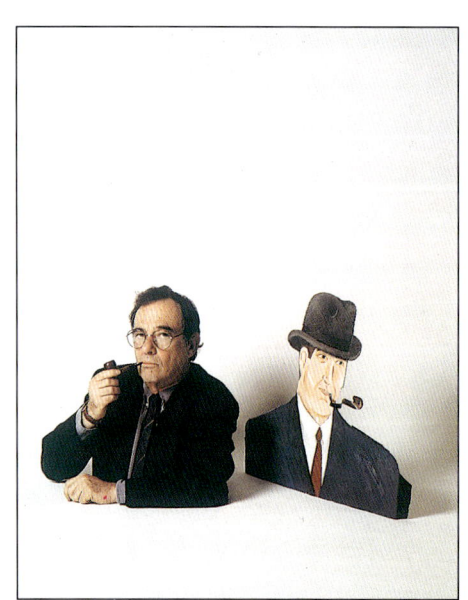

PUBLICATION	Graphis
AWARD	Merit
DESIGN DIRECTOR	B. Martin Pedersen
ART DIRECTORS	B. Martin Pedersen, Randell Pearson, Greg Simpson
DESIGNER	B. Martin Pedersen
PHOTOGRAPHER	Carl Fischer
CATEGORY	Photography/Photojournalism, Portraits
DATE	October 1993

PUBLICATION	Travel & Leisure
AWARD	Gold
DESIGN DIRECTOR	Lloyd Ziff
DESIGNER	Lloyd Ziff
PHOTOGRAPHER	Geof Kern
PHOTO EDITOR	Hazel Hammond
PUBLISHER	American Express Publishing
CATEGORY	Photography/Still Life, Interiors, Travel
DATE	May 1993

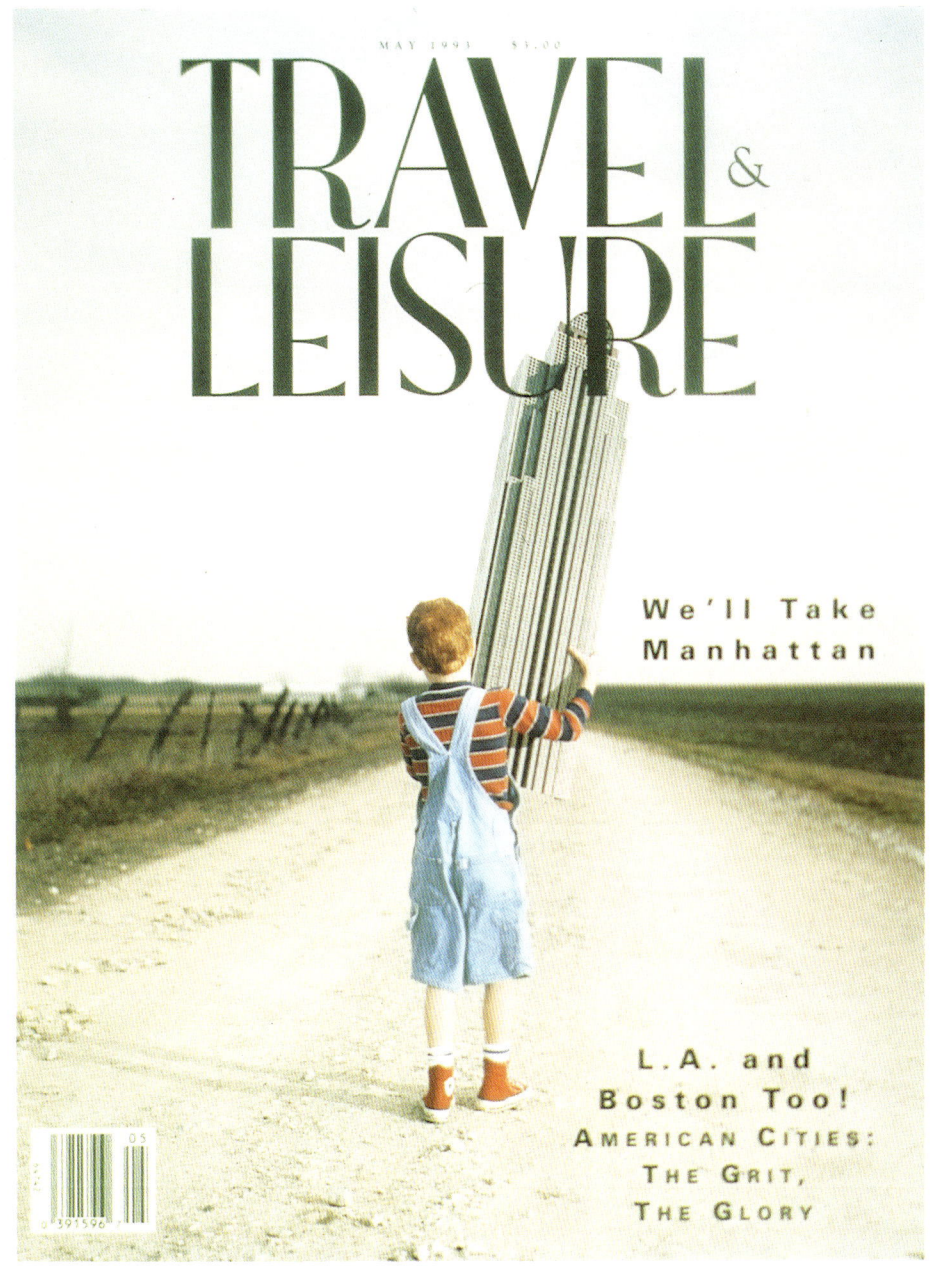

PUBLICATION	Discover
AWARD	Silver
ART DIRECTOR	David Armario
DESIGNER	David Armario
PHOTOGRAPHER	Geof Kern
PHOTO EDITOR	John Barker
PUBLISHER	Disney Magazine Publishing, Inc.
CATEGORY	Photography/Still Life, Interiors, Travel
DATE	June 1993

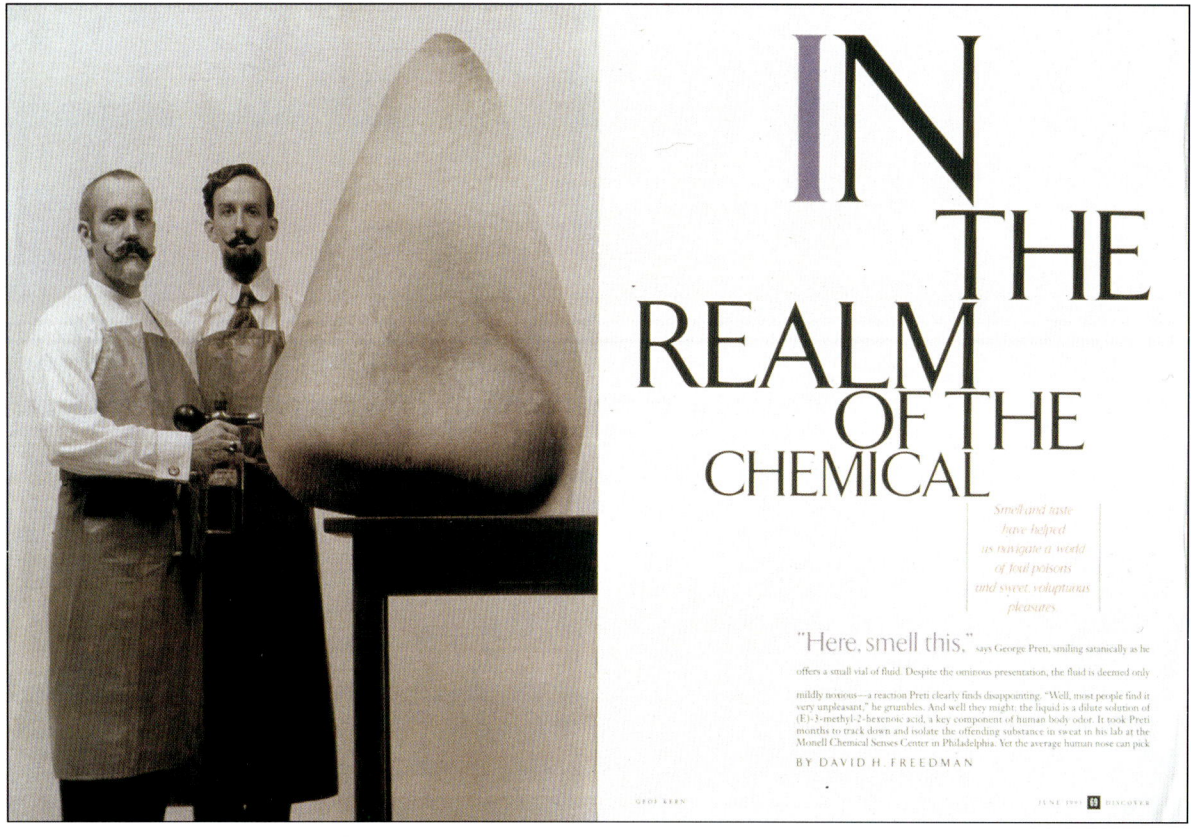

IN THE REALM OF THE CHEMICAL

Smell and taste have helped us navigate a world of foul poisons and sweet, voluptuous pleasures

"Here, smell this," says George Preti, smiling satanically as he offers a small vial of fluid. Despite the ominous presentation, the fluid is deemed only mildly noxious—a reaction Preti clearly finds disappointing. "Well, most people find it very unpleasant," he grumbles. And well they might: the liquid is a dilute solution of (E)-3-methyl-2-hexenoic acid, a key component of human body odor. It took Preti months to track down and isolate the offending substance in sweat in his lab at the Monell Chemical Senses Center in Philadelphia. Yet the average human nose can pick

BY DAVID H. FREEDMAN

PUBLICATION	Discover
AWARD	Merit
ART DIRECTOR	David Armario
DESIGNER	David Armario
PHOTOGRAPHER	Geof Kern
PHOTO EDITOR	John Barker
PUBLISHER	Disney Magazine Publishing, Inc.
CATEGORY	Photography/Still Life, Interiors, Travel
DATE	June 1993

PUBLICATION	Travel & Leisure
AWARD	Merit
DESIGN DIRECTOR	Lloyd Ziff
DESIGNER	Lloyd Ziff
PHOTOGRAPHER	Geof Kern
PHOTO EDITOR	Hazel Hammond
PUBLISHER	American Express Publishing
CATEGORY	Photography/Still Life, Interiors, Travel
DATE	May 1993

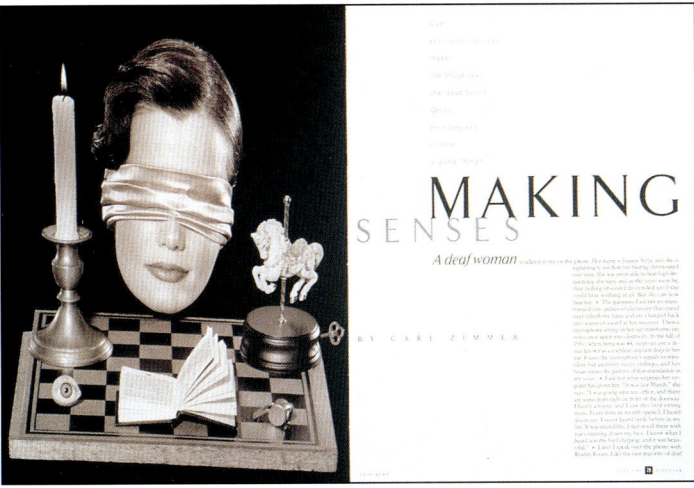

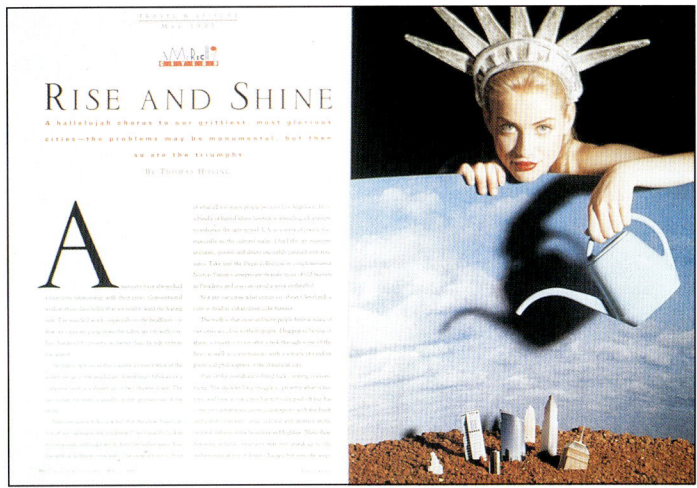

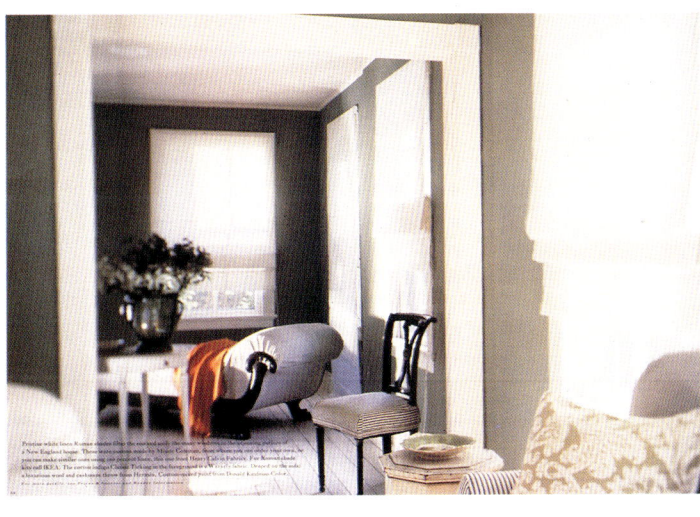

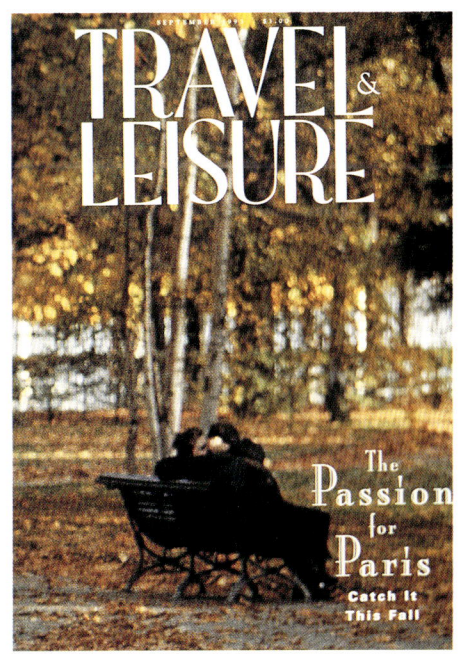

PUBLICATION	House Beautiful
AWARD	Merit
ART DIRECTOR	Andrzej Janerka
DESIGNER	Andrzej Janerka
PHOTOGRAPHER	Jon Jensen
PUBLISHER	The Hearst Corporation
CATEGORY	Photography/Still Life, Interiors, Travel
DATE	January 1993

PUBLICATION	Travel & Leisure
AWARD	Merit
DESIGN DIRECTOR	Lloyd Ziff
DESIGNER	Lloyd Ziff
PHOTOGRAPHER	Hugues Colson
PHOTO EDITOR	Hazel Hammond
PUBLISHER	American Express Publishing
CATEGORY	Photography/Still Life, Interiors, Travel
DATE	September 1993

PUBLICATION   Men's Journal
AWARD   Gold
ART DIRECTOR   Matthew Drace
DESIGNER   Matthew Drace
PHOTOGRAPHER   Raymond Meeks
PUBLISHER   Wenner Media
CATEGORY   Photography Story/Photojournalism, Portraits
DATE   March - April 1993

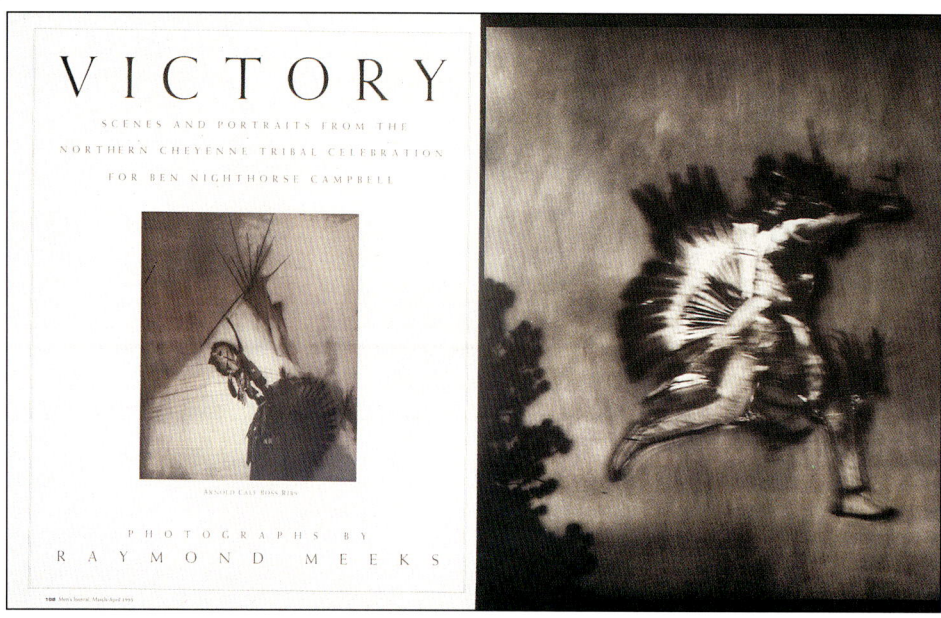

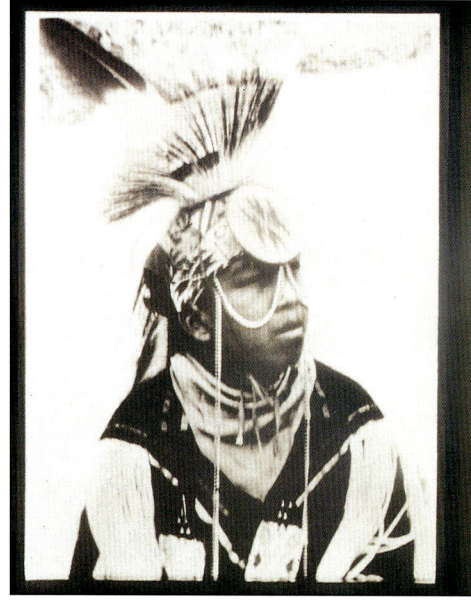

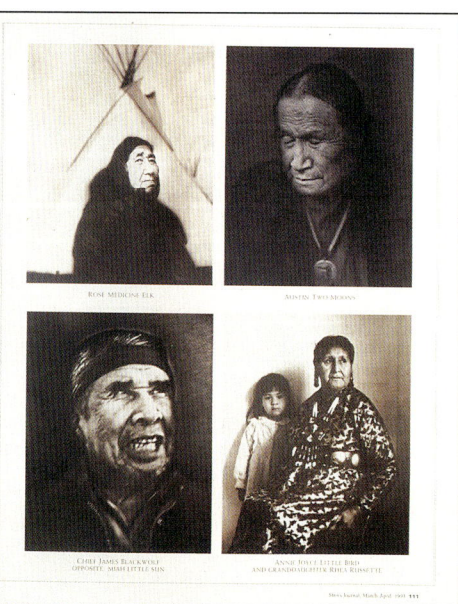

PUBLICATION	Discover
AWARD	Silver
ART DIRECTOR	David Armario
DESIGNERS	David Armario, James Lambertus
PHOTOGRAPHER	Antonin Kratochvil
PHOTO EDITORS	John Barker, Dawn Morishige
PUBLISHER	Disney Magazine Publishing, Inc.
CATEGORY	Photography Story/Photojournalism, Portraits
DATE	March 1993

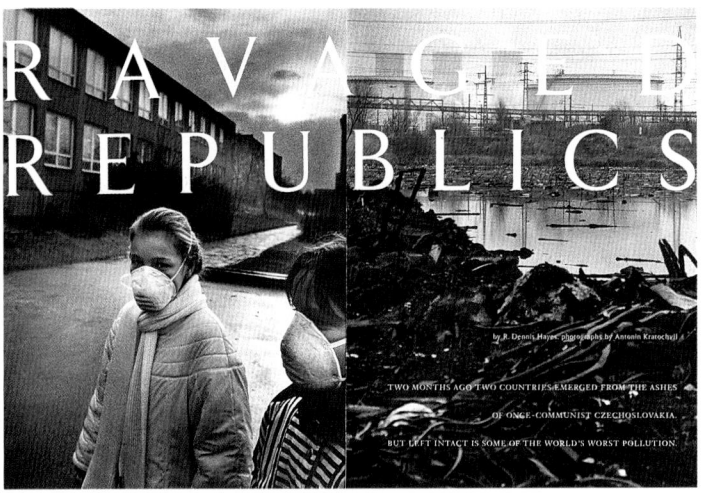

RAVAGED REPUBLICS

by R. Dennis Hayes, photographs by Antonin Kratochvil

TWO MONTHS AGO TWO COUNTRIES EMERGED FROM THE ASHES
OF ONCE-COMMUNIST CZECHOSLOVAKIA.
BUT LEFT INTACT IS SOME OF THE WORLD'S WORST POLLUTION.

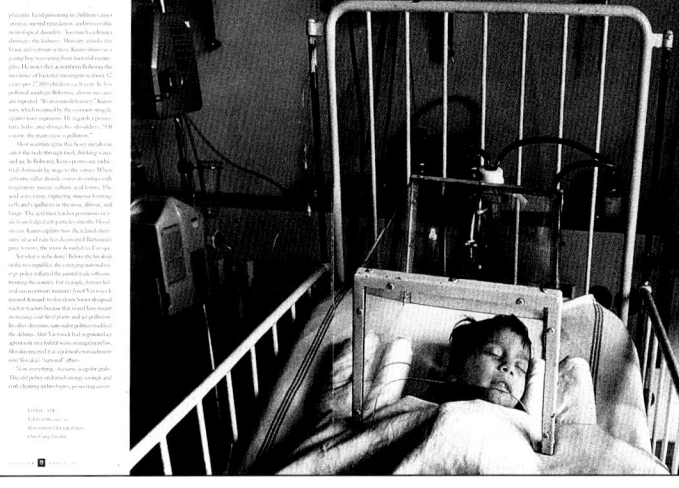

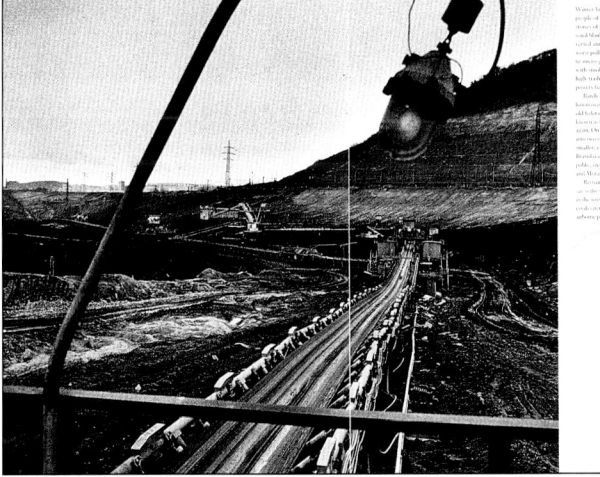

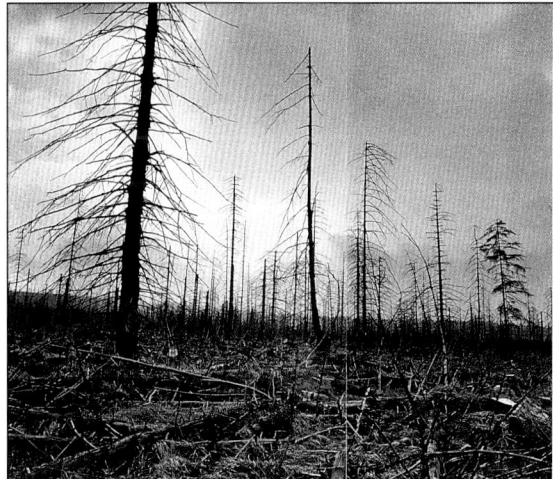

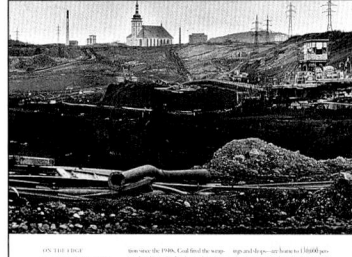

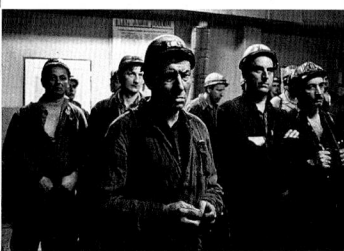

PUBLICATION	Mother Jones
AWARD	Silver
DESIGN DIRECTOR	Kerry Tremain
DESIGNER	Kerry Tremain
PHOTOGRAPHER	James Balog
PHOTO EDITOR	Kerry Tremain
PUBLISHER	Foundation for National Progress
CATEGORY	Photography Story/Photojournalism, Portraits
DATE	July/August 1993

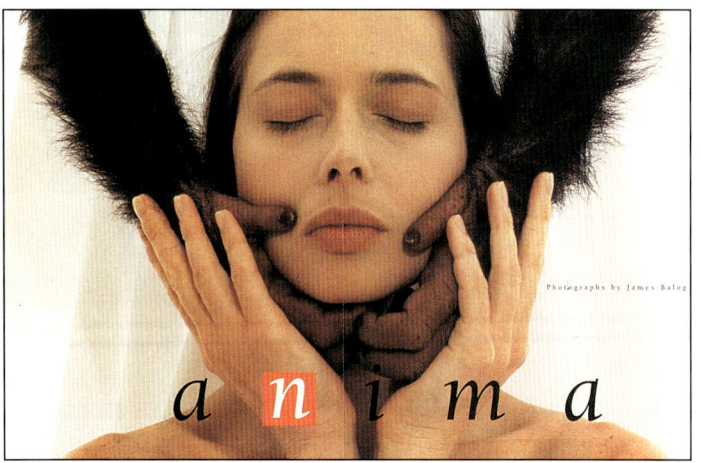

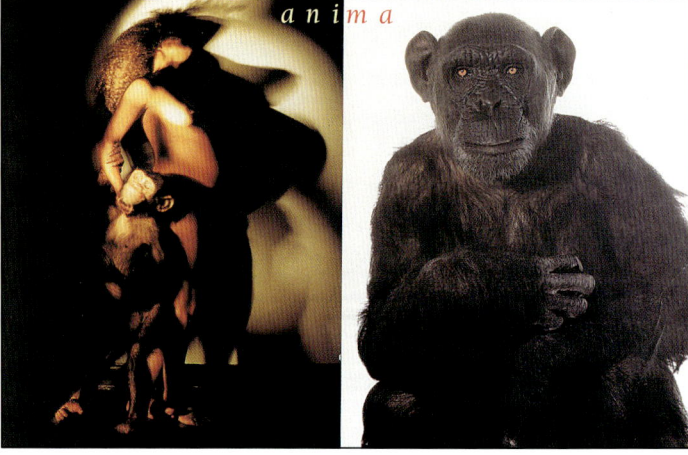

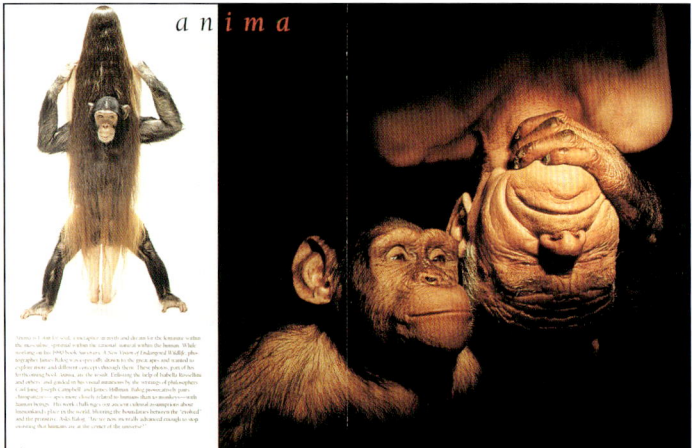

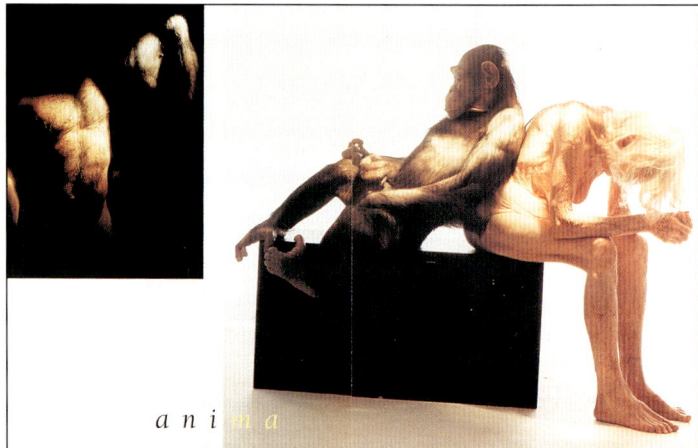

PUBLICATION	Rolling Stone
AWARD	Silver
ART DIRECTOR	Fred Woodward
DESIGNER	Catherine Gilmore-Barnes
PHOTOGRAPHER	Sebastiao Salgado
PHOTO EDITOR	Laurie Kratochvil
PUBLISHER	Wenner Media
CATEGORY	Photography Story/Photojournalism, Portraits
DATE	September 16, 1993

WORKERS OF THE WORLD

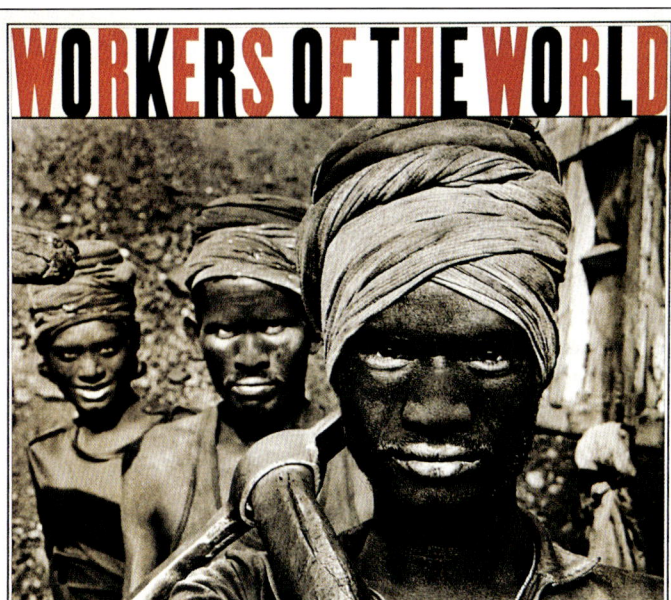

A PORTFOLIO BY SEBASTIÃO SALGADO

IN HIS IMAGES of the world's dispossessed, Sebastião Salgado refuses to choose between the dignity and the misery of his subjects. He simply obliterates the distinction. His photographs of famine victims in Africa, peasants in South America and laborers everywhere rest in a place where journalism and art conspire, one tugging conspicuously at the conscience, while the other secretly rustles the soul.

This peculiar chemistry has made Salgado, 49, world famous. Exhibitions of his work have been mounted in New York City, Paris, Madrid and elsewhere. His photographs have appeared — not illuminating a text but as the text — in prominent European and American publications.

But Salgado's photographs are less frequently displayed in the locales where the images are gathered — a coal mine in India, a tea plantation in Rwanda, sugar-cane fields in Cuba, a sulfur-yielding volcano in Java. In this, his work replicates the transfer of raw material from developing to developed

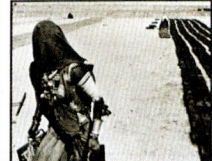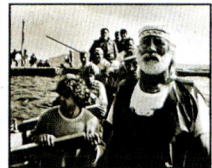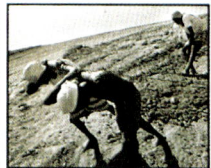

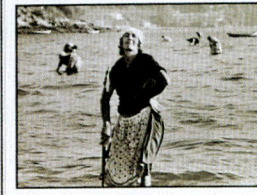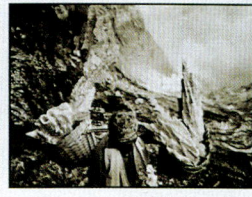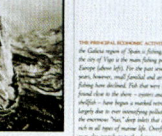

nations, a cycle he documents in his new book, *Workers: An Archaeology of the Industrial Age*, from which these eight images are taken.

Salgado began the project in 1986, traveling to regions of the world where despair is more industrious than tourism. Lingering for days instead of hours, he sought to document the interminable push and pull of manual labor before it is completely displaced by the new age of production. In the process he also continued to reinvigorate photojournalism, itself a victim of the new age of TV and video. Salgado's pictures are testament to the vibrancy of still images.

The only son of a Brazilian cattle rancher, Salgado was trained as an economist. He has described *Workers* as his homage to the traditional working class, particularly that of the poorer Southern Hemisphere. His portraits of these people have an earnestness and simple grace that invests their hard lives with virtue. In certain of Salgado's photographs, labor takes on a nearly religious quality, and the grinding, quotidian struggle of the worker is transformed

into something at once universal and heroic.

Though he often bathes his subjects in a beatific light, Salgado does not obscure reality. His six-year documentation of workers tells us not so much that the labor of blistered

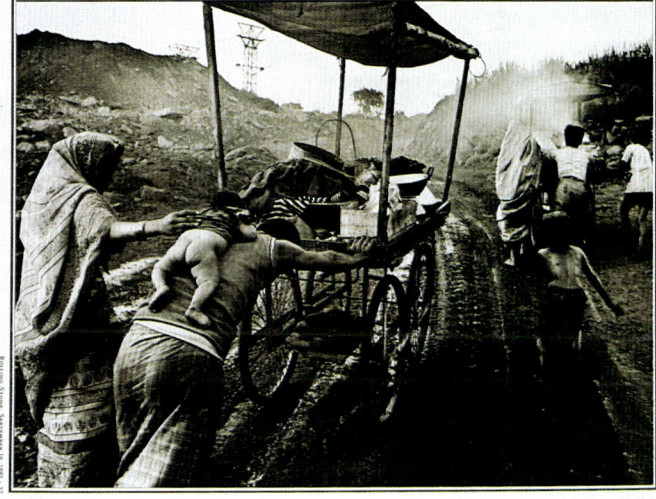

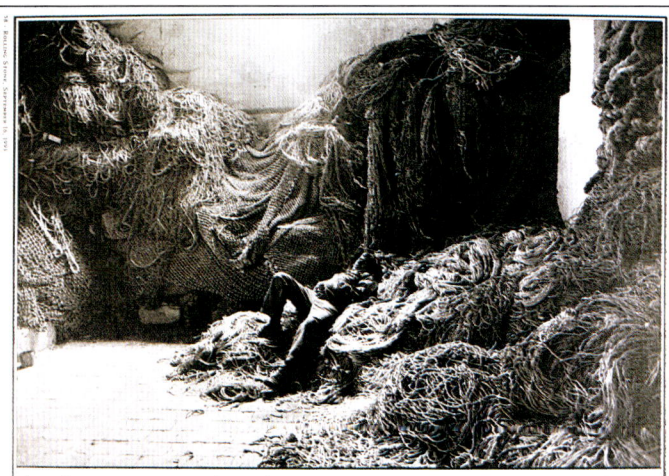

hands, straining muscles and sweat is receding into the past, supplanted by computers and robots, but that such elemental human toil remains very much among us. In seeking to memorialize the past, Salgado's "archaeology" has uncovered the forgotten present.   — FRANCIS WILKINSON

PUBLICATION	The Philadelphia Inquirer Magazine
AWARD	Silver
DESIGN DIRECTOR	Jessica Helfand
ART DIRECTOR	Bert Fox
DESIGNER	Bert Fox
PHOTOGRAPHERS	Carolina Salguero, April Saul, Ron Tarver, Sebastio Salgado
PHOTO EDITOR	Bert Fox
PUBLISHER	The Philadelphia Inquirer
CATEGORY	Photography Story/Photojournalism, Portraits
DATE	July 25/November 14/October 17/April 11, 1993

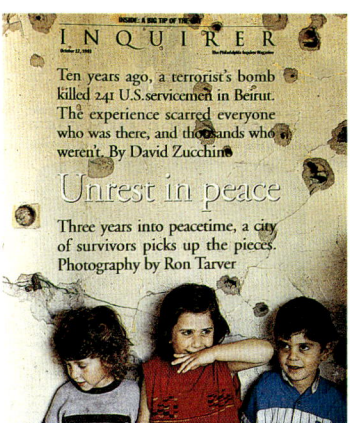

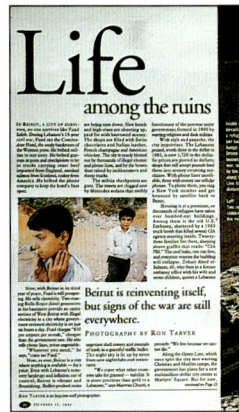

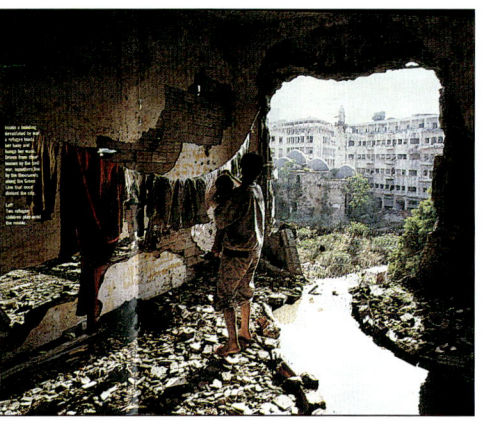

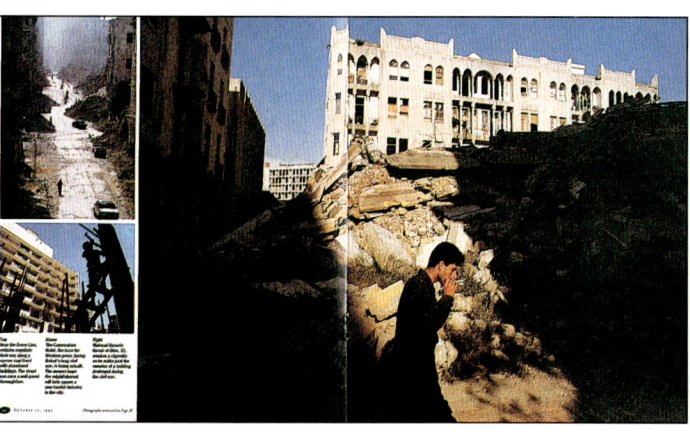

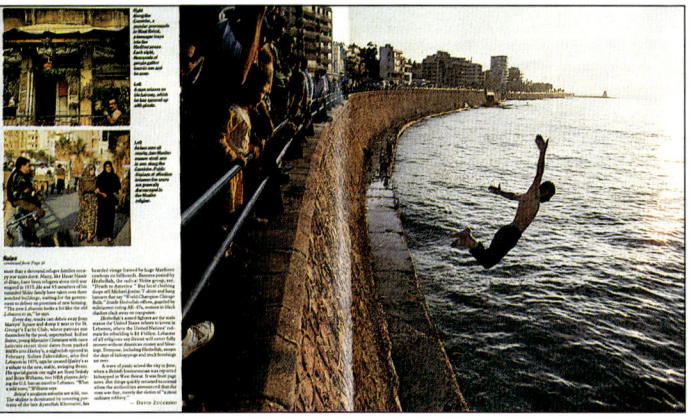

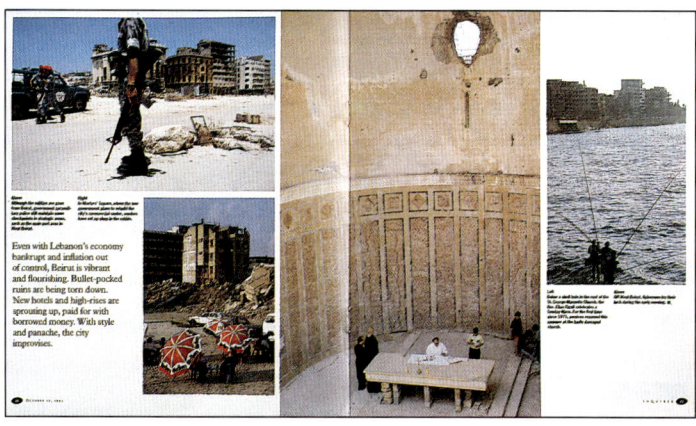

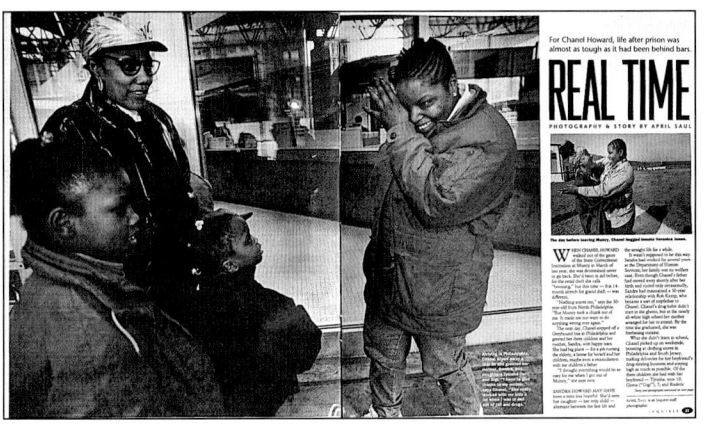

For Chanel Howard, life after prison was almost as tough as it had been behind bars.

REAL TIME

PHOTOGRAPHY & STORY BY APRIL SAUL

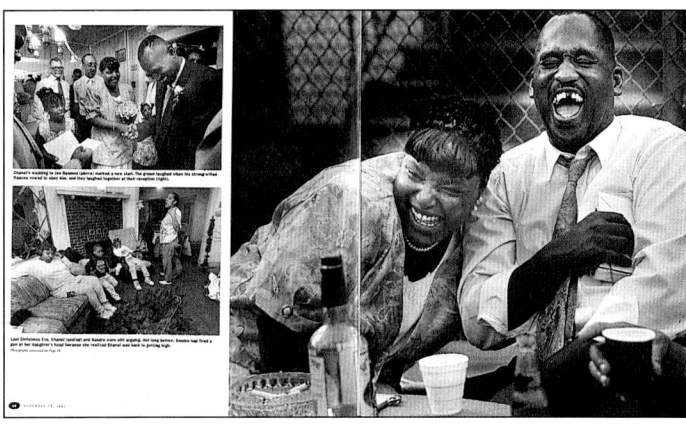

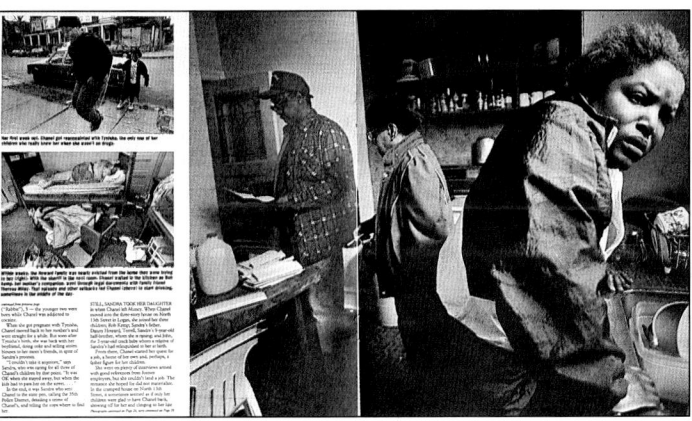

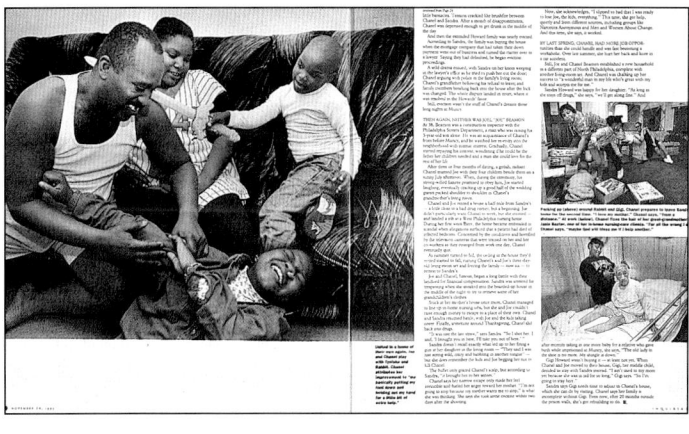

PUBLICATION   The Philadelphia Inquirer Magazine
AWARD   Silver
DESIGN DIRECTOR   Jessica Helfand
ART DIRECTOR   Bert Fox
DESIGNER   Bert Fox
PHOTOGRAPHERS   Carolina Salguero, April Saul, Ron Tarver,
                   Sebastio Salgado
PHOTO EDITOR   Bert Fox
PUBLISHER   The Philadelphia Inquirer
CATEGORY   Photography Story/Photojournalism, Portraits
DATE   July 25/November 14/October 17/April 11, 1993

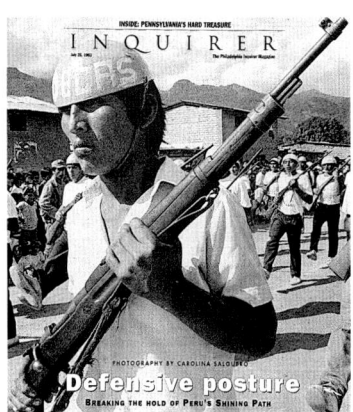

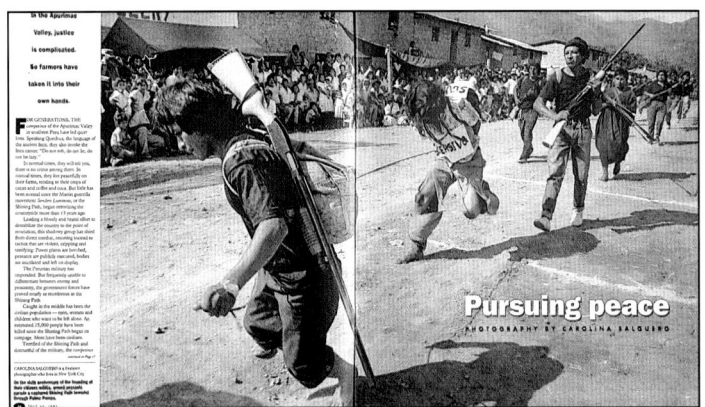

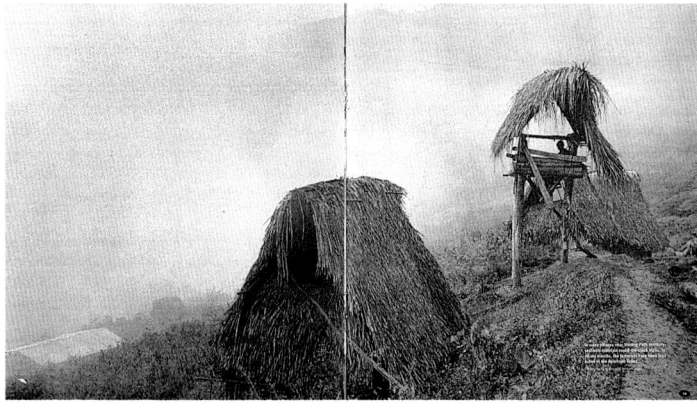

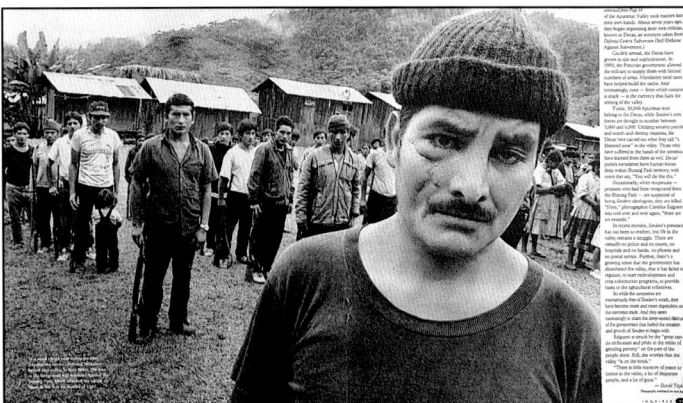

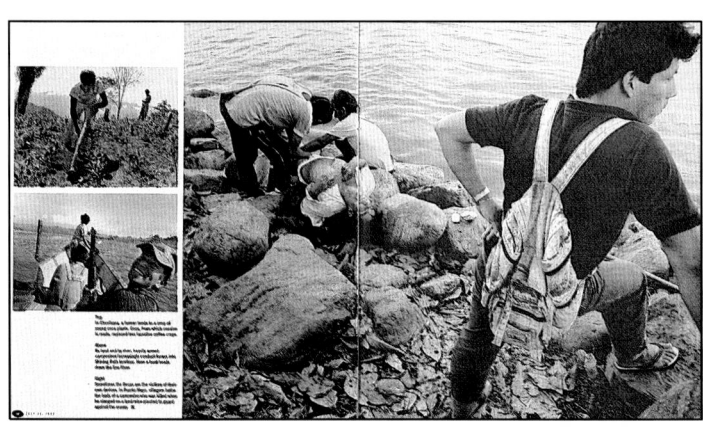

THE OLD FRONT LINE

TEXT AND PHOTOGRAPHS BY J. S. CARTIER

THREE-QUARTERS OF A CENTURY HAS NOT BEEN TIME ENOUGH TO EFFACE THE REMNANTS OF VIOLENCE ALONG A FOUR-HUNDRED-MILE FRONT

It is early fall in France, and the forest is silent and peaceful. A man, dressed in camouflage fatigues and carrying a metal detector and a sawed-off pickax, disappears into the musty underbrush. Here and there holes in the ground are half-filled with dead leaves; strands of rusty barbed wire hang from corkscrew-shaped metal posts. The forest, about forty miles from Paris, is officially called the Bois de la brigade Marine. The French government has given this land to the United States; Americans know it as Belleau Wood. It was here that men of a U.S. Marine Corps brigade, attached to the 2d Infantry Division of the American Expeditionary Forces, fought a desperate battle to keep the German army from reaching Paris in the summer of 1918. Most visitors to the site look at the cemetery and its ornate chapel, the hunting lodge, the captured German 77-mm guns whose wheels have long since rusted away, and the marble monument. Then they drive off to visit the imposing Aisne-Marne monument above Château-Thierry. Meanwhile, the man in camouflage is back, smiling. He has found what he was looking for: uniform buttons and

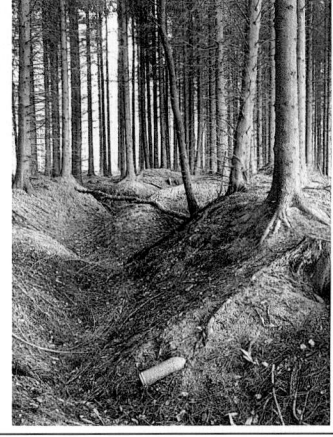

In a corner of the Argonne Forest heavily contested by the French and Germans in the war's final year, the zigzag trenches still yield up the debris of battle, including the shell (left) in the foreground.

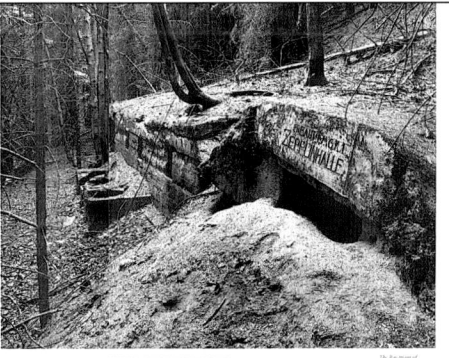

He steps around a French support trench to take in by the chapel and valley beyond. With the remains created by the open topography of Verdun. The concrete "fronds" poured over it can and later turned into a forest has itself grown to take on a life that is man's not apart within.

Fellow at King's College with a research assistant to help identify the vintage we found.

Anna and I returned to New York in January 1992 to print the dozens and I amassed negatives we had made in the few busy months of the project. By the time we returned to Europe the following month, we had developed the system that we stuck with for the rest of the project. First we would sorts ahead of time to the owners of the townships along the old front line, asking for their help in locating sites. In many cases people had been living for so long next to First War vestiges of there had become blend to them and very often could not think of any other first attrib. but a few days we would often they would remember, and we would always tell the villagers that in a very welcome that a certain look and forth on our journey from the North Sea to the Vosges. We did from such routes trips along the front, totaling many thousand miles.

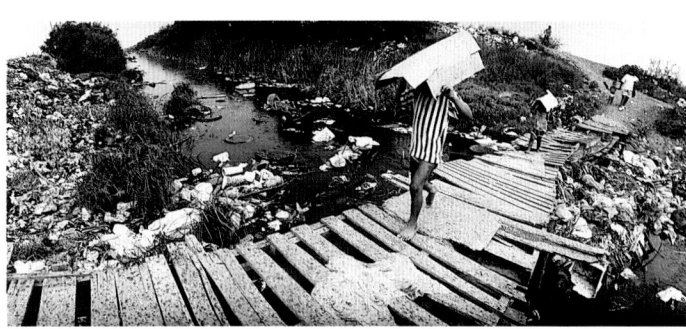

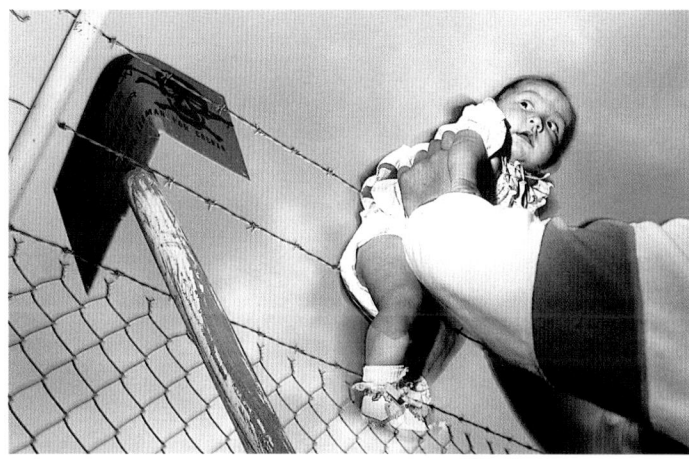

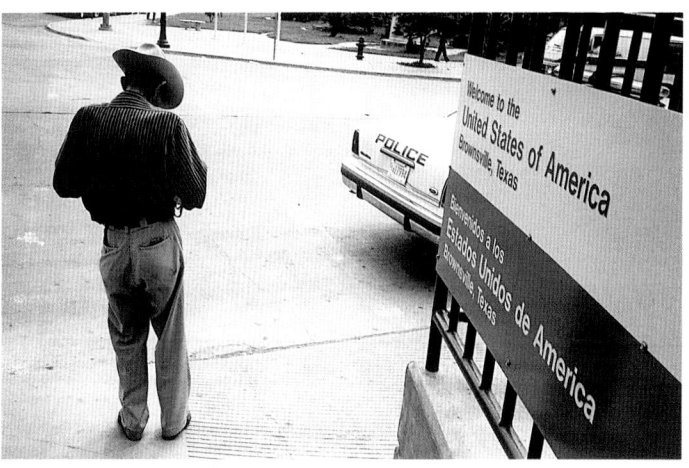

PUBLICATION	American Heritage
AWARD	Merit
ART DIRECTOR	Peter Morance
DESIGNER	Peter Morance
PHOTOGRAPHER	J.S. Cartier
PHOTO EDITOR	Jane Colihan
PUBLISHER	American Heritage
CATEGORY	Photography Story/Photojournalism, Portraits
DATE	November 1993

PUBLICATION	Audubon
AWARD	Merit
ART DIRECTOR	Suzanne Morin
PHOTOGRAPHER	Robb Kendrick
PHOTO EDITOR	Peter Howe
PUBLISHER	National Audubon Society
CATEGORY	Photography Story/Photojournalism, Portraits
DATE	November/December 1993

PUBLICATION	Buzz
AWARD	Merit
DESIGN DIRECTOR	Charles Hess
ART DIRECTOR	Charles Hess
PHOTOGRAPHER	Horace Bristol
PHOTO EDITOR	Charles Hess
PUBLISHER	Buzz, Inc.
CATEGORY	Photography Story/Photojournalism, Portraits
DATE	December 1993

PUBLICATION	Entertainment Weekly
AWARD	Merit
DESIGN DIRECTOR	Michael Grossman
ART DIRECTOR	Mark Michaelson
DESIGNER	Miriam Campiz
PHOTOGRAPHER	Jeffery Newbury
PHOTO EDITORS	Mary Dunn, Doris Brautigan
PUBLISHER	Time Inc.
CATEGORY	Photography Story/Photojournalism, Portraits
DATE	November 30, 1993

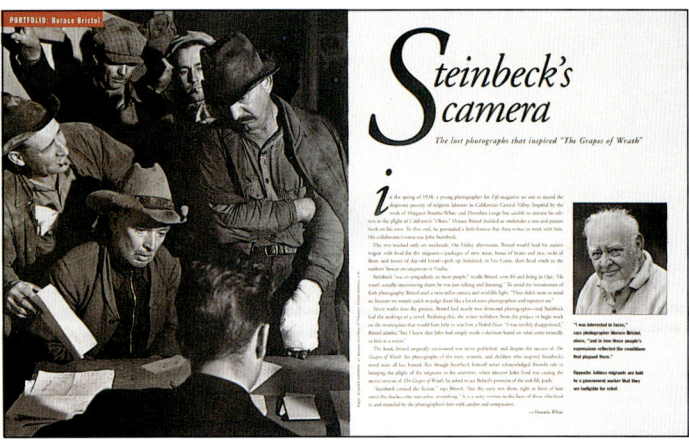

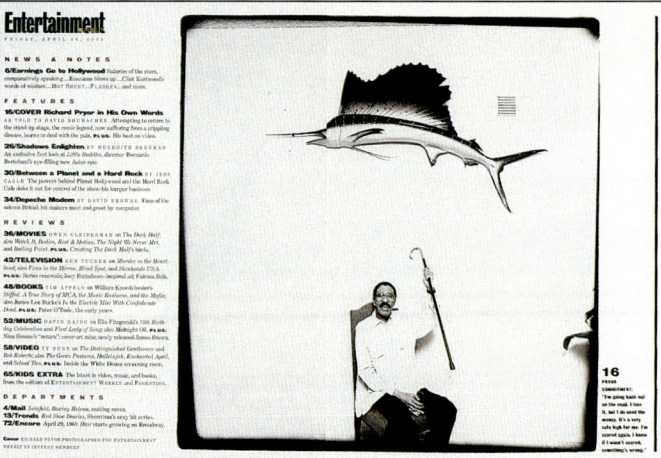

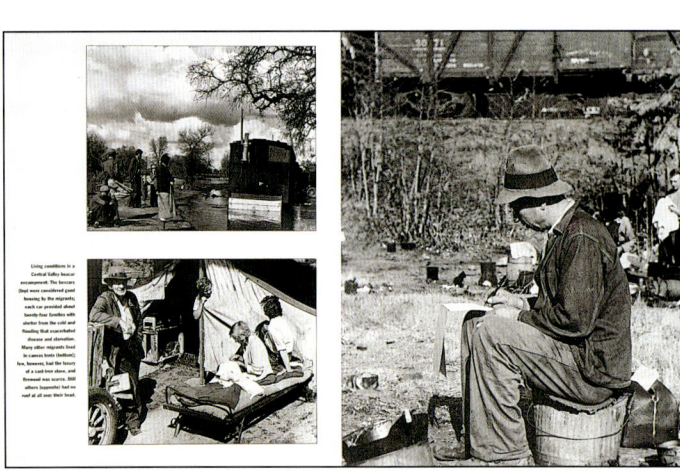

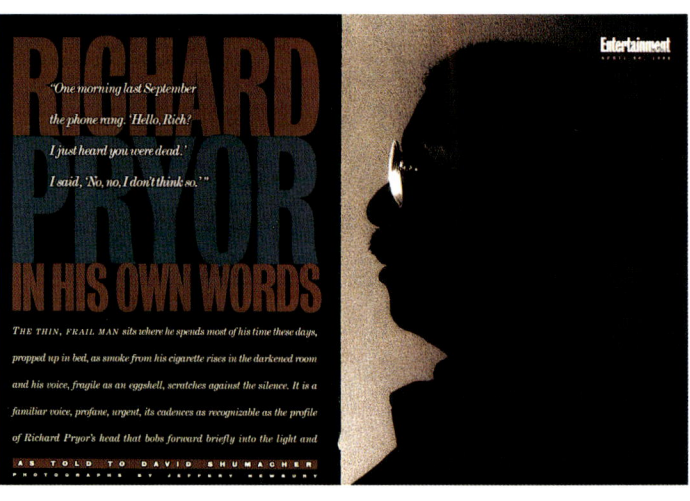

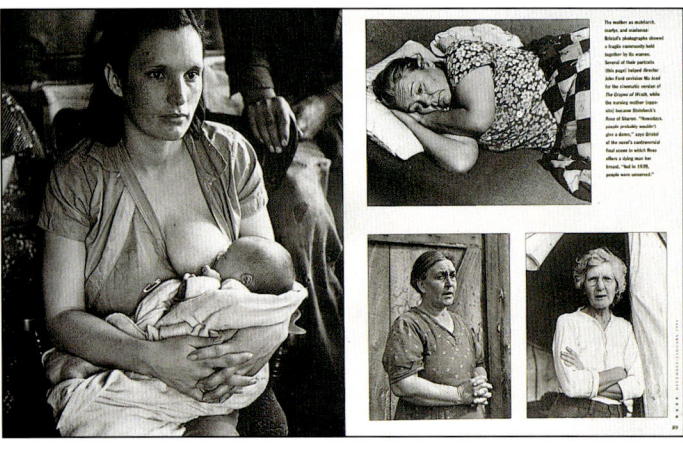

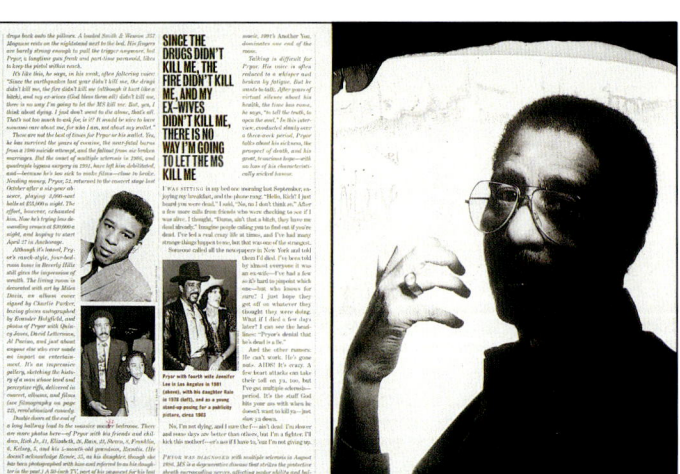

PUBLICATION	GQ
AWARD	Merit
CREATIVE DIRECTOR	Robert Priest
DESIGNER	Dina White
PHOTOGRAPHER	Mary Ellen Mark
PUBLISHER	The Condé Nast Publications Inc.
CATEGORY	Photography Story/Photojournalism, Portraits
DATE	October 1993

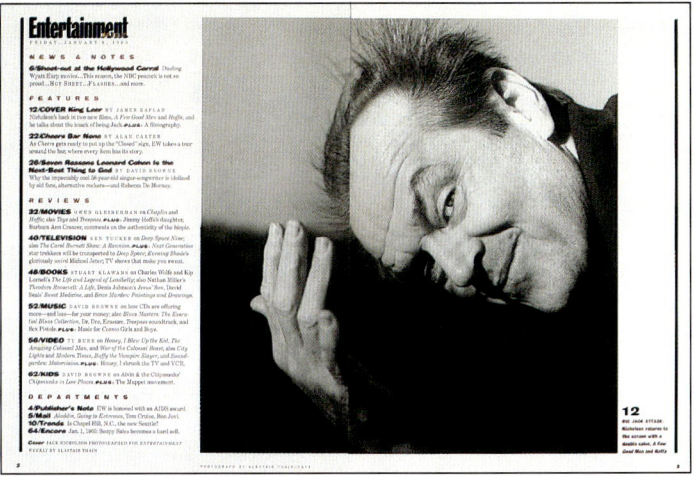

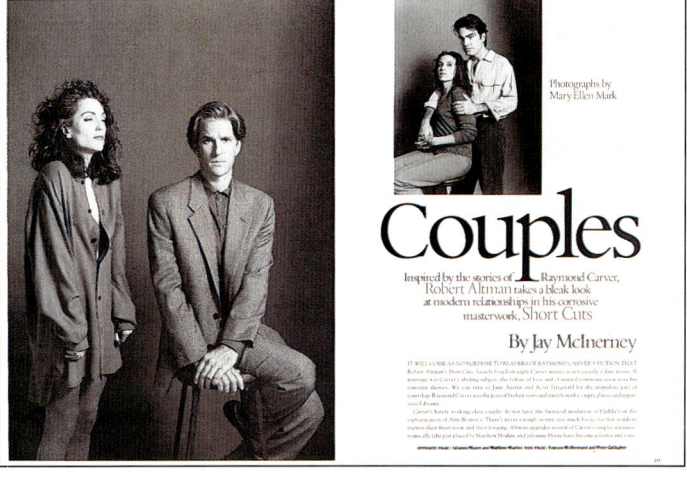

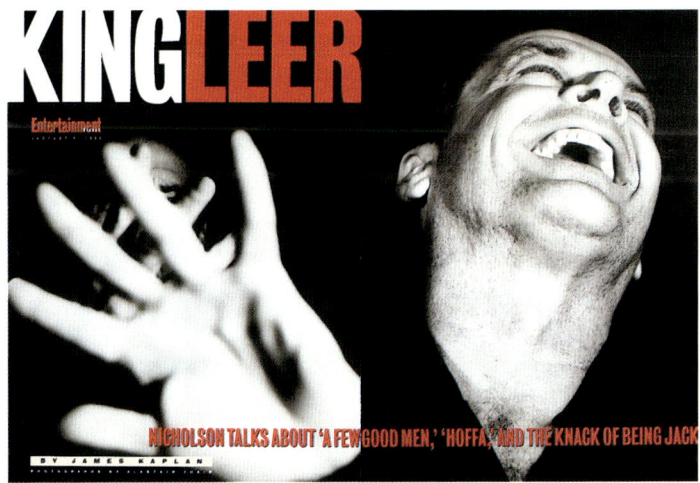

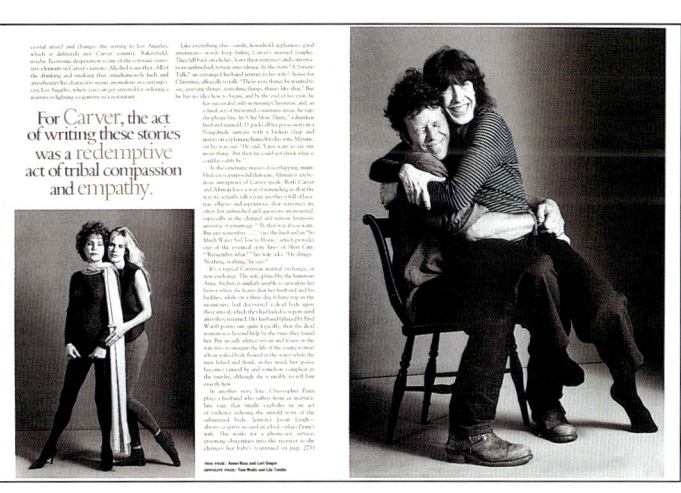

PUBLICATION	Entertainment Weekly
AWARD	Merit
DESIGN DIRECTOR	Michael Grossman
ART DIRECTOR	Mark Michaelson
DESIGNER	Mark Michaelson
PHOTOGRAPHER	Alastair Thain
PHOTO EDITORS	Mary Dunn, Doris Brautigan
PUBLISHER	Time Inc.
CATEGORY	Photography Story/Photojournalism, Portraits
DATE	January 8, 1993

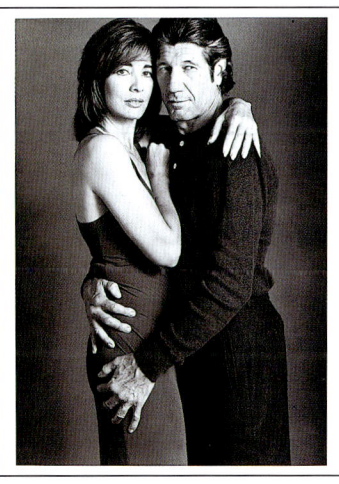

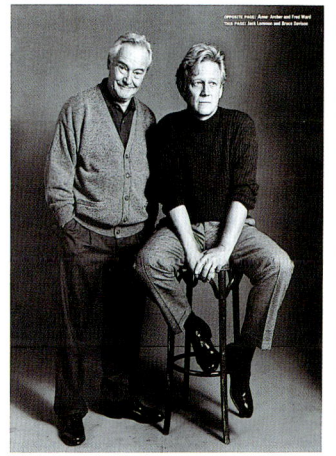

PUBLICATION	Life	PUBLICATION	Martha Stewart Living
AWARD	Merit	AWARD	Merit
DESIGN DIRECTOR	Tom Bentkowski	ART DIRECTOR	Gael Towey
ART DIRECTOR	Tom Bentkowski	DESIGNER	Anne Johnson
DESIGNER	Tom Bentkowski	PHOTOGRAPHERS	Constance Hansen, Guzman
PHOTOGRAPHER	Lynn Johnson	PUBLISHER	Time Inc.
PHOTO EDITORS	David Friend, Bobbi Baker Burrows	CATEGORY	Photography Story/Photojournalism, Portraits
PUBLISHER	Time Inc.	DATE	February 1993
CATEGORY	Photography Story/Photojournalism, Portraits		
DATE	February 1993		

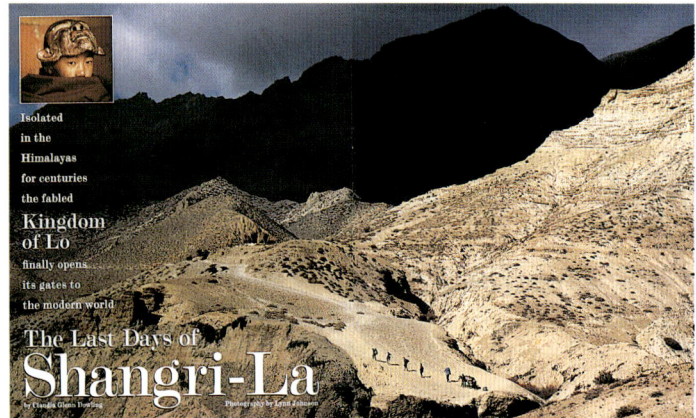

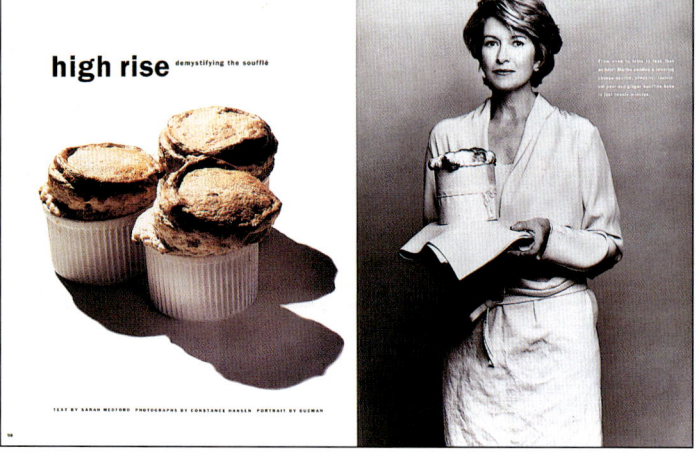

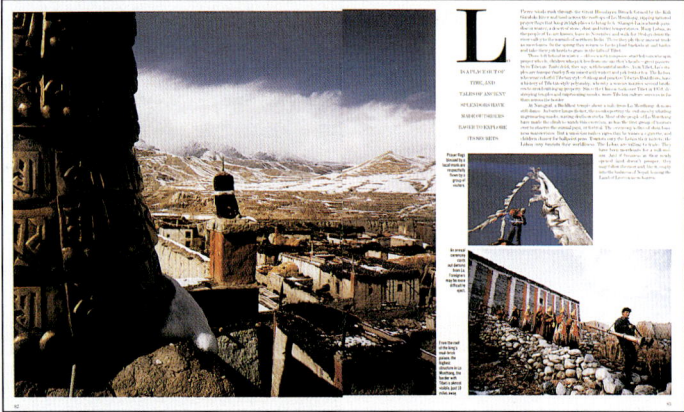

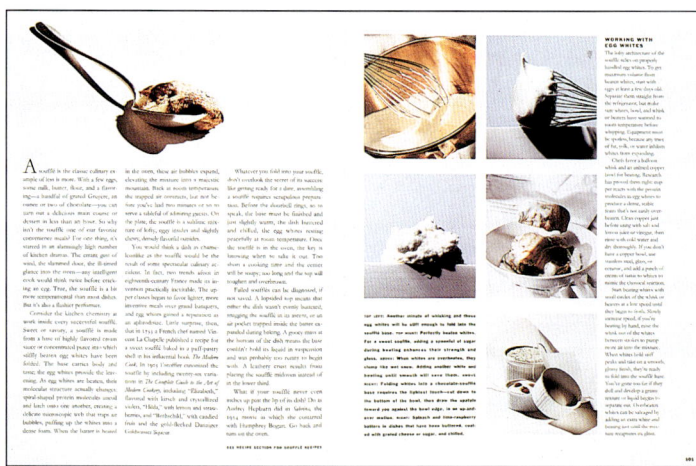

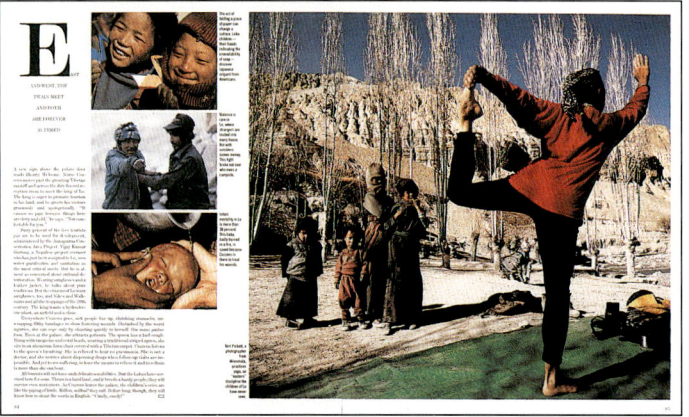

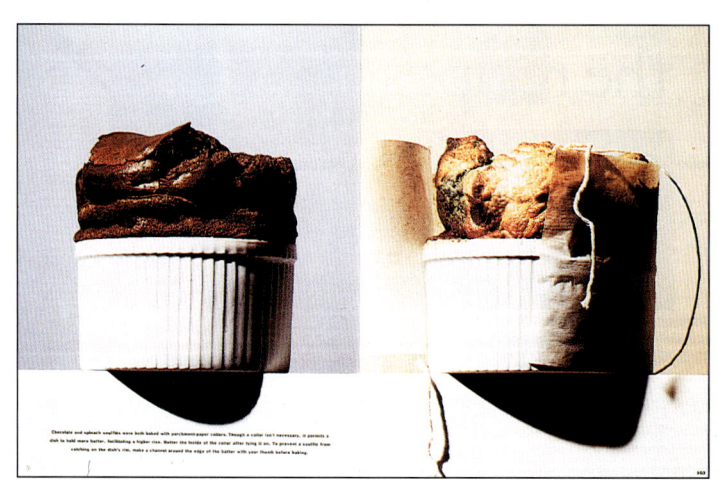

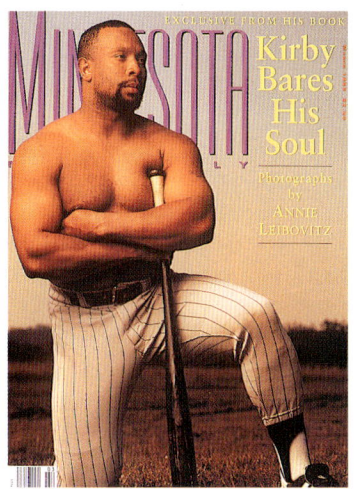

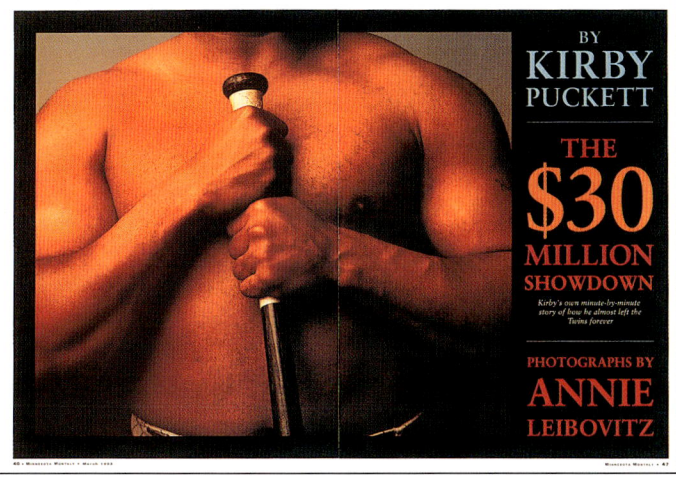

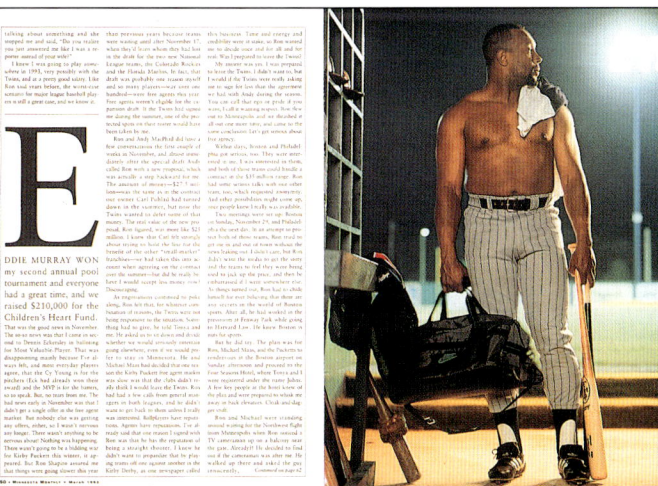

PUBLICATION	Minnesota Monthly
AWARD	Merit
ART DIRECTOR	Mark Shafer
DESIGNERS	Mark Shafer, Brian Donahue
PHOTOGRAPHER	Annie Leibovitz
PHOTO EDITOR	Mark Shafer
PUBLISHER	Minnesota Monthly Publications
CATEGORY	Photography Story/Photojournalism, Portraits
DATE	March 1993

PUBLICATION	Mother Jones
AWARD	Merit
DESIGN DIRECTOR	Kerry Tremain
ART DIRECTOR	Kerry Tremain
DESIGNER	Kerry Tremain
PHOTOGRAPHER	Nicos Economopoulos
PHOTO EDITOR	Kerry Tremain
PUBLISHER	The Foundation for National Progress
CATEGORY	Photography Story/Photojournalism, Portraits
DATE	January/February 1993

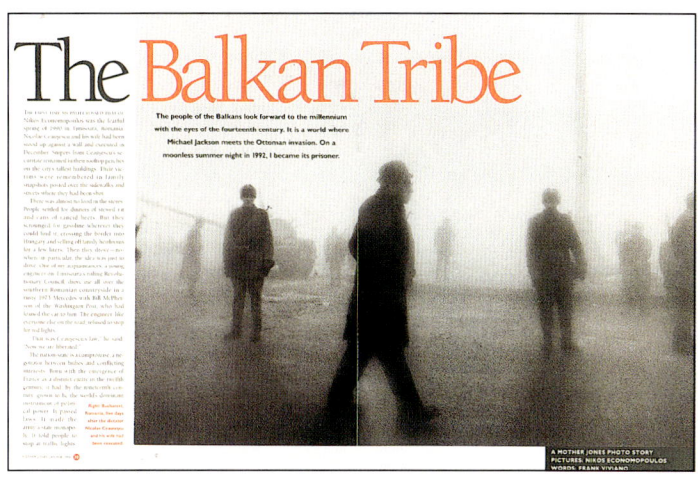

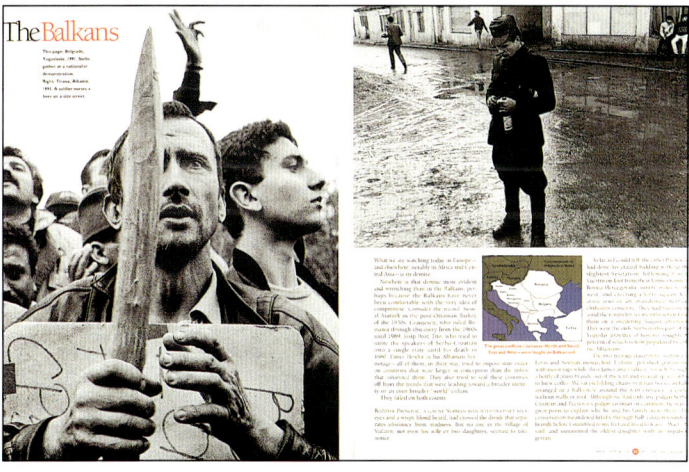

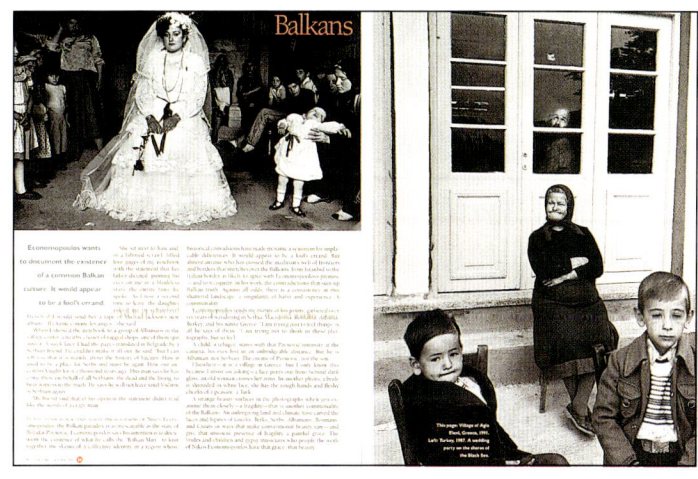

PUBLICATION	Premiere/Special Issue
AWARD	Merit
ART DIRECTOR	Roger Black
DESIGNER	Marianna Ochs
PHOTOGRAPHER	Firooz Zahedi
PHOTO EDITOR	Charlie Holland
PUBLISHER	K-III Magazines
STUDIO	Roger Black, Inc.
CATEGORY	Photography Story/Photojournalism, Portraits
DATE	September 1993

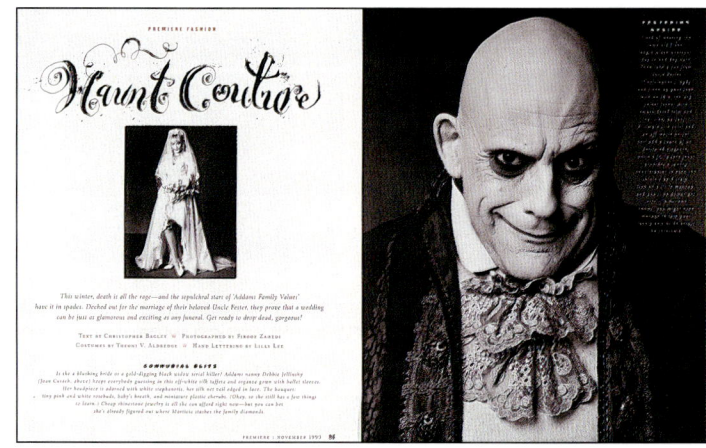

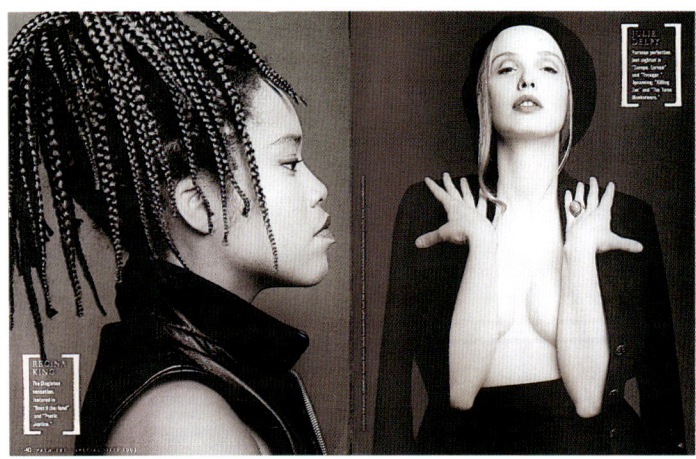

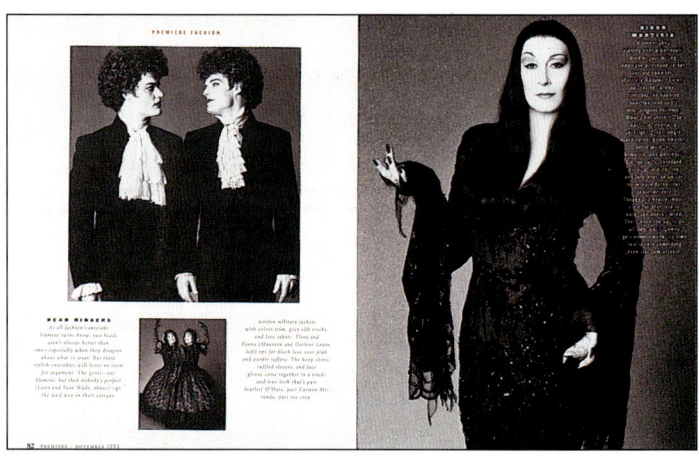

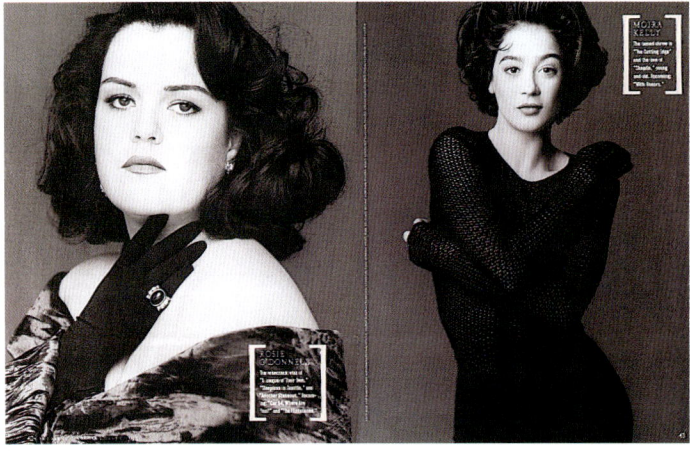

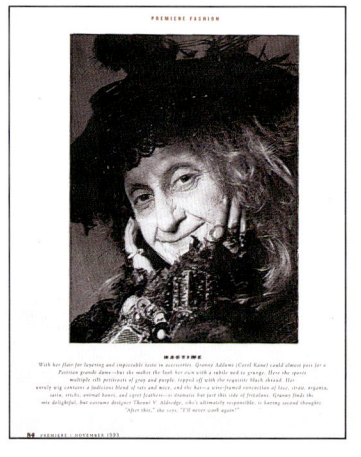

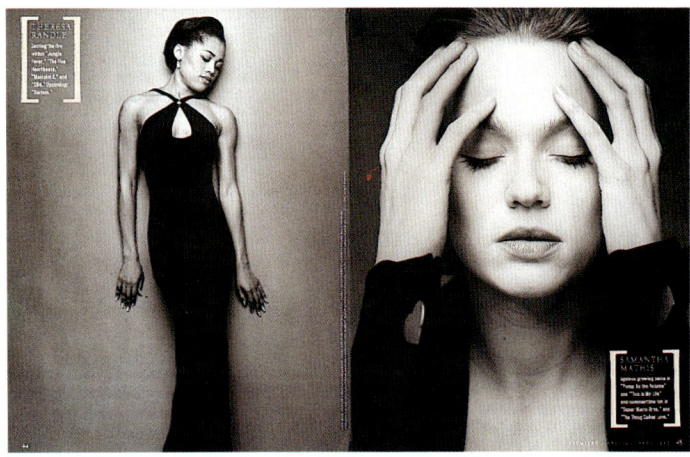

PUBLICATION	Premiere
AWARD	Merit
ART DIRECTOR	John Korpics
DESIGNER	John Korpics
PHOTOGRAPHER	Firooz Zahedi
PHOTO EDITOR	Charlie Holland
PUBLISHER	K-III Magazines
CATEGORY	Photography Story/Photojournalism, Portraits
DATE	November 1993

PUBLICATION	Rolling Stone
AWARD	Merit
ART DIRECTOR	Fred Woodward
DESIGNER	Gail Anderson
PHOTOGRAPHER	Brian Smale
PHOTO EDITOR	Laurie Kratochvil
PUBLISHER	Wenner Media
CATEGORY	Photography Story/Photojournalism, Portraits
DATE	October 14, 1993

PUBLICATION	Rolling Stone
AWARD	Merit
ART DIRECTOR	Fred Woodward
DESIGNER	Debra Bishop
PHOTOGRAPHER	Fred Woodward
PHOTO EDITOR	Laurie Kratochvil
PUBLISHER	Wenner Media
CATEGORY	Photography Story/Photojournalism, Portraits
DATE	April 15, 1993

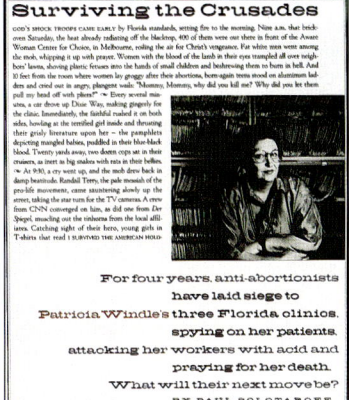

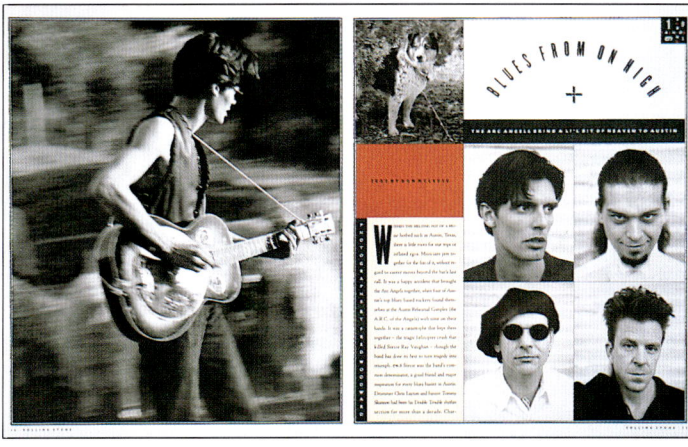

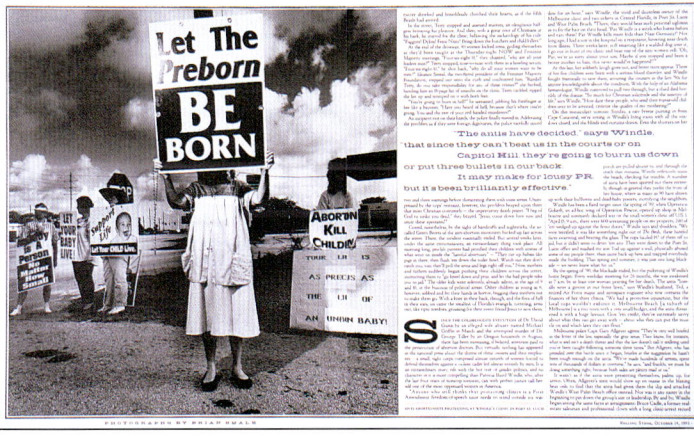

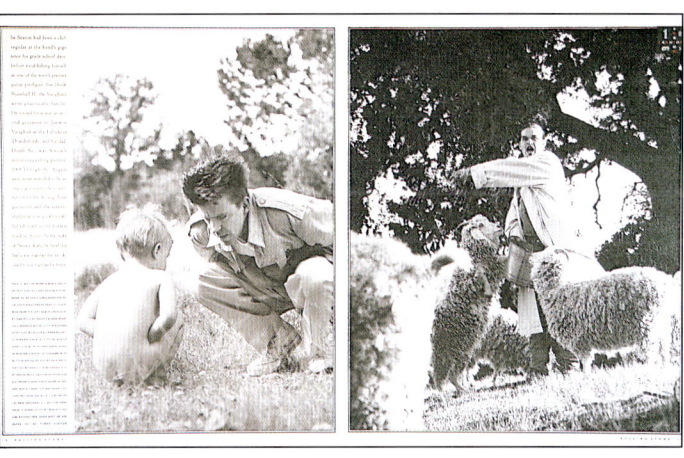

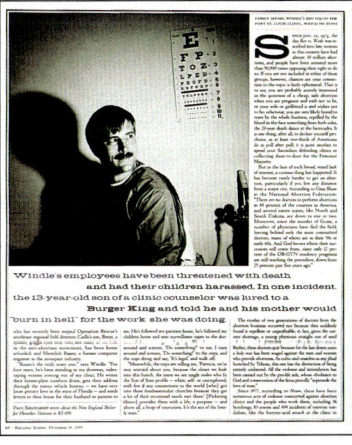

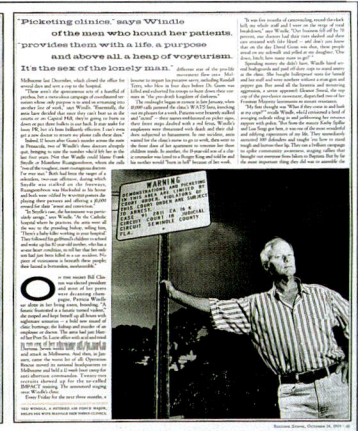

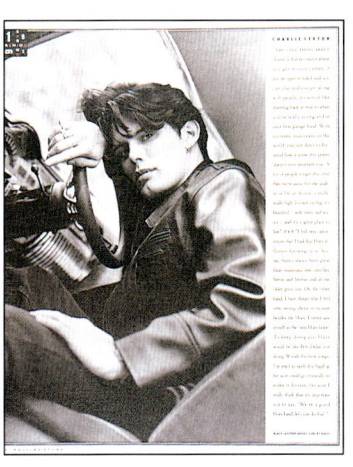

PUBLICATION	Special Report/Whittle
AWARD	Merit
ART DIRECTOR	Jim Phillips
DESIGNER	Joan Thomas
PHOTOGRAPHER	D. Gorton
PHOTO EDITOR	Kathy Getsey
PUBLISHER	Whittle Communications
CATEGORY	Photography Story/Photojournalism, Portraits
DATE	January/February 1993

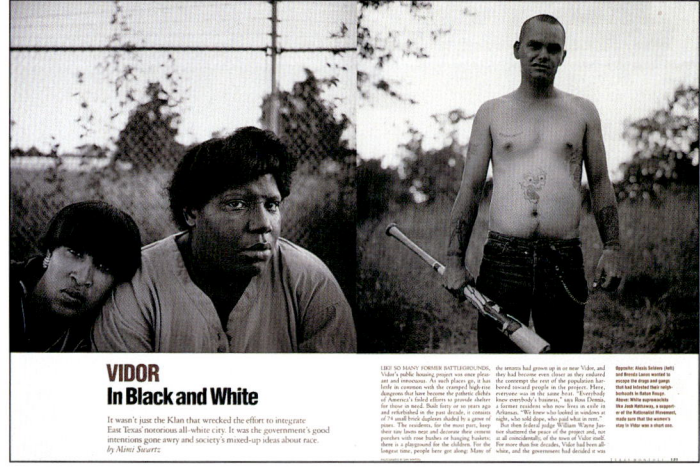

VIDOR
In Black and White

It wasn't just the Klan that wrecked the effort to integrate East Texas' notorious all-white city. It was the government's good intentions gone awry and society's mixed-up ideas about race.
by Almir Swartz

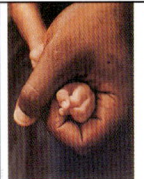
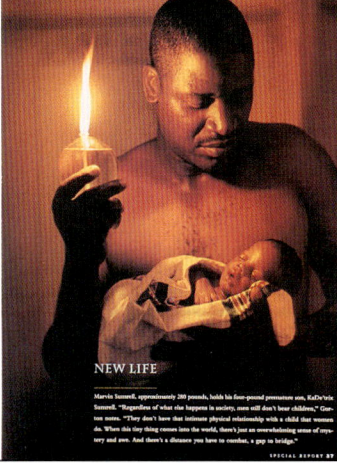

OUR FATHERS

They teach us, they love us, and sometimes they leave us: one photographer's unflinching look at the American dad.

What does it mean to be a father? Photographer—and dad—D. Gorton wasn't sure last year when he began a photographic inquiry into the subject. In search of answers, he photographed fathers from all walks of life and in all stages of parenthood throughout the United States. Of course, he says, the pictures he took reflect the outward changes of the past few generations: Moms are working, and many dads who might have been little more than benevolent bystanders in their children's lives 40 years ago are now more domesticated and involved. Thanks to relatively relaxed attitudes toward divorce and single motherhood, however, other fathers are finding a route they can take to slip out of the picture entirely. And reproductive technologies like artificial insemination and in vitro fertilization may scramble Dad's role in ways we can't even begin to predict.

The death of one of his own children prompted Gorton to push beyond the social and political implications to find the deeper emotional truths of fatherhood. Fathers still feel fulfilled by their children, charmed by them, disappointed by them, and sometimes—murderously angry at them. "I know," says Gorton, "because I've felt all these things."

All the fathers pictured on the following pages, including Gorton himself, have been touched by the changes of the past generation. But in the end, what is most surprising about their stories is not how much has changed, but how much stays the same.

Judy Woodburn

NEW LIFE

Marvin Surrreell, approximately 280 pounds, holds his four-pound premature son, KeDe'trix Surrreell. "Regardless of what else happens in society, men still don't bear children," Gorton notes. "They don't have that intimate physical relationship with a child that women do. When this tiny thing comes into the world, there's just an overwhelming sense of mystery and awe. And there's a distance you have to combat, a gap to bridge."

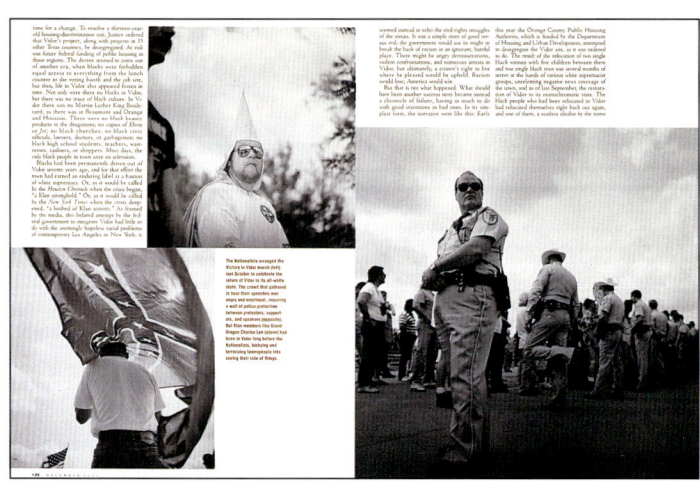

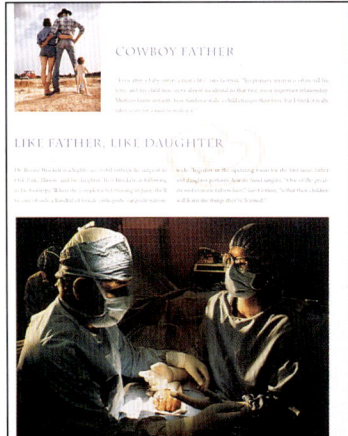

COWBOY FATHER

LIKE FATHER, LIKE DAUGHTER

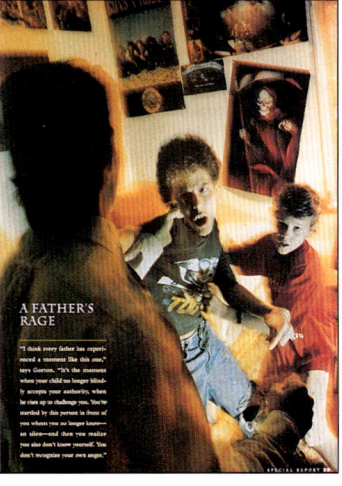

A FATHER'S RAGE

"I think every father has experienced a moment like this one," says Gorton. "It's the moment when your child no longer blindly accepts your authority, when he rises up to challenge you. You're startled by this person in front of you whom you no longer know—an alien—and then you realize you also don't know yourself. You don't recognize your own anger."

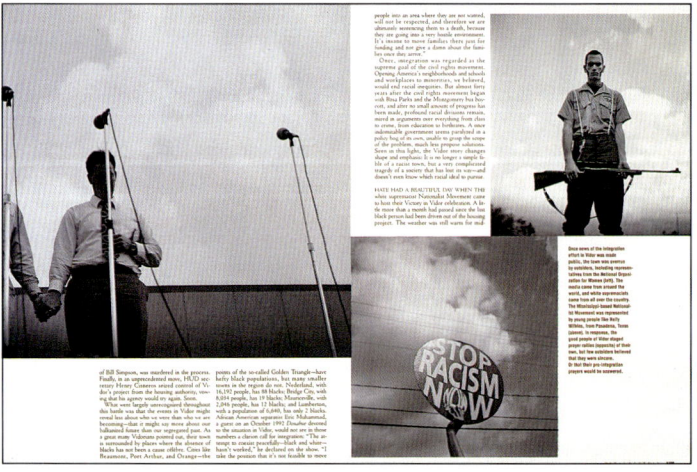

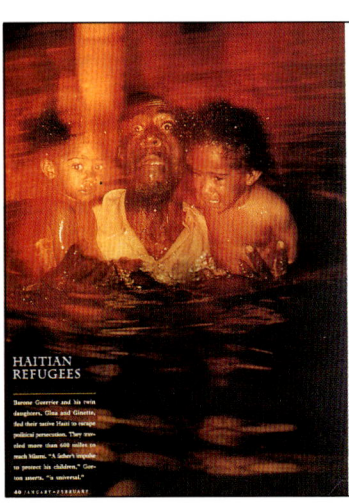

HAITIAN REFUGEES

Baronne Guerrier and his twin daughters, Glaa and Ginette, fled their native Haiti to escape political persecution. They traveled more than 600 miles on much blamesi. "A father's impulse to protect his children," Gorton asserts, "is universal."

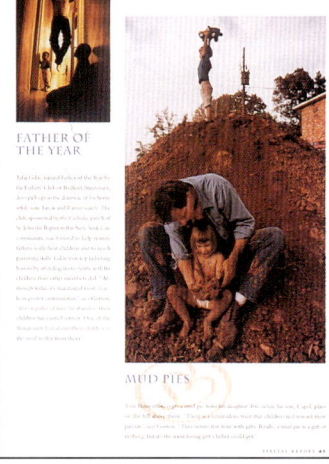

FATHER OF THE YEAR

MUD PIES

PUBLICATION	Texas Monthly
AWARD	Merit
DESIGN DIRECTOR	D.J. Stout
ART DIRECTOR	D.J. Stout
DESIGNER	D.J. Stout
PHOTOGRAPHER	Dan Winters
PHOTO EDITOR	D.J. Stout
PUBLISHER	Texas Monthly
CATEGORY	Photography Story/Photojournalism, Portraits
DATE	December 1993

PUBLICATION	Vibe
AWARD	Merit
DESIGN DIRECTOR	Gary Koepke
ART DIRECTOR	Richard Baker
DESIGNER	Gary Koepke
PHOTOGRAPHER	Dan Winters
PHOTO EDITOR	George Pitts
PUBLISHER	Time Inc. Ventures
STUDIO	Koepke International, Ltd.
CATEGORY	Photography Story/Photojournalism, Portraits
DATE	September 1993

PUBLICATION	Travel Holiday
AWARD	Merit
ART DIRECTOR	Lou DiLorenzo
DESIGNER	Amy Jaffe
PHOTOGRAPHERS	Antonin Kratochvil, Michael Melford, Dennis Marsico, Russell Kaye, Bob Sacha, Joe McNally, Sally Gall, Bob Krist, Karen Kuehn
PHOTO EDITOR	Bill Black
PUBLISHER	Readers Digest Publications
CATEGORY	Photography Story/Photojournalism, Portraits
DATE	December 1993

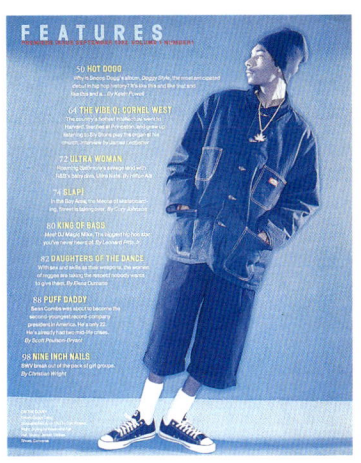

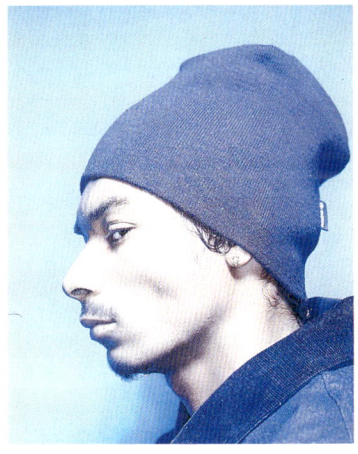

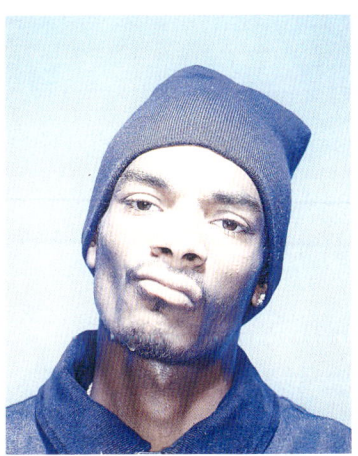

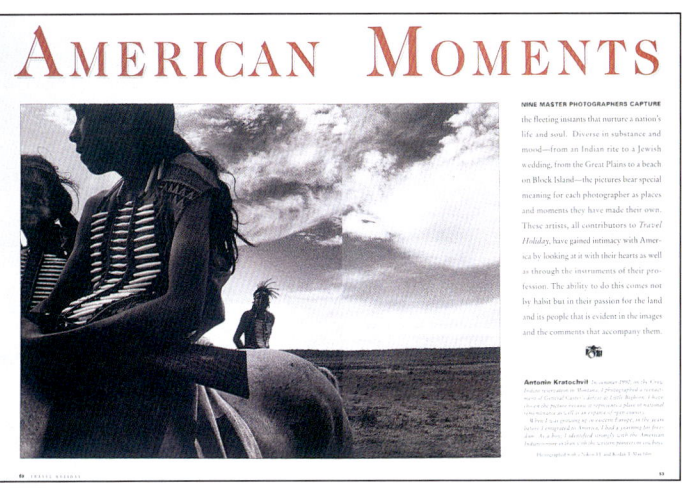

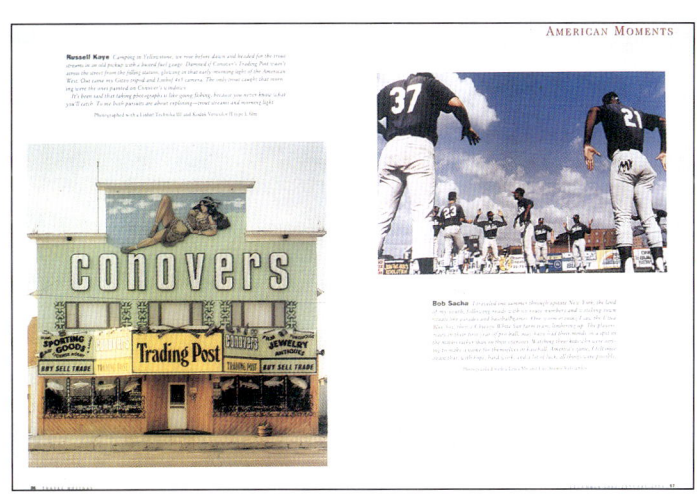

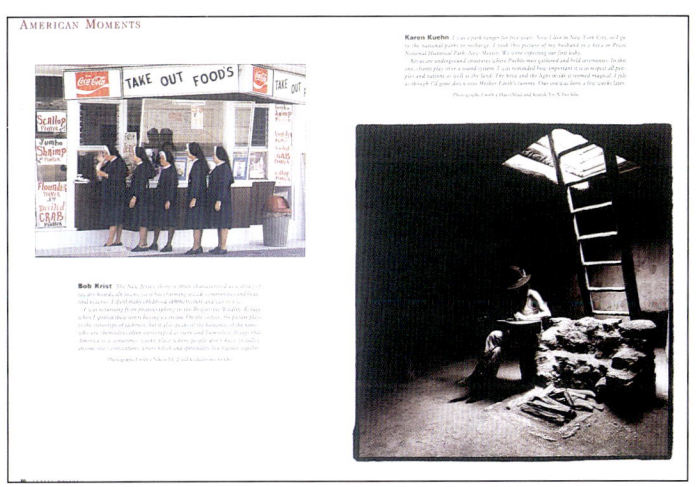

PUBLICATION	The Boston Globe
AWARD	Merit
DESIGN DIRECTOR	Lynn Staley
PHOTOGRAPHER	Various
PHOTO EDITOR	Sue Morrow
PUBLISHER	The Boston Globe
CATEGORY	Photography Story/Photojournalism, Portraits
DATE	October 28, 1993

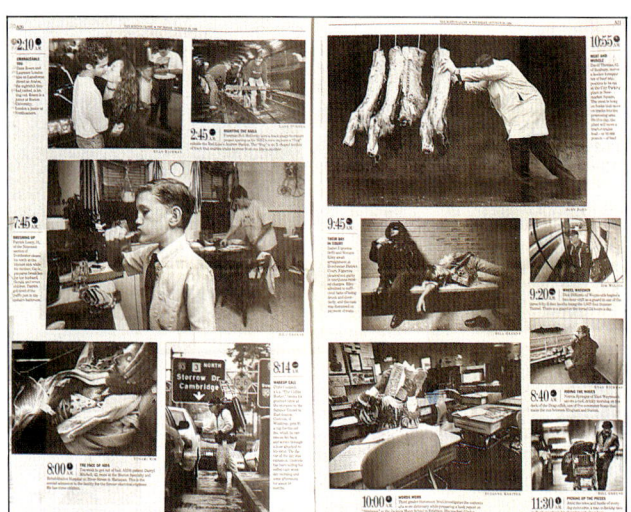

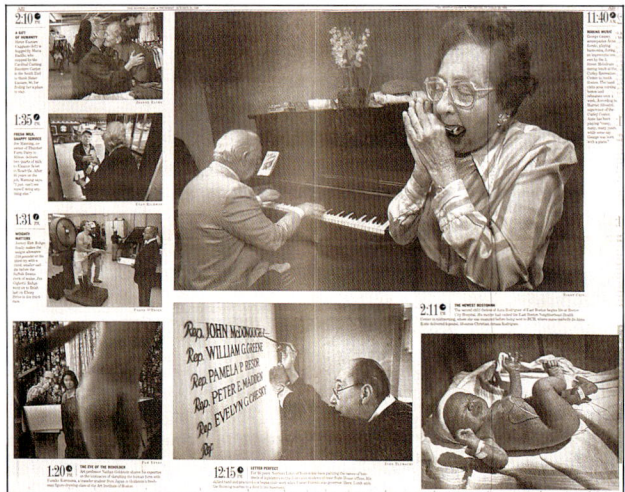

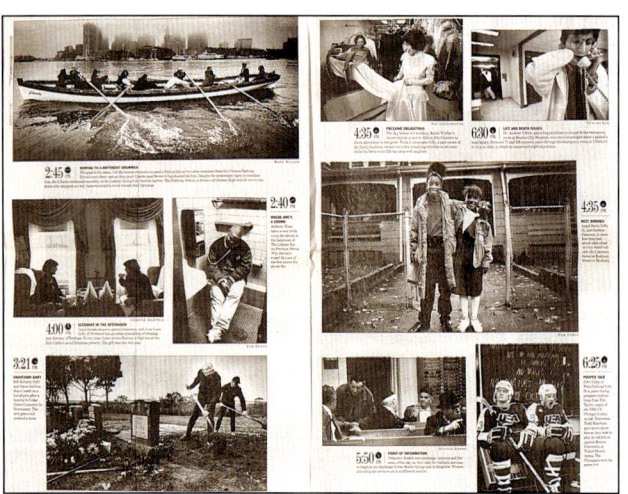

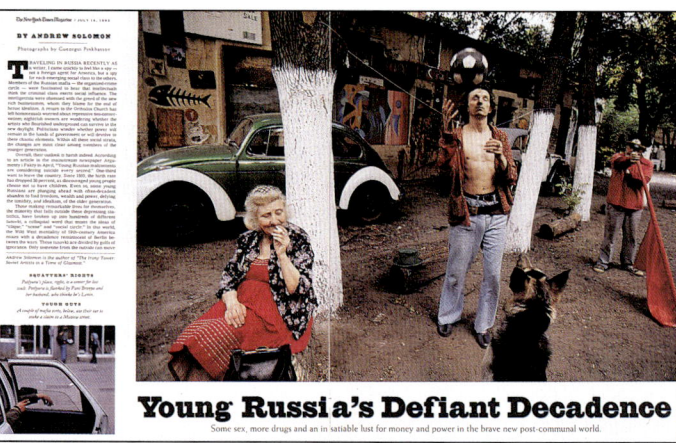

Young Russia's Defiant Decadence

Some sex, more drugs and an insatiable lust for money and power in the brave new post-communal world.

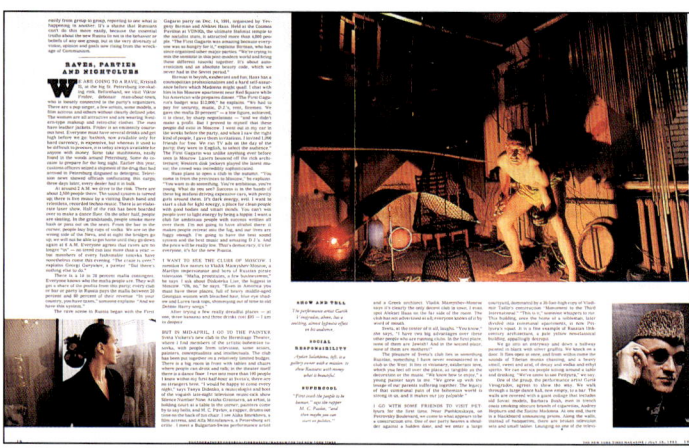

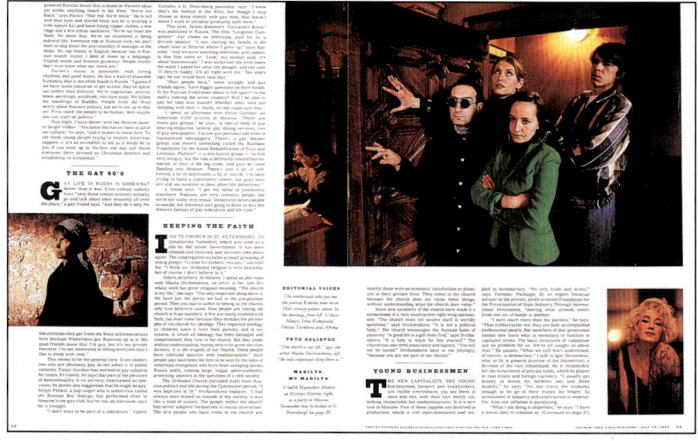

PUBLICATION	The New York Times Magazine
AWARD	Merit
ART DIRECTOR	Janet Froelich
DESIGNER	Kathi Rota
PHOTOGRAPHER	Gueorgui Pinkhassov
PHOTO EDITOR	Kathy Ryan
PUBLISHER	The New York Times
CATEGORY	Photography Story/Photojournalism, Portraits
DATE	July 18, 1993

PUBLICATION   The New York Times Magazine
AWARD   Merit
ART DIRECTOR   Janet Froelich
DESIGNER   Gina Davis
PHOTOGRAPHER   Ellen Binder
PHOTO EDITOR   Kathy Ryan
PUBLISHER   The New York Times
CATEGORY   Photography Story/Photojournalism, Portraits
DATE   October 31, 1993

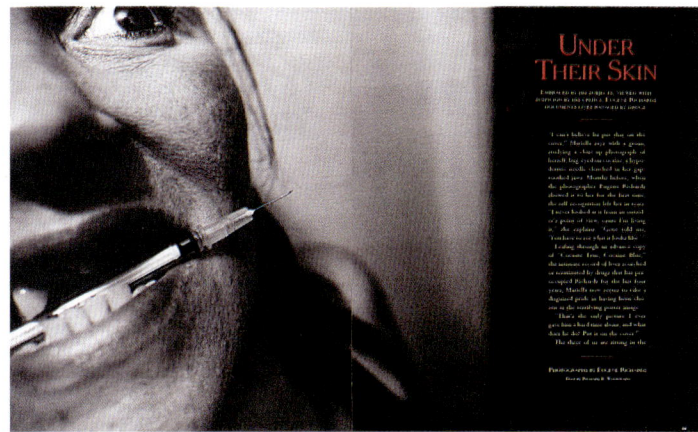

UNDER THEIR SKIN

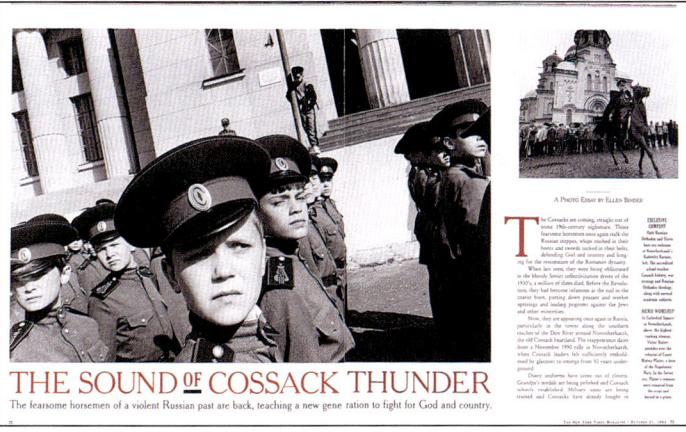

THE SOUND OF COSSACK THUNDER
The fearsome horsemen of a violent Russian past are back, teaching a new generation to fight for God and country.

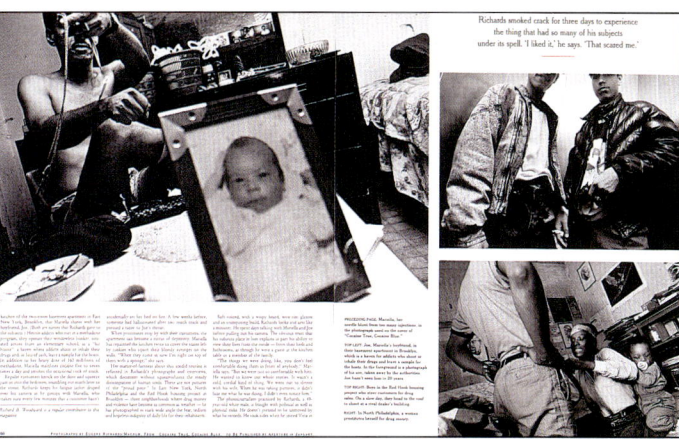

Richards smoked crack for three days to experience the thing that had so many of his subjects under its spell. 'I liked it,' he says. 'That scared me.'

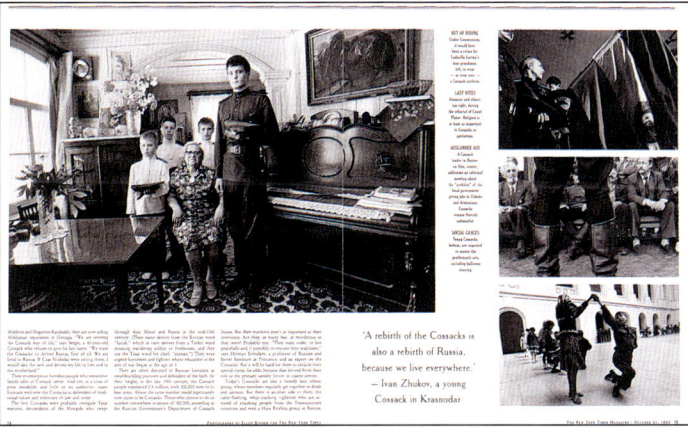

'A rebirth of the Cossacks is also a rebirth of Russia, because we live everywhere.'
— Ivan Zhukov, a young Cossack in Krasnodar

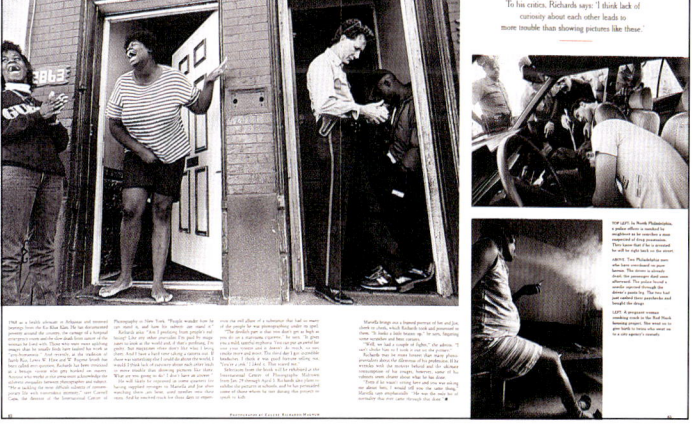

To his critics, Richards says: 'I think lack of curiosity about each other leads to more trouble than showing pictures like these.'

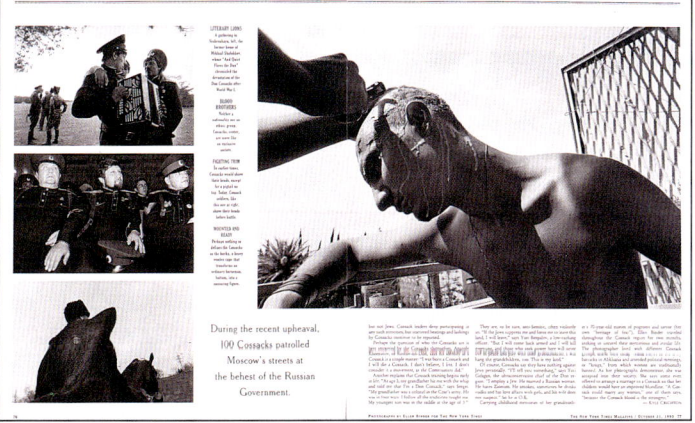

During the recent upheaval, 100 Cossacks patrolled Moscow's streets at the behest of the Russian Government.

PUBLICATION   The New York Times Magazine
AWARD   Merit
ART DIRECTOR   Janet Froelich
DESIGNER   Richard Baker
PHOTOGRAPHER   Eugene Richards
PHOTO EDITOR   Kathy Ryan
PUBLISHER   The New York Times
CATEGORY   Photography Story/Photojournalism, Portraits
DATE   December 5, 1993

PUBLICATION	The Philadelphia Inquirer Magazine
AWARD	Merit
DESIGN DIRECTOR	Jessica Helfand
ART DIRECTOR	Bert Fox
DESIGNER	Bert Fox
PHOTOGRAPHER	J. Kyle Keener
PHOTO EDITOR	Bert Fox
PUBLISHER	The Philadelphia Inquirer
CATEGORY	Photography Story/Photojournalism, Portraits
DATE	December 12, 1993

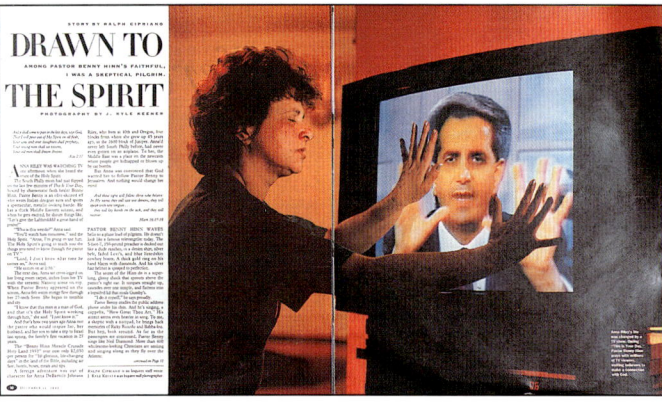

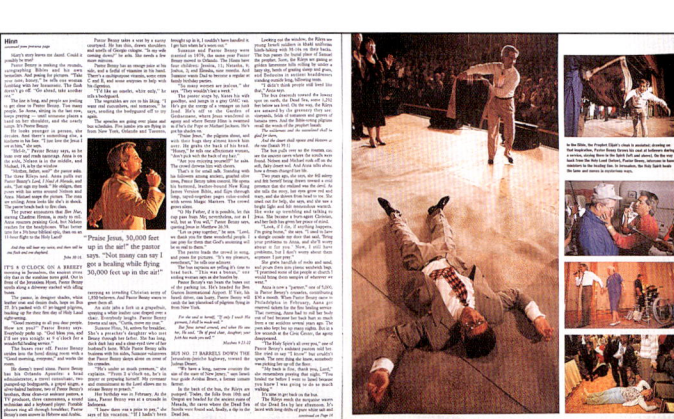

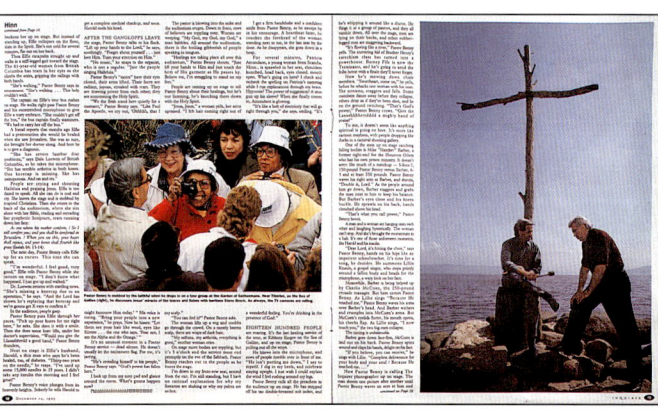

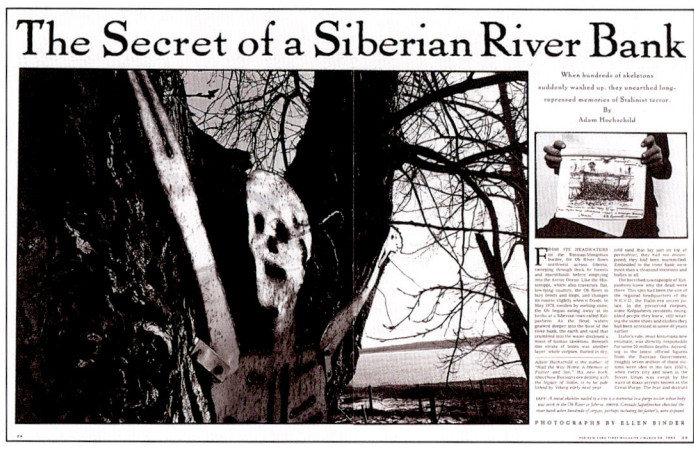

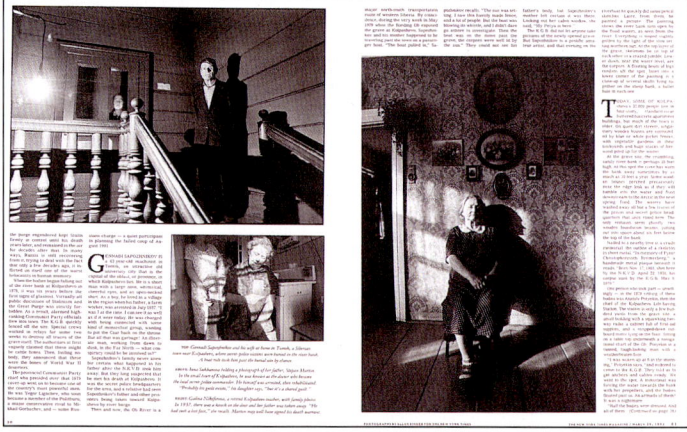

PUBLICATION	The New York Times Magazine
AWARD	Merit
ART DIRECTOR	Janet Froelich
DESIGNER	Kathi Rota
PHOTOGRAPHER	Ellen Binder
PHOTO EDITOR	Kathy Ryan
PUBLISHER	The New York Times
CATEGORY	Photography Story/Photojournalism, Portraits
DATE	March 28, 1993

PUBLICATION Security Management
AWARD Merit
ART DIRECTOR Roy Comiskey
DESIGNER Roy Comiskey
PHOTOGRAPHER Max Hirshfeld
PUBLISHER American Society for Industrial Security
CATEGORY Photography Story/Photojournalism, Portraits
DATE September 1993

PUBLICATION Update
AWARD Merit
DESIGN DIRECTOR Will Kefauver
ART DIRECTOR Ellen Jacob
DESIGNER Elizabeth Chinman
PHOTOGRAPHER C.M. Hardt
PUBLISHER Scholastic, Inc.
CATEGORY Photography Story/Photojournalism, Portraits
DATE February 26, 1993

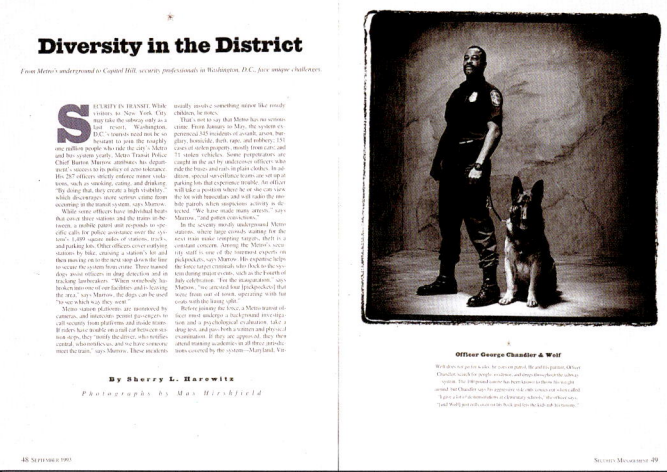

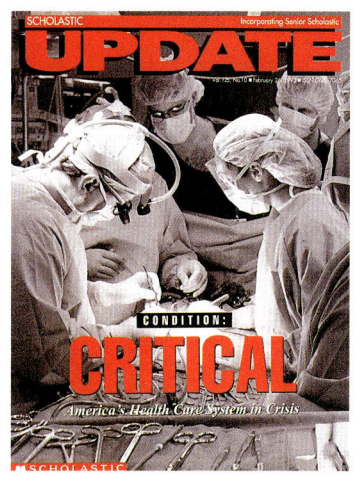

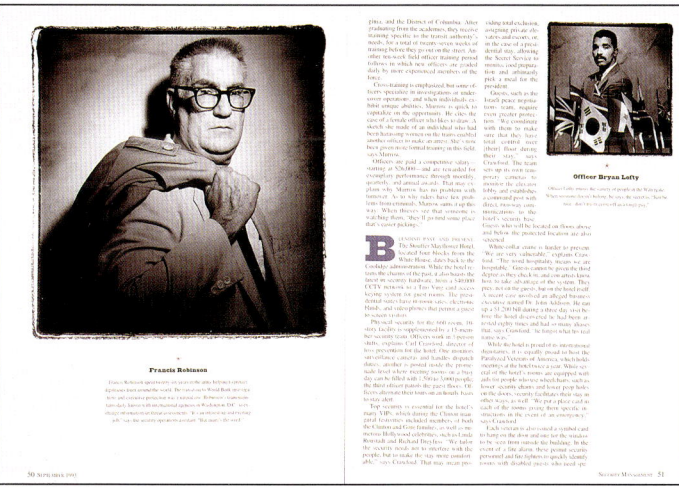

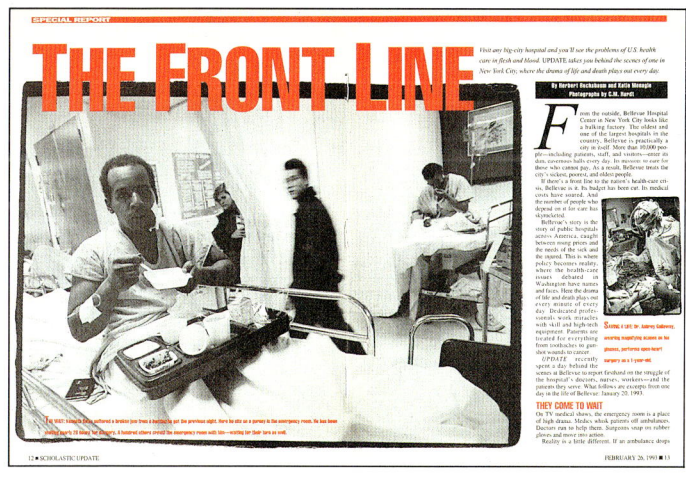

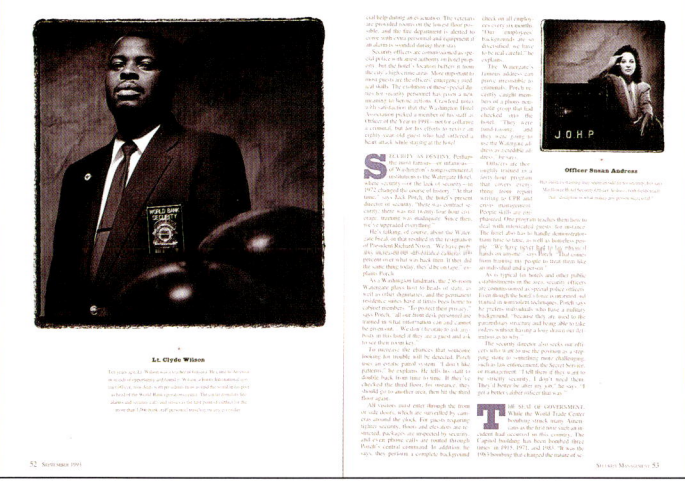

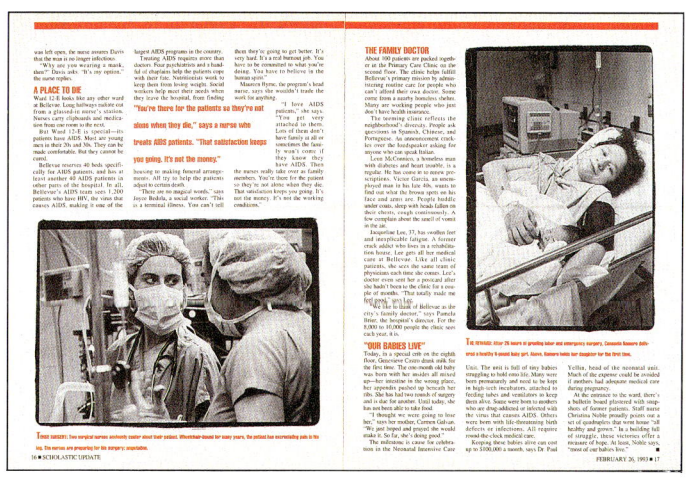

PUBLICATION	Condé Nast Traveler
AWARD	Silver
DESIGN DIRECTOR	Diana LaGuardia
ART DIRECTOR	Christin Gangi
PHOTOGRAPHER	Antonin Kratochvil
PHOTO EDITOR	Kathleen Klech
PUBLISHER	The Condé Nast Publications Inc.
CATEGORY	Photography Story/Still Life, Interiors, Travel
DATE	November 1993

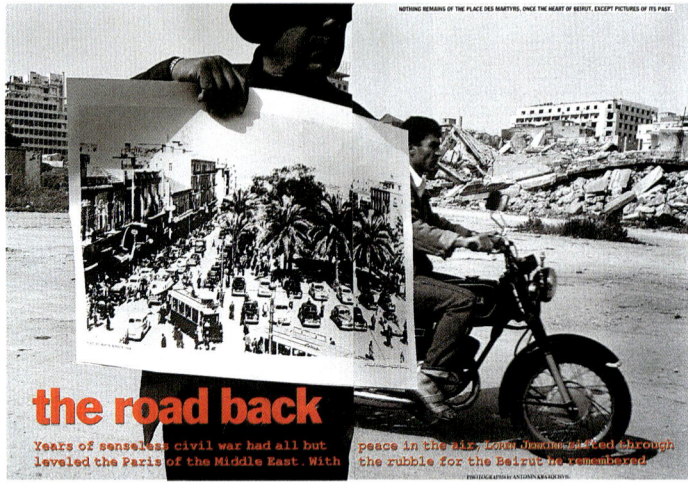

NOTHING REMAINS OF THE PLACE DES MARTYRS, ONCE THE HEART OF BEIRUT, EXCEPT PICTURES OF ITS PAST.

the road back

Years of senseless civil war had all but leveled the Paris of the Middle East. With peace in the air, Town Jonathan Redgehrough the rubble for the Beirut he remembered.

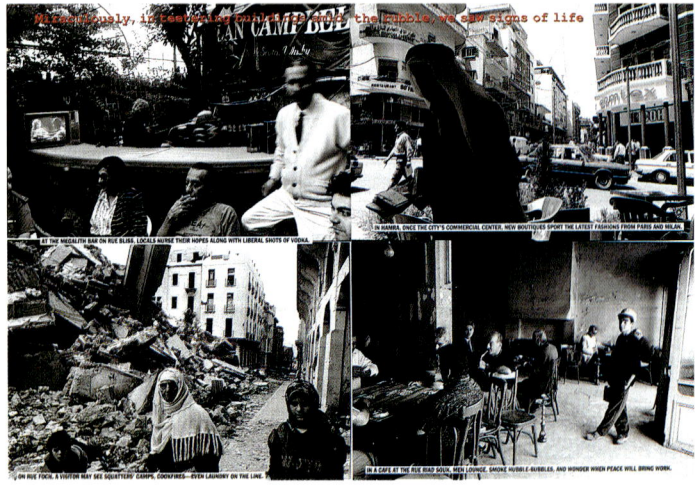

Miraculously, if tentatively, amid the rubble, we saw signs of life

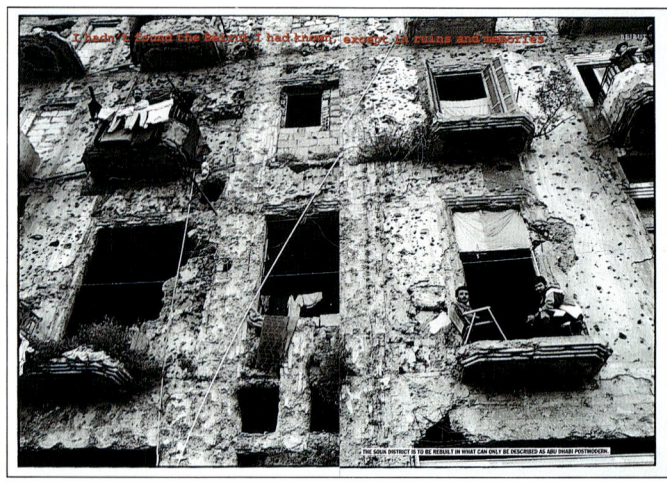

I hadn't found the Beirut I had known, except in ruins and memories

THE SOUK DISTRICT IS TO BE REBUILT IN WHAT CAN ONLY BE DESCRIBED AS ABU DHABI POSTMODERN.

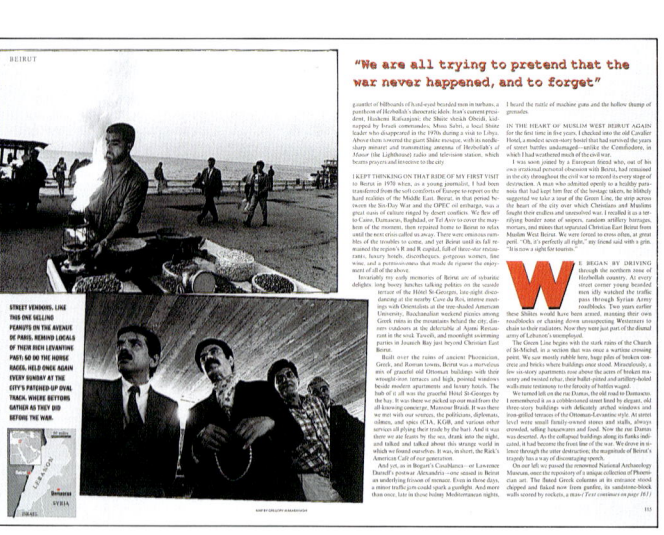

"We are all trying to pretend that the war never happened, and to forget"

STREET VENDORS, LIKE THIS ONE SELLING PEANUTS ON THE AVENUE DE PARIS, REMIND LOCALS OF THEIR RICH LEVANTINE PAST; SO DO THE HORSE RACES, HELD ONCE AGAIN EVERY SUNDAY AT THE CITY'S PATCHED-UP OVAL TRACK, WHERE BETTORS GATHER AS THEY DID BEFORE THE WAR.

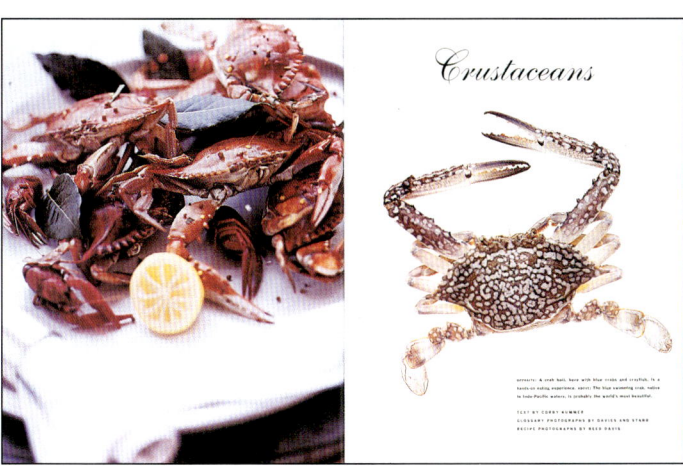

Crustaceans

opposite: A crab boil, here with blue crabs and crayfish, is a feast or eating experience. center: The blue swimming crab, native to Indo-Pacific waters, is probably the world's most beautiful.

TEXT BY CORBY KUMMER
GLOSSARY PHOTOGRAPHS BY DAVIES AND STARR
RECIPE PHOTOGRAPHS BY REED DAVIS

PUBLICATION	Martha Stewart Living
AWARD	Silver
ART DIRECTOR	Gael Towey
DESIGNER	Anne Johnson
PHOTOGRAPHERS	Davies & Starr, Reed Davis
PUBLISHER	Time Inc.
CATEGORY	Photography Story/Still Life, Interiors, Travel
DATE	December 1993

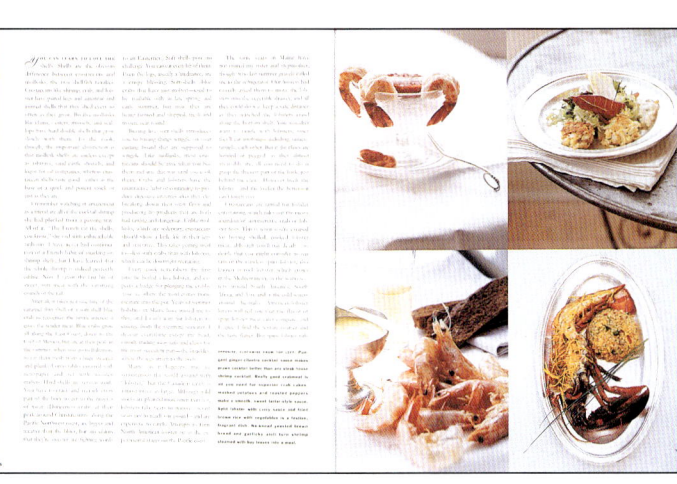

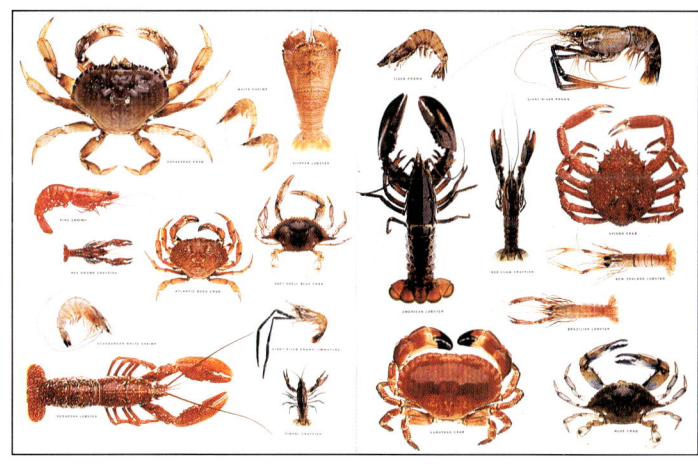

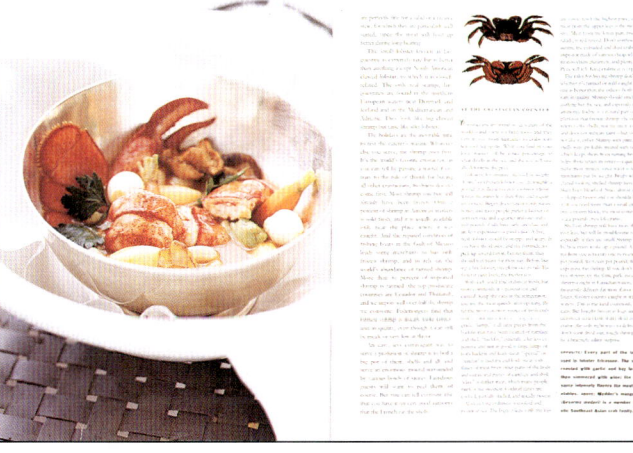

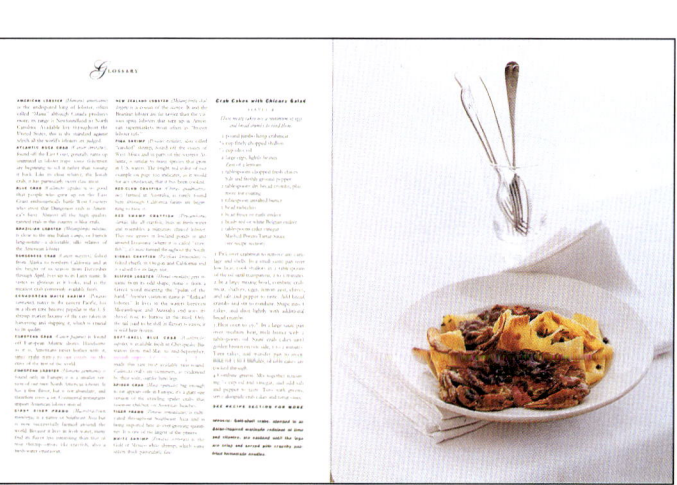

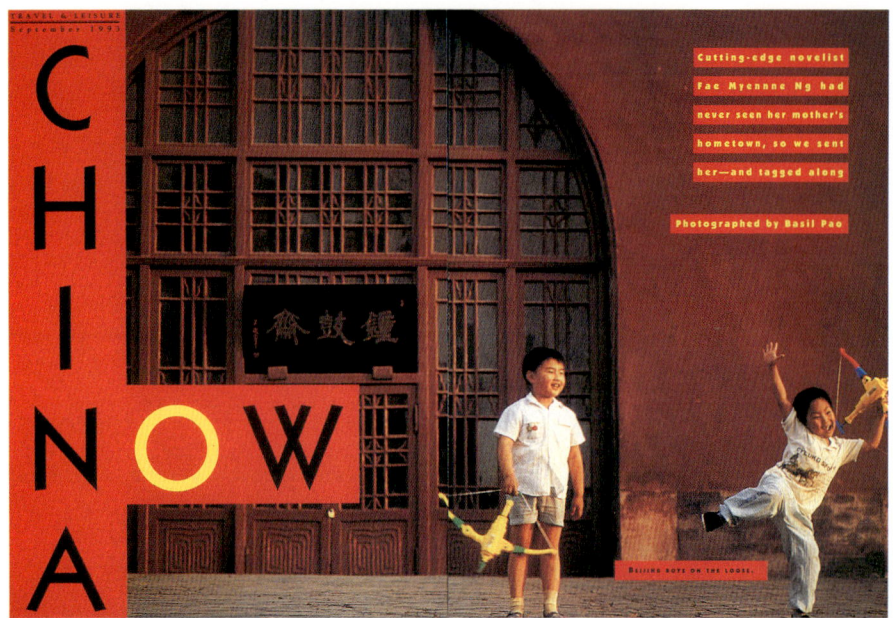

PUBLICATION Travel & Leisure
AWARD Silver
DESIGN DIRECTOR Lloyd Ziff
DESIGNER Lloyd Ziff
ILLUSTRATOR Betty Duke
PHOTOGRAPHER Basil Pao
PUBLISHER American Express
Publishing
CATEGORY Photography Story/
Still Life, Interiors, Travel
DATE September 1993

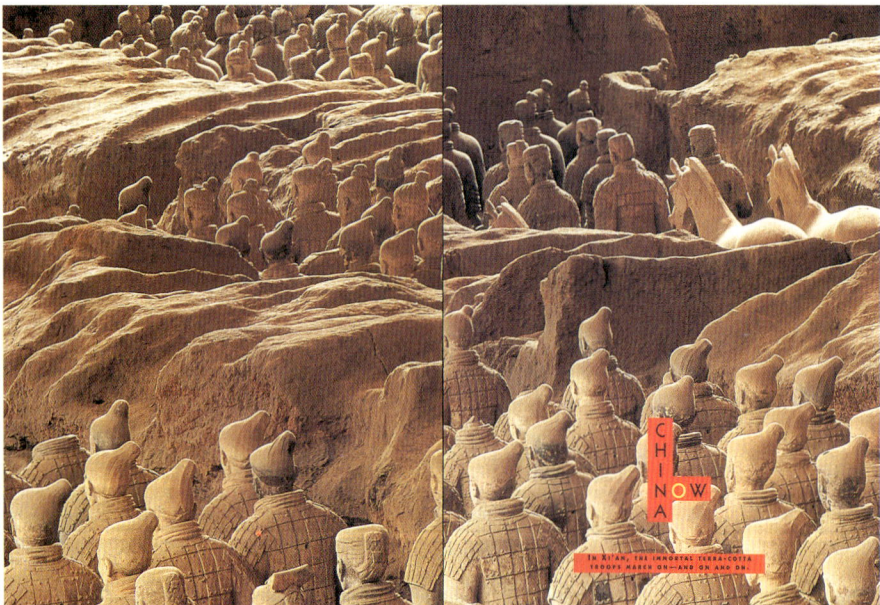

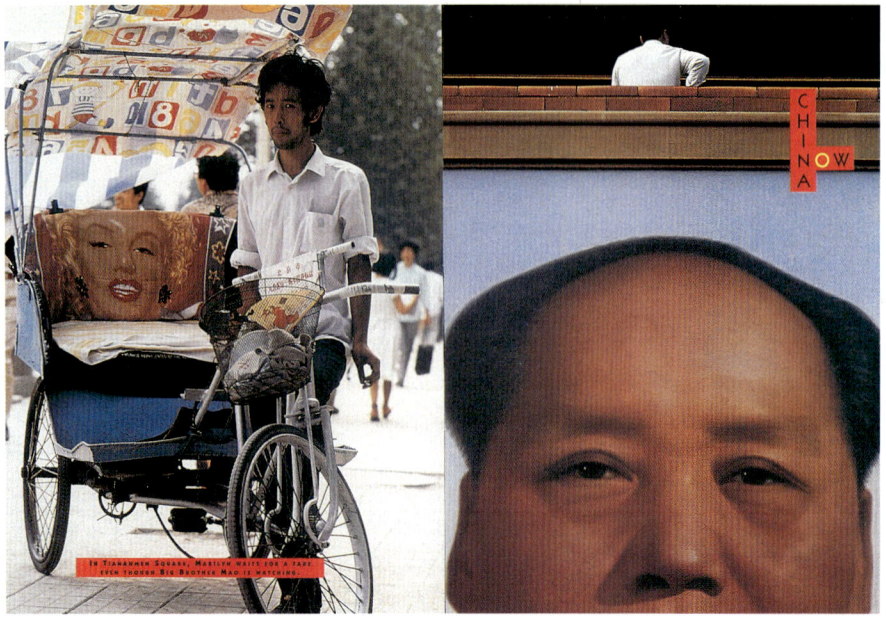

PUBLICATION	Buzz
AWARD	Merit
DESIGN DIRECTOR	Charles Hess
ART DIRECTOR	Charles Hess
PHOTOGRAPHER	Gerhard Yurkovic
PHOTO EDITOR	Pamela Hassell
PUBLISHER	Buzz, Inc.
CATEGORY	Photography Story/Still Life, Interiors, Travel
DATE	August 1993

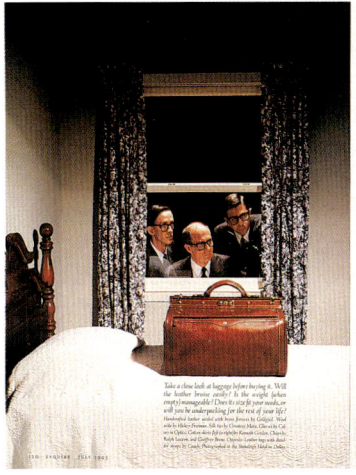

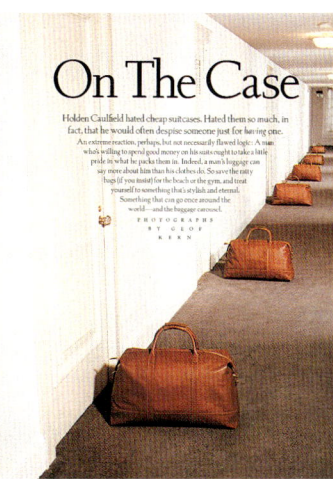

On The Case

Holden Caulfield hated cheap suitcases. Hated them so much, in fact, that he would often despise someone just for having one.

PHOTOGRAPHS BY GEOF KERN

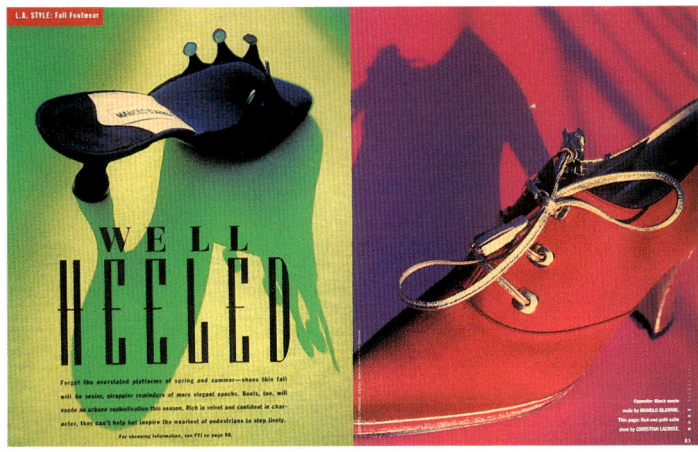

WELL HEELED

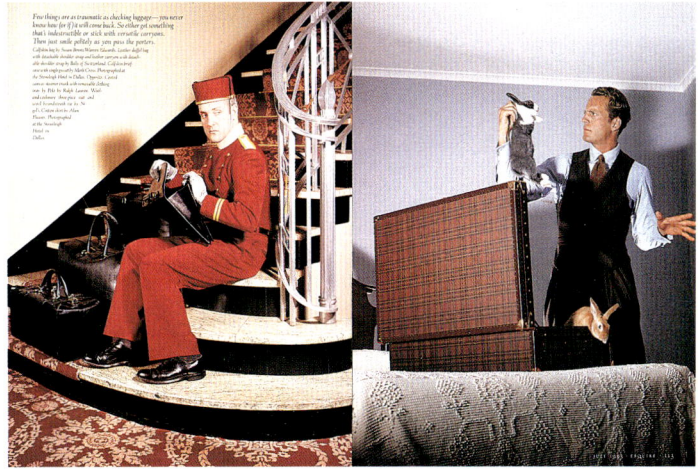

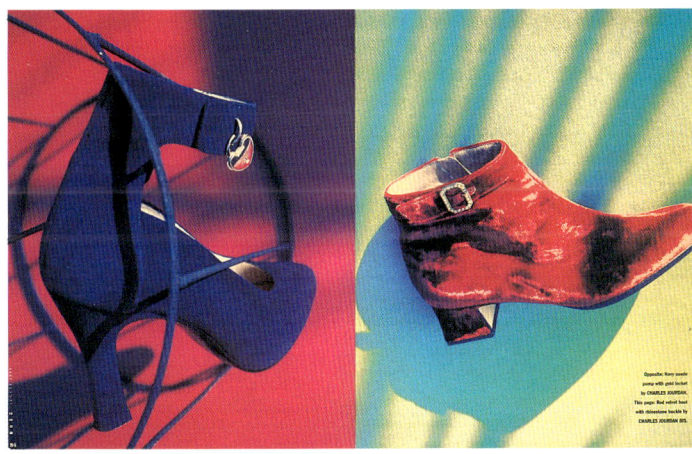

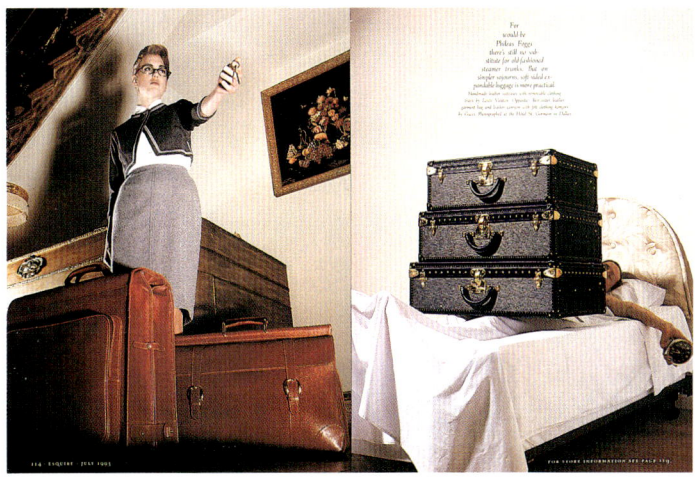

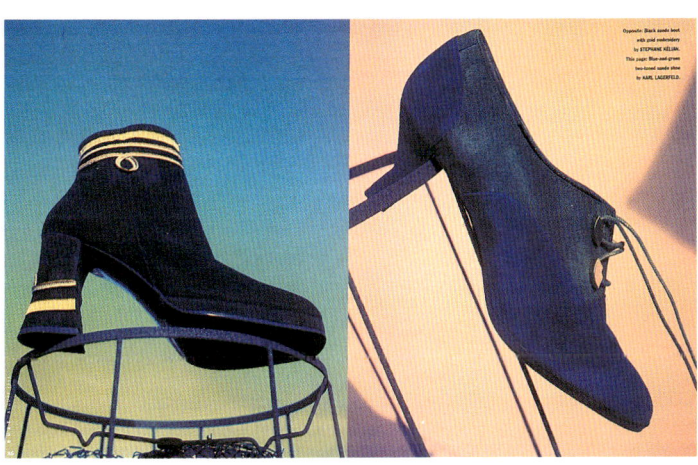

PUBLICATION	Esquire
AWARD	Merit
ART DIRECTOR	Rhonda Rubinstein
DESIGNER	David O'Connor
PHOTOGRAPHER	Geof Kern
PHOTO EDITOR	Betsy Horan
PUBLISHER	The Hearst Corporation
CATEGORY	Photography Story/Still Life, Interiors, Travel
DATE	July 1993

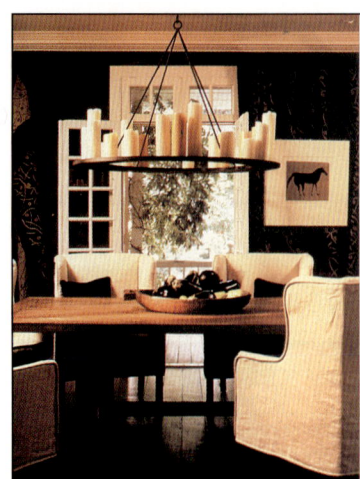

Country with an edge

Nancy Braithwaite cuts through American tradition with a brave, clear eye, distilling form and color, paring away excess, yet guaranteeing comfort

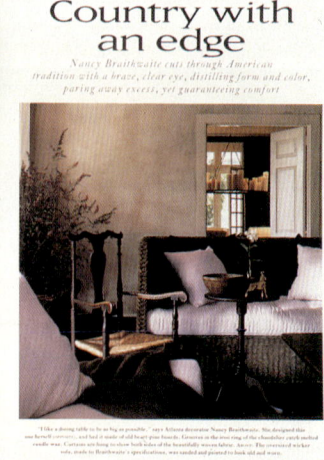

"I like a dining table to be as big as possible," says Atlanta decorator Nancy Braithwaite. She designed this one herself *entirely*, and had it made of old heart pine boards. Greenery in the iron ring of the chandelier circle melted candle wax. Curtains are hung to show both sides of the beautifully woven fabric, *below*. The oversized wicker sofa, made to Braithwaite's specifications, was sanded and painted to look old and worn.

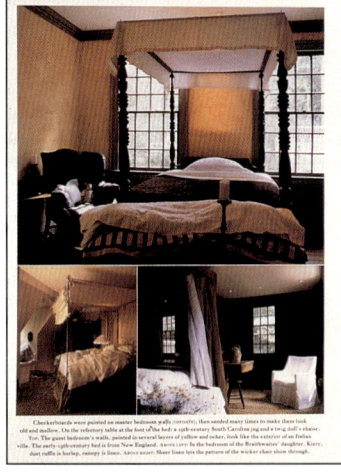

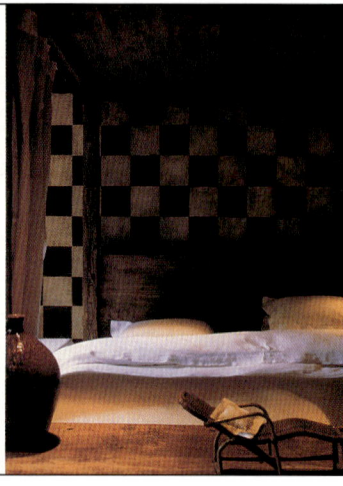

Checkerboards were painted on master bedroom walls *correctly*, then sanded many times to make them look old and mellow. On the refectory table at the foot of the bed a 19th-century South Carolina jug and a twig doll's chaise. *Top*, The guest bedroom's walls, painted in several layers of yellow and ochre, look like the exterior of an Italian villa. The early-19th-century bed is from New England, *bottom left*. In the bedroom of the Braithwaites' daughter, *Kitty*, dust ruffle is burlap, canopy is linen. Antico *mixes*. Sheer linen lets the pattern of the wicker chair show through.

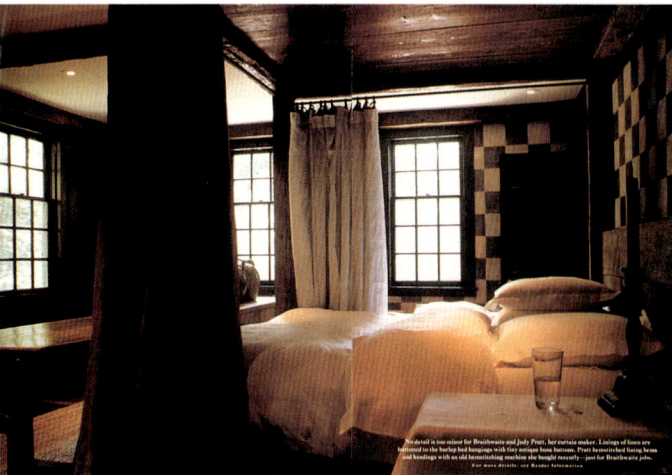

No detail is too minor for Braithwaite and Judy Pratt, her curtain maker. Linings of linen are buttoned to the burlap bed hangings with tiny antique bone buttons. Pratt hemstitched lining hems and bindings with an old hemstitching machine she bought recently—just for Braithwaite jobs.
For more details, see Reader Information.

PUBLICATION	House Beautiful
AWARD	Merit
ART DIRECTOR	Andrzej Janerka
DESIGNER	Andrzej Janerka
PHOTOGRAPHER	Jack Winston
PUBLISHER	The Hearst Corporation
CATEGORY	Photography Story/Still Life, Interiors, Travel
DATE	January 1993

PUBLICATION	Martha Stewart Living
AWARD	Merit
ART DIRECTOR	Gael Towey
DESIGNER	Eric Pike
PHOTOGRAPHER	Maria Robledo
PUBLISHER	Time Inc.
CATEGORY	Photography Story/Still Life, Interiors, Travel
DATE	August 1993

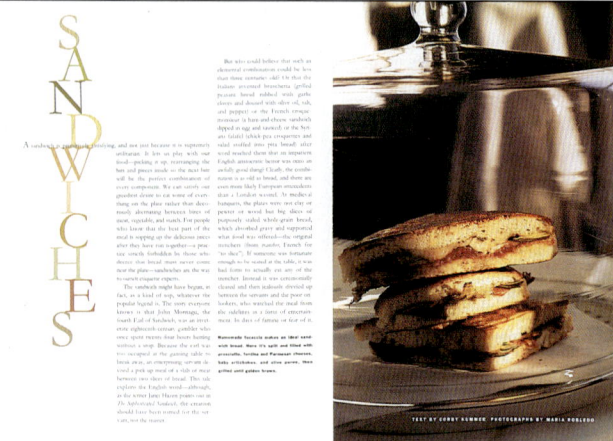

SANDWICHES

TEXT BY COREY KUMMER · PHOTOGRAPHS BY MARIA ROBLEDO

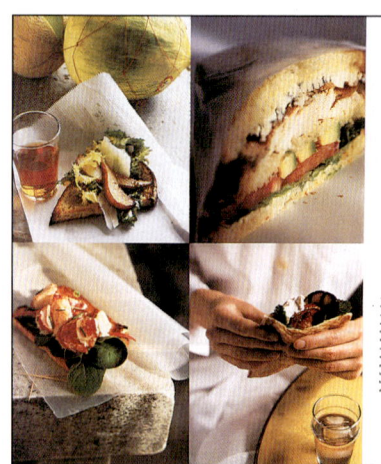

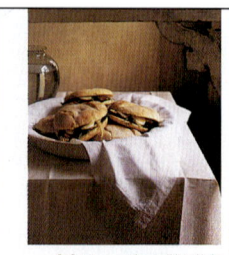

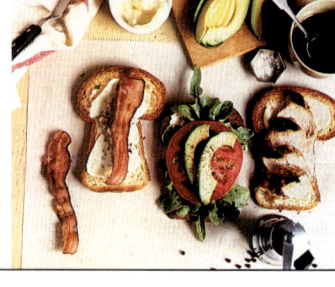

PUBLICATION	Martha Stewart Living
AWARD	Merit
ART DIRECTOR	Gael Towey
DESIGNER	Anne Johnson
PHOTOGRAPHER	Maria Robledo
PUBLISHER	Time Inc.
CATEGORY	Photography Story/Still Life, Interiors, Travel
DATE	April 1993

PUBLICATION	Martha Stewart Living
AWARD	Merit
ART DIRECTOR	Gael Towey
DESIGNER	Gael Towey
PHOTOGRAPHER	Ruven Afandor
PUBLISHER	Time Inc.
CATEGORY	Photography Story/Still Life, Interiors, Travel
DATE	August 1993

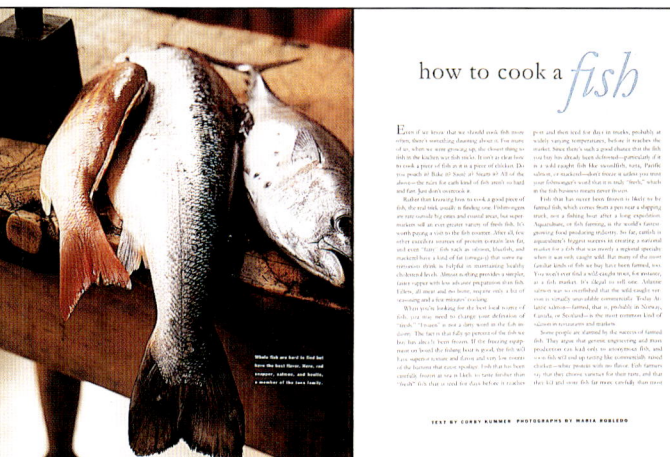

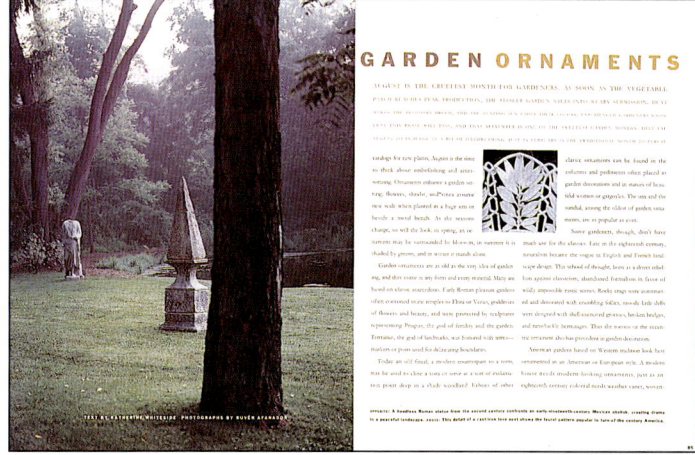

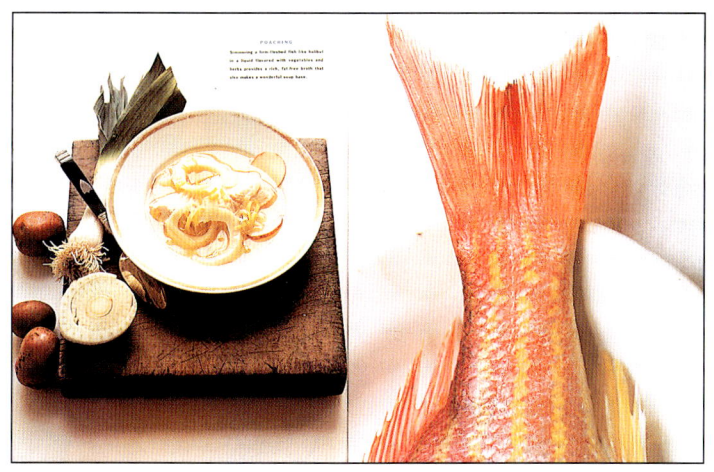

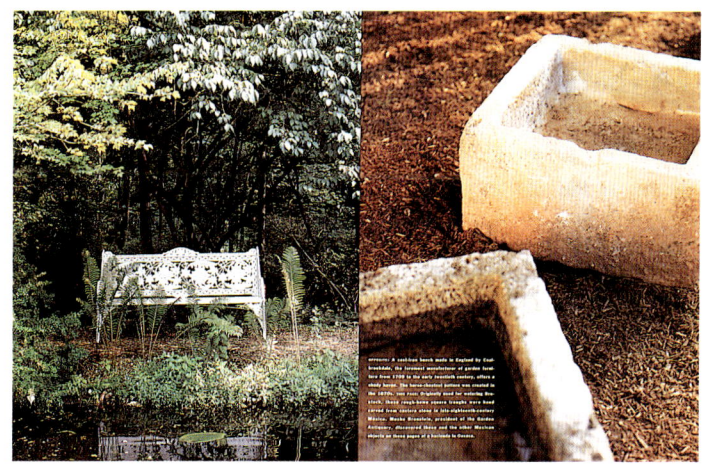

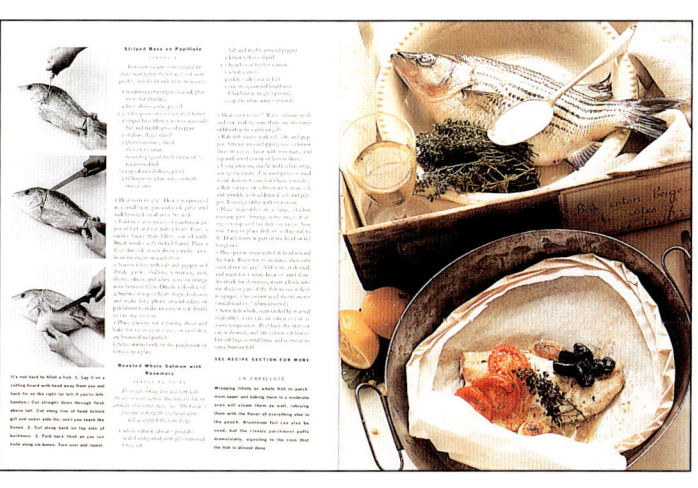

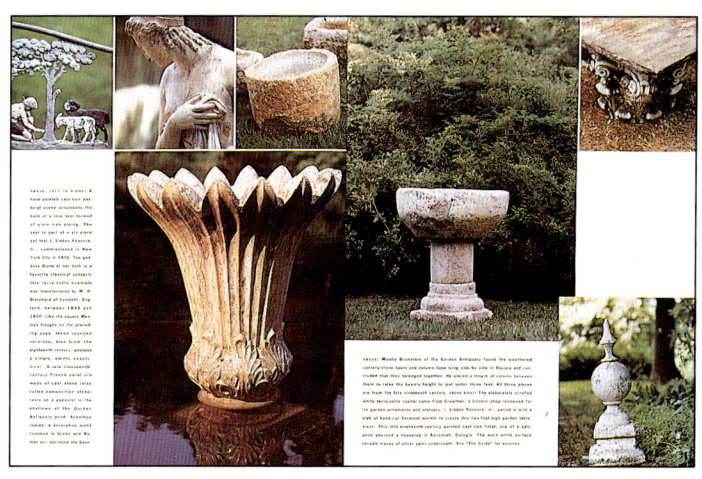

PUBLICATION	Travel & Leisure
AWARD	Merit
DESIGN DIRECTOR	Lloyd Ziff
DESIGNER	Lloyd Ziff
PHOTOGRAPHER	Timothy Hursley
PHOTO EDITOR	Hazel Hammond
PUBLISHER	American Express Publishing
CATEGORY	Photography Story/Still Life, Interiors, Travel
DATE	May 1993

PUBLICATION	Travel & Leisure
AWARD	Merit
DESIGN DIRECTOR	Lloyd Ziff
DESIGNER	Lloyd Ziff
ILLUSTRATOR	Stephen Kelemen
PHOTOGRAPHER	Hugues Colson
PHOTO EDITOR	Hazel Hammond
PUBLISHER	American Express Publishing
CATEGORY	Photography Story/Still Life, Interiors, Travel
DATE	September 1993

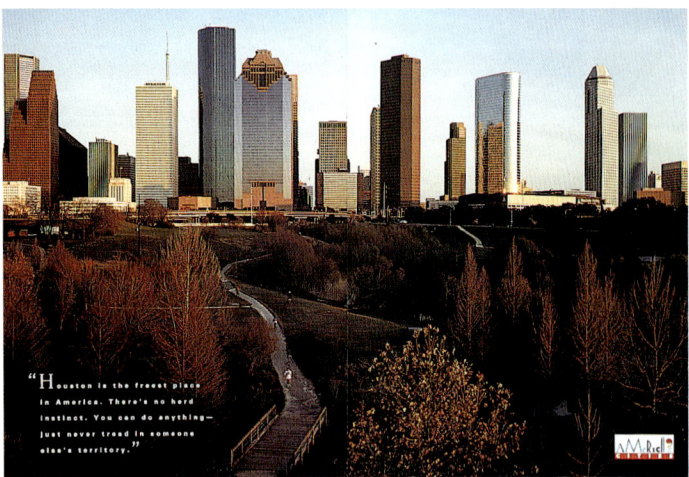

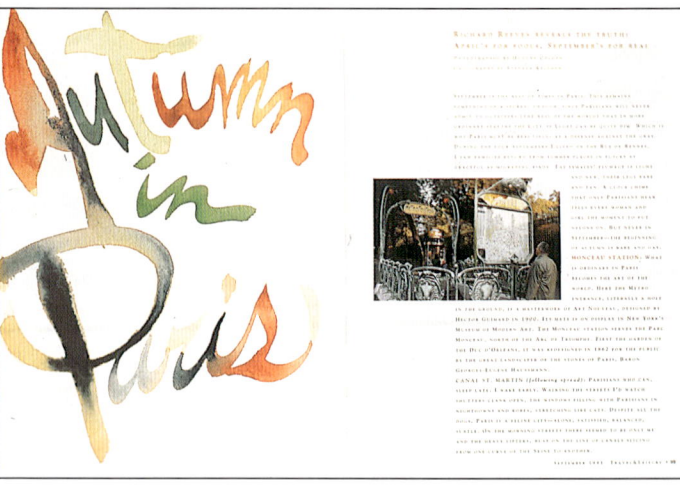

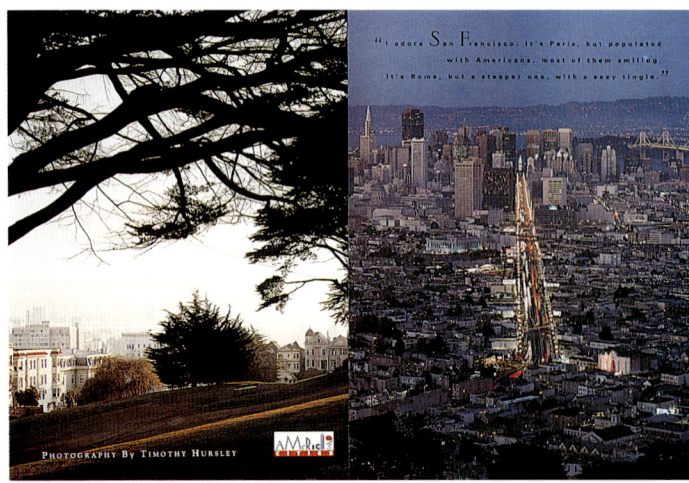

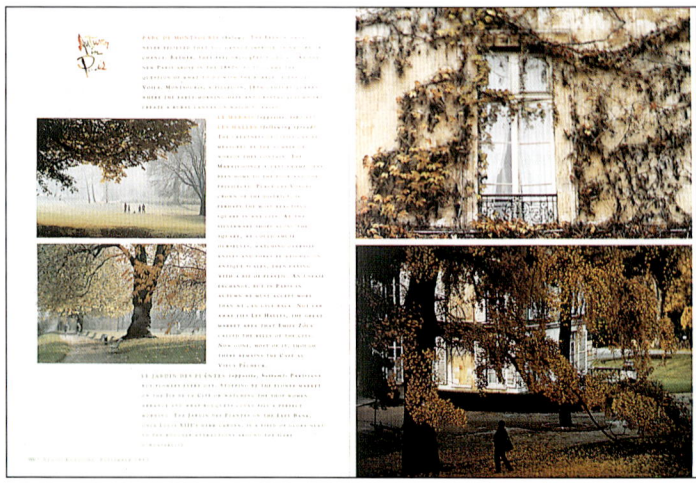

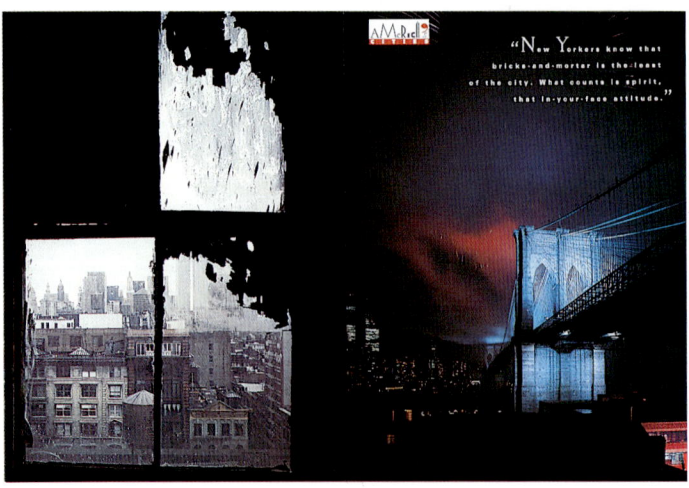

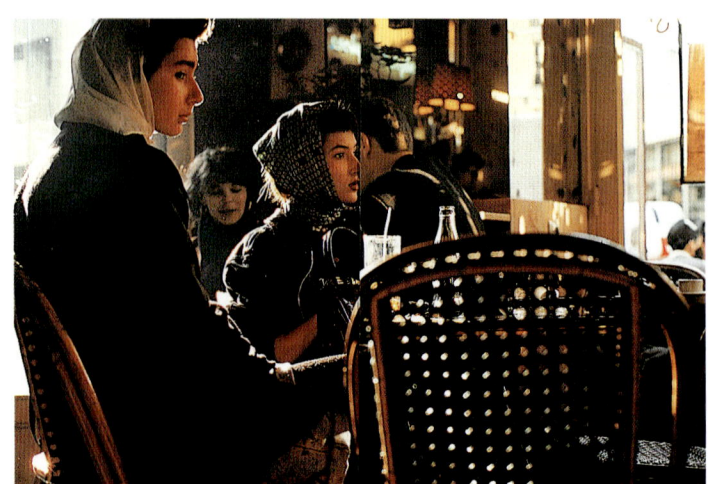

PUBLICATION	Travel & Leisure
AWARD	Merit
DESIGN DIRECTOR	Lloyd Ziff
DESIGNER	Lloyd Ziff
PHOTOGRAPHER	Mitch Epstein
PHOTO EDITOR	Hazel Hammond
PUBLISHER	American Express Publishing
CATEGORY	Photography Story/Still Life, Interiors, Travel
DATE	March 1993

PUBLICATION	Travel & Leisure
AWARD	Merit
DESIGN DIRECTOR	Lloyd Ziff
DESIGNER	Lloyd Ziff
ILLUSTRATOR	Philippe Lardy
PHOTOGRAPHER	Sally Gall
PHOTO EDITOR	Hazel Hammond
PUBLISHER	American Express Publishing
CATEGORY	Photography Story/Still Life, Interiors, Travel
DATE	May 1993

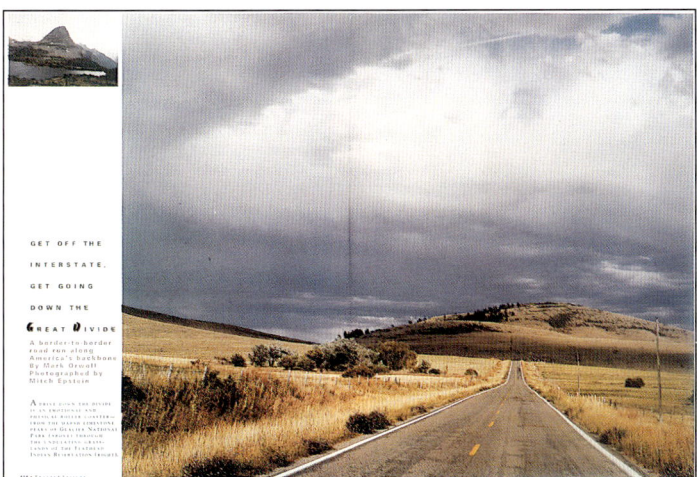

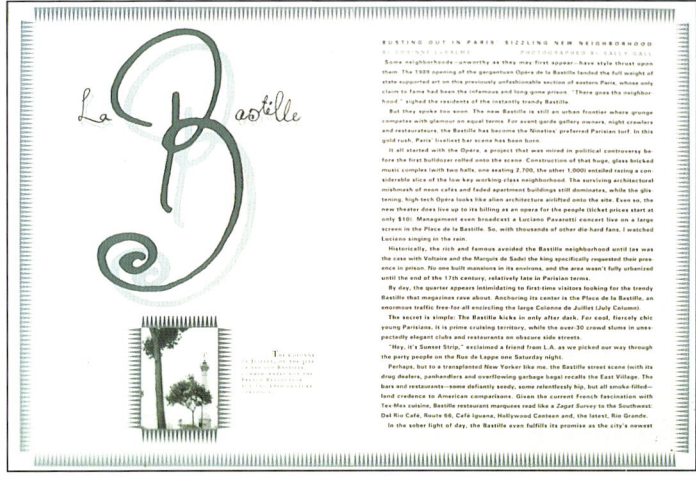

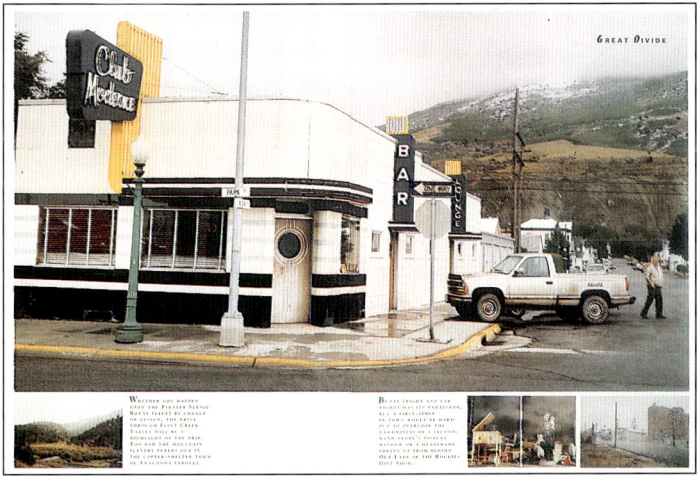

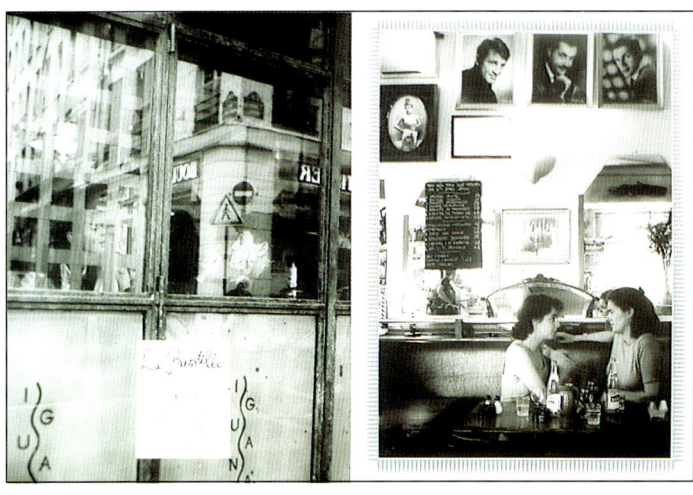

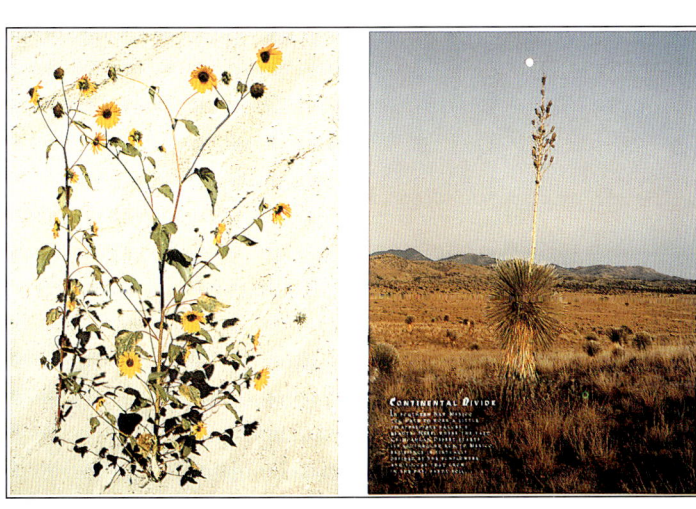

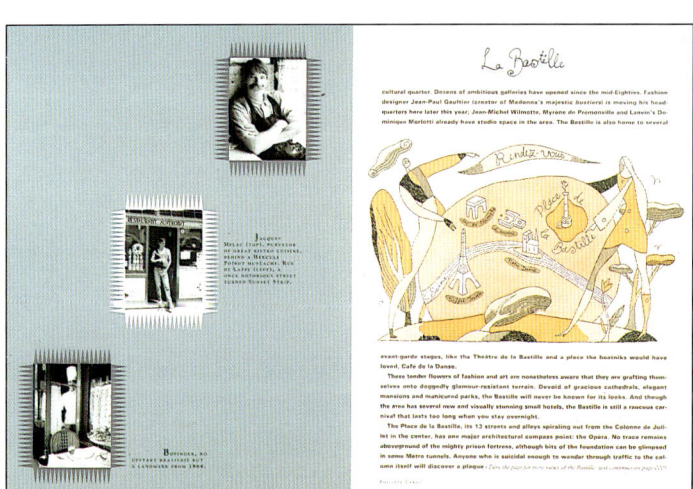

Publication	Travel & Leisure		**Publication**	Elle Décor
Award	Merit		**Award**	Merit
Design Director	Lloyd Ziff		**Art Director**	Caroline Bowyer
Designer	Lloyd Ziff		**Designer**	Caroline Bowyer
Photographer	Maggie Steber		**Photographer**	Bruce Weber
Photo Editor	Hazel Hammond		**Publisher**	Hachette Filipacchi Magazines, Inc.
Publisher	American Express Publishing		**Category**	Photography Story/Still Life, Interiors, Travel
Category	Photography Story/Still Life, Interiors, Travel		**Date**	April/May 1993
Date	April 1993			

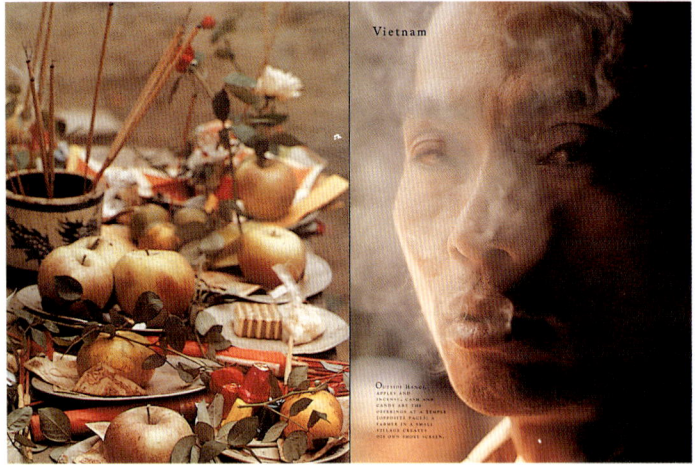

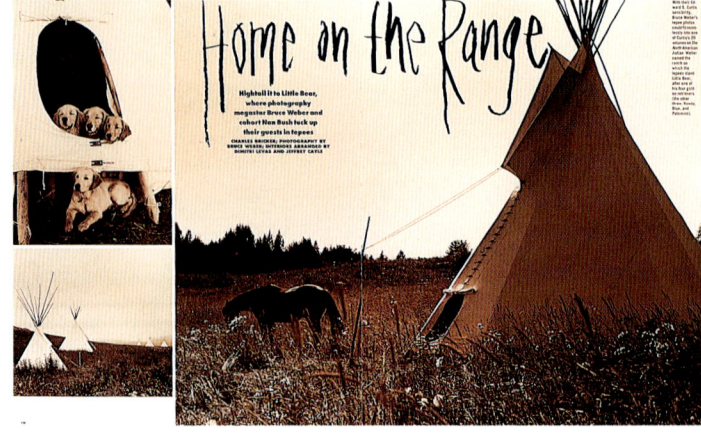

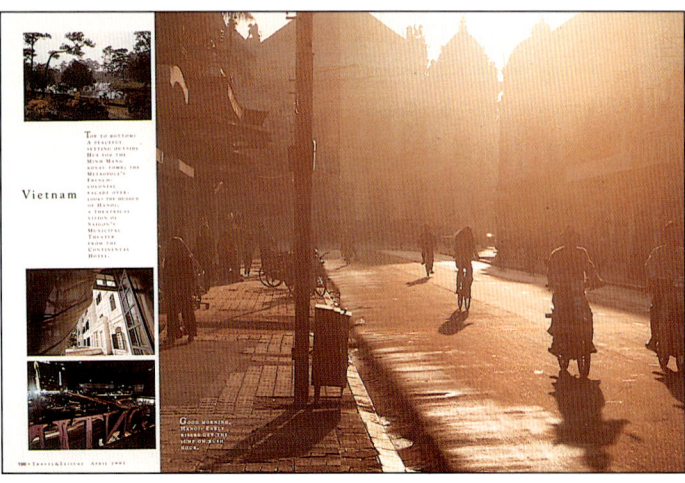

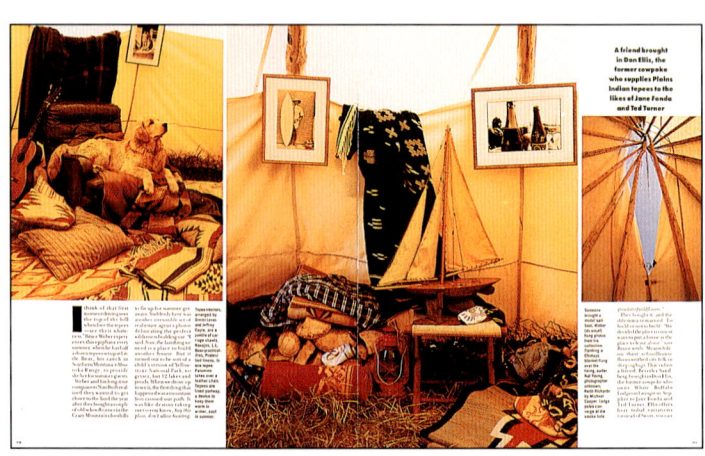

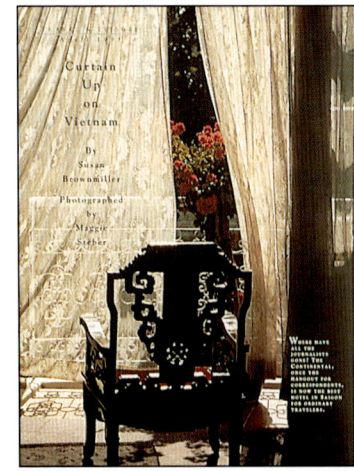

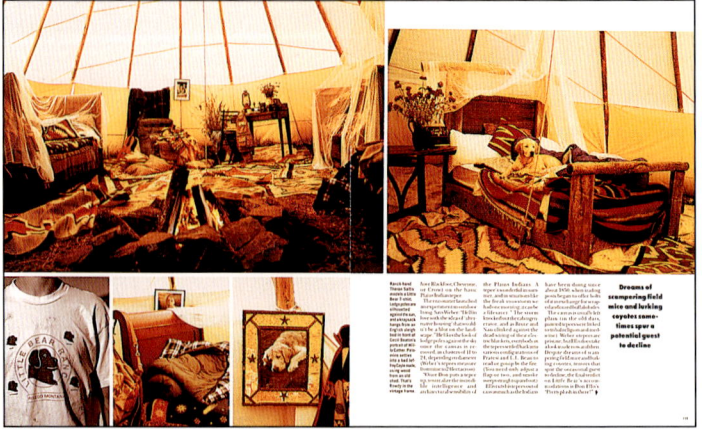

PUBLICATION	The Washington Post Magazine
AWARD	Merit
ART DIRECTOR	Richard Baker
DESIGNER	Richard Baker
PHOTOGRAPHER	Torkil Gudnason
PHOTO EDITOR	Deborah Needleman
PUBLISHER	The Washington Post
CATEGORY	Photography Story/Still Life, Interiors, Travel
DATE	March 7, 1993

PUBLICATION	The New York Times Magazine
AWARD	Merit
ART DIRECTOR	Janet Froelich
DESIGNER	Janet Froelich
PHOTOGRAPHER	Raymond Meier
PHOTO EDITOR	Kathy Ryan
PUBLISHER	The New York Times
CATEGORY	Photography Story/Still Life, Interiors, Travel
DATE	November 5, 1993

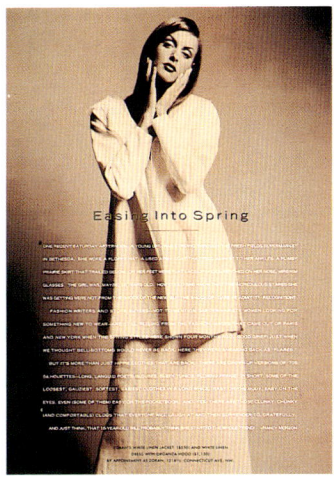

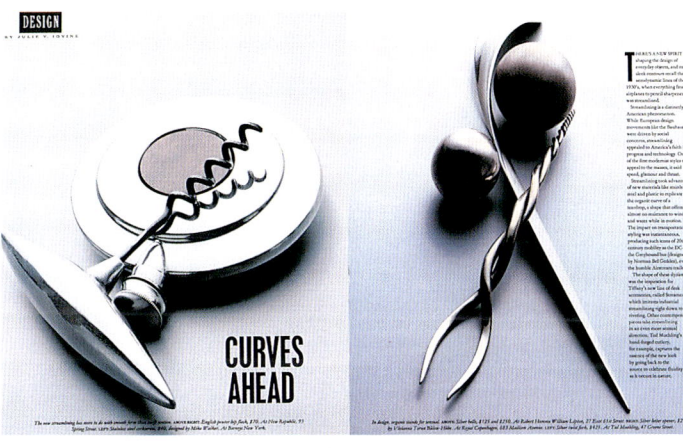

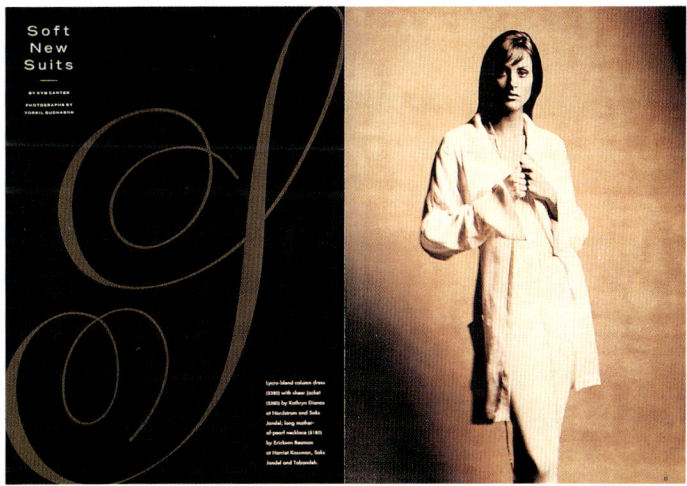

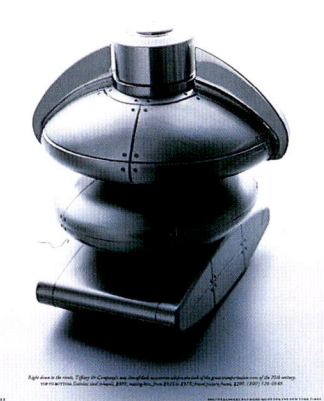

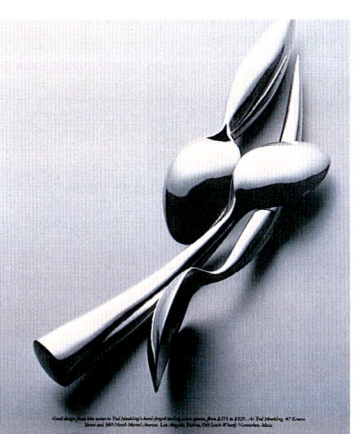

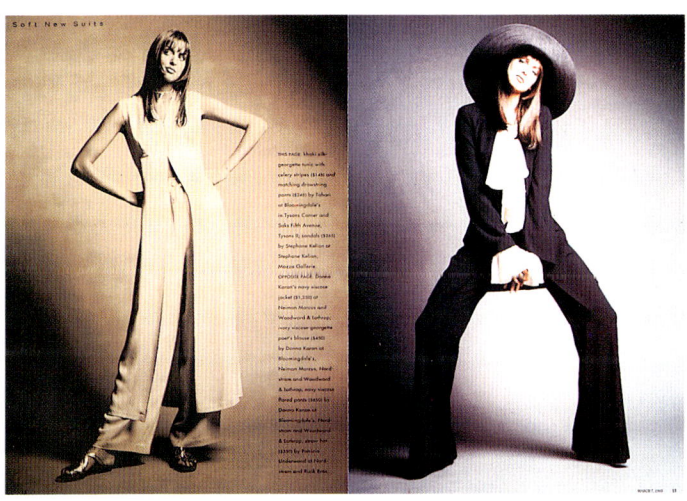

PUBLICATION   The Washington Post Magazine
AWARD   Merit
ART DIRECTOR   Kelly Doe
DESIGNER   Kelly Doe
PHOTOGRAPHER   Russell Kaye
PHOTO EDITOR   Deborah Needleman
PUBLISHER   The Washington Post
CATEGORY   Photography Story/Still Life, Interiors, Travel
DATE   May 23, 1993

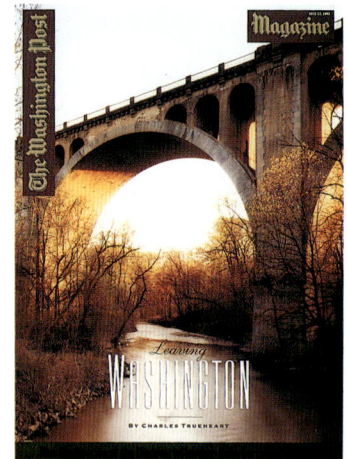

The Washington Post Magazine

Leaving WASHINGTON

BY CHARLES TRUEHEART

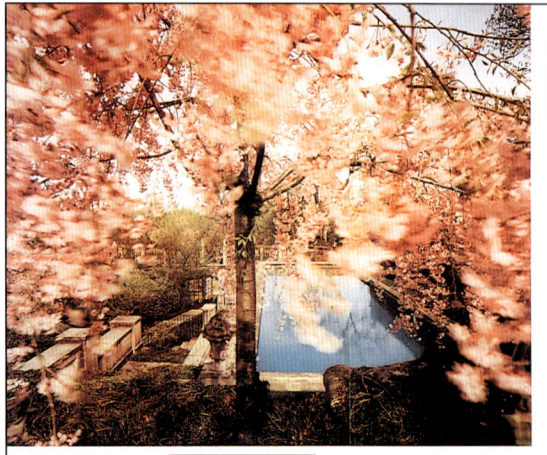

Washington FAREWELL

ALL HIS LIFE, HE'S BEEN
LEAVING AND RETURNING TO THE
CITY. BUT THIS TIME AS HE
PREPARED TO LEAVE, HIS FATHER
LAY DYING. AND THROUGH
HIS SENSE OF LOSS HE FOUND A
SENSE OF PLACE

By Charles Trueheart
Photography by Russell Kaye

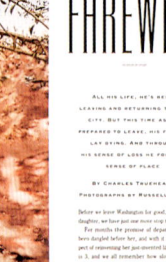
THE DUNBARTON OAKS SWIMMING POOL

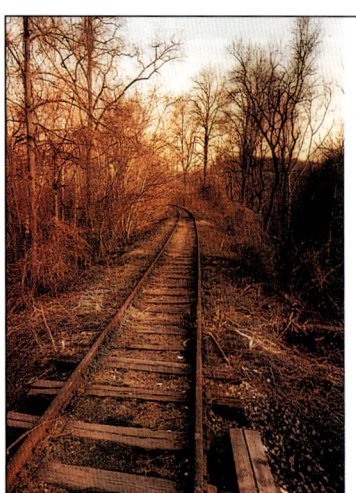

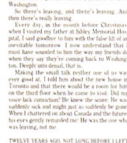
NEAR THE C&O CANAL, a reminder of days gone by

THE INCREDIBLE LIGHTNESS OF FISHING

IF SMALLMOUTH BASS ARE WHAT YOU'RE AFTER, THE JAMES,
POTOMAC AND SHENANDOAH DELIVER ABUNDANCE—
WITH A SIDE ORDER OF SERENITY   BY BILL HEAVEY

Photographs by Russell Kaye

PUBLICATION   The Washington Post Magazine
AWARD   Merit
ART DIRECTOR   Richard Baker
DESIGNER   Kelly Doe
PHOTOGRAPHER   Russell Kaye
PHOTO EDITOR   Karen Tanaka
PUBLISHER   The Washington Post
CATEGORY   Photography Story/Still Life, Interiors, Travel
DATE   March 14, 1993

PUBLICATION	W Magazine
AWARD	Gold
CREATIVE DIRECTOR	Dennis Freedman
DESIGN DIRECTORS	Edward Leida, Jean Griffin
ART DIRECTOR	Kirby Rodriguez
DESIGNERS	Edward Leida, Myla Carver
PHOTOGRAPHER	Perry Ogden
PHOTO EDITOR	Dennis Freedman
PUBLISHER	Fairchild Publications
CATEGORY	Photography Story/Fashion, Beauty
DATE	November 1, 1993

FAR AND AWAY

The wilds of west Ireland are the perfect setting for this season's rough and rugged fashions

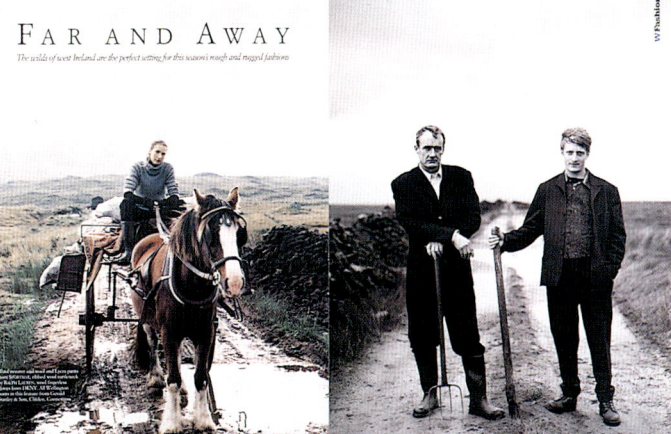

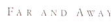
FAR AND AWAY

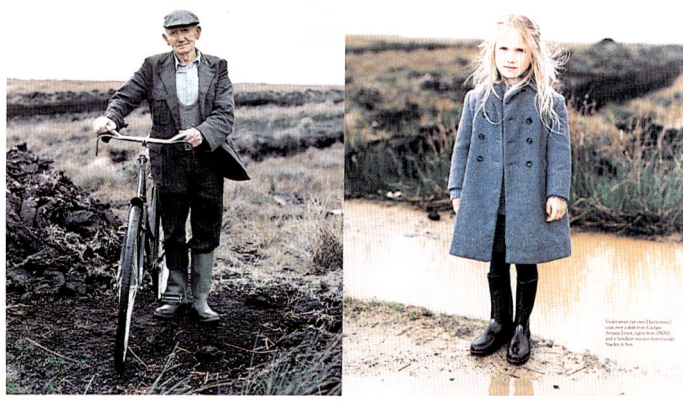

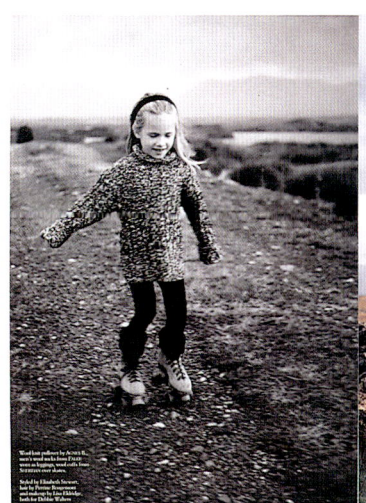

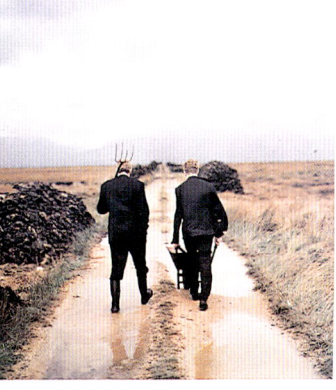
FAR AND AWAY

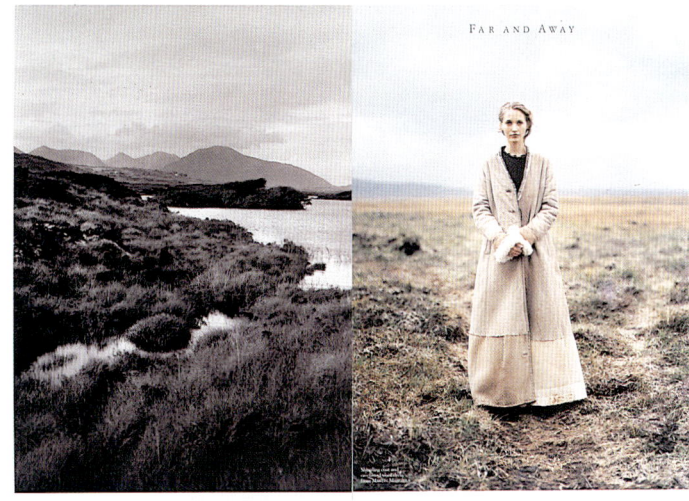
FAR AND AWAY

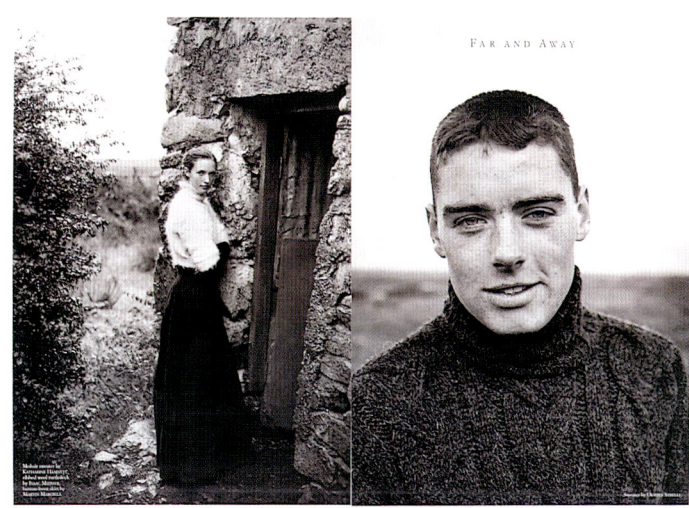
FAR AND AWAY

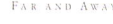
FAR AND AWAY

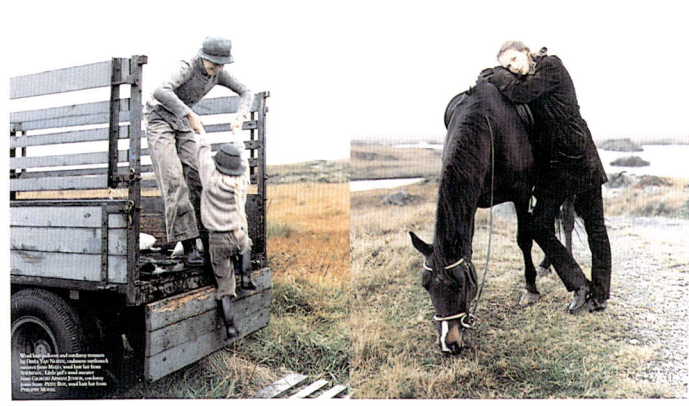

PUBLICATION The New York Times Magazine
AWARD Gold
ART DIRECTOR Janet Froelich
DESIGNER Petra Mercker
PHOTOGRAPHER Kurt Markus
PHOTO EDITOR Kathy Ryan
PUBLISHER The New York Times
CATEGORY Photography Story/Fashion, Beauty
DATE September 12, 1993

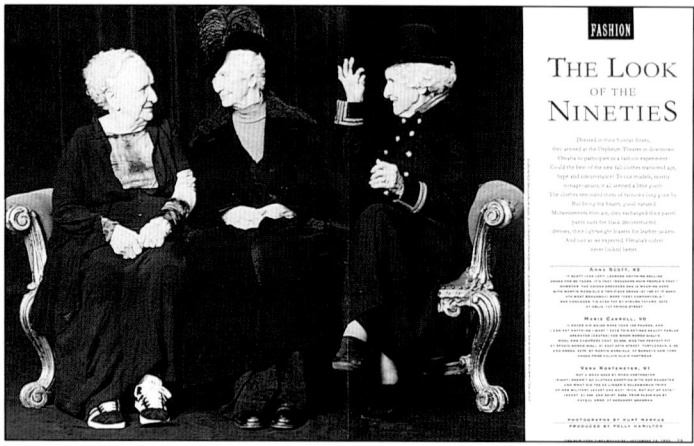

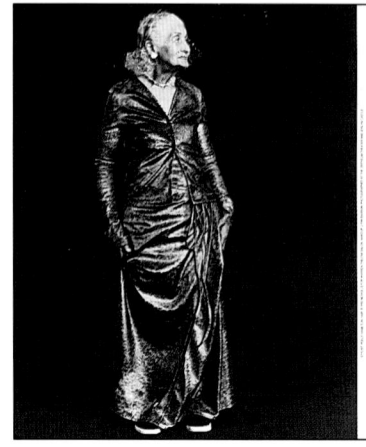
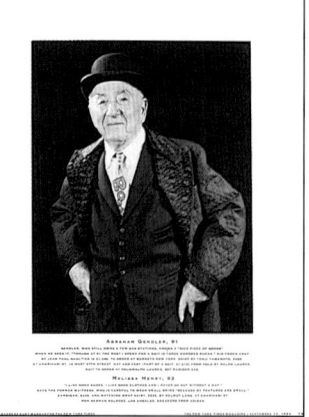
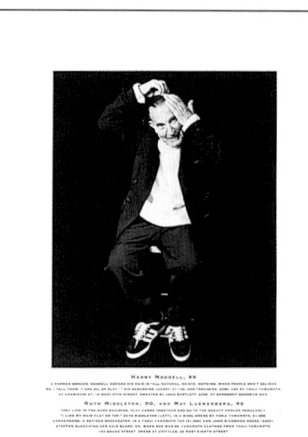
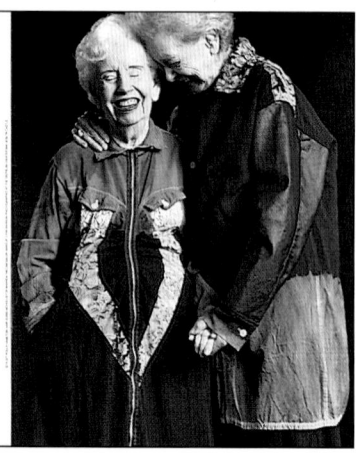

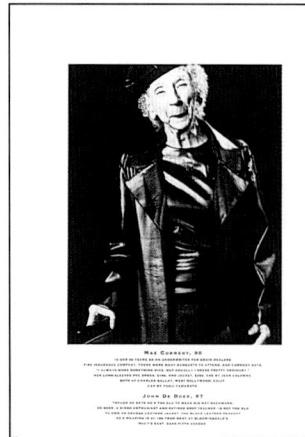
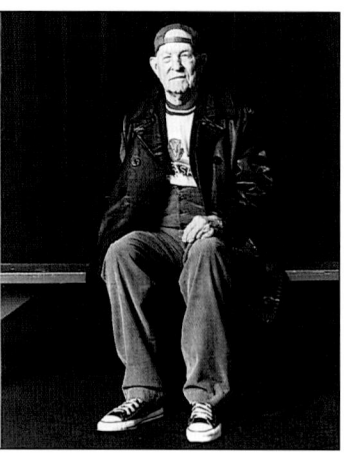
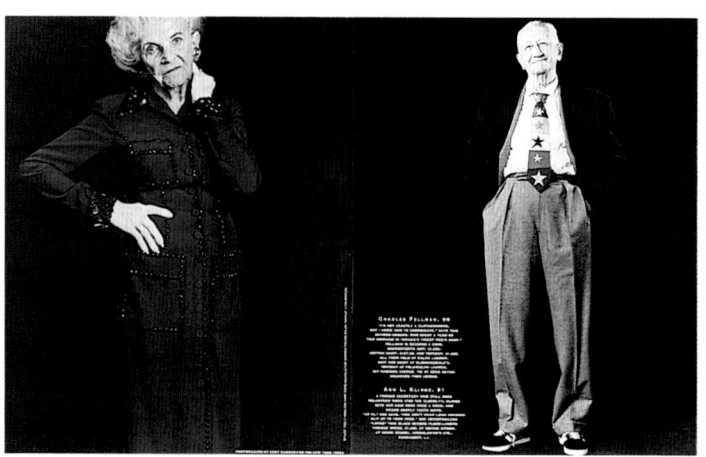

PUBLICATION   Vibe
AWARD   Silver
DESIGN DIRECTOR   Gary Koepke
ART DIRECTOR   Richard Baker
DESIGNER   Richard Baker
PHOTOGRAPHER   Ruven Afanador
PHOTO EDITOR   George Pitts
PUBLISHER   Time Inc. Ventures
STUDIO   Koepke International, Ltd.
CATEGORY   Photography Story/Fashion, Beauty
DATE   September 1993

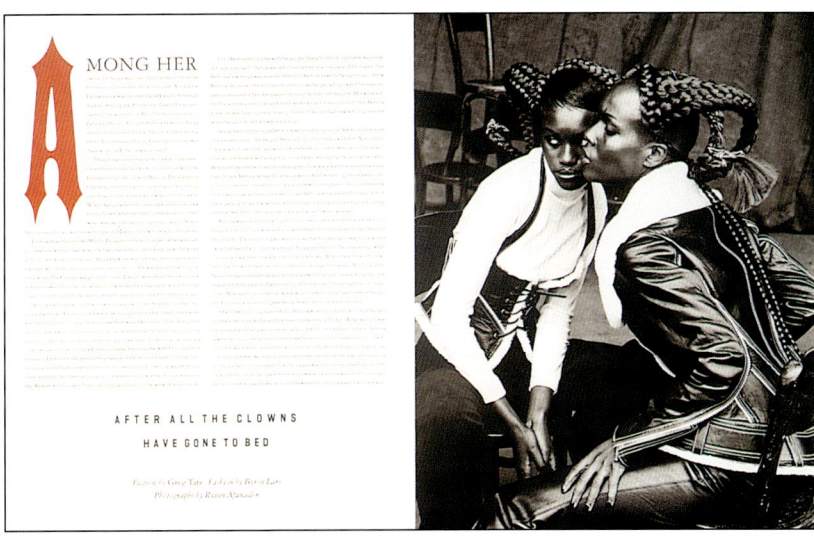

A MONG HER

AFTER ALL THE CLOWNS
HAVE GONE TO BED

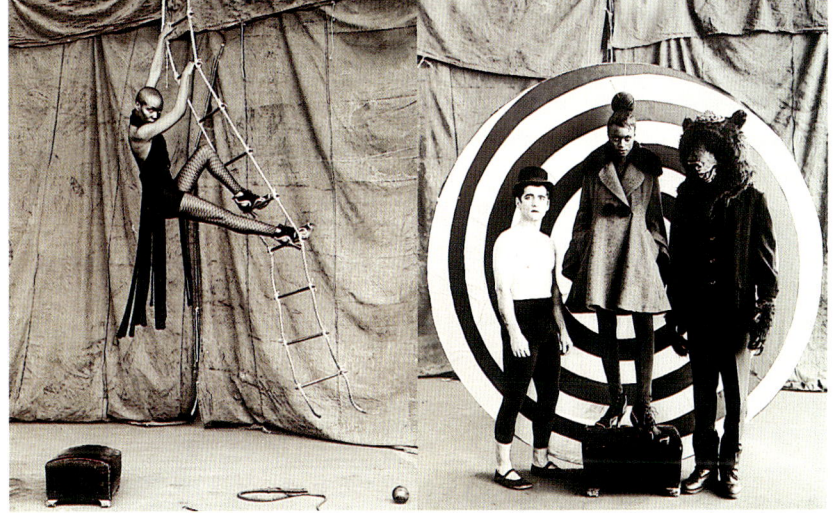

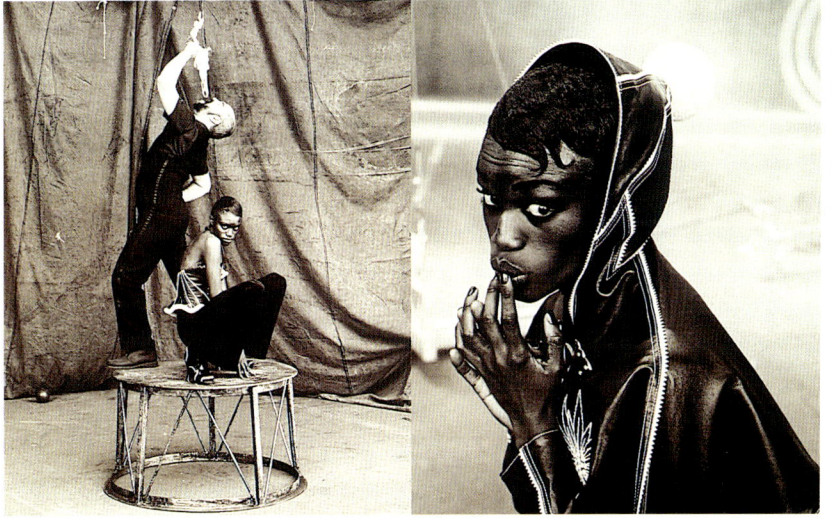

PUBLICATION	Team Leader
AWARD	Silver
DESIGN DIRECTOR	Doug Gottlieb
ART DIRECTOR	Doug Gottlieb
DESIGNER	Doug Gottlieb
PHOTOGRAPHER	Timothy Reagan
PUBLISHER	Fairchild Publications
CATEGORY	Photography Story/Fashion, Beauty
DATE	July 1993

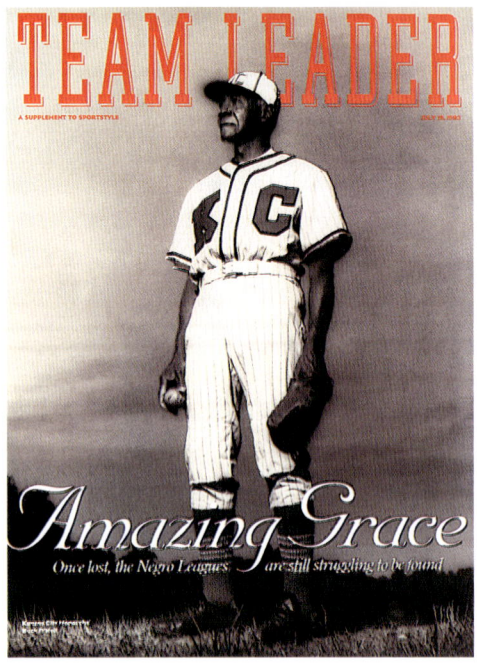

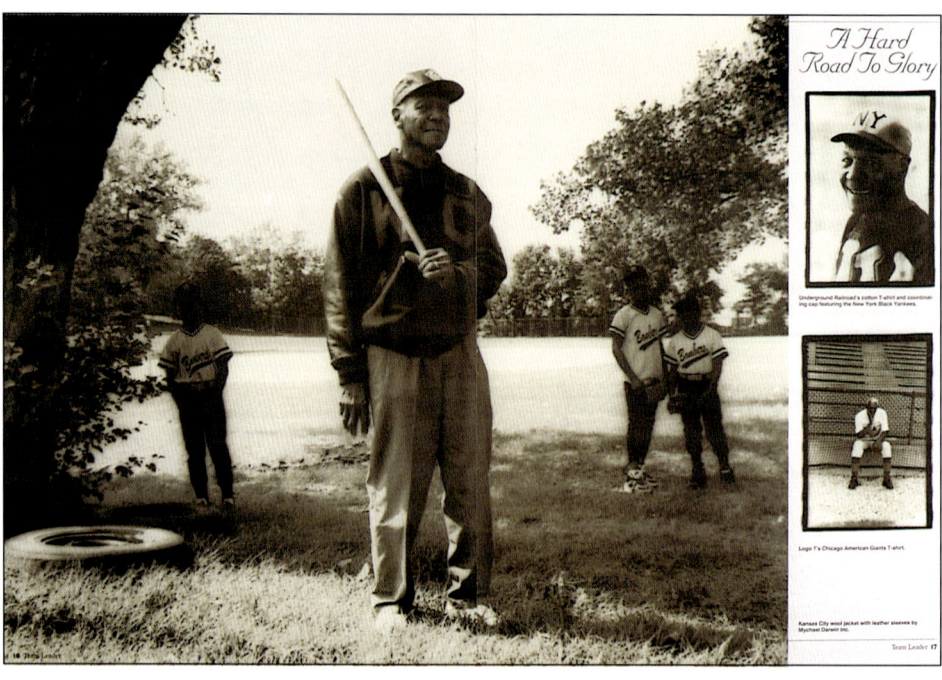

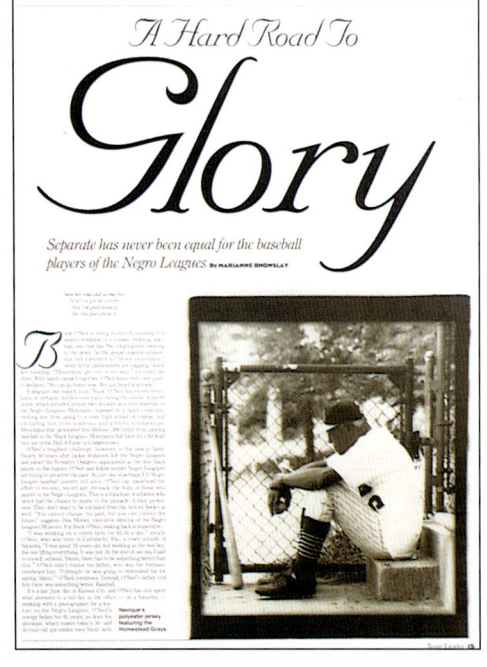

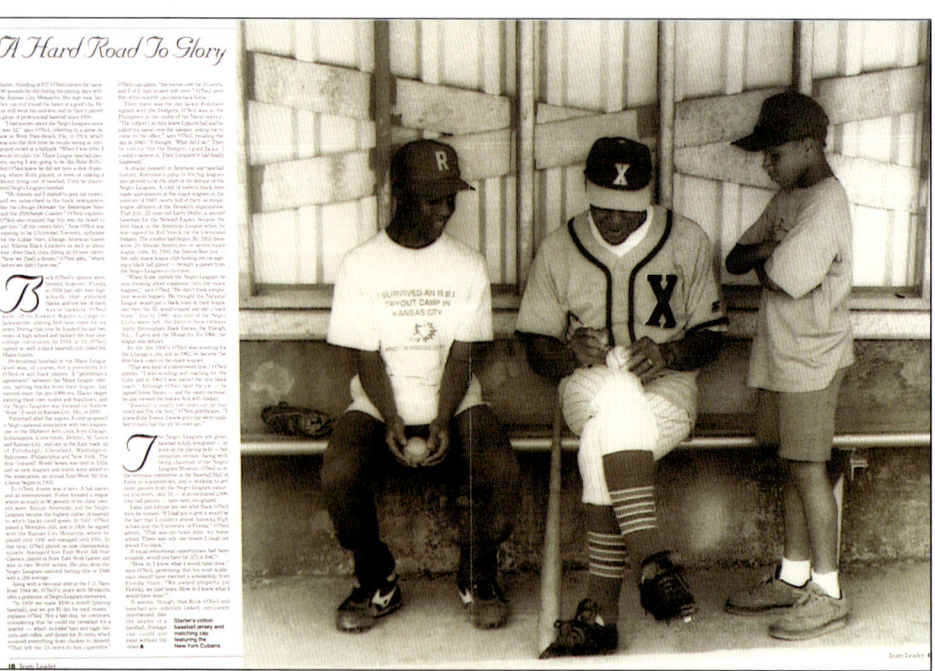

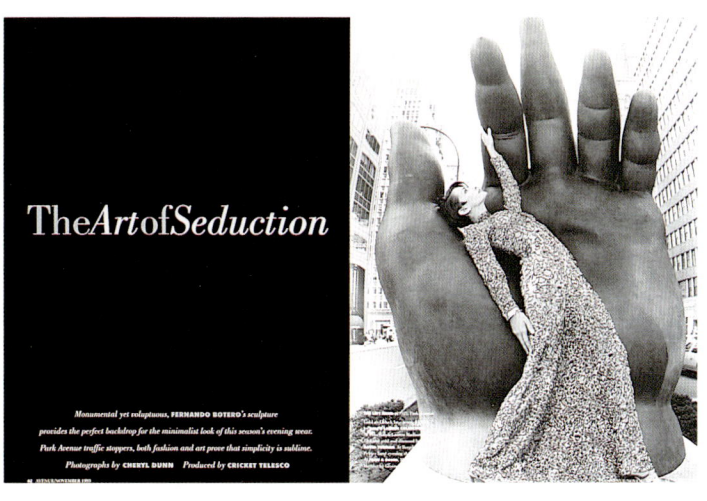

The *Art* of *Seduction*

Monumental yet voluptuous, FERNANDO BOTERO's sculpture provides the perfect backdrop for the minimalist look of this season's evening wear. Park Avenue traffic stoppers, both fashion and art prove that simplicity is sublime.

Photographs by CHERYL DUNN   Produced by CRICKET TELESCO

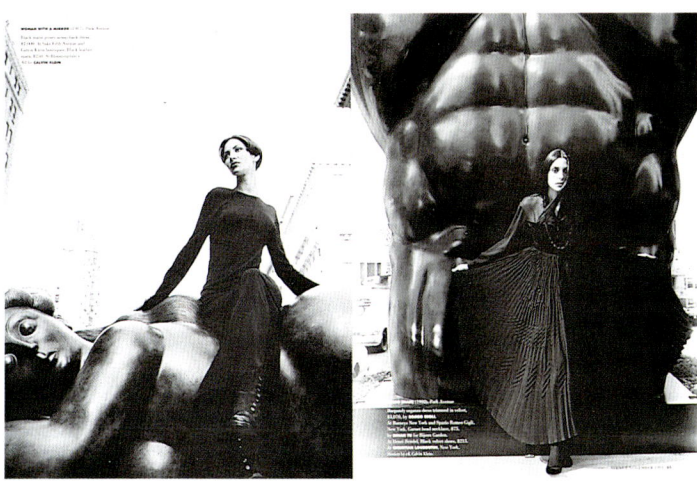

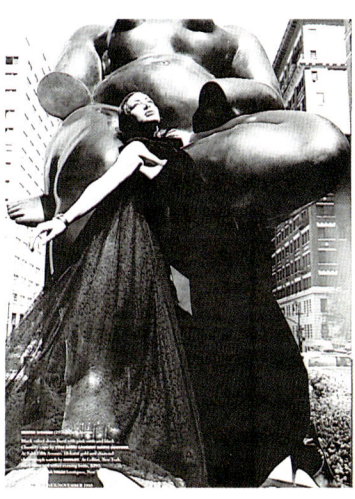

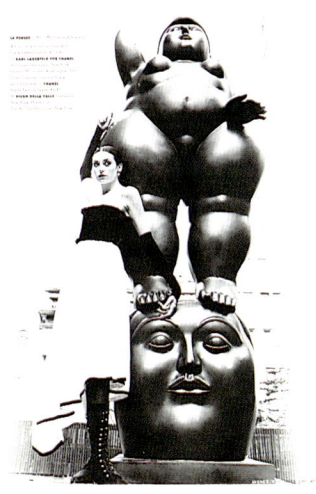

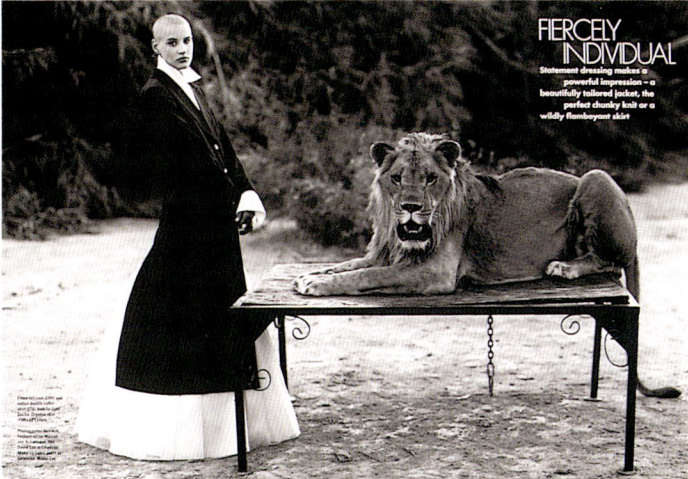

FIERCELY INDIVIDUAL

Statement dressing makes a powerful impression – a beautifully tailored jacket, the perfect chunky knit or a wildly flamboyant skirt

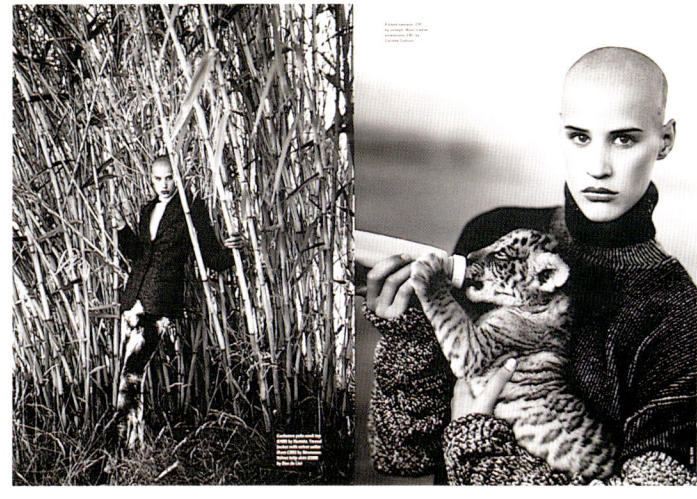

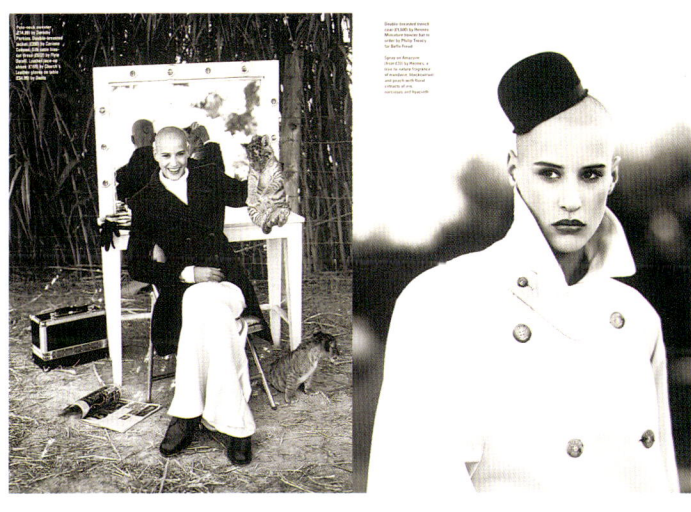

PUBLICATION	Avenue
AWARD	Merit
CREATIVE DIRECTOR	Cricket Telesco
ART DIRECTOR	Lori Ende
DESIGNER	Lori Ende
PHOTOGRAPHER	Cheryl Dunn
PUBLISHER	Avenue Magazine, Inc.
CATEGORY	Photography Story/Fashion, Beauty
DATE	November 1993

PUBLICATION   Men's Journal
AWARD   Merit
ART DIRECTOR   Matthew Drace
DESIGNER   Matthew Drace
PHOTOGRAPHER   Philip Dixon
PHOTO EDITOR   Allyson M. Torrisi
PUBLISHER   Wenner Media
CATEGORY   Photography Story/Fashion, Beauty
DATE   July/August 1993

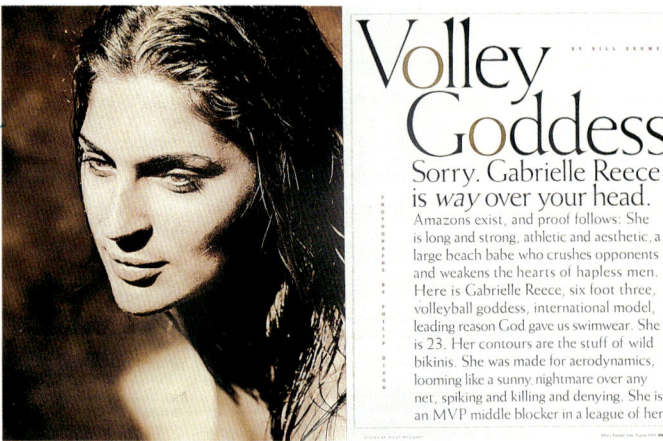

Volley Goddess

Sorry. Gabrielle Reece is *way* over your head.

Amazons exist, and proof follows: She is long and strong, athletic and aesthetic, a large beach babe who crushes opponents and weakens the hearts of hapless men. Here is Gabrielle Reece, six foot three, volleyball goddess, international model, leading reason God gave us swimwear. She is 23. Her contours are the stuff of wild bikinis. She was made for aerodynamics, looming like a sunny, nightmare over any net, spiking and killing and denying. She is an MVP middle blocker in a league of her

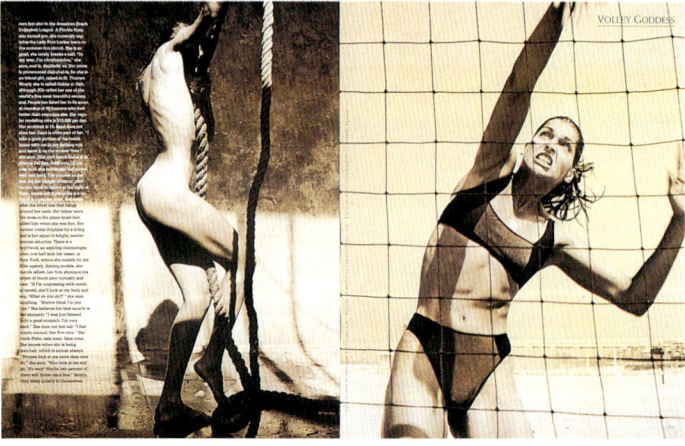

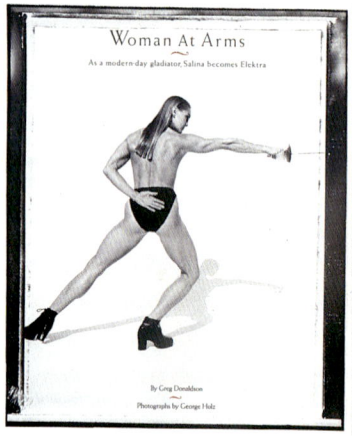

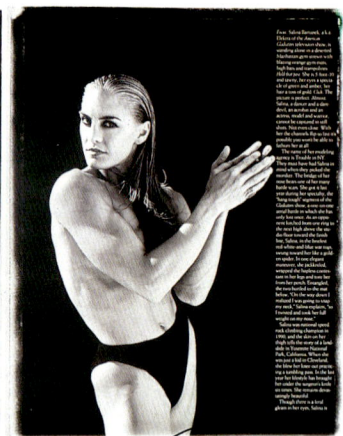

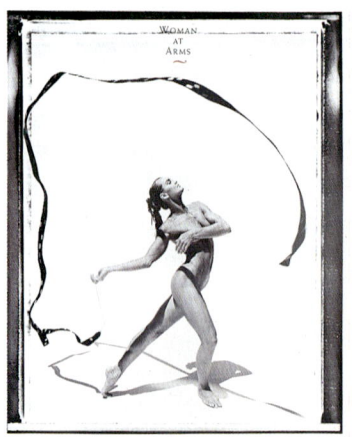

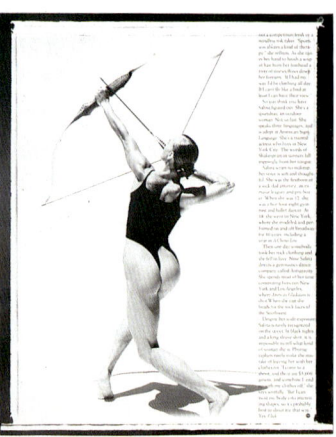

PUBLICATION   Men's Journal
AWARD   Merit
DESIGN DIRECTOR   Matthew Drace
ART DIRECTOR   Matthew Drace
PHOTOGRAPHER   George Holz
PUBLISHER   Wenner Media
CATEGORY   Photography Story/Fashion, Beauty
DATE   November 1993

PUBLICATION	W Magazine
AWARD	Merit
CREATIVE DIRECTOR	Dennis Freedman
DESIGN DIRECTORS	Edward Leida, Jean Griffin
ART DIRECTOR	Kirby Rodriguez
DESIGNERS	Edward Leida, Rosalba Sierra
PHOTOGRAPHER	Raymond Meier
PHOTO EDITOR	Dennis Freedman
PUBLISHER	Fairchild Publications
CATEGORY	Photography Story/Fashion, Beauty
DATE	December 1, 1993

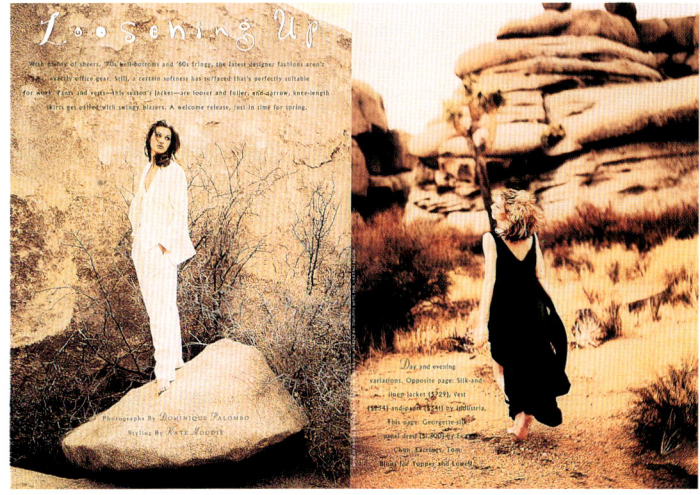

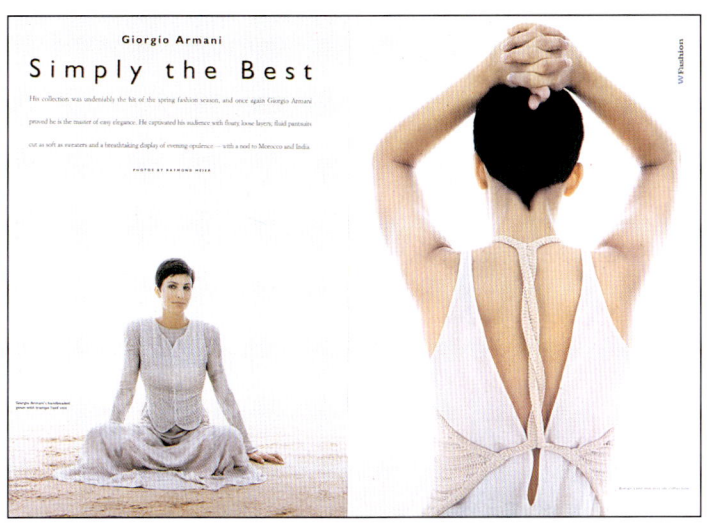

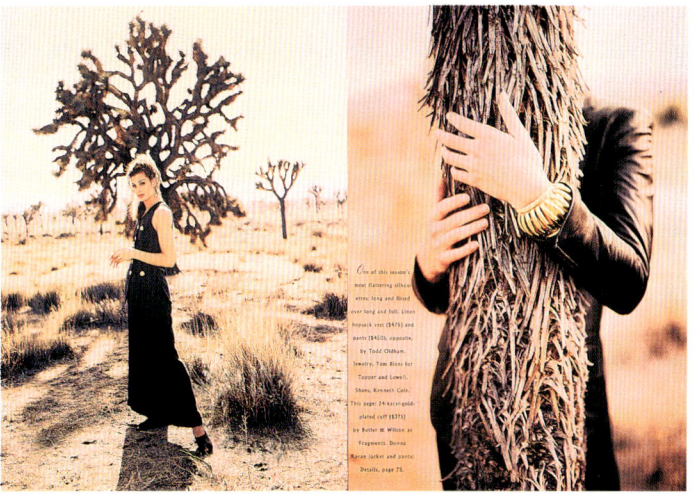

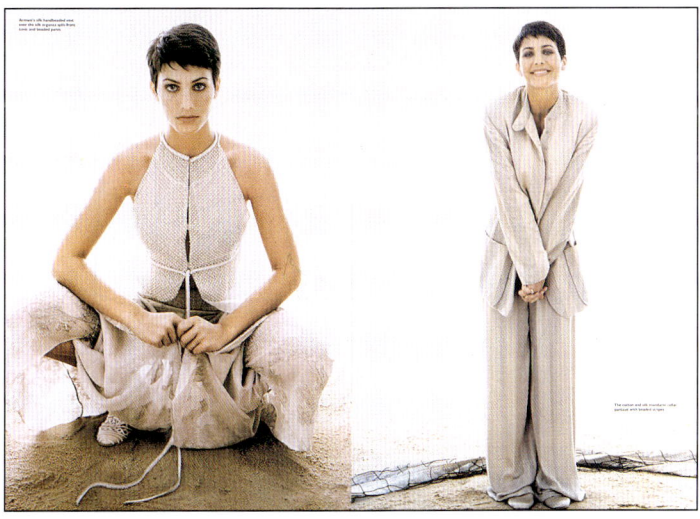

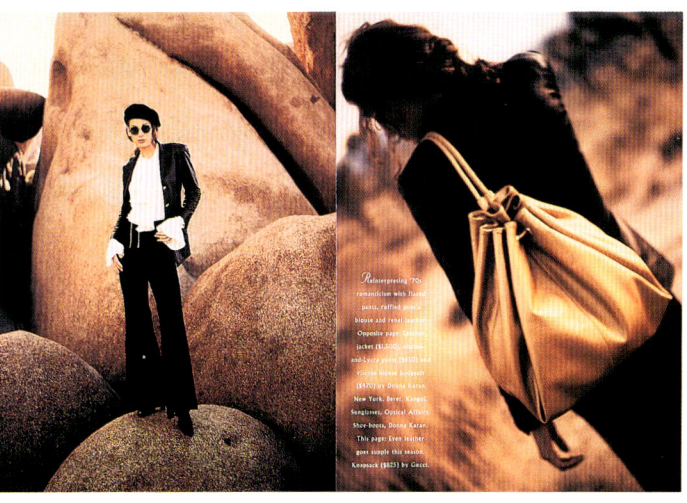

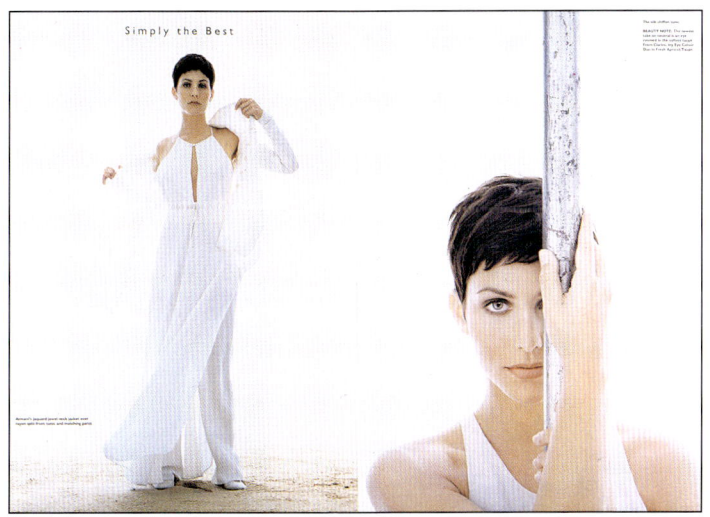

PUBLICATION	Working Woman
AWARD	Merit
ART DIRECTOR	Jolene Cuyler
DESIGNER	Karen Simpson
PHOTOGRAPHER	Dominique Palombo
PHOTO EDITOR	Clare Lissaman
PUBLISHER	Lang Communications
CATEGORY	Photography Story/Fashion, Beauty
DATE	March 1993

PUBLICATION	The Los Angeles Times Magazine
AWARD	Merit
ART DIRECTOR	Nancy Duckworth
DESIGNER	Carol Wakano
PHOTOGRAPHER	Josef Astor
PHOTO EDITOR	Lisa Thackaberry
PUBLISHER	Times Mirror
CATEGORY	Photography Story/Fashion, Beauty

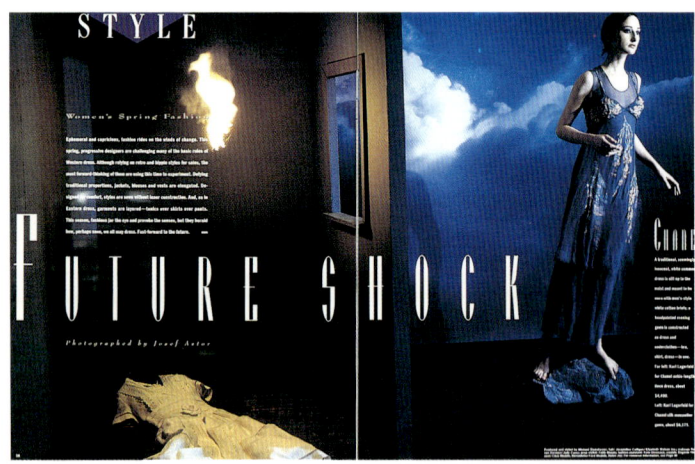

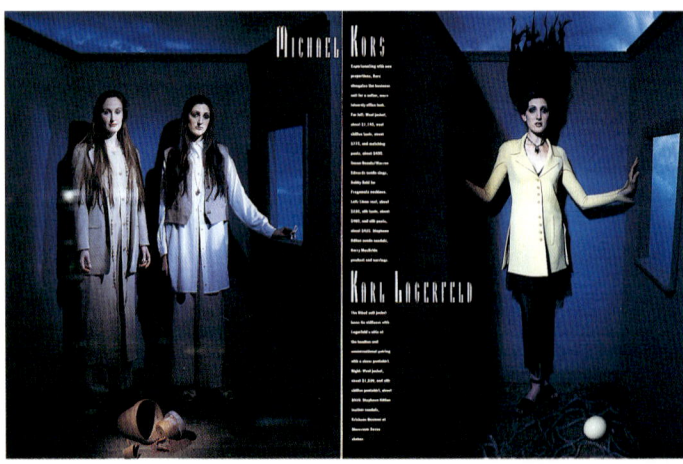

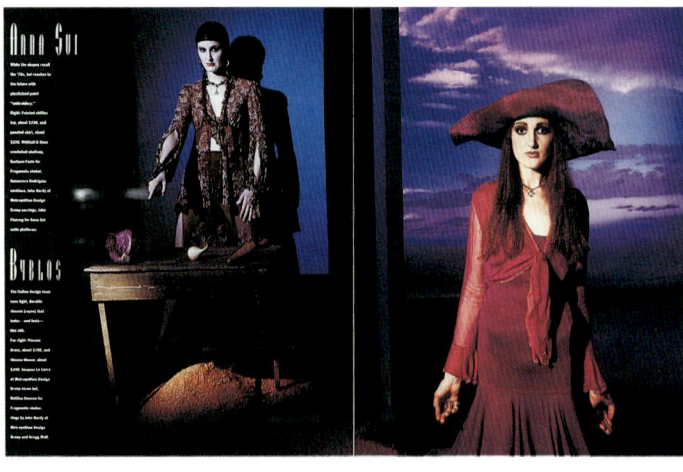

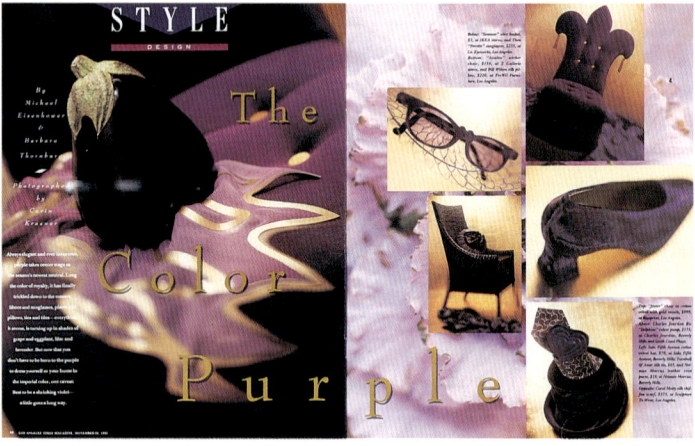

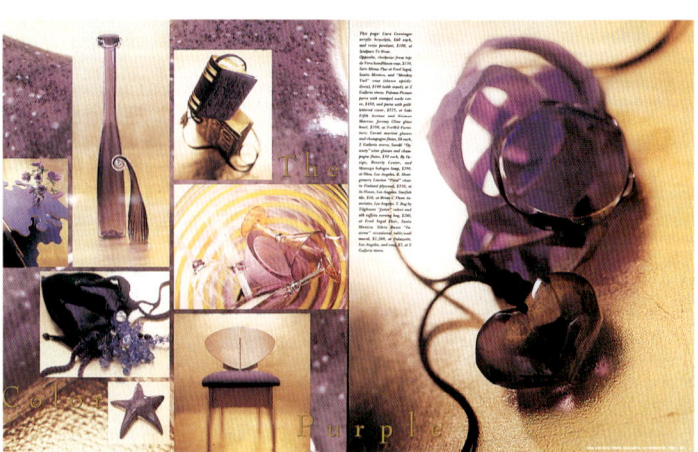

PUBLICATION	The Los Angeles Times Magazine
AWARD	Merit
ART DIRECTOR	Nancy Duckworth
DESIGNER	Nancy Duckworth
PHOTOGRAPHER	Carin Krasner
PHOTO EDITOR	Lisa Thackaberry
PUBLISHER	Times Mirror
CATEGORY	Photography Story/Fashion, Beauty
DATE	November 28, 1993

PUBLICATION	The Los Angeles Times Magazine
AWARD	Merit
ART DIRECTOR	Nancy Duckworth
DESIGNER	Nancy Duckworth
PHOTOGRAPHER	Donna Trope
PHOTO EDITOR	Lisa Thackaberry
PUBLISHER	Times Mirror
CATEGORY	Photography Story/Fashion, Beauty

PUBLICATION	The New York Times Magazine
AWARD	Merit
ART DIRECTOR	Janet Froelich
DESIGNER	Gina Davis
PHOTOGRAPHER	Randall Mesden
PHOTO EDITOR	Kathy Ryan
PUBLISHER	The New York Times
CATEGORY	Photography Story/Fashion, Beauty
DATE	March 28, 1993

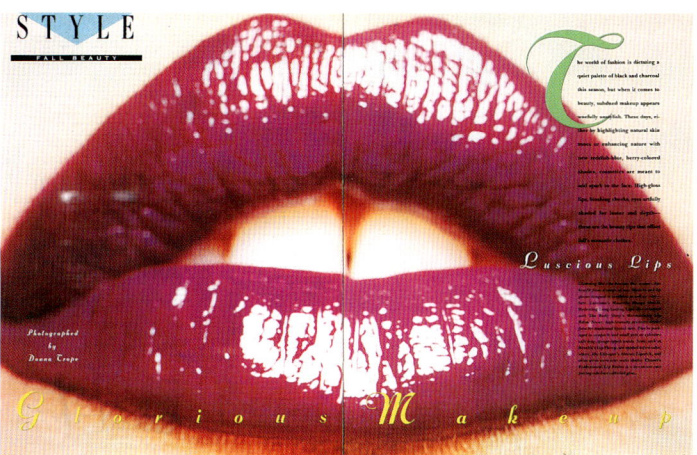

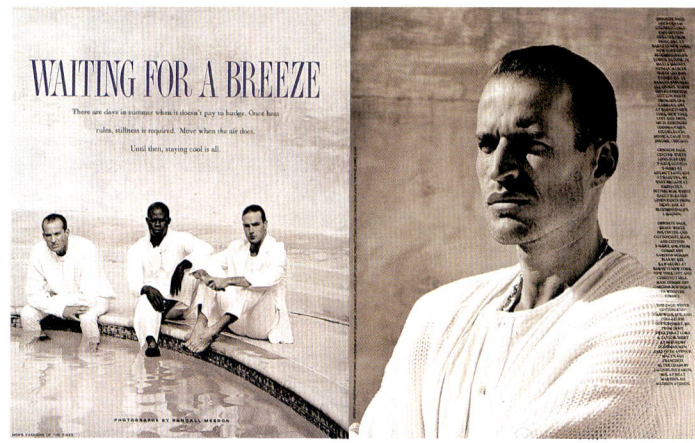

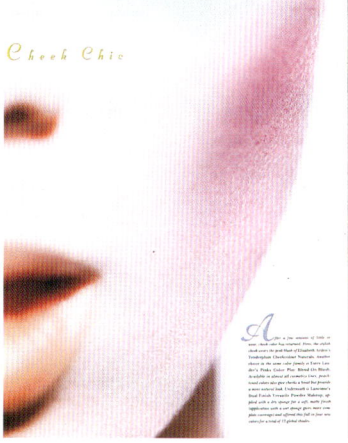

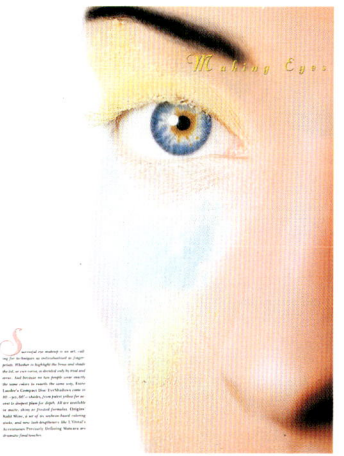

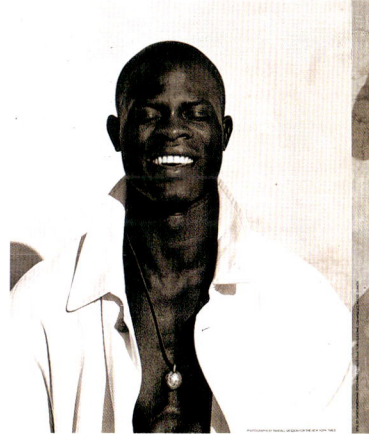

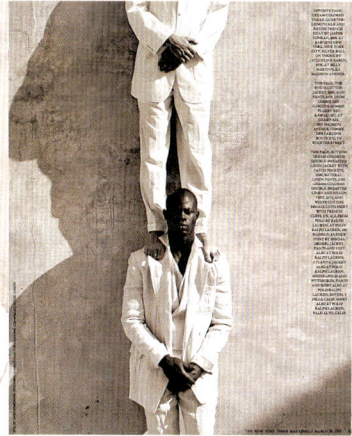

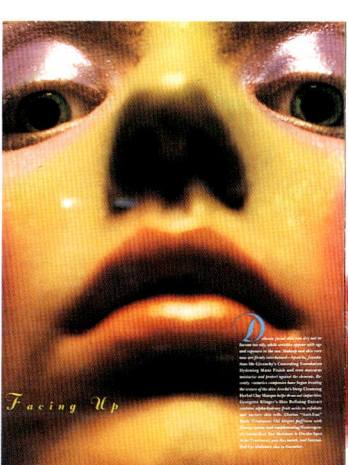

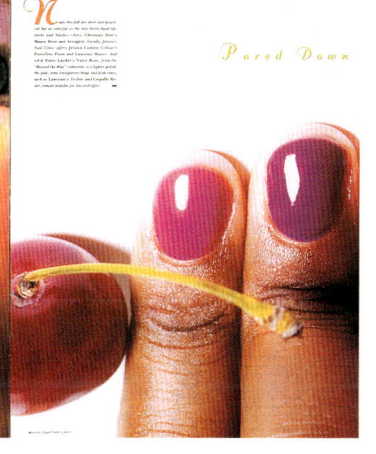

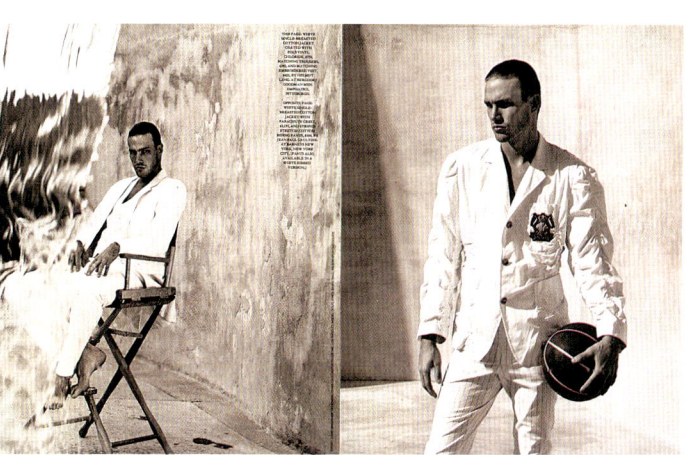

PUBLICATION	Earnshaw's
AWARD	Merit
ART DIRECTOR	Nancy Campbell
DESIGNER	Nancy Campbell
PHOTOGRAPHER	Alexandra Stonehill
PUBLISHER	Earnshaw Publications
CATEGORY	Photography Story/Fashion, Beauty
DATE	March 1993

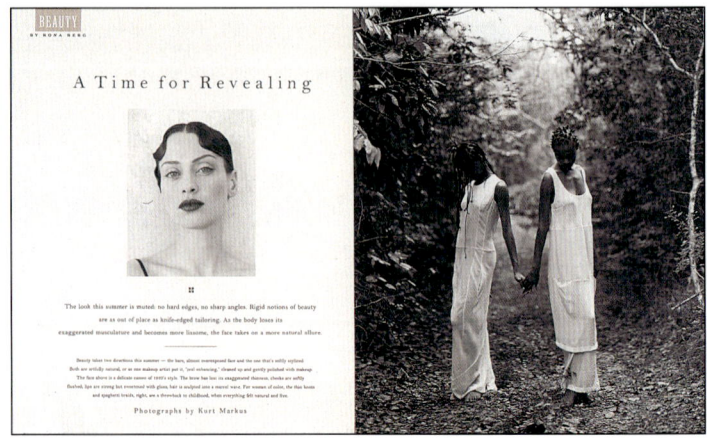

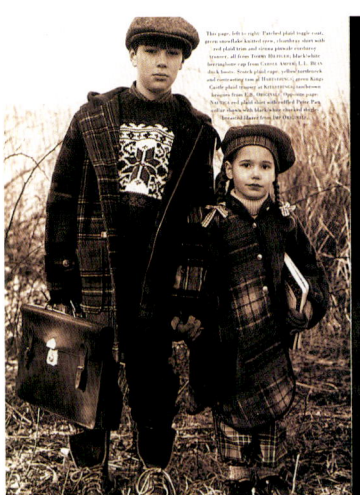
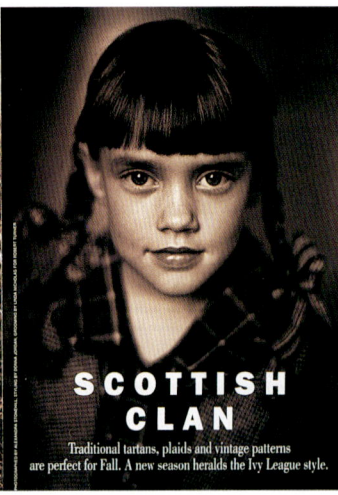

SCOTTISH CLAN

Traditional tartans, plaids and vintage patterns
are perfect for Fall. A new season heralds the Ivy League style.

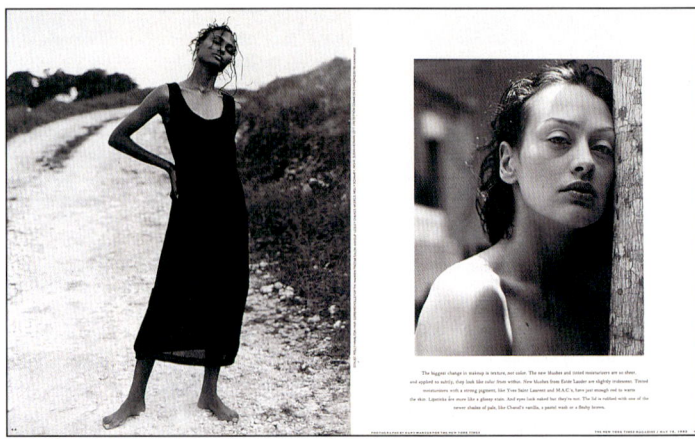

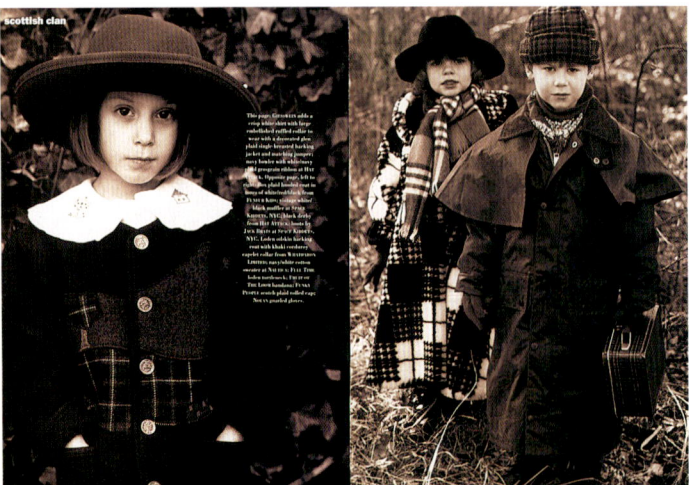

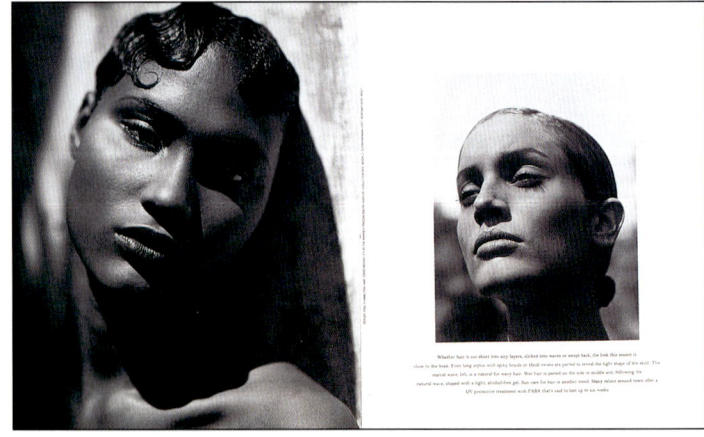

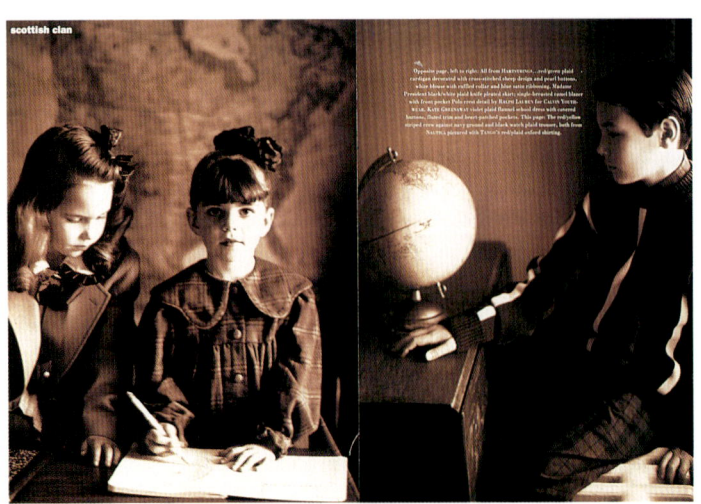

PUBLICATION	The New York Times Magazine
AWARD	Merit
ART DIRECTOR	Janet Froelich
DESIGNER	Gina Davis
PHOTOGRAPHER	Kurt Markus
PHOTO EDITOR	Kathy Ryan
PUBLISHER	The New York Times
CATEGORY	Photography Story/Fashion, Beauty
DATE	May 16, 1993

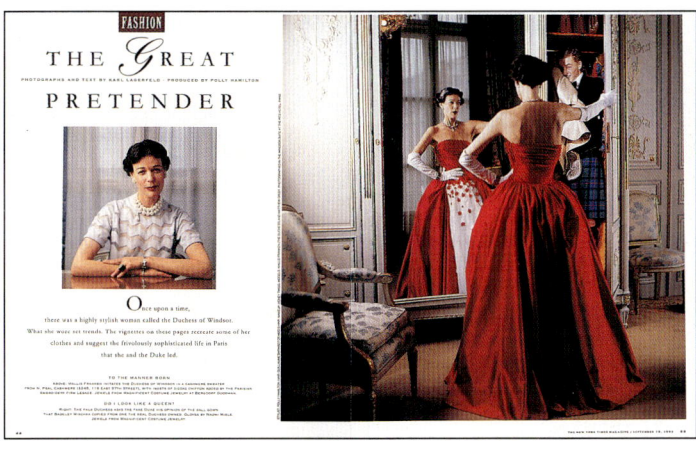

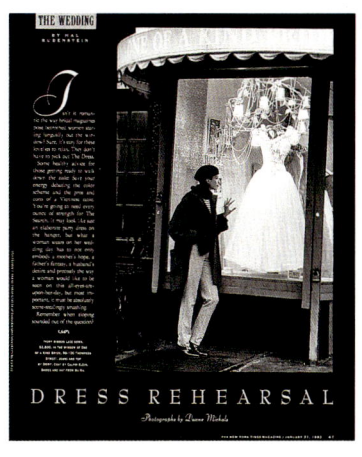

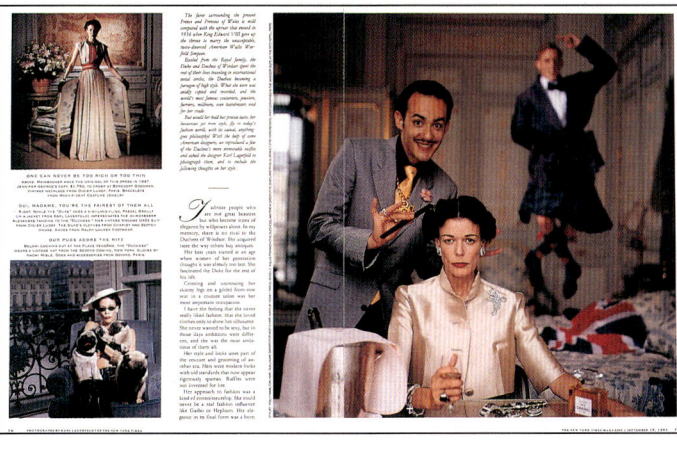

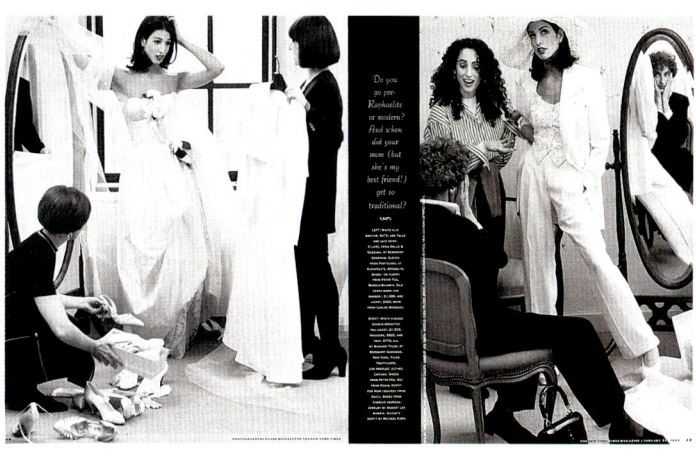

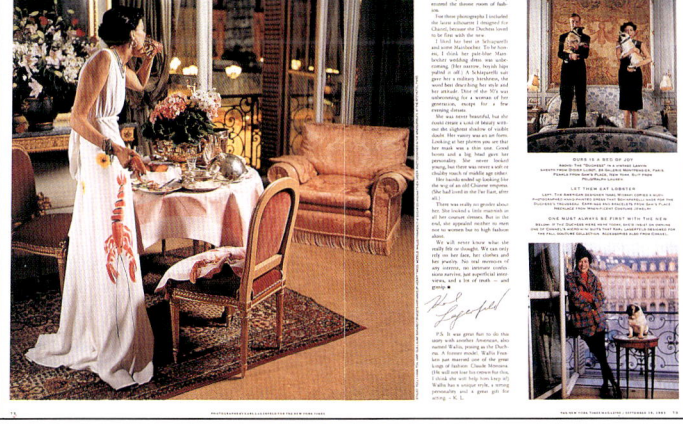

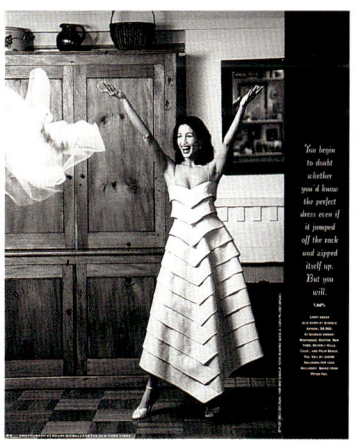

PUBLICATION	The New York Times Magazine
AWARD	Merit
ART DIRECTOR	Janet Froelich
DESIGNER	Petra Mercker
PHOTOGRAPHER	Karl Lagerfeld
PHOTO EDITOR	Kathy Ryan
PUBLISHER	The New York Times
CATEGORY	Photography Story/Fashion, Beauty
DATE	September 19, 1993

PUBLICATION	The New York Times Magazine
AWARD	Merit
ART DIRECTOR	Janet Froelich
DESIGNER	Nancy Harris
PHOTOGRAPHER	Duane Michals
PHOTO EDITOR	Kathy Ryan
PUBLISHER	The New York Times
CATEGORY	Photography Story/Fashion, Beauty
DATE	January 31, 1993

PUBLICATION	Earnshaw's
AWARD	Merit
ART DIRECTOR	Nancy Campbell
DESIGNER	Nancy Campbell
PHOTOGRAPHER	Alexandra Stonehill
PUBLISHER	Earnshaw's Publications
CATEGORY	Photography Story/Fashion, Beauty
DATE	October 1993

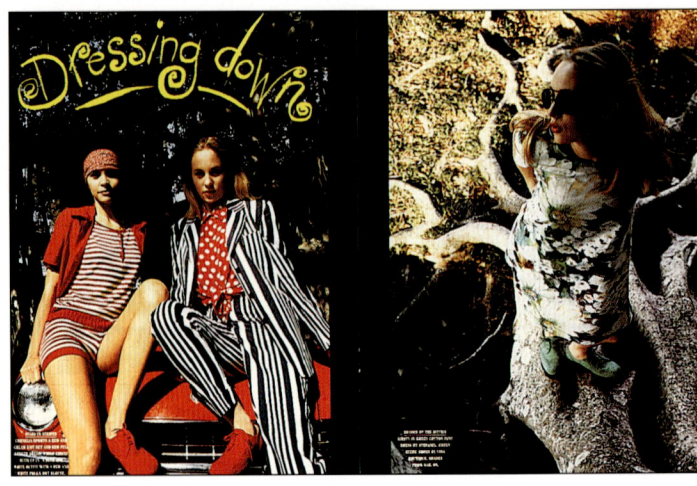

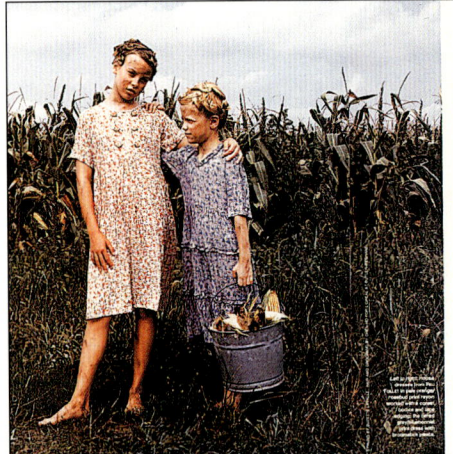

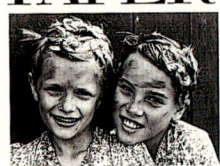

PAPER MOON

Simple clothing drawn from the days of the common worker. The story of Depression days down on the farm. Photographed by Alexandra Stonehill

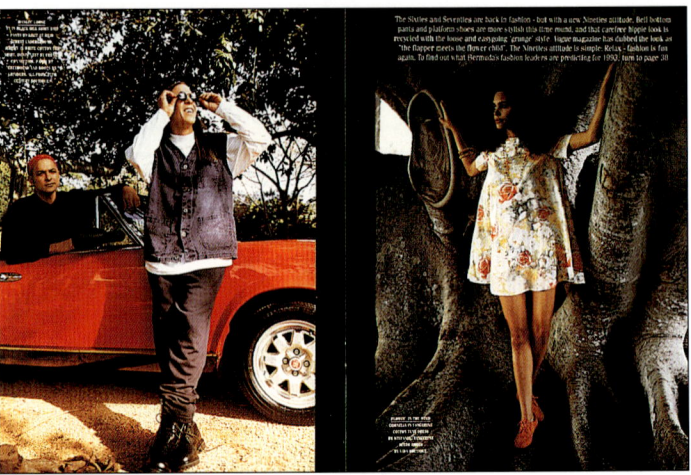

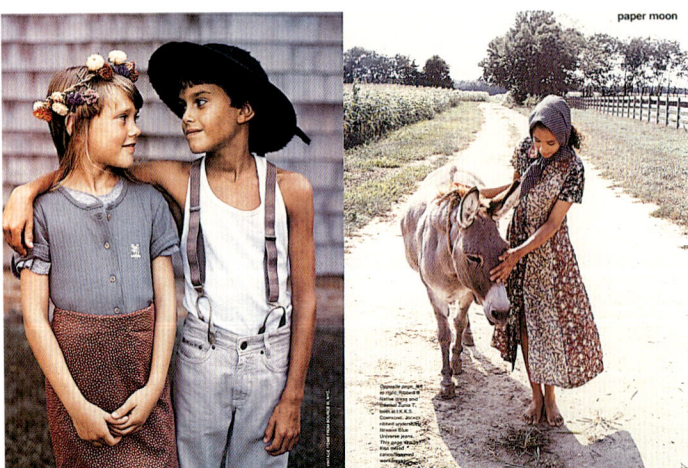

paper moon

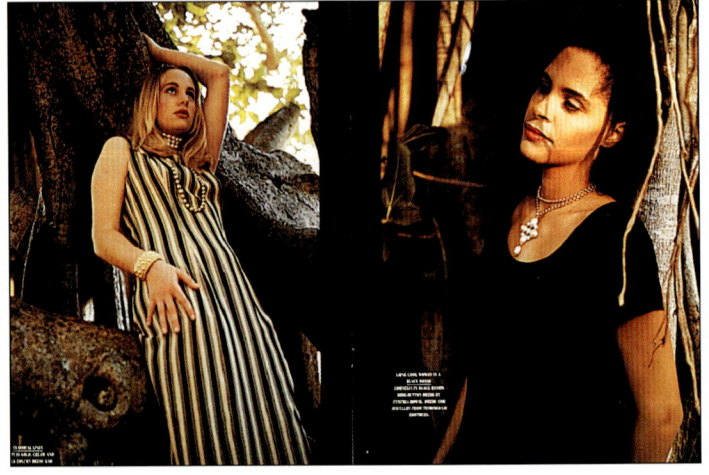

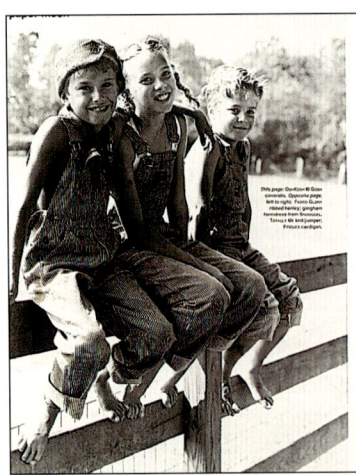

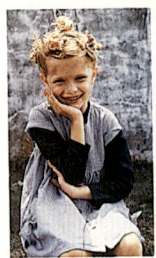

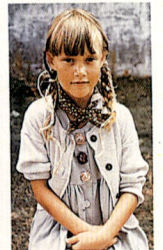

Colors and patterns borrowed from the earth are the inspiration for this authentic kind of clothing

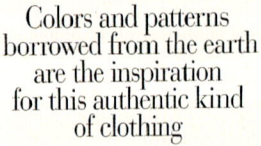

PUBLICATION	RG
AWARD	Merit
ART DIRECTOR	Dana Cooper
DESIGNER	Dana Cooper
PHOTOGRAPHER	Antoine Hunt
PHOTO EDITOR	Dana Cooper
PUBLISHER	Crown Communications
CATEGORY	Photography Story/Fashion, Beauty
DATE	April 1993

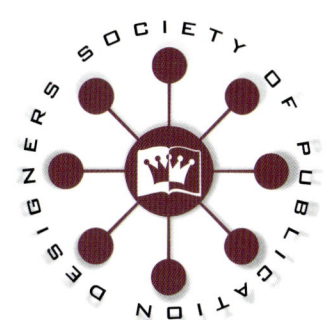

SOCIETY OF PUBLICATION DESIGNERS

INDEX

DESIGNERS

ART

DIRECTORS

DESIGN DIRECTORS

STUDIOS

ILLUSTRATORS

PHOTOGRAPHERS

PHOTO

EDITORS

PUBLISHERS

DESIGNERS

ILLUSTRATORS

PHOTOGRAPHERS

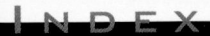

PHOTO EDITORS

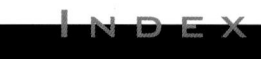

PUBLICATIONS

PUBLISHERS

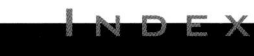

DESIGN FIRM/STUDIO